Recent Advances in Addiction Research

Recent Advances in Addiction Research

Edited by London Stevens

STATES
ACADEMIC PRESS
www.statesacademicpress.com

States Academic Press,
109 South 5th Street,
Brooklyn, NY 11249, USA

Visit us on the World Wide Web at:
www.statesacademicpress.com

ISBN: 978-1-63989-459-8

Trademark Notice: Registered trademark of products or corporate names are used only for explanation and identification without intent to infringe.

Cataloging-in-Publication Data

Recent advances in addiction research / edited by London Stevens.
    p. cm.
Includes bibliographical references and index.
ISBN 978-1-63989-459-8
1. Substance abuse. 2. Psychology, Pathological. 3. Substance abuse--Treatment. I. Stevens, London.
RC564 .R43 2022
362.29--dc23

Table of Contents

Preface

This book was inspired by the evolution of our times; to answer the curiosity of inquisitive minds. Many developments have occurred across the globe in the recent past which has transformed the progress in the field.

Addiction is a brain disorder characterized by the inability to stop using a substance despite knowing that it is causing psychological and physical harm. It is a chronic condition that may arise from taking medications. Many people first engage in an activity voluntarily but addiction can take over and reduce self-control. Addiction can be of two types, namely, substance addiction and non-substance addiction. Most common examples of non-substance addiction are food, gaming, gambling, internet, sex and cell phone. Signs and symptoms of addiction are poor performance at work, declining grades or difficulty at school, a noticeable lack of energy in daily activities, inability to stop using a substance, profound changes in appearance, etc. This book discusses the recent researches in the field of addiction. From theories to research, case studies related to all contemporary topics of relevance to this field have been included herein. This book will serve as a valuable source of reference for graduate and post graduate students.

This book was developed from a mere concept to drafts to chapters and finally compiled together as a complete text to benefit the readers across all nations. To ensure the quality of the content we instilled two significant steps in our procedure. The first was to appoint an editorial team that would verify the data and statistics provided in the book and also select the most appropriate and valuable contributions from the plentiful contributions we received from authors worldwide. The next step was to appoint an expert of the topic as the Editor-in-Chief, who would head the project and finally make the necessary amendments and modifications to make the text reader-friendly. I was then commissioned to examine all the material to present the topics in the most comprehensible and productive format.

I would like to take this opportunity to thank all the contributing authors who were supportive enough to contribute their time and knowledge to this project. I also wish to convey my regards to my family who have been extremely supportive during the entire project.

Editor

Nur transcription factors in stress and addiction

Danae Campos-Melo[†], Danny Galleguillos[†], Natalia Sánchez, Katia Gysling and María E. Andrés*

Nucleus Millennium in Stress and Addiction, Department of Cellular and Molecular Biology, Faculty of Biological Sciences, Pontificia Universidad Católica de Chile, Santiago, Chile

Edited by:
Nicola Maggio, The Chaim Sheba
Medical Center, Israel

Reviewed by:
Ted Abel, University of
Pennsylvania, USA
Izhak Michaelevski, Tel Aviv
University, Israel

*Correspondence:
María E. Andrés, Nucleus
Millennium in Stress and Addiction,
Department of Cellular and
Molecular Biology, Faculty of
Biological Sciences, Pontificia
Universidad Católica de Chile, PO
Box 114D, Santiago 8331150, Chile
e-mail: mandres@bio.puc.cl

The Nur transcription factors Nur77 (NGFI-B, NR4A1), Nurr1 (NR4A2), and Nor-1 (NR4A3) are a sub-family of orphan members of the nuclear receptor superfamily. These transcription factors are products of immediate early genes, whose expression is rapidly and transiently induced in the central nervous system by several types of stimuli. Nur factors are present throughout the hypothalamus-pituitary-adrenal (HPA) axis where are prominently induced in response to stress. Drugs of abuse and stress also induce the expression of Nur factors in nuclei of the motivation/reward circuit of the brain, indicating their participation in the process of drug addiction and in non-hypothalamic responses to stress. Repeated use of addictive drugs and chronic stress induce long-lasting dysregulation of the brain motivation/reward circuit due to reprogramming of gene expression and enduring alterations in neuronal function. Here, we review the data supporting that Nur transcription factors are key players in the molecular basis of the dysregulation of neuronal circuits involved in chronic stress and addiction.

Keywords: Nurr1, Nur77, Nor1, corticotropin releasing factor, addiction, stress, nuclear receptors, gene expression regulation

INTRODUCTION

The transcription factors Nur77 (NGFI-B, NR4A1) (Hazel et al., 1988; Milbrandt, 1988), Nurr1 (NR4A2) (Law et al., 1992) and Nor-1 (NR4A3) (Ohkura et al., 1996) are orphan members of the nuclear receptor superfamily and together conform the Nur subfamily. Nur transcription factors, as members of the nuclear receptor superfamily, share their classic structural organization (**Figure 1A**) encompassing: (a) a non-conserved N-terminal region containing the transcriptional activation function-1 (AF-1), (b) a conserved DNA binding domain (DBD) located in the middle of the proteins, with 90.2% of amino acid sequence identity among all rat Nur factors, and (c) a moderately conserved C-terminal domain, which encloses the ligand-binding domain (LBD) and the ligand-dependent transcriptional activation function 2 or AF-2 (Giguere, 1999). Although Nur transcription factors have a well-recognized LBD structure, their transcriptional activity is not regulated by endogenous ligands as it is for steroid nuclear receptors (Benoit et al., 2004). Crystallographic studies show that the putative ligand-binding pocket of Nurr1 and Nur77 LBDs are filled with side chains of large hydrophobic amino acids, which keep the LBD in a transcriptionally active conformation (Wang et al., 2003; Flaig et al., 2005). Since the binding of ligands does not trigger the transcriptional activity of Nur factors, changes of their expression levels and post-translational modifications appear keys to regulate their activity.

Nur factors behave as immediate early genes, and as such, their mRNA expression is induced independent of protein synthesis in several cell types by multiple kinds of stimuli (Williams and Lau, 1993; Maruyama et al., 1995; Satoh and Kuroda, 2002; Maxwell and Muscat, 2006). Nur factors show some basal expression in specific nuclei of the rodent brain (Zetterstrom et al., 1996b). However, remarkable fast and high induction has been observed for Nur factors in selected brain nuclei or dissociated neurons after physiological, chemical or toxic stimulation (Chan et al., 1993; Honkaniemi et al., 1994; Jacobs et al., 1994; Umemoto et al., 1994; Svenningsson et al., 1995; Imaki et al., 1996; Svenningsson and Fredholm, 1997; Tang et al., 1997; Xing et al., 1997; Honkaniemi and Sharp, 1999; Brosenitsch and Katz, 2001; Ojeda et al., 2003; Maheux et al., 2005). These data strongly support the notion that Nur factors have homeostatic functions and, functioning as immediate-early gene, can also serve as rapid signaling system.

To exert their function as transcriptional regulators, Nur factors bind to nerve-growth-factor inducible gene B (NGFI-B)-responsive element (NBRE) (A/TAAAGGTCA) (Wilson et al., 1991) as monomers (**Figure 1B**) (Wilson et al., 1993a; Paulsen et al., 1995), and to Nur-responsive element (NurRE) (inverted repeated of NBRE-related octanucleotide, AAATG/AC/TCA) (Philips et al., 1997) as homodimers or heterodimers between Nur factors (Philips et al., 1997; Maira et al., 1999). Nur77 and Nurr1, but not Nor-1, can also form heterodimers with RXR retinoid receptor (Perlmann and Jansson, 1995; Zetterstrom et al., 1996a). These heterodimers activate transcription through NBRE elements, where the Nur component binds to the NBRE element,

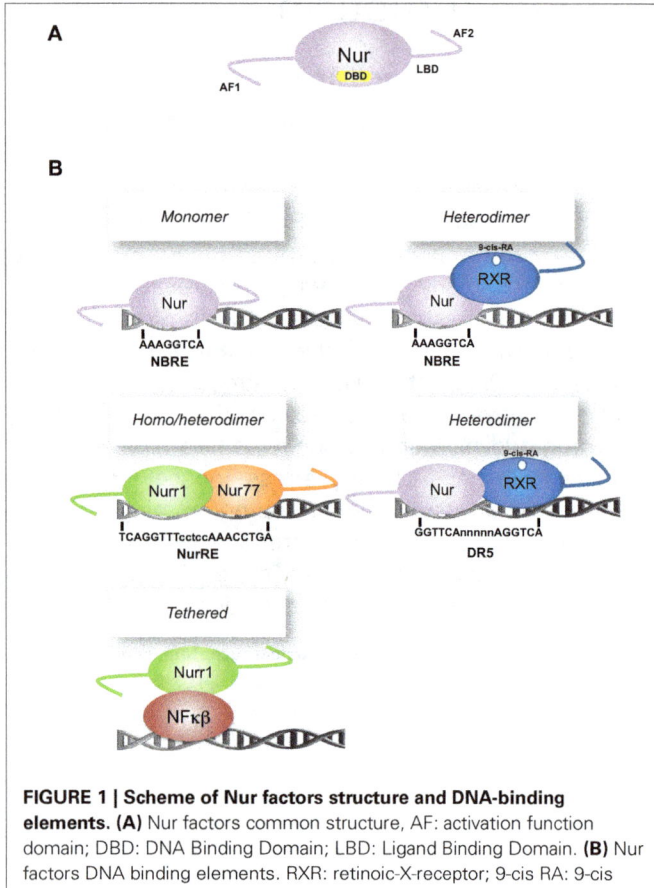

FIGURE 1 | Scheme of Nur factors structure and DNA-binding elements. (A) Nur factors common structure, AF: activation function domain; DBD: DNA Binding Domain; LBD: Ligand Binding Domain. (B) Nur factors DNA binding elements. RXR: retinoic-X-receptor; 9-cis RA: 9-cis retinoic acid.

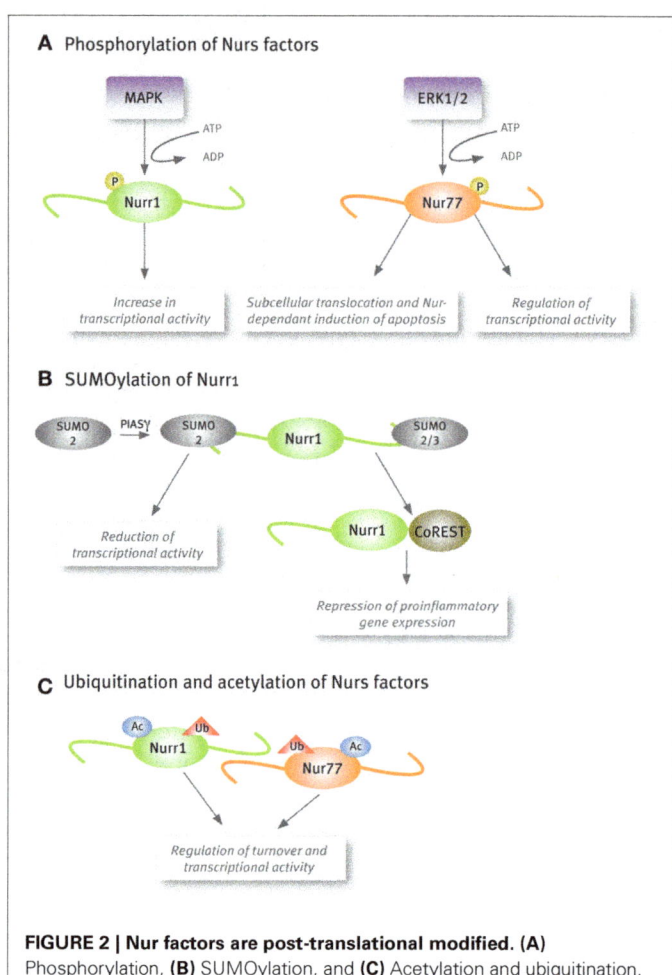

FIGURE 2 | Nur factors are post-translational modified. (A) Phosphorylation, (B) SUMOylation, and (C) Acetylation and ubiquitination.

or through DR5 elements (two direct repeats of the consensus nuclear receptor binding motif separated by five nucleotides, GGTTCAnnnnnAGGTCA). In the case of DR5 elements, both nuclear receptors bind to the DNA (Perlmann and Jansson, 1995). In addition, Nur factors can regulate transcription indirectly by binding to another transcription factor. For instance, Nurr1 represses transcription of inflammatory genes in microglia indirectly by forming a complex with NF-kB transcription factor (Saijo et al., 2009).

Increasing reports show that Nur factors transcriptional activity is regulated by post-translational modifications (**Figure 2**). Phosphorylation of Nur77 by extracellular-signal regulated kinase 2 (ERK2) is required for its transcriptional activity in corticotrophs (Kovalovsky et al., 2002). Similarly, Nurr1 phosphorylation by mitogenic-activated protein kinases increases its transcriptional activity (Nordzell et al., 2004; Sacchetti et al., 2006; Zhang et al., 2007). Phosphorylation of Nur factors plays an important role also in their subcellular translocation and Nur-dependent induction of apoptosis (Katagiri et al., 2000; Slagsvold et al., 2002; Wingate et al., 2006). The post-translational modification SUMOylation has appeared as an important regulatory pathway of Nurr1 transcriptional activity (Galleguillos et al., 2004; Saijo et al., 2009; Arredondo et al., 2013). All Nur factors harbor SUMO consensus motifs in their sequences, but only Nurr1 SUMOylation by SUMO2 and SUMO3 has been

demonstrated. SUMOylation of the N-terminal domain of Nurr1 with SUMO2 reduces its transcriptional activity in promoters harboring more than one NBRE element (Arredondo et al., 2013). Also, SUMOylation with SUMO2 or SUMO3 of the C-terminal of Nurr1 is required to bind the corepressor CoREST and repress pro-inflammatory gene expression (Saijo et al., 2009). Recent work has shown that Nur factors turnover and transcriptional activity are regulated by acetylation (Kang et al., 2010) and ubiquitination (van Tiel et al., 2012; Alvarez-Castelao et al., 2013).

Nur factors are associated to several functions (Maxwell and Muscat, 2006). Some of the functions are exclusive of one factor, like the essential role of Nurr1 in the induction and maintenance of midbrain dopamine neurons (Zetterstrom et al., 1997; Castillo et al., 1998; Saucedo-Cardenas et al., 1998; Kadkhodaei et al., 2009), and Nor-1 requirement for normal embryonic development (Deyoung et al., 2003), inner ear (Ponnio et al., 2002), and hippocampus development (Ponnio and Conneely, 2004). Increasing evidence indicates that all Nur factors play significant roles in inflammatory (McMorrow and Murphy, 2011; van Tiel and de Vries, 2012) and oncogenic processes (Mohan et al., 2012). Increased expression levels of Nur factors have been observed in several types of cancer cell lines and tumors, although the opposite has also been reported. Collected data suggest that Nur77 behaves as a pro-oncogenic factor (Lee et al., 2011). However, the double knockout of Nur77 and Nor-1 induced a fatal acute myeloid leukemia in mice (Mullican et al., 2007), indicating that these nuclear receptors may also play a role as tumor suppressors (Mullican et al., 2007). The apparent controversy or dual role of Nur factors as tumor suppressors and/or pro-oncogenic factors could be explained by a dual role in transcription, behaving as transcriptional activators or repressors. Since Nur factors are transcriptionally active in their native form, less attention has been paid to their role as potential transcriptional repressors. Interestingly, there are several reports showing the interaction of Nur factors with transcriptional corepressors. For example, we showed that PIASγ interacts and represses Nurr1-dependent transcriptional activity (Galleguillos et al., 2004). Nurr1 also interacts with the transcriptional repressors SMRT (Lammi et al., 2008; Jacobs et al., 2009) and CoREST (Saijo et al., 2009). The interaction with SMRT maintains Nurr1 in a transcriptional repressive complex impeding the induction of its dopaminergic target genes (Jacobs et al., 2009). It has also been shown the interaction between Nur77 and SMRT (Sohn et al., 2001). Regarding the role of Nur77 and Nor-1 repressing the expression of target genes, it was shown that abrogation of these transcription factors correlates with an increased expression of MYC oncogene (Boudreaux et al., 2012). In addition, it was demonstrated that MYC is a direct target gene of Nur77/Nor-1, whose expression was strongly repressed in a Nur DNA-binding dependent way (Boudreaux et al., 2012). Nur77 and Nor-1 play also an important role triggering apoptosis in several cell types. Interestingly, this effect is due to the translocation of Nur77/Nor-1 from the nuclei to the mitochondria, where Nur77 triggers cytochrome c release and apoptosis (Li et al., 2000). Through this mechanism, Nur77 and Nor-1 play a central function in the clonal deletion of autoreactive thymocytes (Sohn et al., 2007). Nur77 and Nor-1 colocalize in several cell types, including CNS neurons, and apparently they replace each other in some functions. This colocalization of Nur77 and Nor-1 explain the lack of deleterious effects in the single knockout mice, while lack of both induces a catastrophic deregulation in the immune system. Similarly, colocalization of Nur77 with Nor-1 in the CNS may explain an apparent lack of strong effect of each knockout in the stress and rewarding systems of the brain.

Nur TRANSCRIPTION FACTORS AND DOPAMINERGIC TRANSMISSION

Histological and neurochemical evidence supports the idea that Nur transcription factors are closely associated with dopamine neurotransmission (**Figure 3**, **Table 1**). Nur77 and Nor-1 are expressed in neurons of the striatum, the nucleus accumbens (NAc) and the prefrontal cortex (PFC) (Xiao et al., 1996; Zetterstrom et al., 1996b; Gervais et al., 1999; Werme et al., 2000a,b; Davis and Puhl, 2011), all target nuclei of dopaminergic neurons originated in the ventral midbrain. In these nuclei, a strong control of Nur77 and Nor-1 expression is induced by the stimulation of the dopamine neurons (Chergui et al., 1997); by the administration of dopamine D2 receptor agonists and antagonists (Gervais et al., 1999; Beaudry et al., 2000; Werme et al., 2000b; Langlois et al., 2001; Maheux et al., 2005); by

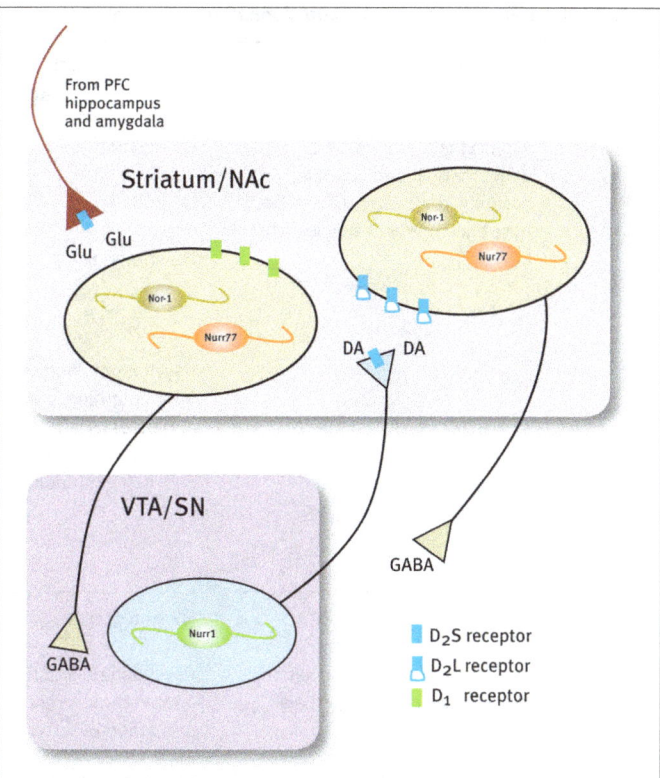

FIGURE 3 | Expression of Nur factors in the in the motivation/reward circuit. Nurr1 is expressed in dopamine neurons of the SN/VTA and Nur77 and Nor-1 are expressed in dopamine-receptive GABAergic neurons of the striatum/NAc. GABAergic projecting neurons in the striatum/NAc are segregated in two populations that express either D1 or D2 receptors (Valjent et al., 2009).

drugs of abuse (Werme et al., 2000a; St-Hilaire et al., 2003b) and after dopamine denervation. Collected data indicate that Nur77 expression is under a tonic inhibitory control exerted by physiological dopamine basal levels through D2 receptor. Acute administration of dopamine D2 agonists decreases Nur77 mRNA levels in the striatum (Gervais et al., 1999), while the opposite is observed after acute dopamine D2 antagonist administration in the striatum, NAc and PFC (Beaudry et al., 2000; Langlois et al., 2001; Maheux et al., 2005). Interestingly, D2 antagonist-dependent induction of Nur77 expression in the striatum and NAc core is preserved after chronic treatment with D2 ligands (Beaudry et al., 2000; Werme et al., 2000b; Mahmoudi et al., 2009, 2013), suggesting that this transcription factor mediates adaptive changes to long-term repetitive dopamine variations (Levesque and Rouillard, 2007).

Studies using dopamine denervation and Nur77 knockout mice have been instrumental to reveal the role of Nur77 as a master factor for adaptations induced by dopaminergic neurotransmission changes. Full lesion of dopamine nigro-striatal pathway and D2 antagonist administration produce a significant up-regulation of both Nur77 and enkephalin mRNA in enkephalin positive neurons of the striatum (Beaudry et al., 2000; St-Hilaire et al., 2003a, 2005). Enkephalin up-regulation induced by D2 antagonists or by dopamine denervation is severely

Table 1 | Nur transcription factors and dopaminergic neurotransmission.

Nur factor	Expression	Effect of DA agonists, antagonists, psychostimulants, and 6-OHDA		KO characteristics
Nur77	High: Striatum, NAc, PFC, olfactory bulb and tubercle, cortex, hippocampal formation, hypothalamus and amygdala[a–e] Low: VTA, SN[a–e]	D1 agonist:	No effects in striatum[f, g]	D2R increases in dorsal striatum[m, n]
		D2 agonist:	mRNA down-regulated in striatum[f, g]	Alterations in the expression of NT and ENK[m, o]
		D2 antagonist:	mRNA up-regulated in striatum, PFC, NAc, VTA, and SN[c, h, i, j, p]	Increased locomotor activity[n]
				Increased sensitivity to low dose of D2 agonist[n]
		Psychostimulants: (amphetamine, cocaine, and others)	mRNA up-regulated in striatum and NAc[e, k, l]	Increased DOPAC in SN and VTA[n]
		D1 and D2 agonists:	mRNA up-regulated in striatum[f]	Decreased cataleptic response after D2R antagonist[m]
		6-OHDA in striatum:	mRNA up-regulated in striatum[f]	Decreased COMT expression[n]
			L-DOPA treatment: complex regulation in striatum[f]	
Nor-1	High: Striatum, NAc, PFC, olfactory bulb and tubercle, cortex, hippocampal formation, hypothalamus and amygdala[a–e] Low: VTA, SN[a–e]	D2 Antagonist:	mRNA up-regulated in striatum, NAc, PFC, VTA and SN[h, p]	Not viable embryos. Embryos die at early stages[q]
		Psychostimulants: (amphetamine, cocaine and others)	mRNA up-regulated in NAc, striatum and cortex[e, l]	
Nurr1	High: VTA, SN[a, b] Low: cortex, hippocampal formation, olfactory bulb, hypothalamus[a, b]	Psychostimulants in drug abusers: (amphetamine, cocaine and others)	mRNA down-regulated in SN and VTA[q, r]	Agenesis DA neurons[t]
		6-OHDA in striatum:	mRNA up-regulated in SN[s]	

DA: dopamine; 6-OHDA: 6-hydroxydopamine; L-DOPA: 3,4-dihydroxyphenylalanine; DOPAC: dihydroxyphenylacetic acid; COMT: catechol-O-methyltransferase; ENK: enkephalin; NT: neurotensin.

[a] *Gofflot et al., 2007*
[b] *Zetterstrom et al., 1996a,b*
[c] *Beaudry et al., 2000*
[d] *Ponnio and Conneely, 2004*
[e] *Werme et al., 2000a,b*
[f] *St-Hilaire et al., 2003a*
[g] *Gervais et al., 1999*
[h] *Maheux et al., 2005*
[i] *Langlois et al., 2001*
[j] *Maheux et al., 2012*
[k] *St-Hilaire et al., 2003b*
[l] *Krasnova et al., 2011*
[m] *Ethier et al., 2004*
[n] *Gilbert et al., 2006*
[o] *St-Hilaire et al., 2006*
[p] *Maheux et al., 2012*
[q] *Nielsen et al., 2008*
[r] *Horvath et al., 2007*
[s] *Ojeda et al., 2003*
[t] *Zetterstrom et al., 1997; Castillo et al., 1998; Saucedo-Cardenas et al., 1998.*

impaired in Nur77 knockout mice (Ethier et al., 2004; St-Hilaire et al., 2006). Moreover, the normalization of enkephalin levels induced by L-DOPA treatment of dopamine denervated animals is not observed in Nur77 knockout mice (St-Hilaire et al., 2006), indicating that Nur77 is essential for this adaptive effect. Interestingly, a recent publication suggests that the D2 control over Nur77 expression in the striatum is due to presynaptic D2 receptors located on glutamatergic terminals coming from the cortex (Maheux et al., 2012). Metabotropic mGlu5 receptor antagonist suppressed D2 antagonist-induced Nur77 expression (Maheux et al., 2012), indicating that glutamate positively controls Nur77 expression in the striatum. These data show that

Nur77 may play an integrative role of multiple signaling in the striatum.

mRNA levels of Nur77 and Nor-1 are extremely low or absent in adult midbrain dopaminergic neurons of substantia nigra (SN) and ventral tegmental area (VTA) in basal conditions (Zetterstrom et al., 1996a,b). However, current data indicate that Nur77 may play an important role regulating dopamine biochemical homeostasis in these nuclei. Nur77-deficient mice show an increase in dopamine D2 receptors in dorsolateral striatum; enhanced spontaneous locomotor activity; greater sensitivity to dopamine D2 receptor agonists and higher levels of DOPAC relative to the wild-type (Gilbert et al., 2006). Remarkably, Nur77 and Nor-1 expression increases significantly in midbrain dopamine neurons after the administration of dopamine D2 receptor antagonists (Maheux et al., 2005).

Unlike Nur77 and Nor-1, Nurr1 is expressed under basal physiological conditions in dopamine neurons of SN and VTA (Xiao et al., 1996; Zetterstrom et al., 1996a; Backman et al., 1999; Ojeda et al., 2003). Strong evidence indicates that Nurr1 is essential for the development of these neurons (Zetterstrom et al., 1997; Castillo et al., 1998; Saucedo-Cardenas et al., 1998). More recently, it was shown that Nurr1 is also critical to maintain midbrain dopamine neurons in the adult (Kadkhodaei et al., 2009). During development, dopamine midbrain precursors do not differentiate into dopaminergic phenotype in the Nurr1 null mice (Zetterstrom et al., 1997; Castillo et al., 1998; Saucedo-Cardenas et al., 1998). Dopaminergic markers like tyrosine hydroxylase (TH), the dopamine transporter (DAT), the vesicular monoamine transporter (VMAT2) and the tyrosine kinase receptor RET (Wallen et al., 2001) are not expressed in the ventral mesencephalon of Nurr1 null mice at birth (reviewed in Smidt et al., 2003; Perlmann and Wallen-Mackenzie, 2004). On the other hand, a progressive decline in the expression of the same genes in the SN and VTA is observed when Nurr1 is ablated in adults (Kadkhodaei et al., 2009, 2013; Galleguillos et al., 2010). Interestingly, it was recently shown that Nurr1 regulates the expression of a set of mitochondria genes (Kadkhodaei et al., 2013). Whether, the role of Nurr1 keeping dopamine neuron fully functional during adulthood and aging is related to the control of genes of the phenotype or mitochondrial genes or both requires further evidence.

The accumulated evidence indicate that Nurr1 regulates the transcription of dopamine phenotype genes (Sakurada et al., 1999; Iwawaki et al., 2000; Sacchetti et al., 2001; Hermanson et al., 2003; Kim et al., 2003; Smits et al., 2003; Galleguillos et al., 2010). Studies in Nurr1-deficient mice (±) indicate that the amount of Nurr1 is important to keep homeostasis during the life of dopamine neurons (Le et al., 1999; Jiang et al., 2005; Eells et al., 2006; Zhang et al., 2012). For instance, aged Nurr1 (±) mice have a significant decrease in rotarod performance and locomotor activity, a motor impairment analogous to Parkinson's disease associated with decreased dopamine levels in the striatum (Jiang et al., 2005). Recently, it was shown that a decreased number of TH positive cells in SN, observed in aged Nurr1 (±) mice, correlates with decreased dopamine release in the striatum (Zhang et al., 2012). Similarly, we showed that inducing a 50% decrease of Nurr1 expression in the SN of adult rats results in a significant decrease of dopamine extracellular levels in the striatum associated with decreased expression of the tyrosine kinase receptor RET (Galleguillos et al., 2010). Nurr1-deficient mice (±) also show some symptoms related to schizophrenia, such as hyperactivity in a novel environment, deficiency in the retention of emotional memory and increased response to swim stress; all symptoms associated with dysfunctions in dopamine neurotransmission (Rojas et al., 2007; Vuillermot et al., 2011). Thus, these data show that Nurr1 controls the expression of dopamine phenotype genes during adulthood. In addition, the data show that survival pathways, which are stressed during aging, require a stronger Nurr1 signaling, that cannot be achieved in Nurr1 heterozygous mice. Remarkably, the amount of Nurr1 protein levels seems to play a significant role controlling the expression of specific sets of target genes. Indeed, the group of Bannon (Johnson et al., 2011), showed that different set of genes are controlled by lower vs. higher Nurr1 level.

How Nurr1 is regulated by dopamine levels and adjusts the expression of target genes accordingly? Accumulated data indicates that Nurr1 expression depends on dopamine signaling, mainly through D2 receptors. D2 receptors are located in soma and dendrites, to regulate firing rate of neurons and presynaptically in axons to regulate dopamine synthesis and release. Drugs of abuse like cocaine decrease Nurr1 in mesencephalon (Bannon et al., 2002, 2004). D2 receptor knockout mice have increased Nurr1 expression in midbrain dopamine neurons (Tseng et al., 2000) and the loss of dopamine in rat striatum induced by 6-hydroxydopamine generates a rapid increase of Nurr1 expression in dopamine neurons of the SN (Ojeda et al., 2003). These data show that dopamine extracellular levels influence the expression of Nurr1 in the SN and VTA. Recent evidence indicates that neuronal firing regulates differentially the expression of Nurr1 and Nur77 in dopamine neurons (Eells et al., 2012). A normal flow of impulses maintains basal expression of Nurr1. Surprisingly, Nur77 was induced with a lower D2 autoreceptor activation in the VTA (Eells et al., 2012). Recently, it was shown that D2 receptors located postsynaptically in GABA projecting neurons of the striatum also regulate dopamine release (Anzalone et al., 2012). Nurr1 and/or Nur77 could be the targets of such a feedback mechanism regulating dopamine homeostasis. The recent findings of Nur77 controlling dopaminergic homeostasis raises several questions regarding the specific role of each Nur factor in dopaminergic gene expression: Are Nur factors redundant or they play particular roles in the adaptation and survival processes of midbrain dopamine neurons during adulthood and aging?

Nur TRANSCRIPTION FACTORS DURING THE STRESS RESPONSE

In response to stressful stimuli, secretory neurons of the paraventricular nucleus (PVN) discharge corticotropin-releasing factor (CRF) that in turn increases both the secretion of adrenocorticotrophin hormone (ACTH) and the transcription of its precursor, the proopiomelanocortin (POMC) gene, in the anterior pituitary. ACTH stimulates the release of glucocorticoids (GCs) and the transcription of genes encoding several steroidogenic enzymes in the adrenal gland. GCs exert diverse effects on target tissues to mobilize energy for the body to deal with the stressor, and also exert a negative feedback through the inhibition of the synthesis and secretion of CRF and POMC (Keller-Wood and Dallman, 1984; Sawchenko and Swanson, 1985; Antoni, 1986; Swanson and Simmons, 1989).

Several lines of evidence indicate that Nur transcription factors play a prominent role in adaptive responses to stress, regulating the transcription of target genes in the hypothalamus-pituitary-adrenal (HPA) axis (**Figure 4**). The evidence indicates that this nuclear receptor subfamily regulates the expression of CRF and POMC in the PVN and pituitary, respectively (Murphy and Conneely, 1997; Drouin et al., 1998). In the adrenal glands, Nur77 and Nor-1 also regulate the expression of steroid-21α-hydroxylase and 3-β-hydroxysteroid dehydrogenase, both enzymes essential for the production of GCs (**Figure 4**) (Wilson et al., 1993b; Fernandez et al., 2000; Bassett et al., 2004).

A complex signaling cascade involving Nur factors is required for POMC regulation. The group of Eduardo Arzt (Kovalovsky et al., 2002) showed that in AtT-20 corticotrophs, CRF induces both Nur77 and Nurr1 expression resulting in POMC transcription through a NurRE site in its promoter. While CRF-mediated induction of Nur factors requires protein kinase A (PKA) and

cAMP signaling, POMC transcriptional induction depends further on MAPK activation. Nur77-dependent induction of POMC transcription required the phosphorylation of Nur77 by MAPK (Kovalovsky et al., 2002). Concordantly, cAMP/PKA signaling enhances DNA binding activity of Nur dimers, but not monomers, and the recruitment of transcriptional coactivators through the AF-1 domain of Nur factors (Maira et al., 2003). Nur transcription factors are also involved in the ending of the stress response. The effect of Nur transcription factors on POMC promoter is antagonized by GCs (Philips et al., 1997; Drouin et al., 1998; Martens et al., 2005; Carpentier et al., 2008). The NurRE element of the POMC gene, which binds Nur dimers, is the target of the repressive effect of GCs. GC receptors bound to ligands directly interact with Nur factors inducing the transrepression of POMC (Martens et al., 2005).

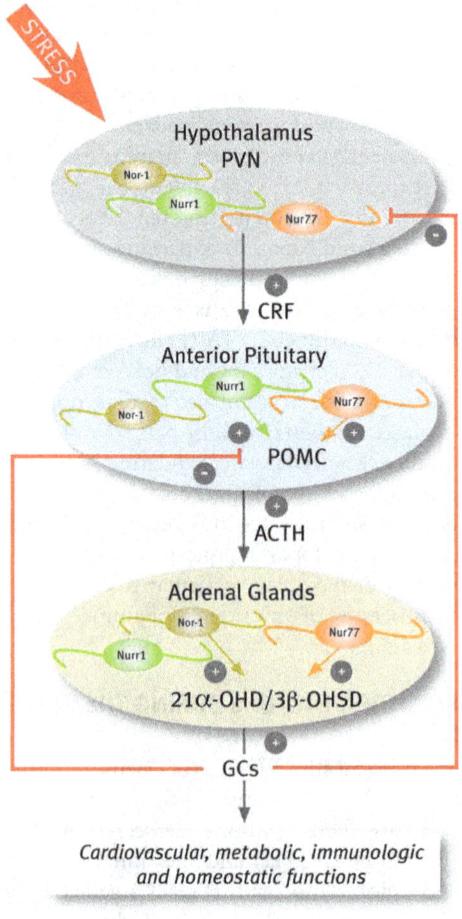

Less is known about the role of Nur factors regulating CRF in the PVN. While Nurr1 is expressed constitutively in the PVN (Saucedo-Cardenas and Conneely, 1996), Nur77 is transiently induced by different types of stressful stimuli (Chan et al., 1993; Honkaniemi et al., 1994; Imaki et al., 1996; Kawasaki et al., 2005), and by central administration of CRF (Parkes et al., 1993). Interestingly, an increased expression of Nur77 occurs in the PVN of virgin and lactating females, but not in pregnant mice stressed either by exposure to a novel environment or forced swimming (Douglas et al., 2003), suggesting a role for sex hormones regulating Nur factors action. In 1997, Murphy and Conneely showed that Nurr1 and Nur77 bind and transactivate the CRF gene (Murphy and Conneely, 1997). The CRF gene promoter harbors a conserved NBRE element (Murphy et al., 1996; Yao and Denver, 2007; Yao et al., 2007), which is required for Nur77-dependent inductive effect of reporters driven by the CRF promoter (Murphy and Conneely, 1997). More recently, Stroth et al. (2011) showed that up-regulation of mRNAs encoding CRF and Nur factors in the PVN during stress depends on Pituitary Adenylate Cyclase Activating Polypeptide (PACAP). Indeed, not only CRF, but also restraint-induced expression of Nur77 and Nurr1 decreases in the pituitary gland of PACAP-deficient mice (Stroth et al., 2011), suggesting a reciprocal regulation between Nur factors and CRF. Normal function of the HPA axis in Nur77 null mutant mice indicates redundancy of Nur factors. Nurr1 mRNA increases in the adrenal gland of Nur77 null mice (Crawford et al., 1995). In addition, Nor-1 and Nur77 play similar, albeit distinct roles in the HPA axis. Similar to Nur77, Nor-1 activates the expression of the gene encoding steroid-21α-hydroxylase (Wilson et al., 1993b; Fernandez et al., 2000) through NBRE elements. In contrast, DNA binding experiments of Nor-1 to NurRE element suggest that Nor-1 is not an efficient substitute of Nur77 activation of POMC gene expression in the pituitary gland (Fernandez et al., 2000).

In addition to its crucial role in the activation of the HPA axis, CRF functions as a neurotransmitter/neuromodulator coordinating extra-hypothalamic aspects of the stress response (Aguilera, 1998; Ziegler and Herman, 2000; Herman et al., 2002). The extra-hypothalamic aspects of the stress response are mediated by interconnected nuclei of the amygdala and the bed nucleus of the stria terminalis (BNST) (Walker et al., 2003). The BNST is the primary integrative center of excitatory and inhibitory inputs regulating the HPA axis during stress (Forray and Gysling,

FIGURE 4 | Scheme of Nur factors expression in the HPA axis.

2004), and mediates anxiety-like behavior resulting of extended threat (Walker et al., 2009). The expression of Nur transcription factors increases in the limbic nuclei associated to the extra-hypothalamic aspects of the stress response, suggesting that Nur factors could also underlie enduring changes induced by chronic stress. For instance, Nor-1 is increased in the somatosensory cortex and amygdala when exposed to novelty stress (Sun et al., 2007). Predator stress increases Nur77 mRNA in prelimbic, infralimbic and, ventral and lateral orbital prefrontal cortexes (Schiltz et al., 2007). Nurr1 expression increases while TH decreases at postnatal day 7 in the VTA of prenatally stressed offspring, which suggest a possible compensatory mechanism that may play Nurr1 to counteract the observed reduction of dopamine levels (Katunar et al., 2009, 2010). In addition, dopamine content decreases within the PFC and midbrain of rats subjected to forced swim test, meanwhile Nurr1 expression increases in the same brain areas (Rojas et al., 2010) supporting a role for Nurr1 counteracting the decrease of dopamine content. Intriguingly, Eells et al. (2002) showed that Nurr1 ($\pm$) mice displayed significantly greater locomotor activity in response to mild stress that correlated with lower dopamine content in mesolimbic and mesocortical circuits (Eells et al., 2002). Taken together the data indicate that Nur factors expression is modulated in limbic circuit during the response to stress. It is unknown what are the genes induced or repressed by Nur factors in the nuclei associated to the extra-hypothalamic aspects of the stress response. One possible target is CRF.

Repeated immobilization stress and chronic mild stress induce CRF expression in the BNST (Stout et al., 2000; Santibanez et al., 2006). We reported that cells expressing CRF in the BNST also express Nur77 (Campos-Melo et al., 2011), even though the expression of Nur77 is wider than CRF in this nucleus. Nur77 expression increases significantly in the dorso-lateral and ventromedial subdivisions of the BNST after acute and repeated immobilization stress (Campos-Melo et al., 2011), same areas where CRF expression increases after repeated immobilization stress (Santibanez et al., 2006). Several years ago, it was shown that the intracerebroventricular injection of CRF increases CRF expression in the PVN (Parkes et al., 1993). A CRF-dependent induction of CRF could be a mechanism of maintaining CRF expression in brain nuclei associated to chronic stress-induced anxiety and depression (Stenzel-Poore et al., 1994; Pelton et al., 1997; Yao and Denver, 2007). In support of this suggestion (Parkes et al., 1993), immunohistochemical data show that CRF neurons are innervated by CRF axons in PVN and amygdala (Moga et al., 1989; Silverman et al., 1989; Moga and Saper, 1994). Similarly, in BNST, positive CRF terminals also innervate CRF neurons (Sakanaka et al., 1986; Veinante et al., 1997). Since CRF induces the expression of Nur77 (Kovalovsky et al., 2002) and Nur77 also is able to induce CRF expression (Murphy and Conneely, 1997), it is possible that Nur77 could mediate the vicious cycle of CRF-dependent CRF induction in the PVN and limbic nuclei, during chronic stress; an hypothesis that requires further investigation.

FUNCTIONAL ROLE OF Nur TRANSCRIPTION FACTORS IN THE ADDICTION PROCESS. PROTECTORS OR INSTIGATORS?

The motivation/reward circuit has its roots in dopamine neurons located in the VTA, which send afferences to the NAc, BNST, septum, amygdala, and PFC. Acute administration of drugs of abuse, which increase dopamine release (Di Chiara and Imperato, 1988), induce the expression of Nur77 and Nor-1 in nuclei of the motivation/reward circuit (**Table 1**) (Werme et al., 2000a; St-Hilaire et al., 2003b; Krasnova et al., 2011). Nur77 and Nor-1 are up-regulated in the NAc, striatum, and cortex after acute administration of cocaine and morphine (Werme et al., 2000a). Similarly, acute administration of methamphetamine upregulates the expression of Nur77 in cortex, striatum and NAc core; and of Nurr1 in the cortex and VTA. Pretreatment with a selective antagonist of D1/D5 dopamine receptors prevents methamphetamine-induced expression of both Nur77 and Nurr1 mRNA, supporting that dopamine-mediated signaling regulates Nur transcription factors expression (Akiyama et al., 2008). In concordance, the simultaneous administration of D1 and D2 agonists increases Nur77 expression in the striatum (St-Hilaire et al., 2003b). However, D1 agonists administered alone do not modify Nur77 expression in the striatum (St-Hilaire et al., 2003a). As analyzed before, substantial data indicate that dopamine D2 antagonists increase, while D2 agonists decrease Nur77 and Nor-1 expression in the striatum (Beaudry et al., 2000; Werme et al., 2000a,b; Langlois et al., 2001; Maheux et al., 2005, 2012; St-Hilaire et al., 2005). How could this paradox be explained? Taken together the available evidence suggests that drugs of abuse would require another neurotransmitter system, besides dopamine, in order to induce Nur77 in GABA projecting neurons of the striatum. Nur77 induction by D2 antagonists in GABA projecting neurons depends on glutamate signaling through mGlu5 receptors (Maheux et al., 2012). Maheux et al. (2012) showed that ablation of the long isoform of dopamine D2 receptors, located postsynaptically do not prevent D2 antagonists-dependent induction of Nur77, indicating that the effect is presynaptic, where the short isoform of the D2 receptor is present. Presynaptic D2 receptors are located in dopaminergic and glutamatergic axons in the striatum. This result was further supported by showing that interrupting glutamate neurotransmission to the striatum by cortex lesion prevented the increase of Nur77 expression induced by D2 antagonists (Maheux et al., 2012). It is tempting to suggest that similarly, drugs of abuse-dependent induction of Nur77 in the striatum and NAc depends, besides dopamine, on glutamate neurotransmission. Dopamine- and glutamate-dependent induction of Nur77 supports a role for Nur77 integrating pre and postsynaptic information in striatal GABA projecting neurons.

The development of compulsive running, associated with a high risk of addictive behavior, correlates with lower Nur77 and Nor1 expression in several nuclei of the motivation/reward circuit, in the addiction-prone Lewis rat strain compared with the less-addiction prone Fisher rats which do not develop compulsive running (Werme et al., 1999). Accordingly, Nur77 null mice show increased locomotor activity, but a similar locomotor sensitization than wild type mice after repeated amphetamine administration (Bourhis et al., 2009). Interestingly, the blockade of amphetamine-induced locomotor sensitization by an RXR antagonist is abolished in Nur77 null mice (Bourhis et al., 2009). Together the data suggest that Nur77 regulates addiction-prone phenotype and sensitization by different mechanisms. The available information regarding Nurr1 protecting or facilitating addictive behaviors is unclear. In one study it was shown that Nurr1 ($\pm$) mice do not develop compulsive running behavior and high ethanol consumption compared to wild type mice (Werme et al., 2003). In another study it was shown that Nurr1 ($\pm$) mice have an increased basal locomotor activity and augmented locomotor response to acute methamphetamine administration (Backman et al., 2003). Mice genetic background, behavioral protocols, among other parameters, may influence these observations. Remarkably, in a recent work it was shown that ablation of the histone deacetylase HDAC3 in the NAc facilitates condition-place preference induced by cocaine (Rogge et al., 2013). This effect was correlated with increased Nurr1 expression in this nucleus, supporting a role for Nurr1 facilitating addiction behaviors (Rogge et al., 2013).

It has been proposed that the persistent behavioral and cognitive effects of chronic intake of drugs of abuse depend on new programs of gene expression triggered by immediate-early genes. Tolerance and sensitization of Nur factors expression in nuclei of the motivation/reward and stress brain circuits suggest that these early genes play a signaling role in the plastic changes underlying long-term adaptations. Studies in cocaine abusers showed a reduction of Nurr1 expression in SN neurons (Nielsen et al., 2008). This decreased expression of Nurr1 correlates with a reduction of DAT expression in the same neurons (Bannon et al., 2002). Similarly, rats chronically treated with cocaine show a down-regulation of the expression of Nurr1 mRNA and protein in the ventral midbrain (Leo et al., 2007). Additionally, chronic use of heroin decreases Nurr1 mRNA to a greater extent with age in the paranigral nucleus of the VTA (Horvath et al., 2007). Nurr1 expression decreases after chronic intake of drugs of abuse, could be an adaptive change to excessive dopamine stimulation, and also could be indicative of Nurr1 role adjusting the expression of dopamine target genes during the addiction process. In this regard, it was shown that an acute methamphetamine challenge to animals pretreated with methamphetamine causes a further decrease in Nurr1 mRNA levels (McCoy et al., 2011), indicating that the signaling system regulating Nurr1 expression adapts to new parameters.

Opposing to a tolerance effect observed for Nurr1; Nur77 seems to adapt to dopamine changes and its levels are still inducible after chronic drug intake. For instance, it has been shown that Nur77 expression increases in the frontal cortex of rats after 10 days of cocaine self-administration (Freeman et al., 2002b) or 14 days in a binge model of cocaine administration (Freeman et al., 2002a), and in the dorsal striatum after 7 days of cocaine self-administration (Lynch et al., 2008). On other hand, it was shown that the expression of several early-genes, including Nur factors, is no longer induced in the striatum after chronic exposure to methamphetamine (McCoy et al., 2011). It is noteworthy that Nor-1 is still significantly induced in the striatum of methamphetamine chronically-treated rats, indicating the capacity of the system to respond in new settings.

Chronic stress also triggers tolerance and sensitization of Nur factors expression. In the PVN, it has been shown that Nur77 is no longer induced after chronic stress stimuli (Umemoto et al., 1994, 1997). In contrast, in the ventral region of the BNST, we observed a higher number of cells expressing Nur77 after repeated immobilization stress compared with acute stress (Campos-Melo et al., 2011). Interestingly, the data of the group of Marta Antonelli (Katunar et al., 2010) suggest that Nurr1 may be the transcription factor setting up the new parameters of the dopamine system after prenatal stress. Using prenatal restraint stress, they showed that Nurr1 is permanently higher in the VTA, but not in the SN, in the offspring of stressed mothers. This increment of Nurr1 expression in the VTA correlates with several changes in the motivation/reward dopamine system that persist to adulthood (Baier et al., 2012). An exciting work indicates that Nur factors integrate stress and drug addiction signaling. Postweaning isolation causes elevation in amphetamine-induced dopamine overflow in Nurr1 ($-$/+) mice, but a reduction in (+/+) mice (Moore et al., 2008). These data demonstrate that a deletion of a single allele of Nurr1, which produced only subtle phenotypic changes, when coupled with a developmental stressor such as postweaning isolation, can dramatically alter mesoaccumbens dopamine neurotransmission (Moore et al., 2008).

CONCLUSIONS

Chronic stress plays a primary role in the origin of several brain pathologies such as anxiety and depression (McCormick and Green, 2013), and facilitates and perpetuates drug addiction (Koob, 2008; Sinha, 2008). Chronic stress and repeated use of addictive drugs induce long-lasting alterations of the motivation/reward circuit and HPA axis (Koob and Le Moal, 2001). The evidence presented points to Nur transcription factors as orchestrators of the molecular bases of the reorganization of these circuits under stressful stimuli and exposure to addictive drugs, since their expression is fast, transient and strongly regulated by dopamine, glutamate, and CRF in the nuclei of the motivation/reward circuit and HPA axis. The features of Nur factors as early genes and orphan nuclear receptors allow them to integrate and transmit fast responses to incoming neurotransmitter signals in neurons. The transient nature of the changes in Nur factor levels suggest that they can re-program the expression of target genes in response to acute and chronic dopamine changes by adjusting their inducibility to the new conditions, as occurring during chronic stress or after repeated exposure to drugs of abuse. Finally, the localization of Nurr1 in dopamine neurons and Nur77/Nor-1 in dopamine-receptive neurons, positions them to translate the dopaminergic information simultaneously to the genome of pre and post-synaptic neurons, allowing an integrative signaling of the motivation/reward circuit. Identifying the intracellular signaling pathways inducing Nur factors expression and their target genes is essential to elucidate their function in normal physiology as well as in addiction and anxiety disorders. These findings might offer novel targets to treat these devastating conditions.

ACKNOWLEDGMENTS

Our work cited in this manuscript was supported by FONDECYT grant N° 3085027 to Danae Campos-Melo, and FONDECYT grants N° 1070349 and 1110352 to María E. Andrés. The Millennium Nucleus in Stress and Addiction is supported by MSI grant N° P10/063-F.

REFERENCES

Aguilera, G. (1998). Corticotropin releasing hormone, receptor regulation and the stress response. *Trends Endocrinol. Metab.* 9, 329–336. doi: 10.1016/S1043-2760(98)00079-4

Akiyama, K., Isao, T., Ide, S., Ishikawa, M., and Saito, A. (2008). mRNA expression of the Nurr1 and NGFI-B nuclear receptor families following acute and chronic administration of methamphetamine. *Prog. Neuropsychopharmacol. Biol. Psychiatry* 32, 1957–1966. doi: 10.1016/j.pnpbp.2008.09.021

Alvarez-Castelao, B., Losada, F., Ahicart, P., and Castano, J. G. (2013). The N-terminal region of Nurr1 (a.a 1-31) is essential for its efficient degradation by the ubiquitin proteasome pathway. *PLoS ONE* 8:e55999. doi: 10.1371/journal.pone.0055999

Antoni, F. A. (1986). Hypothalamic control of adrenocorticotropin secretion: advances since the discovery of 41-residue corticotropin-releasing factor. *Endocr. Rev.* 7, 351–378. doi: 10.1210/edrv-7-4-351

Anzalone, A., Lizardi-Ortiz, J. E., Ramos, M., De M t al. (2012). Dual control of dopamine synthesis and release by presynaptic and postsynaptic dopamine D2 receptors. *J. Neurosci.* 32, 9023–9034. doi: 10.1523/JNEUROSCI.0918-12.2012

Arredondo, C., Orellana, M., Vecchiola, A., Pereira, L. A., Galdames, L., and Andres, M. E. (2013). PIASgamma enhanced SUMO-2 modification of Nurr1 activation-function-1 domain limits Nurr1 transcriptional synergy. *PLoS ONE* 8:e55035. doi: 10.1371/journal.pone.0055035

Backman, C., Perlmann, T., Wallen, A., Hoffer, B. J., and Morales, M. (1999). A selective group of dopaminergic neurons express Nurr1 in the adult mouse brain. *Brain Res.* 851, 125–132. doi: 10.1016/S0006-8993 (99)02149-6

Backman, C., You, Z. B., Perlmann, T., and Hoffer, B. J. (2003). Elevated locomotor activity without altered striatal dopamine contents in Nurr1 heterozygous mice after acute exposure to methamphetamine. *Behav. Brain Res.* 143, 95–100. doi: 10.1016/S0166-4328(03)00029-9

Baier, C. J., Katunar, M. R., Adrover, E., Pallares, M. E., and Antonelli, M. C. (2012). Gestational restraint stress and the

developing dopaminergic system: an overview. *Neurotox. Res.* 22, 16–32. doi: 10.1007/s12640-011-9305-4

Bannon, M. J., Pruetz, B., Barfield, E., and Schmidt, C. J. (2004). Transcription factors specifying dopamine phenotype are decreased in cocaine users. *Neuroreport* 15, 401–404. doi: 10.1097/00001756-200403010-00003

Bannon, M. J., Pruetz, B., Manning-Bog, A. B., Whitty, C. J., Michelhaugh, S. K., Sacchetti, P., et al. (2002). Decreased expression of the transcription factor NURR1 in dopamine neurons of cocaine abusers. *Proc. Natl. Acad. Sci. U.S.A.* 99, 6382–6385. doi: 10.1073/pnas.092654299

Bassett, M. H., Suzuki, T., Sasano, H., De Vries, C. J., Jimenez, P. T., Carr, B. R., et al. (2004). The orphan nuclear receptor NGFIB regulates transcription of 3beta-hydroxysteroid dehydrogenase. implications for the control of adrenal functional zonation. *J. Biol. Chem.* 279, 37622–37630. doi: 10.1074/jbc. M405431200

Beaudry, G., Langlois, M. C., Weppe, I., Rouillard, C., and Levesque, D. (2000). Contrasting patterns and cellular specificity of transcriptional regulation of the nuclear receptor nerve growth factor-inducible B by haloperidol and cloza pine in the rat forebrain. *J. Neurochem.* 75, 1694–1702. doi: 10.1046/j.1471-4159.2000.0751694.x

Benoit, G., Malewicz, M., and Perlmann, T. (2004). Digging deep into the pockets of orphan nuclear receptors: insights from structural studies. *Trends Cell Biol.* 14, 369–376. doi: 10.1016/j.tcb.2004.05.007

Bourhis, E., Maheux, J., Paquet, B., Kagechika, H., Shudo, K., Rompre, P. P., et al. (2009). The transcription factors Nur77 and retinoid X receptors participate in amphetamine-induced locomotor activities. *Psychopharmacology (Berl.)* 202, 635–648. doi: 10.1007/s00213-008-1343-0

Brosenitsch, T. A., and Katz, D. M. (2001). Physiological patterns of electrical stimulation can induce neuronal gene expression by activating N-type calcium channels. *J. Neurosci.* 21, 2571–2579.

Campos-Melo, D., Quiroz, G., Noches, V., Gysling, K., Forray, M. I., and Andres, M. E. (2011). Repeated

immobilization stress increases nur77 expression in the bed nucleus of the stria terminalis. *Neurotox. Res.* 20, 289–300. doi: 10.1007/s12640- 011-9243-1

Carpentier, R., Sacchetti, P., Segard, P., Staels, B., and Lefebvre, P. (2008). The glu- cocorticoid receptor is a co-regulator of the orphan nuclear receptor Nurr1. *J. Neurochem.* 104, 777–789. doi: 10.1111/j.1471-4159.2007.05055.x

Castillo, S. O., Baffi, J. S., Palkovits, M., Goldstein, D. S., Kopin, I. J., Witta, J., et al. (1998). Dopamine biosynthesis is selectively abolished in substantia nigra/ventral tegmental area but not in hypothalamic neurons in mice with targeted disruption of the Nurr1 gene. *Mol. Cell. Neurosci.* 11, 36–46. doi: 10.1006/mcne.1998.0673

Chan, R. K., Brown, E. R., Ericsson, A., Kovacs, K. J., and Sawchenko, P. E. (1993). A comparison of two immediate-early genes, c-fos and NGFI-B, as markers for functional activation in stress-related neuroendocrine circuitry. *J. Neurosci.* 13, 5126–5138.

Chergui, K., Svenningsson, P., Nomikos, G. G., Gonon, F., Fredholm, B. B., and Svensson, T. H. (1997). Increased expression of NGFI-A mRNA in the rat striatum following burst stimulation of the medial forebrain bundle. *Eur. J. Neurosci.* 9, 2370–2382. doi: 10.1111/j.1460-9568.1997.tb01654.x

Crawford, P. A., Sadovsky, Y., Woodson, K., Lee, S. L., and Milbrandt, J. (1995). Adrenocortical function and regulation of the steroid 21-hydroxylase gene in NGFI-B-deficient mice. *Mol. Cell. Biol.* 15, 4331.

Davis, M. I., and Puhl, H. L. 3rd. (2011). Nr4a1-eGFP is a marker of striosome- matrix architecture, development and activity in the extended striatum. *PLoS ONE* 6:e16619. doi: 10.1371/journal.pone.0016619

Deyoung, R. A., Baker, J. C., Cado, D., and Winoto, A. (2003). The orphan steroid receptor Nur77 family member Nor-1 is essential for early mouse embryogenesis. *J. Biol. Chem.* 278, 47104–47109. doi: 10.1074/jbc. M307496200

Di Chiara, G., and Imperato, A. (1988). Drugs abused by humans preferentially increase synaptic dopamine concentrations in the mesolimbic system of freely moving rats. *Proc. Natl. Acad.*

Sci. U.S.A. 85, 5274–5278. doi: 10.1073/pnas.85.14.5274

Douglas, A. J., Brunton, P. J., Bosch, O. J., Russell, J. A., and Neumann, I. D. (2003). Neuroendocrine responses to stress in mice: hyporesponsiveness in pregnancy and parturition. *Endocrinology* 144, 5268–5276. doi: 10.1210/en.2003-0461

Drouin, J., Maira, M., and Philips, A. (1998). Novel mechanism of action for Nur77 and antagonism by glucocorticoids: a convergent mechanism for CRH acti- vation and glucocorticoid repression of POMC gene transcription. *J. Steroid Biochem. Mol. Biol.* 65, 59–63. doi: 10.1016/S0960-0760(97)00180-5

Eells, J. B., Lipska, B. K., Yeung, S. K., Misler, J. A., and Nikodem, V. M. (2002). Nurr1-null heterozygous mice have reduced mesolimbic and mesocortical dopamine levels and increased stress-induced locomotor activity. *Behav. Brain Res.* 136, 267–275. doi: 10.1016/S0166-4328(02)00185-7

Eells, J. B., Misler, J. A., and Nikodem, V. M. (2006). Reduced tyrosine hydroxylase and GTP cyclohydrolase mRNA expression, tyrosine hydroxylase activity, and associated neurochemical alterations in Nurr1-null heterozygous mice. *Brain Res. Bull.* 70, 186–195. doi: 10.1016/j.brainresbull.2006.05.004

Eells, J. B., Wilcots, J., Sisk, S., and Guo-Ross, S. X. (2012). NR4A gene expression is dynamically regulated in the ventral tegmental area dopamine neurons and is related to expression of dopamine neurotransmission genes. *J. Mol. Neurosci.* 46, 545–553. doi: 10.1007/s12031-011-9642-z

Ethier, I., Beaudry, G., St-Hilaire, M., Milbrandt, J., Rouillard, C., and Levesque, D. (2004). The transcription factor NGFI-B (Nur77) and retinoids play a critical role in acute neuroleptic-induced extrapyramidal effect and striatal neuropeptide gene expression. *Neuropsychopharmacology* 29, 335–346. doi: 10.1038/sj.npp.1300318

Fernandez, P. M., Brunel, F., Jimenez, M. A., Saez, J. M., Cereghini, S., and Zakin, M. M. (2000). Nuclear receptors Nor1 and NGFI-B/Nur77 play similar, albeit distinct, roles in the hypothalamo-pituitary-adrenal axis. *Endocrinology* 141, 2392–2400. doi: 10.1210/en.141.7.2392

Forray, M. I., and Gysling, K. (2004). Role of noradrenergic projections to the bed nucleus of the stria terminalis in the regulation of the hypothalamic-pituitary-adrenal axis. *Brain Res. Brain Res. Rev.* 47, 145–160. doi: 10.1016/j.brainresrev.2004.07.011

Freeman, W. M., Brebner, K., Lynch, W. J., Patel, K. M., Robertson, D. J., Roberts, D. C., et al. (2002a). Changes in rat frontal cortex gene expression following chronic cocaine. *Brain Res. Mol. Brain Res.* 104, 11–20. doi: 10.1016/S0169- 328X(02)00197-3

Freeman, W. M., Brebner, K., Patel, K. M., Lynch, W. J., Roberts, D. C., and Vrana, K. E. (2002b). Repeated cocaine self-administration causes multiple changes in rat frontal cortex gene expression. *Neurochem. Res.* 27, 1181–1192. doi: 10.1023/A:1020929526688

Galleguillos, D., Fuentealba, J. A., Gomez, L. M., Saver, M., Gomez, A., Nash, K., et al. (2010). Nurr1 regulates RET expression in dopamine neurons of adult rat midbrain. *J. Neurochem.* 114, 1158–1167. doi: 10.1111/j.1471-4159.2010.06841.x

Galleguillos, D., Vecchiola, A., Fuentealba, J. A., Ojeda, V., Alvarez, K., Gomez, A., et al. (2004). PIASgamma represses the transcriptional activation induced by the nuclear receptor Nurr1. *J. Biol. Chem.* 279, 2005–2011. doi: 10.1074/jbc.M308113200

Gervais, J., Soghomonian, J. J., Richard, D., and Rouillard, C. (1999). Dopamine and serotonin interactions in the modulation of the expression of the immediate-early transcription factor, nerve growth factor-inducible B, in the striatum. *Neuroscience* 91, 1045–1054. doi: 10.1016/S0306-4522(98)00688-5

Giguere, V. (1999). Orphan nuclear receptors: from gene to function. *Endocr. Rev.* 20, 689–725. doi: 10.1210/er.20.5.689

Gilbert, F., Morissette, M., St-Hilaire, M., Paquet, B., Rouillard, C., Di Paolo, T., et al. (2006). Nur77 gene knockout alters dopamine neuron biochem- ical activity and dopamine turnover. *Biol. Psychiatry* 60, 538–547. doi: 10.1016/j.biopsych.2006.04.023

Gofflot, F., Chartoire, N., Vasseur, L., Heikkinen, S., Dembele, D., Le Merrer, J., et al. (2007). Systematic gene expression mapping clusters nuclear recep- tors according to their function in the brain. *Cell* 131, 405–418. doi: 10.1016/j.cell.2007.09.012

Hazel, T. G., Nathans, D., and Lau, L. F. (1988). A gene inducible by serum growth factors encodes a member of the steroid and thyroid hormone receptor super- family. *Proc. Natl. Acad. Sci. U.S.A.* 85, 8444–8448. doi: 10.1073/pnas.85.22.8444

Herman, J. P., Cullinan, W. E., Ziegler, D. R., and Tasker, J. G. (2002). Role of the paraventricular nucleus microenvironment in stress integration. *Eur. J. Neurosci.* 16, 381–385. doi: 10.1046/j.1460-9568.2002.02133.x

Hermanson, E., Joseph, B., Castro, D., Lindqvist, E., Aarnisalo, P., Wallen, A., et al. (2003). Nurr1 regulates dopamine synthesis and storage in MN9D dopamine cells. *Exp. Cell Res.* 288, 324–334. doi: 10.1016/S0014-4827(03) 00216-7

Honkaniemi, J., Kononen, J., Kainu, T., Pyykonen, I., and Pelto-Huikko, M. (1994). Induction of multiple immediate early genes in rat hypothalamic par- aventricular nucleus after stress. *Brain Res. Mol. Brain Res.* 25, 234–241. doi: 10.1016/0169-328X(94)90158-9

Honkaniemi, J., and Sharp, F. R. (1999). Prolonged expression of zinc fin- ger immediate-early gene mRNAs and decreased protein synthesis following kainic acid induced seizures. *Eur. J. Neurosci.* 11, 10–17. doi: 10.1046/j.1460- 9568.1999.00401.x

Horvath, M. C., Kovacs, G. G., Kovari, V., Majtenyi, K., Hurd, Y. L., and Keller, E. (2007). Heroin abuse is characterized by discrete mesolimbic dopamine and opioid abnormalities and exaggerated nuclear receptor-related 1 transcriptional decline with age. *J. Neurosci.* 27, 13371–13375. doi: 10.1523/JNEUROSCI.2398-07.2007

Imaki, T., Shibasaki, T., Chikada, N., Harada, S., Naruse, M., and Demura, H. (1996). Different expression of immediate-early genes in the rat paraventric- ular nucleus induced by stress: relation to corticotropin-releasing factor gene transcription. *Endocr. J.* 43, 629–638. doi: 10.1507/endocrj.43.629

Iwaki, T., Kohno, K., and Kobayashi, K. (2000). Identification of a potential nurr1 response element that activates the tyrosine hydroxylase gene pro- moter in cultured cells. *Biochem. Biophys. Res. Commun.* 274, 590–595. doi: 10.1006/bbrc.2000.3204

Jacobs, F. M., van Erp, S., van der Linden, A. J., von Oerthel, L., Burbach, J. P., and Smidt, M. P. (2009). Pitx3 potentiates Nurr1 in dopamine neuron terminal differentiation through release of SMRT-mediated repression. *Development* 136, 531–540. doi: 10.1242/dev.029769

Jacobs, O., Van Bree, L., Mailleux, P., Zhang, F., Schiffmann, S. N., Halleux, P., et al. (1994). Homolateral cerebrocortical increase of immediate early gene and neurotransmitter messenger RNAs after minimal cortical lesion: blockade by N-methyl-D-aspartate antagonist. *Neuroscience* 59, 827–836. doi: 10.1016/0306- 4522(94)90287-9

Jiang, C., Wan, X., He, Y., Pan, T., Jankovic, J., and Le, W. (2005). Age-dependent dopaminergic dysfunction in Nurr1 knockout mice. *Exp. Neurol.* 191, 154–162. doi: 10.1016/j.expneurol.2004.08.035

Johnson, M. M., Michelhaugh, S. K., Bouhamdan, M., Schmidt, C. J., and Bannon, M. J. (2011). The transcription factor NURR1 exerts concentration-dependent effects on target genes mediating distinct biological processes. *Front. Neurosci.* 5:135. doi: 10.3389/fnins.2011.00135

Kadkhodaei, B., Alvarsson, A., Schintu, N., Ramskold, D., Volakakis, N., Joodmardi, E., et al. (2013). Transcription factor Nurr1 maintains fiber integrity and nuclearencoded mitochondrial gene expression in dopamine neurons. *Proc. Natl. Acad. Sci. U.S.A.* 110, 2360–2365. doi: 10.1073/pnas.1221077110

Kadkhodaei, B., Ito, T., Joodmardi, E., Mattsson, B., Rouillard, C., Carta, M., et al. (2009). Nurr1 is required for maintenance of maturing and adult midbrain dopamine neurons. *J. Neurosci.* 29, 15923–15932. doi: 10.1523/JNEUROSCI.3910-09.2009

Kang, S. A., Na, H., Kang, H. J., Kim, S. H., Lee, M. H., and Lee, M. O. (2010). Regulation of Nur77 protein turnover through acetylation and deacetylation induced by p300 and HDAC1. *Biochem. Pharmacol.* 80, 867–873. doi: 10.1016/j.bcp.2010.04.026

Katagiri, Y., Takeda, K., Yu, Z. X., Ferrans, V. J., Ozato, K., and Guroff, G. (2000). Modulation of retinoid signalling through NGF-induced nuclear export of NGFI-B. *Nat. Cell Biol.* 2, 435–440. doi: 10.1038/35017072

Katunar, M. R., Saez, T., Brusco, A., and Antonelli, M. C. (2009). Immunocytochemical expression of dopamine-related transcription factors Pitx3 and Nurr1 in prenatally stressed adult rats. *J. Neurosci. Res.* 87, 1014–1022. doi: 10.1002/jnr.21911

Katunar, M. R., Saez, T., Brusco, A., and Antonelli, M. C. (2010). Ontogenetic expression of dopamine-related transcription factors and tyrosine hydroxylase in prenatally stressed rats. *Neurotox. Res.* 18, 69–81. doi: 10.1007/s12640-009- 9132-z

Kawasaki, M., Yamaguchi, K., Saito, J., Ozaki, Y., Mera, T., Hashimoto, H., et al. (2005). Expression of immediate early genes and vasopressin heteronuclear RNA in the paraventricular and supraoptic nuclei of rats after acute osmotic stimulus. *J. Neuroendocrinol.* 17, 227–237. doi: 10.1111/j.1365-2826.2005.01297.x

Keller-Wood, M. E., and Dallman, M. F. (1984). Corticosteroid inhibition of ACTH secretion. *Endocr. Rev.* 5, 1–24. doi: 10.1210/edrv-5-1-1

Kim, K. S., Kim, C. H., Hwang, D. Y., Seo, H., Chung, S., Hong, S. J., et al. (2003). Orphan nuclear receptor Nurr1 directly transactivates the promoter activity of the tyrosine hydroxylase gene in a cell-specific manner. *J. Neurochem.* 85, 622–634. doi: 10.1046/j.1471-4159.2003.01671.x

Koob, G. F. (2008). A role for brain stress systems in addiction. *Neuron* 59, 11–34. doi: 10.1016/j.neuron.2008.06.012

Koob, G. F., and Le Moal, M. (2001). Drug addiction, dysregulation of reward, and allostasis. *Neuropsychopharmacology* 24, 97–129. doi: 10.1016/S0893-133X(00)00195-0

Kovalovsky, D., Refojo, D., Liberman, A. C., Hochbaum, D., Pereda, M. P., Coso, O. A., et al. (2002). Activation and induction of NUR77/NURR1 in corticotrophs by CRH/cAMP: involvement of calcium, protein kinase A, and MAPK pathways. *Mol. Endocrinol.* 16, 1638–1651. doi: 10.1210/me. 16.7.1638

Krasnova, I. N., Ladenheim, B., Hodges, A. B., Volkow, N.

D., and Cadet, J. L. (2011). Chronic methamphetamine administration causes differential regula- tion of transcription factors in the rat midbrain. *PLoS ONE* 6:e19179. doi: 10.1371/journal.pone.0019179

Lammi, J., Perlmann, T., and Aarnisalo, P. (2008). Corepressor interaction differ- entiates the permissive and non-permissive retinoid X receptor heterodimers. *Arch. Biochem. Biophys.* 472, 105–114. doi: 10.1016/j.abb.2008.02.003

Langlois, M. C., Beaudry, G., Zekki, H., Rouillard, C., and Levesque, D. (2001). Impact of antipsychotic drug administration on the expression of nuclear recep- tors in the neocortex and striatum of the rat brain. *Neuroscience* 106, 117–128. doi: 10.1016/S0306-4522(01)00248-2

Law, S. W., Conneely, O. M., Demayo, F. J., and O'Malley, B. W. (1992). Identification of a new brain-specific transcription factor, NURR1. *Mol. Endocrinol.* 6, 2129–2135. doi: 10.1210/me.6.12.2129

Le, W., Conneely, O. M., He, Y., Jankovic, J., and Appel, S. H. (1999). Reduced Nurr1 expression increases the vulnerability of mesencephalic dopamine neurons to MPTP-induced injury. *J. Neurochem.* 73, 2218–2221. doi: 10.1046/j.1471-4159.1999.02218.x

Lee, S. O., Li, X., Khan, S., and Safe, S. (2011). Targeting NR4A1 (TR3) in cancer cells and tumors. *Expert Opin. Ther. Targets* 15, 195–206. doi: 10.1517/14728222.2011.547481

Leo, D., di Porzio, U., Racagni, G., Riva, M. A., Fumagalli, F., and Perrone-Capano, C. (2007). Chronic cocaine administration modulates the expression of transcription factors involved in midbrain dopaminergic neuron function. *Exp. Neurol.* 203, 472–480. doi: 10.1016/j.expneurol.2006.08.024

Levesque, D., and Rouillard, C. (2007). Nur77 and retinoid X receptors: crucial factors in dopamine-related neuroadaptation. *Trends Neurosci.* 30, 22–30. doi: 10.1016/j.tins.2006.11.006

Li, H., Kolluri, S. K., Gu, J., Dawson, M. I., Cao, X., Hobbs, P. D., et al. (2000). Cytochrome c release and apoptosis induced by mitochondrial targeting of nuclear orphan receptor TR3. *Science* 289, 1159–1164. doi: 10.1126/sci- ence.289.5482.1159

Lynch, W. J., Girgenti, M. J., Breslin, F. J., Newton, S. S., and Taylor, J. R. (2008). Gene profiling the response to repeated cocaine self-administration in dorsal striatum: a focus on circadian genes. *Brain Res.* 1213, 166–177. doi: 10.1016/j.brainres.2008.02.106

Maheux, J., Ethier, I., Rouillard, C., and Levesque, D. (2005). Induction patterns of transcription factors of the nur family (nurr1, nur77, and nor-1) by typical and atypical antipsychotics in the mouse brain: implication for their mechanism of action. *J. Pharmacol. Exp. Ther.* 313, 460–473. doi: 10.1124/jpet.104.080184

Maheux, J., St-Hilaire, M., Voyer, D., Tirotta, E., Borrelli, E., Rouillard, C., et al. (2012). Dopamine D(2) antagonist-induced striatal Nur77 expression requires activation of mGlu5 receptors by cortical afferents. *Front. Pharmacol.* 3:153. doi: 10.3389/fphar.2012.00153

Mahmoudi, S., Blanchet, P. J., and Levesque, D. (2013). Haloperidol-induced stri- atal Nur77 expression in a non-human primate model of tardive dyskinesia. *Eur. J. Neurosci.* 38, 2192–2198. doi: 10.1111/ejn.12198

Mahmoudi, S., Samadi, P., Gilbert, F., Ouattara, B., Morissette, M., Gregoire, L., et al. (2009). Nur77 mRNA levels and L-Dopa-induced dyskinesias in MPTP monkeys treated with docosahaexaenoic acid. *Neurobiol. Dis.* 36, 213–222. doi: 10.1016/j.nbd.2009.07.017

Maira, M., Martens, C., Batsche, E., Gauthier, Y., and Drouin, J. (2003). Dimer-specific potentiation of NGFI-B (Nur77) transcriptional activity by the protein kinase A pathway and AF-1-dependent coactivator recruitment. *Mol. Cell. Biol.* 23, 763–776. doi: 10.1128/MCB.23.3.763-776.2003

Maira, M., Martens, C., Philips, A., and Drouin, J. (1999). Heterodimerization between members of the Nur subfamily of orphan nuclear receptors as a novel mechanism for gene activation. *Mol. Cell. Biol.* 19, 7549–7557.

Martens, C., Bilodeau, S., Maira, M., Gauthier, Y., and Drouin, J. (2005). Protein-protein interactions and transcriptional antagonism between the subfamily of NGFI-B/Nur77 orphan nuclear receptors and glucocorticoid receptor. *Mol. Endocrinol.* 19,

885–897. doi: 10.1210/me.2004-0333

Maruyama, K., Tsukada, T., Bandoh, S., Sasaki, K., Ohkura, N., and Yamaguchi, K. (1995). Expression of NOR-1 and its closely related members of the steroid/thyroid hormone receptor superfamily in human neuroblastoma cell lines. *Cancer Lett.* 96, 117–122. doi: 10.1016/0304-3835(95)03921-I

Maxwell, M. A., and Muscat, G. E. (2006). The NR4A subgroup: immediate early response genes with pleiotropic physiological roles. *Nucl. Recept. Signal.* 4, e002. doi: 10.1621/nrs.04002

McCormick, C. M., and Green, M. R. (2013). From the stressed adolescent to the anxious and depressed adult: investigations in rodent models. *Neuroscience* 249, 242–257. doi: 10.1016/j.neuroscience.2012.08.063

McCoy, M. T., Jayanthi, S., Wulu, J. A., Beauvais, G., Ladenheim, B., Martin, A., et al. (2011). Chronic methamphetamine exposure suppresses the stri- atal expression of members of multiple families of immediate early genes (IEGs) in the rat: normalization by an acute methamphetamine injection. *Psychopharmacology (Berl.)* 215, 353–365. doi: 10.1007/s00213-010-2146-7

McMorrow, J. P., and Murphy, E. P. (2011). Inflammation: a role for NR4A orphan nuclear receptors? *Biochem. Soc. Trans.* 39, 688–693. doi: 10.1042/BST0390688

Milbrandt, J. (1988). Nerve growth factor induces a gene homologous to the glucocorticoid receptor gene. *Neuron* 1, 183–188. doi: 10.1016/0896-6273(88) 90138-9

Moga, M. M., and Saper, C. B. (1994). Neuropeptide-immunoreactive neurons projecting to the paraventricular hypothalamic nucleus in the rat. *J. Comp. Neurol.* 346, 137–150. doi: 10.1002/cne.903460110

Moga, M. M., Saper, C. B., and Gray, T. S. (1989). Bed nucleus of the stria terminalis: cytoarchitecture, immunohistochemistry, and projection to the parabrachial nucleus in the rat. *J. Comp. Neurol.* 283, 315–332. doi: 10.1002/cne.902830302

Mohan, H. M., Aherne, C. M., Rogers, A. C., Baird, A. W., Winter, D. C., and Murphy, E. P. (2012). Molecular pathways: the role of NR4A orphan

nuclear receptors in cancer. *Clin. Cancer Res.* 18, 3223–3228. doi: 10.1158/1078- 0432.CCR-11-2953

Moore, T. M., Brown, T., Cade, M., and Eells, J. B. (2008). Alterations in amphetamine-stimulated dopamine overflow due to the Nurr1-null het- erozygous genotype and postweaning isolation. *Synapse* 62, 764–774. doi: 10.1002/syn.20550

Mullican, S. E., Zhang, S., Konopleva, M., Ruvolo, V., Andreeff, M., Milbrandt, J., et al. (2007). Abrogation of nuclear receptors Nr4a3 and Nr4a1 leads to development of acute myeloid leukemia. *Nat. Med.* 13, 730–735. doi: 10.1038/nm1579

Murphy, E. P., and Conneely, O. M. (1997). Neuroendocrine regulation of the hypothalamic pituitary adrenal axis by the nurr1/nur77 subfamily of nuclear receptors. *Mol. Endocrinol.* 11, 39–47. doi: 10.1210/me.11.1.39

Murphy, E. P., Dobson, A. D., Keller, C., and Conneely, O. M. (1996). Differential regulation of transcription by the NURR1/NUR77 subfamily of nuclear tran- scription factors. *Gene Expr.* 5, 169–179.

Nielsen, D. A., Ji, F., Yuferov, V., Ho, A., Chen, A., Levran, O., et al. (2008). Genotype patterns that contribute to increased risk for or protection from developing heroin addiction. *Mol. Psychiatry* 13, 417–428. doi: 10.1038/sj.mp.4002147

Nordzell, M., Aarnisalo, P., Benoit, G., Castro, D. S., and Perlmann, T. (2004). Defining an N-terminal activation domain of the orphan nuclear receptor Nurr1. *Biochem. Biophys. Res. Commun.* 313, 205–211. doi: 10.1016/j.bbrc.2003.11.079

Ohkura, N., Ito, M., Tsukada, T., Sasaki, K., Yamaguchi, K., and Miki, K. (1996). Structure, mapping and expression of a human NOR-1 gene, the third mem- ber of the Nur77/NGFI-B family. *Biochim. Biophys. Acta* 1308, 205–214. doi: 10.1016/0167-4781(96)00101-7

Ojeda, V., Fuentealba, J. A., Galleguillos, D., and Andres, M. E. (2003). Rapid increase of Nurr1 expression in the substantia nigra after 6-hydroxydopamine lesion in the striatum of the rat.

J. Neurosci. Res. 73, 686–697. doi: 10.1002/jnr.10705

Parkes, D., Rivest, S., Lee, S., Rivier, C., and Vale, W. (1993). Corticotropin releasing factor activates c-fos, NGFI-B, and corticotropin-releasing factor gene expression within the paraventricular nucleus of the rat hypothalamus. *Mol. Endocrinol.* 7, 1357–1367. doi: 10.1210/me.7.10.1357

Paulsen, R. F., Granas, K., Johnsen, H., Rolseth, V., and Sterri, S. (1995). Three related brain nuclear receptors, NGFI-B, Nurr1, and NOR-1, as transcriptional activators. *J. Mol. Neurosci.* 6, 249–255. doi: 10.1007/BF02736784

Pelton, G. H., Lee, Y., and Davis, M. (1997). Repeated stress, like vasopressin, sensi- tizes the excitatory effects of corticotropin releasing factor on the acoustic startle reflex. *Brain Res.* 778, 381–387. doi: 10.1016/S0006-8993(97)00669-0

Perlmann, T., and Jansson, L. (1995). A novel pathway for vitamin A signaling mediated by RXR heterodimerization with NGFI-B and NURR1. *Genes Dev.* 9, 769–782. doi: 10.1101/gad.9.7.769

Perlmann, T., and Wallen-Mackenzie, A. (2004). Nurr1, an orphan nuclear receptor with essential functions in developing dopamine cells. *Cell Tissue Res.* 318, 45–52. doi: 10.1007/s00441-004-0974-7

Philips, A., Lesage, S., Gingras, R., Maira, M. H., Gauthier, Y., Hugo, P., et al. (1997). Novel dimeric Nur77 signaling mechanism in endocrine and lymphoid cells. *Mol. Cell. Biol.* 17, 5946–5951.

Ponnio, T., Burton, Q., Pereira, F. A., Wu, D. K., and Conneely, O. M. (2002). The nuclear receptor Nor-1 is essential for proliferation of the semicircular canals of the mouse inner ear. *Mol. Cell. Biol.* 22, 935–945. doi: 10.1128/MCB.22.3.935-945.2002

Ponnio, T., and Conneely, O. M. (2004). nor-1 regulates hippocampal axon guidance, pyramidal cell survival, and seizure susceptibility. *Mol. Cell. Biol.* 24, 9070–9078. doi: 10.1128/MCB.24.20.9070-9078.2004

Rogge, G. A., Singh, H., Dang, R., and Wood, M. A. (2013). HDAC3 is a negative regulator of cocaine-context-associated memory formation. *J. Neurosci.* 33, 6623–6632. doi: 10.1523/JNEUROSCI.4472-12.2013

Rojas, P., Joodmardi, E., Hong, Y., Perlmann, T., and Ogren, S. O. (2007). Adult mice with reduced Nurr1 expression: an animal model for schizophrenia. *Mol. Psychiatry* 12, 756–766. doi: 10.1038/sj.mp.4001993

Rojas, P., Joodmardi, E., Perlmann, T., and Ogren, S. O. (2010). Rapid increase of Nurr1 mRNA expression in limbic and cortical brain structures related to cop- ing with depression-like behavior in mice. *J. Neurosci. Res.* 88, 2284–2293. doi: 10.1002/jnr.22377

Sacchetti, P., Carpentier, R., Segard, P., Olive-Cren, C., and Lefebvre, P. (2006). Multiple signaling pathways regulate the transcriptional activity of the orphan nuclear receptor NURR1. *Nucleic Acids Res.* 34, 5515–5527. doi: 10.1093/nar/gkl712

Sacchetti, P., Mitchell, T. R., Granneman, J. G., and Bannon, M. J. (2001). Nurr1 enhances transcription of the human dopamine transporter gene through a novel mechanism. *J. Neurochem.* 76, 1565–1572. doi: 10.1046/j.1471-4159.2001.00181.x

Saijo, K., Winner, B., Carson, C. T., Collier, J. G., Boyer, L., Rosenfeld, M. G., et al. (2009). A Nurr1/CoREST pathway in microglia and astrocytes protects dopaminergic neurons from inflammation-induced death. *Cell* 137, 47–59. doi: 10.1016/j.cell.2009.01.038

Sakanaka, M., Shibasaki, T., and Lederis, K. (1986). Distribution and efferent pro- jections of corticotropin-releasing factor-like immunoreactivity in the rat amyg- daloid complex. *Brain Res.* 382, 213–238. doi: 10.1016/0006-8993(86)91332-6

Sakurada, K., Ohshima-Sakurada, M., Palmer, T. D., and Gage, F. H. (1999). Nurr1, an orphan nuclear receptor, is a transcriptional activator of endogenous tyrosine hydroxylase in neural progenitor cells derived from the adult brain. *Development* 126, 4017–4026.

Santibanez, M., Gysling, K., and Forray, M. I. (2006). Desipramine prevents the sustained increase in corticotropin-releasing hormone-like immunoreactivity induced by repeated immobilization stress in the rat central extended amygdala. *J. Neurosci. Res.* 84, 1270–1281. doi: 10.1002/jnr.21023

Satoh, J., and Kuroda, Y. (2002). The constitutive and inducible expression of Nurr1, a key regulator of dopaminergic

neuronal differentiation, in human neu- ral and non-neural cell lines. *Neuropathology* 22, 219–232. doi: 10.1046/j.1440-1789.2002.00460.x

Saucedo-Cardenas, O., and Conneely, O. M. (1996). Comparative distribution of NURR1 and NUR77 nuclear receptors in the mouse central nervous system. *J. Mol. Neurosci.* 7, 51–63. doi: 10.1007/BF02736848

Saucedo-Cardenas, O., Quintana-Hau, J. D., Le, W. D., Smidt, M. P., Cox, J. J., De Mayo, F., et al. (1998). Nurr1 is essential for the induction of the dopamin-ergic phenotype and the survival of ventral mesencephalic late dopamin- ergic precursor neurons. *Proc. Natl. Acad. Sci. U.S.A.* 95, 4013–4018. doi: 10.1073/pnas.95.7.4013

Sawchenko, P. E., and Swanson, L. W. (1985). Localization, colocalization, and plasticity of corticotropin-releasing factor immunoreactivity in rat brain. *Fed. Proc.* 44, 221–227.

Schiltz, C. A., Kelley, A. E., and Landry, C. F. (2007). Acute stress and nicotine cues interact to unveil locomotor arousal and activity-dependent gene expression in the prefrontal cortex. *Biol. Psychiatry* 61, 127–135. doi: 10.1016/j.biopsych.2006.03.002

Silverman, A. J., Hou-Yu, A., and Chen, W. P. (1989). Corticotropin-releasing factor synapses within the paraventricular nucleus of the hypothalamus. *Neuroendocrinology* 49, 291–299. doi: 10.1159/000125131

Sinha, R. (2008). Chronic stress, drug use, and vulnerability to addiction. *Ann. N.Y. Acad. Sci.* 1141, 105–130. doi: 10.1196/annals.1441.030

Slagsvold, H. H., Ostvold, A. C., Fallgren, A. B., and Paulsen, R. E. (2002). Nuclear receptor and apoptosis initiator NGFI-B is a substrate for kinase ERK2. *Biochem. Biophys. Res. Commun.* 291, 1146–1150. doi: 10.1006/bbrc.2002.6579

Smidt, M. P., Smits, S. M., and Burbach, J. P. (2003). Molecular mechanisms underlying midbrain dopamine neuron development and function. *Eur. J. Pharmacol.* 480, 75–88. doi: 10.1016/j.ejphar.2003.08.094

Smits, S. M., Ponnio, T., Conneely, O. M., Burbach, J. P., and Smidt, M. P. (2003). Involvement of Nurr1 in specifying the neurotransmitter identity of ventral midbrain dopaminergic neurons. *Eur. J. Neurosci.* 18, 1731–1738. doi: 10.1046/j.1460-

9568.2003.02885.x

Sohn, S. J., Thompson, J., and Winoto, A. (2007). Apoptosis during negative selection of autoreactive thymocytes. *Curr. Opin. Immunol.* 19, 510–515. doi: 10.1016/j.coi.2007.06.001

Sohn, Y. C., Kwak, E., Na, Y., Lee, J. W., and Lee, S. K. (2001). Silencing mediator of retinoid and thyroid hormone receptors and activating signal cointegrator-2 as transcriptional coregulators of the orphan nuclear receptor Nur77. *J. Biol. Chem.* 276, 43734–43739. doi: 10.1074/jbc.M107208200

Stenzel-Poore, M. P., Heinrichs, S. C., Rivest, S., Koob, G. F., and Vale, W. W. (1994). Overproduction of corticotropin-releasing factor in transgenic mice: a genetic model of anxiogenic behavior. *J. Neurosci.* 14, 2579–2584.

St-Hilaire, M., Bourhis, E., Levesque, D., and Rouillard, C. (2006). Impaired behavioural and molecular adaptations to dopamine denervation and repeated L-DOPA treatment in Nur77-knockout mice. *Eur. J. Neurosci.* 24, 795–805. doi: 10.1111/j.1460-9568.2006.04954.x

St-Hilaire, M., Landry, E., Levesque, D., and Rouillard, C. (2003a). Denervation and repeated L-DOPA induce a coordinate expression of the transcription factor NGFI-B in striatal projection pathways in hemi-parkinsonian rats. *Neurobiol. Dis.* 14, 98–109. doi: 10.1016/S0969-9961(03)00081-0

St-Hilaire, M., Tremblay, P. O., Levesque, D., Barden, N., and Rouillard, C. (2003b). Effects of cocaine on c-fos and NGFI-B mRNA expression in trans- genic mice underexpressing glucocorticoid receptors. *Neuropsychopharmacology* 28, 478–489. doi: 10.1038/sj.npp.1300067

St-Hilaire, M., Landry, E., Levesque, D., and Rouillard, C. (2005). Denervation and repeated L-DOPA induce complex regulatory changes in neurochemical pheno- types of striatal neurons: implication of a dopamine D1-dependent mechanism. *Neurobiol. Dis.* 20, 450–460. doi: 10.1016/j.nbd.2005.04.001

Stout, S. C., Mortas, P., Owens, M. J., Nemeroff, C. B., and Moreau, J. (2000). Increased corticotropin-releasing factor concentrations in the bed nucleus of the stria terminalis of anhedonic rats. *Eur. J. Pharmacol.* 401, 39–46. doi:

10.1016/S0014-2999(00)00412-X

Stroth, N., Liu, Y., Aguilera, G., and Eiden, L. E. (2011). Pituitary adeny late cyclase-activating polypeptide controls stimulus-transcription coupling in the hypothalamic-pituitary-adrenal axis to mediate sustained hormone secretion during stress. *J. Neuroendocrinol.* 23, 944–955. doi: 10.1111/j.1365-2826.2011.02202.x

Sun, W., Choi, S. H., Park, S. K., Kim, S. J., Noh, M. R., Kim, E. H., et al. (2007). Identification and characterization of novel activity-dependenttran-scription factors in rat cortical neurons. *J. Neurochem.* 100, 269–278. doi: 10.1111/j.1471-4159.2006.04214.x

Svenningsson, P., and Fredholm, B. B. (1997). Caffeine mimics the effect of a dopamine D2/3 receptor agonist on the expression of immediate early genes in globus pallidus. *Neuropharmacology* 36, 1309–1317. doi: 10.1016/S0028-3908(97)00091-9

Svenningsson, P., Nomikos, G. G., and Fredholm, B. B. (1995). Biphasic changes in locomotor behavior and in expression of mRNA for NGFI-A and NGFI- B in rat striatum following acute caffeine administration. *J. Neurosci.* 15, 7612–7624.

Swanson, L. W., and Simmons, D. M. (1989). Differential steroid hormone and neural influences on peptide mRNA levels in CRH cells of the paraventricular nucleus: a hybridization histochemical study in the rat. *J. Comp. Neurol.* 285, 413–435. doi: 10.1002/cne.902850402

Tang, Y. P., Murata, Y., Nagaya, T., Noda, Y., Seo, H., and Nabeshima, T. (1997). NGFI-B, c-fos, and c-jun mRNA expression in mouse brain after acute carbon monoxide intoxication. *J. Cereb. Blood Flow Metab.* 17, 771–780. doi: 10.1097/00004647-199707000-00007

Tseng, K. Y., Roubert, C., Do, L., Rubinstein, M., Kelly, M. A., Grandy, D. K., et al. (2000). Selective increase of Nurr1 mRNA expression in mesencephalic dopaminergic neurons of D2 dopamine receptor-deficient mice. *Brain Res. Mol. Brain Res.* 80, 1–6. doi: 10.1016/S0169-328X(00)00107-8

Umemoto, S., Kawai, Y., and Senba, E. (1994). Differential regulation of IEGs in the rat PVH in single and repeated stress models. *Neuroreport* 6, 201–204. doi: 10.1097/00001756-199412300-00051

Umemoto, S., Kawai, Y., Ueyama, T., and Senba, E. (1997). Chronic glucocorticoid administration as well as repeated stress affects the subsequent acute immo- bilization stress-induced expression of immediate early genes but not that of NGFI-A. *Neuroscience* 80, 763–773. doi: 10.1016/S0306-4522(97)00050-X

Valjent, E., Bertran-Gonzalez, J., Herve, D., Fisone, G., and Girault, J. A. (2009). Looking BAC at striatal signaling: cell-specific analysis in new transgenic mice. *Trends Neurosci.* 32, 538–547. doi: 10.1016/j.tins.2009.06.005

van Tiel, C. M., and de Vries, C. J. (2012). NR4All in the vessel wall. *J. Steroid Biochem. Mol. Biol.* 130, 186–193. doi: 10.1016/j.jsbmb.2011.01.010

van Tiel, C. M., Kurakula, K., Koenis, D. S., van der Wal, E., and de Vries, C. J. (2012). Dual function of Pin1 in NR4A nuclear receptor activation: enhanced activity of NR4As and increased Nur77 protein stability. *Biochim. Biophys. Acta* 1823, 1894–1904. doi: 10.1016/j.bbamcr.2012.06.030

Veinante, P., Stoeckel, M. E., and Freund-Mercier, M. J. (1997). GABA- and peptide-immunoreactivities co-localize in the rat central extended amygdala. *Neuroreport* 8, 2985–2989. doi: 10.1097/00001756-199709080-00035

Vuillermot, S., Joodmardi, E., Perlmann, T., Ove Ogren, S., Feldon, J., and Meyer,(2011). Schizophrenia-relevant behaviors in a genetic mouse model of constitutive Nurr1 deficiency. *Genes Brain Behav.* 10, 589–603. doi: 10.1111/j.1601-183X.2011.00698.x

Walker, D. L., Miles, L. A., and Davis, M. (2009). Selective participation of the bed nucleus of the stria terminalis and CRF in sustained anxiety-like versus phasic fear-like responses. *Prog. Neuropsychopharmacol. Biol. Psychiatry* 33, 1291–1308. doi: 10.1016/j.pnpbp.2009.06.022

Walker, D. L., Toufexis, D. J., and Davis, M. (2003). Role of the bed nucleus of the stria terminalis versus the amygdala in fear, stress, and anxiety. *Eur. J. Pharmacol.* 463, 199–216. doi: 10.1016/S0014-2999(03)01282-2

Wallen, A. A., Castro, D. S., Zetterstrom, R. H., Karlen, M., Olson, L., Ericson, J., et al. (2001). Orphan nuclear receptor Nurr1 is essential for Ret expression in midbrain dopamine neurons and in the brain stem. *Mol. Cell. Neurosci.* 18, 649–663. doi: 10.1006/mcne.2001.1057

Wang, Z., Benoit, G., Liu, J., Prasad, S., Aarnisalo, P., Liu, X., et al. (2003). Structure and function of Nurr1 identifies a class of ligand-independent nuclear receptors. *Nature* 423, 555–560. doi: 10.1038/nature01645

Werme, M., Hermanson, E., Carmine, A., Buervenich, S., Zetterstrom, R. H., Thoren, P., et al. (2003). Decreased ethanol preference and wheel running in Nurr1-deficient mice. *Eur. J. Neurosci.* 17, 2418–2424. doi: 10.1046/j.1460-9568.2003.02666.x

Werme, M., Olson, L., and Brene, S. (2000a). NGFI-B and nor1 mRNAs are upregulated in brain reward pathways by drugs of abuse: different effects in Fischer andLewisrats.*BrainRes.Mol.Brain Res.* 76,18–24.doi:10.1016/S0169-328X(99)00327-7

Werme, M., Ringholm, A., Olson, L., and Brene, S. (2000b). Differential patterns of induction of NGFI-B, Nor1 and c-fos mRNAs in striatal subregions by haloperidol and clozapine. *Brain Res.* 863, 112–119. doi: 10.1016/S0006- 8993(00)02109-0

Werme, M., Thoren, P., Olson, L., and Brene, S. (1999). Addiction-prone Lewis but not Fischer rats develop compulsive running that coincides with downregula-tion of nerve growth factor inducible-B and neuron-derived orphan receptor 1. *J. Neurosci.* 19, 6169–6174.

Williams, G. T., and Lau, L. F. (1993). Activation of the inducible orphan receptor gene nur77 by serum growth factors: dissociation of immediate- early and delayed-early responses. *Mol. Cell. Biol.* 13, 6124–6136. doi: 10.1128/MCB.13.10.6124

Wilson, T. E., Fahrner, T. J., Johnston, M., and Milbrandt, J. (1991). Identification of the DNA binding site for NGFI-B by genetic selection in yeast. *Science* 252, 1296–1300. doi: 10.1126/science.1925541

Wilson, T. E., Fahrner, T. J., and Milbrandt, J. (1993a). The orphan receptors NGFI-B and steroidogenic factor 1 establish monomer binding as a third paradigm of nuclear receptor-DNA interaction. *Mol. Cell. Biol.* 13, 5794–5804. doi: 10.1128/MCB.13.9.5794

Wilson, T. E., Mouw, A. R., Weaver, C. A., Milbrandt, J., and Parker, K. L. (1993b). The orphan nuclear receptor NGFI-B regulates expression of the gene encoding steroid 21-hydroxylase. *Mol. Cell. Biol.* 13, 861–868. doi: 10.1128/MCB.13.2.861

Wingate, A. D., Campbell, D. G., Peggie, M., and Arthur, J. S. (2006). Nur77 is phosphorylated in cells by RSK in response to mitogenic stimulation. *Biochem. J.* 393, 715–724. doi: 10.1042/BJ20050967

Xiao, Q., Castillo, S. O., and Nikodem, V. M. (1996). Distribution of messenger RNAs for the orphan nuclear receptors Nurr1 and Nur77 (NGFI-B) in adult rat brain using *in situ* hybridization. *Neuroscience* 75, 221–230. doi: 10.1016/0306- 4522(96)00159-5

Xing, G., Zhang, L., Zhang, L., Heynen, T., Li, X. L., Smith, M. A., et al. (1997). Rat nurr1 is prominently expressed in perirhinal cortex, and differentially induced in the hippocampal dentate gyrus by electroconvulsive vs. kindled seizures. *Brain Res. Mol. Brain Res.* 47, 251–261. doi: 10.1016/S0169-328X(97)00056-9

Yao, M., and Denver, R. J. (2007). Regulation of vertebrate corticotropin releasing factor genes. *Gen. Comp. Endocrinol.* 153, 200–216. doi: 10.1016/j.ygcen.2007.01.046

Yao, M., Stenzel-Poore, M., and Denver, R. J. (2007). Structural and functional conservation of vertebrate corticotropin-releasing factor genes: evidence for a critical role for a conserved cyclic AMP response element. *Endocrinology* 148, 2518–2531. doi: 10.1210/en.2006-1413

Zetterstrom, R. H., Solomin, L., Jansson, L., Hoffer, B. J., Olson, L., and Perlmann, T. (1997). Dopamine neuron agenesis in Nurr1-deficient mice. *Science* 276, 248–250. doi: 10.1126/science.276.5310.248

Zetterstrom, R. H., Solomin, L., Mitsiadis, T., Olson, L., and Perlmann, T. (1996a). Retinoid X receptor heterodimerization and developmental expression distinguish the orphan nuclear receptors NGFI-B, Nurr1, and Nor1. *Mol. Endocrinol.* 10, 1656–1666. doi: 10.1210/me.10.12.1656

Zetterstrom, R. H., Williams, R., Perlmann, T., and Olson, L. (1996b). Cellular expression of the immediate early transcription factors Nurr1 and NGFI-B suggests a gene regulatory role in several brain regions including the nigrostriatal dopamine system. *Brain Res. Mol. Brain Res.*

41, 111–120. doi: 10.1016/0169-328X(96)00074-5

Zhang, L., Le, W., Xie, W., and Dani, J. A. (2012). Age-related changes in dopamine signaling in Nurr1 deficient mice as a model of Parkinson's disease. *Neurobiol. Aging* 33, 1001.

e1007–1001.e1016. doi: 10.1016/j.neurobiolaging.2011.03.022

Zhang, T., Jia, N., Fei, E., Wang, P., Liao, Z., Ding, L., et al. (2007). Nurr1 is phosphorylated by ERK2 *in vitro* and its phosphorylation upregulates tyro- sine hydroxylase expression in SH-SY5Y cells.

Neurosci. Lett. 423, 118–122. doi: 10.1016/j.neulet.2007.06.041

Ziegler, D. R., and Herman, J. P. (2000). Local integration of glutamate signaling in the hypothalamic paraventricular region: regulation of glucocorticoid stress responses. *Endocrinology* 141, 4801–4804. doi: 10.1210/en.141.12.4801

2

The promises and pitfalls of retrieval-extinction procedures in preventing relapse to drug seeking

Kate Hutton-Bedbrook and Gavan P. McNally*

School of Psychology, The University of New South Wales, Sydney, NSW, Australia

Edited by:
Remi Martin-Fardon, The Scripps Research Institute, USA

Reviewed by:
Osnat Ben-Shahar, University of California Santa Barbara, USA
Alessandra Matzeu, The Scripps Research Institute, USA

*Correspondence:
Gavan P. McNally, School of Psychology, The University of New South Wales, Sydney, NSW 2052, Australia.
e-mail: g.mcnally@unsw.edu.au

Relapse to drug seeking after treatment or a period of abstinence remains a fundamental challenge for drug users. The retrieval – extinction procedure offers promise in augmenting the efficacy of exposure based treatment for drug use and for protecting against relapse to drug seeking. Preceding extinction training with a brief retrieval or reminder trial, retrieval – extinction training, has been shown to reduce reinstatement of extinguished drug seeking in animal models and also to produce profound and long lasting decrements in cue-induced craving in human heroin users. However, the mechanisms that mediate these effects of retrieval – extinction training are unclear. Moreover, under some circumstances, the retrieval – extinction procedure can significantly increase vulnerability to reinstatement in animal models.

Keywords: addiction, reinstatement, relapse, reconsolidation, memory, extinction

Drug addiction involves the compulsive use of drugs despite adverse consequences (Torregrossa and Taylor, 2012). It imposes significant burdens on the individual drug user, their families, and communities. The successful treatment of drug users not only improves the health and well being of the user, but brings significant economic benefit to the broader community via reductions in criminal activity as well as reductions in health services utilization (McCollister and French, 2003). However, the fundamental problem with existing treatments for drug addiction is that they are ineffective at promoting long-term abstinence. The vast majority of drug users will relapse to drug use in the first year following treatment or abstinence (Hunt et al., 1971; Heinz et al., 2008). Relapse is elicited by a number of factors such as stress and negative affect (Shiffman and Waters, 2004), and exposure to drug-related places, people, and cues (Drummond et al., 1995). Unsurprisingly, many treatments have attempted to reduce the power of these factors over drug taking by implementing cue-exposure protocols (Heather and Bradley, 1990; Hammersley, 1992). Typically these treatments involve the non-reinforced exposure to drug-related stimuli and the drugs themselves. For example, the smoker may be exposed to the sight and smell of a burning cigarette, the heroin user to the sight and feel of a loaded syringe and tourniquet. Yet, although these treatments can be successful in reducing responding elicited by such stimuli in the short-term, they yield at best extremely modest long-term efficacy (Conklin and Tiffany, 2002).

In animal models of drug taking, extinction training also produces short-term decrements in drug seeking without long-term protection from reinstatement. Rats, for example, readily learn to self-administer a variety of drugs abused by humans. Drug seeking behavior can be extinguished when the contingency between drug seeking and delivery of the drug reward is broken. However, drug seeking is not permanently lost following extinction. Drug seeking can be reinstated under a number of conditions including following presentations of a drug prime (De Wit and Stewart, 1981), a drug associated stimulus (Davis and Smith, 1976; De Wit and Stewart, 1981), or by a return to the training context when extinction training occurs in a different context (Crombag and Shaham, 2002). In each of these experiments, extinction was achieved by omitting the drug reinforcer as well as any drug associated stimuli. The finding that responding which has been lost via extinction training can be recovered or restored under these different conditions has been interpreted to mean that extinction training does not erase or over write the original drug seeking memory. Rather, extinction training is believed to result in formation of a new memory. This extinction memory competes with the drug seeking memory for expression and for control over motivation and behavior. Specifically, the extinction memory is context-dependent, so that extinction is retrieved, and drug seeking inhibited, only under conditions similar (e.g., context, time) to extinction training (Bouton, 2000).

Due to the apparent failure of standard extinction training to yield long-term behavioral change in humans and other animals, a growing body of literature has begun to focus on the processes of consolidation and reconsolidation of memories in order to promote a permanent change in the original memory and hence a permanent change in behavior. Reconsolidation refers to the process by which a retrieved memory enters into a labile state that requires *de novo* protein synthesis to be "reconsolidated" back into a stable long-term memory. During this labile or active state, that may last as long as 6 h (Nader et al., 2000), the memory is unstable and may be altered, for example to incorporate new information and/or alter its original contents. It is possible to disrupt the memory during this state with pharmacological agents that interfere with the protein synthesis or other cell biological processes required for reconsolidation. For example, pharmacological manipulations may inhibit the reconsolidation of a drug stimulus memory and thereby prevent that stimulus from controlling behavior on later presentations (Lee et al., 2006; Milton et al., 2008). While this approach has provided insights into the molecular mechanisms that underlie memory reconsolidation, there are a number of limitations with translating this approach to a human clinical population. Most importantly, many of these compounds are toxic or have not been approved for human clinical use. Recently, however, a new non-pharmacological approach has been developed that appears to circumvent many of these limitations to human application.

RETRIEVAL – EXTINCTION PROCEDURES

The first evidence for a non-pharmacological disruption of reconsolidation, a "memory retrieval-extinction" procedure, was provided in an animal model of fear, in which a single reactivation trial provided prior to an extinction session prevented later recovery of this fear memory (Monfils et al., 2009). Rats were trained to fear a tone conditioned stimulus (CS) via pairings with a shock unconditioned stimulus (US). The following day the animals were presented with a brief (one tone CS) "reminder" cue followed 10 min, 1, 6, or 24 h later by extinction training that involved a further 18 CS alone presentations; 24 h later the animals were tested for long-term memory and following this for either a renewal or spontaneous recovery test. Rats in both groups showed normal loss of fear during extinction training. Rats that received standard extinction training also showed the normal reinstatement of fear via tests of renewal and spontaneous recovery. The rats that received the retrieval + extinction training did not show any recovery of fear. This retrieval – extinction training prevented the recovery of fear in this model. Retrieval – extinction training also produces relatively permanent fear loss in humans. In normal human subjects, Schiller et al. (2010) reported that a retrieval-extinction procedure rendered experimentally acquired fear resistant to reinstatement and spontaneous recovery. While these findings provide some evidence that the behavioral disruption of reconsolidation may reduce recovery of extinguished fear, it is important to note that there have been some successes (Clem and Huganir, 2010; Rao-Ruiz et al., 2011) and some failures (Chan et al., 2010; Costanzi et al., 2011; Soeter and Kindt, 2011) in replicating these findings.

Recently, Xue et al. (2012) adapted this retrieval – extinction protocol to study its effect on drug seeking in both non-human and human populations. For example, Xue et al., trained rats to self-administer intravenous heroin for 3 h/day for 10 days. The rats readily learned to do so. Then, during extinction, a normal extinction group received 14 daily 195 min extinction sessions whereby responses no longer yielded the drug reward. A Retrieval – extinction group also received 14 daily sessions but these were divided into a 15-min retrieval session followed 10 min later by a longer 180 min extinction session. In both these daily sessions, responding was not reinforced. Both groups showed the normal decline in heroin seeking across the course of extinction training. Later when tested for heroin priming reinstatement, the normal extinction group showed robust reinstatement whereas the retrieval – extinction group did not. Xue et al., were able to report similar effects for the cocaine primed reinstatement of cocaine seeking and spontaneous recovery as well as context-induced reinstatement of cocaine seeking. The effectiveness of the retrieval-extinction procedure in

preventing reinstatement has also been shown in an animal model of alcohol seeking. Millan et al. (2013) trained rats to respond for alcoholic beer. They then extinguished this responding. Whereas rats subjected to normal daily 1 h extinction training sessions later showed a robust context-induced reinstatement of alcohol seeking, rats that had received a 10-min retrieval session prior to a 50-min extinction session did not.

Remarkably, Xue et al. (2012) were able to extend these findings to cue-exposure treatments of heroin addicts in an inpatient treatment setting. On Day 1, participants rated craving levels following exposure to a 5-min video consisting of heroin cues. On Days 2 and 3, the participants were exposed to a 5-min video of heroin cues followed by extinction of these cues 10 min or 6 h later. Blood pressure and heart rate were monitored before and after cue-exposure. In this experiment, normal extinction training (i.e., neutral video followed by heroin cue extinction) produced no significant reduction in cue-induced craving or blood pressure changes. In contrast, the retrieval + extinction group (heroin video followed by heroin cue extinction) showed significant reductions in cue-elicited craving and blood pressure changes. These reductions were also long lasting, persisting up to 6 months following the brief 2 day extinction protocol. It remains to be determined whether the protective effects of this retrieval – extinction manipulation generalize beyond the treatment setting.

NOT MEMORY ERASURE AND NOT ALWAYS PROTECTIVE

The effects of the retrieval-extinction procedure on extinction of drug seeking have been interpreted as a behavioral disruption of the reconsolidation process (Monfils et al., 2009; Schiller and Phelps, 2011; Milton and Everitt, 2012). This is based on the assumption that standard extinction training yields new memory formation that competes with rather than replaces the original memory (Bouton, 1994). When extinction occurs following a retrieval trial, the original memory is assumed to be destabilized and labile allowing the extinction training to directly modify the original memory (Monfils et al., 2009; Torregrossa and Taylor, 2012). According to this interpretation, retrieval-extinction training leads to a change in the original memory that prevents the original memory from supporting reinstatement of drug seeking. Leaving aside the difficulties with making inferences based on the absence of responding (Lattal and Wood, 2013), reconsolidation theory yields two clear predictions about the process and mechanism underlying retrieval-extinction manipulations.

First, a key prediction of reconsolidation theory is that for the retrieval – extinction procedure to be successful, extinction training must occur inside the "reconsolidation window" (Monfils et al., 2009). The reconsolidation window is the hypothetical period of time after memory retrieval during which the memory is destabilized and yet to be reconsolidated. It is this period of destabilization that is purported to enable extinction training to directly modify the original training memory. The evidence in support of this comes from experiments that have shown that extinction training conducted outside the reconsolidation window is ineffective at preventing later reinstatement. For example, Xue et al. (2012) reported that if retrieval preceded extinction training by 6 h in either humans or rats, then it was ineffective at preventing reinstatement. Thus, according to reconsolidation theory, the brief retrieval session must occur prior to extinction in order to disrupt the reconsolidation process. Millan et al. (2013) tested this possibility. Rats were trained to respond for alcoholic beer in daily 1 h sessions. Then responding was extinguished in daily sessions. For the control group, extinction consisted of daily 1 h sessions. For the retrieval – extinction group, extinction consisted of daily 50 min sessions followed 70 min later by a 10-min retrieval session. Recall that Millan et al. (2013) showed previously that the daily 10 min then 50 min sessions (i.e., retrieval + extinction training) yielded a resistance to reinstatement. In this experiment, a reversed extinction + retrieval manipulation likewise yielded a resistance to reinstatement of alcoholic beer seeking. This finding is opposite to that predicted by reconsolidation theory. Reconsolidation theory predicts that the retrieval trial must occur before extinction training in order to reactivate the original memory and allow the new extinction learning to be incorporated prior to reconsolidation (Tronson and Taylor, 2007; Nader and Hardt, 2009; Schiller and Phelps, 2011). It is not possible within this theory for a retrieval trial to act retrospectively on encoding of the extinction memory.

A second key prediction of reconsolidation theory is that the disruption of reconsolidation should be protective. The retrieval – extinction procedure, by directly targeting the original drug taking memories, removes, or severely weakens the basis for reinstatement and so should always protect against reinstatement in animal models and relapse in humans. According to the theory, this manipulation is not only protective but in fact, because it is held to directly alter the original drug seeking memory, it returns the animals to a state similar to that of a naive animal. The available evidence is partly consistent with this. The retrieval – extinction procedure is effective in reducing or abolishing reinstatement across a variety of forms of reinstatement in animal models including spontaneous recovery, drug priming reinstatement, and context-induced reinstatement. However, these forms of reinstatement fail to adequately model a key feature of relapse to drug taking in humans. Such relapse involves drug seeking behavior that yields a drug reward. In the animal models of reinstatement, the drug reward is not available on test. Millan et al. (2013) examined whether the retrieval-extinction procedure would likewise protect animals against reinstatement when the drug reward was contingently available on test. In this experiment rats were trained to respond for alcoholic beer. This responding was then extinguished. For the normal extinction group, extinction training consisted of daily 1 h extinction sessions. For the retrieval – extinction group, extinction training consisted of daily 10 min then 50 min extinction sessions separated by 70 min. Both groups were then tested under a progressive ratio (PR) schedule of reinforcement. The PR test is a widely used measure of the motivation to respond for and consume drug rewards. Importantly, Millan et al. (2013) included a third group on test that had never been trained or extinguished before. This naive group allowed assessment of the possibility that the retrieval – extinction manipulation rendered animals similar to drug naive animals. The PR tests showed that both the normal extinction and retrieval – extinction groups were more motivated to respond for the drug reward than the naive group.

Hence, retrieval – extinction training did not return animals to a state similar to a naive animal. Moreover, these tests showed that the retrieval – extinction manipulation significantly increased the motivation of animals to respond for and consume the drug relative to standard extinction training. These testing conditions model a key feature of relapse to human drug taking. This finding is theoretically interesting because it suggests boundary conditions on the effectiveness of retrieval – extinction training in protecting from reinstatement and it helps identify the precise mechanism of this training. It is practically significant because it may suggest caution in the application of the retrieval – extinction procedure to clinical settings. At minimum, it draws attention within the neuroscience field to the well known clinical possibility that the factors promoting or hindering a lapse may be different to those promoting or hindering relapse to drug taking (Marlatt et al., 1988). These findings were similar to those reported by Ma et al. (2011), where reinstatement of a previously extinguished CPP was augmented in a test 4 weeks after retrieval – extinction training. Taken together, these results suggest that the retrieval-extinction procedure is not always protective against reinstatement and, under some conditions, may actually increase vulnerability to reinstatement.

BEYOND RECONSOLIDATION: UNDERSTANDING HOW MODIFIED EXTINCTION TRAINING PROTOCOLS YIELD LONG LASTING BEHAVIOR CHANGE

Given the profound health, medical, and economic impact of drug use, there is a clear need for new approaches that effectively undermine the persistent propensity of drug users to relapse to drug taking after a period of abstinence and/or extinction. Under some circumstances, retrieval – extinction procedures can produce longer lasting behavioral change than a standard extinction procedure. This extends across a variety of drug reinforcers (heroin, cocaine, alcohol) and different self-administration procedures. Importantly, the protective effects of this retrieval-extinction procedure extend to studies of cravings in human drug users. This generalizability across drug classes and species, as well the procedural simplicity of the retrieval – extinction training, marks the retrieval-extinction procedure as an exciting and promising technique for experimental investigation and therapeutic intervention.

However, at the same time, this technique is poorly understood. The findings reviewed here question both the cause and the consequences of the retrieval – extinction protocol. The finding that a reversed extinction – retrieval manipulation is effective at attenuating some forms of reinstatement is inconsistent with the possibility that this is a behavioral disruption of reconsolidation. The finding that retrieval-extinction may increase vulnerability to reinstatement when testing conditions involves contingent presentations of the reinforcer shows that the retrieval – extinction procedure is not always protective. It is possible that this procedure deepens the learning that normally happens during extinction. Consistent with this is the finding that retrieval – extinction training potentiated extinction-induced changes in PKMζ expression in the amygdala and prefrontal cortex (Xue et al., 2012) and deepened extinction learning can augment resistance to reinstatement (Janak and Corbit, 2011). However, a deepened extinction explanation has difficulty explaining the augmented responding during tests of reacquisition. It is important that the mechanisms for retrieval-extinction training be further investigated. This procedure has great promise as a therapeutic intervention that significantly reduces relapse in drug dependent clinical populations. However, it is clear that the retrieval – extinction procedure is more complicated than previously thought and it may, under some conditions, actually promote relapse.

It is essential that we develop a better understanding of how modified extinction training protocols yield long lasting behavior change.

ACKNOWLEDGMENTS

The preparation of this manuscript was supported by a grant from the National Health and Medical Research Council (APP1047899) and a Future Fellowship from the Australian Research Council (FT120100250).

REFERENCES

Bouton, M. E. (1994). Conditioning, remembering, and forgetting. *J. Exp. Psychol. Anim. Behav. Process.* 20, 219–231.

Bouton, M. E. (2000). A learning theory perspective on lapse, relapse, and the maintenance of behavior change. *Health Psychol.* 19, 57–63.

Chan, W. Y. M., Leung, H. T., Westbrook, R. F., and McNally, G. P. (2010). Effects of recent exposure to a conditioned stimulus on extinction of Pavlovian fear conditioning. *Learn. Mem.* 17, 512–521.

Clem, R. L., and Huganir, R. L. (2010). Calcium-permeable AMPA receptor dynamics mediate fear memory erasure. *Science* 330, 1108–1112.

Conklin, C. A., and Tiffany, S. T. (2002). Applying extinction research and theory to cue-exposure addiction treatments. *Addiction* 97, 155–167.

Costanzi, M., Cannas, S., Saraulli, D., Rossi-Arnaud, C., and Cestari, V. (2011). Extinction after retrieval: effects on the associative and nonassociative components of remote contextual fear memory. *Learn. Mem.* 18, 508–518.

Crombag, H. S., and Shaham, Y. (2002). Renewal of drug seeking by contextual cues after prolonged extinction in rats. *Behav. Neurosci.* 116, 169–173.

Davis, W. M., and Smith, S. G. (1976). Role of conditioned reinforcers in the initiation, maintenance, and extinction of drug-seeking behavior. *Pavlov. J. Biol. Sci.* 11, 222–236.

De Wit, H., and Stewart, J. (1981). Reinstatement of cocaine-reinforced responding in the rat. *Psychopharmacology* 75, 134–143.

Drummond, D. C., Tiffany, S. T., Glautier, S., and Remington, B. (1995). "Cue exposure in understanding and treating addictive behaviour," in *Addictive Behaviours: Cue Exposure Theory and Practice*, eds D. C. Drummond, S. T. Tiffany, S. Glautier, and B. Remington (London: John Wiley & Sons, Inc.), 1–17.

Hammersley, R. (1992). Cue exposure and learning theory. *Addict. Behav.* 17, 297–300.

Heather, N., and Bradley, B. P. (1990). Cue exposure as a practical treatment for addictive disorders: why are we waiting? *Addict. Behav.* 15, 335–337.

Heinz, A., Beck, A., Grüsser, S. M., Grace, A. A., and Wrase, J. (2008). Identifying the neural circuitry of alcohol craving and relapse vulnerability. *Addict. Biol.* 14, 108–118.

Hunt, W. A., Walker Barnett, L., and Branch, L. G. (1971). Relapse rates in addiction programs. *J. Clin. Psychol.* 27, 455–456.

Janak, P. H., and Corbit, L. H. (2011). Deepened extinction following compound stimulus presentation: noradrenergic modulation. *Learn. Mem.* 18, 1–10.

Lattal, K. M., and Wood, M. A. (2013). Epigenetics and persistent memory: implications for reconsolidation and silent extinction beyond the zero. *Nat. Neurosci.* 16, 124–129.

Lee, J. L. C., Milton, A. L., and Everitt, B. J. (2006). Cue-induced cocaine seeking and relapse are reduced by disruption of drug memory reconsolidation. *J. Neurosci.* 26, 5881–5887.

Ma, X., Zhang, J.-J., and Yu, L.-C. (2011). Post-retrieval extinction training enhances or hinders the extinction of morphine-induced conditioned place preference in rats dependent on the retrieval-extinction interval. *Psychopharmacology (Berl.)* 221, 19–26.

Marlatt, G. A., Baer, J. S., Donovan, D. M., and Kivlahan, D. R. (1988). Addictive behaviors: etiology and treatment. *Annu. Rev. Psychol.* 39, 223–252.

McCollister, K. E., and French, M. T. (2003). The relative contribution of outcome domains in the total economic benefit of addiction interventions: a review of first findings. *Addiction* 98, 1647–1649.

Millan, E. Z., Milligan-Saville, J., and McNally, G. P. (2013). Memory retrieval, extinction, and reinstatement of alcohol seeking. *Neurobiol. Learn. Mem.* 101, 26–32.

Milton, A. L., and Everitt, B. J. (2012). Wiping drug memories. *Science* 336, 167–168.

Milton, A. L., Lee, J. L. C., and Everitt, B. J. (2008). Reconsolidation of appetitive memories for both natural and drug reinforcement is dependent on {beta}-adrenergic receptors. *Learn. Mem.* 15, 88–92.

Monfils, M.-H., Cowansage, K. K., Klann, E., and Ledoux, J. E. (2009). Extinction-reconsolidation boundaries: key to persistent attenuation of fear memories. *Science* 324, 951–955.

Nader, K., and Hardt, O. (2009). A single standard for memory: the case for reconsolidation. *Nat. Rev. Neurosci.* 10, 224–234.

Nader, K., Schafe, G. E., and Ledoux, J. E. (2000). Fear memories require protein synthesis in the amygdala for reconsolidation after retrieval. *Nature* 406, 722–726.

Rao-Ruiz, P., Rotaru, D. C., van der Loo, R. J., Mansvelder, H. D., Stiedl, O., Smit, A. B., et al. (2011). Retrieval-specific endocytosis of GluA2-AMPARs underlies adaptive reconsolidation of contextual fear. *Nat. Neurosci.* 14, 1302–1308.

Schiller, D., Monfils, M.-H., Raio, C. M., Johnson, D. C., Ledoux, J. E., and Phelps, E. A. (2010). Preventing the return of fear in humans using reconsolidation update mechanisms. *Nature* 463, 49–53.

Schiller, D., and Phelps, E. A. (2011). Does reconsolidation occur in humans? *Front. Behav. Neurosci.* 5:24. doi:10.3389/fnbeh.2011.00024

Shiffman, S., and Waters, A. J. (2004). Negative affect and smoking lapses: a prospective analysis. *J. Consult. Clin. Psychol.* 72, 192–201.

Soeter, M., and Kindt, M. (2011). Disrupting reconsolidation: pharmacological and behavioral manipulations. *Learn. Mem.* 18, 357–366.

Torregrossa, M. M., and Taylor, J. R. (2012). Learning to forget: manipulating extinction and reconsolidation processes to treat addiction. *Psychopharmacology.* doi:10.1007/s00213-012-2750-9. [Epub ahead of print].

Tronson, N. C., and Taylor, J. R. (2007). Molecular mechanisms of memory reconsolidation. *Nat. Rev. Neurosci.* 8, 262–275.

Xue, Y.-X., Luo, Y.-X., Wu, P., Shi, H.-S., Xue, L.-F., Chen, C., et al. (2012). A memory retrieval-extinction procedure to prevent drug craving and relapse. *Science* 336, 241–245.

3

The role of the glucocorticoids in developing resilience to stress and addiction

Subhashini Srinivasan¹, Masroor Shariff² and Selena E. Bartlett²*

¹ *Ernest Gallo Clinic and Research Center at the University of California San Francisco, Emeryville, CA, USA*
² *Translational Research Institute and Institute for Health and Biomedical Innovation, Queensland University of Technology, Brisbane, QLD, Australia*

Edited by:
Remi Martin-Fardon, The Scripps Research Institute, USA

Reviewed by:
Andrew Lawrence, Florey Neuroscience Institutes, Australia
Leandro Vendruscolo, The Scripps Research Institute, USA

*Correspondence:
Selena E. Bartlett, Faculty of Health, School of Clinical Sciences, Translational Research Institute and Institute for Health and Biomedical Innovation, Queensland University of Technology, Brisbane, QLD 4102, Australia
e-mail: selena.bartlett@qut.edu.au

There is emerging evidence that individuals have the capacity to learn to be resilient by developing protective mechanisms that prevent them from the maladaptive effects of stress that can contribute to addiction. The emerging field of the neuroscience of resilience is beginning to uncover the circuits and molecules that protect against stress-related neuropsychiatric diseases, such as addiction. Glucocorticoids (GCs) are important regulators of basal and stress-related homeostasis in all higher organisms and influence a wide array of genes in almost every organ and tissue. GCs, therefore, are ideally situated to either promote or prevent adaptation to stress. In this review, we will focus on the role of GCs in the hypothalamic-pituitary adrenocortical axis and extra-hypothalamic regions in regulating basal and chronic stress responses. GCs interact with a large number of neurotransmitter and neuropeptide systems that are associated with the development of addiction. Additionally, the review will focus on the orexinergic and cholinergic pathways and highlight their role in stress and addiction. GCs play a key role in promoting the development of resilience or susceptibility and represent important pharmacotherapeutic targets that can reduce the impact of a maladapted stress system for the treatment of stress-induced addiction.

Keywords: addiction, glucocorticoid, stress, resilience, cholinergic, nicotinic acetylcholine receptors, mifepristone, orexin

INTRODUCTION

Susceptibility to developing an addiction is governed by genetics and modified by experience and the environment. Stress plays an important role in increasing susceptibility to addiction. McEwen eloquently wrote that, "human lifetime experiences have a profound impact on the brain, both as a target of stress and allostatic load/overload and as a determinant of physiological and behavioral response to stressors" (1). The ability to cope with stress or resilience (the capacity to bounce back following adversity) significantly predicts whether a person will subsequently develop a stress-related neuropsychiatric disease such as anxiety, depression, and addiction [reviewed in (2)]. A large majority of population have experienced a traumatic event during their lifetime. However, only a small percentage will subsequently experience chronic distress leading to post-traumatic stress disorder (PTSD) or addiction to alcohol or other drugs (3). In most cases, however, people have resilience and do not develop a disease or disorder following exposure to stressors. The emerging field of the neuroscience of resilience is uncovering new circuits and molecules that serve to protect against stress-related neuropsychiatric diseases.

It has often been assumed that resilience is an innate or passive mechanism that cannot be changed. However, research in animals and humans suggest that developing resilience may be a learnt behavior (2). Individuals have the capacity to learn to be resilient by developing mechanisms that protect from the maladaptive effects of stress. Glucocorticoids (GCs), cortisol in humans, or corticosterone in rodents are important regulators

of basal and stress-related homeostasis and have been shown to modulate an array of genes in many organs and tissues (4–6). Thus, GCs are ideally placed to regulate a multitude of signaling pathways activated in response to stress and addiction. In this review, we will focus on the role of GCs in the hypothalamic-pituitary adrenocortical (HPA) axis in regulating basal and chronic stress responses. In addition, we will focus on two systems, the orexinergic and cholinergic systems and their roles in mediating stress and addiction. We will further discuss the emerging interaction between these systems with GCs and in regulation of stress. Lastly, as GCs play a key role in promoting either resilience or susceptibility to stress, we will examine the pharmacotherapeutic opportunities that target GCs for the treatment of stress-induced addiction.

THE ROLE OF THE HPA AXIS AND THE GLUCOCORTICOIDS IN THE NEUROBIOLOGY OF RESILIENCE TO STRESS

The mechanisms that govern an organism's ability to handle stress has been well described in microorganisms that have specialized hubs, called stressosomes, that govern responses to an array of physical and environmental insults (7, 8). The stressosome is a unique structure within the microorganism that precisely orchestrates the molecular machinery that tunes the magnitude of the response to a stressor. The stressosome ultimately ensures the survival of the cell in response to an extensive variety of chemical and physical stressors (7, 8). The mammalian correlate of the "stressosome" is the HPA axis, as it provides a co-ordinated response to acute stress (9). The fundamental components of the central HPA axis are well known and include the corticotropin-releasing hormone (CRH)-secreting neurons of the paraventricular nucleus of the hypothalamus (PVN) (10) that stimulate pituitary adrenocorticotropic hormone (ACTH) and adrenal corticosterone (CORT) secretion (11).

Glucocorticoids are steroid hormones that are secreted by the adrenal glands and are important regulators of homeostasis in basal and stressful conditions. GCs exert their influence through two types of intracellular receptors the type I mineralocorticoid receptor and type II glucocorticoid receptor. Both receptors are expressed throughout the body and exert system-wide effects. In the brain, the high affinity type I mineralocorticoid receptor (also called aldosterone receptor in the kidneys), is expressed predominantly in the hippocampal formation and moderate expression is found in prefrontal cortex (PFC) and amygdala (12–14). The low affinity type II GRs are expressed throughout the brain with highest expression in the PVN and hippocampus and because of its lower affinity to cortisol it plays a key role in stress-related homeostasis when circulating levels of cortisol are high (14–17). GRs and MRs receptors reside in the cytoplasm and mediate classical genomic actions of GCs by acting as nuclear transcriptional activators and repressors (14, 18) and membrane bound GRs mediate the rapid actions of GCs (19, 20). GCs are thus ideally positioned to modulate responses to stress and be activated in the brain during healthy conditions, following acute stress and during adaptation of responses to chronic stress (4, 5, 21).

Glucocorticoids provide inhibitory feedback responses over fast (seconds to minutes) and longer (hours to days) timescales (4, 18, 22–24). The rapid effects involve immediate reduction in miniature EPSC frequency upon application of corticosterone or dexamethasone (synthetic GC) in the PVN (25), and reduced ACTH and corticosterone levels, an effect not observed when membrane impermeable dexamethasone was used, indicating fast feedback inhibition (26). Similar rapid effects of corticosterone on mEPSC in the hippocampus have been observed (27, 28). Thus both short time scale (perhaps non-genomic) and longer time scale (genomic) actions of GC together mediate the inhibitory feedback control. The molecular and neurobiological processes that underpin passive and active resilience are being investigated and candidates are regulators of the HPA axis, molecules involved in the architecture of the synapse and signaling molecules associated with neural plasticity [reviewed by (2)]. GCs represent the end product of the HPA axis and influence many functions of the central nervous system, such as arousal, cognition, mood, sleep, metabolism, and cardiovascular tone, immune, and inflammatory reaction (**Figure 1**).

Repeated traumatic events induce long-lasting behavioral changes that affect cognitive, emotional, and social behaviors that ultimately provide an organism protection or survival. The ability to handle stress may depend on an individual's HPA axis responsiveness that may in turn predict the likelihood of developing neuropsychiatric disorders such as addiction. However, under chronic stress this feedback becomes dysregulated leading to the variety of maladaptive syndromes, such as anxiety and various forms of depressive disorders (1, 5, 29–33) and addiction, including alcohol dependence (34). It has been shown that dysregulation

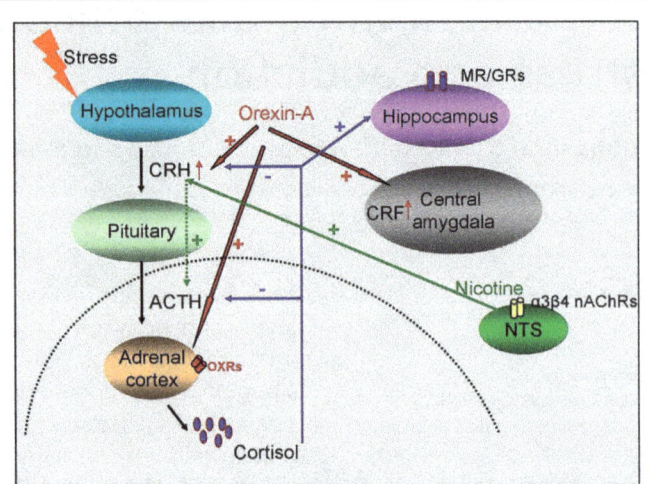

FIGURE 1 | Schematic representation of the interaction between glucocorticoids, orexins, and the cholinergic system in regulating stress responses. Stress activates the release of glucocorticoids from the adrenal gland, which then feedback into the brain and target both the HPA axis and extra-hypothalamic sites like the hippocampus and the amygdala. Orexins also activate the HPA axis and lead to the production of glucocorticoids and stimulate the release of CRF from the PVN of the hypothalamus and the central amygdala. The third player are the nicotinic receptors (nAChRs) which indirectly regulate ACTH release by acting on the PVN.

of the HPA axis by chronic and uncontrollable stress leads to abnormal GC secretion (35, 36). GRs mediate adaptation to stress and regulate termination of the stress response through negative feedback at the level of the HPA axis (30–32). GCs can dynamically regulate tissue sensitivity in a stochastic manner (5) and control the response to chronic stress. GCs regulate tissue and organ sensitivity by modulating GRs signaling, ligand availability, receptor isoform expression, intracellular circulation, and promoter association (30–32).

GLUCOCORTICOID RECEPTORS IN MALADAPTIVE STRESS RESPONSES: THE ROLE OF CHANGES IN PLASTICITY IN THE AMYGDALA

The amygdala is a key brain region that is involved in processing stress, fear, and pavlovian conditioning, and is a site where neuroendocrine signals stimulated by fear and stress interact. It has been proposed that the balance between hippocampal and amygdalar learning is important for determining behavioral stress coping choices. Chronic restraint stress increases dendritic growth and spine density in the basolateral amygdala (BLA) and is in contrast to its role in the hippocampus. The changes in the hippocampus return to baseline during recovery, whereas those in the amygdala are long lasting (37). Neurotrophic factors like BDNF mediate the stress-induced alternations in these brains regions. A recent study demonstrated that increased levels of BDNF are found in response to chronic stress in the BLA, whereas decreased levels were observed in the hippocampus (38). Animals which escape from aggressive interactions seem to have a more robust BDNF expression profile in the hippocampus and less in the amygdala, while the opposite behavior (of stay and face the opponent) have the opposite effect (39). Thus stress activates neurotrophic factors in different brain regions and is thought to be mediated by the GR system. Mice with a targeted genetic deletion of the GR, specifically in the central nucleus of the amygdala (CeA) but not in the forebrain have decreased conditioned fear responses (40). In contrast, targeted forebrain disruption of GRs, excluding the CeA, did not. It is known that the GRs in BLA are involved in consolidation of emotionally arousing and stressful experiences in rodents and humans by interacting with noradrenaline. Human studies have demonstrated that interactions between noradrenergic activity and glucocorticoid stress hormones can bring out disruptions in the neural basis of goal-directed action to habitual stimulus-response learning (41). Recently, it was shown that following acute stress, LTP induction is facilitated in the BLA by both β-adrenergic and GRs activation (42). Taken together, there are circuit specific changes underlying learning during stressful conditions, animals that are susceptible to stress have greater increases in synaptic activity in fear-related circuits such as the amygdala compared to animals that are resilient to stress.

GLUCOCORTICOIDS DRIVE CHANGES IN PLASTICITY IN THE HIPPOCAMPUS AND CORTICAL REGIONS IN RESPONSE TO STRESS

Glucocorticoid receptors in the hippocampus control homeostasis during healthy conditions and then play a role in driving changes in plasticity in response to stressful conditions (43, 44). Early life experiences that ultimately control an individual's HPA responsivity to stressful stimuli are modulated by GR gene expression in the hippocampus and frontal cortex (45). Hippocampal GRs play a role in the formation of long-term inhibitory avoidance memory in rats by inducing the CaMKIIα-BDNF-CREB-dependent neural plasticity pathways (46). In a separate study, chronic exposure to corticosterone resulted in impaired ability to learn response outcomes (47). Memory consolidation is thought to be mediated by the GR, while appraisal and responses to novel information is processed by the MR. Human and rodent studies suggest that under stressful conditions there is a switch from cognitive memory mediated by the hippocampus to habit memory mediated by the caudate nucleus (48, 49). In fact, mice deficient in MR receptors have impaired spatial memory, however they were rescued from further deterioration by stimulus-response memory following stress (50). Similarly, following an acute stressor, GRs are activated and induce synaptic plasticity in the PFC by increasing trafficking and function of NMDARs and AMPARs (51). Furthermore, when the MR was overexpressed in the forebrain of mice using a CAMkIIa promoter driven expression of HA-tagged human MR cDNA, the mice showed improved spatial memory, reduced anxiety without alteration in baseline HPA stress responses (52). There is mounting evidence that GCs participate in the formation of memories in specific circuits that govern stress responses and consequently responses to substances of abuse and alcohol.

GLUCOCORTICOIDS IN THE DEVELOPMENT OF ADDICTION

Chronic exposure to stress leads to alterations in the homeostatic functioning of GCs (29). Furthermore, there is significant dysregulation of the HPA axis following alcohol dependence. It has been shown that acute voluntary ethanol self-administration increases corticosterone levels, in contrast, long-term ethanol exposure in rodents results in a blunted response suggesting the alcohol dependence leads to dysregulation of the HPA axis (53). Transient overexpression of GR in young animals is both necessary and sufficient for bringing about profound changes in the transcriptome in specific brain regions leading to a lifelong increase in vulnerability to anxiety and drugs of abuse (54). The modified transcripts have been implicated in GR and axonal guidance signaling in dentate gyrus and dopamine receptor signaling in nucleus accumbens (NAc) (54). Furthermore, in some individuals, following exposure to stress and psychological trauma, GCs can promote escalated drug-taking behaviors and induce a compromised HPA axis. GCs can cross-sensitize with stimulant drug effects on dopamine transmission within the mesolimbic dopamine reward/reinforcement circuitry (55) and increase susceptibility to developing addictive behaviors (56–58) by increasing the synaptic strength of dopaminergic synapses (59). Importantly, the dopamine responses in the NAc core, but not the shell, have been shown to respond to fluctuating levels of GCs (60). Deficiencies in the GR gene in mice specifically in dopaminergic neurons expressing dopamine D1 receptors that receive dopaminergic input had decreased cocaine self-administration and dopamine cell firing (61). Acute exposure or binge-like ethanol exposure alter GC levels and promote PFC GC-regulated gene expression (62) and neurodegeneration that is dependent on type II GRs (63). GCs induce ethanol associated plasticity of glutamatergic synapses that have been proposed to underlie the development of ethanol dependence, reviewed in (64).

It has been shown that there is a correlation between acute alcohol withdrawal and downregulation of GR mRNA in the PFC, NAc, and bed nucleus of the stria terminalis (BNST), while protracted alcohol abstinence correlated with upregulated GR mRNA in the NAc core, ventral BNST, and CeA (65, 66), reviewed in (67). The transition from initial voluntary drug use to subsequent compulsive drug use has been proposed to reflect a switch from goal-directed to habitual control of action behavior (68). The investigators propose that acute stressors reinstate habitual responding to drug-related cues and repeated stress may promote the transition from voluntary to compulsory drug use. GCs are ideally positioned to regulate a diverse array of systems that modulate the development of addiction. In the following sections, we review the interplay between GCs and the orexinergic and cholinergic systems.

THE OREXINERGIC SYSTEM

The most studied biological functions of orexins/hypocretins are in the central control of feeding, sleep, energy homeostasis, and reward-seeking. Orexin-A and orexin-B (also called hypocretin-1 and -2) interact with two orexin/hypocretin receptor subtypes, the Orexin$_1$ Receptor (OX1R) and Orexin$_2$ Receptor (OX2R) which bind to either or both orexin-A and orexin-B (69, 70). Initial discoveries on the role of orexins came about with identification of deficiencies in the genes either encoding orexin or the OX2R receptor resulting in canine narcolepsy, implicating the role of ORX/Hcrt system in the regulation of sleep and wakefulness (71, 72). Orexin-A and orexin-B have been shown to increase food intake that is blocked by selective antagonists (73, 74). In addition, orexinergic fibers innervate various brain regions involved in energy homeostasis, such as the ventromedial hypothalamic nucleus, the arcuate nucleus, and the PVN of the hypothalamus (75). Orexins regulate autonomic functions, such as regulation of blood pressure and heart rate (76). Thus these neuropeptides are in a unique position to respond to stress.

ROLE OF OREXINS IN STRESS AND ACTIVATION OF THE HPA AXIS

Arousal is an important element of the stress response and the orexin system is a key component of the response to stress. Projections from perifornical nucleus and the dorsomedial nucleus of the hypothalamus are also implicated in addictive behaviors, however their role in arousal and concomitant stress has been the main focus (77). Orexins modulate the HPA axis in response to different stressful stimuli. Prepro-orexin mRNA expression was increased in the lateral hypothalamus (LH) in young rats following immobilization stress and in adult rats following cold stress (78). OX-A activates the HPA axis inducing secretion of ACTH and corticosterone (79). OX-A, but not OX-B, increases glucocorticoid secretion from rat and human adrenal cortices by direct stimulation of adrenocortical cells via OX1R coupled to the adenylate cyclase-dependent cascade (79) (**Figure 1**). Intracerebroventricular (I.C.V) administration of OX-A enhanced ACTH and corticosterone release (80–82). It has been proposed that orexin neurons play an integrative role that links autonomic responses to arousal and/or vigilance during the fight-or-flight response (83) (**Figure 2**).

ROLE OF OREXINS IN ADDICTION

Along with the many functions performed by orexins, the most intriguing is their role in the reward system. Orexin containing neurons project from the LH to the ventral tegmental area (VTA) and NAc, the brain regions that comprise the mesolimbic "reward pathway" (84–86). OXRs have recently been implicated in the motivational drive for addictive substances such as morphine, cocaine (87–91), and alcohol (92–97). The OX1R plays a specific role in ethanol self-administration, cue, and stress-induced relapse, reviewed in (98) with a more limited role for OX2R being shown (99). The orexin system has also been implicated in relapse to drug use. The OX1R plays a role in foot-shock stress-induced reinstatement of cocaine (100, 101) and cue and yohimbine induced reinstatement of ethanol-seeking (94, 96, 102).

The central amygdaloid projections regulate the HPA axis and innervate orexin containing neurons in the lateral hypothalamus. The extended amygdala which includes the CeA, BNST, and the NAc are critical brain areas that process emotional behaviors such as anxiety, fear, stress, and drug addiction. In particular, the CeA and BNST have been shown to play an important role in anxiety-related behaviors and voluntary ethanol consumption (103). The extended amygdala, including the CeA, has been shown to play a critical role in the reinstatement behavior to drugs of abuse. Inactivation of the CeA, but not the BLA, prevents foot-shock-induced reinstatement of cocaine-seeking (104). Dense orexinergic innervation is also observed in all these brain regions (76, 105, 106). These brain regions also express stress peptides such as corticotrophin releasing factor (CRF) and anti-stress peptides such as neuropeptide Y (NPY). Both these neuropeptides have opposing actions in the CeA and regulate ethanol consumption. OX-A

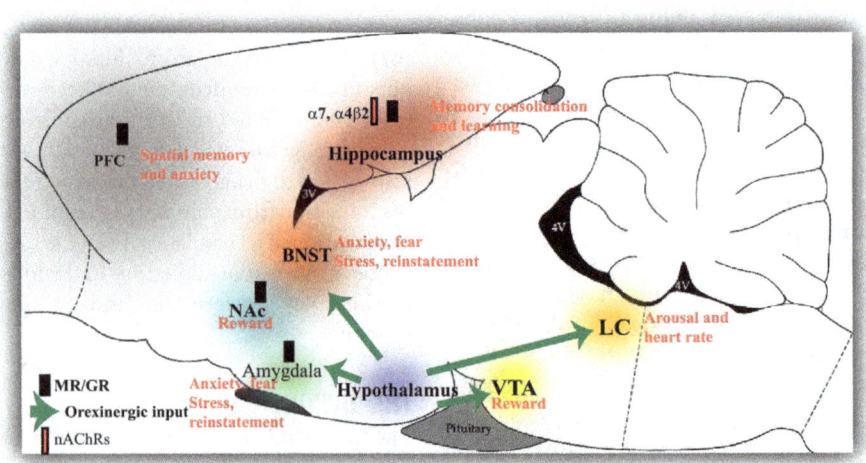

FIGURE 2 | Glucocorticoid, orexinergic, and cholinergic activation of the brain regions involved in stress and drug addiction. Glucocorticoid receptors in the hippocampus and amygdala mediate the effects of stress and consolidation of fearful memories. GCs also modulate alcohol withdrawal in the prefrontal cortex (PFC), nucleus accumbens (NAc), and bed nucleus of the stria terminalis (BNST). Glucocorticoids (GCs) in the hippocampus also negatively regulate the hypothalamus thereby providing a central feedback mechanism. Orexins produced in the hypothalamus activate reward pathways such as the ventral tegmental area (VTA) and the NAc and brain regions involved in stress, fear, and anxiety such as the amygdala and BNST and regulate cardiovascular tone through the locus coeruleus (LC). Both GCs and orexins play similar roles in brain regions implicated in stress and reward. Glucocorticoids have been shown to directly inhibit nicotinic receptor (nAChR) activity in the hippocampus that exert an inhibitory effect on the HPA axis. The nAChRs seem to differentially orchestrate responses to stress.

infusions into the BNST produce anxiety like responses as measured by social interaction test and elevated plus maze test and the effect is mediated by NMDA receptors (107). A recent study also demonstrated that yohimbine activates orexinergic responses, but not adrenergic receptor activity, and depressed excitatory neurotransmission in the BNST that contributed to reinstatement of extinguished cocaine CPP (108). Thus the orexinergic system is involved in mediating stress-induced drug-seeking behavior as it recruits multiple brain regions involved in processing stressful stimuli and addictive behaviors. It is essential to understand the contribution of orexins in the overlap between stress and reward systems. Identifying circuits that mediate stress-induced relapse to drug abuse will be necessary in order to develop targeted pharmacotherapeutic approaches for stress-induced drug relapse. The dual orexin receptor antagonist, suvorexant (109) has successfully completed phase III clinical trials in treating primary insomnia and is currently under FDA review. If approved, this will be the first FDA orexin antagonist available for treating sleep-disorders and has the potential to be repurposed for its efficacy in treating stress and addictive disorders.

INTERACTIONS BETWEEN THE CHOLINERGIC SYSTEM AND HPA AXIS

Allostasis, a process by which homeostasis is regained after stress, occurs by the interaction between the PFC, amygdala, and the hippocampus via the HPA axis (110–113). In this process a number of neurotransmitters and neuromodulators such as acetylcholine, glutamate, and GABA, have been shown to be differentially modulated. Here, we review the involvement of the components of the cholinergic pathway in reacting to, sustaining, and even exacerbating stress.

Components of the cholinergic pathway are – the ligand, acetylcholine (ACh); the enzyme responsible for the breakdown of acetylcholine, acetylcholinesterase (AChE); the enzyme involved in synthesizing ACh, choline acetyltransferase (ChAT); and, the acetylcholine receptors, nicotinic acetylcholine receptor (nAChR), and muscarinic acetylcholine receptor (mAChR). We are focusing specifically on the nicotinic receptor – nAChR – in relation to the cholinergic response to stress. By focusing on the *nAChR-cholinergic pathway*, it is not our purpose to suggest that nAChR is the only or a more important player mediating responses to stress. Rather, it is intended that this review highlights the interactions of the glucocorticoid pathway (mediated via the HPA) and the nAChR-cholinergic pathway in relation to stress.

It is well known that the nAChRs are involved in learning and memory (114, 115). Additionally, the negative effects of chronic stress on memory are also well established (116, 117). Indeed, as early as 1968, the hippocampus was recognized as a target structure for stress hormones (118) with observations that acetylcholine release into the hippocampus (119, 120) increased under various stress models (121). Transgenic mouse knock-out models have shown the importance of the $\alpha 4$ (122), $\beta 3$ (123), and $\beta 4$ (124) nAChR subunits in mediating the anxiogenic effects of stress. Furthermore, the $\alpha 5$ and $\beta 4$ knock-out mice are less sensitive to nicotine (125, 126), a potent anxiolytic agent (127–129) at lower doses (130). Indeed, the $\alpha 7$ and $\alpha 4\beta 2$ nAChRs, which are the primary targets of nicotine, have been shown

to provide a nicotine-mediated neuroprotective effect in stress-induced impairment of hippocampus-dependent memory (131). The hippocampus has been shown to exert an inhibitory effect on the HPA axis (132–136), thus lowering stress. Taken together, the nAChR seem to differentially orchestrate responses to stress via its various subunits.

Activation of the stress response is due to the cascading efflux of CRH, ACTH, and cortisol. Nicotine, a potent ligand at nAChRs, in relatively high doses (2.5–5.0 μg/kg) has been shown to produce a dose-dependent increase in ACTH (137), and its antagonist, mecamylamine, has been shown to block nicotine-stimulated ACTH release (137, 138). In the brain, the region responsible for the CRH-mediated ACTH release is the parvocellular region of the PVN (pcPVN) of the hypothalamus (139, 140). It has, however, been shown that nicotine mediates ACTH release indirectly, via the nicotinic receptors on the nucleus tractus solitarius (NTS) (141, 142). The NTS subsequently mediates action potentials via various afferents to the pcPVN (143, 144). The nAChR in the NTS are found pre-synaptically on glutamatergic projections to the pcPVN (145, 146). Further, the nAChR subunits implicated in the nicotine-mediated effects of ACTH in this pathway are the β_4-containing nAChRs (most likely $\alpha_3\beta_4$*) but not the $\alpha_4\beta_2$ as determined by measurements of mEPSCs in the presence of DHβE, a potent $\alpha_4\beta_2$ inhibitor or cytisine, a potent β_4*-nAChR agonist (146). Therefore, while the $\alpha_4\beta_2$ and α_7 nAChR subunits modulate nicotine-mediated roles elsewhere (131), in the NTS it is a different subtype (146), pointing yet again to a nAChR-based differential modulation to stress (**Figure 1**).

GLUCOCORTICOID INTERACTIONS WITH THE CHOLINERGIC SYSTEM

Glucocorticoids have been shown to directly inhibit nAChR activity (147–149). This is supported by the fact that stress causes a down regulation of the nAChR in the rat cerebral cortex and midbrain (150). Additionally, steroid antagonists have been shown to upregulate nAChR expression (151). That GCs can directly affect nAChR activity via receptor binding or alteration of expression levels can be explained by the presence of glucocorticoid response elements (GRE) on genes transcribing the α_7 subunit of the nAChR – CHRNA7 (152). Indeed, GREs have also been identified on genes for ChAT (153) and AChE (154), components of the cholinergic pathway. Further research is required to study the precise effects of these GREs in this pathway along with investigating if these GRE are also present on other nAChR genes.

Other components of the cholinergic pathway too have been shown to be affected by stress. AChE, responsible for the timely degradation of ACh, has been shown to be regulated via alternative splicing thus modifying neurotransmission (155). Indeed, miRNA post-transcriptional modification of AChE from its usual AChE-S to the read-through form AChE-R alters cholinergic transmission (156). Additionally, post-transcriptional modulation of AChE, again via miRNA, causes hippocampal-related cognitive defects (157). As stated earlier, AChE expression is controlled at the genomic level via the GRE (154) as is ChAT (153). Also, ChAT protein levels were shown to decrease due to chronic stress (158). At the epigenetic level, there is stress-induced epigenetic transcriptional memory of AChE via HDAC4 (159). Interestingly, in this study a GRE was also identified on HDAC4 (159), suggesting a direct epigenetic effect of stress on AChE. All these results point to a multi-faceted mechanism whereby the stress-induced cholinergic response is regulated without the over-articulation of its response that would undoubtedly lead to various stress-related neuropathologies such as PTSD (160, 161), alcohol addiction (162, 163), and addiction to other substances of abuse (164, 165).

In summary, the involvement of the different subtypes of the nAChR in different regions of the brain along with modulation of the cholinergic pathway at various stages such as transcriptional, post-transcriptional, and epigenetic modifications, point to a finely modulated system both temporally and spatially that is attuned to respond to the various stressors that we are faced with in our daily lives. Lastly, while this review has focused on the nAChR and the cholinergic pathway, the involvement of the muscarinic receptor and a myriad other neural circuits cannot be understated. Indeed the ultimate goal of this field of research is to understand sufficiently the intricate interplay between the various pathways and neural circuits that ultimately will enable the alleviation of stress-induced morbidity via development of more effective pharmacotherapeutic strategies against stress.

PHARMACOTHERAPEUTIC STRATEGIES

Ample evidence exists to demonstrate that type II GRs are important therapeutic targets for the treatment of disorders that result from maladaptive stress responses. Mifepristone, also known as RU486, is a derivative of the 19-norprogestin norethindrone and potently competes with type II GRs and progesterone receptors (PRs). Mifepristone has been shown to reduce reinstatement of ethanol-seeking and escalated drinking in two different animal models (66, 166). Furthermore, mifepristone has been shown to be effective at reducing the self-administration of amphetamine

(167), cocaine (168, 169), morphine (170), and ethanol (57, 66, 162, 166, 171–175). A recent study also demonstrates the effectiveness of mifepristone in reducing withdrawal symptoms of alcohol (176). The anti-glucocorticoid activity of mifepristone has made it a potential treatment for Cushing's syndrome (177) and neurological and psychological disorders (178–183). Mifepristone offers a promising way to temporarily reset the stress response system that has become maladapted following chronic and long-term alcohol consumption.

CONCLUSION

Learning to cope with life and/or stress or learning to be susceptible to stress involves dynamic regulation of plasticity in brain circuits that govern stress response pathways. As the brain can be remodeled by experience and neural circuits are adaptable and dynamically regulated, this suggests it is possible to change the brain or learn how to cope with stress and overcome addiction and learn to become more resilient. The molecular pathways and circuits that govern resilience are gradually being uncovered and this will provide opportunities for identifying novel strategies that overcome the impact of addiction on the brain combined with possible novel pharmacotherapeutic strategies that target pro-resilience pathways. In this review, we focused on the role of glucocorticoid hormones, as they have the capacity to provide system-wide feedback during acute and chronic stress and provide a way forward to interrogate and reset brain networks. Understanding the molecular mechanisms that govern mechanisms that the brain utilizes to protect from the deleterious effects of stress will provide exciting new avenues in neuroscience.

ACKNOWLEDGMENTS

This work was supported by funding from the ARC Future Fellowship (Selena E. Bartlett).

REFERENCES

1. McEwen BS. Protection and damage from acute and chronic stress: allostasis and allostatic overload and relevance to the pathophysiology of psychiatric disorders. *Ann N Y Acad Sci* (2004) **1032**:1–7. doi:10.1196/annals.1314.001

2. Russo SJ, Murrough JW, Han MH, Charney DS, Nestler EJ. Neurobiology of resilience. *Nat Neurosci* (2012) **15**:1475–84. doi:10.1038/nn. 3234

3. Nechvatal JM, Lyons DM. Coping changes the brain. *Front Behav Neurosci* (2013) 7:13. doi:10.3389/fnbeh.2013. 00013

4. De Kloet ER, Vreugdenhil E, Oitzl MS, Joels M. Brain corticosteroid receptor balance in health and disease. *Endocr Rev* (1998) **19**:269–301. doi:10.1210/er.19.3.269

5. Kino T. Tissue glucocorticoid sensitivity: beyond stochastic regulation on the diverse actions of glucocorticoids. *Horm Metab Res* (2007) **39**:420–4. doi:10.1055/s-2007-980193

6. McEwen BS, De Kloet ER, Rostene W. Adrenal steroid receptors and actions in the nervous system. *Physiol Rev* (1986) 66: 1121–88.

7. Liebal UW, Millat T, Marles-Wright J, Lewis RJ, Wolkenhauer O. Simulations of stressosome activation emphasize allosteric interactions between RsbR and RsbT. *BMC Syst Biol* (2013) 7:3. doi:10.1186/1752-0509-7-3

8. Marles-Wright J, Grant T, Delumeau O, van Duinen G, Firbank SJ, Lewis PJ, et al. Molecular architecture of the "stressosome," a signal integration and transduction hub. *Science* (2008) **322**:92–6. doi:10.1126/science.1159572

9. Selye H. The significance of the adrenals for adaptation. *Science* (1937) **85**:247–8. doi:10.1126/science.85.2201.247

10. Herman JP, Figueiredo H, Mueller NK, Ulrich-Lai Y, Ostrander MM, Choi DC, et al. Central mechanisms of stress integration: hierarchical circuitry controlling hypothalamo-pituitary-adrenocortical responsiveness. *Front Neuroendocrinol* (2003) **24**:151–80. doi:10.1016/j.yfrne.2003.07.001

11. Ulrich-Lai YM, Herman JP. Neural regulation of endocrine and autonomic stress responses. *Nat Rev Neurosci* (2009) **10**:397–409. doi:10.1038/nrn2647

12. Arriza JL, Simerly RB, Swanson LW, Evans RM. The neuronal mineralocorticoid receptor as a mediator of glucocorticoid response. *Neuron* (1988) **1**:887–900. doi:10.1016/0896-6273(88)90136-5

13. Arriza JL, Weinberger C, Cerelli G, Glaser TM, Handelin BL, Housman DE, et al. Cloning of human mineralocorticoid receptor complementary DNA: structural and functional kinship with the glucocorticoid receptor. *Science* (1987) **237**:268–75. doi:10.1126/science. 3037703

14. Reul JM, de Kloet ER. Two receptor systems for corticosterone in rat brain: microdistribution and differential occupation. *Endocrinology* (1985) **117**:2505–11. doi:10.1210/endo-117-6-2505

15. Aronsson M, Fuxe K, Dong Y, Agnati LF, Okret S, Gustafsson JA. Localization of glucocorticoid receptor mRNA in the male rat brain by in situ hybridization. *Proc Natl Acad Sci U S A* (1988) **85**:9331–5. doi:10.1073/pnas.85.23. 9331

16. Gustafsson JA, Carlstedt-Duke J, Poellinger L, Okret S, Wikstrom AC, Bronnegard M, et al. Biochemistry, molecular biology, and physiology of the glucocorticoid receptor. *Endocr Rev* (1987) **8**:185–234. doi:10.1210/edrv-8-2-185

17. Spencer RL, Young EA, Choo PH, McEwen BS. Adrenal steroid type I and type II receptor binding: estimates of in vivo receptor number, occupancy, and activation with varying level of steroid. *Brain Res* (1990) **514**:37–48. doi:10.1016/0006-8993(90)90433-C

18. Groeneweg FL, Karst H, de Kloet ER, Joels M. Rapid non-genomic effects of corticosteroids and their role in the central stress response. *J Endocrinol* (2011) **209**:153–67. doi:10.1530/JOE-10-0472

19. de Kloet ER, Karst H, Joels M. Corticosteroid hormones in the central stress response: quick-and-slow. *Front Neuroendocrinol* (2008) **29**:268–72. doi:10.1016/j.yfrne.2007.10.002

20. Hinz B, Hirschelmann R. Rapid non-genomic feedback effects of glucocorticoids on CRF-induced ACTH secretion in rats. *Pharm Res* (2000) **17**:1273–7. doi:10.1023/A:1007652908104

21. Sapolsky RM, Romero LM, Munck AU. How do glucocorticoids influence stress responses? Integrating permissive, suppressive, stimulatory, and preparative actions. *Endocr Rev* (2000) **21**:55–89. doi:10.1210/er.21.1.55

22. Grino M, Burgunder JM, Eskay RL, Eiden LE. Onset of glucocorticoid responsiveness of anterior pituitary corticotrophs during development is scheduled by corticotropin-releasing factor. *Endocrinology* (1989) **124**:2686–92. doi:10.1210/endo-124-6-2686

23. Keller-Wood ME, Dallman MF. Corticosteroid inhibition of ACTH secretion. *Endocr Rev* (1984) **5**:1–24. doi:10.1210/edrv-5-1-1

24. Tasker JG, Di S, Malcher-Lopes R. Minireview: rapid glucocorticoid signaling via membrane-associated receptors. *Endocrinology* (2006) **147**:5549–56. doi:10.1210/en.2006-0981

25. Di S, Malcher-Lopes R, Halmos KC, Tasker JG. Nongenomic glucocorticoid inhibition via endocannabinoid release in the hypothalamus: a fast feedback mechanism. *J Neurosci* (2003) **23**:4850–7.

26. Evanson NK, Tasker JG, Hill MN, Hillard CJ, Herman JP. Fast feedback inhibition of the HPA axis by glucocorticoids is mediated by endocannabinoid signaling. *Endocrinology* (2010) **151**:4811–9. doi:10.1210/en.2010-0285

27. Karst H, Berger S, Turiault M, Tronche F, Schutz G, Joels M. Mineralocorticoid receptors are indispensable for nongenomic modulation of hippocampal glutamate transmission by corticosterone. *Proc Natl Acad Sci U S A* (2005) **102**:19204–7. doi:10.1073/pnas.0507572102

28. Qiu S, Champagne DL, Peters M, Catania EH, Weeber EJ, Levitt P, et al. Loss of limbic system-associated membrane protein leads to reduced hippocampal mineralocorticoid receptor expression, impaired synaptic plasticity, and spatial memory deficit. *Biol Psychiatry* (2010) **68**:197–204. doi:10.1016/j.biopsych.2010.02.013

29. Barik J, Marti F, Morel C, Fernandez SP, Lanteri C, Godeheu G, et al. Chronic stress triggers social aversion via glucocorticoid receptor in dopaminoceptive neurons. *Science* (2013) **339**:332–5. doi:10.1126/science.1226767

30. De Kloet ER, Reul JM. Feedback action and tonic influence of corticosteroids on brain function: a concept arising from the heterogeneity of brain receptor systems. *Psychoneuroendocrinology* (1987) **12**:83–105. doi:10.1016/0306-4530(87)90040-0

31. Diorio D, Viau V, Meaney MJ. The role of the medial prefrontal cortex (cingulate gyrus) in the regulation of hypothalamic-pituitary-adrenal responses to stress. *J Neurosci* (1993) **13**:3839–47.

32. Magarinos AM, Somoza G, De Nicola AF. Glucocorticoid negative feedback and glucocorticoid receptors after hippocampectomy in rats. *Horm Metab Res* (1987) **19**:105–9. doi:10.1055/s-2007-1011753

33. McEwen BS, Stellar E. Stress and the individual. Mechanisms leading to disease. *Arch Intern Med* (1993) **153**:2093–101. doi:10.1001/archinte.153.18.2093

34. Koob GF. A role for brain stress systems in addiction.

35. Holsboer F, von Bardeleben U, Wiedemann K, Muller OA, Stalla GK. Serial assessment of corticotropin-releasing hormone response after dexamethasone in depression. Implications for pathophysiology of DST nonsuppression. *Biol Psychiatry* (1987) **22**:228–34. doi:10.1016/0006-3223(87)90237-X

36. Nemeroff CB, Widerlov E, Bissette G, Walleus H, Karlsson I, Eklund K, et al. Elevated concentrations of CSF corticotropin-releasing factor-like immunoreactivity in depressed patients. *Science* (1984) **226**:1342–4. doi:10.1126/science.6334362

37. Vyas A, Mitra R, Shankaranarayana Rao BS, Chattarji S. Chronic stress induces contrasting patterns of dendritic remodeling in hippocampal and amygdaloid neurons. *J Neurosci* (2002) **22**:6810–8.

38. Lakshminarasimhan H, Chattarji S. Stress leads to contrasting effects on the levels of brain derived neurotrophic factor in the hippocampus and amygdala. *PLoS ONE* (2012) 7:e30481. doi:10.1371/journal.pone.0030481

39. Arendt DH, Smith JP, Bastida CC, Prasad MS, Oliver KD, Eyster KM, et al. Contrasting hippocampal and amygdalar expression of genes related to neural plasticity during escape from social aggression. *Physiol Behav* (2012) **107**:670–9. doi:10.1016/j.physbeh.2012.03.005

40. Kolber BJ, Roberts MS, Howell MP, Wozniak DF, Sands MS, Muglia LJ. Central amygdala glucocorticoid receptor action promotes fear-associated CRH activation and conditioning. *Proc Natl Acad Sci U S A* (2008) **105**:12004–9. doi:10.1073/pnas.0803216105

41. Schwabe L, Tegenthoff M, Hoffken O, Wolf OT. Simultaneous glucocorticoid and noradrenergic activity disrupts the neural basis of goal-directed action in the human brain. *J Neurosci* (2012) **32**:10146–55. doi:10.1523/JNEUROSCI.1304-12.2012

42. Sarabdjitsingh RA, Kofink D, Karst H, de Kloet ER, Joels M. Stress-induced enhancement of mouse amygdalar synaptic plasticity depends on glucocorticoid and β-adrenergic activity. *PLoS ONE* (2012) 7:e42143. doi:10.1371/journal.pone.0042143

43. Gourley SL, Swanson AM, Koleske AJ. Corticosteroid-induced neural remodeling predicts behavioral vulnerability and resilience. *J Neurosci* (2013) **33**:3107–12. doi:10.1523/JNEUROSCI.2138-12.2013

44. Lehmann ML, Brachman RA, Martinowich K, Schloesser RJ, Herkenham M. Glucocorticoids orchestrate divergent effects on mood through adult neurogenesis. *J Neurosci* (2013) **33**:2961–72. doi:10.1523/JNEUROSCI.3878-12.2013

45. Meaney MJ, Diorio J, Francis D, Widdowson J, LaPlante P, Caldji C, et al. Early environmental regulation of forebrain glucocorticoid receptor gene expression: implications for adrenocortical responses to stress. *Dev Neurosci* (1996) **18**:49–72. doi:10.1159/000111395

46. Chen DY, Bambah-Mukku D, Pollonini G, Alberini CM. Glucocorticoid receptors recruit the CaMKIIalpha-BDNF-CREB pathways to mediate memory consolidation. *Nat Neurosci* (2012) **15**:1707–14. doi:10.1038/nn.3266

47. Gourley SL, Swanson AM, Jacobs AM, Howell JL, Mo M, Dileone RJ, et al. Action control is mediated by prefrontal BDNF and glucocorticoid receptor binding. *Proc Natl Acad Sci U S A* (2012) **109**:20714–9. doi:10.1073/pnas.1208342109

48. Schwabe L, Oitzl MS, Philippsen C, Richter S, Bohringer A, Wippich W, et al. Stress modulates the use of spatial versus stimulus-response learning strategies in humans. *Learn Mem* (2007) **14**:109–16. doi:10.1101/lm.435807

49. Schwabe L, Schachinger H, de Kloet ER, Oitzl MS. Stress impairs spatial but not early stimulus-response learning. *Behav Brain Res* (2010) **213**:50–5. doi:10.1016/j.bbr

50. ter Horst JP, van der Mark MH, Arp M, Berger S, de Kloet ER, Oitzl MS. Stress or no stress: mineralocorticoid receptors in the forebrain regulate behavioral adaptation. *Neurobiol Learn Mem* (2012) **98**:33–40. doi:10.1016/j.nlm

51. Yuen EY, Liu W, Karatsoreos IN, Ren Y, Feng J, McEwen

BS, et al. Mechanisms for acute stress-induced enhancement of glutamatergic transmission and working memory. *Mol Psychiatry* (2011) **16**:156–70. doi:10.1038/mp.2010.50

52. Lai M, Horsburgh K, Bae SE, Carter RN, Stenvers DJ, Fowler JH, et al. Forebrain mineralocorticoid receptor overexpression enhances memory, reduces anxiety and attenuates neuronal loss in cerebral ischaemia. *Eur J Neurosci* (2007) **25**:1832–42. doi:10.1111/j.1460-9568.2007.05427.x

53. Richardson HN, Lee SY, O'Dell LE, Koob GF, Rivier CL. Alcohol self-administration acutely stimulates the hypothalamic-pituitary-adrenal axis, but alcohol dependence leads to a dampened neuroendocrine state. *Eur J Neurosci* (2008) **28**:1641–53. doi:10.1111/j.1460-9568.2008.06455.x

54. Wei Q, Fentress HM, Hoversten MT, Zhang L, Hebda-Bauer EK, Watson SJ, et al. Early-life forebrain glucocorticoid receptor overexpression increases anxiety behavior and cocaine sensitization. *Biol Psychiatry* (2012) **71**:224–31. doi:10.1016/j.biopsych.2011.07.009

55. de Jong IE, de Kloet ER. Glucocorticoids and vulnerability to psychostimulant drugs: toward substrate and mechanism. *Ann N Y Acad Sci* (2004) **1018**:192–8. doi:10.1196/annals.1296.022

56. Marinelli M, Piazza PV. Interaction between glucocorticoid hormones, stress and psychostimulant drugs. *Eur J Neurosci* (2002) **16**:387–94. doi:10.1046/j.1460-9568.2002.02089.x

57. Roberts AJ, Lessov CN, Phillips TJ. Critical role for glucocorticoid receptors in stress- and ethanol-induced locomotor sensitization. *J Pharmacol Exp Ther* (1995) **275**:790–7.

58. Rouge-Pont F, Marinelli M, Le Moal M, Simon H, Piazza PV. Stress-induced sensitization and glucocorticoids. II. Sensitization of the increase in extracellular dopamine induced by cocaine depends on stress-induced corticosterone secretion. *J Neurosci* (1995) **15**:7189–95.

59. Saal D, Dong Y, Bonci A, Malenka RC. Drugs of abuse and stress trigger a common synaptic adaptation in dopamine neurons. *Neuron* (2003)

37:577–82. doi:10.1016/S0896-6273(03)00021-7

60. Tye SJ, Miller AD, Blaha CD. Differential corticosteroid receptor regulation of mesoaccumbens dopamine efflux during the peak and nadir of the circadian rhythm: a molecular equilibrium in the midbrain? *Synapse* (2009) **63**:982–90. doi:10.1002/syn.20682

61. Ambroggi F, Turiault M, Milet A, Deroche-Gamonet V, Parnaudeau S, Balado E, et al. Stress and addiction: glucocorticoid receptor in dopaminoceptive neurons facilitates cocaine seeking. *Nat Neurosci* (2009) **12**:247–9. doi:10.1038/nn.2282

62. Costin BN, Wolen AR, Fitting S, Shelton KL, Miles MF. Role of adrenal glucocorticoid signaling in prefrontal cortex gene expression and acute behavioral responses to ethanol. *Alcohol Clin Exp Res* (2013) **37**:57–66. doi:10.1111/j.1530-0277.2012.01841.x

63. Cippitelli A, Damadzic R, Hamelink C, Brunnquell M, Thorsell A, Heilig M, et al. Binge-like ethanol consumption increases corticosterone levels and neurodegneration whereas occupancy of type II glucocorticoid receptors with mifepristone is neuroprotective. *Addict Biol* (2012). doi:10.1111/j.1369-1600.2012.00451.x

64. Prendergast MA, Mulholland PJ. Glucocorticoid and polyamine interactions in the plasticity of glutamatergic synapses that contribute to ethanol-associated dependence and neuronal injury. *Addict Biol* (2012) **17**:209–23. doi:10.1111/j.1369-1600.2011.00375.x

65. Little HJ, Croft AP, O'Callaghan MJ, Brooks SP, Wang G, Shaw SG. Selective increases in regional brain glucocorticoid: a novel effect of chronic alcohol. *Neuroscience* (2008) **156**:1017–27. doi:10.1016/j.neuroscience.2008.08.029

66. Vendruscolo LF, Barbier E, Schlosburg JE, Misra KK, Whitfield TW Jr., Logrip ML, et al. Corticosteroid-dependent plasticity mediates compulsive alcohol drinking in rats. *J Neurosci* (2012) **32**:7563–71. doi:10.1523/JNEUROSCI.0069-12.2012

67. Rose AK, Shaw SG, Prendergast MA, Little HJ. The importance of glucocorticoids in alcohol

dependence and neurotoxicity. *Alcohol Clin Exp Res* (2010) **34**:2011–8. doi:10.1111/j.1530-0277.2010.01298.x

68. Yin HH, Mulcare SP, Hilario MR, Clouse E, Holloway T, Davis MI, et al. Dynamic reorganization of striatal circuits during the acquisition and consolidation of a skill. *Nat Neurosci* (2009) **12**:333–41. doi:10.1038/nn.2261

69. de Lecea L, Kilduff TS, Peyron C, Gao X, Foye PE, Danielson PE, et al. The hypocretins: hypothalamus-specific peptides with neuroexcitatory activity. *Proc Natl Acad Sci U S A* (1998) **95**:322–7. doi:10.1073/pnas.95.1.322

70. Sakurai T, Amemiya A, Ishii M, Matsuzaki I, Chemelli RM, Tanaka H, et al. Orexins and orexin receptors: a family of hypothalamic neuropeptides and G protein-coupled receptors that regulate feeding behavior. *Cell* (1998) **92**:573–85. doi:10.1016/S0092-8674(02)09256-5

71. Anaclet C, Parmentier R, Ouk K, Guidon G, Buda C, Sastre JP, et al. Orexin/hypocretin and histamine: distinct roles in the control of wakefulness demonstrated using knock-out mouse models. *J Neurosci* (2009) **29**:14423–38. doi:10.1523/JNEUROSCI.2604-09.2009

72. Chemelli RM, Willie JT, Sinton CM, Elmquist JK, Scammell T, Lee C, et al. Narcolepsy in orexin knockout mice: molecular genetics of sleep regulation. *Cell* (1999) **98**:437–51. doi:10.1016/S0092-8674(00)81973-X

73. Haynes AC, Jackson B, Chapman H, Tadayyon M, Johns A, Porter RA, et al. A selective orexin-1 receptor antagonist reduces food consumption in male and female rats. *Regul Pept* (2000) **96**:45–51. doi:10.1016/S0167-0115(00)00199-3

74. Yamada H, Okumura T, Motomura W, Kobayashi Y, Kohgo Y. Inhibition of food intake by central injection of anti-orexin antibody in fasted rats. *Biochem Biophys Res Commun* (2000) **267**:527–31. doi:10.1006/bbrc.1999.1998

75. Elias CF, Saper CB, Maratos-Flier E, Tritos NA, Lee C, Kelly J, et al. Chemically defined projections linking the mediobasal hypothalamus and the lateral hypothalamic area. *J Comp*

Neurol (1998) **402**:442–59. doi:10.1002/(SICI)1096-9861(19981228)402:4<442::AID-CNE2>3.3.CO;2-I

76. Peyron C, Tighe DK, van den Pol AN, de Lecea L, Heller HC, Sutcliffe JG, et al. Neurons containing hypocretin (orexin) project to multiple neuronal systems. *J Neurosci* (1998) **18**:9996–10015.

77. Harris GC, Aston-Jones G. Arousal and reward: a dichotomy in orexin function. *Trends Neurosci* (2006) **29**:571–7. doi:10.1016/j.tins.2006.08.002

78. Ida T, Nakahara K, Murakami T, Hanada R, Nakazato M, Murakami N. Possible involvement of orexin in the stress reaction in rats. *Biochem Biophys Res Commun* (2000) **270**:318–23. doi:10.1006/bbrc.2000.2412

79. Kagerer SM, Johren O. Interactions of orexins/hypocretins with adrenocortical functions. *Acta Physiol (Oxf)* (2010) **198**:361–71. doi:10.1111/j.1748-1716.2009.02034.x

80. Al-Barazanji KA, Wilson S, Baker J, Jessop DS, Harbuz MS. Central orexin-A activates hypothalamic-pituitary-adrenal axis and stimulates hypothalamic corticotropin releasing factor and arginine vasopressin neurones in conscious rats. *J Neuroendocrinol* (2001) **13**:421–4. doi:10.1046/j.1365-2826.2001.00655.x

81. Jaszberenyi M, Bujdoso E, Pataki I, Telegdy G. Effects of orexins on the hypothalamic-pituitary-adrenal system. *J Neuroendocrinol* (2000) **12**:1174–8. doi:10.1046/j.1365-2826.2000.00572.x

82. Kuru M, Ueta Y, Serino R, Nakazato M, Yamamoto Y, Shibuya I, et al. Centrally administered orexin/hypocretin activates HPA axis in rats. *Neuroreport* (2000) **11**:1977–80. doi:10.1097/00001756-200000660-00034

83. Kuwaki T, Zhang W. Orexin neurons and emotional stress. *Vitam Horm* (2012) **89**:135–58. doi:10.1016/B978-0-12-394623-2.00008-1

84. Di Chiara G, Imperato A. Ethanol preferentially stimulates dopamine release in the nucleus accumbens of freely moving rats. *Eur J Pharmacol* (1985) **115**:131–2. doi:10.1016/0014-2999(85)90598-9

85. Koob GF, Bloom FE. Cellular and molecular mechanisms

of drug dependence. *Science* (1988) **242**:715–23. doi:10. 1126/science.2903550

86. Wise RA, Rompre PP. Brain dopamine and reward. *Annu Rev Psychol* (1989) **40**:191–225. doi:10.1146/annurev.ps.40.0201 89.001203

87. Borgland SL, Taha SA, Sarti F, Fields HL, Bonci A. Orexin A in the VTA is critical for the induction of synaptic plasticity and behavioral sensitization to cocaine. *Neuron* (2006) **49**:589–601. doi:10.1016/ j.neuron.2006.01.016

88. DiLeone RJ, Georgescu D, Nestler EJ. Lateral hypothalamic neuropeptides in reward and drug addiction. *Life Sci* (2003) **73**:759–68. doi:10.1016/S0024-3205(03)00408-9

89. Harris GC, Wimmer M, Aston-Jones G. A role for lateral hypothalamic orexin neurons in reward seeking. *Nature* (2005) **437**:556–9. doi:10.1038/nature04071

90. Paneda C, Winsky-Sommerer R, Boutrel B, de Lecea L. The corticotropin-releasing factor-hypocretin connection: implications in stress response and addiction. *Drug News Perspect* (2005) **18**:250–5. doi:10. 1358/dnp.2005.18.4.908659

91. Pasumarthi RK, Reznikov LR, Fadel J. Activation of orexin neurons by acute nicotine. *Eur J Pharmacol* (2006) **535**:172–6. doi:10.1016/j.ejphar.2006.02.021

92. Dayas CV, McGranahan TM, Martin-Fardon R, Weiss F. Stimuli linked to ethanol availability activate hypothalamic CART and orexin neurons in a reinstatement model of relapse. *Biol Psychiatry* (2008) **63**:152–7. doi:10. 1016/j.biopsych.2007.02.002

93. Jupp B, Krivdic B, Krstew E, Lawrence AJ. The orexin receptor antagonist SB-334867 dissociates the motivational properties of alcohol and sucrose in rats. *Brain Res* (2011) **1391**:54–9. doi:10. 1016/j.brainres.2011.03.045

94. Lawrence AJ, Cowen MS, Yang HJ, Chen F, Oldfield B. The orexin system regulates alcohol-seeking in rats. *Br J Pharmacol* (2006) **148**:752–9. doi:10.1038/sj.bjp.0706789

95. Moorman DE, Aston-Jones G. Orexin-1 receptor antagonism decreases ethanol consumption and preference selectively in high-ethanol – preferring Sprague – Dawley rats. *Alcohol*

(2009) **43**:379–86. doi:10. 1016/j.alcohol.2009.07.002

96. Richards JK, Simms JA, Steensland P, Taha SA, Borgland SL, Bonci A, et al. Inhibition of orexin-1/hypocretin-1 receptors inhibits yohimbine-induced reinstatement of ethanol and sucrose seeking in Long-Evans rats. *Psychopharmacology (Berl)* (2008) **199**:109–17. doi:10.1007/s00213-008-1136-5

97. Srinivasan S, Simms JA, Nielsen CK, Lieske SP, Bito-Onon JJ, Yi H, et al. The dual orexin/hypocretin receptor antagonist, almorexant, in the ventral tegmental area attenuates ethanol self-administration. *PLoS ONE* (2012) **7**:e44726. doi:10.1371/ journal.pone.0044726

98. Kim AK, Brown RM, Lawrence AJ. The role of orexins/hypocretins in alcohol use and abuse: an appetitive-reward relationship. *Front Behav Neurosci* (2012) **6**:78. doi:10.3389/fnbeh.2012.00078

99. Shoblock JR, Welty N, Aluisio L, Fraser I, Motley ST, Morton K, et al. Selective blockade of the orexin-2 receptor attenuates ethanol self-administration, place preference, and reinstatement. *Psychopharmacology (Berl)* (2011) **215**:191–203. doi:10.1007/s00213-010-2127-x

100. Boutrel B, Kenny PJ, Specio SE, Martin-Fardon R, Markou A, Koob GF, et al. Role for hypocretin in mediating stress-induced reinstatement of cocaine-seeking behavior. *Proc Natl Acad Sci U S A* (2005) **102**:19168–73. doi:10.1073/pnas.0507480102

101. Wang B, You ZB, Wise RA. Reinstatement of cocaine seeking by hypocretin (orexin) in the ventral tegmental area: independence from the local corticotropin-releasing factor network. *Biol Psychiatry* (2009) **65**:857–62. doi:10. 1016/j.biopsych.2009.01.018

102. Jupp B, Krstew E, Dezsi G, Lawrence AJ. Discrete cue-conditioned alcohol-seeking after protracted abstinence: pattern of neural activation and involvement of orexin(1) receptors. *Br J Pharmacol* (2011) **162**:880–9. doi:10.1111/j.1476-5381.2010.01088.x

103. Moller C, Wiklund L, Sommer W, Thorsell A, Heilig M. Decreased experimental anxiety and voluntary ethanol consumption in rats following

central but not basolateral amygdala lesions. *Brain Res* (1997) **760**:94–101. doi:10.1016/S0006-8993(97)00308-9

104. McFarland K, Davidge SB, Lapish CC, Kalivas PW. Limbic and motor circuitry underlying footshock-induced reinstatement of cocaine-seeking behavior. *J Neurosci* (2004) **24**:1551–60. doi:10.1523/JNEUROSCI.4177-03.2004

105. Schmidt FM, Arendt E, Steinmetzer A, Bruegel M, Kratzsch J, Strauss M, et al. CSF-hypocretin-1 levels in patients with major depressive disorder compared to healthy controls. *Psychiatry Res* (2011) **190**:240–3. doi: 10.1016/j.psychres.2011.06.004

106. Schmitt O, Usunoff KG, Lazarov NE, Itzev DE, Eipert P, Rolfs A, et al. Orexinergic innervation of the extended amygdala and basal ganglia in the rat. *Brain Struct Funct* (2012) **217**:233–56. doi:10.1007/s00429-011-0343-8

107. Lungwitz EA, Molosh A, Johnson PL, Harvey BP, Dirks RC, Dietrich A, et al. Orexin-A induces anxiety-like behavior through interactions with glutamatergic receptors in the bed nucleus of the stria terminalis of rats. *Physiol Behav* (2012) **107**:726–32. doi:10.1016/ j.physbeh.2012.05.019

108. Conrad KL, Davis AR, Silberman Y, Sheffler DJ, Shields AD, Saleh SA, et al. Yohimbine depresses excitatory transmission in BNST and impairs extinction of cocaine place preference through orexin-dependent, norepinephrine-independent processes. *Neuropsychopharmacology* (2012) **37**:2253–66. doi:10.1038/npp.2012.76

109. Winrow CJ, Gotter AL, Cox CD, Doran SM, Tannenbaum PL, Breslin MJ, et al. Promotion of sleep by suvorexant-a novel dual orexin receptor antagonist. *J Neurogenet* (2011) **25**:52–61. doi: 10.3109/01677063.2011.566953

110. Garrido P, De Blas M, Ronzoni G, Cordero I, Anton M, Gine E, et al. Differential effects of environmental enrichment and isolation housing on the hormonal and neurochemical responses to stress in the prefrontal cortex of the adult rat: relationship to working and emotional memories. *J Neural Transm* (2013) **120**:829–43. doi:10.1007/s00702-012-0935-3

111. Herman JP, Ostrander MM, Mueller NK, Figueiredo H. Limbic system mechanisms of stress regulation: hypothalamo-pituitary-adrenocortical axis. *Prog Neuropsychopharmacol Biol Psychiatry* (2005) **29**:1201–13. doi:10.1016/j.pnpbp.2005.08.006

112. Sullivan RM, Gratton A. Prefrontal cortical regulation of hypothalamic-pituitary-adrenal function in the rat and implications for psychopathology: side matters. *Psychoneuroendocrinology* (2002) **27**:99–114. doi:10.1016/S0306-4530(01)00038-5

113. Weinberg MS, Johnson DC, Bhatt AP, Spencer RL. Medial prefrontal cortex activity can disrupt the expression of stress response habituation. *Neuroscience* (2010) **168**:744–56. doi:10.1016/j.neuroscience.2010.04.006

114. Gold PE. Acetylcholine modulation of neural systems involved in learning and memory. *Neurobiol Learn Mem* (2003) **80**:194–210. doi:10.1016/j.nlm.2003.07.003

115. Levin HS, Rodnitzky RL. Behavioral effects of organophosphate in man. *Clin Toxicol* (1976) **9**:391–403. doi:10.3109/15563657608988138

116. Kim JJ, Diamond DM. The stressed hippocampus, synaptic plasticity and lost memories. *Nat Rev Neurosci* (2002) **3**:453–62.

117. McEwen BS. Effects of adverse experiences for brain structure and function. *Biol Psychiatry* (2000) **48**:721–31. doi:10.1016/S0006-3223(00)00964-1

118. McEwen BS, Weiss JM, Schwartz LS. Selective retention of corticosterone by limbic structures in rat brain. *Nature* (1968) **220**:911–2. doi:10.1038/220911a0

119. Del Arco A, Mora F. Neurotransmitters and prefrontal cortex-limbic system interactions: implications for plasticity and psychiatric disorders. *J Neural Transm* (2009) **116**:941–52. doi:10.1007/s00702-009-0243-8

120. Vizi ES, Kiss JP. Neurochemistry and pharmacology of the major hippocampal transmitter systems: synaptic and nonsynaptic interactions. *Hippocampus* (1998) **8**:566–607. doi:10.1002/(SICI)1098-1063 (1998)8:6<566::AID-HIPO2> 3.0.CO;2-W

121. Imperato A, Puglisi-Allegra S, Casolini P, Angelucci L. Changes in brain dopamine and acetylcholine release during and following stress are independent of the pituitary-adrenocortical axis. *Brain Res* (1991) **538**:111–7. doi:10.1016/0006-8993(91)90384-8

122. Ross SA, Wong JY, Clifford JJ, Kinsella A, Massalas JS, Horne MK, et al. Phenotypic characterization of an alpha 4 neuronal nicotinic acetylcholine receptor subunit knock-out mouse. *J Neurosci* (2000) **20**:6431–41.

123. Booker TK, Butt CM, Wehner JM, Heinemann SF, Collins AC. Decreased anxiety-like behavior in beta3 nicotinic receptor subunit knockout mice. *Pharmacol Biochem Behav* (2007) **87**:146–57. doi:10.1016/j.pbb.2007.04.011

124. Salas R, Pieri F, Fung B, Dani JA, De Biasi M. Altered anxiety-related responses in mutant mice lacking the beta4 subunit of the nicotinic receptor. *J Neurosci* (2003) **23**:6255–63.

125. Salas R, Orr-Urtreger A, Broide RS, Beaudet A, Paylor R, De Biasi M. The nicotinic acetylcholine receptor subunit alpha 5 mediates short-term effects of nicotine in vivo. *Mol Pharmacol* (2003) **63**:1059–66. doi:10.1124/mol.63.5.1059

126. Salas R, Pieri F, De Biasi M. Decreased signs of nicotine withdrawal in mice null for the beta4 nicotinic acetylcholine receptor subunit. *J Neurosci* (2004) **24**:10035–9. doi:10.1523/JNEUROSCI.1939-04.2004

127. Brioni JD, O'Neill AB, Kim DJ, Decker MW. Nicotinic receptor agonists exhibit anxiolytic-like effects on the elevated plus-maze test. *Eur J Pharmacol* (1993) **238**:1–8. doi:10.1016/0014-2999(93)90498-7

128. Cao W, Burkholder T, Wilkins L, Collins AC. A genetic comparison of behavioral actions of ethanol and nicotine in the mirrored chamber. *Pharmacol Biochem Behav* (1993) **45**:803–9. doi:10.1016/0091-3057(93)90124-C

129. Costall B, Kelly ME, Naylor RJ, Onaivi ES. The actions of nicotine and cocaine in a mouse model of anxiety. *Pharmacol Biochem Behav* (1989) **33**:197–203. doi:10.1016/0091-3057(89)90450-4

130. File SE, Cheeta S, Kenny PJ. Neurobiological mechanisms by which nicotine mediates different types of anxiety. *Eur J Pharmacol* (2000) **393**:231–6. doi:10.1016/S0014-2999(99)00889-4

131. Alzoubi KH, Srivareerat M, Tran TT, Alkadhi KA. Role of alpha7- and alpha4beta2-nAChRs in the neuroprotective effect of nicotine in stress-induced impairment of hippocampus-dependent memory. *Int J Neuropsychopharmacol* (2013) **16**:1105–13. doi:10.1017/S1461145712001046

132. Akana SF, Chu A, Soriano L, Dallman MF. Corticosterone exerts site-specific and state-dependent effects in prefrontal cortex and amygdala on regulation of adrenocorticotropic hormone, insulin and fat depots. *J Neuroendocrinol* (2001) **13**:625–37. doi:10.1046/j.1365-2826.2001.00676.x

133. Feldman S, Conforti N, Saphier D. The preoptic area and bed nucleus of the stria terminalis are involved in the effects of the amygdala on adrenocortical secretion. *Neuroscience* (1990) **37**:775–9. doi:10.1016/0306-4522(90)90107-F

134. Herman JP, Schafer MK, Young EA, Thompson R, Douglass J, Akil H, et al. Evidence for hippocampal regulation of neuroendocrine neurons of the hypothalamo-pituitary-adrenocortical axis. *J Neurosci* (1989) **9**:3072–82.

135. Jacobson L, Sapolsky R. The role of the hippocampus in feedback regulation of the hypothalamic-pituitary-adrenocortical axis. *Endocr Rev* (1991) **12**:118–34. doi:10.1210/edrv-12-2-118

136. Sapolsky RM, Krey LC, McEwen BS. Glucocorticoid-sensitive hippocampal neurons are involved in terminating the adrenocortical stress response. *Proc Natl Acad Sci U S A* (1984) **81**:6174–7. doi:10.1073/pnas.81.19.6174

137. Matta SG, Beyer HS, McAllen KM, Sharp BM. Nicotine elevates rat plasma ACTH by a central mechanism. *J Pharmacol Exp Ther* (1987) **243**:217–26.

138. Matta SG, McAllen KM, Sharp BM. Role of the fourth cerebroventricle in mediating rat plasma ACTH responses to intravenous nicotine. *J Pharmacol Exp Ther* (1990) **252**:623–30.

139. Sawchenko PE, Bohn MC. Glucocorticoid receptor-immunoreactivity in C1, C2, and C3 adrenergic neurons that project to the hypothalamus or to the spinal cord in the rat. *J Comp Neurol* (1989) **285**:107–16. doi:10.1002/cne.902850109

140. Swanson LW, Sawchenko PE, Rivier J, Vale WW. Organization of ovine corticotropin-releasing factor immunoreactive cells and fibers in the rat brain: an immunohistochemical study. *Neuroendocrinology* (1983) **36**:165–86. doi:10.1159/000123454

141. Fu Y, Matta SG, Valentine JD, Sharp BM. Adrenocorticotropin response and nicotine-induced norepinephrine secretion in the rat paraventricular nucleus are mediated through brainstem receptors. *Endocrinology* (1997) **138**:1935–43. doi:10.1210/en.138.5.1935

142. Zhao R, Chen H, Sharp BM. Nicotine-induced norepinephrine release in hypothalamic paraventricular nucleus and amygdala is mediated by N-methyl-D-aspartate receptors and nitric oxide in the nucleus tractus solitarius. *J Pharmacol Exp Ther* (2007) **320**:837–44. doi:10.1124/jpet.106.112474

143. Sawchenko PE, Swanson LW. The organization of noradrenergic pathways from the brainstem to the paraventricular and supraoptic nuclei in the rat. *Brain Res* (1982) **257**:275–325.

144. Swanson LW, Sawchenko PE, Berod A, Hartman BK, Helle KB, Vanorden DE. An immunohistochemical study of the organization of catecholaminergic cells and terminal fields in the paraventricular and supraoptic nuclei of the hypothalamus. *J Comp Neurol* (1981) **196**:271–85. doi:10.1002/cne.901960207

145. Kalappa BI, Feng L, Kem WR, Gusev AG, Uteshev VV. Mechanisms of facilitation of synaptic glutamate release by nicotinic agonists in the nucleus of the solitary tract. *Am J Physiol Cell Physiol* (2011) **301**:C347–61. doi:10.1152/ajpcell.00473.2010

146. Smith DV, Uteshev VV. Heterogeneity of nicotinic acetylcholine receptor expression in the caudal nucleus of the solitary tract. *Neuropharmacology* (2008) **54**:445–53. doi:10.1016/j.neuropharm.2007.10.018

147. Bullock AE, Clark AL, Grady SR, Robinson SF, Slobe BS, Marks MJ, et al. Neurosteroids modulate nicotinic receptor function in mouse striatal and thalamic synaptosomes. *J Neurochem* (1997) **68**:2412–23. doi:10.1046/j.1471-4159.1997.68062412.x

148. Ke L, Lukas RJ. Effects of steroid exposure on ligand binding and functional activities of diverse nicotinic acetylcholine receptor subtypes. *J Neurochem* (1996) **67**:1100–12. doi:10.1046/j.1471-4159.1996.67031100.x

149. Shi LJ, He HY, Liu LA, Wang CA. Rapid nongenomic effect of corticosterone on neuronal nicotinic acetylcholine receptor in PC12 cells. *Arch Biochem Biophys* (2001) **394**:145–50. doi:10.1006/abbi.2001.2519

150. Takita M, Muramatsu I. Alteration of brain nicotinic receptors induced by immobilization stress and nicotine in rats. *Brain Res* (1995) **681**:190–2. doi:10.1016/0006-8993(95)00265-R

151. Almeida LE, Pereira EF, Alkondon M, Fawcett WP, Randall WR, Albuquerque EX. The opioid antagonist naltrexone inhibits activity and alters expression of alpha7 and alpha4beta2 nicotinic receptors in hippocampal neurons: implications for smoking cessation programs. *Neuropharmacology* (2000) **39**:2740–55. doi:10.1016/S0028-3908(00)00157-X

152. Leonard S, Gault J, Hopkins J, Logel J, Vianzon R, Short M, et al. Association of promoter variants in the alpha7 nicotinic acetylcholine receptor subunit gene with an inhibitory deficit found in schizophrenia. *Arch Gen Psychiatry* (2002) **59**:1085–96. doi:10.1001/archpsyc.59.12.1085

153. Berse B, Blusztajn JK. Modulation of cholinergic locus expression by glucocorticoids and retinoic acid is cell-type specific. *FEBS Lett* (1997) **410**:175–9. doi:10.1016/S0014-5793(97)00568-1

154. Battaglia M, Ogliari A. Anxiety and panic: from human studies to animal research and back. *Neurosci Biobehav Rev* (2005) **29**:169–79. doi:10.1016/j.neubiorev.2004.06.013

155. Meshorer E, Soreq H. Virtues and woes of AChE alternative splicing in stress-related neuropathologies. *Trends*

Neurosci (2006) **29**:216–24. doi:10.1016/j.tins.2006.02.005

156. Meerson A, Cacheaux L, Goosens KA, Sapolsky RM, Soreq H, Kaufer D. Changes in brain MicroRNAs contribute to cholinergic stress reactions. *J Mol Neurosci* (2010) **40**:47–55. doi:10.1007/s12031-009-9252-1

157. Shaltiel G, Hanan M, Wolf Y, Barbash S, Kovalev E, Shoham S, et al. Hippocampal microRNA-132 mediates stress-inducible cognitive deficits through its acetylcholinesterase target. *Brain Struct Funct* (2013) **218**:59–72. doi:10.1007/s00429-011-0376-z

158. Zhao T, Huang GB, Muna SS, Bagalkot TR, Jin HM, Chae HJ, et al. Effects of chronic social defeat stress on behavior and choline acetyltransferase, 78-kDa glucose-regulated protein, and CCAAT/enhancer-binding protein (C/EBP) homologous protein in adult mice. *Psychopharmacology (Berl)* (2013) **228**:217–30. doi:10.1007/s00213-013-3028-6

159. Sailaja BS, Cohen-Carmon D, Zimmerman G, Soreq H, Meshorer E. Stress-induced epigenetic transcriptional memory of acetylcholinesterase by HDAC4. *Proc Natl Acad Sci U S A* (2012) **109**:E3687–95. doi:10.1073/pnas.1209990110

160. Kaufer D, Friedman A, Seidman S, Soreq H. Acute stress facilitates long-lasting changes in cholinergic gene expression. *Nature* (1998) **393**:373–7. doi:10.1038/30741

161. Pavlovsky L, Bitan Y, Shalev H, Serlin Y, Friedman A. Stress-induced altered cholinergic-glutamatergic interactions in the mouse hippocampus. *Brain Res* (2012) **1472**:99–106. doi:10.1016/j.brainres.2012.05.057

162. Fahlke C, Hard E, Eriksson CJ, Engel JA, Hansen S. Consequence of long-term exposure to corticosterone or dexamethasone on ethanol consumption in the adrenalectomized rat, and the effect of type I and type II corticosteroid receptor antagonists. *Psychopharmacology (Berl)* (1995) **117**:216–24. doi:10.1007/BF02245190

163. Uhart M, Wand GS. Stress, alcohol and drug interaction: an update of human research. *Addict Biol* (2009) **14**:43–64. doi:10.1111/j.1369-1600.2008.00131.x

164. Sinha R. The role of stress in addiction relapse. *Curr Psychiatry Rep* (2007) **9**:388–95. doi:10.1007/s11920-007-0050-6

165. Sinha R, Catapano D, O'Malley S. Stress-induced craving and stress response in cocaine dependent individuals. *Psychopharmacology (Berl)* (1999) **142**:343–51. doi:10.1007/s002130050898

166. Simms JA, Haass-Koffler CL, Bito-Onon J, Li R, Bartlett SE. Mifepristone in the central nucleus of the amygdala reduces yohimbine stress-induced reinstatement of ethanol-seeking. *Neuropsychopharmacology* (2012) **37**:906–18. doi:10.1038/npp.2011.268

167. De Vries TJ, Schoffelmeer AN, Tjon GH, Nestby P, Mulder AH, Vanderschuren LJ. Mifepristone prevents the expression of long-term behavioural sensitization to amphetamine. *Eur J Pharmacol* (1996) **307**:R3–4. doi:10.1016/0014-2999(96)00308-1

168. Deroche-Gamonet V, Sillaber I, Aouizerate B, Izawa R, Jaber M, Ghozland S, et al. The glucocorticoid receptor as a potential target to reduce cocaine abuse. *J Neurosci* (2003) **23**:4785–90.

169. Fiancette JF, Balado E, Piazza PV, Deroche-Gamonet V. Mifepristone and spironolactone differently alter cocaine intravenous self-administration and cocaine-induced locomotion in C57BL/6J mice. *Addict Biol* (2010) **15**:81–7. doi:10.1111/j.1369-1600.2009.00178.x

170. Mesripour A, Hajhashemi V, Rabbani M. Metyrapone and mifepristone reverse recognition memory loss induced by spontaneous morphine withdrawal in mice. *Basic Clin Pharmacol Toxicol* (2008) **102**:377–81. doi:10.1111/j.1742-7843.2007.00183.x

171. Jacquot C, Croft AP, Prendergast MA, Mulholland P, Shaw SG, Little HJ. Effects of the glucocorticoid antagonist, mifepristone, on the consequences of withdrawal from long term alcohol consumption. *Alcohol Clin Exp Res* (2008) **32**:2107–16. doi:10.1111/j.1530-0277.2008.00799.x

172. Koenig HN, Olive MF. The glucocorticoid receptor antagonist mifepristone reduces ethanol intake in rats under limited access conditions. *Psychoneuroendocrinology*

(2004) **29**:999–1003. doi:10.1016/j.psyneuen.2003.09.004

173. Lowery EG, Spanos M, Navarro M, Lyons AM, Hodge CW, Thiele TE. CRF-1 antagonist and CRF-2 agonist decrease binge-like ethanol drinking in C57BL/6J mice independent of the HPA axis. *Neuropsychopharmacology* (2010) **35**:1241–52. doi:10.1038/npp.2009.209

174. O'Callaghan MJ, Croft AP, Jacquot C, Little HJ. The hypothalamopituitary-adrenal axis and alcohol preference. *Brain Res Bull* (2005) **68**:171–8. doi:10.1016/j.brainresbull.2005.08.006

175. Yang X, Wang S, Rice KC, Munro CA, Wand GS. Restraint stress and ethanol consumption in two mouse strains. *Alcohol Clin Exp Res* (2008) **32**:840–52. doi:10.1111/j.1530-0277.2008.00632.x

176. Sharrett-Field L, Butler TR, Berry JN, Reynolds AR, Prendergast MA. Mifepristone pretreatment reduces ethanol withdrawal severity in vivo. *Alcohol Clin Exp Res* (2013):doi:10.1111/acer.12093

177. Johanssen S, Allolio B. Mifepristone (RU 486) in Cushing's syndrome. *Eur J Endocrinol* (2007) **157**:561–9. doi:10.1530/EJE-07-0458

178. DeBattista C, Belanoff J. The use of mifepristone in the treatment of neuropsychiatric disorders. *Trends Endocrinol Metab* (2006) **17**:117–21. doi:10.1016/j.tem.2006.02.006

179. Gallagher P, Watson S, Elizabeth Dye C, Young AH, Nicol Ferrier I. Persistent effects of mifepristone (RU-486) on cortisol levels in bipolar disorder and schizophrenia. *J Psychiatr Res* (2008) **42**:1037–41. doi:10.1016/j.jpsychires.2007.12.005

180. Gallagher P, Watson S, Smith MS, Ferrier IN, Young AH. Effects of adjunctive mifepristone (RU-486) administration on neurocognitive function and symptoms in schizophrenia. *Biol Psychiatry* (2005) **57**:155–61. doi:10.1016/j.biopsych.2004.10.017

181. Gallagher P, Young AH. Mifepristone (RU-486) treatment for depression and psychosis: a review of the therapeutic implications. *Neuropsychiatr Dis Treat* (2006) **2**:33–42.

182. Wulsin AC, Herman JP, Solomon MB. Mifepristone decreases depression-like behavior and modulates neuroendocrine

and central hypothalamic-pituitary-adrenocortical axis responsiveness to stress. *Psychoneuroendocrinology* (2010) **35**:1100–12. doi:10.1016/j.psyneuen.2010.01.011

183. Young AM. Antiglucocorticoid treatments for depression. *Aust N Z J Psychiatry* (2006) **40**:402–5. doi:10.1080/j.1440-1614.2006.01813.x

4

Disruption of maternal parenting circuitry by addictive process: rewiring of reward and stress systems

Helena J. V. Rutherford[1,†] *, Sarah K. Williams[2,†] *, Sheryl Moy[2,3], Linda C. Mayes[1] and Josephine M. Johns[2,3]

[1] Yale Child Study Center, Yale University, New Haven, CT, USA
[2] Department of Psychiatry, University of North Carolina-Chapel Hill, Chapel Hill, NC, USA
[3] Carolina Institute for Developmental Disabilities, University of North Carolina-Chapel Hill, Chapel Hill, NC, USA

Edited by:
Rina Eiden, University at Buffalo, USA

Reviewed by:
Sue Carter, University of Illinois at Chicago, USA
Kelly Lambert, Randolph-Macon College, USA

*Correspondence:

Helena J. V. Rutherford, Yale Child Study Center, Yale University, 230 South Frontage Road, New Haven, CT 06520, USA.
e-mail: helena.rutherford@yale.edu;
Sarah K. Williams, Department of Psychiatry, University of North Carolina-Chapel Hill, 436 Taylor Hall, CB # 7096, Chapel Hill, NC 27599, USA.
e-mail: sarahk_williams@med.unc.edu

[†] Helena J. V. Rutherford and Sarah K. Williams share first-authorship.

Addiction represents a complex interaction between the reward and stress neural circuits, with increasing drug use reflecting a shift from positive reinforcement to negative reinforcement mechanisms in sustaining drug dependence. Preclinical studies have indicated the involvement of regions within the extended amygdala as subserving this transition, especially under stressful conditions. In the addictive situation, the reward system serves to maintain habitual behaviors that are associated with the relief of negative affect, at the cost of attenuating the salience of other rewards. Therefore, addiction reflects the dysregulation between core reward systems, including the prefrontal cortex (PFC), ventral tegmental area (VTA), and nucleus accumbens (NAc), as well as the hypothalamic–pituitary–adrenal axis and extended amygdala of the stress system. Here, we consider the consequences of changes in neural function during or following addiction on parenting, an inherently rewarding process that may be disrupted by addiction. Specifically, we outline the preclinical and human studies that support the dysregulation of reward and stress systems by addiction and the contribution of these systems to parenting. Increasing evidence suggests an important role for the hypothalamus, PFC, VTA, and NAc in parenting, with these same regions being those dysregulated in addiction. Moreover, in addicted adults, we propose that parenting cues trigger stress reactivity rather than reward salience, and this may heighten negative affect states, eliciting both addictive behaviors and the potential for child neglect and abuse.

Keywords: addiction, reward, stress, parenting, preclinical, human

Addiction has been conceptualized as a cyclic process of impairment in self-regulation. Both positive and negative reinforcement mechanisms likely contribute to the maintenance of addiction; the former representing the reward response following initial use, the latter representing continued use for relief of the negative affective state of abstinence. At a neurobiological level, while activation of the brain reward system underscores drug use (i.e., positive reinforcement), the activation of the brain stress system may govern the distress associated with withdrawal (i.e., negative reinforcement). In the addictive situation, the relief of stress by the drug leads to habitual drug use, and the reward system is "co-opted" for purposes of maintaining habitual behavior that is linked to relief of stress or negative emotions. With this co-optation, other more adaptive rewards are not as salient because they are not part of the conditioned stress relief-reward link. Importantly, these rewards include social affiliation and relationships, and this kind of co-optation has profound implications for parenting behaviors among addicted adults, and indeed for their relationships in general. In these instances, relationships may become more stressful for the addicted adult because of the demands for care. Hence, instead of the normative rewards offered by affiliation, the relationship becomes more stressful and serves as a cue for continued compulsive or addictive behavior while perpetuating social or maternal avoidance behavior.

In this paper, we will outline the evidence from preclinical and human studies to address the following propositions outlined in **Figure 1**: (a) addictive processes are a reflection of a dysregulation of the balance between reward systems and the stress response; (b) parenting involves a special adaptation of both reward and stress regulatory neural systems to the relevant cues from offspring that become highly salient for the adult, now a parent; and (c) in the addictive situation, parenting cues are not rewarding but instead stressful. This heightened stress response may promote drug-seeking behaviors rather than parenting behaviors and attending to the infant's needs. We focus on cocaine addiction to explore the evidence for this model.

COCAINE DISRUPTS MATERNAL BEHAVIOR: EVIDENCE FROM RODENT AND HUMAN DATA

Cocaine use and abuse represents a significant public health problem. In 2008, 1.4 million Americans met DSM-IV criteria for drug abuse and dependency for their cocaine addiction (Substance Abuse and Mental Health Services Administration, 2008). Rates of cocaine use in young women have increased, and a number of studies have reported cocaine use during pregnancy (Kuczkowski, 2004). Continued cocaine use into the postpartum period is not uncommon and presents significant problems for parenting practice; specifically, maternal substance abuse is associated

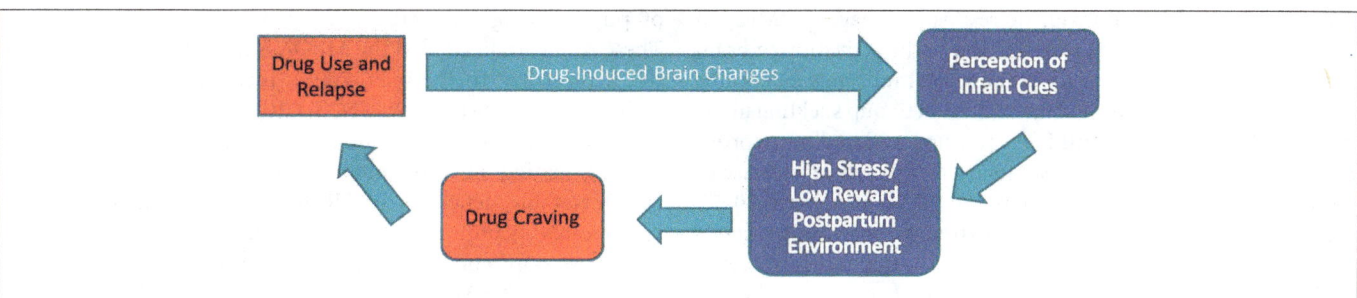

FIGURE 1 | The relationship between addiction and parenting. In our model, addiction represents the dysregulation of stress and reward systems, both of which are adapted to support parenting. In the addicted situation we propose that drug-induced brain changes result in the rewarding value of infant cues being attenuated, replaced by a more stressful neurophysiological response. This stress response to infant cues may increase craving for drugs of abuse, promoting drug seeking and relapse in abstinent mothers, and perpetuates the cycle of neglect.

with significant increases in child neglect (Cash and Wilke, 2003). The complexity of studying cocaine effects on human parenting at behavioral and neurobiological levels is complicated by the breadth of psychosocial and biological variables that are associated with cocaine use and thus, present unique challenges to empirical research. Therefore, we take a complementary approach bridging work from basic science with human studies. Although most mammalian species exhibit some form of parental care toward their young, rodents serve as excellent preclinical models for the study of onset and maintenance of maternal behavior (MB) because, similar to humans, they produce altricial infants requiring an immense commitment in order to ensure survival. The typical rat mother (dam) spends the entire day with pups for 2 weeks postpartum, only leaving the nest to forage for food. Rodents exhibit stereotyped behaviors toward infants (pups) that can be quantified and have behavioral correlates to humans, including nursing and grooming the infant as well as preparing a safe environment for the infant (nest-building). Maternal aggression or defense also emerges during the postpartum period, a behavior that is analogous to "protectiveness" experienced by new human mothers. We begin this paper by considering the empirical support of cocaine disruption to MB in human and rodent studies.

In human studies, the consequences of cocaine exposure and administration on parenting have been explored primarily through observations of mother–child interactions. Within 12–48 h postpartum, mothers who used cocaine during pregnancy responded more passively and were more disengaged from their newborn compared to mothers who were drug-free (Gottwald and Thurman, 1994). Early work with infants suggested that mothers using cocaine during pregnancy evidence reduced expression of positive affect and sensitivity to infant cues, as well as poorer creativity and resourcefulness during dyadic interactions (Burns et al., 1991, 1997). There is some evidence to suggest that while early impairments (e.g., reduced attention toward the infant, shifts in attention away from the infant) in mother–child interactions appear modulated by prenatal cocaine exposure, follow up assessments have shown either a reduction (Mayes et al., 1997) or absence of these same dysfunctions (Ball et al., 1997) suggesting the effects of cocaine exposure may change over time. This has prompted studies to explore the effects of prenatal cocaine exposure on maternal interactions in toddlers too, evidencing maladaptive and hostile interactions of dyads with cocaine

exposure (Johnson et al., 2002; Uhlhorn et al., 2005; Molitor and Mayes, 2010). The consequences of cocaine use during pregnancy have also been explored during feeding episodes. Poorer feeding interactions were reported in mothers who used cocaine during pregnancy and who relapsed postpartum, compared to mothers who had not relapsed (Blackwell et al., 1998). These feeding dyads demonstrated greater conflict (Eiden, 2001) as well as insensitivity (Eiden et al., 2006) between mother and child. It is important to note that impairments in mother–child interactions may also be related to the amount of cocaine consumed during pregnancy (Tronick et al., 2005), as well as postpartum use (Blackwell et al., 1998; Johnson et al., 2002; Eiden et al., 2006). Although to date there are no published neuroimaging studies in cocaine addicted mothers, initial pilot work suggests differential prefrontal cortex (PFC) activation when viewing infant faces in these women compared to mothers with no cocaine use history (Strathearn and Kosten, 2008).

Studies on mother–infant dynamics in the rodent have shown that exposure to cocaine, through acute, intermittent, or chronic treatment regimens, disrupts aspects of MB, with the extent of disruption dependent on dose, duration, time of testing, and treatment regimen (Johns et al., 1994; Nelson et al., 1998). In one commonly used paradigm, dams receive cocaine either chronically on gestation days (GD 1–20; 30 mg/kg) or via single injections during the postpartum period, and are then tested for pup-directed MB following separation and reunion with pups. Either regimen can lead to increased latency and decreased duration of nursing, along with disruptions in licking and nest-building. Cocaine treated dams also exhibit maladaptive maternal aggressive behavior, indicating that social behavior deficits may extend past pup relationships (Johns et al., 1997b; McMurray et al., 2008). These disruptions are not caused by hyperactivity or cocaine withdrawal (Johns et al., 1997b), suggesting instead alterations in motivational or social interaction circuitry.

In contrast to treatment during gestation, repeated exposure to cocaine before pregnancy increases retrieval and licking behaviors in rats and mice early postpartum, suggesting that adult cocaine exposure alters motivational salience and behavior toward later, naturally rewarding stimuli, such as pups (Nephew and Febo, 2010). However, although these mothers were quicker to retrieve pups, they took longer to initiate other MBs, suggesting that the salience may be in having the pup nearby but not in the act of caring for it. Functional magnetic resonance imaging (fMRI) in awake animals has allowed investigation of the activation of brain regions following exposure to rewarding stimuli. Indeed, cocaine pre-exposure also diminished the activation to pup suckling in the medial prefrontal cortex (mPFC), striatum, and auditory cortex, but did not affect baseline dopamine (DA) or percent increase of DA upon exposure to pups in the mPFC (Febo and Ferris, 2007), supporting the important roles in MB and addiction processes these regions hold, a point we will return to later in this review.

Taken together, these findings indicate that cocaine use before, during, and/or after pregnancy can significantly alter MB in the postpartum period. Since MB is not entirely abolished, we propose that these behavioral changes may indicate differences in the reward salience of offspring. Additionally, the transition from pregnancy to the postpartum is inherently stressful to mothers; however, the successful adaptation to this new environment may be considered under the control of allostatic mechanisms. Allostasis has been defined as the active process of responding to challenges from the environment to maintain homeostasis, usually through activation of hormonal stress responses. Successful adaptation to this stressful environment and the ability to respond appropriately to an infant's needs is critical for the infant's survival and thus has been conserved throughout mammalian evolution. It has been proposed that drug addiction can disrupt typical adaptation to stressful non-parenting environments (Le Moal, 2009); however, whether the same is true for the postpartum period remains unclear and offers a potential explanation for the drug-induced deficits described above. The review presented here considers the involvement of neural structures in both the reward and stress systems in parenting (outlined in **Figure 2**).

INITIATION OF MATERNAL BEHAVIOR

Central to this review is the notion that there are significant neurobiological changes subserving the transition to parenthood. These include a variety of structural and neurochemical changes indicating plasticity both at the synaptic and transcriptional regulation levels of control. Throughout this paper we refer to changes in neuronal function, receptor expression, or peptide levels, as a result either from motherhood or drug exposure, as plastic to indicate the dynamic nature of neurons. Critical to the transition to motherhood are significant changes in the function of the hypothalamus and the production of the neuropeptide oxytocin (OT), and therefore we first consider the initiation of MB and the involvement of the hypothalamus and oxytocin before reviewing the stress and reward neural circuitry and their adaptation for parenting.

HYPOTHALAMUS

The medial preoptic area (MPOA) and ventral bed nucleus of the stria terminalis (BNST) are critical for the initiation and maintenance of MB, and represent a directing region controlling the switch to parental behaviors (Numan, 2007). The MPOA has direct connections to the ventral tegmental area (VTA), nucleus accumbens (NAc), mPFC, BNST, and paraventricular nucleus (PVN), allowing it to exert a powerful influence during the postpartum period. Lesions to the MPOA completely abolish retrieval and nest-building behaviors in rats. Nursing is still observed following lesions, though it is diminished, and may be the result

of pups seeking out and attaching to a non-responsive dam. These results indicate that the MPOA is important for the incentive actions in MB (Numan, 2007). Increased MPOA neuronal activation, as measured by c-FOS, CREB, and fMRI, is observed following exposure to pups and pup cues in the first 2 postpartum weeks (Fleming and Korsmit, 1996; Febo et al., 2005; Jin et al., 2005). Notably, deficiency of CREB in mouse mutant lines leads to increases in pup mortality and significant deficits in latency to retrieve pups and in the number of pups brought back to the nest (Jin et al., 2005). DA and serotonin (5-HT) maintain baseline levels in this region across pregnancy, however norepinephrine (NE) is decreased during this period (Olazabal et al., 2004). Overall, the results suggest that CREB activation in the MPOA could be especially important for the initiation and expression of MB. Converging with this in human mothers, individual differences in maternal sensitivity to infant cues revealed differential modulation of the hypothalamus, as well as pituitary and PFC regions, when the mothers were viewing photographs of their own infants, compared to unknown infants (Strathearn et al., 2009). Moreover, in this latter study, maternal OT response following a play interaction correlated with activity in the hypothalamus (as well as the pituitary and ventral striatum).

OXYTOCIN

Oxytocin plays a central role in initiating the onset of MB in several mammalian species, including the rat and human, but its role in maintenance of MB is less clear (Pedersen and Boccia, 2002; Feldman et al., 2007). In the rodent, OT neurons from the PVN project centrally to the main olfactory bulb (MOB), MPOA, NAc, amygdala (AMY), hippocampus, and VTA (see **Figure 3**). OT from the PVN and supraoptic nucleus (SON) project to the pituitary for peripheral release into the bloodstream in response to infant-produced or stressful stimuli (Uvnas-Moberg et al., 2005; Hatton and Wang, 2008). Work using mouse lines null for OT have demonstrated that OT is essential for survival of litters due to effects on milk ejection, but may not be critical for other aspects of maternal responses (Lee et al., 2009). Although OT null-mutants have normal reproductive and nurturing responses (Ferguson et al., 2000, 2001), mouse dams with targeted disruption of the OT receptor gene have significant deficits in pup retrieval, including longer latencies to retrieve each pup and to assume a crouching posture, and shorter time spent crouching over the pups (Takayanagi et al., 2005). Additionally, human mothers with a low functioning OT receptor allele show lower maternal sensitivity in the postpartum (Bakermans-Kranenburg and van Ijzendoorn, 2008). Alterations in OT function have been suggested to underlie maternal deficits in mice with a mutation in *Peg3* (*Paternally expressed gene 3*). Female *Peg3* mutant mice have severe impairments in MB and deficient milk let-down (Champagne et al., 2009). These deficits have been linked to reductions in OT neurons in the hypothalamus and decreased OT binding in the MPOA and lateral septum in *Peg3* mutants (Champagne et al., 2009).

A recent paper by Yoshida et al. (2009) suggested that an underlying mechanism for OT effects on social and anxiety-like behavior is enhanced serotonergic neurotransmission. Central administration of OT to the median raphe nucleus led to significant release of

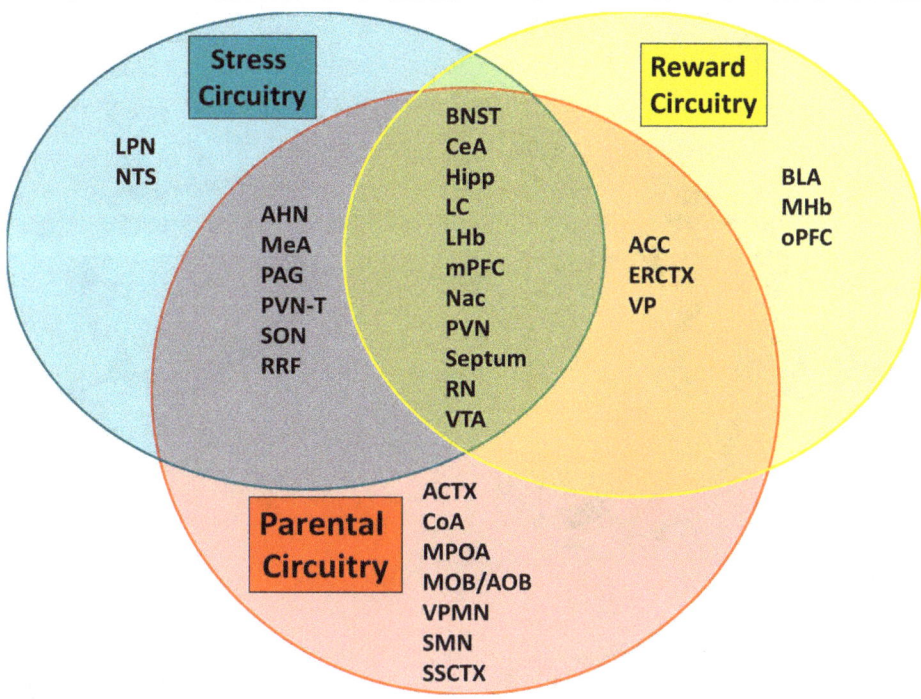

ACC: anterior cingulate cortex
ACTX: auditory cortex
ERCTX: entorhinal cortex
MPFC: medial prefrontal cortex
OPFC: orbito-prefrontal cortex
SSCTX: somatosensory cortex
AOB: accessory olfactory bulb
HIPP: hippocampal formation
LHB: lateral habenula
LS: lateral septum
MHB: medial habenula
MOB: main olfactory bulb
PVN-T: paraventricular nucleus of the thalamus
VP: ventral pallidum
BNST: bed nucleus of stria terminalis
CEA: central nucleus of amygdala
NAC: nucleus accumbens

BLA: basolateral amygdala
COA: cortical amygdala
MEA: medial amygdala
AHN: anterior hypothalamic nucleus
MPOA: medial preoptic area of hypothalamus
PVN: paraventricular nucleus of hypothalamus
SMN: supramammilary body
SON: supraoptic nucleus of hypothalamus
VPMN: ventral premammilary body
PAG: periaquaductal gray
RRF: retrorubial field
VTA: ventral tegmental area
LC : locus coereleus
LPN: lateral parabrachial nucleus
NTS: nucleus tractus solitaris
RN: raphe nuclei

FIGURE 2 | The relationship between neurocircuits of stress, reward, and parenting. Parenting circuitry (red) shares many regions with stress (blue) and reward (yellow). The regions listed in the center have been implicated in all three circuits, suggesting that disruption in regions of one circuit can have profound impact on the functioning of the other connected circuits. It can be seen by the number of regions included in the Parental Circuitry circle that performance of optimal parental care (and the many types of behavior that fall into this category) requires typical functioning of the majority of the brain. Color coding in the legend indicates the anatomical brain systems in which each region belongs.

5-HT in mice (Yoshida et al., 2009). Deletion of the 5-HT$_{1A}$ or $_{1B}$ receptor can alter time spent crouching in the nest, pup retrieval, or other measures of nurturing, and can change maternal effects on the behavioral profiles of offspring (van Velzen and Toth, 2010). Modifications of the serotonin transporter (5-HTT) can confer increased susceptibility to the effects of poor maternal nurturing or other environmental stressors, with long-term consequences for resilience to adverse conditions (Bakermans-Kranenburg and van Ijzendoorn, 2008; Kinnally et al., 2009; Heiming and Sachser, 2010). Enhanced serotonergic neurotransmission by OT could have similar efficacy in the regulation of CREB function relevant to response to stress, exposure to cocaine and other drugs, and to

MB. The reciprocal interactions between the OT and 5-HT signaling pathways in the midbrain and hypothalamus may be severely disrupted following drug use and may contribute to deficits in MB.

Both plasma and brain OT can interact with hypothalamic–pituitary–adrenal (HPA) axis activity (Uvnas-Moberg et al., 2005; Slattery and Neumann, 2008). This information may have implications for human clinical research, as one study recently reported that human mothers who used cocaine during gestation had reduced plasma OT levels and higher perceived stress (Light et al., 2004). The OT system is disrupted by cocaine in several regions, in parallel with behavioral disruptions of MB (Johns et al., 1997a, 2005). For example, the chronic treatment of rat dams with cocaine

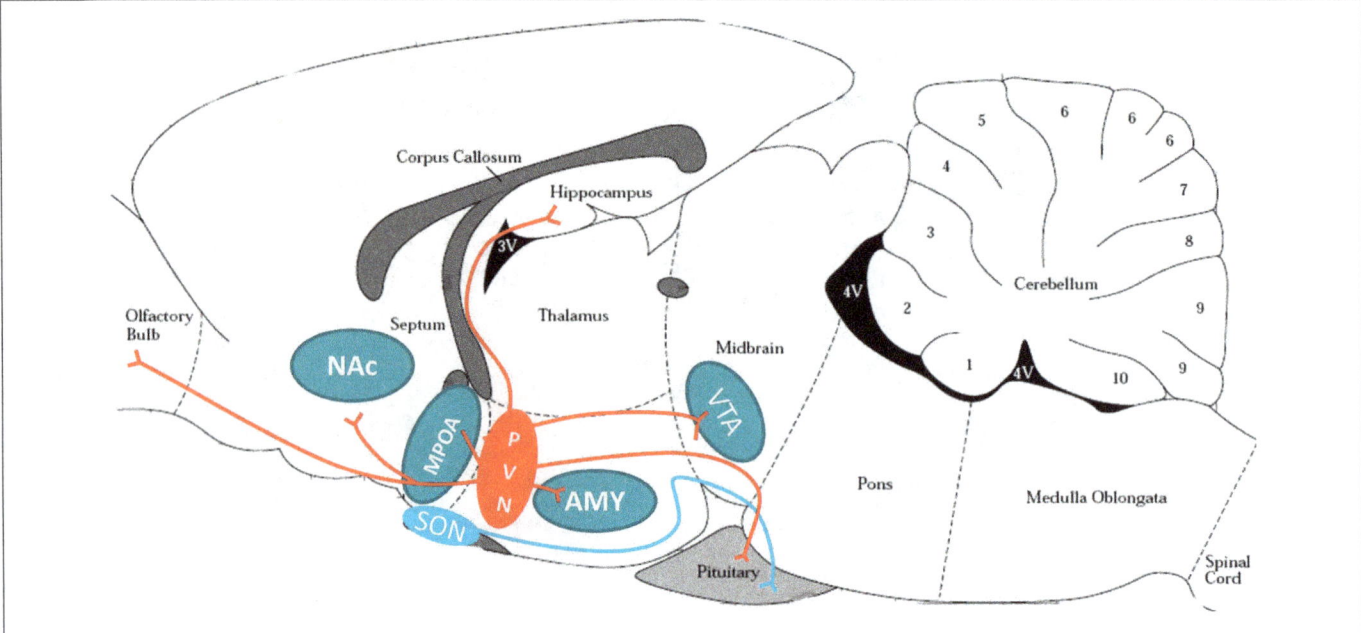

FIGURE 3 | Oxytocinergic projection in the rodent brain. Oxytocin release is anatomically suited to signal in reward, stress, and maternal circuitries. The magnocellular neurons of the PVN (red oval) and SON (blue oval) project to the posterior pituitary to release OT peripherally in response to suckling or stressful stimuli. The parvocellular neurons of the PVN also project to the reward circuitry (VTA and NAc), stress circuitry (hippocampus, AMY, and intra-PVN release), and maternal circuitry (MPOA/BNST and OB), and are believed to be critical for appropriate social interactions. PVN, paraventricular nucleus of hypothalamus; SON, supraoptic nucleus of hypothalamus; VTA, ventral tegmental area; NAc, nucleus accumbens; AMY, amygdala; MPOA, medial preoptic area of the hypothalamus; OB, olfactory bulb. Brain schematic adapted from Paxinos and Watson (1997).

can significantly lower OT levels in the MPOA, hippocampus, and VTA within 24 h of delivery (Johns et al., 1997a). Acute cocaine in the postpartum period can affect OT levels and OT receptors in several brain regions, including lowering levels in the MPOA on postpartum day (PPD) 1, and raising levels in the AMY on PPD 6 (Jarrett et al., 2006; McMurray et al., 2008). Interestingly, OT can also play a role in drug-reward effects. Recent studies in rodent models have shown that OT administration can reduce or block psychostimulant-related responses in tests of conditioned place preference (CPP), self-administration, and reinstatement of drug-seeking behavior (Yang et al., 2010). These data suggest an important role for OT at the intersection of addiction, stress, and MB.

ADAPTION OF THE REWARD SYSTEM FOR PARENTING AND THE IMPACT OF COCAINE

Pups and pup cues have rewarding (motivational) value to rat dams, shown in both CPP and operant responding paradigms (Lee et al., 2000; Mattson and Morrell, 2005). Of particular note, pups often induce CPP greater than the effect of cocaine, indicating the strength of the motivational salience of pups (Seip and Morrell, 2009). However, in rodent studies, as many as 30% of dams prefer a non-pup associated chamber, and these dams exhibit greater locomotor sensitization to cocaine, indicating a subset of the population may be more vulnerable to cocaine's impact on reward circuitry and thus impairments in MB (Mattson and Morrell, 2005; Seip and Morrell, 2007). The circuitry controlling incentive value of reinforcing cues seems to be transiently altered postpartum as dams lack aversive responses (as measured by CPP) after receiving subcutaneous cocaine injections compared to virgin female rats, suggesting that internal physiology can play a major role in the conditioning effects of drugs (Seip et al., 2008).

Multiple reviews of reward circuitry have proposed that DA has a prominent role in drug reward and that the "reward circuit," as presented in **Figure 4**, consists of a midbrain–forebrain pathway that connects the VTA with the NAc and mPFC, with information converging in the NAc to drive locomotor responses toward reward seeking (Koob and Volkow, 2010; Sesack and Grace, 2010). Widespread use of fMRI has also enabled reward circuitry in humans to be investigated, with comparable regions identified, including the orbitofrontal cortex (OFC), amygdala, NAc, as well as the PFC and anterior cingulate cortex (ACC; McClure et al., 2004). A growing literature is emerging that dissects reward-seeking behaviors into independent cognitive processes: "wanting," "liking," and "learning" (Berridge, 2004; Berridge et al., 2009). Liking is defined as the neural reaction underlying sensory pleasure-triggered by immediate receipt of reward. In contrast, "wanting" is defined as the motivational incentive value of the same reward. It has been postulated that dopaminergic signaling described above (VTA/Nac/mPFC) is most important for the "wanting" aspects of behavior. This theory may help explain why, although certain aspects of maternal care are unlikely to have high hedonic impact (i.e., initial nursing, maternal aggression, sleep interruption), mothers still "want" to provide maternal care.

VENTRAL TEGMENTAL AREA

Ventral tegmental area DA neuron activity is responsible for transient and phasic DA release into the NAc (Sombers et al., 2009)

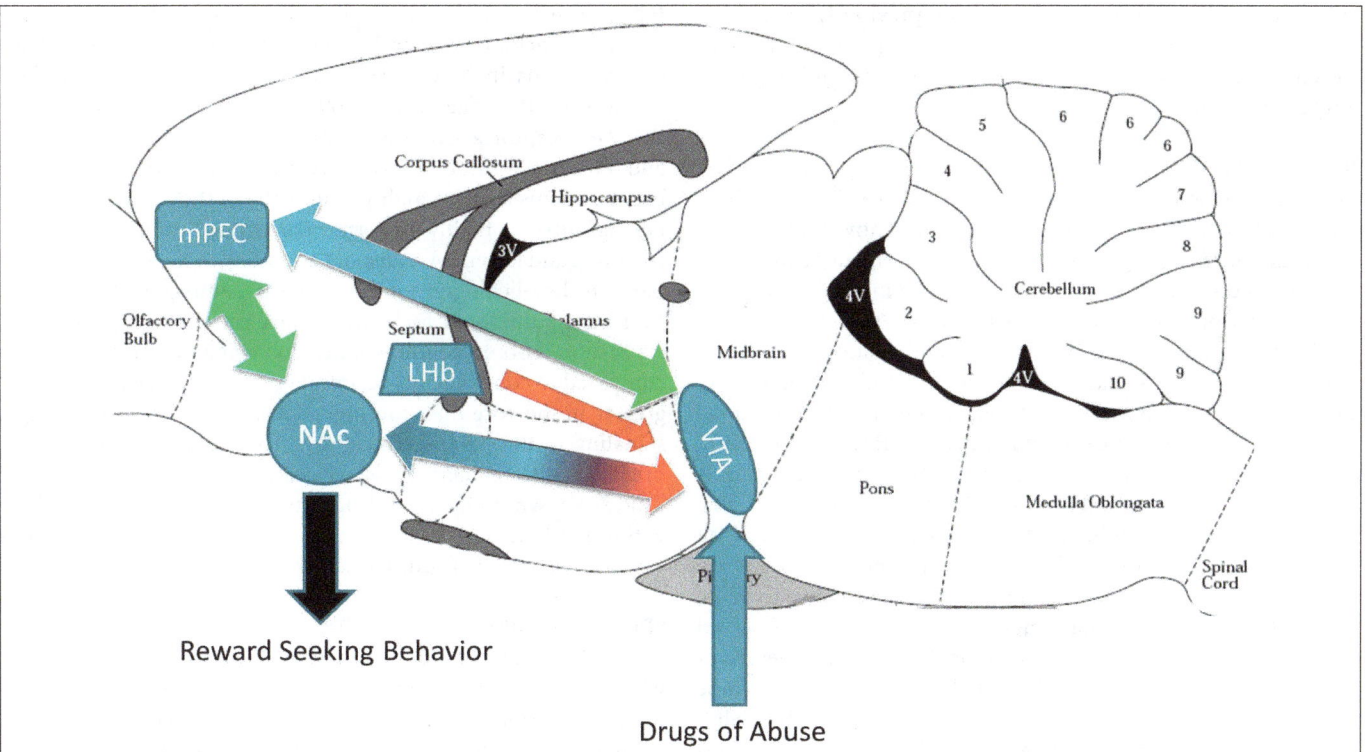

FIGURE 4 | Reward circuitry in the rodent brain. This midline sagittal slice of rodent brain depicts the main brain regions implicated in responding to rewarding stimuli. The ventral tegmental area (VTA) of the midbrain sends dopaminergic projections (blue arrows) to the nucleus accumbens (NAc) and medial prefrontal cortex (mPFC). The NAc (as well as the lateral habenula, LHb) send GABAergic projections (red arrows) to the VTA, while the mPFC sends glutamatergic projections (green arrows) to the VTA. The mPFC and NAc have reciprocal glutamatergic projections. Activity changes in the NAc results in reward seeking or incentive behaviors (black arrow). Brain schematic adapted from Paxinos and Watson (1997).

as well as throughout the reward circuitry, and VTA activity is believed to be crucial for incentive valuation and goal-oriented behaviors (Koob and Volkow, 2010). The VTA consists of DA projection neurons, surrounded by GABAergic interneurons (for review Adell and Artigas, 2004). Cocaine exposure impacts VTA function in ways that may alter its ability to respond to naturally rewarding stimuli. Synaptic levels of 5-HT, NE, and DA are acutely increased by cocaine through its ability to block their transporters, resulting in increased firing rates (Thomas and Malenka, 2003). Cocaine also contributes to increased firing by reducing inhibition, via decreased VTA GABAergic interneuron firing (Steffensen et al., 2008). These cocaine-induced changes do not habituate with repeated exposure; thus, cocaine acutely and chronically increases excitatory tone in the VTA, resulting in higher firing rates (Thomas and Malenka, 2003), potentially creating a threshold for firing that new (infant) stimuli cannot reach. Ovarian hormones enhance cocaine's effect on VTA DA firing in female rats (Zhang et al., 2008), suggesting changes may be accentuated during pregnancy when ovarian hormones are highly upregulated. Importantly, cocaine self-administration causes long-lasting potentiation in the VTA that sucrose self-administration does not (Chen et al., 2008), suggesting that cocaine may prevent further plasticity in the VTA that is needed during the postpartum period.

Evidence from rodent studies supports a role for the DA projection neurons from the VTA in the incentive aspects of MB (Numan, 2007). Lesions of the VTA, or that sever axons from the MPOA to the VTA, disrupt MB (Numan, 2007). Transient inactivation of the VTA, especially through GABA$_A$ receptors, disrupts maternal retrieval, nursing, and CPP for pups (Numan et al., 2009; Seip and Morrell, 2009), while not disrupting cocaine CPP, suggesting that VTA activity is critical for responses to pup stimuli. Mice that are naturally neglectful of their pups show higher basal c-FOS activation, although there is no difference in the number of DA cells in the VTA (Gammie et al., 2008a). This suggests that ignoring pups may be perceived as rewarding for these dams, perhaps due to a reduction in stress. However, whether pup removal decreases stress and increases reward signal in some dams but not others has yet to be directly tested. Electroencephalogram (EEG) and fMRI responses in the VTA are increased by exposure to pups and pup olfactory cues (Febo et al., 2005; Hernandez-Gonzalez et al., 2005). Direct application of OT or opioids in the VTA can facilitate MB (Pedersen et al., 1994; Thompson and Kristal, 1996). Recent evidence has indicated a direct role for OT in regulation of VTA DA cell firing and DA release into the forebrain (Shahrokh et al., 2010). Interestingly, OT antagonists reduce DA release in highly maternal dams, but not in low maternal dams, suggesting there may a "floor" effect on the ability of OT to direct DA cell firing. Taken together, these findings indicate disruption in VTA function can severely affect MB and the rewarding value of pups to dams. Gestational cocaine treatment does not affect basal levels of NE, DA, or DA metabolites in the VTA during the postpartum period; however, basal 5-HT and OT are decreased (Johns et al., 1997a;

Lubin et al., 2003). These data, along with previously mentioned cocaine-induced changes in VTA function, suggest that VTA neurons may be less responsive to OT and thus fire less, although this has yet to be directly tested.

NUCLEUS ACCUMBENS

The NAc, divided into the core and shell, serves several behavioral functions. The shell is involved in the incentive motivational properties of rewarding stimuli via the enhancement of stimulus–reward associations, while the core is involved in the performance components of reward seeking (Di Chiara, 2002; Russo et al., 2010). In humans, the NAc mediates the anticipation and prediction of reward (Knutson and Cooper, 2005), with regional activity varying dependent upon reward magnitude (Haber and Knutson, 2009). The NAc consists primarily of GABAergic projection neurons and interneurons. The major NAc GABAeric efferents project to the lateral hypothalamus, VTA, substantia nigra, brainstem, and ventral pallidum, whose activity is correlated with reward seeking (Koob and Volkow, 2010). Activation of inhibitory DA transmission from the VTA in the NAc in response to acute administration of all major drugs of abuse has been observed (Koob and Volkow, 2010). Cocaine acutely increases levels of inhibitory 5-HT and NE as well (Li et al., 1996). Chronic cocaine exposure upregulates D_1 receptors in the striatum (Ben Shahar et al., 2007), similar to expression in highly maternal dams (Champagne et al., 2004), suggesting that repeated exposure to rewarding stimuli may have similar effects. Although DA transporter expression is unchanged, its activity increases with cocaine consumption (Oleson et al., 2009). Chronic cocaine exposure upregulates 5-HT transporter expression, while not impacting NE transporter expression (Belej et al., 1996). Increases in transporter activity may indicate an attempt of the neurons to return to a level of firing similar to that observed prior to drug use. Cocaine exposure decreases synaptic strength between excitatory PFC afferents to the NAc shell, and causes long-lasting decreased firing in the core (Russo et al., 2010).

The NAc is important for the initiation and maintenance of MB. NAc ablation significantly decreases MB, and specifically lesioning the NAc shell disrupts retrieval behavior without interrupting crouching, licking, or nest-building (Li and Fleming, 2003). The NAc shows increased neuronal activation, through c-FOS expression and fMRI, in response to pups throughout the first postpartum week (Fleming and Korsmit, 1996; Febo et al., 2005). However, no response is observed only to pup cues (Fleming and Korsmit, 1996). In contrast, activation in response to infant cries (relative to white noise) have been observed in human mothers in the regions surrounding the NAc, as well as more extensive cortical and subcortical regions, primarily innervated by dopamine (Lorberbaum et al., 2002).

Lactating rats have lower basal DA in the NAc compared to virgin rats (Olazabal et al., 2004), perhaps allowing greater sensitivity to changes in levels. Real-time *in vivo* voltammetry and microdialysis measurements have shown increased NAc shell DA during nursing, and a direct correlation of DA concentration with duration of licking behavior (Champagne et al., 2004; Afonso et al., 2008). Treatment with DA agonists increases licking specifically in dams that were previously characterized as "low-licking"

(Champagne et al., 2004), suggesting that some threshold must be met to achieve higher licking rates. Similar pharmacological treatments in NAc have been shown to mediate "wanting" of rewards (Berridge et al., 2009). Recently, it has been shown that D_2 receptor activation is important for normal MB (Zhao and Li, 2010). Although D_2 receptor binding does not differ between dams that are highly maternal and those which are low-licking/nursing, highly maternal dams have more D_1 and D_3 receptors and lower DA transporter binding in the NAc shell compared to low-licking/grooming dams (Champagne et al., 2004). In a mouse line bred for maternal neglect, much higher c-FOS expression is observed immediately following the onset of neglect compared to control dams (Gammie et al., 2008a), with the effect greater in the core than the shell. Taken together, dopaminergic signaling in the NAc is critical for MB, and since drug use can drastically alter signaling, this may lead to impaired MB. However, little is known about how drug exposure may impact plasticity within the NAc during pregnancy, parturition, and lactation and this will be a focus of future research.

PREFRONTAL CORTEX

The PFC is involved in a variety of cognitive functions, all of which are critical components in the shift toward drug dependency, addiction, or MB. Understanding the role of the PFC is complex, especially given the wide variation in the degree of cortical parcellation in both human and animal studies (including ACC, OFC, mPFC, and infralimbic) observed across studies (Dalley et al., 2004). The ACC has been associated with the integration and valuation of social information due to its direct connections with AMY, ventral striatum, hypothalamus, periaqueductal gray (PAG), and auditory cortex (Dalley et al., 2004), as well as ordering temporal sequence of behaviors. The OFC, which has a well-established role in decision-making and stimulus–reward relationships, receives input from all sensory modalities as well as the ventral striatum and amygdala. Damage to the OFC may result in changes in anxiety/fear and aggressive behaviors, suggesting its importance in social interactions. The prelimbic and infralimbic cortices, which are subdivisions of the mPFC residing dorsally and ventrally respectively, have been associated with working memory function and attention. However, they play different roles in learning, with the prelimbic cortex contributing to action-outcome associations and the infralimbic contributing to habit formation in rodents. Both the mPFC and OFC have been implicated in controlling impulsivity (Dalley et al., 2004), a point we will return to later. Given that all these functions are critical for appropriate social interactions, understanding how drug use alters their function will highlight how these regions may be involved in altered postpartum behaviors.

Chronic drug use has been tied to deficits in monoamine signaling in the PFC; however it remains unclear whether these deficits are causative or predictive (reviews: Dalley et al., 2008; Koob and Volkow, 2010; Sesack and Grace, 2010). Recent evidence suggests molecular mechanisms underlying drug-induced dysfunction. Glucose metabolism increases following acute cocaine, but decreases following cocaine self-administration, indicating an adapted neuronal response (Hammer Jr. and Cooke, 1994). Cocaine increases blood flow in fMRI studies involving male, female, and lactating rats (Febo et al., 2004; Ferris et al., 2005). This increased "activation" of the mPFC, measured by increased blood flow, may result from increased activity of GABAergic interneurons instead of glutamatergic projection neurons, since cocaine causes a greater VTA-driven inhibition of mPFC projection neurons (Peterson et al., 1990), suggesting an increased inhibition of projection neurons in this area. Cocaine consumption results in hundreds of synaptic plasticity gene expression changes as measured by microarray (Freeman et al., 2010) as well as an upregulation of D_1 receptor and corticotropin releasing factor (CRF) activity (Ben Shahar et al., 2007; Corominas et al., 2010). Taken together, these data suggest multiple mechanisms for a decline in mPFC function through cocaine use. The ACC, OFC, infralimbic, and prelimbic cortex all show increased c-FOS expression in response to cocaine-associated cues compared to saline controls (Ciccocioppo et al., 2001), indicating an important role for drug learning in these areas. Given that these regions are likely responding to cocaine exposure through plastic changes to gene expression, these neurons may not respond with the appropriate amount of neuroplasticity needed for the transition to perform MBs. A single study of cocaine administration prior to pregnancy demonstrated diminished activation to pup suckling in the mPFC, but did not affect baseline DA or percent increase of DA upon exposure to pups in the mPFC (Febo and Ferris, 2007). However, whether cocaine during pregnancy affects the development of plastic changes in the PFC during pregnancy and lactation, similar to those observed in males has yet to be directly tested.

The PFC's role in organizing behavior is critical for the transition to MB, with disruptions to PFC function resulting in deficits to MB. Pharmacological antagonism of sodium channels or activation of GABA in the mPFC has shown that this region is necessary for retrieval behavior of rat dams (Febo et al., 2010). These experiments did not change approach behavior toward pups, only the decision to retrieve them to the nest, indicating a change in motivation not investigatory behaviors. Excitotoxic lesion to the mPFC also disrupts pup retrieval, licking, and the overall pattern or order of MBs, indicating the importance of this region in working memory and attention in the postpartum period (Afonso et al., 2007). Pup suckling increases fMRI response in the medial and lateral PFC and insular cortex of lactating rats, an effect that is dependent on OT (Febo et al., 2005). EEG data suggest that mPFC activity changes in response to pup odors (Hernandez-Gonzalez et al., 2005). As mentioned above, DA contributes to PFC function. DA levels are lower in rats in late pregnancy compared to virgin female rats (Olazabal et al., 2004), which may result in higher overall activity given that DA acts to inhibit activity in the mPFC (Peterson et al., 1990). Recently, high impulsivity has been tied to deficits in MB, which may be associated with alterations in mPFC function (Lovic et al., 2010). Since mPFC DA is an important mediator of impulsivity (Dalley et al., 2008) and can be disrupted by drug abuse, differences in behavioral organization during MB could occur following drug use (although this has yet to be directly tested). Notably, as early as PPD1, the cingulate cortex shows increased c-FOS expression in response to pups, and continues to respond to cues through the first week (Fleming and Korsmit, 1996). Additionally, the infralimbic cortex responds to cues while the prelimbic cortex does not (Fleming and Korsmit,

1996), suggesting the importance of specific regionalization of circuitry.

In human mothers, although widespread activity in the brain is observed when exposed to infant cues, the OFC is emerging as a core region in parenting circuitry, being reliably engaged across studies as well as in different modalities. Activity in the right OFC was greater when mothers listened to infant cries compared to white noise (Lorberbaum et al., 1999, 2002), and bilateral OFC activity increased when mothers viewed photographs of their own child compared to an unfamiliar child (Nitschke et al., 2004). Bridging brain and self-reported mood, this bilateral activity in the OFC has been significantly correlated with positive mood scores while viewing infant faces (Nitschke et al., 2004), with left OFC activity correlating with positive mood and right OFC activity correlating with negative mood scores in a subsequent study (Noriuchi et al., 2008). In this latter report, other regions showed sensitivity to infant familiarity, including the dorsolateral PFC, insula, putamen, and PAG. In preclinical work, the PAG is thought to mediate the immobile stance of nursing since exposure to suckling pups selectively activates PAG to a greater extent than exposure to non-suckling pups (Lonstein and Stern, 1997). The PAG has also been strongly implicated in controlling aggressive behavior in the postpartum period and mediating fearfulness or anxiety (Lonstein et al., 1998). It is worth noting that the lateral OFC (and PAG) responds selectively to cues of maternal attachment, with overlapping regions including striatum, insula, and dorsal ACC responding to cues of maternal and romantic attachment (Bartels and Zeki, 2004). Magnetoencephalography has also demonstrated the role of the OFC to infant cue sensitivity and further suggests that OFC may exert a top-down role on infant face perception (Kringelbach et al., 2008). In a sample containing both parents and non-parents, 130 ms post-stimulus onset there was a significant increase in activity in the mOFC in response to viewing infant faces but not adult faces. Moreover, this early sensitivity to infant faces was not observed in areas traditionally associated with face processing (i.e., fusiform cortex). Nevertheless, after 165 ms from face presentation, a comparable divergence of activity in response to infant and adult faces in fusiform cortex was observed. These findings suggest that the mOFC is not only sensitive to infant cues, but may also modulate subsequent activity in fusiform regions for preferential processing of infant face stimuli.

LATERAL HABENULA

Another forebrain region that can contribute to the MB is the lateral habenula (LHb; Geisler and Trimble, 2008). LHb activity is correlated with the lack of an expected reward as well as stressful stimuli, suggesting a role for processing the saliency and value of rewarding and distressing stimuli. The LHb shows increased c-FOS to acute cocaine and cocaine-associated cues but this response diminishes following repeated exposure (Franklin and Druhan, 2000), suggesting that cocaine exposure disrupts the ability of the LHb to decrease VTA activity. This may be especially important if VTA neurons have reached a level of firing that cannot change further in response to infant stimuli. This structure is activated in response to pups on PPD7 and reacts to pup cues on PPD 10 (Felton et al., 1998). Interestingly, the c-FOS response is diminished in dams that exhibit strong CPP for pups. This may be explained by the role of the LHb in negative reward salience (Mattson and Morrell, 2005). The LHb has also been shown to have both excitatory input and output following MB (Geisler and Trimble, 2008). This is an intriguing area of future research as it may play a critical role in determining the salience of different stimuli during the postpartum.

In summary, a number of core structures have been identified in the reward neural circuitry and we have described the evidence to suggest their adaption to parenting. The modulation of these neurocircuits by cocaine implicates a neurobiological pathway through which substance use can affect parenting behavior. The role of the reward circuitry, specifically mesocorticolimbic DA, has also been implicated in social attachment more broadly in preclinical studies of MB and pair bonding (Insel, 2003). This will be an important avenue for future research to understand how cocaine influences MB as well as the formation and maintenance of maternal attachment.

ADAPTION OF THE STRESS SYSTEM FOR PARENTING AND THE IMPACT OF COCAINE

In addition to the reward neural circuits, there is also significant recruitment of stress neurocircuits in MB across humans and rodents. Moreover, a wealth of behavioral data implicates stress in drug seeking and relapse (Corominas et al., 2010; Koob and Volkow, 2010). Therefore we turn our attention to the neural circuitry of the stress system, its involvement in MB, and modulation by cocaine.

HPA AXIS

The canonical HPA axis stress system seems to play a critical role in the development of drug abuse, while extrahypothalamic stress circuitry [BNST, hippocampus, medial portion of NAc, and central amygdala (CeA)] appears to have a more important role in the motivational effects of both acute withdrawal and stress-induced relapse (Aston-Jones and Harris, 2004; Corominas et al., 2010; Koob and Volkow, 2010). It has been hypothesized that addiction results from a neuroadaptational shift in how rewards are processed, specifically a loss of positive reinforcement and replacement by negative reinforcement within a basal circuit termed the extended amygdala (Koob and Volkow, 2010). This long-lasting shift in how the brain stress systems process similar environmental cues (allostasis) following either drug exposure or repeated stressful events has been defined as allostatic load (McEwen and Gianaros, 2011). Alterations in allostatic load are derived by chronic exposure to psychological or physiological stressors.

Acutely, the HPA axis is activated by a variety of external and internal events (see **Figure 5**). The PVN in the hypothalamus

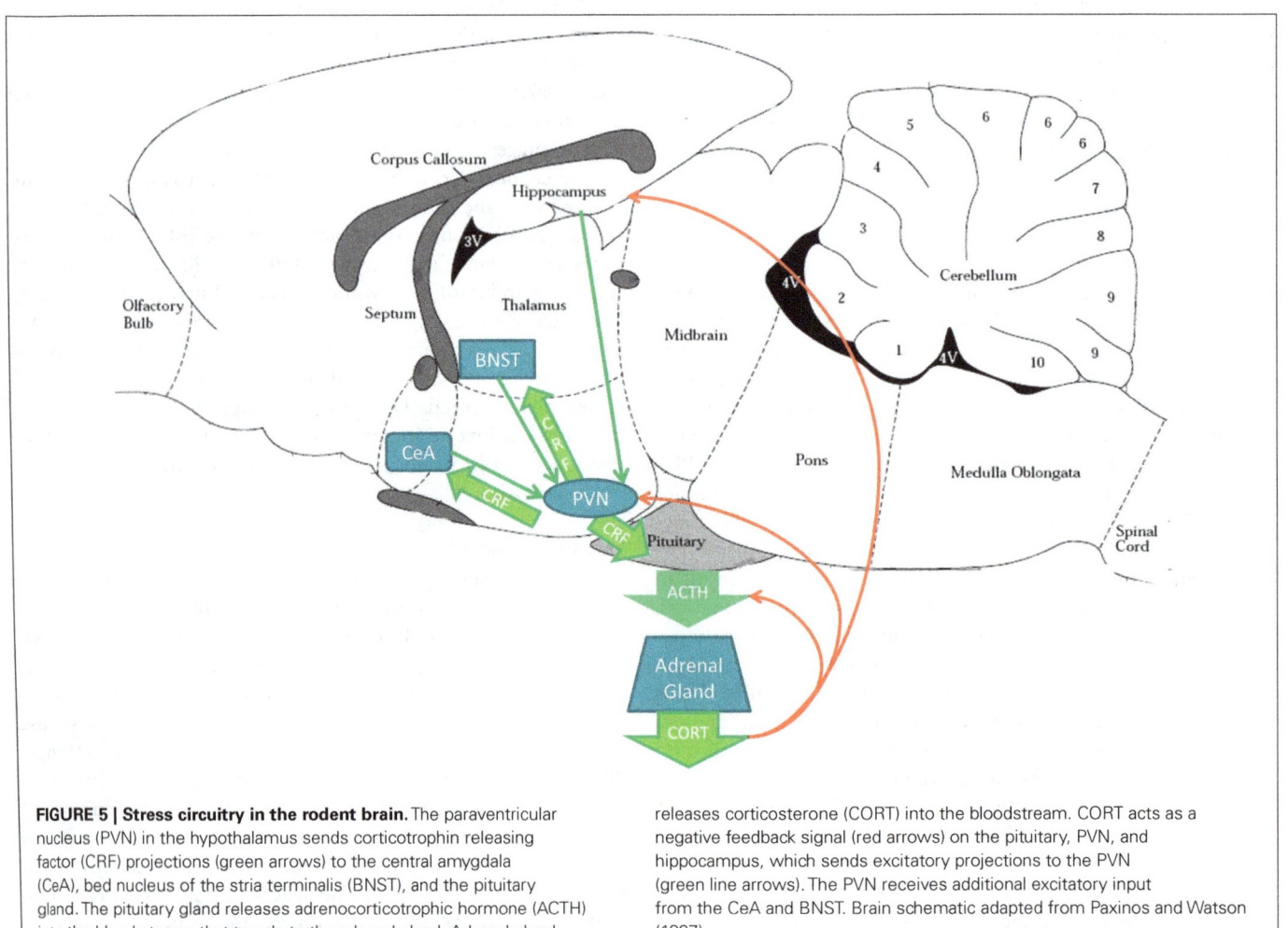

FIGURE 5 | Stress circuitry in the rodent brain. The paraventricular nucleus (PVN) in the hypothalamus sends corticotrophin releasing factor (CRF) projections (green arrows) to the central amygdala (CeA), bed nucleus of the stria terminalis (BNST), and the pituitary gland. The pituitary gland releases adrenocorticotrophic hormone (ACTH) into the blood stream that travels to the adrenal gland. Adrenal gland releases corticosterone (CORT) into the bloodstream. CORT acts as a negative feedback signal (red arrows) on the pituitary, PVN, and hippocampus, which sends excitatory projections to the PVN (green line arrows). The PVN receives additional excitatory input from the CeA and BNST. Brain schematic adapted from Paxinos and Watson (1997).

releases CRF into the hypophyseal blood supply, stimulating release of adrenocorticotropic hormone (ACTH) from the pituitary gland into the circulating blood supply. ACTH acts on the adrenal medulla to release glucocorticoids (GC), i.e., cortisol (humans) or corticosterone (CORT; rodents) into circulation where it exerts numerous physiological effects. Importantly, CORT exerts negative feedback through GC activation in the pituitary, PVN, and hippocampus, returning the system to homeostasis. In addition to release of CRF into the blood, PVN neurons project to other central nervous system sites, such as the BNST, CeA, and VTA (Palkovits et al., 1998; Rodaros et al., 2007), resulting in a variety of neuronal responses in those brain regions (for review see Corominas et al., 2010). The PVN reversibly remodels structurally during pregnancy and lactation to allow greater excitatory input (Panatier and Oliet, 2006), which suggests this is an especially dynamic time for changes in brain stress systems. If drug use alters PVN responsiveness during the postpartum period, this could have deleterious effects given that the PVN also contains cells that produce OT (Slattery and Neumann, 2008), and the PVN has been found to activate in response to pups by PPD7 (Fleming and Korsmit, 1996; Febo et al., 2005).

There is an established bidirectional relationship between substance abuse and stress-related symptomatology in both humans and animal models (Sinha, 2001; Goeders, 2002; Koob and Volkow, 2010). Cocaine acutely activates the HPA axis (Goeders, 2002), a response that is upregulated by female sex hormones (Russo et al., 2003), suggesting that pregnancy, and the accompanying high circulating female steroid hormones, may be an especially sensitive period for cocaine-induced stress hormone effects. Chronic effects depend on the treatment regime; for example, HPA responses neither habituate nor sensitize to daily cocaine administration, although ACTH and CORT responses to binge doses do habituate over repeated exposures (Goeders, 2002). However, self-administration of cocaine causes an increased CORT response and decreased negative feedback that coincides with lower GC receptors in the PVN but not other forebrain regions (Rodaros et al., 2007), indicating other brain centers can exhibit continued response. HPA reactivity is heightened during acute withdrawal and dysregulation persists during protracted abstinence (Goeders, 2002; Corominas et al., 2010). Importantly, chronic cocaine can raise CORT levels significantly during pregnancy (Quinones-Jenab et al., 2000), although the impact on feedback regulation is less clear. Complementary data has shown that stress and HPA signaling can facilitate psychostimulant self-administration (Goeders, 2002), indicating a mechanism that stress may influence later drug seeking in the postpartum.

The role of the HPA stress system in MB is just beginning to be understood, and it is clear that tight regulation is involved throughout the transition from pregnancy, lactation, and weaning. As mentioned above, allostasis or the dynamic response of the HPA and brain stress systems to ever-changing environments, probably plays a critical role, however, the role of allostatic mechanisms are in great need of study. Gestational and postpartum periods are characterized by high basal CORT levels, a hyporesponsive hormonal reaction to stress, and low anxiety levels (Slattery and Neumann, 2008). Changes in maternal stress responses have been correlated with deficits in maternal care (Smith et al., 2004;

Bosch et al., 2007; Chen et al., 2010). Stress during pregnancy can reduce MB in rodents, however, if the rats were prone to have low MB, stress did not affect them, suggesting that optimal care can be reduced only to a certain extent (Champagne and Meaney, 2006). Administering CORT to pregnant or lactating rats decreases nursing and increases neglectful behaviors (Bosch et al., 2007; Brummelte and Galea, 2010). Repeated stressors during the postpartum period can inhibit lactation in rodents, suggesting direct hormonal effects (Lau and Simpson, 2004). Conversely, removing circulating stress hormones reduces but does not abolish MB (Rees et al., 2004). Lactation depends on peripheral OT levels and OT is known to bi-directionally interact with HPA activity, with chronic OT treatment leading to reduced acute stress responses (Uvnas-Moberg et al., 2005), suggesting that OT may help mediate stress hyporesponsiveness in the postpartum period (Slattery and Neumann, 2008).

Many neurotransmitters involved in stress regulation are altered in the early postpartum period, including 5-HT, DA, NE, vasopressin, OT, and CRF (Slattery and Neumann, 2008). These signals act primarily within the PVN to direct stress response, especially CRF and OT release. CRF serves as a "stress" signal not only by activating the HPA axis, but also through signaling to the extended amygdala and VTA, resulting in increased saliency of cues surrounding a stressful event (Gulpinar and Yegen, 2004; Corominas et al., 2010). It has been proposed that postpartum changes in stress responsiveness are caused by the reduction in CRF production in the PVN (Slattery and Neumann, 2008), presumably through high OT levels, which can attenuate upregulation of CRF mRNA in response to stress (Lightman et al., 2001; Windle et al., 2004). In a series of studies using mutant mouse lines, Gammie and colleagues have shown that CRF signaling modulates components of MB (Gammie et al., 2007, 2008b; D'Anna and Gammie, 2009). Targeted disruption of CRFR1 significantly reduced nursing, while CRFR2 knockout dams exhibit reduced maternal aggression in a resident–intruder test. Since exposure to an unfamiliar intruder could be highly stressful for a dam, it is possible that CRF function is especially important for MB related to adverse or anxiogenic conditions. Alterations in CRF-mediated signaling, as observed with repeated cocaine treatment (Corominas et al., 2010), could thus disrupt normal offspring defense. We will now consider the key neural regions which are involved in the stress response, addiction, and parenting; specifically the hippocampus and extended amygdala, before reviewing the important interaction between stress and reward circuitries.

HIPPOCAMPUS

Hippocampal activity exerts an inhibitory influence, via ventral hippocampal neurons' direct connections to the PVN, and regulates release of stress hormones (Herman et al., 2005). The hippocampus has reciprocal excitatory connections, via the entorhinal cortex, with the mPFC, ACC, insular, and other association cortices, suggesting its role in coordinating spatial and social information, as well as contributing to the stress response during pregnancy and lactation. Chronic cocaine exposure alters monoamine signaling as well as several kinase signaling pathways (Dworkin et al., 1995; Freeman et al., 2001), suggesting cocaine may down-regulate the hippocampal formation's ability to temper PVN stress responsiveness.

The hippocampus exhibits increased BOLD signal in response to pup suckling (Febo et al., 2005), and lesions of this area will specifically disrupt MB (Kimble et al., 1967), suggesting perhaps a role for learning safe locations for nursing. The entorhinal cortex, directly adjacent to the hippocampus exhibits the positive BOLD response to pup suckling (Febo et al., 2005), indicating an involvement of social memory. Adult neurogenesis in the hippocampus is decreased in maternally sensitized rats, an effect tied to increased circulating CORT levels (Pawluski and Galea, 2007), and is similar to what is observed following cocaine use (Venkatesan et al., 2007), suggesting that increased CORT from cocaine exposure may decrease neurogenesis even further, although this remains to be tested. Hippocampal monoamine levels do not change throughout pregnancy or following gestational cocaine exposure (Lubin et al., 2003; Olazabal et al., 2004), indicating that potential changes in function may rely on CRF and CORT signaling. In addition, OT levels are decreased in the hippocampus in virgin rats and in the postpartum following chronic gestational cocaine exposure (Johns et al., 1997a; Lubin et al., 2001), which may suggest as interaction with CRF and CORT.

EXTENDED AMYGDALA
The extended amygdala contributes to processing emotions (particularly fear and anxiety), refining the limbic input to motor systems (Alheid, 2003; Koob and Volkow, 2010) and may be involved in the integration of cortical information with the HPA axis function. The extended amygdala consists of the CeA, medial amygdala (MeA), sublenticular extended amygdala, BNST, and medial and caudal portions of the NAc (Alheid, 2003). The CeA and BNST have reciprocal connections with the PVN and are an independent source of CRF (Alheid, 2003). Cocaine exposure results in long-term changes in CRF activity in these regions (Corominas et al., 2010). Chronic cocaine treatment has short and long-term effects on the neuronal response to stress by increasing CRF-dependent activation in the amygdala and BNST in response to stress in males (Kash et al., 2008); however, its effects on females are less clear. Signaling mediated by CRF has been implicated in neuroadaptation during a chronic cocaine regimen and reinstatement of cocaine reward (Corominas et al., 2010). Although a majority of this work has focused on withdrawal from cocaine, it suggests that the chronic exposure alters CRF signaling. Additionally, the conditioned release of NE, which may be altered by cocaine exposure, in the BNST in response to stressors may elevate anxiety which then augments the reward value of drugs through negative reinforcement (Aston-Jones and Harris, 2004; Koob and Volkow, 2010). Overall, these lines of evidence support a role for this region as a critical convergence point between reward and stress circuitry in addiction. Acute cocaine can increase OT in the amygdala (Elliott et al., 2001), while chronic cocaine treatment during pregnancy reduces OT receptor binding in the BNST and amygdala in the early postpartum (Johns et al., 2004; Jarrett et al., 2006).

Disruptions in extended amygdala activity can have major detrimental effects on MB. Activation of the amygdala and BNST regions can lead to decreases in MB (Rasia-Filho et al., 2000; Walker et al., 2003; Bosch et al., 2005). In particular, activation of the MeA

can inhibit dams from approaching pups. Further, mouse dams characterized by maternal neglect have higher c-FOS expression in the MeA and CeA compared to control dams (Numan, 2007; Gammie et al., 2008a). The MeA and cortical amygdala (CeA) are activated by exposure to pups during the first week postpartum, but not by exposure to pup cues (Fleming et al., 1994a; Fleming and Walsh, 1994b; Stack et al., 2002). The basolateral amygdala (BLA) is not activated until PPD3 and responds to cues on PPD10, consistent with its role in cue-learning (Pego et al., 2008). OT in the AMY is important for regulating anxiety and maternal aggressive behavior, and is increased following chronic cocaine exposure (Bosch et al., 2005; McMurray et al., 2008). Given the complex changes occurring in the extended amygdala during the postpartum, it is likely that previous drug use may interrupt the normal course of functional plasticity.

THE INTERACTION OF STRESS AND REWARD CIRCUITS
Importantly, stress alters the reward circuitry. Although the emphasis of stress on reward circuitry function has focused on CRF signaling in the extended amygdala, GC activation is important as well. Chronic stress increases glutamatergic signaling and synaptic function in the NAc shell and the VTA similar to what is observed following psychostimulant exposure (Meshul et al., 1998; Campioni et al., 2009; Lodge and Grace, 2005). Cocaine-induced changes in VTA activity and NAc DA release are dependent on both CRF and CORT (Cleck et al., 2008; Kash et al., 2008). GCs can modulate sensitivity to DA in NAc neurons, especially in lactating rats (Der-Avakian et al., 2006; Byrnes et al., 2007). The role of GCs in sensitizing the NAc to psychostimulants may be especially important, given the large amount of circulating GC during pregnancy and lactation (Byrnes et al., 2007). The transcription factor CREB has been implicated in persistent changes in the brain following exposure to drugs of addiction or stressful environmental events, and is expressed throughout the reward circuitry (Briand and Blendy, 2010). Increased levels of phosphorylated CREB may be an important mechanism in the acute and chronic effects of cocaine administration and sensitization (Briand and Blendy, 2010), and in stress-induced reinstatement of conditioned responses to cocaine (Kreibich and Blendy, 2004). Disruption of *CREB* function can lead to higher sensitivity to the rewarding effects of cocaine, but disrupts potentiation of drug-related behavior following episodes of stress (Dinieri et al., 2009), while *CREB* overexpression can attenuate locomotor effects of cocaine (Kreibich et al., 2009; Briand and Blendy, 2010). Disruption of signaling through CRF receptor 1 can block stress-induced enhancement of conditioned responses to cocaine, as well as stress-elicited increases in phosphorylated CREB (Kreibich et al., 2009). Taken together, these data suggest that cocaine-induced changes in stress signaling may interact synergistically with changes in the reward circuitry to affect maternal response.

Finally it is important to note the proposal that the maintenance of allostatic processes requires the coordinated signaling between the hippocampus, amygdala, and PFC (McEwen and Gianaros, 2011). Since it is clear that these regions are important for reaction to stress and initiation and maintenance of MB, and are negatively impacted by cocaine exposure, they highlight regions that deserve further research in drug-exposed parenting models.

PARENTING CUES AS STRESSFUL CUES IN ADDICTION

As we have reviewed here, the neural circuitry of the reward and stress systems contribute to substance use initiation, as well as continued use and subsequent dependence. Many of the key neural structures within these circuits are also those that are observed in studies of parenting, suggesting that these overlapping neural circuits present as mechanisms through which drugs of abuse can modulate parenting behavior. These findings related to the model presented in the introduction to this review are presented in **Figure 6**. The final component of our model posits that in the addicted situation, infant cues are stressful rather than rewarding, and that heightened levels of stress increases craving for substances of abuse that through past experience have been associated with the relief of negative affect. Therefore, the act of caring for an infant may promote drug-seeking behaviors in currently using mothers, as well as triggering relapse in abstinent mothers.

At a neurobiological level, the relationship between parenting, addiction, and stress is in its infancy. However, substance use has been well associated with stress-related symptomatology (Sinha, 2001), and early on stress has been highlighted as modulating parenting behavior (Webster-Stratton, 1990). Increasing levels of stress in parenting are believed to be related to insufficient resources (e.g., income, emotional stability) to manage the demands of caring for a child, and that this is enhanced in addicted mothers, who report higher levels of stress than non-substance using mothers (Kelley, 1998). This data suggests that addicted mothers may exhibit a maladaptive shift in allostasic control of stress during the postpartum period. Additional research has

evidenced parenting stress as an important mediator to maternal risk factors and their impact on parenting behavior (Suchman and Luthar, 2001). These initial studies support the notion of parenting as a stressor, and we will now consider the relationship between stress and craving which is integral to our model.

Accumulating evidence has shown that individuals with more intense craving when exposed to stress are more likely to relapse, and that drug use affords one means of stress regulation, albeit a maladaptive, self-perpetuating one (Sinha and Li, 2007). In these studies, participants are exposed to an interpersonal stressor and changes in the hemodynamic response are then compared to exposure to a neutral non-stressor condition. In non-substance using individuals, exposure to stress has been shown to increase the hemodynamic response in (1) frontal regions, including the right mPFC and ventral ACC; and (2) limbic and midbrain regions, including the posterior cingulate, left striatum, thalamus, bilateral caudate and putamen, and left hippocampal and parahippocampal regions (Sinha et al., 2004). Further work by the same research group (Sinha et al., 2005) demonstrated that while some changes in the hemodynamic response are common in normal individuals and cocaine-dependent subjects, healthy controls show increased activity in the ACC, while cocaine-dependent participants instead have a decrease in activity in this same region that extended into the lateral frontal cortex. The authors interpret this difference in ACC functioning in relation to differences in emotion regulation and cognitive control between the two groups and the relationship of these functions to addictive behaviors. Replicating their earlier finding, stress exposure increased activity in hippocampal

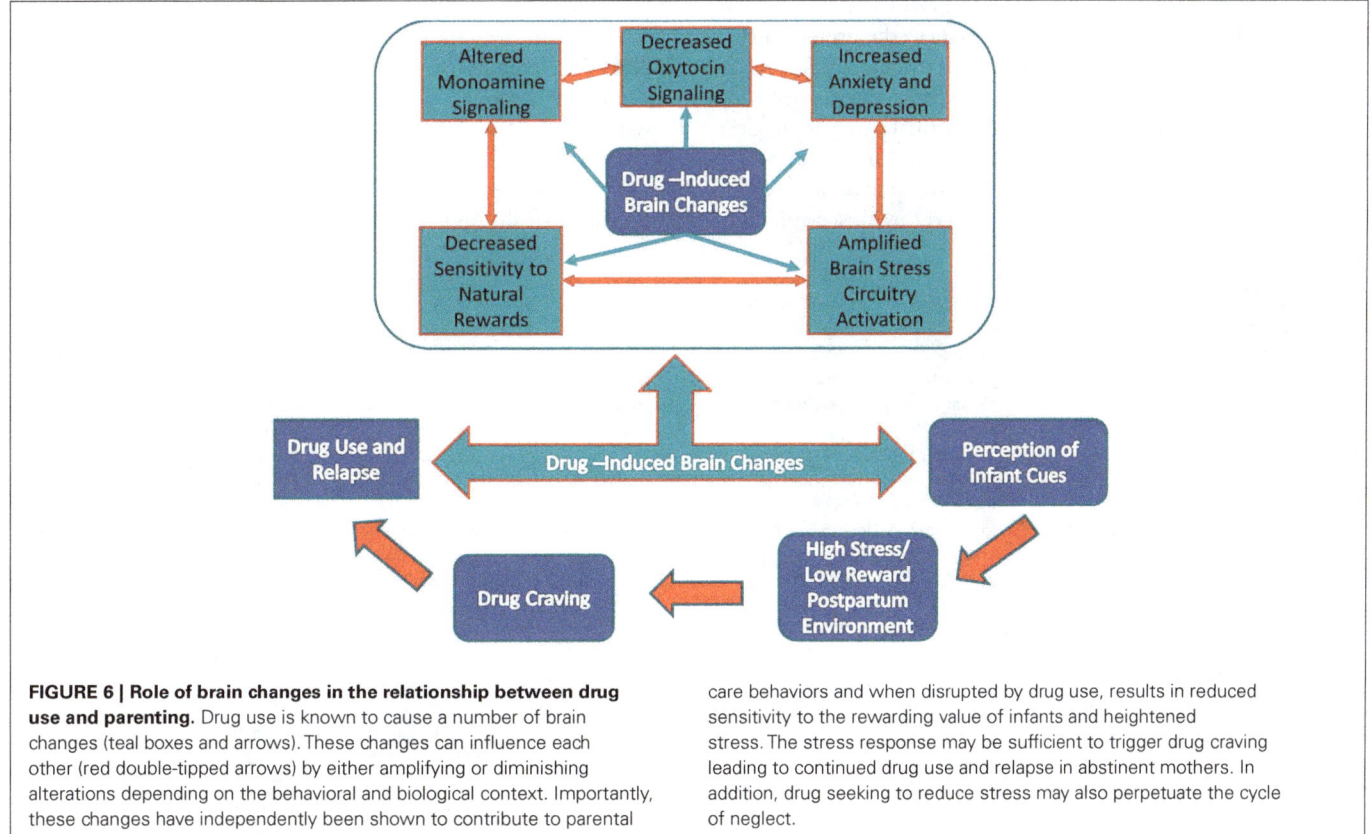

FIGURE 6 | Role of brain changes in the relationship between drug use and parenting. Drug use is known to cause a number of brain changes (teal boxes and arrows). These changes can influence each other (red double-tipped arrows) by either amplifying or diminishing alterations depending on the behavioral and biological context. Importantly, these changes have independently been shown to contribute to parental care behaviors and when disrupted by drug use, results in reduced sensitivity to the rewarding value of infants and heightened stress. The stress response may be sufficient to trigger drug craving leading to continued drug use and relapse in abstinent mothers. In addition, drug seeking to reduce stress may also perpetuate the cycle of neglect.

and parahippocampal regions in healthy controls, but this response was absent in cocaine-dependent participants, who instead showed an increased response in the bilateral dorsal striatum and caudate region. Activity in this latter region positively correlated with self-report craving scores, consistent with this structure's role in addiction. Increasing activity in the right dorsolateral PFC, as well as the left posterior insular and superior temporal sulcus, also correlated with increasing scores on self-report of craving and distress in cocaine-dependent participants. The implications of these findings are that, while addiction modulates the stress response, this modulation of activity correlates with self-reports of drug craving, suggesting a putative link between craving, stress, and addiction. This is further emphasized by finding that increasing activity in regions including the medial PFC, following stress induction, predicts time to relapse, correlating with amount of drug use on each occasion, as well as the number of days drug use has occurred following relapse (Sinha and Li, 2007). A wealth of literature, too large to detail here, has begun to discover the molecular mechanisms and brain activation patterns of similar stress-induced relapse behaviors in animal models. Important to our hypotheses are data suggesting that DA and CRF are critical signaling molecules in the VTA, extended amygdala, and PFC (Erb, 2010; Van den Oever et al., 2010; Wise and Morales, 2010), as well as being associated with alterations in allostatic load.

Finding both that exposure to stress results in brain responses that can differentiate addicted individuals from non-addicted individuals and that neural activity correlates with craving and relapse indicate the importance of vulnerability to stress in the maintenance of addiction. Specifically, these studies indicate that exposure to stress heightens craving which results in drug-seeking behavior and relapse. Bridging these results to the present review, we propose that parenting cues will elicit similar stress reactivity (e.g., Kelley, 1998) which could induce drug-seeking behaviors in the addicted mother, thereby likely contributing to neglectful behavior which is so highly correlated with drug addiction in mothers (e.g., Cash and Wilke, 2003). It is the goal of our ongoing preclinical and human subject studies to explore this empirically.

CONCLUSION

In the review presented here we have identified the contribution of reward and stress pathways to the neural circuitry of parenting, underscoring the modulation of these pathways by addiction. We have described addiction as the dysregulation of the reward and stress systems, the same systems that are adapted for parenting to increase the saliency of infant cues. We propose that in the addictive situation, parenting cues are not as rewarding as they would normally be and could instead be stressful, which with a probable dysregulation of stress adaptation mechanisms, may lead to increased drug seeking and neglectful parenting behavior. While we focused more specifically on cocaine addiction, the principles of this model will likely hold for other addictive processes, owing to the common roles of stress and reward systems in the initiation and maintenance of substance use. Moreover, recognizing early mother–child relationships as a source of stress will be important when considering appropriate therapeutic approaches for prevention as well as treatment of maternal substance abuse (e.g., Pajulo et al., 2006; Suchman et al., 2008). This is emphasized by high relapse rates early postpartum by mothers abstaining from substances of abuse during pregnancy, supporting the notion that the postpartum period presents as a specific time of vulnerability to stress in recent mothers. Indeed, the discussion presented here suggests that therapeutic approaches that target stress regulation may be important for the capacity to parent, maintaining abstinence in addiction, and decreasing the incidence of child abuse and neglect. Potential neurobiological targets could include CRF and OT as they have been shown to be key signaling systems for stress, addiction, and parenting.

ACKNOWLEDGMENTS

The authors were supported by Award Number P01DA022446 (Josephine M. Johns) from the National Institute on Drug Abuse. The content is solely the responsibility of the authors and does not necessarily represent the official views of the National Institute on Drug Abuse or the National Institutes of Health.

REFERENCES

Adell, A., and Artigas, F. (2004). The somatodendritic release of dopamine in the ventral tegmental area and its regulation by afferent transmitter systems. *Neurosci. Biobehav. Rev.* 28, 415–431.

Afonso, V. M., Grella, S. L., Chatterjee, D., and Fleming, A. S. (2008). Previous maternal experience affects accumbal dopaminergic responses to pup-stimuli. *Brain Res.* 1198, 115–123.

Afonso, V. M., Sison, M., Lovic, V., and Fleming, A. S. (2007). Medial prefrontal cortex lesions in the female rat affect sexual and maternal behavior and their sequential organization. *Behav. Neurosci.* 121, 515–526.

Alheid, G. F. (2003). Extended amygdala and basal forebrain. *Ann. N. Y. Acad. Sci.* 985, 185–205.

Aston-Jones, G., and Harris, G. C. (2004). Brain substrates for increased drug seeking during protracted withdrawal. *Neuropharmacology* 47(Suppl. 1), 167–179.

Bakermans-Kranenburg, M. J., and van Ijzendoorn, M. H. (2008). Oxytocin receptor (OXTR) and serotonin transporter (5-HTT) genes associated with observed parenting. *Soc. Cogn. Affect. Neurosci.* 3, 128–134.

Ball, S. A., Mayes, L. C., DeTeso, J. A., and Schottenfeld, R. S. (1997). Maternal attentiveness of cocaine abusers during child-based assessments. *Am. J. Addict.* 6, 135–143.

Bartels, A., and Zeki, S. (2004). The neural correlates of maternal and romantic love. *Neuroimage* 21, 1155–1166.

Belej, T., Manji, D., Sioutis, S., Barros, H. M., and Nobrega, J. N. (1996). Changes in serotonin and norepinephrine uptake sites after chronic cocaine: pre- vs. post-withdrawal effects. *Brain Res.* 736, 287–296.

Ben Shahar, O., Keeley, P., Cook, M., Brake, W., Joyce, M., Nyffeler, M. Heston, R., and Ettenberg, A. (2007). Changes in levels of D1, D2, or NMDA receptors during withdrawal from brief or extended daily access to IV cocaine. *Brain Res.* 1131, 220–228.

Berridge, K. C. (2004). Motivation concepts in behavioral neuroscience. *Physiol. Behav.* 81, 179–209.

Berridge, K. C., Robinson, T. E., and Aldridge, J. W. (2009). Dissecting components of reward: 'liking', 'wanting', and learning. *Curr. Opin. Pharmacol.* 9, 65–73.

Blackwell, P., Kirkhart, K., Schmitt, D., and Kaiser, M. (1998). Cocaine/polydrug-affected dyads: implications for infant cognitive development and mother-infant interaction during the first six postnatal months. *J. Appl. Dev. Psychol.* 19, 235–248.

Bosch, O. J., Meddle, S. L., Beiderbeck, D. I., Douglas, A. J., and Neumann, I. D. (2005). Brain oxytocin correlates with maternal aggression: link to anxiety. *J. Neurosci.* 25, 6807–6815.

Bosch, O. J., Musch, W., Bredewold, R., Slattery, D. A., and Neumann, I. D. (2007). Prenatal stress increases HPA axis activity and impairs maternal care in lactating female offspring: implications for postpartum mood disorder. *Psychoneuroendocrinology* 32, 267–278.

Briand, L. A., and Blendy, J. A. (2010). Molecular and genetic substrates linking stress and addiction. *Brain Res.* 1314, 219–234.

Brummelte, S., and Galea, L. A. (2010). Chronic corticosterone during pregnancy and postpartum affects maternal care, cell proliferation and depressive-like behavior in the dam. *Horm. Behav.* 58, 769–779.

Burns, K., Chethik, L., Burns, W. J., and Clark, R. (1991). Dyadic disturbances in cocaine-abusing mothers and their infants. *J. Clin. Psychol.* 47, 316–319.

Burns, K. A., Chethik, L., Burns, W. J., and Clark, R. (1997). The early relationship of drug abusing mothers and their infants: an assessment at eight to twelve months of age. *J. Clin. Psychol.* 53, 279–287.

Byrnes, E. M., Bridges, R. S., Scanlan, V. F., Babb, J. A., and Byrnes, J. J. (2007). Sensorimotor gating and dopamine function in postpartum rats. *Neuropsychopharmacology* 32, 1021–1031.

Campioni, M. R., Xu, M., and McGehee, D. S. (2009). Stress-induced changes in nucleus accumbens glutamate synaptic plasticity. *J. Neurophysiol.* 101, 3192–3198.

Cash, S. J., and Wilke, D. J. (2003). An ecological model of maternal substance abuse and child neglect: issues, analyses, and recommendations. *Am. J. Orthopsychiatry* 73, 392–404.

Champagne, F. A., Chretien, P., Stevenson, C. W., Zhang, T. Y., Gratton, A., and Meaney, M. J. (2004). Variations in nucleus accumbens dopamine associated with individual differences in maternal behavior in the rat. *J. Neurosci.* 24, 4113–4123.

Champagne, F. A., Curley, J. P., Swaney, W. T., Hasen, N. S., and Keverne, E. B. (2009). Paternal influence on female behavior: the role of Peg3 in exploration, olfaction, and neuroendocrine regulation of maternal behavior of female mice. *Behav. Neurosci.* 123, 469–480.

Champagne, F. A., and Meaney, M. J. (2006). Stress during gestation alters postpartum maternal care and the development of the offspring in a rodent model. *Biol. Psychiatry* 59, 1227–1235.

Chen, B. T., Bowers, M. S., Martin, M., Hopf, F. W., Guillory, A. M., Carelli, R. M., Chou, J. K., and Bonci, A. (2008). Cocaine but not natural reward self-administration nor passive cocaine infusion produces persistent LTP in the VTA. *Neuron* 59, 288–297.

Chen, Y., Holzman, C., Chung, H., Senagore, P., Talge, N. M., and Siler-Khodr, T. (2010). Levels of maternal serum corticotropin-releasing hormone (CRH) at midpregnancy in relation to maternal characteristics. *Psychoneuroendocrinology* 35, 820–832.

Ciccocioppo, R., Sanna, P. P., and Weiss, F. (2001). Cocaine-predictive stimulus induces drug-seeking behavior and neural activation in limbic brain regions after multiple months of abstinence: reversal by D(1) antagonists. *Proc. Natl. Acad. Sci. U.S.A.* 98, 1976–1981.

Cleck, J. N., Ecke, L. E., and Blendy, J. A. (2008). Endocrine and gene expression changes following forced swim stress exposure during cocaine abstinence in mice. *Psychopharmacology (Berl.)* 201, 15–28.

Corominas, M., Roncero, C., and Casas, M. (2010). Corticotropin releasing factor and neuroplasticity in cocaine addiction. *Life Sci.* 86, 1–9.

Dalley, J. W., Cardinal, R. N., and Robbins, T. W. (2004). Prefrontal executive and cognitive functions in rodents: neural and neurochemical substrates. *Neurosci. Biobehav. Rev.* 28, 771–784.

Dalley, J. W., Mar, A. C., Economidou, D., and Robbins, T. W. (2008). Neurobehavioral mechanisms of impulsivity: fronto-striatal systems and functional neurochemistry. *Pharmacol. Biochem. Behav.* 90, 250–260.

D'Anna, K. L., and Gammie, S. C. (2009). Activation of corticotropin-releasing factor receptor 2 in lateral septum negatively regulates maternal defense. *Behav. Neurosci.* 123, 356–368.

Der-Avakian, A., Bland, S. T., Schmid, M. J., Watkins, L. R., Spencer, R. L., and Maier, S. F. (2006). The role of glucocorticoids in the uncontrollable stress-induced potentiation of nucleus accumbens shell dopamine and conditioned place preference responses to morphine. *Psychoneuroendocrinology* 31, 653–663.

Di Chiara, G. (2002). Nucleus accumbens shell and core dopamine: differential role in behavior and addiction. *Behav. Brain Res.* 137, 75–114.

Dinieri, J. A., Nemeth, C. L., Parsegian, A., Carle, T., Gurevich, V. V., Gurevich, E., Neve, R. L., Nestler, E. J., and Carlezon, W. A. Jr. (2009). Altered sensitivity to rewarding and aversive drugs in mice with inducible disruption of cAMP response element-binding protein function within the nucleus accumbens. *J. Neurosci.* 29, 1855–1859.

Dworkin, S. I., Co, C., and Smith, J. E. (1995). Rat brain neurotransmitter turnover rates altered during withdrawal from chronic cocaine administration. *Brain Res.* 682, 116–126.

Eiden, R. D. (2001). Maternal substance use and mother–infant feeding interactions. *Infant Ment. Health J.* 22, 497–511.

Eiden, R. D., Stevens, A., Schuetze, P., and Dombkowski, L. E. (2006). A conceptual model for maternal behavior among polydrug cocaine-using mothers: the role of postnatal cocaine use and maternal depression. *Psychol. Addict. Behav.* 20, 1–10.

Elliott, J. C., Lubin, D. A., Walker, C. H., and Johns, J. M. (2001). Acute cocaine alters oxytocin levels in the medial preoptic area and amygdala in lactating rat dams: implications for cocaine-induced changes in maternal behavior and maternal aggression. *Neuropeptides* 35, 127–134.

Erb, S. (2010). Evaluation of the relationship between anxiety during withdrawal and stress-induced reinstatement of cocaine seeking. *Prog. Neuropsychopharmacol. Biol. Psychiatry* 34, 798–807.

Febo, M., Felix-Ortiz, A. C., and Johnson, T. R. (2010). Inactivation or inhibition of neuronal activity in the medial prefrontal cortex largely reduces pup retrieval and grouping in maternal rats. *Brain Res.* 1325, 77–88.

Febo, M., and Ferris, C. F. (2007). Development of cocaine sensitization before pregnancy affects subsequent maternal retrieval of pups and prefrontal cortical activity during nursing. *Neuroscience* 148, 400–412.

Febo, M., Numan, M., and Ferris, C. F. (2005). Functional magnetic resonance imaging shows oxytocin activates brain regions associated with mother-pup bonding during suckling. *J. Neurosci.* 25, 11637–11644.

Febo, M., Segarra, A. C., Nair, G., Schmidt, K., Duong, T. Q., and Ferris, C. F. (2004). The neural consequences of repeated cocaine exposure revealed by functional MRI in awake rats. *Neuropsychopharmacology* 30, 936–943.

Feldman, R., Weller, A., Zagoory-Sharon, O., and Levine, A. (2007). Evidence for a neuroendocrinological foundation of human affiliation: plasma oxytocin levels across pregnancy and the postpartum period predict mother-infant bonding. *Psychol. Sci.* 18, 965–970.

Felton, T. M., Linton, L., Rosenblatt, J. S., and Morrell, J. I. (1998). Intact neurons of the lateral habenular nucleus are necessary for the non-hormonal, pup-mediated display of maternal behavior in sensitized virgin female rats. *Behav. Neurosci.* 112, 1458–1465.

Ferguson, J. N., Aldag, J. M., Insel, T. R., and Young, L. J. (2001). Oxytocin in the medial amygdala is essential for social recognition in the mouse. *J. Neurosci.* 21, 8278–8285.

Ferguson, J. N., Young, L. J., Hearn, E. F., Matzuk, M. M., Insel, T. R., and Winslow, J. T. (2000). Social amnesia in mice lacking the oxytocin gene. *Nat. Genet.* 25, 284–288.

Ferris, C. F., Kulkarni, P., Sullivan, J. M. Jr., Harder, J. A., Messenger, T. L., and Febo, M. (2005). Pup suckling is more rewarding than cocaine: evidence from functional magnetic resonance imaging and three-dimensional computational analysis. *J. Neurosci.* 25, 149–156.

Fleming, A. S., and Korsmit, M. (1996). Plasticity in the maternal circuit: effects of maternal experience on Fos-Lir in hypothalamic, limbic, and cortical structures in the postpartum rat. *Behav. Neurosci.* 110, 567–582.

Fleming, A. S., Suh, E. J., Korsmit, M., and Rusak, B. (1994a). Activation of Fos-like immunoreactivity in the medial preoptic area and limbic structures by maternal and social interactions in rats. *Behav. Neurosci.* 108, 724–734.

Fleming, A. S., and Walsh, C. (1994b). Neuropsychology of maternal behavior in the rat: c-fos expression during mother-litter interactions. *Psychoneuroendocrinology* 19, 429–443.

Franklin, T. R., and Druhan, J. P. (2000). Expression of Fos-related antigens in the nucleus accumbens and associated regions following exposure to a cocaine-paired environment. *Eur. J. Neurosci.* 12, 2097–2106.

Freeman, W. M., Brebner, K., Lynch, W. J., Robertson, D. J., Roberts, D. C., and Vrana, K. E. (2001). Cocaine-responsive gene expression changes in rat hippocampus. *Neuroscience* 108, 371–380.

Freeman, W. M., Lull, M. E., Patel, K. M., Brucklacher, R. M., Morgan, D., Roberts, D. C., and Vrana, K. E. (2010). Gene expression changes in the medial prefrontal cortex and nucleus accumbens following abstinence from cocaine self-administration. *BMC Neurosci.* 11, 29. doi: 10.1186/1471-2202-11-29

Gammie, S. C., Bethea, E. D., and Stevenson, S. A. (2007). Altered maternal profiles in corticotropin-releasing factor receptor 1 deficient mice. *BMC Neurosci.* 8, 17. doi: 10.1186/1471-2202-8-17

Gammie, S. C., Edelmann, M. N., Mandel-Brehm, C., D'Anna, K. L., Auger, A. P., and Stevenson, S. A. (2008a). Altered dopamine signaling in naturally occurring maternal neglect. *PLoS ONE* 3, e1974. doi: 10.1371/journal.pone.0001974

Gammie, S. C., Seasholtz, A. F., and Stevenson, S. A. (2008b). Deletion of corticotropin-releasing factor binding protein selectively impairs maternal, but not intermale aggression. *Neuroscience* 157, 502–512.

Geisler, S., and Trimble, M. (2008). The lateral habenula: no longer neglected. *CNS Spectr.* 13, 484–489.

Goeders, N. E. (2002). Stress and cocaine addiction. *J. Pharmacol. Exp. Ther.* 301, 785–789.

Gottwald, S. R., and Thurman, S. K. (1994). The effects of prenatal cocaine exposure on mother–infant interaction and infant arousal in the newborn period. *Topics Early Child. Spec. Educ.* 14, 217–231.

Gulpinar, M. A., and Yegen, B. C. (2004). The physiology of learning and memory: role of peptides and stress. *Curr. Protein Pept. Sci.* 5, 457–473.

Haber, S. N., and Knutson, B. (2009). The reward circuit: linking primate anatomy and human imaging. *Neuropsychopharmacology* 35, 4–26.

Hammer, R. P. Jr., and Cooke, E. S. (1994). Gradual tolerance of metabolic activity is produced in mesolimbic regions by chronic cocaine treatment, while subsequent cocaine challenge activates extrapyramidal regions of rat brain. *J. Neurosci.* 14, 4289–4298.

Hatton, G. I., and Wang, Y. F. (2008). Neural mechanisms underlying the milk ejection burst and reflex. *Prog. Brain Res.* 170, 155–166.

Heiming, R. S., and Sachser, N. (2010). Consequences of serotonin transporter genotype and early adversity on behavioral profile – pathology or adaptation? *Front. Neurosci.* 4:187. doi: 10.3389/fnins.2010.00187

Herman, J. P., Ostrander, M. M., Mueller, N. K., and Figueiredo, H. (2005). Limbic system mechanisms of stress regulation: hypothalamo-pituitary-adrenocortical axis. *Prog. Neuropsychopharmacol. Biol. Psychiatry* 29, 1201–1213.

Hernandez-Gonzalez, M., Prieto-Beracoechea, C., Navarro-Meza, M.,

Ramos-Guevara, J. P., Reyes-Cortes, R., and Guevara, M. A. (2005). Prefrontal and tegmental electrical activity during olfactory stimulation in virgin and lactating rats. *Physiol. Behav.* 83, 749–758.

Insel, T. R. (2003). Is social attachment an addictive disorder? *Physiol. Behav.* 79, 351–357.

Jarrett, T. M., McMurray, M. S., Walker, C. H., and Johns, J. M. (2006). Cocaine treatment alters oxytocin receptor binding but not mRNA production in postpartum rat dams. *Neuropeptides* 40, 161–167.

Jin, S. H., Blendy, J. A., and Thomas, S. A. (2005). Cyclic AMP response element-binding protein is required for normal maternal nurturing behavior. *Neuroscience* 133, 647–655.

Johns, J. M., Elliott, D. L., Hofler, V. E., Joyner, P. W., McMurray, M. S., and Jarrett, T. M., Haslup, A. M., Middleton, C. L., Elliott, J. C., and Walker, C. H. (2005). Cocaine treatment and prenatal environment interact to disrupt intergenerational maternal behavior in rats. *Behav. Neurosci.* 119, 1605–1618.

Johns, J. M., Lubin, D. A., Walker, C. H., Joyner, P., Middleton, C., Hofler, V., and McMurray, M. (2004). Gestational treatment with cocaine and fluoxetine alters oxytocin receptor number and binding affinity in lactating rat dams. *Int. J. Dev. Neurosci.* 22, 321–328.

Johns, J. M., Lubin, D. A., Walker, C. H., Meter, K. E., and Mason, G. A. (1997a). Chronic gestational cocaine treatment decreases oxytocin levels in the medial preoptic area, ventral tegmental area and hippocampus in Sprague-Dawley rats. *Neuropeptides* 31, 439–443.

Johns, J. M., Noonan, L. R., Zimmerman, L. I., Li, L., and Pedersen, C. A. (1997b). Effects of short- and long- term withdrawal from gestational cocaine treatment on maternal behavior and aggression in Sprague-Dawley rats. *Dev. Neurosci.* 19, 368–374.

Johns, J. M., Noonan, L. R., Zimmerman, L. I., Li, L., and Pedersen, C. A. (1994). Effects of chronic and acute cocaine treatment on the onset of maternal behavior and aggression in Sprague-Dawley rats. *Behav. Neurosci.* 108, 107–112.

Johnson, A. L., Morrow, C. E., Accornero, V. H., Xue, L., Anthony, J. C., and Bandstra, E. S. (2002). Maternal cocaine use: estimated effects on mother-child play interactions in the preschool period. *J. Dev. Behav. Pediatr.* 23, 191–202.

Kash, T. L., Nobis, W. P., Matthews, R. T., and Winder, D. G. (2008). Dopamine enhances fast excitatory synaptic transmission in the extended amygdala by a CRF-R1-dependent process. *J. Neurosci.* 28, 13856–13865.

Kelley, S. J. (1998). Stress and coping behaviors of substance-abusing mothers. *J. Soc. Pediatr. Nurs.* 3, 103–110.

Kimble, D. P., Rogers, L., and Hendrickson, C. W. (1967). Hippocampal lesions disrupt maternal, not sexual behavior in the albino rat. *J. Comp. Physiol. Psychol.* 63, 401–407.

Kinnally, E. L., Tarara, E. R., Mason, W. A., Mendoza, S. P., Abel, K., Lyons, L. A., and Capitanio, J. P. (2009). Serotonin transporter expression is predicted by early life stress and is associated with disinhibited behavior in infant rhesus macaques. *Genes Brain Behav.* 9, 45–52.

Knutson, B., and Cooper, J. C. (2005). Functional magnetic resonance imaging of reward prediction. *Curr. Opin. Neurol.* 18, 411–417.

Koob, G. F., and Volkow, N. D. (2010). Neurocircuitry of addiction. *Neuropsychopharmacology* 35, 217–238.

Kreibich, A. S., and Blendy, J. A. (2004). cAMP response element-binding protein is required for stress but not cocaine-induced reinstatement. *J. Neurosci.* 24, 6686–6692.

Kreibich, A. S., Briand, L., Cleck, J. N., Ecke, L., Rice, K. C., and Blendy, J. A. (2009). Stress-induced potentiation of cocaine reward: a role for CRF R1 and CREB. *Neuropsychopharmacology* 34, 2609–2617.

Kringelbach, M. L., Lehtonen, A., Squire, S., Harvey, A. G., Craske, M. G., Holliday, I. E., Green, A. L., Aziz, T. Z., Hansen, P. C., Cornelissen, P. L., and Stein, A. (2008). A specific and rapid neural signature for parental instinct. *PLoS ONE* 3, e1664. doi: 10.1371/journal.pone.0001664

Kuczkowski, K. (2004). The cocaine abusing parturient: a review of anesthetic considerations. *Can. J. Anesth.* 51, 145–154.

Lau, C., and Simpson, C. (2004). Animal models for the study of the effect of prolonged stress on lactation in rats. *Physiol. Behav.* 82, 193–197.

Le Moal, M. (2009). Drug abuse: vulnerability and transition to addiction. *Pharmacopsychiatry* 42, S42–S55.

Lee, A., Clancy, S., and Fleming, A. S. (2000). Mother rats bar-press for pups: effects of lesions of the mpoa and limbic sites on maternal behavior and operant responding for pup- reinforcement. *Behav. Brain Res.* 108, 215–231. [Corrected and republished article originally

printed in *Behav. Brain Res.* 1999; 100, 15–31].

Lee, H. J., Macbeth, A. H., Pagani, J. H., and Young, W. S. III. (2009). Oxytocin: the great facilitator of life. *Prog. Neurobiol.* 88, 127–151.

Li, M., and Fleming, A. S. (2003). The nucleus accumbens shell is critical for normal expression of pup-retrieval in postpartum female rats. *Behav. Brain Res.* 145, 99–111.

Li, M. Y., Yan, Q. S., Coffey, L. L., and Reith, M. E. (1996). Extracellular dopamine, norepinephrine, and serotonin in the nucleus accumbens of freely moving rats during intracerebral dialysis with cocaine and other monoamine uptake blockers. *J. Neurochem.* 66, 559–568.

Light, K. C., Grewen, K. M., Amico, J. A., Boccia, M., Brownley, K. A., and Johns, J. M. (2004). Deficits in plasma oxytocin responses and increased negative affect, stress, and blood pressure in mothers with cocaine exposure during pregnancy. *Addict. Behav.* 29, 1541–1564.

Lightman, S. L., Windle, R. J., Wood, S. A., Kershaw, Y. M., Shanks, N., and Ingram, C. D. (2001). Peripartum plasticity within the hypothalamo-pituitary-adrenal axis. *Prog. Brain Res.* 133, 111–129.

Lodge, D. J., and Grace, A. A. (2005). Acute and chronic corticotropin-releasing factor 1 receptor blockade inhibits cocaine-induced dopamine release: correlation with dopamine neuron activity. *J. Pharmacol. Exp. Ther.* 314, 201–206.

Lonstein, J. S., Simmons, D. A., and Stern, J. M. (1998). Functions of the caudal periaqueductal gray in lactating rats: kyphosis, lordosis, maternal aggression, and fearfulness. *Behav. Neurosci.* 112, 1502–1518.

Lonstein, J. S., and Stern, J. M. (1997). Role of the midbrain periaqueductal gray in maternal nurturance and aggression: c-fos and electrolytic lesion studies in lactating rats. *J. Neurosci.* 17, 3364–3378.

Lorberbaum, J. P., Newman, J. D., Dubno, J. R., Horwitz, A. R., Nahas, Z., Teneback, C. C., Bloomer, C. W., Bohning, D. E., Vincent, D., Johnson, M. R., Emmanuel, N., Brawman-Mintzer, O., Book, S. W., Lydiard, R. B., Ballenger, J. C., and George, M. S. (1999). Feasibility of using fMRI to study mothers responding to infant cries. *Depress. Anxiety* 10, 99–104.

Lorberbaum, J. P., Newman, J. D., Horwitz, A. R., Dubno, J. R., Lydiard, R. B., Hamner, M. B., Bohning, D. E., and George, M. S. (2002). A potential role for thalamocingulate circuitry in human maternal behavior. *Biol. Psychiatry* 51, 431–445.

Lovic, V., Palombo, D. J., and Fleming, A. S. (2010). Impulsive rats are less maternal. *Dev. Psychobiol.* 53, 13–22.

Lubin, D. A., Cannon, J. B., Black, M. C., Brown, L. E., and Johns, J. M. (2003). Effects of chronic cocaine on monoamine levels in discrete brain structures of lactating rat dams. *Pharmacol. Biochem. Behav.* 74, 449–454.

Lubin, D. A., Meter, K. E., Walker, C. H., and Johns, J. M. (2001). Effects of chronic cocaine administration on aggressive behavior in virgin rats. *Prog. Neuropsychopharmacol. Biol. Psychol.* 25, 1421–1433.

Mattson, B. J., and Morrell, J. I. (2005). Preference for cocaine- versus pup-associated cues differentially activates neurons expressing either Fos or cocaine- and amphetamine-regulated transcript in lactating, maternal rodents. *Neuroscience* 135, 315–328.

Mayes, L. C., Feldman, R., Granger, R. H., Haynes, O. M., Bornstein, M. H., and Schottenfeld, R. (1997). The effects of polydrug use with and without cocaine on mother-infant interaction at 3 and 6 months. *Infant Behav. Dev.* 20, 489–502.

McClure, S. M., York, M. K., and Montague, P. R. (2004). The neural substrates of reward processing in humans: the modern role of fMRI. *Neuroscientist* 10, 260–268.

McEwen, B. S., and Gianaros, P. J. (2011). Stress- and allostasis-induced brain plasticity. *Annu. Rev. Med.* 62, 431–445.

McMurray, M. S., Joyner, P. W., Middleton, C. W., Jarrett, T. M., Elliott, D. L., Black, M. A., Hofler, V. E., Walker, C. H., and Johns, J. M. (2008). Intergenerational effects of cocaine on maternal aggressive behavior and brain oxytocin in rat dams. *Stress* 11, 398–410.

Meshul, C. K., Noguchi, K., Emre, N., and Ellison, G. (1998). Cocaine-induced changes in glutamate and GABA immunolabeling within rat habenula and nucleus accumbens. *Synapse* 30, 211–220.

Molitor, A., and Mayes, L. C. (2010). Problematic dyadic interaction among toddlers and their polydrug-cocaine-using mothers. *Infant Ment. Health J.* 31, 121–140.

Nelson, C. J., Meter, K. E., Walker, C. H., Ayers, A. A., and Johns, J. M. (1998). A dose–response study of chronic cocaine on maternal behavior in rats. *Neurotoxicol. Teratol.* 20, 657–660.

Nephew, B. C., and Febo, M. (2010). Effect of cocaine sensitization prior to pregnancy on maternal care and aggression in the rat.

Psychopharmacology (Berl.) 209, 127–135.

Nitschke, J. B., Nelson, E. E., Rusch, B. D., Fox, A. S., Oakes, T. R., and Davidson, R. J. (2004). Orbitofrontal cortex tracks positive mood in mothers viewing pictures of their newborn infants. *Neuroimage* 21, 583–592.

Noriuchi, M., Kikuchi, Y., and Senoo, A. (2008). The functional neuroanatomy of maternal love: mother's response to infant's attachment behaviors. *Biol. Psychiatry* 63, 415–423.

Numan, M. (2007). Motivational systems and the neural circuitry of maternal behavior in the rat. *Dev. Psychobiol.* 49, 12–21.

Numan, M., Stolzenberg, D. S., Dellevigne, A. A., Correnti, C. M., and Numan, M. J. (2009). Temporary inactivation of ventral tegmental area neurons with either muscimol or baclofen reversibly disrupts maternal behavior in rats through different underlying mechanisms. *Behav. Neurosci.* 123, 740–751.

Olazabal, D. E., Abercrombie, E., Rosenblatt, J. S., and Morrell, J. I. (2004). The content of dopamine, serotonin, and their metabolites in the neural circuit that mediates maternal behavior in juvenile and adult rats. *Brain Res. Bull.* 63, 259–268.

Oleson, E. B., Talluri, S., Childers, S. R., Smith, J. E., Roberts, D. C., Bonin, K. D., and Budygin, E. A. (2009). Dopamine uptake changes associated with cocaine self-administration. *Neuropsychopharmacology* 34, 1174–1184.

Pajulo, M., Suchman, N., Kalland, M., and Mayes, L. (2006). Enhancing the effectiveness of residential treatment for substance abusing pregnant and parenting women: focus on maternal reflective functioning and mother-child relationship. *Infant Ment. Health J.* 27, 448.

Palkovits, M., Young, W. S. III, Kovacs, K., Toth, Z., and Makara, G. B. (1998). Alterations in corticotropin-releasing hormone gene expression of central amygdaloid neurons following long-term paraventricular lesions and adrenalectomy. *Neuroscience* 85, 135–147.

Panatier, A., and Oliet, S. H. (2006). Neuron-glia interactions in the hypothalamus. *Neuron Glia Biol.* 2, 51–58.

Pawluski, J. L., and Galea, L. A. (2007). Reproductive experience alters hippocampal neurogenesis during the postpartum period in the dam. *Neuroscience* 149, 53–67.

Paxinos, G., and Watson, C. (1997). "The Rat Brain", in *Stereotaxic Coordinates*. San Diego: Academic Press.

Pedersen, C. A., and Boccia, M. L. (2002). Oxytocin links mothering received, mothering bestowed and adult stress responses. *Stress* 5, 259–267.

Pedersen, C. A., Caldwell, J. D., Walker, C., Ayers, G., and Mason, G. A. (1994). Oxytocin activates the postpartum onset of rat maternal behavior in the ventral tegmental and medial preoptic areas. *Behav. Neurosci.* 108, 1163–1171.

Pego, J. M., Morgado, P., Pinto, L. G., Cerqueira, J. J., Almeida, O. F., and Sousa, N. (2008). Dissociation of the morphological correlates of stress-induced anxiety and fear. *Eur. J. Neurosci.* 27, 1503–1516.

Peterson, S. L., Olsta, S. A., and Matthews, R. T. (1990). Cocaine enhances medial prefrontal cortex neuron response to ventral tegmental area activation. *Brain Res. Bull.* 24, 267–273.

Quinones-Jenab, V., Krey, L. C., Schlussman, S. D., Ho, A., and Kreek, M. J. (2000). Chronic 'binge' pattern cocaine alters the neuroendocrine profile of pregnant rats. *Neurosci. Lett.* 282, 120–122.

Rasia-Filho, A. A., Londero, R. G., and Achaval, M. (2000). Functional activities of the amygdala: an overview. *J. Psychiatry Neurosci.* 25, 14–23.

Rees, S. L., Panesar, S., Steiner, M., and Fleming, A. S. (2004). The effects of adrenalectomy and corticosterone replacement on maternal behavior in the postpartum rat. *Horm. Behav.* 46, 411–419.

Rodaros, D., Caruana, D. A., Amir, S., and Stewart, J. (2007). Corticotropin-releasing factor projections from limbic forebrain and paraventricular nucleus of the hypothalamus to the region of the ventral tegmental area. *Neuroscience* 150, 8–13.

Russo, S. J., Dietz, D. M., Dumitriu, D., Morrison, J. H., Malenka, R. C., and Nestler, E. J. (2010). The addicted synapse: mechanisms of synaptic and structural plasticity in nucleus accumbens. *Trends Neurosci.* 33, 267–276.

Russo, S. J., Festa, E. D., Fabian, S. J., Gazi, F. M., Kraish, M., Jenab, S., and Quiñones-Jenab, V. (2003). Gonadal hormones differentially modulate cocaine-induced conditioned place preference in male and female rats. *Neuroscience* 120, 523–533.

Seip, K. M., and Morrell, J. I. (2007). Increasing the incentive salience of cocaine challenges preference for pup- over cocaine-associated stimuli during early postpartum: place preference and locomotor analyses in the lactating female rat. *Psychopharmacology (Berl.)* 194, 309–319.

Seip, K. M., and Morrell, J. I. (2009). Transient inactivation of the ventral tegmental area selectively disrupts the expression of conditioned place preference for pup- but not cocaine-paired contexts. *Behav. Neurosci.* 123, 1325–1338.

Seip, K. M., Pereira, M., Wansaw, M. P., Reiss, J. I., Dziopa, E. I., and Morrell, J. I. (2008). Incentive salience of cocaine across the postpartum period of the female rat. *Psychopharmacology (Berl.)* 199, 119–130.

Sesack, S. R., and Grace, A. A. (2010). Cortico-basal ganglia reward network: microcircuitry. *Neuropsychopharmacology* 35, 27–47.

Shahrokh, D. K., Zhang, T. Y., Diorio, J., Gratton, A., and Meaney, M. J. (2010). Oxytocin-dopamine interactions mediate variations in maternal behavior in the rat. *Endocrinology* 151, 2276–2286.

Sinha, R. (2001). How does stress increase risk of drug abuse and relapse? *Psychopharmacologia* 158, 343–359.

Sinha, R., Lacadie, C., Skudlarski, P., Fulbright, R., Rounsaville, B., Kosten, T., and Wexler, B. E. (2005). Neural activity associated with stress-induced cocaine craving: a functional magnetic resonance imaging study. *Psychopharmacology (Berl.)* 183, 171–180.

Sinha, R., Lacadie, C., Skudlarski, P., and Wexler, B. E. (2004). Neural circuits underlying emotional distress in humans. *Ann. N. Y. Acad. Sci.* 1032, 254–257.

Sinha, R., and Li, C. S. R. (2007). Imaging stress- and cue-induced drug and alcohol craving: association with relapse and clinical implications. *Drug Alcohol Rev.* 26, 25–31.

Slattery, D. A., and Neumann, I. D. (2008). No stress please! Mechanisms of stress hyporesponsiveness of the maternal brain. *J. Physiol.* 586, 377–385.

Smith, J. W., Seckl, J. R., Evans, A. T., Costall, B., and Smythe, J. W. (2004). Gestational stress induces post-partum depression-like behaviour and alters maternal care in rats. *Psychoneuroendocrinology* 29, 227–244.

Sombers, L. A., Beyene, M., Carelli, R. M., and Wightman, R. M. (2009). Synaptic overflow of dopamine in the nucleus accumbens arises from neuronal activity in the ventral tegmental area. *J. Neurosci.* 29, 1735–1742.

Stack, E. C., Balakrishnan, R., Numan, M. J., and Numan, M. (2002). A functional neuroanatomical investigation of the role of the medial preoptic area in neural circuits regulating maternal behavior. *Behav. Brain Res.* 131, 17–36.

Steffensen, S. C., Taylor, S. R., Horton, M. L., Barber, E. N., Lyle, L. T., Stobbs, S. H., and Allison, D. W. (2008). Cocaine disinhibits dopamine neurons in the ventral tegmental area via use-dependent blockade of GABA neuron voltage-sensitive sodium channels. *Eur. J. Neurosci.* 28, 2028–2040.

Strathearn, L., Fonagy, P., Amico, J., and Montague, P. R. (2009). Adult attachment predicts maternal brain and oxytocin response to infant cues. *Neuropsychopharmacology* 34, 2655–2666.

Strathearn, L., and Kosten, T. R. (2008). Does chronic cocaine use affect a mother's brain response to baby face cues? A pilot fMRI study. *The College on Problems of Drug Dependence 70th Annual Scientific Meeting.*

Substance Abuse and Mental Health Services Administration. (2008). Results from the 2007 National Survey on Drug Use and Health: National Findings (Office of Applied Studies, NSDUH Series H-34, DHHS Publication No. SMA 08-4343). Rockville, MD.

Suchman, N., Decoste, C., Castiglioni, N., Legow, N., and Mayes, L. (2008). THE MOTHERS AND TODDLERS PROGRAM: preliminary findings from an attachment-based parenting intervention for substance-abusing mothers. *Psychoanal. Psychol.* 25.

Suchman, N. E., and Luthar, S. S. (2001). The mediating role of parenting stress in methadone-maintained mothers' parenting. *Parent Sci. Pract.* 1, 285–315.

Takayanagi, Y., Yoshida, M., Bielsky, I. F., Ross, H. E., Kawamata, M., Onaka, T., Yanagisawa, T., Kimura, T., Matzuk, M. M., Young, L. J., and Nishimori, K. (2005). Pervasive social deficits, but normal parturition, in oxytocin receptor-deficient mice. *Proc. Natl. Acad. Sci. U.S.A.* 102, 16096–16101.

Thomas, M. J., and Malenka, R. C. (2003). Synaptic plasticity in the mesolimbic dopamine system. *Philos. Trans. R. Soc. Lond. B Biol. Sci.* 358, 815–819.

Thompson, A. C., and Kristal, M. B. (1996). Opioid stimulation in the ventral tegmental area facilitates the onset of maternal behavior in rats. *Brain Res.* 743, 184–201.

Tronick, E. Z., Messinger, D. S., Weinberg, M. K., Lester, B. M., LaGasse, L., Seifer, R., Bauer, C. R., Shankaran, S., Bada, H., Wright, L. L., Poole, K., and Liu, J. (2005). Cocaine exposure is associated with subtle compromises of infants' and mothers' social-emotional behavior and dyadic features of their interaction in the face-to-face still-face paradigm. *Dev. Psychol.* 41, 711–722.

Uhlhorn, S. B., Messinger, D. S., and Bauer, C. R. (2005). Cocaine exposure and mother-toddler social play. *Infant Behav. Dev.* 28, 62–73.

Uvnas-Moberg, K., Arn, I., and Magnusson, D. (2005). The psychobiology of emotion: the role of the oxytocinergic system. *Int. J. Behav. Med.* 12, 59–65.

Van den Oever, M. C., Spijker, S., Smit, A. B., and De Vries, T. J. (2010). Prefrontal cortex plasticity mechanisms in drug seeking and relapse. *Neurosci. Biobehav. Rev.* 25, 276–284.

van Velzen, A., and Toth, M. (2010). Role of maternal 5-HT(1A) receptor in programming offspring emotional and physical development. *Genes Brain Behav.* 9, 877–885.

Venkatesan, A., Nath, A., Ming, G. L., and Song, H. (2007). Adult hippocampal neurogenesis: regulation by HIV and drugs of abuse. *Cell Mol. Life Sci.* 64, 2120–2132.

Walker, D. L., Toufexis, D. J., and Davis, M. (2003). Role of the bed nucleus of the stria terminalis versus the amygdala in fear, stress, and anxiety. *Eur. J. Pharmacol.* 463, 199–216.

Webster-Stratton, C. (1990). Stress: a potential disruptor of parent perceptions and family interactions. *J. Clin. Child Adolesc. Psychol.* 19, 302–312.

Windle, R. J., Kershaw, Y. M., Shanks, N., Wood, S. A., Lightman, S. L., and Ingram, C. D. (2004). Oxytocin attenuates stress-induced c-fos mRNA expression in specific forebrain regions associated with modulation of hypothalamo-pituitary-adrenal activity. *J. Neurosci.* 24, 2974–2982.

Wise, R. A., and Morales, M. (2010). A ventral tegmental CRF-glutamate-dopamine interaction in addiction. *Brain Res.* 1314, 38–43.

Yang, J. Y., Qi, J., Han, W. Y., Wang, F., and Wu, C. F. (2010). Inhibitory role of oxytocin in psychostimulant-induced psychological dependence and its effects on dopaminergic and glutamatergic transmission. *Acta Pharmacol. Sin.* 31, 1071–1074.

Yoshida, M., Takayanagi, Y., Inoue, K., Kimura, T., Young, L. J., Onaka, T., and Nishimori, K. (2009). Evidence that oxytocin exerts anxiolytic effects via oxytocin receptor expressed in serotonergic neurons in mice. *J. Neurosci.* 29, 2259–2271.

Zhang, D., Yang, S., Yang, C., Jin, G., and Zhen, X. (2008). Estrogen regulates responses of dopamine neurons in the ventral tegmental area to cocaine. *Psychopharmacology (Berl.)* 199, 625–635.

Zhao, C., and Li, M. (2010). c-Fos identification of neuroanatomical sites associated with haloperidol and clozapine disruption of maternal behavior in the rat. *Neuroscience* 166, 1043–1055.

Conflict of Interest Statement: The authors declare that the research was conducted in the absence of any commercial or financial relationships that could be construed as a potential conflict of interest.

5

Homers at the interface between reward and pain

Ilona Obara[1,2]*, Scott P. Goulding[1], Adam T. Gould[1], Kevin D. Lominac[1], Jia-Hua Hu[3], Ping Wu Zhang[3], Georg von Jonquieres[4], Marlin Dehoff[3], Bo Xiao[3], Peter H. Seeburg[5], Paul F. Worley[3], Matthias Klugmann[4] and Karen K. Szumlinski[1]

[1] Department of Psychology, Neuroscience Research Institute, University of California at Santa Barbara, Santa Barbara, CA, USA
[2] School of Medicine, Pharmacy and Health, Queen's Campus, University of Durham, Stockton on Tees, UK
[3] Department of Neuroscience, Johns Hopkins University School of Medicine, Baltimore, MD, USA
[4] Translational Neuroscience Facility, School of Medical Sciences, UNSW Kensington Campus, University of New South Wales, Sydney, NSW, Australia
[5] Department of Molecular Neurobiology, Max Planck Institute Medical Research, Heidelberg, Germany

Edited by:
Remi Martin-Fardon, The Scripps Research Institute, USA

Reviewed by:
Scott Edwards, The Scripps Research Institute, USA
Thomas J. Martin, Wake Forest University Health Sciences, USA

*Correspondence:
Ilona Obara, School of Medicine, Pharmacy and Health, Queen's Campus, University of Durham, Stockton on Tees TS17 6BH, UK
e-mail: ilona.obara@durham.ac.uk

Pain alters opioid reinforcement, presumably *via* neuroadaptations within ascending pain pathways interacting with the limbic system. Nerve injury increases expression of glutamate receptors and their associated Homer scaffolding proteins throughout the pain processing pathway. Homer proteins, and their associated glutamate receptors, regulate behavioral sensitivity to various addictive drugs. Thus, we investigated a potential role for Homers in the interactions between pain and drug reward in mice. Chronic constriction injury (CCI) of the sciatic nerve elevated Homer1b/c and/or Homer2a/b expression within all mesolimbic structures examined and for the most part, the Homer increases coincided with elevated mGluR5, GluN2A/B, and the activational state of various down-stream kinases. Behaviorally, CCI mice showed pain hypersensitivity and a conditioned place-aversion (CPA) at a low heroin dose that supported conditioned place-preference (CPP) in naïve controls. Null mutations of *Homer1a*, *Homer1*, and *Homer2*, as well as transgenic disruption of mGluR5-Homer interactions, either attenuated or completely blocked low-dose heroin CPP, and none of the CCI mutant strains exhibited heroin-induced CPA. However, heroin CPP did not depend upon full Homer1c expression within the nucleus accumbens (NAC), as CPP occurred in controls infused locally with small hairpin RNA-Homer1c, although intra-NAC and/or intrathecal cDNA-Homer1c, -Homer1a, and -Homer2b infusions (to best mimic CCI's effects) were sufficient to blunt heroin CPP in uninjured mice. However, arguing against a simple role for CCI-induced increases in either spinal or NAC Homer expression for heroin CPA, cDNA infusion of our various cDNA constructs either did not affect (intrathecal) or attenuated (NAC) heroin CPA. Together, these data implicate increases in glutamate receptor/Homer/kinase activity within limbic structures, perhaps outside the NAC, as possibly critical for switching the incentive motivational properties of heroin following nerve injury, which has relevance for opioid psychopharmacology in individuals suffering from neuropathic pain.

Keywords: Homer proteins, Group1 metabotropic glutamate receptors, NMDA receptors, neuropathic pain, heroin, nucleus accumbens, conditioned place-preference, conditioned place-aversion

INTRODUCTION

Comorbidity exists between chronic pain and motivational disturbances (e.g., Doth et al., 2010; Ohayon and Schatzberg, 2010; Jarcho et al., 2012; Oluigbo et al., 2012), and a cause-effect relationship between chronic pain and a blunted motivational state is apparent also in animal studies (c.f., Niikura et al., 2010). The pain processing pathway interacts at multiple levels with brain structures embedded within mesocorticolimbic subcircuits underpinning subjective responses to, as well as the incentive value of, stimuli (both appetitive or noxious), including subregions of the prefrontal cortex (PFC), nuclei of the amygdala (AMY), the ventral tegmental area (VTA), and subregions of the nucleus accumbens (NAC) (c.f., Leknes and Tracey, 2008; Becker et al., 2012). While the neurocircuitry underpinning pain perception and the subjective pain response is known to involve activation within several frontal cortical subregions and thalamus (c.f., Leknes and Tracey, 2008; Oluigbo et al., 2012), the precise neurocircuitry involved in pain-induced alterations in motivation are less well understood (Becker et al., 2012).

Patients' hypersensitivity to pain stimuli correlates with increases in PFC-NAC connectivity in recent neuroimaging studies and, importantly, heighted connectivity is predictive of affective pain, as well as pain severity in humans (e.g., Baliki et al., 2010, 2012). In animal and human studies, noxious stimuli, including chronic constriction injury (CCI) of the sciatic nerve, alters the activational state of mesocorticolimbic circuit (e.g., Kuroda et al., 1995; Rodella et al., 1998; Narita et al., 2003, 2005; Ozaki et al., 2003, 2004; Wood et al., 2007). Thus, injury-induced mesocorticolimbic anomalies are theorized to underpin the negative affective aspects of pain, as well as the impairments in motivation often observed in individuals suffering from chronic somatic pain (c.f., Leknes and Tracey, 2008; Becker et al., 2012; Oluigbo et al., 2012). In support of an interaction between a chronic pain state and drug reinforcement/reward, there is an absence of both opioid drug- and psychomotor stimulant-induced conditioned place-preference (CPP) in animal models of inflammatory or neuropathic pain (c.f., Niikura et al., 2010), which is consistent with very little evidence for the clinical diagnosis of addiction in individuals undergoing pharmacotherapy for chronic pain symptoms (e.g., Niikura et al., 2010; Minozzi et al., 2013). However, pain symptoms augment opioid drug consumption under operant procedures in animal models, which is theorized to reflect a compensation for a depressed mesocorticolimbic circuit (Colpaert et al., 1982, 2001; Dib and Duclaux, 1982; Lyness et al., 1989; Martin et al., 2007, 2011), fitting with extant CPP data indicating blunted drug-conditioned reward following nerve injury (c.f., Niikura et al., 2010).

Glutamate neuroadaptations within the mesocorticolimbic system are theorized to contribute significantly to drug reward/reinforcement in various addiction-related animal models (e.g., Szumlinski et al., 2008; Kalivas, 2009; Olive et al., 2012). As noxious, painful stimuli augment glutamatergic neurotransmission both at the spinal and supraspinal levels and glutamatergic hyperactivity is considered an active mediator of pain symptomatology (c.f., Chiechio and Nicoletti, 2012; Harris and Clauw, 2012; Wozniak et al., 2012; Osikowicz et al., 2013), the present study employed a combination of immunoblotting and behavioral genetic approaches to test the hypothesis that injury-induced increases in mesocorticolimbic glutamate transmission contribute to a blunted motivational state within the confines of a heroin CPP model of drug reward.

MATERIALS AND METHODS
SUBJECTS
Subjects included adult male C57BL/6J (B6) mice (8 weeks of age; 25–30 g; the Jackson Laboratories, Bar Harbor, ME, USA), as well as several strains of constitutive gene knock-out (KO) mice that were available at the time of study, including *Homer1a* KO (Hu et al., 2012), *Homer1* KO (Yuan et al., 2003), and *Homer2* KO (Shin et al., 2003) mice. Knock-in (KI) mice expressing mutant mGluR5 with a phenylalanine (F) to arginine (R) switch at position 1128 that markedly reduces mGluR5-Homer interactions (*Grm5*$^{R/R}$; Cozzoli et al., 2009) were also employed. All the above mutant strains were bred in-house at UCSB from mating of heterozygous breeder pairs (B6 × 129Xi/SvJ background) and male wild-type (WT), heterozygous (HET), and homozygous KO/KI littermate pups were employed in all studies. For the KO/KI strains bred in-house, mice were selected from a minimum of four different litters within each replicate and testing began at 7–8 weeks of age. Experimental protocols were approved by the IACUCs of our respective institutions and were consistent with the guidelines provided by NIH and the Committee for Research and Ethical Issues of IASP.

NEUROPATHIC PAIN, INFLAMMATORY PAIN, AND PAIN THRESHOLD ASSESSMENT
The procedures for inducing peripheral neuropathy by CCI of the sciatic nerve were identical to those described recently by our

group (Obara et al., 2013). The total length of nerve affected was 3–4 mm. Mechanical and cold hypersensitivity at the plantar surface of the hind paw ipsilateral to the injury was assessed, respectively, using von Frey filaments (0.07–6 g; Stoelting, Wood Dale, IL, USA) and the acetone test (50 μl) before nerve injury (as one index of basal pain threshold), and on days 3, 7, and/or 14 post-CCI (e.g., Obara et al., 2003, 2013; Osikowicz et al., 2008).

IMMUNOBLOTTING
At 1 or 2 weeks after nerve injury, the entire NAC, the VTA, the entire AMY, and the PFC (anterior cingulate, prelimbic, and infralimbic cortices) were dissected from B6 mice ($n = 6$–8/group/timepoint) over ice, homogenized in a buffer containing both protease and phosphatase inhibitors and subjected to conventional immunoblotting procedures (20 μg protein/lane) as described previously by our group (e.g., Goulding et al., 2011; Obara et al., 2013). The details regarding the antibodies employed to detect protein levels of Homer1b/c, Homer2a/b, mGluR1, mGluR5, GluN2A, GluN2B, PI3K, p(Tyr)PI3K p85α binding motif, ERK1/2, p(Tyr204)ERK1/2, PKCε, p(Ser729)PKCε, and calnexin (loading and transfer control) are provided in the legend for **Figure 2**. The data for neuropathic animals at the different time-points post-injury were expressed as a percent change from the mean signal of the uninjured controls for each individual membrane ($n = 3$–4/membrane) as published previously (e.g., Obara et al., 2013).

HEROIN-INDUCED PLACE-CONDITIONING
Mice were assayed for the development of heroin place-conditioning, starting at 14 days post-nerve injury. The apparatus and procedures for heroin place-conditioning were similar to those employed in our previous studies of drug-conditioned reward in mice (e.g., Penzner et al., 2008) and proceeded in the following four sequential phases: habituation, preconditioning test (Pre-Test), conditioning, postconditioning test (Post-test). All sessions were 15 min in duration and animals received no injections during the habituation, Pre-Test, or Post-Test sessions when they had free-access to both compartments of the apparatus. For conditioning, mice received four alternating pairings of distinct compartments with either intraperitoneal heroin (0.01–3 mg/kg; vol = 0.01 ml/kg) or an equivalent volume of saline in an unbiased fashion. Locomotor activity was monitored during all free-access sessions, as well as on the first and fourth saline/heroin conditioning session to index spontaneous and heroin-induced changes in ambulation, respectively. An increase in heroin-induced locomotion from injections 1–4 indicated the presence of locomotor sensitization. The time spent in the drug-paired vs. -unpaired compartment on the Post-Test served to index place-conditioning. The dose-response study of B6 mice employed 8–9/mice/group/dose, while the sample sizes employed in the single-dose study of mutant mice were: 11–15 mice/group/genotype for *Homer1a* KO, 11–3 mice/group/genotype for *Homer1* KO, 8–15 mice/group/genotype for *Homer2* KO, and 12–18 mice/group/genotype for *Grm5*$^{R/R}$ mutant.

SURGICAL PROCEDURES AND AAV INFUSION
The procedure for generating neurotropic chimeric AAV1/2 vectors carrying the renilla green fluorescent protein (hrGFP) cDNA

or the hemagglutinin (HA) tag fused to the coding region of rat *Homer1c*, and *Homer2b* have been described in detail elsewhere (e.g., Klugmann et al., 2005) and the AAV-cDNA constructs were identical to those employed previously (e.g., Klugmann et al., 2005; Tappe et al., 2006; Cozzoli et al., 2009; Goulding et al., 2011; Ary et al., 2013). The design of the AAV constructs for expression of small hairpin RNAs (shRNA) against Homer1c were described in detail in Klugmann and Szumlinski (2008). Briefly, we used a bicistronic expression cassette entailing the human U6 promoter to drive the shRNA, followed by the hrGFP reporter under the control of the chicken-beta actin (CBA) promoter for identification of transduced neurons. The shRNA-Homer1c construct was the same as that used in a recently published report, in which we demonstrated approximately 50% protein knock-down within the brain at 3 weeks post-infusion (Ary et al., 2013). AAV-shEGFP-CBA-hrGFP was used as a generic control (GFP) in our AAV studies. The surgical procedures for intra-NAC AAV infusion (0.5 μl/side) were identical to those used in previous studies (e.g., Cozzoli et al., 2009) and resulted in placement of microinjectors within the boundaries of the NAC (see **Figure 5A**). Studies examining behavioral response in heroin-induced place-preference test after intrathecal AAV infusion employed mice whose neuropathic pain symptoms and AAV transduction patterns within spinal cord were described before (Obara et al., 2013). Following either intracranial or intrathecal infusion, animals were left undisturbed for 3 weeks when AAV-mediated transgene expression peaks to remain at maximally stable levels prior to behavioral testing (e.g., Klugmann et al., 2005; Klugmann and Szumlinski, 2008). Sample sizes employed in the statistical analyses of the data ranged from 8 to 11 mice/group/AAV for both the NAC and spinal cord study.

STATISTICAL ANALYSIS

Behavioral and biochemical results are presented as means ± SEM ($n = 8$–12/group). Immunoblotting data were analyzed by one-way analyses of variance (ANOVA) with Tukey's multiple comparison *post hoc* tests and these results are presented in **Table 1**. Behavioral results were analyzed by two-way ANOVA and significant interactions were followed up by an analysis for simple effects and Bonferroni's multiple comparison *post hoc* tests, when appropriate. To confirm significant place-conditioning, *a priori* dependent-sample *t*-tests were conducted for the time spent in the heroin-paired vs. -unpaired compartment, separately for each treatment group/genotype. $\alpha = 0.05$ for all analyses and the results of the statistical analyses for the behavioral assays are presented in their corresponding figure legends.

RESULTS

CCI ELEVATES MESOCORTICOLIMBIC PROTEIN EXPRESSION AND ABOLISHES HEROIN CPP

Chronic constriction injury of the sciatic nerve increased mechanical and cold hypersensitivity in B6 mice (**Figures 1A,B**). This hypersensitivity was associated with increased expression of the majority of our proteins of interest within all four mesocorticolimbic structures investigated (as indicated in **Figure 1C**), with regional distinctions in the magnitude and/or time-course of the observed protein changes (**Figure 2**; see **Table 1**). In the PFC (**Figure 2A**), CCI increased Homer1b/c, Homer2a/b,

GluN2A, and p(Tyr)p85α at both time-points post-injury, while those for mGluR1a, GluN2B, and pPKCε were time-dependent. In the NAC (**Figure 2B**), CCI increased Homer1b/c, GluN2A, and pPKCε at both time-points, while kinase activation increased time-dependently and the rise in mGluR5 was transient. In the AMY (**Figure 2C**), the rise in mGluR5 was also transient; however, CCI increased Homer1b/c, GluN2B, PKCε, pPKCε, and p(Tyr)p85α both time-points and ERK levels increased time-dependently. Unfortunately, we could not detect a reliable signal for mGluR1a within our AMY samples. Finally, in the VTA (**Figure 2D**), CCI increased Homer2a/b, and GluN2A at both time-points, the rise in GluN2B, pPKCε, and the pPKCε:PKCε ratio increased time-dependently and the rise in p(Tyr)p85α and ERK were transient.

We next assayed for CCI-induced changes in heroin-conditioned reward in B6 mice as an index of motivation. All but the lowest heroin dose elicited a significant CPP in injury-naïve B6 controls (**Figure 3**). In contrast, no heroin dose elicited CPP in injured B6 mice and the 0.1-mg/kg dose elicited a significant conditioned place-aversion (CPA). The injury-induced abolishment of CPP did not reflect impairments in motor activity as group differences were not observed regarding: (1) spontaneous locomotor activity (data not shown; total distance traveled during Habituation, Pre-Test, or Post-Test; *t*-tests, $p > 0.05$); (2) saline- or heroin-induced locomotor activity on injection 1 or 4; or (3) the expression of heroin-induced locomotor sensitization, which was observed only at the 3-mg/kg dose [data not shown; Heroin effect: $F_{(2,48)} = 25.76$, $p = 0.001$; Heroin × Injection: $F_{(2,48)} = 2.87$, $p = 0.07$].

GENOTYPE × PAIN INTERACTIONS IN HEROIN CPP

Given the CCI-induced rise in Homer expression throughout the mesocorticolimbic system, we next assayed for low-dose heroin-induced place-conditioning in naïve and CCI *Homer1a*, *Homer1*, and *Homer2* null mutant mice, as well as in transgenic mice with a disrupted mGluR5-Homer interaction ($Grm5^{R/R}$). The 0.1-mg/kg heroin dose elicited a significant CPP in injury-naïve WT mice from all strains and this CPP was absent in all homozygous mutant littermate animals (**Figure 4**, left). Consistent with the above data from B6 mice, the 0.1-mg/kg heroin dose elicited a significant CPA in all CCI WT mice, but this too was attenuated or prevented in all homozygous mutant mouse lines (**Figure 4**, right). Such data pose a necessary role for Homer1a induction, as well as scaffolding by constitutively expressed (coiled-coil) CC-Homer proteins and their interaction with mGluR5 as critical for both heroin-related appetitive and aversive learning.

AAV-MEDIATED HOMER GENE TRANSFER AND INJURY-INDUCED CPA

The pattern of AAV-mediated neuronal transduction within the NAC was consistent with that reported previously by our group (e.g., Cozzoli et al., 2009; Goulding et al., 2011), with little spread beyond the infusion site (**Figures 5A,A″**). Intra-NAC cDNA-Homer1c and shRNA-Homer1c infusion potentiated and inhibited, respectively, both mechanical and cold hypersensitivity following CCI, but the effect was more pronounced in the von Frey test (**Figure 5B**). Neither Homer manipulation influenced basal

Table 1 | Statistical results of the one-way ANOVAs conducted on the immunoblotting data ($\alpha = 0.05$) and follow-up Tukey's multiple comparison *post hoc* tests, where appropriate.

Region	Protein	Results	
		ANOVA	***Post hoc***
PFC	mGluR1a	$F_{(2,23)} = 10.53, p = 0.0007$	CCI 2 weeks > CNT = CCI 1 week
	mGluR5	$F_{(2,23)} = 3.80, p = 0.04$	
	GluN2A	$F_{(2,21)} = 6.47, p = 0.0007$	CCI 1 week = CCI 2 weeks > CNT
	GluN2B	$F_{(2,23)} = 10.39, p = 0.0007$	CCI 2 weeks > CNT = CCI 1 week
	Homer1b/c	$F_{(2,21)} = 13.67, p = 0.0002$	CCI 1 week = CCI 2 weeks > CNT
	Homer2a/b	$F_{(2,19)} = 12.51, p = 0.0005$	CCI 1 week = CCI 2 weeks > CNT
	PKCε	$F_{(2,23)} = 0.32, p = 0.73$	
	pPKCε	$F_{(2,17)} = 3.94, p = 0.04$	CCI 2 weeks > CNT = CCI 1 week
	pPKCε:PKCε ratio	$F_{(2,17)} = 2.06, p = 0.16$	
	PI3K	$F_{(2,17)} = 0.37, p = 0.69$	
	P(Tyr)p85α	$F_{(2,19)} = 8.22, p = 0.003$	CCI 1 week = CCI 2 weeks > CNT
	ERK	$F_{(2,20)} = 0.06, p = 0.94$	
	pERK	$F_{(2,20)} = 0.06, p = 0.95$	
	pERK:ERK ratio	$F_{(2,17)} = 0.01, p = 0.98$	
NAC	mGluR1a	$F_{(2,17)} = 1.45, p = 0.26$	
	mGluR5	$F_{(2,17)} = 6.97, p = 0.0007$	CCI 1 week > CNT = CCI 2 weeks
	GluN2A	$F_{(2,17)} = 10.52, p = 0.001$	CCI 1 week = CCI 2 weeks > CNT
	GluN2B	$F_{(2,17)} = 1.62, p = 0.23$	
	Homer1b/c	$F_{(2,17)} = 7.96, p = 0.004$	CCI 1 week = CCI 2 weeks > CNT
	Homer2a/b	$F_{(2,17)} = 0.24, p = 0.78$	
	PKCε	$F_{(2,17)} = 1.71, p = 0.21$	
	pPKCε	$F_{(2,17)} = 7.31, p = 0.006$	CCI 1 week = CCI 2 weeks > CNT
	pPKCε:PKCε ratio	$F_{(2,17)} = 7.28, p = 0.006$	CCI 2 weeks > CNT = CCI 1 week
	PI3K	$F_{(2,17)} = 0.29, p = 0.74$	
	P(Tyr)p85α	$F_{(2,17)} = 12.25, p = 0.0007$	CCI 2 weeks > CNT = CCI 1 week
	ERK	$F_{(2,17)} = 1.04, p = 0.38$	
	pERK	$F_{(2,17)} = 0.42, p = 0.67$	
	pERK:ERK ratio	$F_{(2,17)} = 7.68, p = 0.005$	CCI 2 weeks > CNT = CCI 1 week
AMY	mGluR1a	–	
	mGluR5	$F_{(2,17)} = 12.59, p = 0.0006$	CCI 1 week > CNT = CCI 2 weeks
	GluN2A	$F_{(2,17)} = 1.26, p = 0.31$	
	GluN2B	$F_{(2,17)} = 13.16, p = 0.0005$	CCI 1 week = CCI 2 weeks > CNT
	Homer1b/c	$F_{(2,17)} = 14.41, p = 0.0003$	CCI 1 week = CCI 2 weeks > CNT
	Homer2a/b	$F_{(2,17)} = 0.15, p = 0.86$	
	PKCε	$F_{(2,17)} = 12.65, p = 0.0006$	CCI 1 week = CCI 2 weeks > CNT
	pPKCε	$F_{(2,17)} = 16.43, p = 0.0002$	CCI 1 week = CCI 2 weeks > CNT
	pPKCε:PKCε ratio	$F_{(2,17)} = 0.38, p = 0.68$	
	PI3K	$F_{(2,17)} = 0.45, p = 0.64$	
	P(Tyr)p85α	$F_{(2,17)} = 13.85, p = 0.0004$	CCI 1 week = CCI 2 weeks > CNT
	ERK	$F_{(2,17)} = 3.83, p = 0.04$	CCI 2 weeks > CNT = CCI 1 week
	pERK	$F_{(2,17)} = 0.65, p = 0.54$	
	pERK:ERK ratio	$F_{(2,17)} = 1.69, p = 0.21$	
VTA	mGluR1a	$F_{(2,17)} = 3.63, p = 0.05$	CCI 1 week = CCI 2 weeks > CNT
	mGluR5	$F_{(2,17)} = 0.42, p = 0.66$	
	GluN2A	$F_{(2,17)} = 5.08, p = 0.02$	CCI 1 week = CCI 2 weeks > CNT
	GluN2B	$F_{(2,17)} = 6.19, p = 0.01$	CCI 2 weeks > CNT = CCI 1 week
	Homer1b/c	$F_{(2,17)} = 1.68, p = 0.22$	
	Homer2a/b	$F_{(2,17)} = 6.99, p = 0.007$	
	PKCε	$F_{(2,17)} = 0.17, p = 0.84$	

(Continued)

Table 1 | Continued

Region	Protein	Results	
		ANOVA	*Post hoc*
	pPKCε	$F_{(2,17)} = 6.29$, $p = 0.01$	CCI 2 weeks > CNT = CCI 1 week
	pPKCε:PKCε ratio	$F_{(2,17)} = 6.22$, p = 0.01	CCI 2 weeks > CNT = CCI 1 week
	PI3K	$F_{(2,17)} = 2.82$, $p = 0.09$	
	P(Tyr)p85α	$F_{(2,17)} = 3.87$, $p = 0.04$	CCI 1 week > CNT = CCI 2 weeks
	ERK	$F_{(2,17)} = 5.31$, $p = 0.02$	CCI 1 week > CNT = CCI 2 weeks
	pERK	$F_{(2,17)} = 0.08$, $p = 0.92$	
	pERK:ERK ratio	$F_{(2,17)} = 2$, $p = 0.005$	

*The data are summarized in **Figure 2** and sample sizes ranged from 6 to 8 mice/group.*

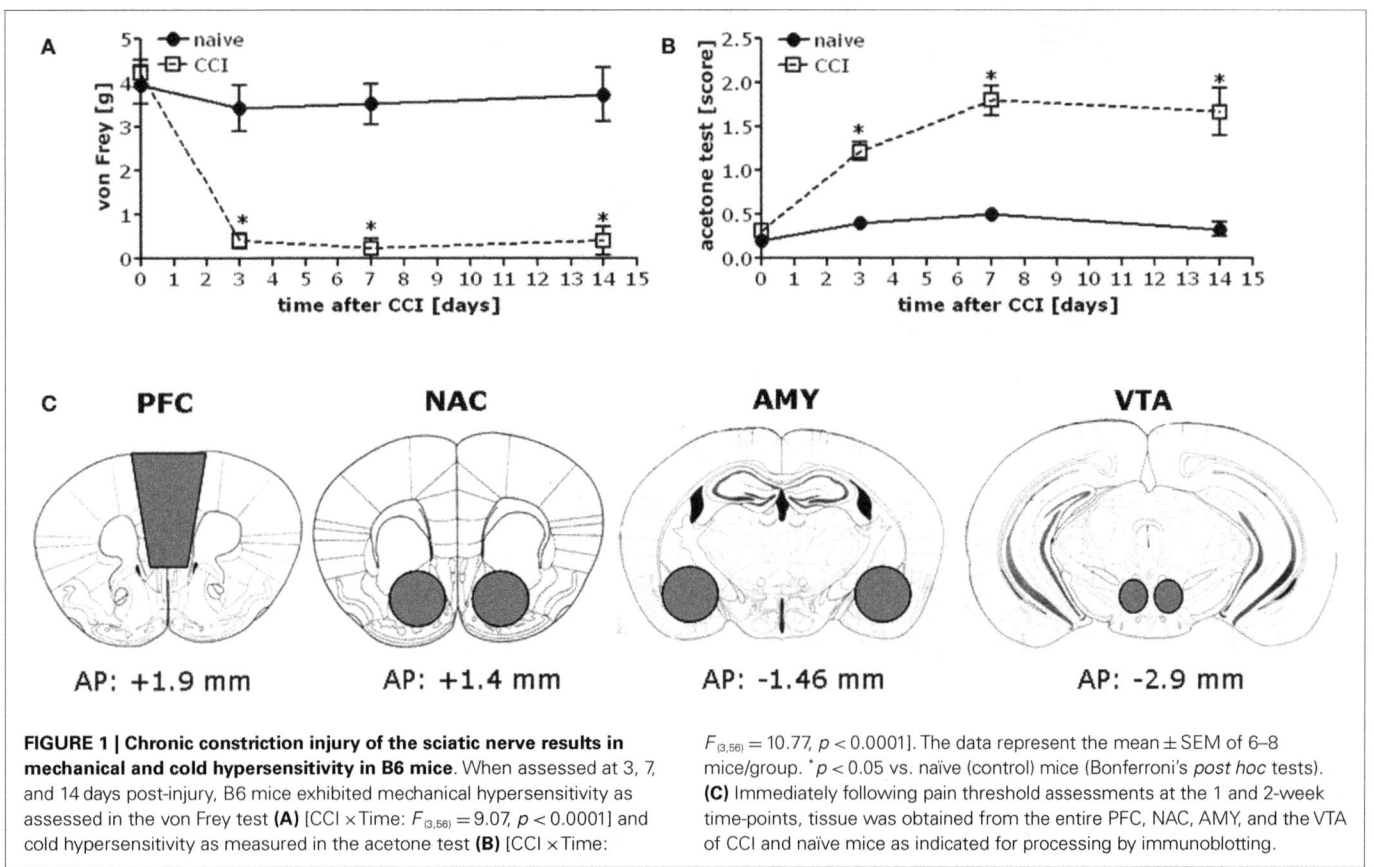

FIGURE 1 | Chronic constriction injury of the sciatic nerve results in mechanical and cold hypersensitivity in B6 mice. When assessed at 3, 7, and 14 days post-injury, B6 mice exhibited mechanical hypersensitivity as assessed in the von Frey test **(A)** [CCI ×Time: $F_{(3,56)} = 9.07$, $p < 0.0001$] and cold hypersensitivity as measured in the acetone test **(B)** [CCI ×Time:

$F_{(3,56)} = 10.77$, $p < 0.0001$]. The data represent the mean ± SEM of 6–8 mice/group. *$p < 0.05$ vs. naïve (control) mice (Bonferroni's *post hoc* tests). **(C)** Immediately following pain threshold assessments at the 1 and 2-week time-points, tissue was obtained from the entire PFC, NAC, AMY, and the VTA of CCI and naïve mice as indicated for processing by immunoblotting.

pain threshold to mechanical and cold stimuli (**Figure 5B**) nor did they alter simple spinal pain reflex assessed in the tail-flick test (**Figure 5C**).

While intra-NAC shRNA-Homer1c did not influence heroin CPP in injury-naïve animals, it prevented injury-induced heroin CPA (**Figure 5D**, left). In contrast to shRNA-Homer1c infusion, intra-NAC cDNA-Homer1c infusion prevented heroin-induced place-conditioning in both naïve and injured groups (**Figure 5D**, right).

Intrathecal infusion of cDNA-Homer1c and -Homer2b potentiates, while that of cDNA-Homer1a attenuates, CCI-induced pain hypersensitivity (Obara et al., 2013). Thus, we determined

whether or not spinal Homer expression might also regulate heroin place-conditioning. Intrathecal infusion of all three AAV-cDNAs blunted heroin CPP in injury-naïve mice (**Figure 6**, left). In this study, the heroin CPA exhibited by GFP-infused CCI mice was not as robust as that observed in the experiments above; nevertheless, none of the AAV-cDNAs influenced the extent or direction of behavior exhibited by CCI animals (**Figure 6**, right).

DISCUSSION

Pain-associated affective and motivational blunting is hypothesized to involve injury-induced changes in mesocorticolimbic

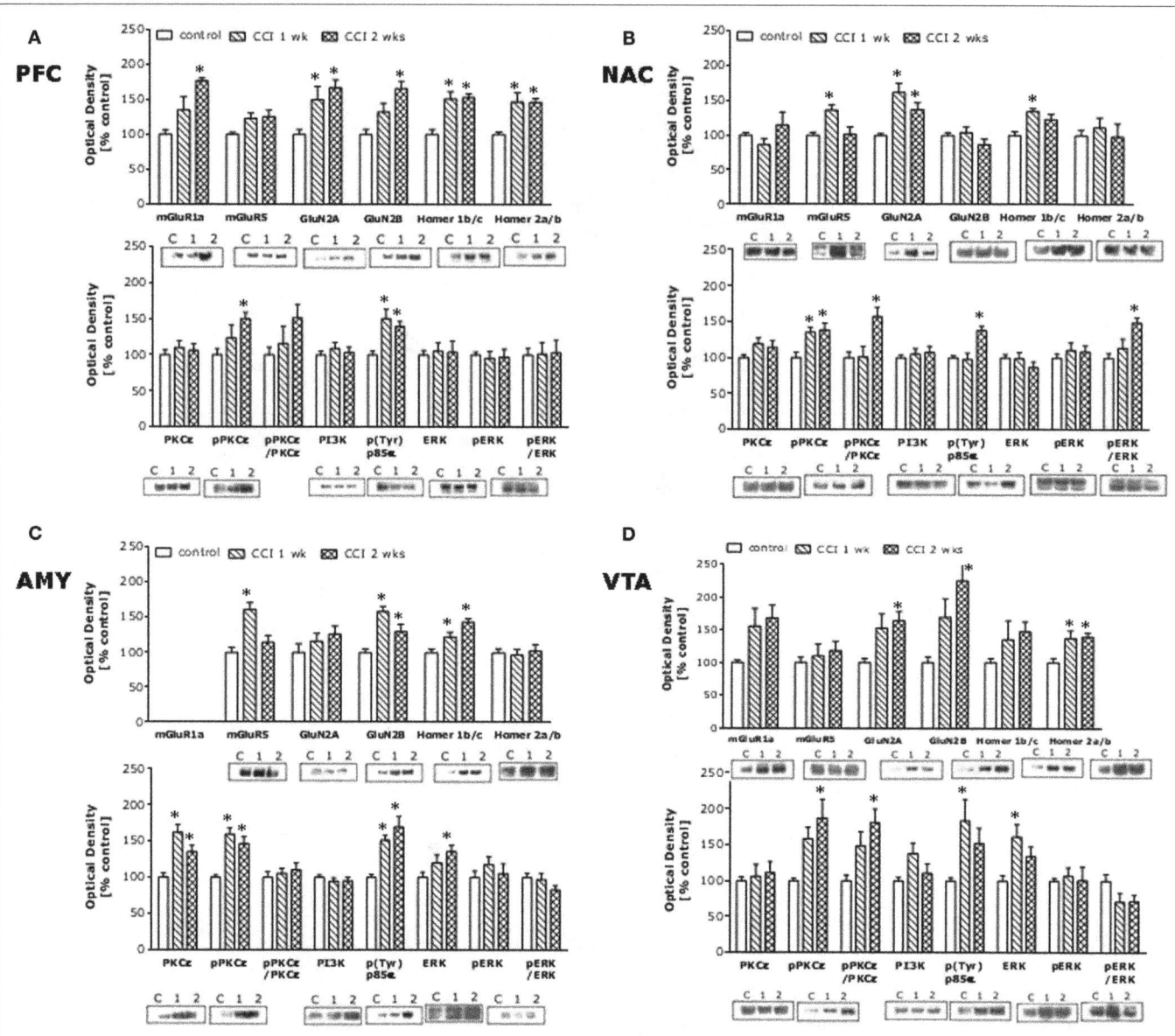

FIGURE 2 | Chronic constriction injury of the sciatic nerve augments glutamate-related protein expression throughout the mesocorticolimbic circuit. Summary of the changes in protein expression observed within the PFC **(A)**, NAC **(B)**, AMY **(C)**, and VTA **(D)** in sciatic nerve-ligated mice (CCI) sacrificed at 1 or 2 weeks following injury, as well as in naïve controls. The following rabbit polyclonal antibodies were used: anti-Homer 2a/b and anti-Homer 1b/c (Dr. Paul F. Worley, Johns Hopkins University School of Medicine; 1:1000 dilution), anti-mGluR5 (Upstate, Lake Placid, NY, USA; 1:1000 dilution), anti-GluN2A and anti-GluN2A (Calbiochem, San Diego, CA, USA; 1:1000 dilution), anti-PI3K antibody (Upstate; 1:1000 dilution), and anti-p-(Tyr) PI3K p85α binding motif (Cell Signaling Technology, Beverly, MA, USA; 1:250 dilution), anti-ERK1/2 (Santa Cruz Biotechnology, Santa Cruz, CA, USA; 1:500 dilution), anti-PKCε and anti-p(Ser729)PKCε (Santa Cruz

Biotechnology; 1:1000 dilution). Anti-mGluR1a (Upstate; 1:1000 dilution) and anti-p(Tyr204)ERK1/2 (Santa Cruz Biotechnology; 1:1000) mouse polyclonal antibodies were also used. A rabbit anti-calnexin monoclonal antibody (Stressgen, Victoria, BC, Canada; 1:1000 dilution) was used as a loading and transfer control. Immunoreactive bands were detected using enhanced chemiluminescence and immunoreactivity quantified using Image J (NIH, Bethesda, MD, USA). The data for neuropathic animals at the different time-points post-CCI were expressed as a percent change from the mean signal of the uninjured controls for each individual membrane ($n = 3$–4/membrane). The data represent the mean $\pm$ SEM of 6–8 mice/group and detailed results of the statistical analyses of these data are presented in **Table 1**. $^{*}p < 0.05$ vs. naïve (control) mice (see **Table 1**; one-way ANOVA followed by Tukey's *post hoc* tests).

function (c.f., Leknes and Tracey, 2008; Becker et al., 2012; Oluigbo et al., 2012). Thus, the present study characterized CCI-induced changes glutamate receptor expression/signaling within four major components of the mesocorticolimbic system

and then assayed the functional relevance of mGluR5 interactions with its scaffolding molecule Homer (Shiraishi-Yamaguchi and Furuichi, 2007) for pain-elicited changes in heroin's incentive motivational properties.

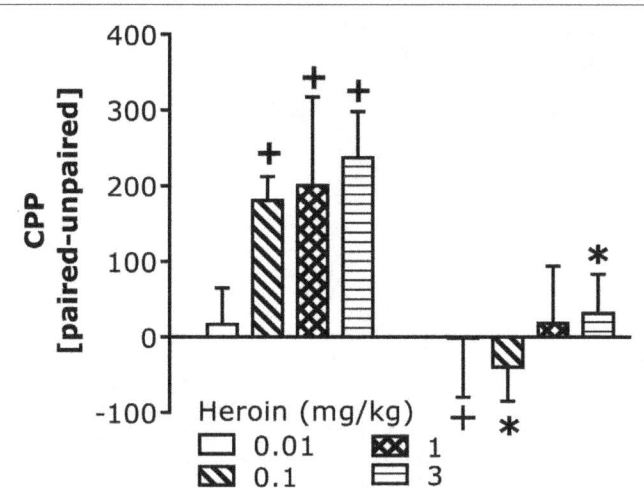

FIGURE 3 | Chronic constriction injury perturbs heroin-induced CPP in B6 mice. Summary of the difference in the time spent (in seconds) between the heroin-paired and -unpaired compartment on a test for place-conditioning conducted 24 h following conditioning with 0.01, 0.1, 1, and 3 mg/kg heroin in B6 mice. CCI significantly altered heroin CPP [CCI × Heroin: $F_{(1,58)} = 11.67$, $p = 0.001$]. Deconstruction of the interaction along with Heroin Dose factor indicated no CCI effects at the lowest dose of heroin, but group differences at all other doses [0.01 mg/kg: $t_{(14)} = 0.20$, $p = 0.42$; 0.1 mg/kg: $t_{(16)} = 4.63$, $p = 0.0001$; 1 mg/kg: $t_{(14)} = 1.31$, $p = 0.11$; 3 mg/kg: $t_{(14)} = 2.58$, $p = 0.01$]. To confirm the presence or absence of place-conditioning in each group, t-tests were conducted and verified significant CPP in control naïve mice at doses of 0.1 mg/kg heroin or greater [0.1 mg/kg: $t_{(8)} = 5.60$, $p = 0.001$; 1 mg/kg: $t_{(7)} = 2.58$, $p = 0.04$; 3 mg/kg: $t_{(7)} = 3.90$, $p = 0.006$], while the 0.01-mg/kg dose produced a significant CPA in CCI mice [$t_{(9)} = 3.97$, $p = 0.004$]. No significant conditioning was observed in CCI mice at the other heroin doses ($p > 0.05$). The data represent the mean ± SEM of 8–9 animals/group/dose. *$p < 0.05$ vs. naïve control; +$p < 0.05$ vs. 0 min (Bonferroni's *post hoc* tests or t-test).

NEUROPATHY AUGMENTS INDICES OF MESOCORTICOLIMBIC GLUTAMATE TRANSMISSION

Chronic constriction injury-induced hypersensitivity was associated with up-regulated mesocorticolimbic glutamate receptor and CC-Homer expression, as well as increased indices of ERK, PI3K, and/or PKCε activity. The present PFC data replicate our earlier study (Obara et al., 2013), indicating that injury up-regulates glutamate receptor signaling within a forebrain region important for volitional control over behavior, cognition, and emotion (c.f., Arnsten and Rubia, 2012; Depue, 2012). CCI-induced increases in protein expression were observed also within VTA, NAC, and AMY, with some regional differences that are not to be unexpected. However, CCI elevated Homer1b/c levels and PI3K activation in all mesocorticolimbic regions examined. Homer proteins are involved in the recruitment of PI3K-enhancer to Group1 mGluRs to induce PI3K activity (Rong et al., 2003). PI3K induction, at least within spinal cord, contributes to the development of neuropathic pain hypersensitivity (Xu et al., 2011). As an intra-NAC infusion of cDNA-Homer1c was sufficient to promote CCI-induced pain hypersensitivity, injury-induced increases in mesocorticolimbic Homer-dependent PI3K activity may contribute significantly to somatic and affective pain chronification following peripheral nerve injury. Indeed, certain AMY subregions receive direct and indirect nociceptive input from spinal cord, brainstem, thalamus, and cortex (c.f., Leknes and Tracey, 2008; Becker et al., 2012). Moreover, central sensitization, via signaling pathways involving ERK, PKCs, and PI3K, occurs within this structure in various models of chronic pain (c.f., Neugebauer et al., 2004; Neugebauer, 2006; Fu et al., 2008; Tappe-Theodor et al., 2011). Our observation of up-regulated protein expression within AMY could reflect a central sensitization of mesocorticolimbic activity that would be predicted to elicit negative emotional disturbances characteristic of chronic pain sufferers.

While we failed to detect a significant reduction in VTA ERK activity following CCI, previous studies indicated reduced VTA ERK activation and *c-fos* expression following injury, which was interpreted to reflect blunted VTA responsiveness and theorized to contribute to pain-induced amotivational states (e.g., Narita et al., 2003, 2004; Ozaki et al., 2004). However, CCI elevated our other indices of signaling within VTA, most notably GluN2 subunits, Homer2a/b, activated PKCε, and PI3K, which would be predicted to elevate, rather than depress, *basal* activity of mesolimbic dopamine neurons to heighten the saliency of both conditioned and unconditioned pain cues (Berridge, 2007; Bromberg-Martin et al., 2010). Indeed, these present immunoblotting results are consistent with human neuroimaging data indicating correlations between heightened PFC-NAC connectivity and pain chronification (Baliki et al., 2010, 2012). Thus, injury-induced plasticity within corticofugal glutamatergic and mesocorticolimbic dopaminergic projections might heighten PFC-NAC connectivity predictive of somatic and affective pain chronification. In support of this notion, NAC Homer1c expression bi-directionally altered CCI-induced pain symptoms, with increased Homer1c promoting nociception in CCI mice (see below).

HEROIN CPP AND HOMER-mGluR5 INTERACTIONS

In all experiments, repeated low-dose (0.1 mg/kg) heroin consistently supported CPP in injury-naïve WT mice. Remarkably, this low-dose heroin CPP was attenuated or absent in injury-naïve mice from all four mutant strains. Opioids and their withdrawal alter *Homer1* gene products within the PFC and AMY (Ammon et al., 2003; Kuntz et al., 2008) and recently, polymorphisms in *Homer1*, as well as changes in striatal and AMY *Homer1* mRNA expression, were reported in post-mortem studies of heroin addicts (Okvist et al., 2011; Jacobs et al., 2012). While constitutive *Homer2* deletion does not impact heroin-induced locomotor activity (Szumlinski et al., 2004), to the best of our knowledge, these data are the first to describe the heroin reward phenotype produced by constitutive deletion of different *Homer* genes or transgenic disruption of mGluR5-Homer interactions. That null mutations of *Homer1a* and *Homer1* (the latter of which eliminates both inducible and CC Homer1 isoforms; see Yuan et al., 2003) produced a more pronounced effect upon conditioning than *Homer2* deletion argues a more critical role for *Homer1* gene products, particularly Homer1a, in this form of heroin-related learning. Moreover, the fact that *Grm5^{R/R}* mice not only failed to exhibit heroin CPP, but tended toward CPA, argues further that the interaction between *Homer1* gene products and mGluR5 is fundamental to the motivational valence of low-dose heroin, which is worthy

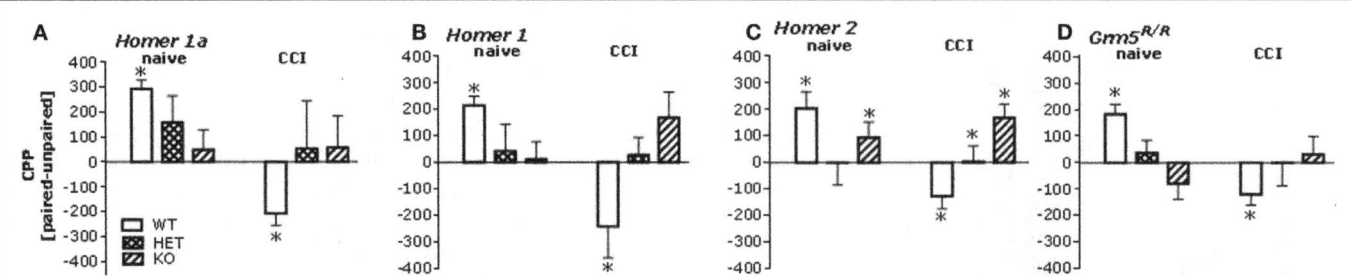

FIGURE 4 | Mutations affecting mGluR5-Homer interactions blunt heroin CPP and reverse the effects of CCI upon heroin CPA. Summary of the difference in the time spent in the heroin-paired and -unpaired compartments (CPP) following conditioning with 0.1 mg/kg heroin in mice with constitutive deletion of *Homer1a*, *Homer1*, or *Homer2*, and in mice expressing the *Grm5^{R/R}* transgene. Analysis of the data from all of the mutant animals revealed significant Genotype × CCI interactions [*Homer1a*: $F_{(2,64)} = 3.50$, $p = 0.04$; *Homer1*: $F_{(2,67)} = 6.10$, $p = 0.004$; *Homer2*: $F_{(2,66)} = 4.14$, $p = 0.02$; *Grm5^{R/R}*: $F_{(2,101)} = 6.71$, $p = 0.002$]. **(A)** In uninjured mice from the *Homer1a* study, a priori *t*-tests (time on paired vs. unpaired side) confirmed significant CPP in *Homer1a* WT [$t_{(10)} = 8.43$, $p < 0.0001$; $n = 11$], but no place-conditioning was evidence in their HET or KO counterparts (*t*-tests, *p*'s > 0.50, $n = 13$–15). In CCI mice from the Homer1a study, CPA was apparent in WT controls ($t_{(10)} = 2.81$, $p = 0.02$; $n = 11$), but again no conditioning was apparent in their HET or KO counterparts (*t*-tests, $p > 0.65$;

$n = 8$–12). **(B)** As observed in the *Homer1a* study, heroin elicited CPP and CPA, respectively in uninjured and CCI *Homer1* WT mice [naïve: $t_{(9)} = 6.12$, $p < 0.0001$; CCI: $t_{(10)} = 2.34$, $p = 0.04$], while no significant place-conditioning was apparent under either condition in HET or KO mice ($n = 11$–13; *t*-tests, $p > 0.12$). **(C)** Heroin elicited CPP and CPA, respectively, in uninjured and CCI *Homer2* WT mice [naïve: $t_{(9)} = 3.18$, $p = 0.01$; CCI: $t_{(7)} = 2.76$, $p = 0.03$]. No place-conditioning was apparent in HET mice under either condition ($n = 15$; *t*-tests, $p > 0.90$). While uninjured *Homer2* KO mice did not exhibit CPP ($n = 11$; *t*-test, $p = 0.15$), CPP, not CPA, was apparent in their CCI counterparts [$t_{(7)} = 3.27$, $p = 0.01$]. **(D)** Heroin elicited also CPP and CPA, respectively, in naïve and CCI mice *Grm5^{F/F}* mice (i.e., WT) [naïve: $t_{(21)} = 4.90$, $p < 0.0001$; CCI: $t_{(18)} = 3.00$, $p = 0.08$], while no significant place-conditioning was apparent in Grm5F/R or Grm5R/R mutants ($n = 12$–18; *t*-tests, $p > 0.20$). *$p < 0.05$ Paired vs. unpaired (i.e., conditioning; *t*-tests); +$p < 0.05$ vs. WT control (Tukey's *post hoc* tests).

of further exploration. The *Grm5^{R/R}* data are interesting as the effect of mGluR5 antagonism upon opioid-induced CPP is inconsistent (Popik and Wróbel, 2002; McGeehan and Olive, 2003; van der Kam et al., 2009). As the *Grm5^{R/R}* mutation does not impact total receptor expression (Cozzoli et al., 2009), the present behavioral observations implicate intracellular signaling processes that are known to be modulated by dynamic changes in Homer1a/CC-Homer interactions with mGluR5 in the positive incentive motivational properties of heroin-paired cue/contexts. Such signaling processes include (but are not likely limited to): altered regulation of voltage-gated ion channels, constitutive mGluR5 activity, induction of PI3K activity, and mGluR-dependent regulation of NMDA receptor current (c.f., Shiraishi-Yamaguchi and Furuichi, 2007). While the precise biochemical mechanisms mediating the blunted heroin CPP exhibited by *Homer* mutant and *Grm5^{R/R}* mice obviously require detailed study that are beyond the scope of this report, the results of larger-scale dose-response studies of cocaine or alcohol CPP argue that this heroin phenotype does not reflect a mere impairment of associative learning processes (Szumlinski et al., 2004, 2005; Datko et al., 2008; Goulding et al., 2009). Unfortunately, cessation of breeding programs for the various mutant lines precludes a full dose-response analysis of heroin CPP. Thus, it remains to be determined whether or not the blunted low-dose heroin CPP observed in injury-naïve *Homer1a/1/2* or *Grm5^{R/R}* mutant mice reflects changes in the sensitivity or efficacy of heroin to elicit conditioned reward or if the blunted CPP extends to any other measure of heroin reward/reinforcement. However, arguing against increased sensitivity to heroin intoxication as a mechanism underpinning the blunted heroin CPP, all mutant lines exhibited WT-levels of heroin-induced locomotion throughout testing.

Interestingly, *Homer1* deletion abolished low-dose heroin CPP, while intra-NAC shRNA-Homer1c infusion had absolutely no effect. These data indicate either that: (1) the neural locus mediating the CPP effect of *Homer1* deletion resides outside the NAC or (2) the CPP effect of *Homer1* deletion reflect an absence of inducible, rather than constitutively expressed, *Homer1* gene products. As the effects of *Homer1a* deletion mirrored those of *Homer1* deletion argues in favor of the latter possibility. However, based on suggestions of regional differences in heroin-induced changes in *Homer1* mRNA within PFC, AMY, and dorsal striatum (Kuntz et al., 2008; Okvist et al., 2011; Jacobs et al., 2012), *Homer1* gene products in these other addiction-relevant brain regions may contribute more so to the conditioned incentive motivational properties of low-dose heroin. It is interesting to note, however, that intra-NAC cDNA-Homer1c, as well as intrathecal cDNA-Homer1a, -Homer1c, and -Homer2b infusion, in injury-naïve mice was sufficient to block heroin CPP. The result for the NAC may be counterintuitive based on the findings from the KO studies, but, as argued below, may reflect a facilitation of low-dose heroin hyperalgesia that renders the heroin experience more aversive.

INJURY-INDUCED HEROIN CPA ALSO REQUIRES INTACT mGluR5-HOMER INTERACTIONS

Most notable and distinct from the results of earlier CPP studies in injured animals (c.f., Niikura et al., 2010), neuropathic B6 mice exhibited CPA in response to 0.1 mg/kg heroin – a dose of heroin that supported CPP in uninjured animals. In WT mice, CCI clearly augmented pain symptoms prior to heroin conditioning (see also Obara et al., 2013), supporting a causal

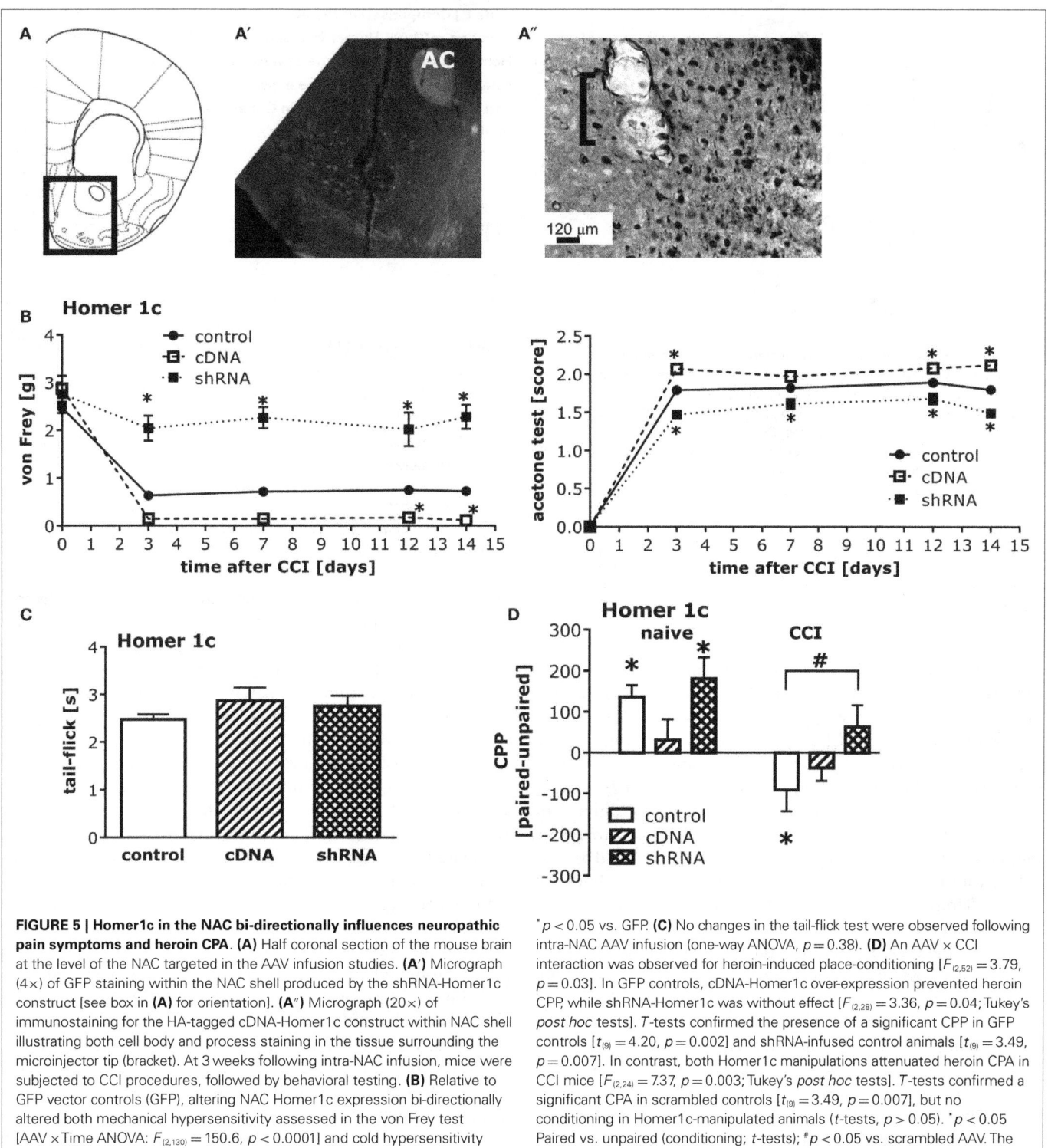

FIGURE 5 | Homer1c in the NAC bi-directionally influences neuropathic pain symptoms and heroin CPA. **(A)** Half coronal section of the mouse brain at the level of the NAC targeted in the AAV infusion studies. **(A′)** Micrograph (4×) of GFP staining within the NAC shell produced by the shRNA-Homer1c construct [see box in **(A)** for orientation]. **(A″)** Micrograph (20×) of immunostaining for the HA-tagged cDNA-Homer1c construct within NAC shell illustrating both cell body and process staining in the tissue surrounding the microinjector tip (bracket). At 3 weeks following intra-NAC infusion, mice were subjected to CCI procedures, followed by behavioral testing. **(B)** Relative to GFP vector controls (GFP), altering NAC Homer1c expression bi-directionally altered both mechanical hypersensitivity assessed in the von Frey test [AAV × Time ANOVA: $F_{(2,130)} = 150.6$, $p < 0.0001$] and cold hypersensitivity assessed in the acetone test [AAV × Time ANOVA: $F_{(2,130)} = 93.27$, $p < 0.0001$].

$^*p < 0.05$ vs. GFP. **(C)** No changes in the tail-flick test were observed following intra-NAC AAV infusion (one-way ANOVA, $p = 0.38$). **(D)** An AAV × CCI interaction was observed for heroin-induced place-conditioning [$F_{(2,52)} = 3.79$, $p = 0.03$]. In GFP controls, cDNA-Homer1c over-expression prevented heroin CPP, while shRNA-Homer1c was without effect [$F_{(2,28)} = 3.36$, $p = 0.04$; Tukey's *post hoc* tests]. *T*-tests confirmed the presence of a significant CPP in GFP controls [$t_{(9)} = 4.20$, $p = 0.002$] and shRNA-infused control animals [$t_{(9)} = 3.49$, $p = 0.007$]. In contrast, both Homer1c manipulations attenuated heroin CPA in CCI mice [$F_{(2,24)} = 7.37$, $p = 0.003$; Tukey's *post hoc* tests]. *T*-tests confirmed a significant CPA in scrambled controls [$t_{(9)} = 3.49$, $p = 0.007$], but no conditioning in Homer1c-manipulated animals (*t*-tests, $p > 0.05$). $^*p < 0.05$ Paired vs. unpaired (conditioning; *t*-tests); $^\#p < 0.05$ vs. scrambled AAV. The data represent the mean ± SEM of 8–11 mice/AAV/condition.

relation between pain symptomatology and low-dose heroin aversion. In further support of a direct cause-effect relation between pain and heroin aversion, cDNA-Homer1 infusion into either the NAC or spinal cord augments pain hypersensitivity and abolishes heroin CPP in injury-naive animals. Furthermore, intra-NAC

shRNA-Homer1c infusion, a manipulation that reduced pain hypersensitivity following CCI, prevented subsequent heroin CPA. However, neither intra-NAC nor intrathecal cDNA-Homer1c infusion potentiated heroin CPA in CCI animals. In fact, NAC cDNA-Homer1c transduction in CCI mice attenuated heroin CPA,

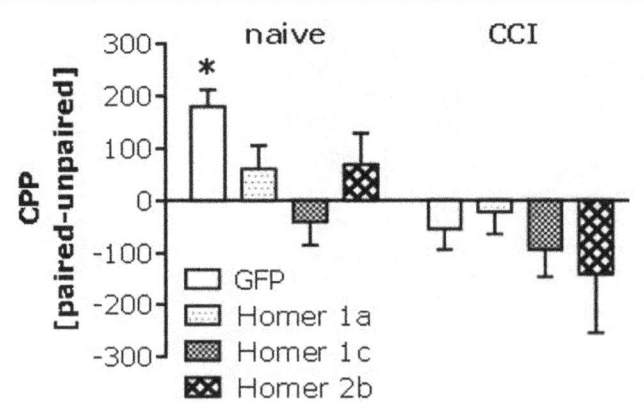

FIGURE 6 | Spinal Homer over-expression alters heroin-induced place-conditioning. Summary of the effects of intrathecal administration of AAVs carrying cDNA for Homer1a, Homer1c, or Homer2b upon place-conditioning elicited by 0.1 mg/kg in naïve (control) and CCI mice. Analyses of these data revealed a main CCI effect [$F_{(1,70)} = 12.82$, $p = 0.001$], but interaction with the AAV factor ($p = 0.28$). *A priori* t-tests confirmed a significant CPP in naïve mice infused with GFP [$t_{(8)} = 5.60$, $p = 0.001$], but no CPP in any of the cDNA-infused naïve groups (t-tests, p's > 0.05). In this study, we observed only a modest CPA in CCI-GFP controls [$t_{(8)} = 2.05$, $p = 0.08$], as well as in cDNA-Homer1c infused CCI mice [$t_{(9)} = 1.84$, $p = 0.09$], while no evidence for conditioning was observed in cDNA-Homer1a or cDNA-Homer2b CCI mice (p's > 0.20). The data represent the mean ± SEM of 8–10 mice/AAV/condition. *$p < 0.05$ Paired vs. unpaired (conditioning; t-tests).

Table 2 | Comparison of the effects of constitutive gene mutations affecting mGluR5-Homer interactions or AAV-mediated changes in Homer expression upon the development of neuropathic pain symptoms following CCI, the expression of a low-dose heroin CPP, and the heroin CPA observed in CCI animals (present study; Obara et al., 2013)[1].

Gene manipulation	CCI pain symptoms	Heroin CPP	CCI-induced heroin CPA
CONSTITUTIVE GENE MUTATION			
Homer1a KO	↑[1]	↓	↓
Homer1 KO	No effect[1]	↓	↓
Homer2 KO	No effect[1]	↓	↓ (Full reversal)
Grm5[R/R]	↑[1]	↓	↓
AAV-MEDIATED GENE TRANSFER			
NAC cDNA-Homer1c	↑	↓	↓
NAC shRNA-Homer1c	↓	No effect	↓
IT cDNA-Homer1a	↓[1]	↓	No effect
IT cDNA-Homer1c	↑[1]	↓	No effect
IT cDNA-Homer2b	↑[1]	↓	No effect

CCI, chronic constriction injury of the sciatic nerve; CPA, conditioned place-aversion; CPP, conditioned place-preference; IT, intrathecal; NAC, intra-nucleus accumbens.

although the magnitude of place-conditioning was not statistically different from GFP-infused CCI controls. These data, coupled with the lack of any significant cDNA effect in our spinal cord study (where weak CPA was observed in CCI mice) argue against a ceiling effect limiting the expression of CCI-induced CPA. Arguably, however, the fact that the effects of cDNA-Homer infusion upon heroin place-conditioning were not additive with those produced by CCI alone might be interpreted to reflect mechanistic interdependency, an interpretation that would be consistent with the notion that CCI-induced increases in glutamate receptor/Homer expression are neuroadaptations that promote dysphoric states.

Indeed, the present data from the studies of transgenic mice support this possibility as no evidence for CCI-induced heroin CPA was apparent in any mutant strain; in fact, both *Homer1* and *Homer2* KO mice exhibited conditioned approach behavior following nerve injury. That both *Homer1a* deletion and the *Grm5*[R/R] transgene exacerbate neuropathic pain symptoms, while neither *Homer1* nor *Homer2* deletion influence pain hypersensitivity (Obara et al., 2013), argues that the severity of neuropathic pain symptoms is not a determinant of CCI-induced deficits in heroin CPP (**Table 2**). CCI-induced neuropathy likely involves temporally dynamic changes in inducible vs. constitutive Homer expression, with early post-injury elevations in inducible Homers facilitating synaptic rearrangement that is later maintained by injury-induced increases in CC-Homer expression (e.g., Miletic et al., 2005, 2009; Miyabe et al., 2006; Tappe et al., 2006; Ma et al., 2009; Obara et al., 2013). Thus, the genetic interruption

of the temporal dynamics of the interplay between inducible and CC-Homer protein expression at glutamate receptors, and likely other Homer-interacting molecules, while not always sufficient to prevent neuroplasticity within pain pathways, appears to be sufficient to prevent whatever mesocorticolimbic neuroplasticity mediating CCI-induced deficits in heroin-conditioned reward. Given the present data, it becomes important to characterize more systematically: (1) how heroin dose interacts with a chronic pain state to influence drug reward/reinforcement and to relate these interactions to the expression of different Homer isoforms, as well as their major interacting partners throughout the central nervous system; (2) to extrapolate findings for heroin to prescription opioid drugs employed in pain management, and importantly; (3) to examine the relevance of injury-induced changes in glutamate receptor/Homer expression for the incentive motivational properties of opioid and other non-opioid analgesic drugs (e.g., cannabinoids). Arguably, such lines of investigation will enable a better understanding of the molecular and cellular processes mediating pain-induced dysphoria, which has relevance not only for therapeutic intervention of pain-induced negative affective states, but also individual vulnerability to develop abuse or addiction during pain management with opioid or non-opioid drugs with high abuse potential.

ACKNOWLEDGMENTS

This research was supported by funds from UCSB, as well as NIH grants DA024038 and AA016650 to Karen K. Szumlinski, NIH grants DA11742 and DA10309 to Paul F. Worley, and by funds from UNSW, as well as the Australian Research Council Future Fellowship to Matthias Klugmann.

REFERENCES

Ammon, S., Mayer, P., Riechert, U., Tischmeyer, H., and Hollt, V. (2003). Microarray analysis of genes expressed in the frontal cortex of rats chronically treated with morphine and after naloxone precipitated withdrawal. *Brain Res. Mol. Brain Res.* 112, 113–125. doi:10.1016/S0169-328X(03)00057-3

Arnsten, A. F., and Rubia, K. (2012). Neurobiological circuits regulating attention, cognitive control, motivation, and emotion: disruptions in neurodevelopmental psychiatric disorders. *J. Am. Acad. Child Adolesc. Psychiatry* 51, 356–367. doi:10.1016/j.jaac.2012.01.008

Ary, A. W., Lominac, K. D., Wroten, M. G., Williams, A. R., Campbell, R. R., Ben-Shahar, O., et al. (2013). Imbalances in prefrontal cortex CC-Homer1 versus CC-Homer2 expression promote cocaine preference. *J. Neurosci.* 33, 8101–8113. doi:10.1523/JNEUROSCI.1727-12.2013

Baliki, M. N., Geha, P. Y., Fields, H. L., and Apkarian, A. V. (2010). Predicting value of pain and analgesia: nucleus accumbens response to noxious stimuli changes in the presence of chronic pain. *Neuron* 66, 149–160. doi:10.1016/j.neuron.2010.03.002

Baliki, M. N., Petre, B., Torbey, S., Herrmann, K. M., Huang, L., Schnitzer, T. J., et al. (2012). Corticostriatal functional connectivity predicts transition to chronic back pain. *Nat. Neurosci.* 15, 1117–1119. doi:10.1038/nn.3153

Becker, S., Gandhi, W., and Schweinhardt, P. (2012). Cerebral interactions of pain and reward and their relevance for chronic pain. *Neurosci. Lett.* 520, 182–187. doi:10.1016/j.neulet.2012.03.013

Berridge, K. C. (2007). The debate over dopamine's role in reward: the case for incentive salience. *Psychopharmacology (Berl.)* 191, 391–431. doi:10.1007/s00213-006-0578-x

Bromberg-Martin, E. S., Matsumoto, M., and Hikosaka, O. (2010). Dopamine in motivational control: rewarding, aversive, and alerting. *Neuron* 68, 815–834. doi:10.1016/j.neuron.2010.11.022

Chiechio, S., and Nicoletti, F. (2012). Metabotropic glutamate receptors and the control of chronic pain. *Curr. Opin. Pharmacol.* 12, 28–34. doi:10.1016/j.coph.2011.10.010

Colpaert, F. C., Meert, T., De Witte, P., and Schmitt, P. (1982). Further evidence validating adjuvant arthritis as an experimental model of chronic pain in the rat. *Life Sci.* 31, 67–75. doi:10.1016/0024-3205(82)90402-7

Colpaert, F. C., Taraye, J. P., Alliaga, M., Bruins Slot, L. A., Attal, N., and Koek, W. (2001). Opioid self-administration as a measure of chronic nociceptive pain in arthritic rats. *Pain* 91, 33–45. doi:10.1016/S0304-3959(00)00413-9

Cozzoli, D. K., Goulding, S. P., Zhang, P. W., Xiao, B., Hu, J. H., Ary, A. W., et al. (2009). Binge drinking upregulates accumbens mGluR5-Homer2-PI3K signaling: functional implications for alcoholism. *J. Neurosci.* 29, 8655–8668. doi:10.1523/JNEUROSCI.5900-08.2009

Datko, M. C., Hu, J.-H., Williams, M., Reyes, C., Seeburg, P. H., Schwarz, M. K., et al. (2008). The induction of Homer1a is necessary for cocaine-induced neuroplasticity. *Soc. Neurosci. Abstr.* 767.10.

Depue, B. E. (2012). A neuroanatomical model of prefrontal inhibitory modulation of memory retrieval. *Neurosci. Biobehav. Rev.* 36, 1382–1399. doi:10.1016/j.neubiorev.2012.02.012

Dib, B., and Duclaux, R. (1982). Intracerebroventricular self-injection of morphine in response to pain in the rat. *Pain* 13, 395–406. doi:10.1016/0304-3959(82)90008-2

Doth, A. H., Hansson, P. T., Jensen, M. P., and Taylor, R. S. (2010). The burden of neuropathic pain: a systematic review and meta-analysis of health utilities. *Pain* 149, 338–344. doi:10.1016/j.pain.2010.02.034

Fu, Y., Han, J., Ishola, T., Scerbo, M., Adwanikar, H., Ramsey, C., et al. (2008). PKA and ERK, but not PKC, in the amygdala contribute to pain-related synaptic plasticity and behavior. *Mol. Pain* 4, 26. doi:10.1186/1744-8069-4-26

Goulding, S. P., Bergin, M., Hu, J. H., Worley, P. F., and Szumlinski, K. K. (2009). Evidence that the negative regulator of Group1 mGluR function Daughter of Homer (DOH) is necessary for high-dose alcohol reward in mice. *Alcohol. Clin. Exp. Res.* 33(Suppl. 1), 75A.

Goulding, S. P., Obara, I., Lominac, K. D., Gould, A. T., Miller, B. W., Klugmann, M., et al. (2011). Accumbens Homer2-mediated signaling: a factor contributing to mouse strain differences in alcohol drinking? *Genes Brain Behav.* 10, 111–126. doi:10.1111/j.1601-183X.2010.00647.x

Harris, R. E., and Clauw, D. J. (2012). Imaging central neurochemical alterations in chronic pain with proton magnetic resonance spectroscopy. *Neurosci. Lett.* 520, 192–196. doi:10.1016/j.neulet.2012.03.042

Hu, J. H., Yang, L., Kammermeier, P. J., Moore, C. G., Brakeman, P. R., Tu, J., et al. (2012). Preso1 dynamically regulates group I metabotropic glutamate receptors. *Nat. Neurosci.* 15, 836–844. doi:10.1038/nn.3103

Jacobs, M. M., Okvist, A., Horvath, M., Keller, E., Bannon, M. J., Morgello, S., et al. (2012). Dopamine receptor D1 and postsynaptic density gene variants associate with opiate abuse and striatal expression levels. *Mol. Psychiatry* (in press). doi:10.1038/mp.2012.140

Jarcho, J. M., Mayer, E. A., Jiang, Z. K., Feier, N. A., and London, E. D. (2012). Pain, affective symptoms, and cognitive deficits in patients with cerebral dopamine dysfunction. *Pain* 153, 744–754. doi:10.1016/j.pain.2012.01.002

Kalivas, P. W. (2009). The glutamate homeostasis hypothesis of addiction. *Nat. Rev. Neurosci.* 10, 561–572. doi:10.1038/nrn2515

Klugmann, M., Symes, C. W., Leichtlein, C. B., Klaussner, B. K., Dunning, J., Fong, D., et al. (2005). AAV-mediated hippocampal expression of short and long Homer 1 proteins differentially affect cognition and seizure activity in adult rats. *Mol. Cell. Neurosci.* 28, 347–360. doi:10.1016/j.mcn.2004.10.002

Klugmann, M., and Szumlinski, K. K. (2008). Targeting Homer genes using adeno-associated viral vector: lessons learned from behavioural and neurochemical studies. *Behav. Pharmacol.* 19, 485–500. doi:10.1097/FBP.0b013e32830c369f

Kuntz, K. L., Patel, K. M., Grigson, P. S., Freeman, W. M., and Vrana, K. E. (2008). Heroin self-administration: II. CNS gene expression following withdrawal and cue-induced drug-seeking behavior. *Pharmacol. Biochem. Behav.* 90, 349–356. doi:10.1016/j.pbb.2008.03.019

Kuroda, R., Yorimae, A., Yamada, Y., Nakatani, J., and Takatsuji, K. (1995). c-Fos expression after formalin injection into the face in the cat. *Stereotact. Funct. Neurosurg.* 65, 152–156. doi:10.1159/000098686

Leknes, S., and Tracey, I. (2008). A common neurobiology for pain and pleasure. *Nat. Rev. Neurosci.* 9, 314–320. doi:10.1038/nrn2333

Lyness, W. H., Smith, F. L., Heavner, J. E., Iacono, C. U., and Garvin, R. D. (1989). Morphine self-administration in the rat during adjuvant-induced arthritis. *Life Sci.* 45, 2217–2224. doi:10.1016/0024-3205(89)90062-3

Ma, Z. L., Zhu, W., Zhang, W., and Gu, X. P. (2009). Effect of the synaptic scaffolding protein Homer1a on chronic compression of dorsal root ganglion. *Ann. Clin. Lab. Sci.* 39, 71–75.

Martin, T. J., Buechler, N. L., Kim, S. A., Ewan, E. E., Xiao, R., and Childers, S. R. (2011). Involvement of the lateral amygdala in the antiallodynic and reinforcing effects of heroin in rats after peripheral nerve injury. *Anesthesiology* 114, 633–642. doi:10.1097/ALN.0b013e318209aba7

Martin, T. J., Kim, S. A., Buechler, N. L., Porreca, F., and Eisenach, J. C. (2007). Opioid self-administration in the nerve injured rat: relevance of antiallodynic effects to drug consumption and effects of intrathecal analgesics. *Anesthesiology* 106, 312–322. doi:10.1097/00000542-200702000-00020

McGeehan, A. J., and Olive, M. F. (2003). The mGluR5 antagonist MPEP reduces the conditioned rewarding effects of cocaine but not other drugs of abuse. *Synapse* 47, 240–242. doi:10.1002/syn.10166

Miletic, G., Driver, A. M., Miyabe-Nishiwaki, T., and Miletic, V. (2009). Early changes in Homer1 proteins in the spinal dorsal horn are associated with loose ligation of the rat sciatic nerve. *Anesth. Analg.* 109, 2000–2007. doi:10.1213/ANE.0b013e3181beea9b

Miletic, G., Miyabe, T., Gebhardt, K. J., and Miletic, V. (2005). Increased levels of Homer1b/c and Shank1a in the post-synaptic density of spinal dorsal horn neurons are associated with neuropathic pain in rats. *Neurosci. Lett.* 386, 189–193. doi:10.1016/j.neulet.2005.06.007

Minozzi, S., Amato, L., and Davoli, M. (2013). Development of dependence following treatment with opioid analgesics for pain relief: a systematic review. *Addiction* 108, 688–698. doi:10.1111/j.1360-0443.2012.04005.x

Miyabe, T., Miletic, G., and Miletic, V. (2006). Loose ligation of the sciatic nerve in rats elicits transient up-regulation of Homer1a gene expression in the spinal dorsal horn. *Neurosci. Lett.* 398, 296–299. doi:10.1016/j.neulet.2006.01.011

Narita, M., Kishimoto, Y., Ise, Y., Yajima, Y., Misawa, K., and Suzuki, T. (2005). Direct evidence for the involvement of the mesolimbic kappa-opioid system in the morphine-induced rewarding effect under an inflammatory pain-like state. *Neuropsychopharmacology* 30, 111–118. doi:10.1038/sj.npp.1300527

Narita, M., Oe, K., Kato, H., Shibasaki, M., Narita, M., Yajima, Y., et al. (2004). Implication of spinal protein kinase C in the suppression of morphine-induced rewarding effect under a neuropathic pain-like state in mice. *Neuroscience* 125, 545–551. doi:10.1016/j.neuroscience.2004.02.022

Narita, M., Ozaki, S., Narita, M., Ise, Y., Yajima, Y., and Suzuki, T. (2003). Change in the expression of c-fos in the rat brain following sciatic nerve ligation. *Neurosci. Lett.* 352, 231–233. doi:10.1016/j.neulet.2003.08.052

Neugebauer, V. (2006). "Subcortical processing of nociceptive information: basal ganglia and amygdala," in *Pain*, eds F. Cervero and T. S. Jensen (Amsterdam: Elsevier), 141–158.

Neugebauer, V., Li, W., Bird, G. C., and Han, J. S. (2004). The amygdala and persistent pain. *Neuroscientist* 10, 221–234. doi:10.1177/1073858403261077

Niikura, K., Narita, M., Butelman, E. R., Kreek, M. J., and Suzuki, T. (2010). Neuropathic and chronic pain stimuli downregulate central mu-opioid and dopaminergic transmission. *Trends Pharmacol. Sci.* 31, 299–305. doi:10.1016/j.tips.2010.04.003

Obara, I., Goulding, S. P., Hu, J. H., Klugmann, M., Worley, P. F., and Szumlinski, K. K. (2013). Nerve injury-induced changes in Homer/glutamate receptor signaling contribute to development and maintenance of neuropathic pain. *Pain* (in press). doi:10.1016/j.pain.2013.03.035

Obara, I., Mika, J., Schafer, M. K., and Przewlocka, B. (2003). Antagonists of the kappa-opioid receptor enhance allodynia in rats and mice after sciatic nerve ligation. *Br. J. Pharmacol.* 140, 538–546. doi:10.1038/sj.bjp.0705427

Ohayon, M. M., and Schatzberg, A. F. (2010). Chronic pain and major depressive disorder in the general population. *J. Psychiatr. Res.* 44, 454–461. doi:10.1016/j.jpsychires.2009.10.013

Okvist, A., Fagergren, P., Whittard, J., Garcia-Osta, A., Drakenberg, K., Horvath, M. C., et al. (2011). Dysregulated postsynaptic density and endocytic zone in the amygdala of human heroin and cocaine abusers. *Biol. Psychiatry* 69, 245–252. doi:10.1016/j.biopsych.2010.09.037

Olive, M. F., Cleva, R. M., Kalivas, P. W., and Malcolm, R. J. (2012). Glutamatergic medications for the treatment of drug and behavioral addictions. *Pharmacol. Biochem. Behav.* 100, 801–810. doi:10.1016/j.pbb.2011.04.015

Oluigbo, C. O., Salma, A., and Rezai, A. R. (2012). Targeting the affective and cognitive aspects of chronic neuropathic pain using basal forebrain neuromodulation: rationale, review and proposal. *J. Clin. Neurosci.* 19, 1216–1221. doi:10.1016/j.jocn.2012.04.002

Osikowicz, M., Mika, J., Makuch, W., and Przewlocka, B. (2008). Glutamate receptor ligands attenuate allodynia and hyperalgesia and potentiate morphine effects in a mouse model of neuropathic pain. *Pain* 139, 117–126.

Osikowicz, M., Mika, J., and Przewlocka, B. (2013). The glutamatergic system as a target for neuropathic pain relief. *Exp. Physiol.* 98, 372–384. doi:10.1113/expphysiol.2012.069922

Ozaki, S., Narita, M., Narita, M., Iino, M., Miyoshi, K., and Suzuki, T. (2003). Suppression of the morphine-induced rewarding effect and G-protein activation in the lower midbrain following nerve injury in the mouse: involvement of G-protein-coupled receptor kinase 2. *Neuroscience* 116, 89–97. doi:10.1016/S0306-4522(02)00699-1

Ozaki, S., Narita, M., Narita, M., Ozaki, M., Khotib, J., and Suzuki, T. (2004). Role of extracellular signal-regulated kinase in the ventaral tegmental area in the suppression of the morphine-induced rewarding effect in mice with sciatic nerve ligation. *J. Neurochem.* 88, 1389–1397. doi:10.1046/j.1471-4159.2003.02272.x

Penzner, J. H., Thompson, D. L., Arth, C., Fowler, J. K., Ary, A. W., and Szumlinski, K. K. (2008). Protracted "anti-addictive" phenotype produced in C57BL/6J mice by adolescent phenylpropanolamine treatment. *Addict. Biol.* 13, 310–325. doi:10.1111/j.1369-1600.2008.00101.x

Popik, P., and Wróbel, M. (2002). Morphine conditioned reward is inhibited by MPEP, the mGluR5 antagonist. *Neuropharmacology* 43, 1210–1217. doi:10.1016/S0028-3908(02)00309-X

Rodella, L., Rezzani, R., Gioia, G., Tredici, G., and Bianchi, R. (1998). Expression of fos immunoreactivity in the rat supraspinal regions following noxious visceral stimulation. *Brain Res. Bull.* 47, 357–366. doi:10.1016/S0361-9230(98)00123-3

Rong, R., Ahn, J. Y., Huang, H., Nagata, E., Kalman, D., Kapp, J. A., et al. (2003). PI3 kinase enhancer-Homer complex couples mGluRI to PI3 kinase, preventing neuronal apoptosis. *Nat. Neurosci.* 6, 1153–1161. doi:10.1038/nn1134

Shin, D. M., Dehoff, M., Luo, X., Kang, S. H., Tu, J., Nayak, S. K., et al. (2003). Homer 2 tunes G protein-coupled receptors stimulus intensity by regulating RGS proteins and PLCbeta GAP activities. *J. Cell Biol.* 162, 293–303. doi:10.1083/jcb.200210109

Shiraishi-Yamaguchi, Y., and Furuichi, T. (2007). The Homer family proteins. *Genome Biol.* 8, 206. doi:10.1186/gb-2007-8-2-206

Szumlinski, K. K., Ary, A. W., and Lominac, K. D. (2008). Homers regulate drug-induced neuroplasticity: implications for addiction. *Biochem. Pharmacol.* 75, 112–133. doi:10.1016/j.bcp.2007.07.031

Szumlinski, K. K., Dehoff, M. H., Kang, S. H., Frys, K. A., Lominac, K. D., Rohrer, J., et al. (2004). Homer proteins regulate vulnerability to cocaine. *Neuron* 43, 401–413. doi:10.1016/j.neuron.2004.07.019

Szumlinski, K. K., Lominac, K. D., Oleson, E. B., Walker, J. K., Mason, A., Dehoff, M. H., et al. (2005). Homer2 is necessary for ethanol-induced neuroplasticity. *J. Neurosci.* 25, 7054–7061. doi:10.1523/JNEUROSCI.1529-05.2005

Tappe, A., Klugmann, M., Luo, C., Hirlinger, D., Agarwal, N., Benrath, J., et al. (2006). Synaptic scaffolding protein Homer1a protects against chronic inflammatory pain. *Nat. Med.* 12, 677–681. doi:10.1038/nm1406

Tappe-Theodor, A., Fu, Y., Kuner, R., and Neugebauer, V. (2011). Homer1a signaling in the amygdala counteracts pain-related synaptic plasticity, mGluR1 function and pain behaviors. *Mol. Pain* 7, 38. doi:10.1186/1744-8069-7-38

van der Kam, E. L., De Vry, J., and Tzschentke, T. M. (2009). 2-Methyl-6-(phenylethynyl)-pyridine (MPEP) potentiates ketamine and heroin reward as assessed by acquisition, extinction, and reinstatement of conditioned place preference in the rat. *Eur. J. Pharmacol.* 606, 94–101. doi:10.1016/j.ejphar.2008.12.042

Wood, P. B., Schweinhardt, P., Jaeger, E., Dagher, A., Hakyemez, H., Rabiner, E. A., et al. (2007). Fibromyalgia patients show an abnormal dopamine response to pain. *Eur. J. Neurosci.* 25, 3576–3582. doi:10.1111/j.1460-9568.2007.05623.x

Wozniak, K. M., Rojas, C., Wu, Y., and Slusher, B. S. (2012). The role of glutamate signaling in pain processes and its regulation by GCP II inhibition. *Curr. Med. Chem.* 19, 1323–1334. doi:10.2174/092986712799462630

Xu, Q., Fitzsimmons, B., Steinauer, J., O'Neill, A., Newton, A. C., Hua, X. Y., et al. (2011). Spinal phosphinositide 3-kinase-Akt-mammalian target of rapamycin signaling cascades in inflammation-induced hyperalgesia. *J. Neurosci.* 31, 2113–2124. doi:10.1523/JNEUROSCI.2139-10.2011

Yuan, J. P., Kiselyov, K., Shin, D. M., Chen, J., Shcheynikov, N., Kang, S. H., et al. (2003). Homer binds TRPC family channels and is required for gating of TRPC1 by IP3 receptors. *Cell* 114, 777–789. doi:10.1016/S0092-8674(03)00716-5

6

Dare to delay? The impacts of adolescent alcohol and marijuana use onset on cognition, brain structure, and function

Krista M. Lisdahl*, Erika R. Gilbart, Natasha E. Wright and Skyler Shollenbarger

Department of Psychology, University of Wisconsin-Milwaukee, Milwaukee, WI, USA

Edited by:
Remi Martin-Fardon, The Scripps Research Institute, USA

Reviewed by:
Susan F. Tapert, University of California San Diego, USA
Carmelo Mario Vicario, University of Queensland, Italy

*Correspondence:
Krista M. Lisdahl, University of Wisconsin-Milwaukee, 2241 East Hartford Avenue, Milwaukee, WI 53211, USA
e-mail: krista.medina@gmail.com

Throughout the world, drug and alcohol use has a clear adolescent onset (Degenhardt et al., 2008). Alcohol continues to be the most popular drug among teens and emerging adults, with almost a third of 12th graders and 40% of college students reporting recent binge drinking (Johnston et al., 2009, 2010), and marijuana (MJ) is the second most popular drug in teens (Johnston et al., 2010). The initiation of drug use is consistent with an overall increase in risk-taking behaviors during adolescence that coincides with significant neurodevelopmental changes in both gray and white matter (Giedd et al., 1996a; Paus et al., 1999; Sowell et al., 1999, 2002, 2004; Gogtay et al., 2004; Barnea-Goraly et al., 2005; Lenroot and Giedd, 2006). Animal studies have suggested that compared to adults, adolescents may be particularly vulnerable to the neurotoxic effects of drugs, especially alcohol and MJ (see Schneider and Koch, 2003; Barron et al., 2005; Monti et al., 2005; Cha et al., 2006; Rubino et al., 2009; Spear, 2010). In this review, we will provide a detailed overview of studies that examined the impact of early adolescent onset of alcohol and MJ use on neurocognition (e.g., Ehrenreich et al., 1999; Wilson et al., 2000; Tapert et al., 2002a; Hartley et al., 2004; Fried et al., 2005; Townshend and Duka, 2005; Medina et al., 2007a; McQueeny et al., 2009; Gruber et al., 2011, 2012; Hanson et al., 2011; Lisdahl and Price, 2012), with a special emphasis on recent prospective longitudinal studies (e.g., White et al., 2011; Hicks et al., 2012; Meier et al., 2012). Finally, we will explore potential clinical and public health implications of these findings.

Keywords: adolescence, MRI, alcohol, binge drinking, marijuana, neuropsychology, cognition, age onset

INTRODUCTION

Throughout the world, drug and alcohol use has a clear adolescent onset (Degenhardt et al., 2008). Alcohol continues to be the most popular drug among teens and young adults, with almost a third of 12th graders and 40% of college students reporting recent binge drinking (four standard alcohol drinks on an occasion in females and five drinks for males; Johnston et al., 2010, 2011). Further, the majority of teens (58%) drinkers also use marijuana (MJ) (Martin et al., 1996), contributing to frequent comorbidity between alcohol and MJ use disorders (Agosti et al., 2002). Indeed, MJ is the second most popular drug and is on the rise in teens, with up to 25% reporting past year use (Johnston et al., 2011). Given this, studies examining the neurocognitive consequences of alcohol and MJ use in youth have gained attention in the scientific literature. This review will present current research regarding the neurocognitive consequences of alcohol, especially binge drinking, and MJ use during the teenage years. Studies utilizing neuropsychological assessment, structural and functional neuroimaging will be reviewed, the impact of teenage drug use onset will be discussed and recommendations for future research will be presented.

Adolescence is a dynamic time marked by increased risk-taking behaviors including substance use (Spear, 2000; Gardener and Steinberg, 2005; Eaton et al., 2006; Casey et al., 2008) that coincide with significant neurodevelopmental changes. Brain regions associated with executive functioning (e.g., problem solving, planning, working memory, and emotional regulation), including the prefrontal cortex (PFC), parietal cortex, and cerebellum, continue to undergo gray matter synaptic pruning into the mid-20s (Giedd et al., 1996a; Sowell et al., 1999, 2002, 2004; Gogtay et al., 2004; Lenroot and Giedd, 2006). White matter volume and integrity increases into the early thirties, yielding improvements in efficient neural conductivity (Giedd et al., 1999; Paus et al., 1999; Barnea-Goraly et al., 2005; Jernigan and Gamst, 2005; Nagel et al., 2006). Scholars have emphasized that it may not be the late maturation of the PFC alone that is responsible for increased risk-taking behavior during adolescence, but rather it is due to differential developmental trajectories of the PFC compared to limbic system. During the teen years, the limbic system develops earlier than the PFC (Giedd et al., 1996b; Galvan et al., 2006; Casey et al., 2008). Indeed, as the PFC undergoes neuronal maturation, greater top-down control of the limbic system results in improved inhibitory control and affective processing as an adolescent becomes an adult (Casey et al., 1997, 2005, 2008; Monk et al., 2003; Liston et al., 2006). It should also be noted that there are gender differences in the timing and rate of neurodevelopment (see Lenroot and Giedd, 2010 for review). More specifically, gray matter volumes peak in executive centers earlier for girls, indicating that females undergo synaptic pruning earlier and there are greater age-related white matter increases in males; overall, this results in relatively larger brain volumes in boys compared to girls (Giedd et al., 1996b; Nagel et al., 2006; Lenroot et al., 2007; Lenroot and Giedd, 2010). This neuromaturation may represent a sensitive period during which exposure to drugs may have a greater impact on neurocognition compared to adult exposure.

IMPACT OF ADOLESCENT VS. ADULT AGE OF ALCOHOL USE ONSET ON NEUROCOGNITION

Animal studies have suggested that compared to adults, adolescents may be particularly vulnerable to the neurotoxic effects of early alcohol use onset (AUO) (see Barron et al., 2005; Monti et al., 2005; Spear, 2010 for previous reviews). In humans, addiction specialists have attempted to categorize subtypes of alcohol dependence. One model subdivides alcohol-dependent individuals into Type I and II alcohol-dependent groups (Cloninger, 1987), with Type II alcoholics demonstrating an early AUO (before age 25), earlier treatment attempts, increased novelty seeking, and strong family history of substance-use disorders (SUD; von Knorring et al., 1985; Gilligan et al., 1988; Sullivan et al., 1990). Research examining this typology has revealed that emerging adult AUO (<22–25 years old) is associated with increased childhood behavioral problems, impulsivity, poor decision-making, increased mood disorders, aggressiveness, severity of substance-use problems, more rapid progression from regular drinking to AUD, unique patterns of cerebral blood flow in the PFC, hyperarousal and poor sensorimotor gating, and increased comorbidity with externalizing disorders and ADHD (Varma et al., 1994; Johnson et al., 2000; Demir et al., 2002; Bjork et al., 2004; Dawe et al., 2004; Dom et al., 2006a,b; Pardo et al., 2007; Chen et al., 2011; Lee et al., 2011; Wilens et al., 2011). Specifically, DeWit et al. (2000) reported that the odds of developing lifetime alcohol dependence increase by 14% with each increasing year of AUO.

Several of these symptoms, including impulsivity, poor decision making, externalizing symptoms, aggressiveness, sensation seeking are associated with PFC function, which is continuing to develop during the teenage and emerging adult years (see Kolb et al., 2012; Lenroot and Giedd, 2010 for review). Therefore, it has been hypothesized that PFC dysfunction places individuals at risk for early substance use and early AUO further disrupts PFC development, defining a sensitive period for increased neurocognitive effects in adolescents with AUD. In order to test this model, the Minnesota Twin Family Study examined the impact of premorbid personality and adolescent AUO on personality changes through adolescence into emerging adulthood (Hicks et al., 2010, 2012). These investigations found that behavioral disinhibition prior to AUO significantly predicted age of AUO (no onset, adult onset, adolescent onset who stopped using and adolescent onset with continued symptoms of AUD), with increased disinhibition predicting earlier AUO especially in males (Hicks et al., 2010, 2012). Further, early AUO uniquely predicted lack of maturation in behavioral disinhibition compared to other subgroups (Hicks et al., 2012; see **Figure 1**). Further, this study found that adolescents who stopped drinking had significant recovery in both behavioral disinhibition and negative emotionality (Hicks et al.,

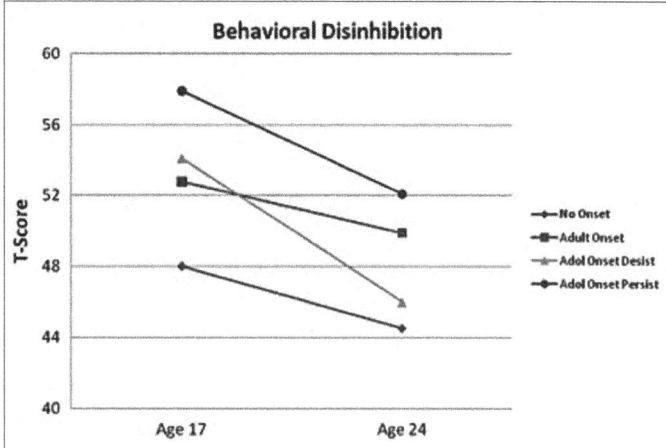

FIGURE 1 | The figure depicts the mean behavioral disinhibition scores for the alcohol-dependent groups (no onset, *n* = 1211; adult onset, *n* = 545; adolescent onset-desist, *n* = 71; and adolescent onset-persist, *n* = 149) at ages 17 and 24 (scores are in a *T*-score metric; mean = 50, SD = 10).

2012), suggesting potential recovery of PFC function with abstinence. Other studies examining the impact of adolescent AUO vs. adult AUO have demonstrated that sensitivity to punishment, disinhibition, and increased likelihood of developing an AUD in teenage AUO (Lyvers et al., 2009, 2011).

BINGE OR HEAVY ALCOHOL USE AND NEUROCOGNITION IN YOUTH

Given the alarming rates of binge drinking in both teenagers and young adults, especially college students (Johnston et al., 2009, 2010), it is important to determine whether binge drinking (defined as four standard alcohol drinks on an occasion in females and five drinks for males), even in the absence of an AUD, is associated with cognition and brain changes. This risky drinking pattern has induced neuronal damage and long-lasting behavioral deficits in adolescent and adult animals (Monti et al., 2005; see Barron et al., 2005; Spear, 2010; Coleman et al., 2011). Still, there have been relatively few human studies to date that specifically examine the effects of intermittent binge drinking in adolescents and emerging adults. Thus far, those studies have reported cognitive deficits associated with binge drinking in otherwise healthy teens and emerging adults, including poorer sustained attention (Hartley et al., 2004), memory (Hartley et al., 2004; Scaife and Duka, 2009; Parada et al., 2011), spatial working memory (Townshend and Duka, 2005; Scaife and Duka, 2009), psychomotor speed (Hartley et al., 2004), working memory (Parada et al., 2012), perseverative responding (Parada et al., 2012), and response inhibition and rule acquisition in females (Townshend and Duka, 2005; Scaife and Duka, 2009), although two studies actually found faster motor responding during a visuospatial task (Townshend and Duka, 2005; Scaife and Duka, 2009). Given the high rates of binge drinking in high school and college students, these results are of great concern and these cognitive problems may be, at least in part, to blame for the lower grades seen in heavy drinking students.

Evidence also suggests underlying structural and functional brain changes associated with binge drinking in adolescents and emerging adults. Using diffusion tensor imaging (DTI), an MRI technique that quantifies white matter integrity, McQueeny et al. (2009) found that teenage binge drinking was associated with significantly reduced white matter quality in several brain regions that connect the brain stem, motor areas, limbic regions, and cortex including the PFC (i.e., the corpus callosum, superior longitudinal fasciculus, corona radiata, internal and external capsules, and commissural, limbic, brainstem, and cortical projection fibers). Greater symptoms of hangover and increased estimated peak BAC estimates were significantly correlated with poorer white matter integrity in white matter tracts connecting the two hemispheres, frontal lobe, and cerebellar tracts.

Alterations in macro-structure of cortical and subcortical gray matter have also been reported. Although binge drinking was not directly assessed, we (Medina et al., 2010) found that increased overall quantity of alcohol use during the past year was significantly related to smaller cerebellar vermis volumes in substance-using teens. In a follow-up study, our group demonstrated that greater number of drinks per binge in the past 3 months significantly predicted reduced bilateral white and gray matter volumes in the cerebellum in 106 otherwise healthy teens (Lisdahl et al., 2013; see **Figure 2**). Squeglia et al. (2012) examined cortical thickness in 59 teenagers (ages 16–19) with and without binge-drinking history. Gender significantly moderated the effects of recent binge drinking on PFC and cingulate cortex thickness, with female binge drinkers demonstrating thicker cortices compared to non-drinkers and males demonstrating cortical thinning. In the females, thicker prefrontal cortices were associated with poorer visuospatial, inhibition, and attentional functioning suggesting potential disruption of healthy adolescent PFC pruning in the binge-drinking teens.

Functional changes in brain activation have also been associated with intermittent binge drinking in youth. Event-related potential (ERP) studies have found abnormal signal in anterior and inferior PFC regions to working memory and response inhibition tasks in emerging adults with a history of at least 2 years of intermittent binge drinking (Crego et al., 2010; López-Caneda et al., 2012). Maurage et al. (2009) reported that increases in binge drinking during the first year of college was associated with increasing delays in P1, N2, and P3b latency, areas underlying perceptual, attentional, and executive functioning. This is consistent with Ehlers et al. (2007) who reported smaller P300 amplitudes and latency in adolescents and emerging adults with a binge-drinking history. Research utilizing electroencephalography (EEG) found increased spectral power in delta and fast-beta bands in binge-drinking emerging adults, which is consistent with findings reported in adults with alcohol dependence (Courtney and Polich, 2010).

In a teenage sample, Schweinsburg et al. (2010a) found that binge drinkers had abnormal brain response during a verbal encoding functional magnetic resonance imaging (fMRI) task. Further, unlike the controls, the binge drinkers failed to engage the hippocampus during novel verbal encoding. In a similar sample of 95 adolescents, Squeglia et al. (2011) reported significant gender differences in binge-drinking effects on a spatial working memory task. Female binge drinkers had blunted activation in frontal,

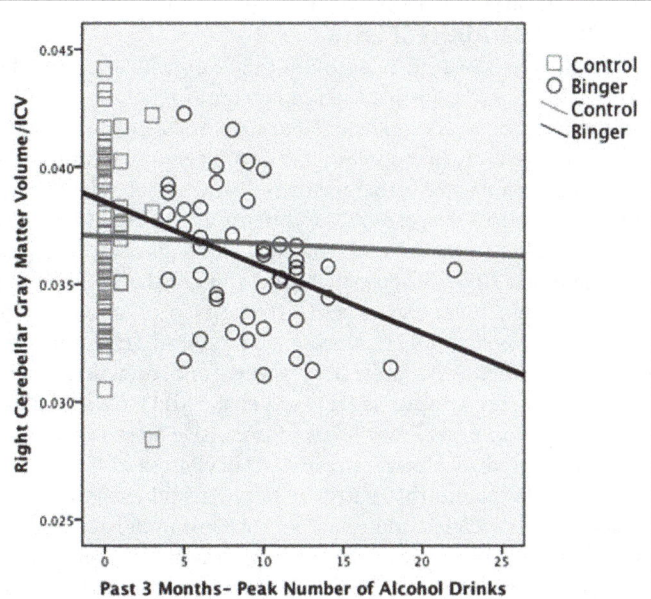

FIGURE 2 | Reduced right hemisphere cerebellar gray matter volume (corrected for intracranial volume) associated with peak number of alcohol drinks consumed in the past 3 months in binge drinking (*n* = 46) and control (*n* = 60) adolescents (adapted from Lisdahl et al., 2013).

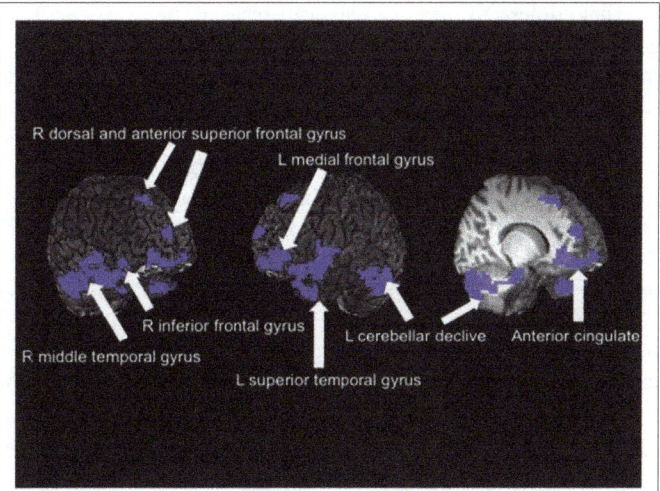

FIGURE 3 | Significant fMRI clusters predicted by the interaction between gender and binge-drinking status (*N* = 95). Areas in blue indicate where female binge drinkers demonstrated significantly reduced BOLD response during the spatial working memory task compared to female controls, while male binge drinkers demonstrated increased BOLD response (adapted from Squeglia et al., 2011).

temporal, and cerebellar cortices compared to controls while males demonstrated the opposite pattern (see **Figure 3**). Other groups have reported blunted amygdala, striatal, and insular activity to emotional cues and decision-making tasks in adolescent binge drinkers compared to social drinkers (Gilman et al., 2012; Xiao et al., 2012).

NEUROCOGNITIVE CONSEQUENCES OF ALCOHOL USE DISORDERS IN ADOLESCENTS

Converging lines of evidence suggest that even with substantially shorter periods of exposure, adolescent onset of AUD is associated with neurocognitive deficits. Neuropsychological studies have found that AUD during adolescence and emerging adulthood is associated with poorer verbal memory (Brown et al., 2000; Hanson et al., 2011; Thoma et al., 2011), attention (Tapert and Brown, 1999; Koskinen et al., 2011; Thoma et al., 2011), processing speed (Thoma et al., 2011), visuospatial functioning (Sher et al., 1997; Giancola et al., 1998; Tapert et al., 2002a; Hanson et al., 2011), language (Moss et al., 1994), executive functioning (Hanson et al., 2011; White et al., 2011), and exacerbation of antisocial personality behavior disorder symptoms (Howard et al., 2011). One longitudinal study found that lower levels of impulsive behavior in early adolescence predicted lower rates of AUD in young adulthood; furthermore, they found that past year heavy drinking significantly prospectively predicted additional increases in impulsivity in the following year (White et al., 2011). Withdrawal symptoms seem to be particularly sensitive predictors of cognitive deficits, including poorer visuospatial functioning and memory retrieval (Brown and Tapert, 1999; Brown et al., 2000; Tapert et al., 2002a; Hanson et al., 2011).

Studies utilizing high-resolution MRI have revealed structural abnormalities in teens with AUD, including reduced hippocampal (De Bellis et al., 2000; Nagel et al., 2005; Medina et al., 2007c) and PFC (De Bellis et al., 2005; Medina et al., 2008) volumes, suggesting that adolescent onset of AUD can result in neuronal atrophy, especially in brain regions underlying executive functioning and memory. Using fMRI to assess blood flow changes during cognitive tasks, Tapert et al. (2004) have shown that despite similar behavioral performance on a spatial working memory task, adolescents with AUD have increased brain response in parietal and blunted response in occipital, PFC, and cerebellar regions. Park et al. (2011) found reduced fMRI activation in bilateral frontal and precentral, left superior temporal and parietal cortices, and left cerebellar cortex and increased right uncus activation during a verbal working memory task in teenage males with AUD compared to healthy controls. These results indicate that the adolescent brain may be able to partially compensate for alcohol-induced neuronal insult by relying on other areas to successfully complete the task.

Gender differences in AUD effects have also been reported. Caldwell et al. (2005) found that, after controlling for average BAC, females with AUD demonstrated reduced PFC response compared to gender-matched controls, while the males showed the opposite pattern. Overall, females demonstrated more alcohol-related abnormalities in the PFC compared to males, which was consistent with our structural findings (Medina et al., 2008). Further, young adult women with AUD who underwent a similar fMRI spatial working memory task demonstrated overall blunted brain activation along with poorer behavioral performance (Tapert et al., 2001). In conclusion, emerging adult females with AUD may no longer be able to compensate as effectively as adolescents, demonstrating additional performance decrements with continued alcohol use into early adulthood.

Taken together, these studies suggest that both intermittent binge drinking and the development of AUD can result in

significant cognitive, structural, and functional brain changes in both male and female adolescents and emerging adults. Given the fact that approximately 40% of college students engage in binge drinking, this is a major concern. Combined with other alcohol-related consequences (e.g., hangover, poor sleep, emotional stress, legal issues, relationship conflict), these cognitive problems may reduce performance in the classroom. Indeed, studies have found that problematic binge drinking has been predictive of a poorer end-of-semester grade point average (Read et al., 2007).

IMPACT OF ADOLESCENT VS. ADULT AGE OF MARIJUANA USE ONSET ON NEUROCOGNITION

Similar to alcohol findings, preclinical studies have found increased cellular changes associated with THC (delta-9-tetrahydrocannabinol; i.e., one of the major psychoactive compounds in MJ) exposure during adolescence compared to adulthood (e.g., Schneider and Koch, 2003; O'Shea et al., 2004; Cha et al., 2006; Quinn et al., 2008; Rubino et al., 2008). Thus far, human findings suggest that earlier MJ use onset (MUO), typically defined as use starting before 16–18 years old, is associated with more severe cognitive consequences. Converging lines of evidence suggest that regular use of MJ starting before 18 is associated with increased deficits in poorer attention (Ehrenreich et al., 1999), visual search (Huestegge et al., 2002), reduced overall or verbal IQ (Pope et al., 2003; Meier et al., 2012), and executive functioning (Fontes et al., 2011; Solowij et al., 2012). In a thorough study targeting executive functioning, Fontes et al. (2011) compared teenage ($n = 49$) to adult ($n = 55$) MUO matched for IQ, years of daily use, current MJ use, lifetime consumption, and length of abstinence. They found that early onset MJ users had significantly poorer sustained attention, cognitive inhibition, and abstract reasoning (see **Figure 4**).

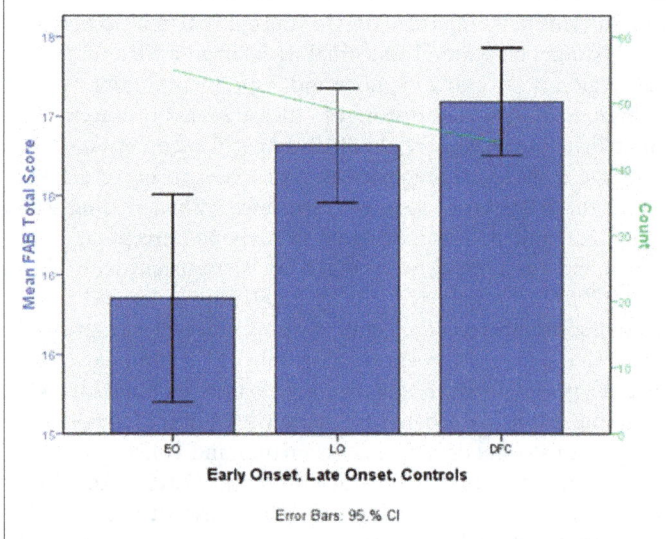

FIGURE 4 | Deficits in mean total Frontal Assessment Battery (FAB) total score in early adolescent MJ use onset (EO, $n = 49$), late adult onset (LO, $n = 55$), and control groups (DFC, $n = 44$) (scores are in a T-score metric; mean = 50, SD = 10 with lower scores indicating impairment; adapted from Fontes et al., 2011).

Perhaps the most notable study to date on this topic examined the impact of regular MJ use on IQ and neuropsychological functioning in a longitudinal sample of 1,037 individuals followed from birth to age 38 (Meier et al., 2012). After matching for total number of MJ dependence symptoms, the adolescent MUO demonstrated the most robust change in IQ, who as a group demonstrated a drop from childhood "average" to adult "low-average" full-scale IQ. Indeed, the adolescent MUO individuals never achieved their predicted trajectory in IQ, even with sustained abstinence in adulthood.

Increased structural and functional brain changes associated with adolescent MUO have also been reported. In one of the earliest studies, Wilson et al. (2000) found reduced overall cortical gray matter and increased white matter volumes in participants with adolescent MUO compared to later onset of use. Lopez-Larson et al. (2011) found significant correlations between earlier MUO and decreased right superior PFC cortical thickness in 18 current MJ users. Adolescent onset MJ use has also been linked with increased PFC white matter diffusivity and increased impulsivity compared to later onset in a sample of well-matched MJ users (Gruber et al., 2011; see **Figure 5**). Functional MRI studies have reported abnormal brain activation abnormalities in early vs. late MUO in PFC and parietal regions (Becker et al., 2010a; Jager et al., 2010; Gruber et al., 2012), although one study did not report age of onset effects on a verbal encoding task (Becker et al., 2010b). [See **Figure 6** to examine PFC activation differences between adolescent and adult MUO groups on an inhibitory control fMRI task (Gruber et al., 2012)].

In summary, the brain appears to be particularly vulnerable to adolescent MJ exposure. The PFC continues to mature into early adulthood and may be particularly sensitive to adolescent MJ exposure, as early MUO samples have demonstrated executive dysfunction (Fontes et al., 2011; Gruber et al., 2011; Solowij et al., 2012), structural damage (Churchwell et al., 2010; Gruber et al., 2011; Lopez-Larson et al., 2011), and abnormal brain activation (Jager et al., 2010; Gruber et al., 2012) in the PFC.

HEAVY MARIJUANA USE AND NEUROCOGNITION IN ADOLESCENTS AND EMERGING ADULTS

Consistent with the age of onset data, converging lines of evidence is building to suggest that chronic MJ during the teenage years is associated with neurocognitive deficits. For example, in a longitudinal study following adolescents with SUD over time, Tapert et al. (2002b) found that greater cumulative MJ use over an 8-year follow-up period was associated with poorer attention functioning. Tait et al. (2011) found that after controlling for potentially confounding variables, continued MJ use over an 8-year period was associated with decrements in verbal memory. Other studies conducted in adolescents with minimal psychiatric comorbidities have suggested cognitive deficits associated with regular adolescent MJ use, including processing speed (Fried et al., 2005; Medina et al., 2007a; Lisdahl and Price, 2012), complex attention (Tapert et al., 2002a; Harvey et al., 2007; Medina et al., 2007a; Hanson et al., 2010b; Mathias et al., 2011; Lisdahl and Price, 2012), memory (Schwartz et al., 1989; Fried et al., 2005; Harvey et al., 2007; Medina et al., 2007a; McHale and Hunt, 2008; Hanson et al., 2010b; Solowij et al., 2011; Tait et al., 2011; Thoma et al., 2011), executive functioning, especially cognitive disinhibition (Harvey et al., 2007; Medina et al., 2007a; McHale and Hunt, 2008; Hanson et al., 2010b; Mathias et al., 2011; Gonzalez et al., 2012; Grant et al., 2012; Lisdahl and Price, 2012; Schuster et al., 2012; Solowij et al., 2012), and risky sexual behavior (Schuster et al., 2012).

We (Medina et al., 2007a) compared neuropsychological functioning in a sample of demographically matched healthy controls and MJ-using adolescents without comorbid psychiatric disorders who underwent 28 days of monitored abstinence. After controlling for alcohol use, adolescent MJ users demonstrated deficits in complex attention, verbal story learning, sequencing ability, and slower psychomotor speed compared to controls (Medina et al., 2007a). In a follow-up study that included 59 teens and emerging adult MJ users and controls, we found a similar pattern of cognitive deficits in the MJ users who demonstrated

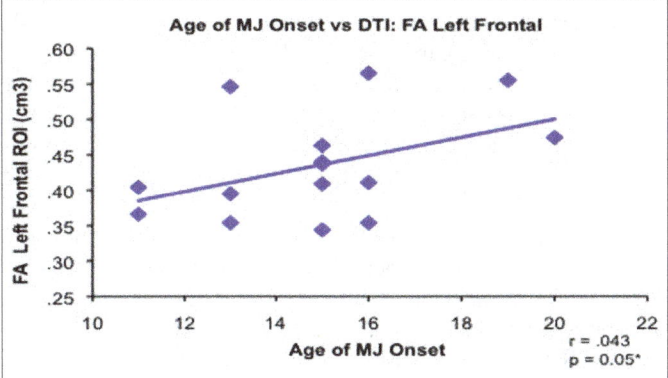

FIGURE 5 | Bivariate relationship between younger age of regular marijuana (MJ) use onset (range 11–20 years of age) and decreased white matter integrity (reduced FA measured by diffusion tensor imaging) in 15 MJ users in the left frontal region of interest (adapted from Gruber et al., 2011).

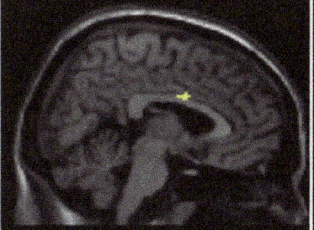 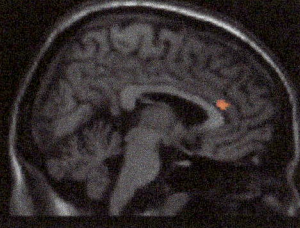

FIGURE 6 | Whole brain inhibitory processing results demonstrating significant differences between adolescent early onset (n = 9) and late adult onset (n = 14) MJ users, early onset MJ users demonstrated increased middle right cingulum and decreased anterior cingulate BOLD response to an inhibitory processing (multisource interference task, MSIT) fMRI task (adapted from Gruber et al., 2012).

poorer complex attention, slower psychomotor speed, and reduced inhibitory control (Lisdahl and Price, 2012; see **Figure 7**).

Increasingly, studies utilizing neuroimaging methods to assess brain structure have reported consequences of chronic MJ use in adolescents. Our group has examined brain volumes in a subsample of adolescent MJ users without comorbid psychiatric, developmental, or neurologic conditions (ages 16–19) and healthy controls. Thus far, we found that adolescent MJ users (who also had heavy alcohol use) did not significantly differ from healthy controls in their hippocampal volumes, although correlations between hippocampal volumes and verbal memory were abnormal compared to the controls (Medina et al., 2007c). In 16 MJ users and 16 healthy controls without comorbid psychiatric disorders we found marginal MJ group-by-gender interactions in predicting PFC volume; female MJ users demonstrated comparatively larger volumes, while male users had smaller volumes compared to same-gender controls (Medina et al., 2009). MJ group status and total PFC volume interacted in predicting executive functioning; among the MJ users (especially the girls), larger PFC volumes were associated with poorer executive functioning, while the opposite pattern was seen among the controls, suggesting that larger PFC volumes in the MJ users was detrimental. More recently, increased posterior inferior cerebellar vermis volumes in adolescent MJ users and increased left amygdala volumes in female MJ users were observed compared to controls, suggesting disruption in affective processing circuitry (Jarvis et al., 2008; Medina et al., 2010; McQueeny et al., 2011).

Recently other groups have reported decreased cortical thickness in right caudal middle frontal, bilateral insula, and bilateral superior frontal cortices and increased cortical thickness in lingual, temporal, inferior parietal, and paracentral regions (Lopez-Larson et al., 2011), decreased right medial orbitofrontal cortex volume (Churchwell et al., 2010), and reduced bilateral hippocampal volumes (Ashtari et al., 2011) in adolescent MJ users without comorbid psychiatric conditions compared to healthy controls.

The above structural alterations were associated with increased executive dysfunction (Medina et al., 2009, 2010; Churchwell et al., 2010), mood symptoms (McQueeny et al., 2011), and verbal memory deficits (Ashtari et al., 2011). Adolescent MJ users have also demonstrated reduced cerebral blood flow in temporal, insular, and PFC regions after 4 weeks of monitored abstinence, which may also underlie observed cognitive deficits (Jacobus et al., 2012).

Micro-structural and neurochemical abnormalities have also been reported in otherwise healthy adolescent MJ users. Recent use of magnetic resonance spectroscopy (MRS) has revealed neurochemical alterations in adolescent MJ users, including reduced anterior cingulate glutamate, N-acetyl aspartate, creatine, and *myo*-inositol (Prescot et al., 2011), lower global *myo*-inositol/creatine ratios in subcortical gray matter structures, and reduced *myo*-inositol in white matter (Silveri et al., 2011) suggesting an early neurochemical response to neuronal toxicity and disruption of microglia activity.

Subtle white matter abnormalities have also been observed in adolescent and emerging adult MJ users. Our group found that increased depressive symptoms in MJ users was associated with smaller global white matter volume (Medina et al., 2007b), suggesting that MJ use during adolescence may disrupt white matter connections between areas involved in mood regulation. Using DTI, Bava et al. (2009) found that MJ users had significantly poorer white matter integrity, measured by lower fractional anisotropy (FA) in 10 brain regions, especially in regions underlying executive functioning and working memory. Increased FA was also seen in regions underlying vision, suggesting possible over-recruitment of these brain regions in adolescent MJ users compared to controls. With one exception (DeLisi et al., 2006), these results are consistent with other studies that have demonstrated reduced white matter integrity in adolescent and young adult MJ users who initiated use during adolescence (Arnone et al., 2008; Ashtari et al., 2009; Gruber et al., 2011).

There is also converging evidence of inefficient brain activation patterns in adolescent and emerging adult MJ users compared to healthy controls. Studies utilizing fMRI and PET with adolescents have found abnormal PFC, limbic, parietal, and cerebellar activation patterns in MJ users in response to finger tapping (Lopez-Larson et al., 2012), attentional control (Abdullaev et al., 2010), verbal working memory (Jacobsen et al., 2007; Jager et al., 2010), verbal encoding (Becker et al., 2010b), spatial working memory (Schweinsburg et al., 2008, 2010b; Smith et al., 2010), cognitive inhibition (Tapert et al., 2007), and monetary decision-making (Vaidya et al., 2012) tasks. For example, Jager et al. (2010) reported that MJ-using teenage boys (ages 13–19) demonstrated excessive activation in executive (PFC) regions during a verbal working memory task, especially during initial encoding, compared to non-using healthy controls. Consistent with this finding, our laboratory (Tapert et al., 2007) found that after controlling for alcohol use, MJ users demonstrated increased executive (right dorsolateral PFC, bilateral medial frontal), working memory (parietal), and visual (occipital) activation during inhibitory "no-go" trials (i.e., tests of impulse control), compared to normal controls, even though they had marginally poorer performance. Further, teen MJ users with lighter use histories demonstrated the greatest brain activation to both the cognitive inhibition and

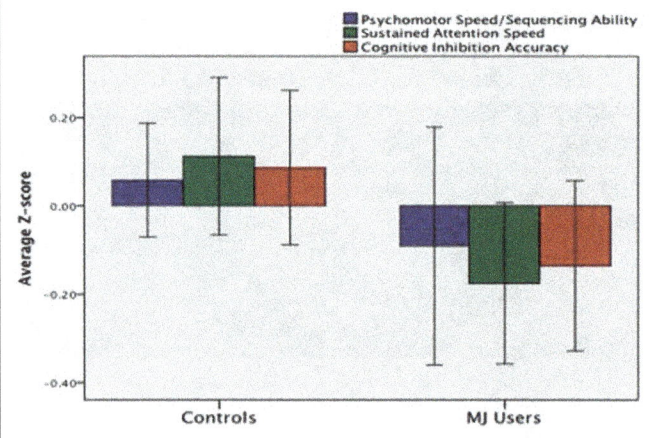

FIGURE 7 | Deficits in mean z-score psychomotor speed, sustained attention, and cognitive inhibition were observed in emerging MJ (n = 23) users compared to normal controls (n = 35) following a minimum of 1 week of abstinence (adapted from Lisdahl and Price, 2012).

spatial working memory tasks (Tapert et al., 2007; Schweinsburg et al., 2008), while teens with more intense use histories (earlier onset, longer duration, increased lifetime use) had lower activation than controls. A recent functional connectivity study found increased connectivity between PFC and occipitoparietal regions in adolescent MJ users as cognitive control demands increased (Harding et al., 2012). These findings suggests that during *initial* MJ exposure the brain may successfully compensate by recruiting additional neuronal resources, although this compensation may falter with more problematic and increased MJ use patterns.

Taken together, the above studies suggest that regular MJ use during adolescence may lead to structural changes such as abnormal gray matter pruning patterns and reduced white matter myelination. These changes have been associated with poor neuronal efficiency and poorer cognitive functioning, especially psychomotor speed, executive functioning, emotional control, and learning and memory, even after a month of monitored abstinence. Given the high rates of MJ use in teens and emerging adults, this may mean a large proportion of youth are experiencing cognitive difficulties that may negatively impact their performance. Indeed, we have found increased school difficulty and reduced grades in MJ-using teens (Medina et al., 2007a) (**Table 1**).

POTENTIAL LIMITATIONS OF THE EXISTING LITERATURE

It is important to note some limitations of the above research. Although several of the above studies did control for family history of SUD and excluded subjects with Axis I comorbid psychiatric disorders, it is still difficult to determine whether the brain and cognitive abnormalities may have predated the onset of adolescent drug use. Risk factors associated with early drug experimentation (such as poor cognitive inhibition, attention problems, conduct disorder, and family history of SUD) are themselves related to subtle cognitive and brain abnormalities (Aronowitz et al., 1994; Tapert and Brown, 2000; Tapert et al., 2002a; Nigg et al., 2004; Schweinsburg et al., 2004; Hill et al., 2007a,b; Spadoni et al., 2008; Ridenour et al., 2009; Hanson et al., 2010a) and at least some evidence exists suggesting preexisting brain abnormalities predate and predict the onset of substance use (e.g., Cheetham et al., 2012). It is notable, however, that prospective longitudinal studies have provided evidence for additional cognitive and brain abnormalities following the onset of regular alcohol or MJ use that are above and beyond premorbid differences in personality, cognition, and brain structure (Maurage et al., 2009; White et al., 2011; Hicks et al., 2012; Meier et al., 2012). Still, additional longitudinal research in teenagers prior to alcohol and MJ exposure, especially in at-risk comorbid samples, is needed to explore the influence of early drug use on adolescent neurodevelopment.

RECOVERY OF FUNCTION WITH ABSTINENCE? A MESSAGE OF HOPE

There is even less research available to help determine whether sustained abstinence from alcohol and MJ results in recovery of cognitive functions, although findings to date are hopeful. For example, Hanson et al. (2011) reported that having greater days of abstinence from alcohol and drugs at a 10-year follow-up was associated with improved executive functioning, even controlling for baseline executive functioning and education. In our binge-drinking sample, increased abstinence was associated with

larger bilateral cerebellar volumes (Lisdahl et al., 2013). In adolescent MJ users, short-term memory impairments mildly recovered following 3–6 weeks of MJ abstinence (Schwartz et al., 1989; Hanson et al., 2010b), although another study found that adolescent MJ users who abstained for a minimum of 3 months did not demonstrate any cognitive deficits compared to controls (Fried et al., 2005) and in one prospective longitudinal study individuals who began using MJ early never returned to their predicted IQ trajectory even with sustained abstinence in adulthood (Meier et al., 2012). Few fMRI studies have examined recovery of function; in a cross-sectional study, recent MJ users demonstrated increased activation in brain regions underlying executive control and attention, such as the insula and PFC, compared to abstinent ex-users (Schweinsburg et al., 2010b). This preliminary evidence suggests that the inefficient brain response seen in teenage MJ users may begin to normalize after several weeks of abstinence. In sum, these results suggest there may be subtle recovery of cognitive functioning with increasing lengths of abstinence from MJ and alcohol. Additional research is necessary to examine whether complete recovery of neurocognitive functioning occurs in adolescents with sustained abstinence, or if their neurocognitive trajectory is subtly altered into adulthood. Still, these preliminary findings can be utilized to help increase motivation for abstinence in alcohol and MJ-using youth, as it is expected that with continued abstinence they will experience at least minimal improvements in attention, verbal memory, and neuronal processing speed.

CONCLUSION AND RECOMMENDATIONS
INCREASE PSYCHOEDUCATION, SCREENING, AND PERSONALIZED FEEDBACK

Alarming numbers of adolescents and emerging adults regularly binge drink and use MJ (Johnston et al., 2009, 2010). Animal and human research suggests that adolescence may be a vulnerable period for drug exposure due to critical neurodevelopmental processes that peak during this period. Indeed, adolescents and emerging adults who initiate binge drinking or use MJ regularly tend to show inferior cognitive skills compared to teens that abstain or use lightly or Compared to individuals who begin substance use in adulthood. This review paper outlined several studies that suggest binge drinking, AUD, and chronic MJ use during the teenage and early adult years results in gray and white matter micro- and macro-structural abnormalities that are oftentimes correlated with cognitive deficits. Evidence is also mounting that heavy teenage alcohol and MJ use may disrupt brain function, leading to inefficient neuronal activation early on and diminished activation with continued heavy use into emerging adulthood. Additional research is needed to examine the impact of these neurocognitive deficits on treatment outcomes in order to individualize treatment and prevention campaigns (e.g., Feldstein Ewing et al., 2012).

These findings have significant clinical impact as even subtle brain abnormalities and cognitive problems in teens and young adults may lead to important psychosocial consequences. Combined negative impacts of drug and alcohol-related consequences (such as hangovers or emotional stress), sleep deprivation caused by drug use (Cohen-Zion et al., 2009), and acute effects of being intoxicated at school may lead to even more pronounced cognitive problems in *current* alcohol and MJ-using college students. Youth may miss information presented in class or on the job due to poorer

Table 1 | Human studies reporting neurocognitive effects of regular alcohol and marijuana exposure in adolescents and emerging adults (organized by cognitive, structural, or functional consequences and clustered according to functional outcomes).

Alcohol use disorder studies	Teenage onset worse?	Cognitive deficits	Brain structure abnormalities	Brain function abnormalities
Hicks et al. (2012)	Yes	↑ behavioral disinhibition		
Lyvers et al. (2009)	Yes	↑ reward sensitivity; disinhibition		
Lyvers et al. (2011)	Yes	↑ reward sensitivity; disinhibition		
Brown et al. (2000)		↓ verbal memory		
Hanson et al. (2011)		↓ verbal memory		
Thoma et al. (2011)		↓ processing speed		
Koskinen et al. (2011)		↓ attention		
Tapert and Brown (1999)		↓ attention		
Giancola et al. (1998)		↓ visuospatial ability		
Sher et al. (1997)		↓ visuospatial ability		
Tapert et al. (2002a)		↓ visuospatial ability		
Moss et al. (1994)		↓ language		
White et al. (2011)		↓ executive functioning, inhibition		
Howard et al. (2011)		↑ antisocial personality disorder symptoms		
De Bellis et al. (2000)			↓ HC volume	
Nagel et al. (2005)			↓ left HC volume	
Medina et al. (2007a)			↓ left HC volume	
Medina et al. (2010)			↓ cerebellar vermis GM volume	
De Bellis et al. (2005)			↓ PFC volume	
Medina et al. (2008)			↓ PFC volume	
Caldwell et al. (2005)				Females: ↓ superior frontal, temporal, cingulate, fusiform BOLD response during SWM task; Males opposite pattern.
Park et al. (2011)				↓ PFC, temporal, parietal, cerebellar, ↑ uncus fMRI BOLD during VWM task in males
Tapert et al. (2004)				↓ PFC, occipital, cerebellar, ↑ parietal fMRI BOLD during SWM task
Tapert et al. (2001)				↓ PFC, parietal fMRI BOLD during SWM task in females

(Continued)

Table 1 | Continued

Binge-drinking studies	Teenage onset worse?	Cognitive findings	Brain structure findings	Brain function findings
Hartley et al. (2004)		↓ sustained attention, memory, psychomotor speed		
Parada et al. (2011)		↓ verbal memory, working memory, perseverative responding		
Scaife and Duka (2009)		↓ verbal memory, SWM, cognitive inhibition		
Townshend and Duka (2005)		↓ SWM, cognitive inhibition, rule acquisition		
Lisdahl et al. (2013)			↓ L/R cerebellar GM and WM volumes	
McQueeny et al. (2009)			↓ white matter integrity DTI (CC, superior longitudinal fasciculus, corona radiate, internal/external capsules)	
Squeglia et al. (2012)			Females: ↑ PFC/cingulate thickness; Males: ↓ PFC/cingulate thickness	
Courtney and Polich (2010)				↑ EEG spectral power in delta and fast beta bands
Crego et al. (2010)				↓ ERP in anterior/inferior PFC
Ehlers et al. (2007)				↓ P300 ERP amplitude
López-Caneda et al. (2012)				↑ go-P3 ERP in right inferior PFC
Maurage et al. (2009)				↓ P1, N2, P3b ERP latency
Gilman et al. (2012)				↓ NAcc, amygdala fMRI BOLD during emotional cues task after consuming alcohol
Schweinsburg et al. (2010a)				↓ HC fMRI BOLD during verbal encoding task
Squeglia et al. (2011)				Females: ↓ PFC, temporal, and cerebellar BOLD during SWM fMRI task. Males: opposite pattern.
Xiao et al. (2012)				↑ amygdala, insula fMRI BOLD during IGT task

Marijuana studies	Teenage onset worse?	Cognitive findings	Brain structure findings	Brain function findings
Meier et al. (2012)	Yes	↓ IQ		
Pope et al. (2003)	Yes	↓ IQ		
Ehrenreich et al. (1999)	Yes	↓ attention		

(Continued)

Table 1 | Continued

Marijuana studies	Teenage onset worse?	Cognitive findings	Brain structure findings	Brain function findings
Huestegge et al. (2002)	Yes	↓ visual search		
Fontes et al. (2011)	Yes	↓ executive functioning		
Solowij et al. (2012)	Yes	↓ executive functioning		
Churchwell et al. (2010)	Yes		↓ PFC volume	
Gruber et al. (2011)	Yes	↑ impulsivity	↓ WM integrity in PFC	
Lopez-Larson et al. (2011)	Yes		↓ superior PFC thickness	
Wilson et al. (2000)	Yes		↓ total GM; ↑ total WM	
Becker et al. (2010a)	Yes			↑ left superior PFC fMRI BOLD during working memory task in early onset
Becker et al. (2010b)	No			↑ left parahippocampal gyrus, fMRI BOLD during learning task in all MJ users
Gruber et al. (2012)	Yes			↓ anterior cingulate fMRI BOLD during inhibition task in early onset
Jager et al. (2010)	Yes			↑ PFC fMRI BOLD during novel stimuli presentation in working memory task in early onset
Fried et al. (2005)		↓ processing speed verbal memory		
Hanson et al. (2010b)		↓ complex attention, verbal memory		
Harvey et al. (2007)		↓ complex attention, verbal memory; executive functioning		
Lisdahl and Price (2012)		↓ complex attention processing speed, sequencing ability, cognitive inhibition		
Medina et al. (2007a)		↓ complex attention processing speed, verbal memory, sequencing ability		
Mathias et al. (2011)		↓ complex attention, executive functioning		
Tapert et al. (2002a)		↓ complex attention		
McHale and Hunt (2008)		↓ verbal memory, executive functioning		
Schwartz et al. (1989)		↓ verbal memory		
Solowij et al. (2011)		↓ verbal memory; executive functioning		

(Continued)

Table 1 | Continued

Marijuana studies	Teenage onset worse?	Cognitive findings	Brain structure findings	Brain function findings
Tait et al. (2011)		↓ verbal memory		
Thoma et al. (2011)		↓ verbal memory		
Gonzalez et al. (2012)		↓ executive functioning		
Grant et al. (2012)		↓ executive functioning		
Schuster et al. (2012)		↓ executive functioning; ↑ risky sexual behavior		
McQueeny et al. (2011)		↑ depressive symptoms	Females: ↑ left amygdala	
Medina et al. (2007b)		↑ depressive symptoms	↓ global WM	
Jarvis et al. (2008)			↑ amygdala volume	
Ashtari et al. (2011)		↓ verbal memory	↓ HC volume	
Medina et al. (2007b)			↑ left HC volume	
Churchwell et al. (2010)		↓ executive functioning	↓ right medial orbitofrontal cortex volume	
Lopez-Larson et al. (2011)			↓ right caudal, middle frontal, inula, superior frontal thickness; ↑ lingual, temporal, inferior parietal, paracentral thickness	
Medina et al. (2010)		↓ executive functioning	↑ inferior cerebellar vermis volume	
Medina et al. (2009)		↓ executive functioning	Females: ↑ inferior PFC volume	
Arnone et al. (2008)			↓ WM integrity (corpus collosum)	
Ashtari et al. (2009)			↓ WM integrity (arcuate fasciculus)	
Bava et al. (2009)			↓ white matter integrity in 10 regions (especially PFC, parietal cortex); ↑ WM integrity in occipital cortex	
DeLisi et al. (2006)			No WM differences detected	
Prescot et al. (2011)			↓ ACC glutamate, N-acetyl aspartate, creatine, *myo*-inositol	
Silveri et al. (2011)			↓ subcortical GM *myo*-inositol/creatine; WM *myo*-inositol	
Abdullaev et al. (2010)				↑ PFC fMRI BOLD during attentional control task

(Continued)

Table 1 | Continued

Marijuana studies	Teenage onset worse?	Cognitive findings	Brain structure findings	Brain function findings
Harding et al. (2012)				↑ PFC and occipitoparietal connectivity as task demands increase
Jacobsen et al. (2007)				↓ PFC, parietal connectivity during verbal working memory task while undergoing nicotine withdrawal
Jacobus et al. (2012)				↓ cerebral blood flow in temporal lobe, insula, and PFC
Jager et al. (2010)				↑ PFC fMRI BOLD during verbal encoding task in males
Lopez-Larson et al. (2012)				↓ cingulate gyrus, cerebellar fMRI BOLD during finger tapping task
Schweinsburg et al. (2008)				↓ PFC, occipital, ↑ parietal fMRI BOLD during SWM task
Schweinsburg et al. (2010b)				↑ PFC, insula, ↓ precentral fMRI BOLD during SWM task in recent MJ users vs. abstinent users
Smith et al. (2010)				↑ inferior, middle PFC fMRI BOLD during SWM task
Tapert et al. (2007)				↑ PFC, parietal, occipital fMRI BOLD during inhibitory processing task
Vaidya et al. (2012)				↑ ventral medial PFC, cerebellar PET rCBF during IGT task

Teenage onset worse? = "yes" – analysis revealed that teenage age of onset (< 16, 17, or 18 years of age) was associated with significantly poorer neurocognitive outcome; if "no" – onset was not associated with outcome; if left blank – age of onset analysis was not conducted in this study. GM, gray matter; WM, white matter; PFC, prefrontal cortex; HC, hippocampus; SWM, spatial working memory; VWM, verbal working memory; IGT, Iowa Gambling task.

processing speed, initial learning, complex attention, and working memory. Indeed, researchers have found that substance-induced cognitive disadvantage may lead to lower than expected school performance, increased school problems, risky decision-making, and poorer emotional regulation (Lynskey and Hall, 2000; Medina et al., 2007a; Kloos et al., 2009).

It is critical to disseminate these findings to high school and college students, young military enlistees, therapists, teachers, child psychiatrists, pediatricians, and parents to help minimize regular alcohol and MJ consumption in youth. Fortunately, high-quality psychoeducation materials regarding the effects of alcohol and drugs on the brain, including pamphlets designed for teens and young adults, are available at no cost through the National Institute on Drug Abuse[1], the National Institute on Alcohol Abuse and Alcoholism[2], teen-centered sites like the www.thecoolspot.gov and www.drugfreeamerica.org, and university websites such as Teen Safe[3], which has an excellent parent resource center. Still, we may improve outcomes by providing more personalized feedback about

drugs and alcohol health effects (see Larimer and Cronce, 2007). To date, however, no systematic individualized feedback programs have integrated information regarding the effects of drugs on neurocognition. At this time, more global feedback focused on group, or normative, performance results could be integrated. For example, adolescents who engage in heavy drinking could be told that, "Teens who drank more than nine alcohol drinks in one occasion had 1.8 cubic centimeters less cerebellar brain volume than teens who drank three or fewer drinks when drinking, on average. The cerebellum is important for coordination and thinking skills" (Lisdahl et al., 2013). Youth who engage in weekly MJ use could be told "even with similar verbal intelligence and reading ability, MJ users scored more than half a standard deviation lower on an executive functioning task, achieved a half-point lower GPA, and were more likely to demonstrate behavioral problems in school (26 vs. 0%) compared to peers who did not regularly use MJ" (Medina et al., 2007a). This normative feedback could be developed further and disseminated more globally by services aimed at health education and drug prevention in youth. One potential opportunity is to integrate this information more thoroughly into existing computerized programs such as CRAFFT screening tool (Knight et al., 2002), which asks six questions and reveals a teen's risk for

[1] www.nida.nih.gov
[2] www.niaaa.nih.gov
[3] www.Teen-Safe.org

problematic, abusive, or dependent use patterns[4]. After retrieving your score, the computerized program provides potential impact of your use on health, including brain function. After taking the screening tool, physicians and therapists could then utilize brief motivational interviewing to help educate youth further about the negative effects of alcohol and MJ use on the brain. Taken further, therapists could order neuropsychological testing and give truly individualized feedback regarding the student's cognitive functioning.

DEVELOP INTERVENTIONS TO IMPROVE NEUROCOGNITION: EXERCISE?

Treatments that may reverse substance-induced neurocognitive damage in youth are needed. Some potential candidates include cognitive rehabilitation (see Macher and Earleywine, 2012) or exercise. In animals, physical activity has been linked to decreased inflammatory response and oxidative stress at moderate levels (Radak et al., 2007; Sim et al., 2008; Sakurai et al., 2009), increased c-FOS expression (Sim et al., 2008), and improved catecholaminergic (dopamine, norepinephrine, and epinephrine) function in brain regions including the PFC (Heyes et al., 1985; Elam et al., 1987; Chaouloff, 1989; Dunn and Dishman, 1991; Dunn et al., 1996; Waters et al., 2005). Several human studies have concluded that activity and cardiorespiratory fitness have positive effects on brain health and neuronal plasticity, although the vast majority of the studies have been conducted in older adults (Brisswalter et al., 2002; Cotman and Berchtold, 2002; Colcombe and Kramer, 2003; Colcombe et al., 2004, 2006; Heyn et al., 2004; Kramer and Erickson, 2007; Boecker et al., 2008; Hillman et al., 2008; Ma, 2008; Ploughman, 2008; Coelho et al., 2013). Given ongoing neurodevelopment and fewer comorbid problems like vascular disease in youth, these findings may not directly generalize to teens.

Although research has shown that physical activity is associated with improved mood, decreased drug use, and increased grade point in adolescents (Winnail et al., 1995; Field et al., 2001; Audrain-McGovern et al., 2006), very few studies have directly examined the neurocognitive benefits of physical activity in adolescents. In meta-analyses (Etnier et al., 1997; Sibley and Etnier, 2003), low to large (0.24–0.77) effect sizes for the impact of activity on perceptual skills, academic achievement, and verbal tests in adolescents have been reported; however, higher-order executive functioning or brain structure were not measured. Research examining the impact of acute effects of exercise or improved fitness in healthy emerging adults have found superior executive control (Dustman et al., 1990; Hillman et al., 2003; Themanson

and Hillman, 2006; Themanson et al., 2006; Ferris et al., 2007), increased cerebral blood flow (Pereira et al., 2007; Timinkul et al., 2008), and improved white matter integrity (Marks et al., 2007). In sum, there is at least preliminary evidence that increased physical activity is associated improved neurocognitive functioning, especially executive functioning, in otherwise healthy young adults without cerebrovascular disease. Perhaps most promising, recent research has suggested that exercise interventions may reverse neuronal damage in binge drinking adolescent animals (Helfer et al., 2009) and brief interventions to increase exercise may help reduce drug use and increase physical activity in adolescents (Werch et al., 2005). Additional research is needed to examine how physical activity impacts neurocognition in adolescent drug users, but there is optimism that this is an ideal time to intervene. Indeed, physical activity during the this sensitive stage of ongoing neurodevelopment (ages 15–25) has been associated with superior information processing in elderly men, after controlling for their current level of activity (Dik et al., 2003). Therefore, there is an opportunity to intervene early during the school years to reduce drug use, reverse neurocognitive damage, and perhaps instill lifelong exercise habits that may actually improve aging.

SUMMARY: DELAY THE ONSET

Adolescence has been named the "gateway to adult health outcomes" (Raphael, 2013) and presents a golden opportunity for public policy intervention to significantly improve health outcomes that last throughout adulthood. However, this sensitive period is also associated with the onset of binge drinking and MJ use, which negatively impacts cognition, brain structure, and function in otherwise healthy teens and young adults. Early age of onset (before age 18) has been linked with the greatest neurocognitive deficits. Therefore, general psychoeducation coupled with personalized feedback regarding effects of chronic drug use on thinking abilities and brain health need to be integrated into current prevention, screening, and treatment programs. Interventions geared toward lowering alcohol and drug exposure in teens and young adults that have shown evidence of efficacy need to be implemented more aggressively in schools and college campuses to not only reduce symptoms of drug abuse and dependence, but *delay the onset of regular use* from early teen years to early adult years in order to prevent long-term neuronal damage and ensure optimal brain health and cognitive functioning in youth.

ACKNOWLEDGMENTS

During manuscript preparation, Dr. Lisdahl was supported by the NIDA-funded grant R01DA030354.

---

[4]http://www.ceasar.org/teens/test.php

REFERENCES

Abdullaev, Y., Posner, M. I., Nunnally, R., and Dishion, T. J. (2010). Functional MRI evidence for inefficient attentional control in adolescent chronic cannabis abuse. *Behav. Brain Res.* 215, 45–57. doi:10.1016/j.bbr.2010.06.023

Agosti, V., Nunes, E., and Levin, F. (2002). Rates of psychiatric comorbidity among U.S. residents with lifetime cannabis dependence. *Am. J. Drug Alcohol Abuse* 28, 643–652. doi:10.1081/ADA-120015873

Arnone, D., Barrick, T. R., Chengappa, S., Mackay, C. E., Clark, C. A., and Abou-Saleh, M. T. (2008). Corpus callosum damage in heavy marijuana use: preliminary evidence from diffusion tensor tractography and tract-based spatial statistics. *Neuroimage* 41, 1067–1074. doi:10.1016/j.neuroimage.2008.02.064

Aronowitz, B., Liebowitz, M. R., Hollander, E., Fazzini, E., Durlach-Misteli, C., Frenkel, M., et al. (1994). Neuropsychiatric and neuropsychological findings in conduct disorder and attention-deficit hyperactivity disorder. *J. Neuropsychiatry Clin. Neurosci.* 6, 245–249.

Ashtari, M., Avants, B., Cyckowski, L., Cervellione, K. L., Roofeh, D., Cook, P., et al. (2011). Medial temporal structures and memory functions in adolescents with heavy cannabis use. *J. Psychiatr. Res.* 45, 1055–1066. doi:10.1016/j.jpsychires.2011.01.004

Ashtari, M., Cervellione, K., Cottone, J., Ardekani, B. A., Sevy, S., and Kumra, S. (2009). Diffusion abnormalities in adolescents and young adults with a history of heavy cannabis use. *J. Psychiatr. Res.* 43, 189–204. doi:10.1016/j.jpsychires.2008.12.002

Audrain-McGovern, J., Rodriguez, D., Wileyto, E. P., Schmitz, K. H., and Shields, P. G. (2006). Effect of team sport participation on genetic predisposition to adolescent smoking progression. *Arch. Gen. Psychiatry* 63, 433–441. doi:10.1001/archpsyc.63.4.433

Barnea-Goraly, N., Menon, V., Eckert, M., Tamm, L., Bammer, R., Karchemskiy, A., et al. (2005). White matter development during childhood and adolescence: a cross-sectional diffusion tensor imaging study. *Cereb. Cortex* 15, 1848–1854. doi:10.1093/cercor/bhi062

Barron, S., White, A., Swartzwelder, H. S., Bell, R. L., Rodd, Z. A., Slawecki, C. J., et al. (2005). Adolescent vulnerabilities to chronic alcohol or nicotine exposure: findings from rodent models. *Alcohol. Clin. Exp. Res.* 29, 1720–1725. doi:10.1097/01.alc.0000179220.79356.e5

Bava, S., Frank, L. R., McQueeny, T., Schweinsburg, B. C., Schweinsburg, A. D., and Tapert, S. F. (2009). Altered white matter microstructure in adolescent substance users. *Psychiatry Res.* 173, 228–237. doi:10.1016/j.pscychresns.2009.04.005

Becker, B., Wagner, D., Gouzoulis-Mayfrank, E., Spuentrup, E., and Daumann, J. (2010a). The impact of early-onset cannabis use on functional brain correlates of working memory. *Prog. Neuropsychopharmacol. Biol. Psychiatry* 34, 837–845. doi:10.1016/j.pnpbp.2010.03.032

Becker, B., Wagner, D., Gouzoulis-Mayfrank, E., Spuentrup, E., and Daumann, J. (2010b). Altered parahippocampal functioning in cannabis users is related to the frequency of use. *Psychopharmacology (Berl.)* 209, 361–374. doi:10.1007/s00213-010-1805-z

Bjork, J. M., Hommer, D. W., Grant, S. J., and Danube, C. (2004). Impulsivity in abstinent alcohol-dependent patients: relation to control subjects and type 1-/type 2-like traits. *Alcohol* 34, 133–150. doi:10.1016/j.alcohol.2004.06.012

Boecker, H., Henriksen, G., Sprenger, T., Miederer, I., Willoch, F., Valet, M., et al. (2008). Positron emission tomography ligand activation studies in the sports sciences: measuring neurochemistry in vivo. *Methods* 45, 307–318. doi:10.1016/j.ymeth.2008.07.003

Brisswalter, J., Collardeau, M., and René, A. (2002). Effects of acute physical exercise characteristics on cognitive performance. *Sports Med.* 32, 555–566. doi:10.2165/00007256-200232090-00002

Brown, S. A., and Tapert, S. F. (1999). Neuropsychological correlates of adolescent substance abuse: four-year outcomes. *J. Int. Neuropsychol. Soc.* 5, 481–493. doi:10.1017/S1355617799566010

Brown, S. A., Tapert, S. F., Granholm, E., and Delis, D. C. (2000). Neurocognitive functioning of adolescents: effects of protracted alcohol use. *Alcohol. Clin. Exp. Res.* 24, 164–171. doi:10.1111/j.1530-0277.2000.tb04586.x

Caldwell, L. C., Schweinsburg, A. D., Nagel, B. J., Barlett, V. C., Brown, S. A., and Tapert, S. F. (2005). Gender and adolescent alcohol use disorders on BOLD (blood oxygen level dependent) response to spatial working memory. *Alcohol Alcohol.* 40, 194–200. doi:10.1093/alcalc/agh134

Casey, B. J., Galvan, A., and Hare, T. A. (2005). Changes in cerebral functional organization during cognitive development. *Curr. Opin. Neurobiol.* 15, 239–244. doi:10.1016/j.conb.2005.03.012

Casey, B. J., Getz, S., and Galvan, A. (2008). The adolescent brain. *Dev. Rev.* 28, 62–77. doi:10.1016/j.dr.2007.08.003

Casey, B. J., Trainor, R. J., Orendi, J. L., Schubert, A. B., Nystrom, L. E., Giedd, J. N., et al. (1997). A developmental functional MRI study of prefrontal activation during performance of a go-no-go task. *J. Cogn. Neurosci.* 9, 835–847. doi:10.1162/jocn.1997.9.6.835

Cha, Y. M., White, A. M., Kuhn, C. M., Wilson, W. A., and Swartzwelder, H. S. (2006). Differential effects of delta(9)-THC on learning in adolescent and adult rats. *Pharmacol. Biochem. Behav.* 83, 448–455. doi:10.1016/j.pbb.2006.03.006

Chaouloff, F. (1989). Physical exercise and brain monoamines: a review. *Acta Physiol. Scand.* 137, 1–13. doi:10.1111/j.1748-1716.1989.tb08715.x

Cheetham, A., Allen, N. B., Whittle, S., Simmons, J. G., Yücel, M., and Lubman, D. I. (2012). Orbitofrontal volumes in early adolescence predict initiation of cannabis use: a 4-year longitudinal and prospective study. *Biol. Psychiatry* 71, 684–692. doi:10.1016/j.biopsych.2011.10.029

Chen, Y. C., Prescott, C. A., Walsh, D., Patterson, D. G., Riley, B. P., Kendler, K. S., et al. (2011). Different phenotypic and genotypic presentations in alcohol dependence: age at onset matters. *J. Stud. Alcohol Drugs* 72, 752–762.

Churchwell, J. C., Lopez-Larson, M., and Yurgelun-Todd, D. A. (2010). Altered frontal cortical volume and decision making in adolescent cannabis users. *Front. Psychol.* 1:225. doi:10.3389/fpsyg.2010.00225

Cloninger, C. R. (1987). Neurogenetic adaptive mechanisms in alcoholism. *Science* 236, 410–416. doi:10.1126/science.2882604

Coelho, F. G., Gobbi, S., Andreatto, C. A., Corazza, D. I., Pedroso, R. V., and Santos-Galduróz, R. F. (2013). Physical exercise modulates peripheral levels of brain-derived neurotrophic factor (BDNF): a systematic review of experimental studies in the elderly. *Arch. Gerontol. Geriatr.* 56, 10–15. doi:10.1016/j.archger.2012.06.003

Cohen-Zion, M., Drummond, S. P. A., Padula, C. B., Winward, J., Kanady, J., Medina, K. L., et al. (2009). Sleep architecture in adolescent marijuana and alcohol users during acute and extended abstinence. *Addict. Behav.* 34, 967–969. doi:10.1016/j.addbeh.2009.05.011

Colcombe, S., and Kramer, A. F. (2003). Fitness effects on the cognitive function of older adults: a meta-analytic study. *Psychol. Sci.* 14, 125–130. doi:10.1111/1467-9280.t01-1-01430

Colcombe, S. J., Erickson, K. I., Scalf, P. E., Kim, J. S., Prakash, R., McAuley, E., et al. (2006). Aerobic exercise training increases brain volume in aging humans. *J. Gerontol. A Biol. Sci. Med. Sci.* 61, 1166–1170. doi:10.1093/gerona/61.11.1166

Colcombe, S. J., Kramer, A. F., Erickson, K. I., Scalf, P., McAuley, E., Cohen, N. J., et al. (2004). Cardiovascular fitness, cortical plasticity, and aging. *Proc. Natl. Acad. Sci. U.S.A.* 101, 3316–3321. doi:10.1073/pnas.0400266101

Coleman, L. G. Jr., He, J., Lee, J., Styner, M., and Crews, F. T. (2011). Adolescent binge drinking alters adult brain neurotransmitter gene expression, behavior, brain regional volumes, and neurochemistry in mice. *Alcohol. Clin. Exp. Res.* 35, 671–688. doi:10.1111/j.1530-0277.2010.01385.x

Cotman, C. W., and Berchtold, N. C. (2002). Exercise: a behavioral intervention to enhance brain health and plasticity. *Trends Neurosci.* 25, 295–301. doi:10.1016/S0166-2236(02)02143-4

Courtney, K. E., and Polich, J. (2010). Binge drinking effects on EEG in young adult humans. *Int. J. Environ.* Res. Public Health 7, 2325–2336. doi:10.3390/ijerph7052325

Crego, A., Rodriguez-Holguín, S., Parada, M., Mota, N., Corral, M., and Cadaveira, F. (2010). Reduced anterior prefrontal cortex activation in young binge drinkers during a visual working memory task. *Drug Alcohol Depend.* 109, 45–56. doi:10.1016/j.drugalcdep.2009.11.020

Dawe, S., Gullo, M. J., and Loxton, N. J. (2004). Reward drive and rash impulsiveness as dimensions of impulsivity: implications for substance misuse. *Addict. Behav.* 29, 1389–1405. doi:10.1016/j.addbeh.2004.06.004

De Bellis, M. D., Clark, D. B., Beers, S. R., Soloff, P. H., Boring, A. M., Hall, J., et al. (2000). Hippocampal volume in adolescent-onset alcohol use disorders. *Am. J. Psychiatry* 157, 737–744. doi:10.1176/appi.ajp.157.5.737

De Bellis, M. D., Narasimhan, A., Thatcher, D. L., Keshavan, M. S., Soloff, P., and Clark, D. B. (2005). Prefrontal cortex, thalamus and cerebellar volumes in adolescents and young adults with adolescent onset alcohol use disorders and comorbid mental disorders. *Alcohol. Clin. Exp. Res.* 29, 1590–1600. doi:10.1097/01.alc.0000179368.87886.76

Degenhardt, L., Chiu, W. T., Sampson, N., Kessler, R. C., Anthony, J. C., Angermeyer, M., et al. (2008). Toward a global view of alcohol, tobacco, cannabis, and cocaine use: findings from the WHO World Mental Health Surveys. *PLoS Med.* 5:e141. doi:10.1371/journal.pmed.0050141

DeLisi, L. E., Bertisch, H. C., Szulc, K. U., Majcher, M., Brown, K., Bappal, A., et al. (2006). A preliminary DTI study showing no brain structural change associated with adolescent cannabis use. *Harm. Reduct. J.* 3, 17. doi:10.1186/1477-7517-3-17

Demir, B., Ulug, B., Lay Ergün, E., and Erbas, B. (2002). Regional cerebral blood flow and neuropsychological functioning in early and late onset alcoholism. *Psychiatry Res.* 115, 115–125. doi:10.1016/S0925-4927(02)00071-9

DeWit, D. J., Adlaf, E. M., Offord, D. R., and Ogborne, A. C. (2000). Age at first alcohol use: a risk factor for the development of alcohol disorders. *Am. J. Psychiatry* 157, 745–750. doi:10.1176/appi.ajp.157.5.745

Dik, M., Deeg, D. J., Visser, M., and Jonker, C. (2003). Early life physical activity and cognition at old age. *J. Clin. Exp. Neuropsychol.* 25, 643–653. doi:10.1076/jcen.25.5.643.14583

Dom, G., Hulstijn, W., and Sabbe, B. (2006a). Differences in impulsivity and sensation seeking between early- and late-onset alcoholics. *Addict. Behav.* 31, 298–308. doi:10.1016/j.addbeh.2005.05.009

Dom, G., D'haene, P., Hulstijn, W., and Sabbe, B. (2006b). Impulsivity in abstinent early- and late-onset alcoholics: differences in self-report measures and a discounting task. *Addiction* 101, 50–59. doi:10.1111/j.1360-0443.2005.01270.x

Dunn, A. L., and Dishman, R. K. (1991). Exercise and the neurobiology of depression. *Exerc. Sport Sci. Rev.* 19, 41–98. doi:10.1249/00003677-199101000-00002

Dunn, A. L., Reigle, T. G., Youngstedt, S. D., Armstrong, R. B., and Dishman, R. K. (1996). Brain norepinephrine and metabolites after treadmill training and wheel running in rats. *Med. Sci. Sports Exerc.* 28, 204–209. doi:10.1097/00005768-199602000-00008

Dustman, R. E., Emmerson, R. Y., Ruhling, R. O., Shearer, D. E., Steinhaus, L. A., Johnson, S. C., et al. (1990). Age and fitness effects on EEG, ERPs, visual sensitivity, and cognition. *Neurobiol. Aging* 11, 193–200. doi:10.1016/0197-4580(90)90545-B

Eaton, L. K., Kann, L., Kinchen, S., Ross, J., Hawkins, J., Harris, W. A., et al. (2006). Youth risk behavior surveillance – United States, 2005, surveillance summaries. *MMWR Surveill. Summ.* 55, 1–108.

Ehlers, C. L., Phillips, E., Finnerman, G., Gilder, D., Lau, P., and Criado, J. (2007). P3 components and adolescent binge drinking in Southwest California Indians. *Neurotoxicol. Teratol.* 29, 153–163. doi:10.1016/j.ntt.2006.11.013

Ehrenreich, H., Rinn, T., Kunert, H. J., Moeller, M. R., Poser, W., Schilling, L., et al. (1999). Specific attentional dysfunction in adults following early start of marijuana use. *Psychopharmacology (Berl.)* 142, 295–301. doi:10.1007/s002130050892

Elam, M., Svensson, T. H., and Thorén, P. (1987). Brain monoamine metabolism is altered in rats following spontaneous, long-distance running. *Acta Physiol. Scand.* 130, 313–316. doi:10.1111/j.1748-1716.1987.tb08142.x

Etnier, J., Salazar, W., Landers, D., Petruzzello, S., Han, M., and Nowell, P. (1997). The influence of physical fitness and exercise upon cognitive functioning: a meta-analysis. *J. Sport Exerc. Psychol.* 19, 249–277.

Feldstein Ewing, S. W., Mead, H. K., Yezhuvath, U., Dewitt, S., Hutchison, K. E., and Filbey, F. M. (2012). A preliminary examination of how serotonergic polymorphisms influence brain response following an adolescent cannabis intervention. *Psychiatry Res.* 204, 112–116. doi:10.1016/j.pscychresns.2012.10.011

Ferris, L. T., Williams, J. S., and Shen, C. L. (2007). The effect of acute exercise on serum brain-derived neurotrophic factor levels and cognitive function. *Med. Sci. Sports Exerc.* 39, 728–734. doi:10.1249/mss.0b013e31802f04c7

Field, T., Diego, M., and Sanders, C. E. (2001). Exercise is positively related to adolescents' relationships and academics. *Adolescence* 36, 105–110.

Fontes, M. A., Bolla, K. I., Cunha, P. J., Almeida, P. P., Jungerman, F., Laranjeira, R. R., et al. (2011). Cannabis use before age 15 and subsequent executive functioning. *Br. J. Psychiatry* 198, 442–447. doi:10.1192/bjp.bp.110.077479

Fried, P. A., Watkinson, B., and Gray, R. (2005). Neurocognitive consequences of marihuana-a comparison with pre-drug performance. *Neurotoxicol. Teratol.* 27, 231–239. doi:10.1016/j.ntt.2004.11.003

Galvan, A., Hare, T. A., Parra, C. E., Penn, J., Voss, H., Glover, G., et al. (2006). Earlier development of the accumbens relative to orbitofrontal cortex might underlie risk-taking behavior in adolescents. *J. Neurosci.* 26, 6885–6892. doi:10.1523/JNEUROSCI.1062-06.2006

Gardener, M., and Steinberg, L. (2005). Peer influence on risk taking, risk preference, and risky decision making in adolescence and adulthood: an experimental study. *Dev. Psychol.* 41, 625–635. doi:10.1037/0012-1649.41.4.625

Giancola, P. R., Mezzich, A. C., and Tarter, R. E. (1998). Disruptive, delinquent and aggressive behavior in female adolescents with a psychoactive substance use disorder: relation to executive cognitive functioning. *J. Stud. Alcohol* 59, 560–567.

Giedd, J. N., Blumenthal, J., Jeffries, N. O., Castellanos, F. X., Liu, H., Zijdenbos, A., et al. (1999). Brain development during childhood and adolescence: a longitudinal MRI study. *Nat. Neurosci.* 2, 861–863. doi:10.1038/13158

Giedd, J. N., Snell, J. W., Lange, N., Rajapakse, J. C., Casey, B. J.,

Kozuch, P. L., et al. (1996a). Quantitative magnetic resonance imaging of human brain development: ages 4-18. *Cereb. Cortex* 6, 551–560. doi:10.1093/cercor/6.4.551

Giedd, J. N., Vaituzis, A. C., Hamburger, S. D., Lange, N., Rajapakse, J. C., Kaysen, D., et al. (1996b). Quantitative MRI of the temporal lobe, amygdala, and hippocampus in normal human development: ages 4-18 years. *J. Comp. Neurol.* 366, 223–230. doi:10.1002/(SICI)1096-9861(19960304)366:2<223::AID-CNE3>;3.0.CO;2-7

Gilligan, S. B., Reich, T., and Cloninger, C. R. (1988). Alcohol-related symptoms in heterogeneous families of hospitalized alcoholics. *Alcohol. Clin. Exp. Res.* 12, 671–678. doi:10.1111/j.1530-0277.1988.tb00263.x

Gilman, J. M., Ramchandani, V. A., Crouss, T., and Hommer, D. W. (2012). Subjective and neural responses to intravenous alcohol in young adults with light and heavy drinking patterns. *Neuropsychopharmacology* 37, 467–477. doi:10.1038/npp.2011.206

Gogtay, N., Giedd, J. N., Lusk, L., Hayashi, K. M., Greenstein, D., Vaituzis, A. C., et al. (2004). Dynamic mapping of human cortical development during childhood through early adulthood. *Proc. Natl. Acad. Sci. U.S.A* 101, 8174–8179. doi:10.1073/pnas.0402680101

Gonzalez, R., Schuster, R. M., Mermelstein, R. J., Vassileva, J., Martin, E. M., and Diviak, K. R. (2012). Performance of young adult cannabis users on neurocognitive measures of impulsive behavior and their relationship to symptoms of cannabis use disorders. *J. Clin. Exp. Neuropsychol.* 34, 962–976. doi:10.1080/13803395.2012.703642

Grant, J. E., Chamberlain, S. R., Schreiber, L., and Odlaug, B. L. (2012). Neuropsychological deficits associated with cannabis use in young adults. *Drug Alcohol Depend.* 121, 159–162. doi:10.1016/j.drugalcdep.2011.08.015

Gruber, S. A., Dahlgren, M. K., Sagar, K. A., Gönenc, A., and Killgore, W. D. (2012). Age of onset of marijuana use impacts inhibitory processing. *Neurosci. Lett.* 511, 89–94. doi:10.1016/j.neulet.2012.01.039

Gruber, S. A., Silveri, M. M., Dahlgren, M. K., and Yurgelun-Todd, D. (2011). Why so impulsive? White matter alterations are associated with impulsivity in chronic marijuana smokers. *Exp. Clin.*

Psychopharmacol. 19, 231–242. doi:10.1037/a0023034

Hanson, K. L., Medina, K. L., Nagel, B. J., Spadoni, A. D., Gorlick, A., and Tapert, S. F. (2010a). Hippocampal volumes in adolescents with and without a family history of alcoholism. *Am. J. Drug Alcohol Abuse* 36, 161–167. doi:10.3109/00952991003736397

Hanson, K. L., Winward, J. L., Schweinsburg, A. D., Medina, K. L., Brown, S. A., and Tapert, S. F. (2010b). Longitudinal study of cognition among adolescent marijuana users over three weeks of abstinence. *Addict. Behav.* 35, 970–976. doi:10.1016/j.addbeh.2010.06.012

Hanson, K. L., Medina, K. L., Padula, C. B., Tapert, S. F., and Brown, S. A. (2011). How does adolescent alcohol and drug use affect neuropsychological functioning in young adulthood: 10-year outcomes. *J. Child Adolesc. Subst. Abuse* 20, 135–154.

Harding, I. H., Solowij, N., Harrison, B. J., Takagi, M., Lorenzetti, V., Lubman, D. I., et al. (2012). Functional connectivity in brain networks underlying cognitive control in chronic cannabis users. *Neuropsychopharmacology* 37, 1923–1933. doi:10.1038/npp.2012.39

Hartley, D. E., Elsabagh, S., and File, S. E. (2004). Binge drinking and sex: effects on mood and cognitive function in healthy young volunteers. *Pharmacol. Biochem. Behav.* 78, 611–619. doi:10.1016/j.pbb.2004.04.027

Harvey, M. A., Sellman, J. D., Porter, R. J., and Frampton, C. M. (2007). The relationship between non-acute adolescent marijuana use and cognition. *Drug Alcohol Rev.* 26, 309–319. doi:10.1080/09595230701247772

Helfer, J. L., Goodlett, C. R., Greenough, W. T., and Klintsova, A. Y. (2009). The effects of exercise on adolescent hippocampal neurogenesis in a rat model of binge alcohol exposure during the brain growth spurt. *Brain Res.* 19, 1–11. doi:10.1016/j.brainres.2009.07.090

Heyes, M. P., Garnett, E. S., and Coates, G. (1985). Central dopaminergic activity influences rats ability to exercise. *Life Sci.* 36, 671–677. doi:10.1016/0024-3205(85)90172-9

Heyn, P., Abreu, B. C., and Ottenbacher, K. J. (2004). The effects of exercise training on elderly persons with cognitive impairment and dementia: a meta-analysis. *Arch. Phys. Med. Rehabil.* 85, 1694–1704. doi:10.1016/j.apmr.2004.03.019

Hicks, B. M., Durbin, C. E., Blonigen, D. M., Iacono, W. G., and McGue,

M. (2012). Relationship between personality change and the onset and course of alcohol dependence in young adulthood. *Addiction* 107, 540–548. doi:10.1111/j.1360-0443.2011.03617.x

Hicks, B. M., Iacono, W. G., and McGue, M. (2010). Consequences of an adolescent onset and persistent course of alcohol dependence in men: adolescent risk factors and adult outcomes. *Alcohol. Clin. Exp. Res.* 34, 819–833. doi:10.1111/j.1530-0277.2010.01154.x

Hill, S. Y., Muddasani, S., Prasad, K., Nutche, J., Steinhauer, S. R., Scanlon, J., et al. (2007a). Cerebellar volume in offspring from multiplex alcohol dependence families. *Biol. Psychiatry* 61, 41–47. doi:10.1016/j.biopsych.2006.01.007

Hill, S. Y., Kostelnik, B., Holmes, B., Goradia, D., McDermott, M., Diwadkar, V., et al. (2007b). fMRI BOLD response to the eyes task in offspring from multiplex alcohol dependence families. *Alcohol. Clin. Exp. Res.* 31, 2028–2035. doi:10.1111/j.1530-0277.2007.00535.x

Hillman, C. H., Erickson, K. I., and Kramer, A. F. (2008). Be smart, exercise your heart: exercise effects on brain and cognition. *Nat. Rev. Neurosci.* 9, 58–65. doi:10.1038/nrn2298

Hillman, C. H., Snook, E. M., and Jerome, G. J. (2003). Acute cardiovascular exercise and executive control function. *Int. J. Psychophysiol.* 48, 307–314. doi:10.1016/S0167-8760(03)00080-1

Howard, R., Finn, P., Jose, P., and Gallagher, J. (2011). Adolescent-onset alcohol abuse exacerbates the influence of childhood conduct disorder on late adolescent and early adult antisocial behaviour. *J. Forens. Psychiatry Psychol.* 23, 7–22. doi:10.1080/14789949.2011.641996

Huestegge, L., Radach, R., Kunert, H. J., and Heller, D. (2002). Visual search in long-term cannabis users with early age of onset. *Prog. Brain Res.* 140, 377–394. doi:10.1016/S0079-6123(02)40064-7

Jacobsen, L. K., Pugh, K. R., Constable, R. T., Westerveld, M., and Mencl, W. E. (2007). Functional correlates of verbal memory deficits emerging during nicotine withdrawal in abstinent adolescent marijuana users. *Biol. Psychiatry* 61, 31–40. doi:10.1016/j.biopsych.2006.02.014

Jacobus, J., Goldenberg, D., Wierenga, C. E., Tolentino, N. J., Liu, T. T., and Tapert, S. F. (2012). Altered cerebral blood flow and neurocognitive correlates in adolescent cannabis

users. *Psychopharmacology (Berl.)* 222, 675–684. doi:10.1007/s00213-012-2674-4

Jager, G., Block, R. I., Luijten, M., and Ramsey, N. F. (2010). Cannabis use and memory brain function in adolescent boys: a cross-sectional multicenter functional magnetic resonance imaging study. *J. Am. Acad. Child Adolesc. Psychiatry* 49, 561–572. doi:10.1016/j.jaac.2010.02.001

Jarvis, K., DelBello, M. P., Mills, N., Elman, I., Strakowski, S. M., and Adler, C. M. (2008). Neuroanatomic comparison of bipolar adolescents with and without cannabis use disorders. *J. Child Adolesc. Psychopharmacol.* 18, 557–563. doi:10.1089/cap.2008.033

Jernigan, T., and Gamst, A. (2005). Changes in volume with age: consistency and interpretation of observed effects. *Neurobiol. Aging* 26, 1271–1274. doi:10.1016/j.neurobiolaging.2005.05.016

Johnson, B. A., Cloninger, C. R., Roache, J. D., Bordnick, P. S., and Ruiz, P. (2000). Age of onset as a discriminator between alcoholic subtypes in a treatment-seeking outpatient population. *Am. J. Addict.* 9, 17–27. doi:10.1080/10550490050172191

Johnston, L. D., O'Malley, P. M., Bachman, J. G., and Schulenberg, J. E. (2009). *Monitoring the Future National Survey Results on Drug Use, 1975–2008: Volume II, College Students and Adults Ages 19–50* (NIH Publication No. 09-7403). Bethesda, MD: National Institute on Drug Abuse.

Johnston, L. D., O'Malley, P. M., Bachman, J. G., and Schulenberg, J. E. (2010). *Monitoring the Future National Results on Adolescent Drug Use: Overview of Key Findings, 2009* (NIH Publication No. 10-7583). Bethesda, MD: National Institute on Drug Abuse.

Johnston, L. D., O'Malley, P. M., Bachman, J. G., and Schulenberg, J. E. (2011). *Marijuana use Continues to Rise Among U.S. Teens, While Alcohol use Hits Historic Lows.* Ann Arbor, MI: University of Michigan News Service.

Kloos, A., Weller, R. A., Chan, R., and Weller, E. B. (2009). Gender differences in adolescent substance abuse. *Curr. Psychiatry Rep.* 11, 120–126. doi:10.1007/s11920-009-0019-8

Knight, J. R., Sherritt, L., Shrier, L. A., Harris, S. K., and Chang, G. (2002). Validity of the CRAFFT substance abuse screening test among adolescent clinic patients. *Arch. Pediatr. Adolesc. Med.* 156, 607–614.

Kolb, B., Mychasiuk, R., Muhammad, A., Li, Y., Frost, D. O., and Gibb, R. (2012). Experience and the developing prefrontal cortex. *Proc. Natl. Acad. Sci. U.S.A.* 16, 109. doi:10.1073/pnas.1121251109

Koskinen, S. M., Ahveninen, J., Kujala, T., Kaprio, J., O'Donnell, B. F., Osipova, D., et al. (2011). A longitudinal twin study of effects of adolescent alcohol abuse on the neurophysiology of attention and orienting. *Alcohol. Clin. Exp. Res.* 35, 1339–1350. doi:10.1111/j.1530-0277.2011.01470.x

Kramer, A. F., and Erickson, K. I. (2007). Capitalizing on cortical plasticity: influence of physical activity on cognition and brain function. *Trends Cogn. Sci. (Regul. Ed.)* 11, 342–348. doi:10.1016/j.tics.2007.06.009

Larimer, M. E., and Cronce, J. M. (2007). Identification, prevention, and treatment revisited: individual-focused college drinking prevention strategies 1999-2006. *Addict. Behav.* 32, 2439–2468. doi:10.1016/j.addbeh.2007.05.006

Lee, S. S., Humphreys, K. L., Flory, K., Liu, R., and Glass, K. (2011). Prospective association of childhood attention-deficit/hyperactivity disorder (ADHD) and substance use and abuse/dependence: a meta-analytic review. *Clin. Psychol. Rev.* 31, 328–341. doi:10.1016/j.cpr.2011.01.006

Lenroot, R. K., and Giedd, J. N. (2006). Brain development in children and adolescents: insights from anatomical magnetic resonance imaging. *Neurosci. Biobehav. Rev.* 30, 718–729. doi:10.1016/j.neubiorev.2006.06.001

Lenroot, R. K., and Giedd, J. N. (2010). Sex differences in the adolescent brain. *Brain Cogn.* 72, 46–55. doi:10.1016/j.bandc.2009.10.008

Lenroot, R. K., Gogtay, N., Greenstein, D. K., Wells, E. M., Wallace, G. L., Clasen, L. S., et al. (2007). Sexual dimorphism of brain developmental trajectories during childhood and adolescence. *Neuroimage* 36, 1065–1073. doi:10.1016/j.neuroimage.2007.03.053

Lisdahl, K. M., and Price, J. S. (2012). Increased marijuana use and gender predict poorer cognitive functioning in healthy emerging adults. *J. Int. Neuropsychol. Soc.* 18, 678–688. doi:10.1017/S1355617712000276

Lisdahl, K. M., Thayer, R., Squeglia, L., McQueeny, T. M., and Tapert, S. T. (2013). Cerebellar structure in adolescent binge drinkers. *Psychiatry Res.* 211, 17–23. doi:10.1016/j.pscychresns.2012.07.009

Liston, C., Watts, R., Tottenham, N., Davidson, M. C., Niogi, S., Ulug, A. M., et al. (2006). Frontostriatal microstructure modulates efficient recruitment of cognitive control. *Cereb. Cortex* 16, 553–560. doi:10.1093/cercor/bhj003

López-Caneda, E., Cadaveira, F., Crego, A., Gómez-Suárez, A., Corral, M., Parada, M., et al. (2012). Hyperactivation of right inferior frontal cortex in young binge drinkers during response inhibition: a follow-up study. *Addiction* 107, 1796–1808. doi:10.1111/j.1360-0443.2012.03908.x

Lopez-Larson, M. P., Bogorodzki, P., Rogowska, J., McGlade, E., King, J. B., Terry, J., et al. (2011). Altered prefrontal and insular cortical thickness in adolescent marijuana users. *Behav. Brain Res.* 220, 164–172. doi:10.1016/j.bbr.2011.02.001

Lopez-Larson, M. P., Rogowska, J., Bogorodzki, P., Bueler, C. E., McGlade, E. C., and Yurgelun-Todd, D. A. (2012). Corticocerebellar abnormalities in adolescents with heavy marijuana use. *Psychiatry Res.* 202, 224–232. doi:10.1016/j.pscychresns.2011.11.005

Lynskey, M., and Hall, W. (2000). The effects of adolescent cannabis use on educational attainment: a review. *Addiction* 95, 1621–1630. doi:10.1046/j.1360-0443.2000.951116213.x

Lyvers, M., Czerczyk, C., Follent, A., and Lodge, P. (2009). Disinhibition and reward sensitivity in relation to alcohol consumption by university undergraduates. *Addict. Res. Theory* 17, 668–677.

Lyvers, M., Duff, H., and Hasking, P. (2011). Risky alcohol use and age of onset of regular alcohol consumption in relation to frontal lobe indices, reward sensitivity and rash impulsiveness. *Addict. Res. Theory* 19, 251–259.

Ma, Q. (2008). Beneficial effects of moderate voluntary physical exercise and its biological mechanisms on brain health. *Neurosci. Bull.* 24, 265–270. doi:10.1007/s12264-008-0402-1

Macher, R. B., and Earleywine, M. (2012). Enhancing neuropsychological performance in chronic cannabis users: the role of motivation. *J. Clin. Exp. Neuropsychol.* 34, 405–415. doi:10.1080/13803395.2011.646957

Marks, B. L., Madden, D. J., Bucur, B., Provenzale, J. M., White, L. E., Cabeza, R., et al. (2007). Role of aerobic fitness and aging on cerebral white matter integrity. *Ann.*

N. Y. Acad. Sci. 1097, 171–174. doi:10.1196/annals.1379.022

Martin, C. S., Kaczynski, N. A., Maisto, S. A., and Tarter, R. E. (1996). Polydrug use in adolescent drinkers with and without DSM-IV alcohol abuse and dependence. *Alcohol. Clin. Exp. Res.* 20, 1099–1108. doi:10.1111/j.1530-0277.1996.tb01953.x

Mathias, C. W., Blumenthal, T. D., Dawes, M. A., Liguori, A., Richard, D. M., Bray, B., et al. (2011). Failure to sustain prepulse inhibition in adolescent marijuana users. *Drug Alcohol Depend.* 116, 110–116. doi:10.1016/j.drugalcdep.2010.11.020

Maurage, P. M., Pesenti, M., Philippot, P., Joassin, F., and Campanella, S. (2009). Latent deleterious effects of binge drinking over a short period of time revealed only by electrophysiological measures. *J. Psychiatry Neurosci.* 34, 111–118.

McHale, S., and Hunt, N. (2008). Executive function deficits in short-term abstinent cannabis users. *Hum. Psychopharmacol.* 23, 409–415. doi:10.1002/hup.941

McQueeny, T., Schweinsburg, B. C., Schweinsburg, A. D., Jacobus, J., Bava, S., Frank, L. R., et al. (2009). Altered white matter integrity in adolescent binge drinkers. *Alcohol. Clin. Exp. Res.* 33, 1278–1285. doi:10.1111/j.1530-0277.2009.00953.x

McQueeny, T. M., Padula, C., Price, J., Medina, K. L., Logan, P., and Tapert, S. F. (2011). Gender effects on amygdala morphometry in adolescent marijuana users. *Behav. Brain Res.* 224, 128–134. doi:10.1016/j.bbr.2011.05.031

Medina, K. L., Hanson, K., Schweinsburg, A. D., Cohen-Zion, M., Nagel, B. J., and Tapert, S. F. (2007a). Neuropsychological functioning in adolescent marijuana users: subtle deficits detectable after 30 days of abstinence. *J. Int. Neuropsychol. Soc.* 13, 807–820. doi:10.1017/S1355617707071032

Medina, K. L., Nagel, B. J., McQueeny, T., Park, A., and Tapert, S. F. (2007b). Depressive symptoms in adolescents: associations with white matter volume and marijuana use. *J. Child Psychol. Psychiatry* 48, 592–600. doi:10.1111/j.1469-7610.2007.01728.x

Medina, K. L., Schweinsburg, A. D., Cohen-Zion, M., Nagel, B. J., and Tapert, S. F. (2007c). Effects of alcohol and combined marijuana and alcohol use during adolescence on hippocampal asymmetry.

Neurotoxicol. Teratol. 29, 141–152. doi:10.1016/j.ntt.2006.10.010

Medina, K. L., McQueeny, T., Nagel, B. J., Hanson, K., Schweinsburg, A. D., and Tapert, S. F. (2008). Prefrontal cortex volumes in adolescents with alcohol use disorders: unique gender effects. *Alcohol. Clin. Exp. Res.* 32, 386–394. doi:10.1111/j.1530-0277.2007.00602.x

Medina, K. L., McQueeny, T., Nagel, B. J., Hanson, K. L., Yang, T., and Tapert, S. F. (2009). Prefrontal morphometry in abstinent adolescent marijuana users: subtle gender effects. *Addict. Biol.* 14, 457–468. doi:10.1111/j.1369-1600.2009.00166.x

Medina, K. L., Nagel, B. J., and Tapert, S. F. (2010). Cerebellar vermis abnormality in adolescent marijuana users. *Psychiatry Res.* 182, 152–159. doi:10.1016/j.pscychresns.2009.12.004

Meier, M. H., Caspi, A., Ambler, A., Harrington, H., Houts, R., Keefe, R. S., et al. (2012). Persistent cannabis users show neuropsychological decline from childhood to midlife. *Proc. Natl. Acad. Sci. U.S.A.* 109, E2657–E2664. doi:10.1073/pnas.1206820109

Monk, C. S., McClure, E. B., Nelson, E. E., Zarahn, E., Bilder, R. M., Leibenluft, E., et al. (2003). Adolescent immaturity in attention-related brain engagement to emotional facial expressions. *Neuroimage* 20, 420–428. doi:10.1016/S1053-8119(03)00355-0

Monti, P. M., Miranda, R., Nixon, K., Sher, K. J., Swartzwelder, H. S., Tapert, S. F., et al. (2005). Adolescence: booze, brains, and behavior. *Alcohol. Clin. Exp. Res.* 29, 207–220. doi:10.1097/01.ALC.0000153551.11000.F3

Moss, H. B., Kirisci, L., Gordon, H. W., and Tarter, R. E. (1994). A neuropsychologic profile of adolescent alcoholics. *Alcohol. Clin. Exp. Res.* 18, 159–163. doi:10.1111/j.1530-0277.1994.tb00897.x

Nagel, B. J., Medina, K. L., Yoshii, J., Schweinsburg, A. D., Moadab, I., and Tapert, S. F. (2006). Age related changes in prefrontal white matter volume across adolescence. *Neuroreport* 17, 1427–1431. doi:10.1097/01.wnr.0000233099.97784.45

Nagel, B. J., Schweinsburg, A. D., Phan, V., and Tapert, S. F. (2005). Reduced hippocampal volume among adolescents with alcohol use disorders without psychiatric comorbidity. *Psychiatry Res.* 139, 181–190. doi:10.1016/j.pscychresns.2005.05.008

Nigg, J. T., Glass, J. M., Wong, M. M., Poon, E., Jester, J. M., Fitzgerald, H. E., et al. (2004). Neuropsychological executive functioning in children at elevated risk for alcoholism: findings in early adolescence. *J. Abnorm. Psychol.* 113, 302–314. doi:10.1037/0021-843X.113.2.302

O'Shea, M., Singh, M. E., McGregor, I. S., and Mallet, P. E. (2004). Chronic cannabinoid exposure produces lasting memory impairment and increased anxiety in adolescent but not adult rats. *J. Psychopharmacol.* 18, 502–508. doi:10.1177/0269881104047277

Parada, M., Corral, M., Caamaño-Isorna, F., Mota, N., Crego, A., Holguín, S. R., et al. (2011). Binge drinking and declarative memory in university students. *Alcohol. Clin. Exp. Res.* 35, 1475–1484. doi:10.1111/j.1530-0277.2011.01484.x

Parada, M., Corral, M., Mota, N., Crego, A., Rodríguez Holguín, S., and Cadaveira, F. (2012). Executive functioning and alcohol binge drinking in university students. *Addict. Behav.* 37, 167–172. doi:10.1016/j.addbeh.2011.09.015

Pardo, Y., Aguilar, R., Molinuevo, B., and Torrubia, R. (2007). Alcohol use as a behavioural sign of disinhibition: evidence from J.A. Gray's model of personality. *Addict. Behav.* 32, 2398–2403. doi:10.1016/j.addbeh.2007.02.010

Park, M. S., Sohn, S., Park, J. E., Kim, S. H., Yu, I. K., and Sohn, J. H. (2011). Brain functions associated with verbal working memory tasks among young males with alcohol use disorders. *Scand. J. Psychol.* 52, 1–7. doi:10.1111/j.1467-9450.2010.00848.x

Paus, T., Zijdenbos, A., Worsley, K., Collins, D. L., Blumenthal, J., Giedd, J. N., et al. (1999). Structural maturation of neural pathways in children and adolescents: in vivo study. *Science* 283, 1908–1911. doi:10.1126/science.283.5409.1908

Pereira, A. C., Huddleston, D. E., Brickman, A. M., Sosunov, A. A., Hen, R., McKhann, G. M., et al. (2007). An in vivo correlate of exercise-induced neurogenesis in the adult dentate gyrus. *Proc. Natl. Acad. Sci. U.S.A.* 104, 5638–5643. doi:10.1073/pnas.0611721104

Ploughman, M. (2008). Exercise is brain food: the effects of physical activity on cognitive function. *Dev. Neurorehabil.* 11, 236–240. doi:10.1080/17518420801997007

Pope, H. Jr., Gruber, A., Hudson, J., Cohane, G., Huestis, M., and

Yurgelun-Todd, D. (2003). Early-onset cannabis use and cognitive deficits: what is the nature of the association? *Drug Alcohol Depend.* 69, 303.

Prescot, A. P., Locatelli, A. E., Renshaw, P. F., and Yurgelun-Todd, D. A. (2011). Neurochemical alterations in adolescent chronic marijuana smokers: a proton MRS study. *Neuroimage* 57, 69–75. doi:10.1016/j.neuroimage.2011.02.044

Quinn, H. R., Matsumoto, I., Callaghan, P. D., Long, L. E., Arnold, J. C., Gunasekaran, N., et al. (2008). Adolescent rats find repeated Δ9-THC less aversive than adult rats but display greater residual cognitive deficits and changes in hippocampal protein expression following exposure. *Neuropsychopharmacology* 33, 1113–1126. doi:10.1038/sj.npp.1301475

Radak, Z., Kumagai, S., Taylor, A. W., Naito, H., and Goto, S. (2007). Effects of exercise on brain function: role of free radicals. *Appl. Physiol. Nutr. Metab.* 32, 942–946. doi:10.1139/H07-081

Raphael, D. (2013). Adolescence as a gateway to adult health outcomes. *Maturitas* 75, 137–141. doi:10.1016/j.maturitas.2013.03.013

Read, J. P., Merrill, J. E., Kahler, C. W., and Strong, D. R. (2007). Predicting functional outcomes among college drinkers: reliability and predictive validity of the Young Adult Alcohol Consequences Questionnaire. *Addict. Behav.* 32, 2597–2610. doi:10.1016/j.addbeh.2007.06.021

Ridenour, T. A., Tarter, R. E., Reynolds, M., Mezzich, A., Kirisci, L., and Vanyukov, M. (2009). Neurobehavior disinhibition, parental substance use disorder, neighborhood quality and development of cannabis use disorder in boys. *Drug Alcohol Depend.* 102, 71–77. doi:10.1016/j.drugalcdep.2009.01.009

Rubino, T., Realini, N., Braida, D., Guidi, S., Capurro, V., Viganò, D., et al. (2009). Changes in hippocampal morphology and neuroplasticity induced by adolescent THC treatment are associated with cognitive impairment in adulthood. *Hippocampus* 19, 763–772. doi:10.1002/hipo.20554

Rubino, T., Vigano, D., Realini, N., Guidali, C., Braida, D., Capurro, V., et al. (2008). Chronic delta 9-tetrahydrocannabinol during adolescence provokes sex-dependent changes in the emotional profile in adult rats: behavioral and biochemical correlates.

Neuropsychopharmacology 33, 2760–2771. doi:10.1038/sj.npp.1301664

Sakurai, T., Izawa, T., Kizaki, T., Ogasawara, J. E., Shirato, K., Imaizumi, K., et al. (2009). Exercise training decreases expression of inflammation-related adipokines through reduction of oxidative stress in rat white adipose tissue. *Biochem. Biophys. Res. Commun.* 379, 605–609. doi:10.1016/j.bbrc.2008.12.127

Scaife, J. C., and Duka, T. (2009). Behavioural measures of frontal lobe function in a population of young social drinkers with binge drinking pattern. *Pharmacol. Biochem. Behav.* 93, 354–362. doi:10.1016/j.pbb.2009.05.015

Schneider, M., and Koch, M. (2003). Chronic pubertal but not adult chronic cannabinoid treatment impairs sensorimotor gating, recognition memory and performance in a progressive ratio task in adult rats. *Neuropsychopharmacology* 28, 1760–1790. doi:10.1038/sj.npp.1300225

Schuster, R. M., Crane, N. A., Mermelstein, R., and Gonzalez, R. (2012). The influence of inhibitory control and episodic memory on the risky sexual behavior of young adult cannabis users. *J. Int. Neuropsychol. Soc.* 18, 827–833. doi:10.1017/S1355617712000586

Schwartz, R. H., Gruenewald, P. J., Klitzner, M., and Fedio, P. (1989). Short-term memory impairment in cannabis-dependent adolescents. *Am. J. Dis. Child.* 143, 1214–1219.

Schweinsburg, A. D., McQueeny, T., Nagel, B. J., Eyler, L. T., and Tapert, S. F. (2010a). A preliminary study of functional magnetic resonance imaging response during verbal encoding among adolescent binge drinkers. *Alcohol* 44, 111–117. doi:10.1016/j.alcohol.2009.09.032

Schweinsburg, A. D., Schweinsburg, B. C., Medina, K. L., McQueeny, T., Brown, S. A., and Tapert, S. F. (2010b). The influence of recency of use on fMRI response during spatial working memory in adolescent marijuana users. *J. Psychoactive Drugs* 42, 401–412. doi:10.1080/02791072.2010.10400703

Schweinsburg, A. D., Nagel, B. J., Schweinsburg, B. C., Park, A., Theilmann, R. J., and Tapert, S. F. (2008). Abstinent adolescent marijuana users show altered fMRI response during spatial working memory. *Psychiatry Res.* 163, 40–51. doi:10.1016/j.pscychresns.2007.04.018

Schweinsburg, A. D., Paulus, M. P., Barlett, V. C., Killeen, L. A., Caldwell, L. C., Pulido, C., et al. (2004). An FMRI study of response inhibition in youths with a family history of alcoholism. *Ann. N. Y. Acad. Sci.* 1021, 391–394. doi:10.1196/annals.1308.050

Sher, K. J., Martin, E. D., Wood, P. K., and Rutledge, P. C. (1997). Alcohol use disorders and neuropsychological functioning in first-year undergraduates. *Exp. Clin. Psychopharmacol.* 5, 304–315. doi:10.1037/1064-1297.5.3.304

Sibley, B., and Etnier, J. (2003). The relationship between physical activity and cognition in children: a meta-analysis. *Pediatr. Exerc. Sci.* 15, 243–256.

Silveri, M. M., Jensen, J. E., Rosso, I. M., Sneider, J. T., and Yurgelun-Todd, D. A. (2011). Preliminary evidence for white matter metabolite differences in marijuana-dependent young men using 2D J-resolved magnetic resonance spectroscopic imaging at 4 Tesla. *Psychiatry Res.* 191, 201–211. doi:10.1016/j.pscychresns.2010.10.005

Sim, Y. J., Kim, H., Shin, M. S., Chang, H. K., Shin, M. C., Ko, I. G., et al. (2008). Effect of postnatal treadmill exercise on c-Fos expression in the hippocampus of rat pups born from the alcohol-intoxicated mothers. *Brain Dev.* 30, 118–125. doi:10.1016/j.braindev.2007.07.003

Smith, A. M., Longo, C. A., Fried, P. A., Hogan, M. J., and Cameron, I. (2010). Effects of marijuana on visuospatial working memory: an fMRI study in young adults. *Psychopharmacology (Berl.)* 210, 429–438. doi:10.1007/s00213-010-1841-8

Solowij, N., Jones, K. A., Rozman, M. E., Davis, S. M., Ciarrochi, J., Heaven, P. C., et al. (2011). Verbal learning and memory in adolescent cannabis users, alcohol users and non-users. *Psychopharmacology (Berl.)* 216, 131–144. doi:10.1007/s00213-011-2203-x

Solowij, N., Jones, K. A., Rozman, M. E., Davis, S. M., Ciarrochi, J., Heaven, P. C., et al. (2012). Reflection impulsivity in adolescent cannabis users: a comparison with alcohol-using and non-substance-using adolescents. *Psychopharmacology (Berl.)* 219, 575–586. doi:10.1007/s00213-011-2486-y

Sowell, E. R., Thompson, P., Leonard, C. M., Welcome, S. E., Kan, E., and Toga, A. W. (2004). Longitudinal mapping of cortical thickness and brain growth in normal children. *J. Neurosci.* 24, 8223–8231. doi:10.1523/JNEUROSCI.1798-04.2004

Sowell, E. R., Thompson, P. M., Holmes, C. J., Jernigan, T. L., and Toga, A. W. (1999). In vivo evidence for post adolescent brain maturation in frontal and striatal regions. *Nat. Neurosci.* 2, 859–861. doi:10.1038/13154

Sowell, E. R., Trauner, D. A., Gamst, A., and Jernigan, T. L. (2002). Development of cortical and subcortical brain structures in childhood and adolescence: a structural MRI study. *Dev. Med. Child Neurol.* 44, 4–16. doi:10.1017/S0012162201001591

Spadoni, A. D., Norman, A. L., Schweinsburg, A. D., and Tapert, S. F. (2008). Effects of family history of alcohol use disorders on spatial working memory BOLD response in adolescents. *Alcohol. Clin. Exp. Res.* 32, 1135–1145. doi:10.1111/j.1530-0277.2008.00694.x

Spear, L. P. (2000). *The Adolescent Brain and Age-Related Behavioral Manifestations.* New York, NY: Norton & Company, Inc.

Spear, L. P. (2010). The behavioral neuroscience of adolescence. *Neurosci. Biobehav. Rev.* 24, 417–463. doi:10.1016/S0149-7634(00)00014-2

Squeglia, L. M., Schweinsburg, A. D., Pulido, C., and Tapert, S. F. (2011). Adolescent binge drinking linked to abnormal spatial working memory brain activation: differential gender effects. *Alcohol. Clin. Exp. Res.* 35, 1831–1841. doi:10.1111/j.1530-0277.2011.01527.x

Squeglia, L. M., Sorg, S. F., Schweinsburg, A. D., Wetherill, R. R., Pulido, C., and Tapert, S. F. (2012). Binge drinking differentially affects adolescent male and female brain morphometry. *Psychopharmacology (Berl.)* 220, 529–539. doi:10.1007/s00213-011-2500-4

Sullivan, J. L., Baenziger, J. C., Wagner, D. L., Rauscher, F. P., Nurnberger, J. I. Jr., and Holmes, J. S. (1990). Platelet MAO in subtypes of alcoholism. *Biol. Psychiatry* 27, 911–922. doi:10.1016/0006-3223(90)90473-F

Tait, R. J., Mackinnon, A., and Christensen, H. (2011). Cannabis use and cognitive function: 8-year trajectory in a young adult cohort. *Addiction* 106, 2195–2203. doi:10.1111/j.1360-0443.2011.03574.x

Tapert, S. F., Baratta, M. V., Abrantes, A. M., and Brown, S. A. (2002a). Attention dysfunction predicts substance involvement in community youths. *J. Am. Acad. Child Adolesc. Psychiatry* 41, 680–686. doi:10.1097/00004583-200206000-00007

Tapert, S. F., Granholm, E., Leedy, N. G., and Brown, S. A. (2002b). Substance use and withdrawal: neuropsychological functioning over 8 years in youth. *J. Int. Neuropsychol. Soc.* 8, 873–883. doi:10.1017/S1355617702870011

Themanson, J. R., Hillman, C. H., and Curtin, J. J. (2006). Age and physical activity influences on action monitoring during task switching. *Neurobiol. Aging* 27, 1335–1345. doi:10.1016/j.neurobiolaging.2005.07.002

Tapert, S. F., Brown, G. G., Kindermann, S. S., Cheung, E. H., Frank, L. R., and Brown, S. A. (2001). fMRI measurement of brain dysfunction in alcohol-dependent young women. *Alcohol. Clin. Exp. Res.* 25, 236–245. doi:10.1111/j.1530-0277.2001.tb02204.x

Tapert, S. F., and Brown, S. A. (1999). Neuropsychological correlates of adolescent substance abuse: four year outcomes. *J. Int. Neuropsychol. Soc.* 5, 481–493. doi:10.1017/S1355617799566010

Tapert, S. F., and Brown, S. A. (2000). Substance dependence, family history of alcohol dependence, and neuropsychological functioning in adolescence. *Addiction* 95, 1043–1053. doi:10.1046/j.1360-0443.2000.95710436.x

Tapert, S. F., Schweinsburg, A. D., Barlett, V. C., Brown, S. A., Frank, L. R., Brown, G. G., et al. (2004). Blood oxygen level dependent response and spatial working memory in adolescents with alcohol use disorders. *Alcohol. Clin. Exp. Res.* 28, 1577–1586. doi:10.1097/01.ALC.0000141812.81234.A6

Tapert, S. F., Schweinsburg, A. D., Drummond, S. P., Paulus, M. P., Brown, S. A., Yang, T. T., et al. (2007). Functional MRI of inhibitory processing in abstinent adolescent marijuana users. *Psychopharmacology (Berl.)* 194, 173–183. doi:10.1007/s00213-007-0823-y

Themanson, J. R., and Hillman, C. H. (2006). Cardiorespiratory fitness and acute aerobic exercise effects on neuroelectric and behavioral measures of action monitoring. *Neuroscience* 141, 757–767. doi:10.1016/j.neuroscience.2006.04.004

Thoma, R. J., Monnig, M. A., Lysne, P. A., Ruhl, D. A., Pommy, J. A., Bogenschutz, M., et al. (2011). Adolescent substance abuse: the effects of alcohol and marijuana on neuropsychological performance. *Alcohol. Clin. Exp. Res.*

35, 39–46. doi:10.1111/j.1530-0277.2010.01320.x

Timinkul, A., Kato, M., Omori, T., Deocaris, C. C., Ito, A., Kizuka, T., et al. (2008). Enhancing effect of cerebral blood volume by mild exercise in healthy young men: a near-infrared spectroscopy study. *Neurosci. Res.* 61, 242–248. doi:10.1016/j.neures.2008.03.012

Townshend, J. M., and Duka, T. (2005). Binge drinking, cognitive performance and mood in a population of young social drinkers. *Alcohol. Clin. Exp. Res.* 29, 317–325. doi:10.1097/01.ALC.0000156453.05028.F5

Vaidya, J. G., Block, R. I., O'Leary, D. S., Ponto, L. B., Ghoneim, M. M., and Bechara, A. (2012). Effects of chronic marijuana use on brain activity during monetary decision-making. *Neuropsychopharmacology* 37, 618–629. doi:10.1038/npp.2011.227

Varma, V. K., Basu, D., Malhotra, A., Sharma, A., and Mattoo, S. K. (1994). Correlates of early- and late-onset alcohol dependence. *Addict. Behav.* 19, 609–619. doi:10.1016/0306-4603(94)90016-7

von Knorring, A.-L., Bohman, M., von Knorring, L., and Oreland, L. (1985). Platelet MAO activity as a biological marker in subgroups of alcoholism. *Acta Psychiatr. Scand.* 72, 51–58. doi:10.1111/j.1600-0447.1985.tb02570.x

Waters, R. P., Emerson, A. J., Watt, M. J., Forster, G. L., Swallow, J. G., and Summers, C. H. (2005). Stress induces rapid changes in central catecholaminergic activity in Anolis carolinensis: restraint and forced physical activity. *Brain Res. Bull.* 67, 210–218. doi:10.1016/j.brainresbull.2005.06.029

Werch, C. C., Moore, M. J., DiClemente, C. C., Bledsoe, R., and Jobli, E. (2005). A multihealth behavior intervention integrating physical activity and substance use prevention for adolescents. *Prev. Sci.* 6, 213–226. doi:10.1007/s11121-005-0012-3

White, H. R., Marmorstein, N. R., Crews, F. T., Bates, M. E., Mun, E. Y., and Loeber, R. (2011). Associations between heavy drinking and changes in impulsive behavior among adolescent boys. *Alcohol. Clin. Exp. Res.* 35, 295–303. doi:10.1111/j.1530-0277.2010.01345.x

Wilens, T. E., Martelon, M., Joshi, G., Bateman, C., Fried, R., Petty, C., et al. (2011). Does ADHD predict substance-use disorders? A 10-year follow-up study of young adults with ADHD. *J. Am.* *Acad. Child Adolesc. Psychiatry* 50, 543–553. doi:10.1016/j.jaac.2011.01.021

Wilson, W., Mathew, R., Turkington, T., Hawk, T., Coleman, R. E., and Provenzale, J. (2000). Brain morphological changes and early marijuana use: a magnetic resonance and positron emission tomography study. *J. Addict. Dis.* 19, 1–22. doi:10.1300/J069v19n01_01

Winnail, S. D., Valois, R. F., McKeown, R. E., Saunders, R. P., and Pate, R. R. (1995). Relationship between physical activity level and cigarette, smokeless tobacco, and marijuana use among public high school adolescents. *J. Sch. Health* 65, 438–442. doi:10.1111/j.1746-1561.1995.tb08209.x

Xiao, L., Bechara, A., Gong, Q., Huang, X., Li, X., Xue, G., et al. (2012). Abnormal affective decision making revealed in adolescent binge drinkers using a functional magnetic resonance imaging study. *Psychol. Addict. Behav.* doi:10.1037/a0027892. [Epub ahead of print].

7

Kappa-opioid receptor signaling in the striatum as a potential modulator of dopamine transmission in cocaine dependence

Pierre Trifilieff [1,2] and Diana Martinez [1]*

[1] New York State Psychiatric Institute, Columbia University, New York, NY, USA
[2] NutriNeuro, UMR 1286 INRA, University Bordeaux 2, Bordeaux, France

Edited by:
Nicholas W. Gilpin, Louisiana State University Health Sciences Center New Orleans, USA

Reviewed by:
Raj Sevak, University of California Los Angeles, USA
Luigi Janiri, Università Cattolica del S. Cuore, Italy

*Correspondence:
Diana Martinez, New York State Psychiatric Institute, Columbia University, 1051 Riverside Drive #32, New York, NY 10032, USA
e-mail: dm437@columbia.edu

Cocaine addiction is accompanied by a decrease in striatal dopamine signaling, measured as a decrease in dopamine D2 receptor binding as well as blunted dopamine release in the striatum. These alterations in dopamine transmission have clinical relevance, and have been shown to correlate with cocaine-seeking behavior and response to treatment for cocaine dependence. However, the mechanisms contributing to the hypodopaminergic state in cocaine addiction remain unknown. Here we review the positron emission tomography (PET) imaging studies showing alterations in D2 receptor binding potential and dopamine transmission in cocaine abusers and their significance in cocaine-seeking behavior. Based on animal and human studies, we propose that the kappa receptor/dynorphin system, because of its impact on dopamine transmission and upregulation following cocaine exposure, could contribute to the hypodopaminergic state reported in cocaine addiction, and could thus be a relevant target for treatment development.

Keywords: imaging, kappa opioid receptor, dopamine, cocaine dependence, striatum, dopamine receptor

INTRODUCTION

Studies imaging the neurochemistry associated with cocaine addiction in humans have largely focused on dopamine signaling in the striatum. These studies show that pre-synaptic dopamine release, in response to the administration of a stimulant, is reduced in cocaine abusers compared to healthy controls. This has important implications for this disorder, since the reduction in dopamine release has been shown to correlate with increased cocaine-seeking behavior. Importantly, the imaging studies were performed at about 14 days abstinence, which has clinical relevance, since previous studies have shown that cocaine abusers who achieve 2 weeks of abstinence have a better treatment response compared to those who do not (Bisaga et al., 2010; Oliveto et al., 2012). Thus, a better understanding of the mechanisms behind blunted dopamine release would be expected to have implications for treatment development. Among the possible mechanisms that are known to regulate striatal dopamine release is dynorphin acting at the kappa receptor. Kappa receptor activation in the striatum has been shown to inhibit stimulant-induced dopamine release, in addition to striatal dopamine levels and dopamine neurons activity (for review, see Koob and Le Moal, 2008; Muschamp and Carlezon, 2013). Furthermore, studies in humans and animals show that dynorphin is significantly upregulated following chronic cocaine exposure, and that this effect is long lasting (for review, see Koob and Le Moal, 2008; Muschamp and Carlezon, 2013), which could account for the decrease in dopamine signaling seen after 2 weeks of abstinence in the human imaging studies. Here, we review the data suggesting that the cocaine-induced elevation in dynorphin may contribute to the hypodopaminergic state observed in cocaine addiction.

PET IMAGING OF DOPAMINE TRANSMISSION IN COCAINE ADDICTION

PRINCIPLES OF PET IMAGING

Positron emission tomography (PET) allows imaging of the neurochemistry associated with drug and alcohol addiction in the human brain. This imaging modality uses radionuclide-labeled ligands that bind to a specific receptor, and the radioligands used most frequently in addiction research label the dopamine receptors. Radiotracers that label the dopamine type 2 family of receptors (referred to as D2) can also be used to measure changes in extracellular dopamine. This is performed by imaging with radiotracers that are sensitive to changes in extracellular dopamine, and obtaining scans before and after the administration of a psychostimulant (such as amphetamine or methylphenidate). These stimulants increase extracellular dopamine levels, which results in a reduction of dopamine receptors that are available to bind to the radiotracer, shown in **Figure 1**. For reasons that are not completely understood, this method can be used with most D2 receptor radiotracers but not with radiotracers that bind to the D1 receptor. Thus, imaging studies using the D2 receptor radiotracers (such as [11C]raclopride or [18F]fallypride) can be used to measure changes in endogenous dopamine, whereas radiotracers that label the D1 receptor (such as [11C]NNC112 or [11C]SCH23390) cannot (Abi-Dargham et al., 1999; Chou et al., 1999; Laruelle, 2000; Martinez and Narendran, 2010).

The main outcome measure in radioligand imaging studies is receptor binding to the radiotracer, referred to as BPND, defined as the ratio of specific to non-specific binding (Innis et al., 2007). The change in extracellular dopamine resulting from stimulant

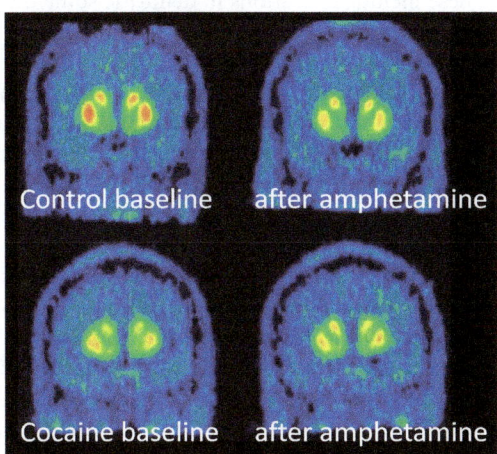

FIGURE 1 | PET scans in a healthy control and cocaine-dependent subject. The comparison of the top panels (pre- and post-amphetamine administration) in the healthy control shows that radiotracer ([11C]raclopride) binding is reduced in the striatum following amphetamine. The cocaine-dependent subject (bottom panel) has have lower D2 receptors compared the control in the baseline condition. In addition, the cocaine abuses has less radiotracer displacement (Δ BPND) following amphetamine. Adapted from Trifilieff and Martinez "Cocaine: Mechanism and Effects in the Brain" in "The Effects of Drug Abuse on the Human Nervous System" M. Kuhar and B. Madras editors, 2012, publisher Neuroscience-Net, LLC.

administration is measured by comparing baseline BPND (pre-stimulant administration) and BPND following the stimulant. This is used to derive the percent change in BPND, or ΔBPND, defined as [(BPNDbaseline – BPNDchallenge)/BPNDbaseline]. Previous studies in non-human primates have shown that ΔBPND correlates linearly with changes in extracellular dopamine, measured with microdialysis (Breier et al., 1997; Endres et al., 1997; Laruelle et al., 1997). Thus, ΔBPND provides an indirect measure of stimulant-induced pre-synaptic dopamine release, and can be used to characterize the alterations in dopamine signaling that occur in cocaine dependence.

PET IMAGING OF DOPAMINE RECEPTORS IN COCAINE ADDICTION

To date, six studies have been performed imaging the D2 receptor in cocaine abusers, and these consistently show a decrease in binding in the striatum compared to matched controls (Volkow et al., 1990, 1993, 1997; Martinez et al., 2004, 2009a, 2011). The decrease is about 15–20% and occurs in both the ventral and dorsal striatum. Importantly, animals with low D2 receptor levels in the striatum, prior to drug exposure, display greater cocaine self-administration (Morgan et al., 2002; Czoty et al., 2004; Nader et al., 2006; Dalley et al., 2007). Imaging studies in humans show that low striatal D2 receptor binding in cocaine abusers in the striatum correlates with decreases in glucose metabolism in the orbito-frontal cortex and cingulate gyrus, which process drive and affect, and may lead to continued drug-taking behavior (Volkow et al., 1993, 1999). Several authors have proposed that changes in D2 receptor binding in addiction could reflect behavioral vulnerability to drug self-administration, such as lack of cognitive control or increased

impulsivity (Everitt et al., 2008; Dalley et al., 2011; Groman and Jentsch, 2012).

One PET imaging study has measured D1 receptor binding in cocaine abuse (Martinez et al., 2009b). This study showed no difference in D1 receptor binding in cocaine abusers compared to controls, which is consistent with a post-mortem study of striatal D1 receptor mRNA (Meador-Woodruff et al., 1993). However, the imaging study also showed that, within the cocaine-dependent subjects, low D1 receptor binding in the ventral striatum was associated with greater choices to self-administer cocaine. Thus, this finding may represent a phenotype in which low D1 receptor binding in the limbic striatum is associated with a greater vulnerability to the reinforcing effects of cocaine. This is in agreement with pharmacologic studies in humans showing that stimulation of D1 receptors reduces, whereas blockade of the D1 receptor enhances, the reinforcing effects of cocaine (Haney et al., 1999, 2001). Taken together, these studies indicate that decreased signaling at the D1 receptor may be associated with more cocaine-taking behavior.

PET IMAGING DOPAMINE RELEASE IN COCAINE ABUSERS

Imaging studies measuring pre-synaptic dopamine release show that cocaine dependence is associated with a reduction in responsiveness of the dopamine system to a stimulant challenge. For example, in healthy human volunteers, the administration of a psychostimulant produces a decrease in [11C]raclopride binding (ΔBPND) of 15–20% (Volkow et al., 1994; Drevets et al., 2001; Martinez et al., 2003; Munro et al., 2006), but in cocaine abusers the decrease in [11C]raclopride binding is significantly blunted (Volkow et al., 1997; Malison et al., 1999; Martinez et al., 2007b, 2011). Thus, four studies have shown that cocaine dependence is associated with reduced [11C]raclopride displacement following stimulant administration compared to healthy controls, which represents a reduction in pre-synaptic dopamine release. PET imaging studies also show that cocaine abuse is associated with both decreased [18F]DOPA uptake and striatal vesicular monoamine transporter 2 binding, which provide measures of pre-synaptic dopamine stores (Wu et al., 1997; Narendran et al., 2012).

In addition to a reduction in stimulant-induced dopamine release, PET imaging has also shown that dopamine levels in the resting condition (without any stimulant administration) are reduced in cocaine dependence. This is performed by imaging the D2 receptors before and after acute depletion of endogenous dopamine using alpha-methyl-para-tyrosine (AMPT). Thus, imaging after AMPT administration results in an increase in [11C]raclopride binding, as opposed to the decrease seen after stimulant administration (Martinez et al., 2009a). AMPT administration resulted in an increase of $11.1 \pm 4.4\%$ in [11C]raclopride binding in the striatum for healthy controls, but only $5.7 \pm 5.9\%$ for cocaine-dependent volunteers (Martinez et al., 2009a), indicating that basal dopamine levels are decreased in cocaine abuse.

Taken together, imaging studies in cocaine abuse consistently show a reduction in striatal dopamine transmission, compared to healthy controls, measured as decreased pre-synaptic dopamine release (Volkow et al., 1997; Malison et al., 1999; Martinez et al., 2007b, 2011) and reduced baseline levels of endogenous dopamine (Martinez et al., 2009a). Similar findings have been shown in rodents (Parsons et al., 1991; Robertson et al., 1991; Rossetti et al., 1992; Weiss et al., 1992; Gerrits et al., 2002) and non-human primates (Castner et al., 2000; Kirkland Henry et al., 2009). Thus, cocaine dependence is associated with a hypodopaminergic state, which correlates with behaviors that contribute to addiction and relapse (Melis et al., 2005). Importantly, the PET scans showing blunted dopamine release were obtained after about 2 weeks of abstinence, to avoid the acute effect of cocaine on dopamine signaling, and due to the clinical relevance of this time point. Previous studies have shown that cocaine abusers who can achieve 2 weeks of abstinence have a better treatment response compared to those who do not (Bisaga et al., 2010; Oliveto et al., 2012).

SIGNIFICANCE OF THE HYPODOPAMINERGIC STATE IN COCAINE ABUSE

The impact of dopamine transmission on addiction has been demonstrated for decades, but its actual role in mediating the reinforcing effects of drugs of abuse remains under debate. Dopamine does not appear to only signal "reward" (drug or natural rewards), although dopamine neurons fire in response to the receipt of a reward, and during the expectation of a reward. However, dopamine signaling more likely mediates the reinforcing effects of natural rewards and abused drugs, and makes the behavior required to obtain the reward more likely to be repeated (Schultz, 2006; Berridge, 2007; Wise, 2008; Salamone and Correa, 2012). However, the imaging studies in cocaine dependence consistently show that pre-synaptic dopamine is reduced compared to controls, indicating that this disorder is associated with a hypodopaminergic state. This plays a crucial role in drug-seeking and taking, even after prolonged drug-free periods (Melis et al., 2005).

The imaging studies in human cocaine abusers show that blunted dopamine release correlates with an increase in cocaine self-administration (Martinez et al., 2007b, 2011). These studies showed that low dopamine release in cocaine abusers, measured as ΔBPND, was associated with the decision to take cocaine in the presence of competing non-drug reinforcers. The inability of the cocaine-dependent subjects with low dopamine release to alter their behavior can be viewed as an inability to respond to alternative sources of reward. This is consistent with the theory that decreased dopamine function in addiction results in a decreased interest to non-drug-related stimuli and increased susceptibility to the drug of choice (Melis et al., 2005).

These studies raise the question regarding the mechanism behind this decrease in pre-synaptic dopamine release. Previous studies in animals have shown that cocaine exposure results in reduced burst firing of the dopamine neurons of the ventral tegmental area (Brodie and Dunwiddie, 1990; Lacey et al., 1990; Ackerman and White, 1992; Gao et al., 1998). Decreases in extracellular dopamine levels in the nucleus accumbens have also been reported following cocaine withdrawal (Parsons et al., 1991; Robertson et al., 1991; Rossetti et al., 1992; Weiss et al., 1992). Cocaine administration has also been shown to alter the sensitivity of D2 autoreceptors of the midbrain (Gao et al., 1998; Lee et al., 1999; Marinelli et al., 2003), which could reduce pre-synaptic dopamine release. In addition to these functional changes in dopamine signaling, animal studies have also shown that cocaine exposure produces morphological changes in dopamine

neurons. These include alterations in dendritic spine density and morphology and a reduction in the size of the dopamine neurons of the ventral tegmental area (Melis et al., 2005).

Presently, it is unknown whether these changes occur in the human brain. Human studies of the dopamine transporter (DAT), which can serve as a marker for the integrity of the dopamine neurons (Fusar-Poli and Meyer-Lindenberg, 2013), show that the DAT is increased in post-mortem studies of cocaine abusers (Little et al., 1993, 1999). However, imaging studies show that the DAT is increased for a short time period following the cessation of cocaine use, but soon return to control levels (Volkow et al., 1996; Wang et al., 1997; Malison et al., 1998). But measuring DAT binding alone is unlikely to reveal morphological alterations of the dopamine neurons, and other means for investigating this with imaging in humans are not yet available. With respect to the dopamine receptors in the midbrain, one study in methamphetamine abusers and another in cocaine abusers showed that D3 receptor binding is elevated in the substantia nigra/ventral tegmental area (SN/VTA) compared to controls (Matuskey et al., 2011; Boileau et al., 2012). The specific role of the D3 receptor in the modulation of dopamine transmission and its function as an autoreceptor are still highly debated (Sokoloff et al., 2006). However, considering the possible implication of this receptor in modulating dopamine synthesis and release (for review, Gross and Drescher, 2012), an increase in D3 receptor levels in SN/VTA may contribute to the hypodopaminergic state observed in addiction.

In addition to alterations in the dopamine neurons themselves, it is possible that other neurotransmitter systems may be regulating the dopamine system. Candidates include the glutamatergic, GABAergic, serotoninergic, or noradrenergic afferents to the dopamine and striatal neurons, which have been reviewed previously (Melis et al., 2005; Gerfen and Surmeier, 2011). In this review, we focus on the kappa/dynorphin system as a potential modulator of dopamine release in cocaine abuse for the following reasons: (1) among the neurotransmitters that modulate dopamine transmission, evidence from human and animal studies show that cocaine exposure significantly upregulates kappa/dynorphin signaling (for review, see Wee and Koob, 2010; Muschamp and Carlezon, 2013); (2) in the striatum, dynorphin signaling strongly regulates dopamine signaling and animal studies show that activation of the kappa system reduces pre-synaptic dopamine release (Koob and Le Moal, 2008; Muschamp and Carlezon, 2013). Thus, elevated striatal dynorphin activity at the kappa receptor could be a compensatory adaptation that inhibits psychostimulant-induced dopamine release (Koob and Le Moal, 2008; Muschamp and Carlezon, 2013).

DYNORPHIN AND KAPPA RECEPTORS
KAPPA RECEPTOR/DYNORPHIN SIGNALING

Dynorphin (DYN) is the class of peptides cleaved from prodynorphin, which include dynorphin A and B (and others) which have a high affinity for the kappa receptor (KOR) (Chen et al., 2007). Currently, only one KOR subtype (type 1) has been cloned, and while types 2 and 3 have been hypothesized, they have yet to be fully characterized (Shippenberg et al., 2007). KOR selective agonists and antagonists have been developed in recent years, allowing investigation into the neurochemical and behavioral effects of the

DYN/KOR system. The KOR agonists include the arylacetamides U69593 and U50488, and salvinorin A, a naturally occurring alkaloid found in the plant *Salvia divinorum* (Von Voigtlander and Lewis, 1982; Lahti et al., 1985; Roth et al., 2002). The selective KOR antagonists include nor-binaltorphimine (nor-BNI), 5′-guanidinonaltrindole (GNTI), and JDTic (Endoh et al., 1992; Jones and Portoghese, 2000; Carroll et al., 2004). Activation of the KOR is aversive in both humans and animals, and KOR agonists are not self-administered by animals (Mucha and Herz, 1985; Tang and Collins, 1985; Pfeiffer et al., 1986; Bals-Kubik et al., 1993; Walsh et al., 2001; Wadenberg, 2003), although the same cannot be said of some humans.

KOR signaling is complex and agonists have been shown to activate, inhibit and/or have no effect on downstream signaling (i.e., cAMP, IP3/DAG, and Ca^{2+}) depending on experimental conditions (Tejeda et al., 2012). It is likely that KOR agonists display inverted U-shape effects, because of KOR ability to recruit both inhibitory $G\beta\gamma$, $G\alpha_i$, $G\alpha_o$, $G\alpha_z$, and $G\alpha_{16}$, and stimulatory, $G\alpha_s$, G-proteins (Law et al., 2000; Tejeda et al., 2012). Nanomolar ligand concentrations result in the recruitment of inhibitory G-proteins and a decrease in membrane excitability as well as transmitter release via stimulation of K^+-channel activity (Grudt and Williams, 1993) and inhibition of Ca^{2+}-channel and presynaptic release machinery activity (Gross et al., 1990; Iremonger and Bains, 2009). In contrast, sub-nanomolar ligand concentrations may result in coupling of KOR to $G\alpha$s and produce opposite effects (Crain and Shen, 1996; Tejeda et al., 2012). It should be noted that KOR activity can modulate D2 autoreceptor-dependent decrease in dopamine release by signaling interaction (Jackisch et al., 1994; Acri et al., 2001; Fuentealba et al., 2006).

KAPPA RECEPTOR/DYNORPHIN IN DIRECT AND INDIRECT PATHWAYS OF THE STRIATUM

The medium spiny neurons (MSNs) can be categorized into at least two subgroups according to their projections sites and the proteins they express (Gerfen, 2000; Gerfen and Surmeier, 2011). The "direct" or striatonigral pathway made up of MSNs that project monosynaptically to the medial globus pallidus and back to the dopamine neuron cell bodies of the substantia nigra. MSNs from the direct pathway express the dopaminergic D1 receptor, M4 muscarinic acetylcholine receptor, substance P, and dynorphin. The indirect striatopallidal pathway is composed of MSNs that project to the lateral globus pallidus, which reach the substantia nigra through synaptic relays through the lateral globus pallidus and subthalamic nucleus. These MSNs express the dopaminergic D2 receptor, adenosine receptors and enkephalin. It should be noted that the segregation of these two populations of MSNs has been established in the dorsal striatum, but that several studies show that a subpopulation of MSNs in the NAc seem to co-express D1 and D2 receptors (George and O'Dowd, 2007; Valjent et al., 2009). Dopamine can activate or inhibit cyclic AMP-dependent signaling through D1 receptor and D2 receptor respectively, as we will review below. Therefore, dopamine is likely to have differential effects on D1- and D2-expressing MSNs and recent data suggest that, cocaine administration activate signaling pathways in D1-expressing, but actively inhibits them in D2-expressing MSNs (McClung et al., 2004; Bateup et al., 2010), which could account for the imbalance between direct and indirect pathways in addiction (Lobo et al., 2010; Pascoli et al., 2012).

D1 receptors recruit adenylyl cyclase through activation of the stimulatory $G\alpha_s$ protein and consequently stimulate the production of adenosine 3′, 5′-monophosphate (cAMP) which leads to the activation of protein kinase A (PKA)-dependent signaling pathways. In contrast, D2 receptor inhibits adenylyl cyclase and cAMP/PKA pathways by recruiting inhibitory $G\alpha_i$. Accordingly, cocaine activates PKA signaling pathway mainly through activation of D1 receptor and manipulation of this pathway alters behavioral responses to cocaine (Girault, 2012). One of the downstream targets of PKA is the transcription factor CREB. Interestingly, whereas overexpression of CREB in the nucleus accumbens reduces the rewarding properties of cocaine, overexpression of a dominant-negative form enhances it (Carlezon et al., 1998; Walters and Blendy, 2001; McClung and Nestler, 2008) suggesting that activation of CREB could counteract the postsynaptic effects of cocaine and therefore decrease behavioral response to cocaine. One of the downstream genes regulated by CREB in the nucleus accumbens encodes preprodynorphin, the precursor gene product of dynorphin (McClung and Nestler, 2008). Activation of the kappa receptor decreases cocaine-induced dopamine release (for review, see Wee and Koob, 2010; Muschamp and Carlezon, 2013). Accordingly, stimulation of the D1 receptor elevates dynorphin expression, which can be blocked with receptor antagonists (Liu and Graybiel, 1998). Thus, it has been proposed that activation of the D1/PKA/CREB pathway could be counteracting the effects of cocaine through synthesis and release of dynorphin (for review, see Wee and Koob, 2010; Muschamp and Carlezon, 2013), shown in **Figure 2**.

KAPPA RECEPTOR/DYNORPHIN AND DOPAMINE SIGNALING

The DYN/KOR receptor system has been shown to play a significant role in regulating striatal dopamine transmission. DYN immunoreactive axon terminals originating from D1 receptor-expressing MSNs are found in the caudate, putamen, and nucleus accumbens (Hurd and Herkenham, 1995; Van Bockstaele et al., 1995). The KOR is expressed both pre- and post-synaptically on dopamine neurons, and the pre-synaptic KOR is apposed to DAT on the dopamine axon terminals, indicating that this system closely regulates the mesoaccumbal dopamine neurons (Svingos et al., 2001).

A number of animal studies have shown that the administration of a KOR agonist reduces dopamine levels in the striatum and dopamine neuron activity in the nucleus accumbens and ventral tegmental area (Di Chiara and Imperato, 1988; Heijna et al., 1990, 1992; Donzanti et al., 1992; Spanagel et al., 1992; Maisonneuve et al., 1994; Xi et al., 1998; Thompson et al., 2000; Margolis et al., 2003; Zhang et al., 2004b). In fact, KOR activation reduces basal dopamine levels as well as stimulant-induced dopamine release (cocaine) (Spanagel et al., 1990; Maisonneuve et al., 1994; Carlezon et al., 2006; Gehrke et al., 2008). Reverse dialysis into the nucleus accumbens reduces extracellular dopamine (Donzanti et al., 1992; Zhang et al., 2004a). Notably, this effect is seen when the KOR agonist is administered into the striatum, whereas administration into the VTA appears to be species dependent (Spanagel et al., 1992; Chefer et al., 2005; Ford et al., 2006; Margolis et al., 2006).

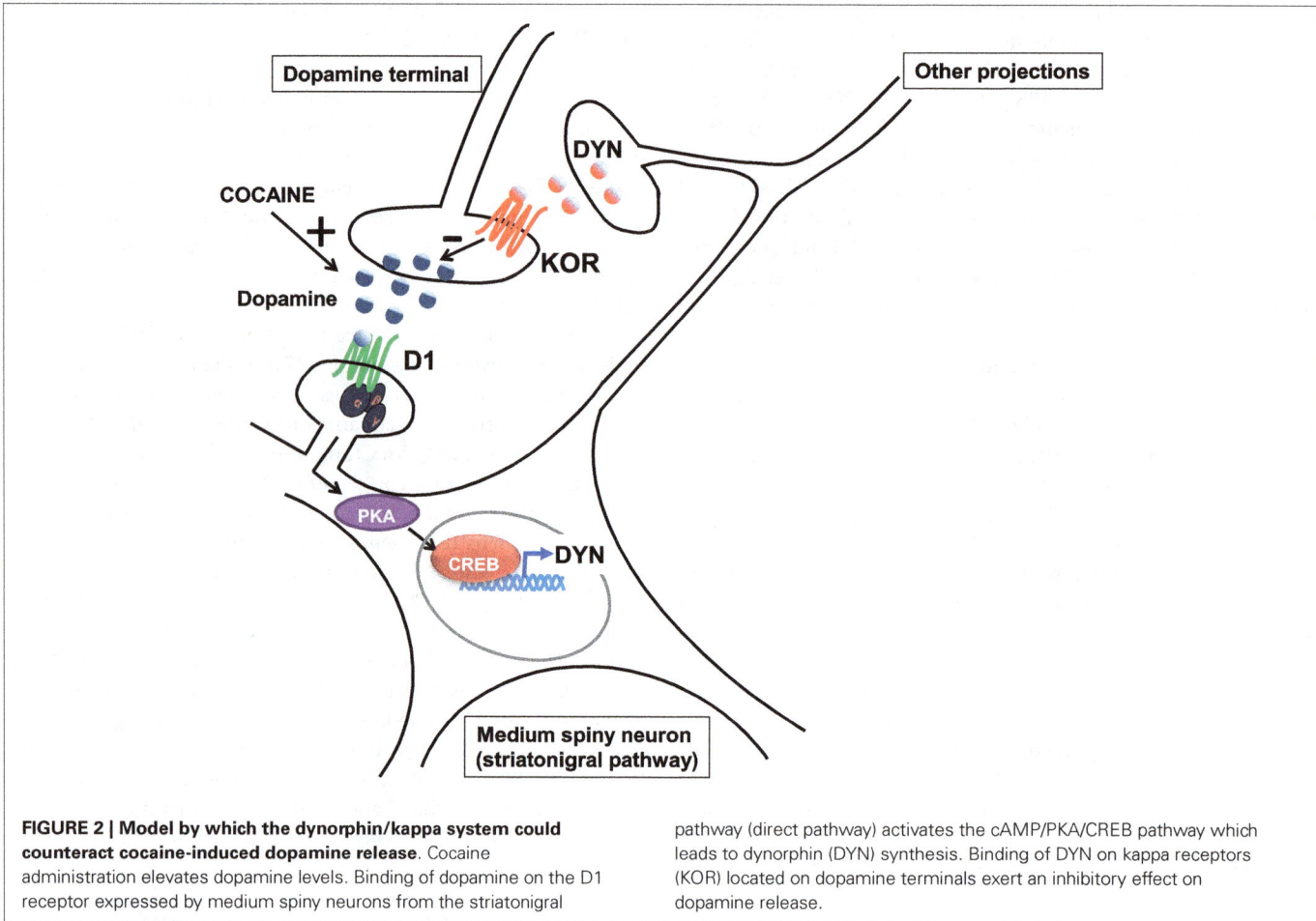

FIGURE 2 | Model by which the dynorphin/kappa system could counteract cocaine-induced dopamine release. Cocaine administration elevates dopamine levels. Binding of dopamine on the D1 receptor expressed by medium spiny neurons from the striatonigral pathway (direct pathway) activates the cAMP/PKA/CREB pathway which leads to dynorphin (DYN) synthesis. Binding of DYN on kappa receptors (KOR) located on dopamine terminals exert an inhibitory effect on dopamine release.

KOR activation has been shown to inhibit electrically evoked [³H]dopamine release in the nucleus accumbens (Heijna et al., 1992; Yokoo et al., 1992), which also shows that activation of this receptor reduces striatal dopamine transmission. More recently, Chefer et al. (2005) showed that the deletion of KOR is associated with an enhancement of basal dopamine release. Alternatively, KOR antagonists stimulate the release of dopamine in the striatum (Maisonneuve et al., 1994; You et al., 1999; Beardsley et al., 2005). Lastly, repeated KOR agonist administration reduces striatal D2 receptor density (Izenwasser et al., 1998). These findings show that DYN/KOR signaling exerts inhibitory control over dopamine release and dopamine receptor signaling in the striatum (Bruijnzeel, 2009; Wee and Koob, 2010) and demonstrate that excessive KOR activation significantly reduces striatal dopamine transmission, independent of the modality used to measure dopamine transmission.

Notably, imaging studies show that, in addition to cocaine dependence, addiction to other substances of abuse also results in blunted pre-synaptic dopamine release, measured with PET. This finding has also been reported in studies of alcohol, methamphetamine, opiate, and tobacco dependence (Martinez et al., 2007a, 2012; Busto et al., 2009; Wang et al., 2012). While some studies have shown that the DYN/KOR system plays a role in these disorders as well (for review, see Wee and Koob, 2010; Koob, 2013), the

effect of drug exposure on KOR and DYN is less clear and may even be down-regulated in methamphetamine and opiate dependence (Drakenberg et al., 2006; Frankel et al., 2007). Further studies are needed to clarify the interaction between the DYN/KOR system and dopamine signaling in these disorders.

KAPPA RECEPTOR/DYNORPHIN SYSTEM IN COCAINE ABUSE

Three post-mortem studies have been performed investigating KOR binding in cocaine abuse. The first of these, by Hurd and Herkenham (1993), showed a twofold increase in KOR binding in the caudate, but not the putamen or ventral striatum, in cocaine-dependent subjects compared to control subjects. Mash and Staley (1999) used *in vitro* autoradiography and ligand binding to map KOR in the brains of cocaine abusers and showed a twofold increase in the anterior and ventral sectors of the caudate and putamen, and nucleus accumbens compared to controls. Similar results were reported by Staley et al. (1997) who used radiolabeling to measure the KOR and reported a significant increase in KOR in the caudate, putamen, and nucleus accumbens in cocaine exposed compared to control brain tissue. These studies demonstrate that cocaine abuse or dependence is associated with a significant upregulation of the KOR in the striatum. However, to date, no human *in vivo* imaging studies of the KOR have been published in cocaine abuse. While previous PET studies imaged the mu opioid receptor in cocaine dependence (Zubieta et al., 1996; Gorelick et al., 2008), PET imaging of the KOR has not been previously possible due to the lack of an appropriate radiotracer. Therefore, correlations with clinical outcomes, such as cocaine-seeking behavior could not be performed. In addition, these post-mortem studies did not measure markers of dopamine transmission (such as receptor density or dopamine levels), so that it remains unknown whether the increase in KOR signaling coincides with a reduction in dopamine signaling largely described in PET imaging studies. Measuring both KOR binding and dopamine transmission in the same individuals will require the development of new radiotracers for KOR.

COCAINE ADMINISTRATION AND DYNORPHIN

A number of animal studies have shown that repeated cocaine administration increases levels of DYN, prodynorphin mRNA, and preprodynorphin mRNA. The initial studies measured peptide levels and showed that chronic dosing of cocaine increased striatal dynorphin levels by 40–100% (Sivam, 1989; Smiley et al., 1990). Further studies measuring prodynorphin and preprodynorphin mRNA, instead of peptide levels, have replicated these findings. Daunais et al. (Daunais et al., 1993, 1995; Daunais and McGinty, 1995, 1996) showed that cocaine self-administration increases preprodynorphin mRNA in the caudate/putamen by more than 100%. Similar results have been reported in studies by other groups as well, where the administration of cocaine has been shown to increase preprodynorphin mRNA levels 50–100% in the caudate/putamen of rats and mice (Yuferov et al., 2001; Zhou et al., 2002; Jenab et al., 2003; Schlussman et al., 2003, 2005; Zhang et al., 2013). Spangler et al. (1993, 1996) demonstrated that cocaine increased prodynorphin mRNA in the caudate/putamen by 40%, and that these levels remained elevated for days. Overall, the above studies in rodents consistently report that cocaine administration increases DYN, prodynorphin, and preprodynorphin mRNA with levels ranging from about 40 to 100%. Previous studies have shown that the levels of DYN peptide and prodynorphin/preprodynorphin mRNAs correlate with each other, suggesting that increases in mRNAs closely reflect increases in the peptide itself (Li et al., 1988; Sivam, 1996).

These findings in rodents have been replicated in studies of rhesus monkeys and humans. Fagergren et al. (2003) performed a study in rhesus monkeys who self-administered cocaine and showed that prodynorphin mRNA levels were increased in the dorsolateral caudate (83%), central caudate (34%), and the dorsal putamen (194%). In humans, Hurd and Herkenham (1993) first reported that cocaine abuse was associated with an increase in preprodynorphin mRNA in the putamen and caudate in a post-mortem study of cocaine abusing subjects compared to control subjects. More recently, Frankel et al. (2008) measured DYN peptide levels in a post-mortem study of cocaine abusers and controls subjects, and reported a significant increase in DYN in the caudate and a trend toward a significant increase in the putamen compared to control subjects. A very large increase was seen in the ventral pallidum but no difference was seen in the thalamus, frontal, temporal, parietal, and occipital cortices. Taken together, these studies indicate that cocaine exposure increases striatal DYN signaling at the kappa receptor in rodents, non-human primates,

and humans. Considering the effect of DYN on dopamine signaling, it is likely that the sustained increase in DYN levels by cocaine exposure participates to the hypodopaminergic state described in cocaine abusers.

Theses findings in human and animal studies suggest that treatments that target KOR signaling would modulate cocaine-seeking behavior. However, animal studies exploring the effect of KOR agonist or antagonist administration on cocaine self-administration are mixed (for review, see Wee and Koob, 2010; Butelman et al., 2012). Partly, this effect depends on the reinforcement schedule used, doses of drug administered, and timing of the effect, since changes in KOR/DYN have a slow onset (Wee et al., 2009; Knoll et al., 2011). Moreover, the DYN/KOR system appears to play a more significant role in mediating the aversive effects that occur with cocaine exposure.

KAPPA RECEPTOR/DYNORPHIN AND STRESSED-INDUCED COCAINE-SEEKING BEHAVIOR

Animal studies have investigated the relationship between KOR activation and stress-induced cocaine-seeking behavior. DYN is released in response to physical stress in the striatum, amygdala, and hippocampus (Shirayama et al., 2004; Land et al., 2008), and blockade of the KOR reduces the effects of stress on cocaine-seeking behavior. McLaughlin et al. (2003) showed that swim stress and social defeat stress both significantly enhance conditioned place preference (CPP) for cocaine in mice. This effect was blocked by KOR antagonist administration and was not seen in prodynorphin knock-out mice (McLaughlin et al., 2003, 2006). In addition, the administration of a KOR agonist prior to cocaine conditioning was shown to be as effective as stress in potentiating subsequent cocaine-induced CPP (McLaughlin et al., 2006). Beardsley et al. (2005) showed that lever pressing for cocaine is reinstated in rodents following uncontrollable footshock, and that this effect is blocked by the administration of JDTic, a KOR antagonist. Along these same lines, Redila and Chavkin (2008) showed that intermittent foot shock, forced swim, and KOR agonist administration all reinstate cocaine CPP in mice. This effect was blocked with pre-treatment with the KOR antagonist nor-BNI, and did not occur in mice lacking either the KOR or prodynorphin. Carey et al. (2007) also showed that pre-treatment with a KOR antagonist blocked stress-induced reinstatement of cocaine CPP.

These studies show that signaling at the KOR plays a significant role in cocaine-seeking behavior following stress. Recent studies have also shown that DYN signaling and corticotropin releasing factor (CRF) function together to increase the negative reinforcing effects of cocaine (Koob et al., 2004). Land et al. (2008) used a phospho-selective antibody for the activated form of KOR and showed that both physical stress and CRF administration resulted in DYN-dependent activation of the KOR. Valdez et al. (2007) showed that, in monkeys, cocaine-seeking behavior is reinstated by the administration of a KOR agonist, and that this effect is blocked by CRF antagonist administration. KOR agonists stimulate the HPA axis in rodents and humans (Ur et al., 1997; Laorden et al., 2000), and it has previously been reported that KOR activation elicits CRF release (Nikolarakis et al., 1986; Song and Takemori, 1992) and vice-versa (Land et al., 2008).

Studies in human cocaine abusers have also shown that stress increases the risk of drug abuse and relapse (De La Garza et al., 2009). The pharmacological or psychological activation of the hypothalamic pituitary adrenal axis has been shown to increase craving in addition to the probability of increased cocaine use (Elman et al., 2003; Shoptaw et al., 2004; Elman and Lukas, 2005). Sinha and colleagues have shown that stress imagery increases anxiety and craving for cocaine (Sinha et al., 1999, 2006; Fox et al., 2006). Importantly, this group has also shown that stress-induced cocaine craving is associated with a shorter time to relapse in cocaine-dependent subjects following discharge from inpatient treatment (Sinha et al., 2006). To date, the imaging studies in addiction have not focused on stress-induced reinstatement of cocaine-seeking behavior, and future research should focus on the role of dopamine and KOR signaling and stress.

Thus, DYN/KOR signaling appears to play a crucial role in reinstating drug-seeking behavior by mediating the negative effects associated with drug cessation and stress-induced drug taking (Koob and Le Moal, 2008; Muschamp and Carlezon, 2013).

CONCLUSION

The data presented here suggest that blunted striatal dopamine release measured with imaging in cocaine dependence may be associated with an upregulation of DYN. Acting at the KOR of the dopamine terminals, KOR activation would be expected to produce a decrease in striatal dopamine release. Post-mortem studies in cocaine abusers and animal studies show that both KOR and DYN are upregulated following chronic cocaine exposure, and that this effect is long lasting (Spangler et al., 1993, 1996). In addition, the imaging studies in cocaine abusers show that blunted dopamine release is associated with an increased risk of relapse while animal studies show that activation of the KOR increases cocaine self-administration. However, studies have not been conducted measuring KOR and striatal dopamine signaling in human cocaine abusers concurrently. Thus, future studies imaging the KOR in cocaine abusers and correlating their level directly with dopamine transmission, and with relevant clinical outcomes, is needed.

Chronic cocaine exposure induces CREB phosphorylation and changes in gene expression, which increase expression of prodynorphin mRNA in the nucleus accumbens in addition to other factors. As described above, excessive DYN signaling results in a decrease in extracellular dopamine release, which has been shown in the imaging studies of human cocaine abusers. These findings suggest that increasing signaling at the dopamine receptors may be an appropriate treatment approach, but clinical studies using dopamine agonists have not shown efficacy (Amato et al., 2011). Thus, pharmacologic manipulations that increase endogenous dopamine may be of use, particularly since imaging studies show that intact dopamine signaling is predictive of a positive treatment response. The data reviewed here suggest that KOR antagonists would be expected to counteract the effects of DYN upregulation and may restore pre-synaptic dopamine release. In addition, KOR antagonists have very limited, if any, nervous system side effects (Kreek et al., 2012) and block stress-induced cocaine self-administration in animal studies. Together, these findings suggest that KOR antagonists may provide an important avenue for future treatment development for cocaine addiction (Muschamp and Carlezon, 2013).

REFERENCES

Abi-Dargham, A., Simpson, N., Kegeles, L., Parsey, R., Hwang, D. R., Anjilvel, S., et al. (1999). PET studies of binding competition between endogenous dopamine and the D1 radiotracer [11C]NNC 756. *Synapse* 32, 93–109. doi:10.1002/(SICI)1098-2396(199905)32:2<93::AID-SYN3>3.0.CO;2-C

Ackerman, J. M., and White, F. J. (1992). Decreased activity of rat A10 dopamine neurons following withdrawal from repeated cocaine. *Eur. J. Pharmacol.* 218, 171–173. doi:10.1016/0014-2999(92)90161-V

Acri, J. B., Thompson, A. C., and Shippenberg, T. (2001). Modulation of pre- and post-synaptic dopamine D2 receptor function by the selective kappa-opioid receptor agonist U69593. *Synapse* 39, 343–350. doi:10.1002/1098-2396(20010315)39:4<343::AID-SYN1018>3.0.CO;2-Q

Amato, L., Minozzi, S., Pani, P. P., Solimini, R., Vecchi, S., Zuccaro, P., et al. (2011). Dopamine agonists for the treatment of cocaine dependence. *Cochrane Database Syst. Rev.* CD003352.

Bals-Kubik, R., Ableitner, A., Herz, A., and Shippenberg, T. S. (1993). Neuroanatomical sites mediating the motivational effects of opioids as mapped by the conditioned place preference paradigm in rats. *J. Pharmacol. Exp. Ther.* 264, 489–495.

Bateup, H. S., Santini, E., Shen, W., Birnbaum, S., Valjent, E., Surmeier, D. J., et al. (2010). Distinct subclasses of medium spiny neurons differentially regulate striatal motor behaviors. *Proc. Natl. Acad. Sci. U.S.A.* 107, 14845–14850. doi:10.1073/pnas.1009874107

Beardsley, P. M., Howard, J. L., Shelton, K. L., and Carroll, F. I. (2005). Differential effects of the novel kappa opioid receptor antagonist, JDTic, on reinstatement of cocaine-seeking induced by footshock stressors vs. cocaine primes and its antidepressant-like effects in rats. *Psychopharmacology (Berl.)* 183, 118–126. doi:10.1007/s00213-005-0167-4

Berridge, K. C. (2007). The debate over dopamine's role in reward: the case for incentive salience. *Psychopharmacology (Berl.)* 191, 391–431. doi:10.1007/s00213-006-0578-x

Bisaga, A., Aharonovich, E., Cheng, W. Y., Levin, F. R., Mariani, J. J., Raby, W. N., et al. (2010). A placebo-controlled trial of memantine for cocaine dependence with high-value voucher incentives during a pre-randomization lead-in period. *Drug Alcohol Depend.* 111, 97–104. doi:10.1016/j.drugalcdep.2010.04.006

Boileau, I., Payer, D., Houle, S., Behzadi, A., Rusjan, P. M., Tong, J., et al. (2012). Higher binding of the dopamine D3 receptor-preferring ligand [11C]-(+)-propyl-hexahydro-naphtho-oxazin in methamphetamine polydrug users: a positron emission tomography study. *J. Neurosci.* 32, 1353–1359. doi:10.1523/JNEUROSCI.4371-11.2012

Breier, A., Su, T. P., Saunders, R., Carson, R. E., Kolachana, B. S., Debartolomeis, A., et al. (1997). Schizophrenia is associated with elevated amphetamine-induced synaptic dopamine concentrations: evidence from a novel positron emission tomography method. *Proc. Natl. Acad. Sci. U.S.A.* 94, 2569–2574. doi:10.1073/pnas.94.6.2569

Brodie, M. S., and Dunwiddie, T. V. (1990). Cocaine effects in the ventral tegmental area: evidence for an indirect dopaminergic mechanism of action. *Naunyn Schmiedebergs Arch. Pharmacol.* 342, 660–665. doi:10.1007/BF00175709

Bruijnzeel, A. W. (2009). kappa-Opioid receptor signaling and brain reward function. *Brain Res. Rev.* 62, 127–146. doi:10.1016/j.brainresrev.2009.09.008

Busto, U. E., Redden, L., Mayberg, H., Kapur, S., Houle, S., and Zawertailo, L. A. (2009). Dopaminergic activity in depressed smokers: a positron emission tomography study. *Synapse* 63, 681–689. doi:10.1002/syn.20646

Butelman, E. R., Yuferov, V., and Kreek, M. J. (2012). kappa-Opioid receptor/dynorphin system: genetic and pharmacotherapeutic implications for addiction. *Trends Neurosci.* 35, 587–596. doi:10.1016/j.tins.2012.05.005

Kappa-opioid receptor signaling in the striatum as a potential modulator of dopamine transmission in cocaine...

85

Carey, A. N., Borozny, K., Aldrich, J. V., and McLaughlin, J. P. (2007). Reinstatement of cocaine place-conditioning prevented by the peptide kappa-opioid receptor antagonist arodyn. *Eur. J. Pharmacol.* 569, 84–89. doi:10.1016/j.ejphar.2007.05.007

Carlezon, W. A. Jr., Beguin, C., Dinieri, J. A., Baumann, M. H., Richards, M. R., Todtenkopf, M. S., et al. (2006). Depressive-like effects of the kappa-opioid receptor agonist salvinorin A on behavior and neurochemistry in rats. *J. Pharmacol. Exp. Ther.* 316, 440–447. doi:10.1124/jpet.105.092304

Carlezon, W. A. Jr., Thome, J., Olson, V. G., Lane-Ladd, S. B., Brodkin, E. S., Hiroi, N., et al. (1998). Regulation of cocaine reward by CREB. *Science* 282, 2272–2275. doi:10.1126/science.282.5397.2272

Carroll, I., Thomas, J. B., Dykstra, L. A., Granger, A. L., Allen, R. M., Howard, J. L., et al. (2004). Pharmacological properties of JDTic: a novel kappa-opioid receptor antagonist. *Eur. J. Pharmacol.* 501, 111–119. doi:10.1016/j.ejphar.2004.08.028

Castner, S. A., Al-Tikriti, M. S., Baldwin, R. M., Seibyl, J. P., Innis, R. B., and Goldman-Rakic, P. S. (2000). Behavioral changes and [123I]IBZM equilibrium SPECT measurement of amphetamine-induced dopamine release in rhesus monkeys exposed to subchronic amphetamine. *Neuropsychopharmacology* 22, 4–13. doi:10.1016/S0893-133X(99)00080-9

Chefer, V. I., Czyzyk, T., Bolan, E. A., Moron, J., Pintar, J. E., and Shippenberg, T. S. (2005). Endogenous kappa-opioid receptor systems regulate mesoaccumbal dopamine dynamics and vulnerability to cocaine. *J. Neurosci.* 25, 5029–5037. doi:10.1523/JNEUROSCI.0854-05.2005

Chen, Y., Chen, C., and Liu-Chen, L. Y. (2007). Dynorphin peptides differentially regulate the human kappa opioid receptor. *Life Sci.* 80, 1439–1448. doi:10.1016/j.lfs.2007.01.018

Chou, Y. H., Karlsson, P., Halldin, C., Olsson, H., and Farde, L. (1999). A PET study of D(1)-like dopamine receptor ligand binding during altered endogenous dopamine levels in the primate brain. *Psychopharmacology (Berl.)* 146, 220–227. doi:10.1007/s002130051110

Crain, S. M., and Shen, K. F. (1996). Modulatory effects of Gs-coupled excitatory opioid receptor functions on opioid analgesia, tolerance, and dependence. *Neurochem. Res.* 21, 1347–1351. doi:10.1007/BF02532375

Czoty, P. W., Morgan, D., Shannon, E. E., Gage, H. D., and Nader, M. A. (2004). Characterization of dopamine D1 and D2 receptor function in socially housed cynomolgus monkeys self-administering cocaine. *Psychopharmacology (Berl.)* 174, 381–388. doi:10.1007/s00213-003-1752-z

Dalley, J. W., Everitt, B. J., and Robbins, T. W. (2011). Impulsivity, compulsivity, and top-down cognitive control. *Neuron* 69, 680–694. doi:10.1016/j.neuron.2011.01.020

Dalley, J. W., Fryer, T. D., Brichard, L., Robinson, E. S., Theobald, D. E., Laane, K., et al. (2007). Nucleus accumbens D2/3 receptors predict trait impulsivity and cocaine reinforcement. *Science* 315, 1267–1270. doi:10.1126/science.1137073

Daunais, J. B., and McGinty, J. F. (1995). Cocaine binges differentially alter striatal preprodynorphin and zif/268 mRNAs. *Brain Res. Mol. Brain Res.* 29, 201–210. doi:10.1016/0169-328X(94)00246-B

Daunais, J. B., and McGinty, J. F. (1996). The effects of D1 or D2 dopamine receptor blockade on zif/268 and preprodynorphin gene expression in rat forebrain following a short-term cocaine binge. *Brain Res. Mol. Brain Res.* 35, 237–248. doi:10.1016/0169-328X(95)00226-I

Daunais, J. B., Roberts, D. C., and McGinty, J. F. (1993). Cocaine self-administration increases preprodynorphin, but not c-fos, mRNA in rat striatum. *Neuroreport* 4, 543–546. doi:10.1097/00001756-199305000-00020

Daunais, J. B., Roberts, D. C., and McGinty, J. F. (1995). Short-term cocaine self administration alters striatal gene expression. *Brain Res. Bull.* 37, 523–527. doi:10.1016/0361-9230(95)00049-K

De La Garza, R. II, Ashbrook, L. H., Evans, S. E., Jacobsen, C. A., Kalechstein, A. D., and Newton, T. F. (2009). Influence of verbal recall of a recent stress experience on anxiety and desire for cocaine in non-treatment seeking, cocaine-addicted volunteers. *Am. J. Addict.* 18, 481–487. doi:10.3109/10550490903205876

Di Chiara, G., and Imperato, A. (1988). Opposite effects of mu and kappa opiate agonists on dopamine release in the nucleus accumbens and in the dorsal caudate of freely moving rats. *J. Pharmacol. Exp. Ther.* 244, 1067–1080.

Donzanti, B. A., Althaus, J. S., Payson, M. M., and Von Voigtlander, P. F. (1992). Kappa agonist-induced reduction in dopamine release: site of action and tolerance. *Res. Commun. Chem. Pathol. Pharmacol.* 78, 193–210.

Drakenberg, K., Nikoshkov, A., Horvath, M. C., Fagergren, P., Gharibyan, A., Saarelainen, K., et al. (2006). Mu opioid receptor A118G polymorphism in association with striatal opioid neuropeptide gene expression in heroin abusers. *Proc. Natl. Acad. Sci. U.S.A.* 103, 7883–7888. doi:10.1073/pnas.0600871103

Drevets, W. C., Gautier, C., Price, J. C., Kupfer, D. J., Kinahan, P. E., Grace, A. A., et al. (2001). Amphetamine-induced dopamine release in human ventral striatum correlates with euphoria. *Biol. Psychiatry* 49, 81–96. doi:10.1016/S0006-3223(00)01038-6

Elman, I., and Lukas, S. E. (2005). Effects of cortisol and cocaine on plasma prolactin and growth hormone levels in cocaine-dependent volunteers. *Addict. Behav.* 30, 859–864. doi:10.1016/j.addbeh.2004.08.019

Elman, I., Lukas, S. E., Karlsgodt, K. H., Gasic, G. P., and Breiter, H. C. (2003). Acute cortisol administration triggers craving in individuals with cocaine dependence. *Psychopharmacol. Bull.* 37, 84–89.

Endoh, T., Matsuura, H., Tanaka, C., and Nagase, H. (1992). Norbinaltorphimine: a potent and selective kappa-opioid receptor antagonist with long-lasting activity in vivo. *Arch. Int. Pharmacodyn. Ther.* 316, 30–42.

Endres, C. J., Kolachana, B. S., Saunders, R. C., Su, T., Weinberger, D., Breier, A., et al. (1997). Kinetic modeling of [C-11]raclopride: combined PET-microdialysis studies. *J. Cereb. Blood Flow Metab.* 17, 932–942. doi:10.1097/00004647-199709000-00002

Everitt, B. J., Belin, D., Economidou, D., Pelloux, Y., Dalley, J. W., and Robbins, T. W. (2008). Review. Neural mechanisms underlying the vulnerability to develop compulsive drug-seeking habits and addiction. *Philos. Trans. R. Soc. Lond. B Biol. Sci.* 363, 3125–3135. doi:10.1098/rstb.2008.0089

Fagergren, P., Smith, H. R., Daunais, J. B., Nader, M. A., Porrino, L. J., and Hurd, Y. L. (2003). Temporal upregulation of prodynorphin mRNA in the primate striatum after cocaine self-administration. *Eur. J. Neurosci.* 17, 2212–2218. doi:10.1046/j.1460-9568.2003.02636.x

Ford, C. P., Mark, G. P., and Williams, J. T. (2006). Properties and opioid inhibition of mesolimbic dopamine neurons vary according to target location. *J. Neurosci.* 26, 2788–2797. doi:10.1523/JNEUROSCI.4331-05.2006

Fox, H. C., Garcia, M. Jr., Kemp, K., Milivojevic, V., Kreek, M. J., and Sinha, R. (2006). Gender differences in cardiovascular and corticoadrenal response to stress and drug cues in cocaine dependent individuals. *Psychopharmacology (Berl.)* 185, 348–357. doi:10.1007/s00213-005-0303-1

Frankel, P. S., Alburges, M. E., Bush, L., Hanson, G. R., and Kish, S. J. (2007). Brain levels of neuropeptides in human chronic methamphetamine users. *Neuropharmacology* 53, 447–454. doi:10.1016/j.neuropharm.2007.06.009

Frankel, P. S., Alburges, M. E., Bush, L., Hanson, G. R., and Kish, S. J. (2008). Striatal and ventral pallidum dynorphin concentrations are markedly increased in human chronic cocaine users. *Neuropharmacology* 55, 41–46. doi:10.1016/j.neuropharm.2008.04.019

Fuentealba, J. A., Gysling, K., Magendzo, K., and Andres, M. E. (2006). Repeated administration of the selective kappa-opioid receptor agonist U-69593 increases stimulated dopamine extracellular levels in the rat nucleus accumbens. *J. Neurosci. Res.* 84, 450–459. doi:10.1002/jnr.20890

Fusar-Poli, P., and Meyer-Lindenberg, A. (2013). Striatal presynaptic dopamine in schizophrenia, part I: meta-analysis of dopamine active transporter (DAT) density. *Schizophr. Bull.* 39, 22–32. doi:10.1093/schbul/sbr111

Gao, W. Y., Lee, T. H., King, G. R., and Ellinwood, E. H. (1998). Alterations in baseline activity and quinpirole sensitivity in putative dopamine neurons in the substantia nigra and ventral tegmental area after withdrawal from cocaine pretreatment. *Neuropsychopharmacology* 18, 222–232. doi:10.1016/S0893-133X(97)00132-2

Gehrke, B. J., Chefer, V. I., and Shippenberg, T. S. (2008). Effects of acute and repeated administration of salvinorin A on dopamine function in the rat dorsal striatum. *Psychopharmacology (Berl.)* 197, 509–517. doi:10.1007/s00213-007-1067-6

George, S. R., and O'Dowd, B. F. (2007). A novel dopamine receptor signaling unit in brain: heterooligomers of D1 and D2 dopamine receptors. *ScientificWorldJournal* 7, 58–63. doi:10.1100/tsw.2007.223

Gerfen, C. R. (2000). Molecular effects of dopamine on striatal-projection pathways. *Trends Neurosci.* 23, S64–S70. doi:10.1016/S1471-1931(00)00019-7

Gerfen, C. R., and Surmeier, D. J. (2011). Modulation of striatal projection systems by dopamine. *Annu. Rev. Neurosci.* 34, 441–466. doi:10.1146/annurev-neuro-061010-113641

Gerrits, M. A., Petromilli, P., Westenberg, H. G., Di Chiara, G., and Van Ree, J. M. (2002). Decrease in basal dopamine levels in the nucleus accumbens shell during daily drug-seeking behaviour in rats. *Brain Res.* 924, 141–150. doi:10.1016/S0006-8993(01)03105-5

Girault, J. A. (2012). Signaling in striatal neurons: the phosphoproteins of reward, addiction, and dyskinesia. *Prog. Mol. Biol. Transl. Sci.* 106, 33–62. doi:10.1016/B978-0-12-396456-4.00006-7

Gorelick, D. A., Kim, Y. K., Bencherif, B., Boyd, S. J., Nelson, R., Copersino, M. L., et al. (2008). Brain mu-opioid receptor binding: relationship to relapse to cocaine use after monitored abstinence. *Psychopharmacology (Berl.)* 200, 475–486. doi:10.1007/s00213-008-1225-5

Groman, S. M., and Jentsch, J. D. (2012). Cognitive control and the dopamine D(2)-like receptor: a dimensional understanding of addiction. *Depress. Anxiety* 29, 295–306. doi:10.1002/da.20897

Gross, G., and Drescher, K. (2012). "The role of dopamine D(3) receptors in antipsychotic activity and cognitive functions," in *Handbook of Experimental Pharmacology*, eds M. Geyer and G. Gross (Heidelberg: Springer), 167–210.

Gross, R. A., Moises, H. C., Uhler, M. D., and Macdonald, R. L. (1990). Dynorphin A and cAMP-dependent protein kinase independently regulate neuronal calcium currents. *Proc. Natl. Acad. Sci. U.S.A.* 87, 7025–7029. doi:10.1073/pnas.87.18.7025

Grudt, T. J., and Williams, J. T. (1993). kappa-Opioid receptors also increase potassium conductance. *Proc. Natl. Acad. Sci. U.S.A.* 90, 11429–11432. doi:10.1073/pnas.90.23.11429

Haney, M., Collins, E. D., Ward, A. S., Foltin, R. W., and Fischman, M. W. (1999). Effect of a selective dopamine D1 agonist (ABT-431) on smoked cocaine self-administration in humans. *Psychopharmacology (Berl.)* 143, 102–110. doi:10.1007/s002130050925

Haney, M., Ward, A. S., Foltin, R. W., and Fischman, M. W. (2001). Effects of ecopipam, a selective dopamine D1 antagonist, on smoked cocaine self-administration by humans. *Psychopharmacology (Berl.)* 155, 330–337. doi:10.1007/s002130100725

Heijna, M. H., Bakker, J. M., Hogenboom, F., Mulder, A. H., and Schoffelmeer, A. N. (1992). Opioid receptors and inhibition of dopamine-sensitive adenylate cyclase in slices of rat brain regions receiving a dense dopaminergic input. *Eur. J. Pharmacol.* 229, 197–202. doi:10.1016/0014-2999(92)90555-I

Heijna, M. H., Padt, M., Hogenboom, F., Portoghese, P. S., Mulder, A. H., and Schoffelmeer, A. N. (1990). Opioid receptor-mediated inhibition of dopamine and acetylcholine release from slices of rat nucleus accumbens, olfactory tubercle and frontal cortex. *Eur. J. Pharmacol.* 181, 267–278. doi:10.1016/0014-2999(90)90088-N

Hurd, Y. L., and Herkenham, M. (1993). Molecular alterations in the neostriatum of human cocaine addicts. *Synapse* 13, 357–369. doi:10.1002/syn.890130408

Hurd, Y. L., and Herkenham, M. (1995). The human neostriatum shows compartmentalization of neuropeptide gene expression in dorsal and ventral regions: an in situ hybridization histochemical analysis. *Neuroscience* 64, 571–586. doi:10.1016/0306-4522(94)00417-4

Innis, R. B., Cunningham, V. J., Delforge, J., Fujita, M., Gjedde, A., Gunn, R. N., et al. (2007). Consensus nomenclature for in vivo imaging of reversibly binding radioligands. *J. Cereb. Blood Flow Metab.* 27, 1533–1539. doi:10.1038/sj.jcbfm.9600493

Iremonger, K. J., and Bains, J. S. (2009). Retrograde opioid signaling regulates glutamatergic transmission in the hypothalamus. *J. Neurosci.* 29, 7349–7358. doi:10.1523/JNEUROSCI.0381-09.2009

Izenwasser, S., Acri, J. B., Kunko, P. M., and Shippenberg, T. (1998). Repeated treatment with the selective kappa opioid agonist U-69593 produces a marked depletion of dopamine D2 receptors. *Synapse* 30, 275–283. doi:10.1002/(SICI)1098-2396(199811)30:3<275::AID-SYN5>3.0.CO;2-8

Jackisch, R., Hotz, H., Allgaier, C., and Hertting, G. (1994). Presynaptic opioid receptors on dopaminergic nerves in the rabbit caudate nucleus: coupling to pertussis toxin-sensitive G-proteins and interaction with D2 autoreceptors? *Naunyn Schmiedebergs Arch. Pharmacol.* 349, 250–258. doi:10.1007/BF00169291

Jenab, S., Festa, E. D., Russo, S. J., Wu, H. B., Inturrisi, C. E., and Quinones-Jenab, V. (2003). MK-801 attenuates cocaine induction of c-fos and pre-prodynorphin mRNA levels in Fischer rats. *Brain Res. Mol. Brain Res.* 117, 237–239. doi:10.1016/S0169-328X(03)00319-X

Jones, R. M., and Portoghese, P. S. (2000). 5'-Guanidinonaltrindole, a highly selective and potent kappa-opioid receptor antagonist. *Eur. J. Pharmacol.* 396, 49–52. doi:10.1016/S0014-2999(00)00208-9

Kirkland Henry, P., Davis, M., and Howell, L. L. (2009). Effects of cocaine self-administration history under limited and extended access conditions on in vivo striatal dopamine neurochemistry and acoustic startle in rhesus monkeys. *Psychopharmacology (Berl.)* 205, 237–247. doi:10.1007/s00213-009-1534-3

Knoll, A. T., Muschamp, J. W., Sillivan, S. E., Ferguson, D., Dietz, D. M., Meloni, E. G., et al. (2011). Kappa opioid receptor signaling in the basolateral amygdala regulates conditioned fear and anxiety in rats. *Biol. Psychiatry* 70, 425–433. doi:10.1016/j.biopsych.2011.03.017

Koob, G. F. (2013). Theoretical frameworks and mechanistic aspects of alcohol addiction: alcohol addiction as a reward deficit disorder. *Curr. Top. Behav. Neurosci.* 13, 3–30. doi:10.1007/7854_2011_129

Koob, G. F., Ahmed, S. H., Boutrel, B., Chen, S. A., Kenny, P. J., Markou, A., et al. (2004). Neurobiological mechanisms in the transition from drug use to drug dependence. *Neurosci. Biobehav. Rev.* 27, 739–749. doi:10.1016/j.neubiorev.2003.11.007

Koob, G. F., and Le Moal, M. (2008). Addiction and the brain antireward system. *Annu. Rev. Psychol.* 59, 29–53. doi:10.1146/annurev.psych.59.103006.093548

Kreek, M. J., Levran, O., Reed, B., Schlussman, S. D., Zhou, Y., and Butelman, E. R. (2012). Opiate addiction and cocaine addiction: underlying molecular neurobiology and genetics. *J. Clin. Invest.* 122, 3387–3393. doi:10.1172/JCI60390

Lacey, M. G., Mercuri, N. B., and North, R. A. (1990). Actions of cocaine on rat dopaminergic neurones in vitro. *Br. J. Pharmacol.* 99, 731–735. doi:10.1111/j.1476-5381.1990.tb12998.x

Lahti, R. A., Mickelson, M. M., McCall, J. M., and Von Voigtlander, P. F. (1985). [3H]U-69593 a highly selective ligand for the opioid kappa receptor. *Eur. J. Pharmacol.* 109, 281–284. doi:10.1016/0014-2999(85)90431-5

Land, B. B., Bruchas, M. R., Lemos, J. C., Xu, M., Melief, E. J., and Chavkin, C. (2008). The dysphoric component of stress is encoded by activation of the dynorphin kappa-opioid system. *J. Neurosci.* 28, 407–414. doi:10.1523/JNEUROSCI.4458-07.2008

Laorden, M. L., Castells, M. T., Martinez, M. D., Martinez, P. J., and Milanes, M. V. (2000). Activation of c-fos expression in hypothalamic nuclei by mu- and kappa-receptor agonists: correlation with catecholaminergic activity in the hypothalamic paraventricular nucleus. *Endocrinology* 141, 1366–1376. doi:10.1210/en.141.4.1366

Laruelle, M. (2000). Imaging synaptic neurotransmission with in vivo binding competition techniques: a critical review. *J. Cereb. Blood Flow Metab.* 20, 423–451. doi:10.1097/00004647-200003000-00001

Laruelle, M., Iyer, R. N., Al-Tikriti, M. S., Zea-Ponce, Y., Malison, R., Zoghbi, S. S., et al. (1997). Microdialysis and SPECT measurements of amphetamine-induced dopamine release in nonhuman primates. *Synapse* 25, 1–14. doi:10.1002/(SICI)1098-2396(199701)25:1<1::AID-SYN1>3.0.CO;2-H

Law, P. Y., Wong, Y. H., and Loh, H. H. (2000). Molecular mechanisms and regulation of opioid receptor signaling. *Annu. Rev. Pharmacol. Toxicol.* 40, 389–430. doi:10.1146/annurev.pharmtox.40.1.389

Lee, T. H., Gao, W. Y., Davidson, C., and Ellinwood, E. H. (1999). Altered activity of midbrain dopamine neurons following 7-day withdrawal from chronic cocaine abuse is normalized by D2 receptor stimulation during the early withdrawal phase. *Neuropsychopharmacology* 21, 127–136. doi:10.1016/S0893-133X(99)00011-1

Li, S. J., Sivam, S. P., McGinty, J. F., Jiang, H. K., Douglass, J., Calavetta, L., et al. (1988). Regulation of the metabolism of striatal dynorphin by the dopaminergic system. *J. Pharmacol. Exp. Ther.* 246, 403–408.

Little, K. Y., Kirkman, J. A., Carroll, F. I., Clark, T. B., and Duncan, G. E. (1993). Cocaine use increases [3H]WIN 35428 binding sites in human striatum. *Brain Res.* 628, 17–25. doi:10.1016/0006-8993(93)90932-D

Little, K. Y., Zhang, L., Desmond, T., Frey, K. A., Dalack, G. W., and Cassin, B. J. (1999). Striatal dopaminergic abnormalities in human cocaine users. *Am. J. Psychiatry* 156, 238–245.

Liu, F. C., and Graybiel, A. M. (1998). Dopamine and calcium signal interactions in the developing striatum: control by kinetics of CREB phosphorylation. *Adv. Pharmacol.* 42, 682–686. doi:10.1016/S1054-3589(08)60840-6

Lobo, M. K., Covington, H. E. III, Chaudhury, D., Friedman, A. K., Sun, H., Damez-Werno, D., et al. (2010). Cell type-specific loss of BDNF signaling mimics optogenetic control of cocaine reward. *Science* 330, 385–390. doi:10.1126/science.1188472

Maisonneuve, I. M., Archer, S., and Glick, S. D. (1994). U50,488, a kappa agonist, attenuates cocaine-induced increases in extracellular dopamine in the nucleus accumbens of rats. *Neurosci. Lett.* 181, 57–60. doi:10.1016/0304-3940(94)90559-2

Malison, R. T., Best, S. E., Van Dyck, C. H., McCance, E. F., Wallace, E. A., Laruelle, M., et al. (1998). Elevated striatal dopamine transporters during acute cocaine abstinence as measured by [123I] beta-CIT SPECT. *Am. J. Psychiatry* 155, 832–834.

Malison, R. T., Mechanic, K. Y., Klummp, H., Baldwin, R. M., Kosten, T. R., Seibyl, J. P., et al. (1999). Reduced amphetamine-stimulated dopamine release in cocaine addicts as measured by [123I]IBZM SPECT. *J. Nucl. Med.* 40, 110.

Margolis, E. B., Hjelmstad, G. O., Bonci, A., and Fields, H. L. (2003). Kappa-opioid agonists directly inhibit midbrain dopaminergic neurons. *J. Neurosci.* 23, 9981–9986.

Margolis, E. B., Lock, H., Chefer, V. I., Shippenberg, T. S., Hjelmstad, G. O., and Fields, H. L. (2006). Kappa opioids selectively control dopaminergic neurons projecting to the prefrontal cortex. *Proc. Natl. Acad. Sci. U.S.A.* 103, 2938–2942. doi:10.1073/pnas.0511159103

Marinelli, M., Cooper, D. C., Baker, L. K., and White, F. J. (2003). Impulse activity of midbrain dopamine neurons modulates drug-seeking behavior. *Psychopharmacology (Berl.)* 168, 84–98. doi:10.1007/s00213-003-1491-1

Martinez, D., Broft, A., Foltin, R. W., Slifstein, M., Hwang, D. R., Huang, Y., et al. (2004). Cocaine dependence and d2 receptor availability in the functional subdivisions of the striatum: relationship with cocaine-seeking behavior. *Neuropsychopharmacology* 29, 1190–1202. doi:10.1038/sj.npp.1300420

Martinez, D., Carpenter, K. M., Liu, F., Slifstein, M., Broft, A., Friedman, A. C., et al. (2011). Imaging dopamine transmission in cocaine dependence: link between neurochemistry and response to treatment. *Am. J. Psychiatry* 168, 634–641. doi:10.1176/appi.ajp.2010.10050748

Martinez, D., Greene, K., Broft, A., Kumar, D., Liu, F., Narendran, R., et al. (2009a). Lower level of endogenous dopamine in patients with cocaine dependence: findings from PET imaging of D(2)/D(3) receptors following acute dopamine depletion. *Am. J. Psychiatry* 166, 1170–1177. doi:10.1176/appi.ajp.2009.08121801

Martinez, D., Slifstein, M., Narendran, R., Foltin, R. W., Broft, A., Hwang, D. R., et al. (2009b). Dopamine D1 receptors in cocaine dependence measured with PET and the choice to self-administer cocaine. *Neuropsychopharmacology* 34, 1774–1782. doi:10.1038/npp.2008.235

Martinez, D., Kim, J. H., Krystal, J., and Abi-Dargham, A. (2007a). Imaging the neurochemistry of alcohol and substance abuse. *Neuroimaging Clin. N. Am.* 17, 539–555. doi:10.1016/j.nic.2007.07.004

Martinez, D., Narendran, R., Foltin, R. W., Slifstein, M., Hwang, D. R., Broft, A., et al. (2007b). Amphetamine-induced dopamine release: markedly blunted in cocaine dependence and predictive of the choice to self-administer cocaine. *Am. J. Psychiatry* 164, 622–629. doi:10.1176/appi.ajp.164.4.622

Martinez, D., and Narendran, R. (2010). Imaging neurotransmitter release by drugs of abuse. *Curr. Top. Behav. Neurosci.* 3, 219–245. doi:10.1007/7854_2009_34

Martinez, D., Saccone, P. A., Liu, F., Slifstein, M., Orlowska, D., Grassetti, A., et al. (2012). Deficits in dopamine D(2) receptors and presynaptic dopamine in heroin dependence: commonalities and differences with other types of addiction. *Biol. Psychiatry* 71, 192–198. doi:10.1016/j.biopsych.2011.08.024

Martinez, D., Slifstein, M., Broft, A., Mawlawi, O., Hwang, D. R., Huang, Y., et al. (2003). Imaging human mesolimbic dopamine transmission with positron emission tomography. Part II: amphetamine-induced dopamine release in the functional subdivisions of the striatum. *J. Cereb. Blood Flow Metab.* 23, 285–300. doi:10.1097/00004647-200303000-00004

Mash, D. C., and Staley, J. K. (1999). D3 dopamine and kappa opioid receptor alterations in human brain of cocaine-overdose victims. *Ann. N. Y. Acad. Sci.* 877, 507–522. doi:10.1111/j.1749-6632.1999.tb09286.x

Matuskey, D., Gallezot, J., Keunpoong, L., Zheng, M., Lin, S., Carson, R., et al. (2011). Subcortical D3/D2 receptor binding in cocaine dependent humans. *J. Nucl. Med.* 52, 1284.

McClung, C. A., and Nestler, E. J. (2008). Neuroplasticity mediated by altered gene expression. *Neuropsychopharmacology* 33, 3–17. doi:10.1038/sj.npp.1301544

McClung, C. A., Ulery, P. G., Perrotti, L. I., Zachariou, V., Berton, O., and Nestler, E. J. (2004). DeltaFosB: a molecular switch for long-term adaptation in the brain. *Brain Res. Mol. Brain Res.* 132, 146–154. doi:10.1016/j.molbrainres.2004.05.014

McLaughlin, J. P., Land, B. B., Li, S., Pintar, J. E., and Chavkin, C. (2006). Prior activation of kappa opioid receptors by U50,488 mimics repeated forced swim stress to potentiate cocaine place preference conditioning. *Neuropsychopharmacology* 31, 787–794. doi:10.1038/sj.npp.1300860

McLaughlin, J. P., Marton-Popovici, M., and Chavkin, C. (2003). Kappa opioid receptor antagonism and prodynorphin gene disruption block stress-induced behavioral responses. *J. Neurosci.* 23, 5674–5683.

Meador-Woodruff, J. H., Little, K. Y., Damask, S. P., Mansour, A., and Watson, S. J. (1993). Effects of cocaine on dopamine receptor gene expression: a study in the postmortem human brain. *Biol. Psychiatry* 34, 348–355. doi:10.1016/0006-3223(93)90178-G

Melis, M., Spiga, S., and Diana, M. (2005). The dopamine hypothesis of drug addiction: hypodopaminergic state. *Int. Rev. Neurobiol.* 63, 101–154. doi:10.1016/S0074-7742(05)63005-X

Morgan, D., Grant, K. A., Gage, H. D., Mach, R. H., Kaplan, J. R., Prioleau, O., et al. (2002). Social dominance in monkeys: dopamine D2 receptors and cocaine self-administration. *Nat. Neurosci.* 5, 169–174. doi:10.1038/nn798

Mucha, R. F., and Herz, A. (1985). Motivational properties of kappa and mu opioid receptor agonists studied with place and taste preference conditioning. *Psychopharmacology (Berl.)* 86, 274–280. doi:10.1007/BF00432213

Munro, C. A., McCaul, M. E., Wong, D. F., Oswald, L. M., Zhou, Y., Brasic, J., et al. (2006). Sex differences in striatal dopamine release in healthy adults. *Biol. Psychiatry* 59, 966–974. doi:10.1016/j.biopsych.2006.01.008

Muschamp, J. W., and Carlezon, W. A. Jr. (2013). Roles of nucleus accumbens CREB and dynorphin in dysregulation of motivation. *Cold Spring Harb. Perspect. Med.* doi:10.1101/cshperspect.a012005. [Epub ahead of print].

Nader, M. A., Morgan, D., Gage, H. D., Nader, S. H., Calhoun, T. L., Buchheimer, N., et al. (2006). PET imaging of dopamine D2 receptors during chronic cocaine self-administration in monkeys. *Nat. Neurosci.* 9, 1050–1056. doi:10.1038/nn1737

Narendran, R., Lopresti, B. J., Martinez, D., Mason, N. S., Himes, M., May, M. A., et al. (2012). In vivo evidence for low striatal vesicular monoamine transporter 2 (VMAT2) availability in cocaine abusers. *Am. J. Psychiatry* 169, 55–63. doi:10.1176/appi.ajp.2011.11010126

Nikolarakis, K. E., Almeida, O. F., and Herz, A. (1986). Stimulation of hypothalamic beta-endorphin and dynorphin release by corticotropin-releasing factor (in vitro). *Brain Res.* 399, 152–155. doi:10.1016/0006-8993(86)90610-4

Oliveto, A., Poling, J., Mancino, M. J., Williams, D. K., Thostenson, J., Pruzinsky, R., et al. (2012). Sertraline delays relapse in recently abstinent cocaine-dependent patients with depressive symptoms. *Addiction* 107, 131–141. doi:10.1111/j.1360-0443.2011.03552.x

Parsons, L. H., Smith, A. D., and Justice, J. B. Jr. (1991). Basal extracellular dopamine is decreased in the rat nucleus accumbens during abstinence from chronic cocaine. *Synapse* 9, 60–65. doi:10.1002/syn.890090109

Pascoli, V., Turiault, M., and Luscher, C. (2012). Reversal of cocaine-evoked synaptic potentiation resets drug-induced adaptive behaviour. *Nature* 481, 71–75. doi:10.1038/nature10709

Pfeiffer, A., Brantl, V., Herz, A., and Emrich, H. M. (1986). Psychotomimesis mediated by kappa opiate receptors. *Science* 233, 774–776. doi:10.1126/science.3016896

Redila, V. A., and Chavkin, C. (2008). Stress-induced reinstatement of cocaine seeking is mediated by the kappa opioid system. *Psychopharmacology (Berl.)* 200, 59–70. doi:10.1007/s00213-008-1122-y

Robertson, M. W., Leslie, C. A., and Bennett, J. P. Jr. (1991). Apparent synaptic dopamine deficiency induced by withdrawal from chronic cocaine treatment. *Brain Res.* 538, 337–339. doi:10.1016/0006-8993(91)90451-Z

Rossetti, Z. L., Melis, F., Carboni, S., and Gessa, G. L. (1992). Dramatic depletion of mesolimbic extracellular dopamine after withdrawal from morphine, alcohol or cocaine: a common neurochemical substrate for drug dependence. *Ann. N. Y. Acad. Sci.* 654, 513–516. doi:10.1111/j.1749-6632.1992.tb26016.x

Roth, B. L., Baner, K., Westkaemper, R., Siebert, D., Rice, K. C., Steinberg, S., et al. (2002). Salvinorin A: a potent naturally occurring nonnitrogenous kappa opioid selective agonist. *Proc. Natl. Acad. Sci. U.S.A.* 99, 11934–11939. doi:10.1073/pnas.182234399

Salamone, J. D., and Correa, M. (2012). The mysterious motivational functions of mesolimbic dopamine. *Neuron* 76, 470–485. doi:10.1016/j.neuron.2012.10.021

Schlussman, S. D., Zhang, Y., Yuferov, V., Laforge, K. S., Ho, A., and Kreek, M. J. (2003). Acute 'binge' cocaine administration elevates dynorphin mRNA in the caudate putamen of C57BL/6J but not 129/J mice. *Brain Res.* 974, 249–253. doi:10.1016/S0006-8993(03)02561-7

Schlussman, S. D., Zhou, Y., Bailey, A., Ho, A., and Kreek, M. J. (2005). Steady-dose and escalating-dose "binge" administration of cocaine alter expression of behavioral stereotypy and striatal preprodynorphin mRNA levels in rats. *Brain Res. Bull.* 67, 169–175. doi:10.1016/j.brainresbull.2005.04.018

Schultz, W. (2006). Behavioral theories and the neurophysiology of reward. *Annu. Rev. Psychol.* 57, 87–115. doi:10.1146/annurev.psych.56.091103.070229

Shippenberg, T. S., Zapata, A., and Chefer, V. I. (2007). Dynorphin and the pathophysiology of drug addiction. *Pharmacol. Ther.* 116, 306–321. doi:10.1016/j.pharmthera.2007.06.011

Shirayama, Y., Ishida, H., Iwata, M., Hazama, G. I., Kawahara, R., and Duman, R. S. (2004). Stress increases dynorphin immunoreactivity in limbic brain regions and dynorphin antagonism produces antidepressant-like

effects. *J. Neurochem.* 90, 1258–1268. doi:10.1111/j.1471-4159.2004.02589.x

Shoptaw, S., Majewska, M. D., Wilkins, J., Twitchell, G., Yang, X., and Ling, W. (2004). Participants receiving dehydroepiandrosterone during treatment for cocaine dependence show high rates of cocaine use in a placebo-controlled pilot study. *Exp. Clin. Psychopharmacol.* 12, 126–135. doi:10.1037/1064-1297.12.2.126

Sinha, R., Catapano, D., and O'Malley, S. (1999). Stress-induced craving and stress response in cocaine dependent individuals. *Psychopharmacology (Berl.)* 142, 343–351. doi:10.1007/s002130050898

Sinha, R., Garcia, M., Paliwal, P., Kreek, M. J., and Rounsaville, B. J. (2006). Stress-induced cocaine craving and hypothalamic-pituitary-adrenal responses are predictive of cocaine relapse outcomes. *Arch. Gen. Psychiatry* 63, 324–331. doi:10.1001/archpsyc.63.3.324

Sivam, S. P. (1989). Cocaine selectively increases striatonigral dynorphin levels by a dopaminergic mechanism. *J. Pharmacol. Exp. Ther.* 250, 818–824.

Sivam, S. P. (1996). Dopaminergic regulation of striatonigral tachykinin and dynorphin gene expression: a study with the dopamine uptake inhibitor GBR-12909. *Brain Res. Mol. Brain Res.* 35, 197–210. doi:10.1016/0169-328X(95)00216-F

Smiley, P. L., Johnson, M., Bush, L., Gibb, J. W., and Hanson, G. R. (1990). Effects of cocaine on extrapyramidal and limbic dynorphin systems. *J. Pharmacol. Exp. Ther.* 253, 938–943.

Sokoloff, P., Diaz, J., Le Foll, B., Guillin, O., Leriche, L., Bezard, E., et al. (2006). The dopamine D3 receptor: a therapeutic target for the treatment of neuropsychiatric disorders. *CNS Neurol. Disord. Drug Targets* 5, 25–43.

Song, Z. H., and Takemori, A. E. (1992). Stimulation by corticotropin-releasing factor of the release of immunoreactive dynorphin A from mouse spinal cords in vitro. *Eur. J. Pharmacol.* 222, 27–32. doi:10.1016/0014-2999(92)90458-G

Spanagel, R., Herz, A., and Shippenberg, T. (1992). Opposing tonically active endogenous opioid systems modulate the mesolimbic dopaminergic pathway. *Proc. Natl. Acad. Sci. U.S.A.* 89, 2046–2050. doi:10.1073/pnas.89.6.2046

Spanagel, R., Herz, A., and Shippenberg, T. S. (1990). The effects of opioid peptides on dopamine release in the nucleus accumbens: an in vivo

microdialysis study. *J. Neurochem.* 55, 1734–1740. doi:10.1111/j.1471-4159.1990.tb04963.x

Spangler, R., Ho, A., Zhou, Y., Maggos, C. E., Yuferov, V., and Kreek, M. J. (1996). Regulation of kappa opioid receptor mRNA in the rat brain by "binge" pattern cocaine administration and correlation with preprodynorphin mRNA. *Brain Res. Mol. Brain Res.* 38, 71–76. doi:10.1016/0169-328X(95)00319-N

Spangler, R., Unterwald, E., and Kreek, M. (1993). Binge cocaine administration induces a sustained increase of prodynorphin mRNA in rat caudate-putamen. *Brain Res. Mol. Brain Res.* 19, 323–327. doi:10.1016/0169-328X(93)90133-A

Staley, J. K., Rothman, R. B., Rice, K. C., Partilla, J., and Mash, D. C. (1997). Kappa2 opioid receptors in limbic areas of the human brain are upregulated by cocaine in fatal overdose victims. *J. Neurosci.* 17, 8225–8233.

Svingos, A., Chavkin, C., Colago, E., and Pickel, V. (2001). Major coexpression of k-opioid receptors and the dopamine transporter in nucleus accumbens axonal profiles. *Synapse* 42, 185–192. doi:10.1002/syn.10005

Tang, A. H., and Collins, R. J. (1985). Behavioral effects of a novel kappa opioid analgesic, U-50488, in rats and rhesus monkeys. *Psychopharmacology (Berl.)* 85, 309–314. doi:10.1007/BF00428193

Tejeda, H. A., Shippenberg, T. S., and Henriksson, R. (2012). The dynorphin/kappa-opioid receptor system and its role in psychiatric disorders. *Cell. Mol. Life Sci.* 69, 857–896. doi:10.1007/s00018-011-0844-x

Thompson, A., Zapata, A., Justice, J., Vaughan, R., Sharpe, L., and Shippenberg, T. (2000). Kappa-opioid receptor activation modifies dopamine uptake in the nucleus accumbens and opposes the effects of cocaine. *J. Neurosci.* 20, 9333–9340.

Ur, E., Wright, D. M., Bouloux, P. M., and Grossman, A. (1997). The effects of spiradoline (U-62066E), a kappa-opioid receptor agonist, on neuroendocrine function in man. *Br. J. Pharmacol.* 120, 781–784. doi:10.1038/sj.bjp.0700971

Valdez, G. R., Platt, D. M., Rowlett, J. K., Ruedi-Bettschen, D., and Spealman, R. D. (2007). Kappa agonist-induced reinstatement of cocaine seeking in squirrel monkeys: a role for opioid and stress-related mechanisms. *J. Pharmacol. Exp. Ther.* 323, 525–533. doi:10.1124/jpet.107.125484

Valjent, E., Bertran-Gonzalez, J., Herve, D., Fisone, G., and Girault, J. A. (2009). Looking BAC at striatal signaling: cell-specific analysis in new transgenic mice. *Trends Neurosci.* 32, 538–547. doi:10.1016/j.tins.2009.06.005

Van Bockstaele, E. J., Gracy, K. N., and Pickel, V. M. (1995). Dynorphin-immunoreactive neurons in the rat nucleus accumbens: ultrastructure and synaptic input from terminals containing substance P and/or dynorphin. *J. Comp. Neurol.* 351, 117–133. doi:10.1002/cne.903510111

Volkow, N. D., Fowler, J. S., Wang, G. J., Hitzemann, R., Logan, J., Schlyer, D. J., et al. (1993). Decreased dopamine D2 receptor availability is associated with reduced frontal metabolism in cocaine abusers. *Synapse* 14, 169–177. doi:10.1002/syn.890140210

Volkow, N. D., Fowler, J. S., Wolf, A. P., Schlyer, D., Shiue, C. Y., Alpert, R., et al. (1990). Effects of chronic cocaine abuse on postsynaptic dopamine receptors. *Am. J. Psychiatry* 147, 719–724.

Volkow, N. D., Wang, G. J., Fowler, J. S., Hitzemann, R., Angrist, B., Gatley, S. J., et al. (1999). Association of methylphenidate-induced craving with changes in right striatoorbitofrontal metabolism in cocaine abusers: implications in addiction. *Am. J. Psychiatry* 156, 19–26.

Volkow, N. D., Wang, G. J., Fowler, J. S., Logan, J., Gatley, S. J., Hitzemann, R., et al. (1997). Decreased striatal dopaminergic responsiveness in detoxified cocaine-dependent subjects. *Nature* 386, 830–833. doi:10.1038/386830a0

Volkow, N. D., Wang, G. J., Fowler, J. S., Logan, J., Hitzemann, R., Ding, Y. S., et al. (1996). Decreases in dopamine receptors but not in dopamine transporters in alcoholics. *Alcohol. Clin. Exp. Res.* 20, 1594–1598.

Volkow, N. D., Wang, G.-J., Fowler, J. S., Logan, J., Schlyer, D., Hitzemann, R., et al. (1994). Imaging endogenous dopamine competition with [11C]raclopride in the human brain. *Synapse* 16, 255–262. doi:10.1002/syn.890160402

Von Voigtlander, P. F., and Lewis, R. A. (1982). U-50,488, a selective kappa opioid agonist: comparison to other reputed kappa agonists. *Prog. Neuropsychopharmacol. Biol. Psychiatry* 6, 467–470. doi:10.1016/S0278-5846(82)80130-9

Wadenberg, M. L. (2003). A review of the properties of spiradoline: a potent and selective kappa-opioid receptor agonist. *CNS Drug Rev.* 9, 187–198. doi:10.1111/j.1527-3458.2003.tb00248.x

Walsh, S. L., Geter-Douglas, B., Strain, E. C., and Bigelow, G. E. (2001). Enadoline and butorphanol: evaluation of kappa-agonists on cocaine pharmacodynamics and cocaine self-administration in humans. *J. Pharmacol. Exp. Ther.* 299, 147–158.

Walters, C. L., and Blendy, J. A. (2001). Different requirements for cAMP response element binding protein in positive and negative reinforcing properties of drugs of abuse. *J. Neurosci.* 21, 9438–9444.

Wang, G. J., Smith, L., Volkow, N. D., Telang, F., Logan, J., Tomasi, D., et al. (2012). Decreased dopamine activity predicts relapse in methamphetamine abusers. *Mol. Psychiatry* 17, 918–925. doi:10.1038/mp.2011.86

Wang, G. J., Volkow, N. D., Fowler, J. S., Fischman, M., Foltin, R., Abumrad, N. N., et al. (1997). Cocaine abusers do not show loss of dopamine transporters with age. *Life Sci.* 61, 1059–1065. doi:10.1016/S0024-3205(97)00614-0

Wee, S., and Koob, G. F. (2010). The role of the dynorphin-kappa opioid system in the reinforcing effects of drugs of abuse. *Psychopharmacology (Berl.)* 210, 121–135. doi:10.1007/s00213-010-1825-8

Wee, S., Orio, L., Ghirmai, S., Cashman, J. R., and Koob, G. F. (2009). Inhibition of kappa opioid receptors attenuated increased cocaine intake in rats with extended access to cocaine. *Psychopharmacology (Berl.)* 205, 565–575. doi:10.1007/s00213-009-1563-y

Weiss, F., Paulus, M. P., Lorang, M. T., and Koob, G. F. (1992). Increases in extracellular dopamine in the nucleus accumbens by cocaine are inversely related to basal levels: effects of acute and repeated administration. *J. Neurosci.* 12, 4372–4380.

Wise, R. A. (2008). Dopamine and reward: the anhedonia hypothesis 30 years on. *Neurotox. Res.* 14, 169–183. doi:10.1007/BF03033808

Wu, J. C., Bell, K., Najafi, A., Widmark, C., Keator, D., Tang, C., et al. (1997). Decreasing striatal 6-FDOPA uptake with increasing duration of cocaine withdrawal. *Neuropsychopharmacology* 17, 402–409. doi:10.1016/S0893-133X(97)00089-4

Xi, Z. X., Fuller, S. A., and Stein, E. A. (1998). Dopamine release in the nucleus accumbens during heroin self-administration is modulated by kappa opioid receptors: an in vivo fast-cyclic voltammetry

study. *J. Pharmacol. Exp. Ther.* 284, 151–161.

Yokoo, H., Yamada, S., Yoshida, M., Tanaka, M., and Nishi, S. (1992). Attenuation of the inhibitory effect of dynorphin on dopamine release in the rat nucleus accumbens by repeated treatment with methamphetamine. *Eur. J. Pharmacol.* 222, 43–47. doi:10.1016/0014-2999(92)90461-C

You, Z. B., Herrera-Marschitz, M., and Terenius, L. (1999). Modulation of neurotransmitter release in the basal ganglia of the rat brain by dynorphin peptides. *J. Pharmacol. Exp. Ther.* 290, 1307–1315.

Yuferov, V., Zhou, Y., Laforge, K. S., Spangler, R., Ho, A., and Kreek, M. J. (2001). Elevation of guinea pig brain preprodynorphin mRNA expression and hypothalamic-pituitary-adrenal axis activity by "binge" pattern cocaine administration. *Brain Res. Bull.* 55, 65–70. doi:10.1016/S0361-9230(01)00496-8

Zhang, Y., Butelman, E. R., Schlussman, S. D., Ho, A., and Kreek, M. J. (2004a). Effect of the endogenous kappa opioid agonist dynorphin A(1-17) on cocaine-evoked increases in striatal dopamine levels and cocaine-induced place preference in C57BL/6J mice. *Psychopharmacology (Berl.)* 172, 422–429. doi:10.1007/s00213-003-1688-3

Zhang, Y., Butelman, E. R., Schlussman, S. D., Ho, A., and Kreek, M. J. (2004b). Effect of the kappa opioid agonist R-84760 on cocaine-induced increases in striatal dopamine levels and cocaine-induced place preference in C57BL/6J mice. *Psychopharmacology (Berl.)* 173, 146–152. doi:10.1007/s00213-003-1716-3

Zhang, Y., Schlussman, S. D., Rabkin, J., Butelman, E. R., Ho, A., and Kreek, M. J. (2013). Chronic escalating cocaine exposure, abstinence/withdrawal, and chronic re-exposure: effects on striatal dopamine and opioid systems in C57BL/6J mice. *Neuropharmacology* 67, 259–266. doi:10.1016/j.neuropharm.2012.10.015

Zhou, Y., Spangler, R., Schlussman, S. D., Yuferov, V. P., Sora, I., Ho, A., et al. (2002). Effects of acute "binge" cocaine on preprodynorphin, preproenkephalin, proopiomelanocortin, and corticotropin-releasing hormone receptor mRNA levels in the striatum and hypothalamic-pituitary-adrenal axis of mu-opioid receptor knockout mice. *Synapse* 45, 220–229. doi:10.1002/syn.10101

Zubieta, J. K., Gorelick, D. A., Stauffer, R., Ravert, H. T., Dannals, R. F., and Frost, J. J. (1996). Increased mu opioid receptor binding detected by PET in cocaine-dependent men is associated with cocaine craving. *Nat. Med.* 2, 1225–1229. doi:10.1038/nm1196-1225

8

Addiction is a reward deficit and stress surfeit disorder

George F. Koob*

Committee on the Neurobiology of Addictive Disorders, The Scripps Research Institute, La Jolla, CA, USA

Edited by:
Nicholas W. Gilpin, LSUHSC-New Orleans, USA

Reviewed by:
Benjamin Boutrel, Lausanne University Hospital, Switzerland
Glenn Valdez, Grand Valley State University, USA

*Correspondence:
George F. Koob, Committee on the Neurobiology of Addictive Disorders, The Scripps Research Institute, 10550 North Torrey Pines Road, SP30-2400, La Jolla, CA 92037, USA
e-mail: gkoob@scripps.edu

Drug addiction can be defined by a three-stage cycle – *binge/intoxication*, *withdrawal/negative affect*, and *preoccupation/anticipation* – that involves allostatic changes in the brain reward and stress systems. Two primary sources of reinforcement, positive and negative reinforcement, have been hypothesized to play a role in this allostatic process. The negative emotional state that drives negative reinforcement is hypothesized to derive from dysregulation of key neurochemical elements involved in the brain reward and stress systems. Specific neurochemical elements in these structures include not only decreases in reward system function (within-system opponent processes) but also recruitment of the brain stress systems mediated by corticotropin-releasing factor (CRF) and dynorphin-κ opioid systems in the ventral striatum, extended amygdala, and frontal cortex (both between-system opponent processes). CRF antagonists block anxiety-like responses associated with withdrawal, block increases in reward thresholds produced by withdrawal from drugs of abuse, and block compulsive-like drug taking during extended access. Excessive drug taking also engages the activation of CRF in the medial prefrontal cortex, paralleled by deficits in executive function that may facilitate the transition to compulsive-like responding. Neuropeptide Y, a powerful anti-stress neurotransmitter, has a profile of action on compulsive-like responding for ethanol similar to a CRF_1 antagonist. Blockade of the κ opioid system can also block dysphoric-like effects associated with withdrawal from drugs of abuse and block the development of compulsive-like responding during extended access to drugs of abuse, suggesting another powerful brain stress system that contributes to compulsive drug seeking. The loss of reward function and recruitment of brain systems provide a powerful neurochemical basis that drives the compulsivity of addiction.

Keywords: opponent process, extended amygdala, corticotropin-releasing factor, dynorphin, reward, compulsive, withdrawal, prefrontal cortex

WHAT IS ADDICTION?

Addiction can be defined as a chronic, relapsing disorder that has been characterized by (i) a compulsion to seek and take drugs, (ii) loss of control over drug intake, and (iii) emergence of a negative emotional state (e.g., dysphoria, anxiety, and irritability) that defines a motivational withdrawal syndrome when access to the drug is prevented (1). The occasional, limited, recreational use of a drug is clinically distinct from escalated drug use, the loss of control over drug intake, and the emergence of compulsive drug-seeking behavior that characterize addiction.

Addiction has been conceptualized as a three-stage cycle – *binge/intoxication*, *withdrawal/negative affect*, and *preoccupation/anticipation* – that worsens over time and involves allostatic changes in the brain reward and stress systems. Two primary sources of reinforcement, positive and negative reinforcement, have been hypothesized to play a role in this allostatic process. Positive reinforcement is defined as the process by which presentation of a stimulus increases the probability of a response; negative reinforcement is defined as the process by which removal of an aversive stimulus (or negative emotional state of withdrawal in the case of addiction) increases the probability of a response. Reward is operationally defined similarly to positive reinforcement as any stimulus that increases the probability of a response but also has a positive hedonic effect. Different theoretical perspectives from experimental psychology (positive and negative reinforcement frameworks), social psychology (self-regulation failure framework), and neurobiology (counteradaptation and sensitization frameworks) can be superimposed on the stages of the addiction cycle (1). These stages are thought to feed into each other, become more intense, and ultimately lead to the pathological state known as *addiction* (**Figure 1**). The neural substrates for the two sources of reinforcement that play a key role in the allostatic neuroadaptations derive from two key motivational systems required for survival: the brain reward and brain stress systems.

BRAIN REWARD SYSTEMS

Comprehension of a brain reward system was greatly facilitated by the discovery of electrical brain stimulation reward by Olds and Milner (2). Brain stimulation reward involves widespread neurocircuitry throughout the brain, but the most sensitive sites include the trajectory of the medial forebrain bundle that connects the ventral tegmental area with the basal forebrain [(2–4); **Figure 2**]. All drugs of abuse acutely decrease brain stimulation reward thresholds [i.e., increase or facilitate reward; (5)]. When drugs are administered chronically, withdrawal from drugs of abuse increases reward thresholds (decrease reward). Although

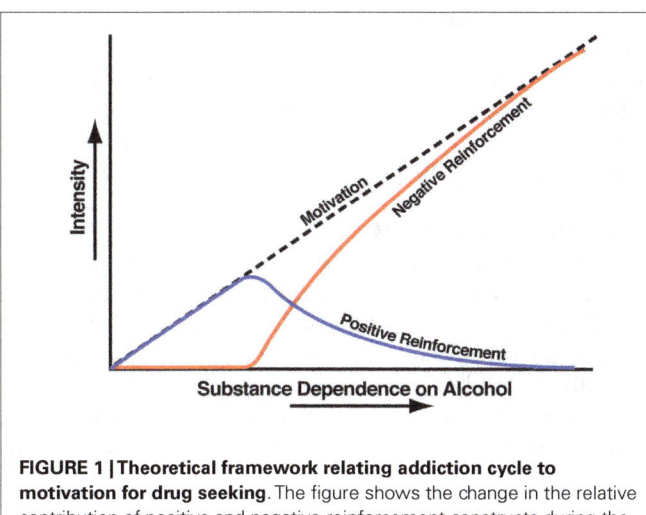

FIGURE 1 | Theoretical framework relating addiction cycle to motivation for drug seeking. The figure shows the change in the relative contribution of positive and negative reinforcement constructs during the development of substance dependence [taken with permission from Ref. (61)].

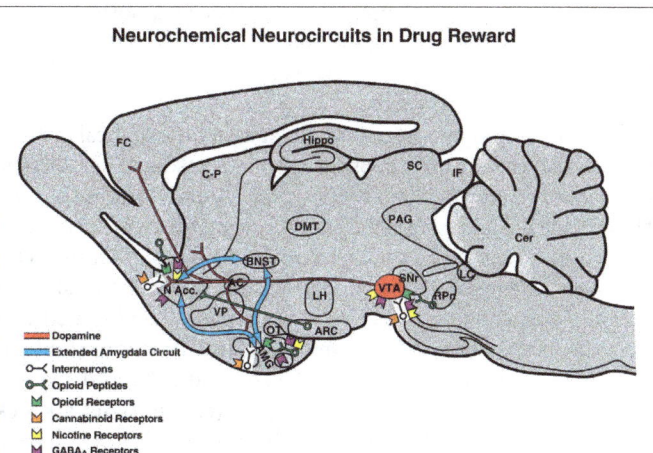

FIGURE 2 | Neurotransmitter pathways and receptor systems implicated in the acute reinforcing effects of drugs of abuse within the medial forebrain bundle. A sagittal rodent brain section is shown. The medial forebrain bundle represents ascending and descending projections between the ventral forebrain (nucleus accumbens, olfactory tubercle, and septal area) and ventral midbrain (ventral tegmental area; not shown in figure for clarity). Cocaine and amphetamines increase dopamine levels in the nucleus accumbens and amygdala via direct actions on dopamine terminals. Opioids activate endogenous opioid receptors in the ventral tegmental area, nucleus accumbens, and amygdala. Opioids also facilitate the release of dopamine in the nucleus accumbens via actions either in the ventral tegmental area or nucleus accumbens but are also hypothesized to activate elements independent of the dopamine system. Alcohol activates GABA$_A$ receptors or enhances GABA release in the ventral tegmental area, nucleus accumbens, and amygdala. Alcohol is also hypothesized to facilitate the release of opioid peptides in the ventral tegmental area, nucleus accumbens, and central nucleus of the amygdala. Alcohol facilitates the release of dopamine in the nucleus accumbens via an action either in the ventral tegmental area or nucleus accumbens. Nicotine activates nicotinic acetylcholine receptors in the ventral tegmental area, nucleus accumbens, and amygdala either directly or indirectly via actions on interneurons. Cannabinoids activate cannabinoid CB$_1$ receptors in the ventral tegmental area, nucleus accumbens, and amygdala. Cannabinoids facilitate the release of dopamine in the nucleus accumbens via an unknown mechanism, either in the ventral tegmental area or nucleus accumbens. The blue arrows represent the interactions within the extended amygdala system hypothesized to play a key role in psychostimulant reinforcement. AC, anterior commissure; AMG, amygdala; ARC, arcuate nucleus; BNST, bed nucleus of the stria terminalis; Cer, cerebellum; C-P, caudate-putamen; DMT, dorsomedial thalamus; FC, frontal cortex; Hippo, hippocampus; IF, inferior colliculus; LC, locus coeruleus; LH, lateral hypothalamus; MFB, medial forebrain bundle; N Acc., nucleus accumbens; OT, olfactory tract; PAG, periaqueductal gray; RPn, reticular pontine nucleus; SC, superior colliculus; SNr, substantia nigra pars reticulata; VP, ventral pallidum; VTA, ventral tegmental area [taken with permission from Ref. (183)].

much emphasis was initially placed on the role of ascending monoamine systems, particularly the dopamine system, in the medial forebrain bundle in mediating brain stimulation reward, other non-dopaminergic systems in the medial forebrain bundle clearly play a key role (6–8). Indeed, the role of dopamine is hypothesized to be more indirect. Many studies suggest that activation of the mesolimbic dopamine system attaches incentive salience to stimuli in the environment (9–11) to drive the performance of goal-directed behavior (12) or activation in general (13, 14), and work concerning the acute reinforcing effects of drugs of abuse supports this hypothesis.

Our knowledge of the neurochemical substrates that mediate the acute reinforcing effects of drugs of abuse has contributed significantly to our knowledge of the brain reward system. These substrates include connections of the medial forebrain bundle reward system with primary contributions from the ventral tegmental area, nucleus accumbens, and amygdala. Much evidence supports the hypothesis that psychostimulant drugs dramatically activate the mesolimbic dopamine system (projections from the ventral tegmental area to the nucleus accumbens) during limited-access drug self-administration and that this mechanism is critical for mediating the rewarding effects of cocaine, amphetamines, and nicotine. However, evidence supports both dopamine-dependent and dopamine-independent neural substrates for opioid and alcohol reward (15–17). Serotonin systems, particularly those involving serotonin 5-HT$_{1B}$ receptor activation in the nucleus accumbens, have also been implicated in the acute reinforcing effects of psychostimulant drugs, whereas μ-opioid receptors in both the nucleus accumbens and ventral tegmental area mediate the reinforcing effects of opioids. Opioid peptides in the ventral striatum and amygdala have been hypothesized to mediate the acute reinforcing effects of ethanol self-administration, largely based on the effects of opioid antagonists. Inhibitory γ-aminobutyric acid (GABA) systems are activated both pre- and postsynaptically in the amygdala by ethanol at intoxicating doses, and GABA receptor

antagonists block ethanol self-administration [for comprehensive reviews, see (16, 17)].

For the *binge/intoxication stage* of the addiction cycle, studies of the acute reinforcing effects of drugs of abuse *per se* have identified key neurobiological substrates. Evidence is strong for a role for dopamine in the acute reinforcing actions of psychostimulants, opioid peptide receptors in the acute reinforcing effects of opioids, and GABA and opioid peptides in the acute reinforcing actions of alcohol. Important anatomical circuits include the mesocorticolimbic dopamine system that originates in the ventral tegmental area and local opioid peptide systems, both of which converge on the nucleus accumbens (17).

BRAIN STRESS SYSTEMS

The brain stress systems can be defined as neurochemical systems that are activated during exposure to acute stressors or in a chronic state of stress and mediate species-typical behavioral responses. These behavioral responses in animals range from freezing to flight and typically have face and predictive validity for similar behavior responses in humans. For example, animals exposed to a stressor will show an enhanced freezing response to a conditioned fear stimulus, an enhanced startle response to a startle stimulus, avoidance of open areas, open arms, or height, and enhanced species-typical responses to an aversive stimulus (e.g., burying a shock probe in the defensive burying test). Key neuronal/neurochemical systems with circumscribed neurocircuitry that mediate behavioral responses to stressors include glucocorticoids, corticotropin-releasing factor (CRF), norepinephrine, and dynorphin, and key neurochemical systems that act in opposition to the brain stress systems include neuropeptide Y (NPY), nociceptin, and endocannabinoids [for reviews, see (18–20)]. For the purposes of this review, two brain stress systems with prominent roles in driving the dark side of addiction will be considered: CRF and dynorphin.

CORTICOTROPIN-RELEASING FACTOR

Corticotropin-releasing factor is a 41-amino-acid polypeptide that controls hormonal, sympathetic, and behavioral responses to stressors (21, 22). Central administration of CRF mimics the behavioral response to activation and stress in rodents, and administration of competitive CRF receptor antagonists generally has anti-stress effects [for reviews, see (23–26)]. Two major CRF receptors have been identified, with CRF_1 receptor activation associated with increased stress responsiveness (27) and CRF_2 receptor activation associated with decreases in feeding and decreases in stress responsiveness (28, 29), although there is some controversy in this area (30). CRF neurons are present in the neocortex, the extended amygdala, the medial septum, the hypothalamus, the thalamus, the cerebellum, and autonomic midbrain and hindbrain nuclei (31). Extensive research has been performed on CRF neurons in the paraventricular nucleus of the hypothalamus (PVN), central nucleus of the amygdala (CeA), and bed nucleus of the stria terminalis (BNST), demonstrating a key role for PVN CRF neurons in controlling the pituitary adrenal response to stress (32) and a key role for BNST and CeA CRF in mediating the negative affective responses to stress and drug withdrawal (33).

The neuroanatomical entity termed the extended amygdala (34) may represent a common anatomical substrate that integrates brain arousal-stress systems with hedonic processing systems to produce the neuroadaptations associated with the development of addiction (see below). The extended amygdala is composed of the CeA, BNST, and a transition zone in the medial (shell) subregion of the nucleus accumbens. Each of these regions has cytoarchitectural and circuitry similarities (34). The extended amygdala receives numerous afferents from limbic structures, such as the basolateral amygdala and hippocampus, and sends efferents to the medial part of the ventral pallidum and a large projection to the lateral hypothalamus, thus further defining the specific brain areas that interface classical limbic (emotional) structures with the extrapyramidal motor system (35). CRF in the extended amygdala has long been hypothesized to play a key role not only in fear conditioning (36, 37) but also in the emotional component of pain processing (38).

DYNORPHIN-κ OPIOID SYSTEM

Dynorphins are opioid peptides that derive from the prodynorphin precursor and contain the leucine (leu)-enkephalin sequence at the N-terminal portion of the molecule and are the presumed endogenous ligands for the κ opioid receptor (39). Dynorphins are widely distributed in the central nervous system (40) and play a role in neuroendocrine regulation, pain regulation, motor activity, cardiovascular function, respiration, temperature regulation, feeding behavior, and stress responsivity (41). Dynorphins bind to all three opioid receptors but show a preference for κ receptors (39). Dynorphin-κ receptor system activation produces some actions that are similar to other opioids (analgesia) but others opposite to those of μ opioid receptors in the motivational domain. Dynorphins produce aversive dysphoric-like effects in animals and humans and have been hypothesized to mediate negative emotional states (42–45).

Dopamine receptor activation in the nucleus accumbens shell stimulates a cascade of events that ultimately lead to cyclic adenosine monophosphate response element-binding protein (CREB) phosphorylation and subsequent alterations in gene expression, notably the activation of the expression of prodynorphin mRNA. Subsequent activation of dynorphin systems has been hypothesized to feed back to decrease dopamine release in the mesolimbic dopamine system (46–50) and glutamate release in the nucleus accumbens (51, 52). Both of these changes may contribute to the dysphoric syndrome associated with cocaine dependence. *In vivo* microdialysis studies have also provided evidence that κ opioid receptors located in the prefrontal cortex (PFC) and ventral tegmental area also regulate the basal activity of mesocortical dopamine neurons (53, 54). In the extended amygdala, enhanced dynorphin action may also activate brain stress responses, such as CRF (55), or CRF in turn may activate dynorphin (56, 57).

DYNAMIC CHANGES IN REWARD: OPPONENT PROCESS

Changes in reinforcement were inextricably linked with hedonic, affective, or emotional states in addiction in the context of temporal dynamics by Solomon's opponent-process theory of motivation. Solomon and Corbit (58) postulated that hedonic, affective, or emotional states, once initiated, are automatically modulated by the central nervous system through mechanisms that reduce the intensity of hedonic feelings. The *a-process* includes affective or hedonic habituation (or tolerance), and the *b-process* includes affective or hedonic withdrawal (abstinence). The *a-process* in drug use consists of positive hedonic responses, occurs shortly after the presentation of a stimulus, correlates closely with the intensity, quality, and duration of the reinforcer, and shows tolerance. In contrast, the *b-process* in drug use appears after the *a-process* has terminated, consists of negative hedonic responses, and is sluggish in onset, slow to build up to an asymptote, slow to decay, and gets larger with repeated exposure. The thesis we have elaborated is that there is a neurocircuitry change in specific neurochemical systems that account for the *b-process*. Such opponent processes are hypothesized to begin early in drug taking, reflecting not only deficits in brain reward system function but also the recruitment of brain stress systems. Furthermore, we hypothesize that the recruitment of brain stress systems forms one of the major sources of negative reinforcement in addiction. Finally, we have hypothesized that such changes result not in a return to homeostasis of reward/stress function but in allostasis of reward/stress function that continues to drive the addiction process (**Figure 3**).

Allostasis, originally conceptualized to explain persistent morbidity of arousal and autonomic function, can be defined as "stability through change." Allostasis involves a feed-forward mechanism rather than the negative feedback mechanisms of homeostasis, with continuous reevaluation of need and continuous readjustment of all parameters toward new set points. An *allostatic state* has been defined as a state of chronic deviation of the regulatory system from its normal (homeostatic) operating level (15). *Allostatic load* was defined as the "long-term cost of allostasis that accumulates over time and reflects the accumulation of damage that can lead to pathological states" (59).

Opponent process-like negative emotional states have been characterized in humans by acute and protracted abstinence

from all major drugs of abuse (60–62). Similar results have been observed in animal models with all major drugs of abuse using intracranial self-stimulation (ICSS) as a measure of hedonic tone. Withdrawal from chronic cocaine (63), amphetamine (64), opioids (65), cannabinoids (66), nicotine (67), and ethanol (68) leads to increases in reward threshold during acute abstinence, and some of these elevations in threshold can last for up to 1 week (69). These observations lend credence to the hypothesis that opponent processes in the hedonic domain have an identifiable neurobiological basis and provide an impetus for defining the mechanisms involved. Understanding the mechanisms that drive this increase in reward thresholds is key to understanding the mechanisms that drive negative reinforcement in addiction.

Such elevations in reward threshold begin rapidly and can be observed within a single session of self-administration (70), bearing a striking resemblance to human subjective reports of acute withdrawal. Dysphoria-like responses also accompany acute opioid and ethanol withdrawal (71, 72). Here, naloxone administration following single injections of morphine increased reward thresholds, measured by ICSS, and increased thresholds with repeated morphine and naloxone-induced withdrawal experience (71). Similar results were observed during repeated acute withdrawal from ethanol (72).

NEUROADAPTATIONS RESPONSIBLE FOR OPPONENT PROCESS

One hypothesis is that drug addiction progresses from a source of positive reinforcement that may indeed involve a form of sensitization of incentive salience, as argued by Robinson and Berridge (9), to sensitization of opponent processes that set up a powerful negative reinforcement process. A further elaboration of this hypothesis is that there are both within- and between-system neuroadaptations to excessive activation of the reward system at the neurocircuitry level. Within-system neuroadaptations are defined as the process by which the primary cellular response element to the drug (circuit A) itself adapts to neutralize the drug's effects. Persistence of the opposing effects after the drug disappears produces adaptation. A between-system neuroadaptation is a circuitry change, in which B circuits (i.e., the stress or anti-reward circuits) are activated by circuit A (i.e., the reward circuit). In the present treatise, within-system neuroadaptations can dynamically interact with a between-system neuroadaptation, in which circuit B (i.e., the anti-reward circuit) is activated either in parallel or in series to suppress the activity of circuit A (see below).

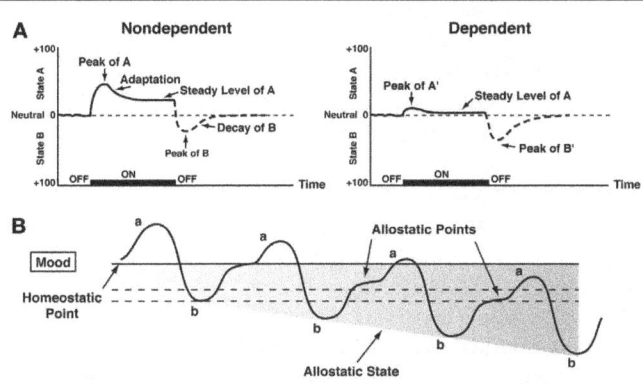

FIGURE 3 | (A) The standard pattern of affective dynamics produced by (*left*) a relatively novel unconditioned stimulus (i.e., in a non-dependent state) and (*right*) a familiar, frequently repeated unconditioned stimulus (i.e., in a dependent state) [taken with permission from Ref. (184)]. **(B)** The changes in the affective stimulus (state) in an individual with repeated frequent drug use that may represent a transition to an allostatic state in the brain reward systems and, by extrapolation, a transition to addiction. Note that the apparent *b-process* never returns to the original homeostatic level before drug taking is reinitiated, thus creating a greater and greater allostatic state in the brain reward system. In other words, the counteradaptive opponent-process (*b-process*) does not balance the activational process (*a-process*) but in fact shows a residual hysteresis. While these changes are exaggerated and condensed over time in the present conceptualization, the hypothesis here is that even during post-detoxification, a period of "protracted abstinence," the reward system is still bearing allostatic changes. In the non-dependent state, reward experiences are normal, and the brain stress systems are not greatly engaged. During the transition to the state known as addiction, the brain reward system is in a major underactivated state while the brain stress system is highly activated [taken with permission from Ref. (15)].

ANIMAL MODELS OF THE TRANSITION TO AN ADDICTION-LIKE STATE AS DEFINED BY ESCALATION IN DRUG SELF-ADMINISTRATION WITH PROLONGED ACCESS

A progressive increase in the frequency and intensity of drug use is one of the major behavioral phenomena that characterize the development of addiction and has face validity with the criteria of the *Diagnostic and Statistical Manual of Mental Disorders*, 4th edition (DSM-IV): "The substance is often taken in larger amounts and over a longer period than was intended" (American Psychological Association, 1994). A framework with which to model the transition from drug use to drug addiction can be found in recent animal models of prolonged access to intravenous cocaine self-administration. Historically, animal models of cocaine self-administration involved the establishment of stable behavior from day to day to allow the reliable interpretation of data provided by within-subject designs aimed at exploring the neuropharmacological and neurobiological bases of the reinforcing effects of acute cocaine. Up until 1998, after the acquisition of self-administration, rats were typically allowed access to cocaine for 3 h or less per day to establish highly stable levels of intake and patterns of responding between daily sessions. This was a useful paradigm for exploring the neurobiological substrates for the acute reinforcing effects of drugs of abuse.

However, in an effort to explore the possibility that differential access to drugs of abuse may have more face validity for the compulsive-like responding observed in addiction, animals have been allowed extended access to all major drugs of abuse (**Figure 4**). Increased intake was observed in the extended-access group for intravenous cocaine, methamphetamine, heroin, and nicotine and oral alcohol during extended access and dependence (73–79). For example, when animals were allowed access for 1 and 6 h to different doses of cocaine, after escalation, both the long-access (LgA) and short-access (ShA) animals titrated their cocaine intake, but LgA rats consistently self-administered almost twice as much cocaine at any dose tested, further suggesting an upward shift in the set point for cocaine reward in the escalated animals (80–82).

Consistent with the hypothesis that extended access to drugs of abuse produces compulsive-like responding, in which animals will "continue to respond in the face of adverse consequences" (another DSM-IV criteria for Substance Dependence), animals with extended access that show escalation in self-administration also show increased responding on a progressive-ratio schedule of reinforcement [(83–85); **Figure 5**]. Changes in the reinforcing and incentive effects of drug intake that are consistent with the increases in progressive-ratio responding have been observed following extended access and include increased drug-induced reinstatement after extinction, a decreased latency to goal time in a runway model for drug reward, and responding in the face of punishment (86–92). Altogether, these results suggest that drug taking with extended-access changes the motivation to seek the drug. Some have argued that enhanced drug taking reflects a sensitization of reward (93), but studies of locomotor sensitization suggest that locomotor sensitization occurs independently of escalation (94–96). The increased brain reward thresholds and neuropharmacological studies outlined below argue for a reward deficit state that drives the increased drug taking during extended access.

ANIMALS ESCALATE THEIR INTAKE OF DRUGS WITH EXTENDED ACCESS, WITH A PARALLEL INCREASE IN REWARD THRESHOLDS

The hypothesis that compulsive cocaine use is accompanied by a chronic perturbation in brain reward homeostasis has been tested in animal models of escalation in drug intake with prolonged access combined with measures of brain stimulation reward thresholds. Animals implanted with intravenous catheters and allowed differential access to intravenous self-administration of cocaine showed increases in cocaine self-administration from day

to day in the LgA group (6 h; LgA) but not in the ShA group (1 h; ShA). The differential exposure to cocaine self-administration had dramatic effects on reward thresholds that progressively increased in LgA rats but not ShA or control rats across successive self-administration sessions (97). Elevations in baseline reward thresholds temporally preceded and were highly correlated with escalation in cocaine intake (**Figure 6**). Post-session elevations in reward thresholds failed to return to baseline levels before the onset of each subsequent self-administration session, thereby deviating more and more from control levels. The progressive elevation in reward thresholds was associated with a dramatic escalation in cocaine consumption that was observed previously (97). Similar results have been observed with extended access to methamphetamine (98) and heroin (99). Rats allowed 6 h access to methamphetamine or 23 h access to heroin also showed a time-dependent increase in reward thresholds that paralleled the increases in heroin intake (**Figure 6**). Similar results of parallel increases in brain reward thresholds with escalation of nicotine intake have been observed with extended access to nicotine (100).

BRAIN REWARD SYSTEM SUBSTRATES FOR THE NEGATIVE REINFORCEMENT ASSOCIATED WITH ADDICTION (WITHIN-SYSTEM NEUROADAPTATIONS)

The *withdrawal/negative affect* stage can be defined as the presence of motivational signs of withdrawal in humans, including chronic irritability, physical pain, emotional pain [i.e., hyperkatifeia; (101)], malaise, dysphoria, alexithymia, and loss of motivation for natural rewards. It is characterized in animals by increases in reward thresholds during withdrawal from all major drugs of abuse. More compelling, as noted above, in animal models of the transition to addiction, similar changes in brain reward thresholds occur that temporally precede and are highly correlated with escalation in drug intake (97–99). Such acute withdrawal is associated with decreased activity of the mesocorticolimbic dopamine system, reflected by electrophysiological recordings and *in vivo* microdialysis [(102–104); **Figure 7**].

Human imaging studies of individuals with addiction during withdrawal or protracted abstinence have generated results that are consistent with animal studies. There are decreases in dopamine D_2 receptors (hypothesized to reflect hypodopaminergic functioning), hyporesponsiveness to dopamine challenge (105), and hypoactivity of the orbitofrontal-infralimbic cortex system (105). These are hypothesized to be within-system neuroadaptations that may reflect presynaptic release or postsynaptic receptor plasticity.

In the context of chronic alcohol administration, multiple molecular mechanisms have been hypothesized to counteract the acute effects of ethanol that could be considered within-system neuroadaptations. For example, chronic ethanol decreases γ-aminobutyric acid (GABA) receptor function, possibly through downregulation of the α_1 subunit (106, 107). Chronic ethanol also decreases the acute inhibition of adenosine reuptake [i.e., tolerance develops to the inhibition of adenosine by ethanol; (108)]. Perhaps more relevant to the present treatise, whereas acute ethanol activates adenylate cyclase, withdrawal from chronic ethanol decreases CREB phosphorylation in the amygdala and is linked to decreases in the function of NPY and anxiety-like responses observed during acute ethanol withdrawal (109, 110).

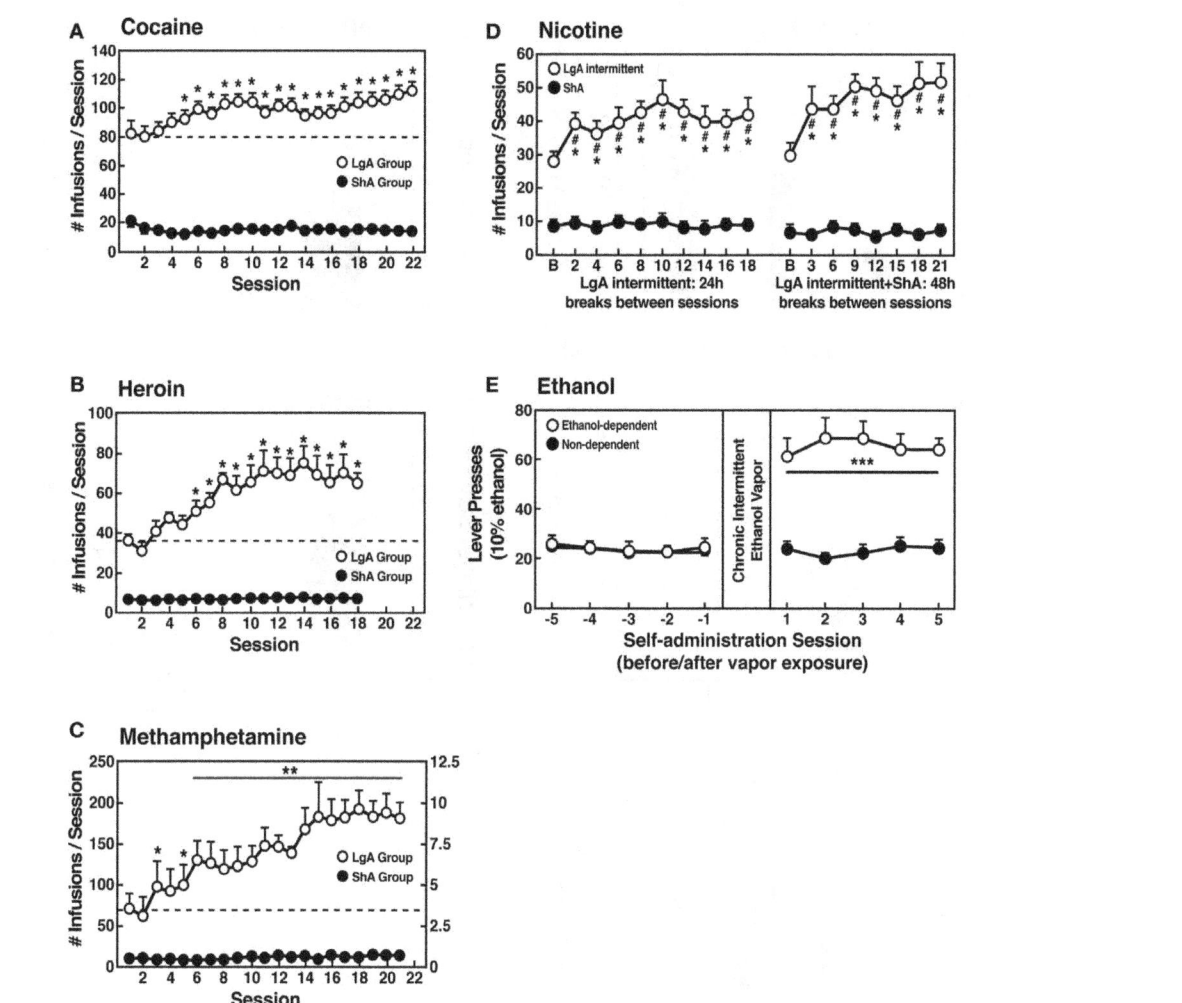

FIGURE 4 | (A) Effect of drug availability on cocaine intake (mean ± SEM). In long-access (LgA) rats (n = 12) but not short-access (ShA) rats (n = 12), the mean total cocaine intake started to increase significantly from session 5 (p < 0.05; sessions 5–22 compared with session 1) and continued to increase thereafter (p < 0.05; session 5 compared with sessions 8–10, 12, 13, and 17–22) [taken with permission from Ref. (74)]. **(B)** Effect of drug availability on total intravenous heroin self-infusions (mean ± SEM). During the escalation phase, rats had access to heroin (40 μg per infusion) for 1 h (ShA rats, n = 5–6) or 11 h per session (LgA rats, n = 5–6). Regular 1 h (ShA rats) or 11 h (LgA rats) sessions of heroin self-administration were performed 6 days a week. The dotted line indicates the mean ± SEM number of heroin self-infusions in LgA rats during the first 11 h session. *p < 0.05, different from the first session (paired t-test) [taken with permission from Ref. (73)]. **(C)** Effect of extended access to intravenous methamphetamine on self-administration as a function of daily sessions in rats trained to self-administer 0.05 mg/kg/infusion of intravenous methamphetamine during the 6 h session. ShA, 1 h session (n = 6). LgA, 6 h session (0.05 mg/kg/infusion, n = 4). **p < 0.01, compared with day 1 [taken with permission from Ref. (75)]. **(D)** Nicotine intake

(mean ± SEM) in rats that self-administered nicotine under a fixed-ratio (FR) 1 schedule in either 21 h (LgA) or 1 h (ShA) sessions. LgA rats increased their nicotine intake on an intermittent schedule with 24–48 h breaks between sessions, whereas LgA rats on a daily schedule did not. The left shows the total number of nicotine infusions per session when the intermittent schedule included 24 h breaks between sessions. The right shows the total number of nicotine infusions per session when the intermittent schedule included 48 h breaks between sessions. *p < 0.05, compared with baseline; *p < 0.05, compared with daily self-administration group. n = 10 per group [taken with permission from Ref. (185)]. **(E)** Ethanol self-administration in ethanol-dependent and non-dependent animals. The induction of ethanol dependence and correlation of limited ethanol self-administration before and excessive drinking after dependence induction following chronic intermittent ethanol vapor exposure is shown. ***p < 0.001, significant group × test session interaction. With all drugs, escalation is defined as a significant increase in drug intake within-subjects in extended-access groups, with no significant changes within-subjects in limited-access groups [taken with permission from Ref. (186)].

BRAIN STRESS SYSTEM SUBSTRATES FOR THE NEGATIVE REINFORCEMENT ASSOCIATED WITH ADDICTION (BETWEEN-SYSTEM NEUROADAPTATIONS)

Brain neurochemical systems involved in arousal-stress modulation have been hypothesized to be engaged within the neurocircuitry of the brain stress systems in an attempt to overcome the chronic presence of the perturbing drug and restore normal function despite the presence of drug (18). Both the hypothalamic-pituitary-adrenal (HPA) axis and extrahypothalamic brain stress system mediated by CRF are dysregulated by

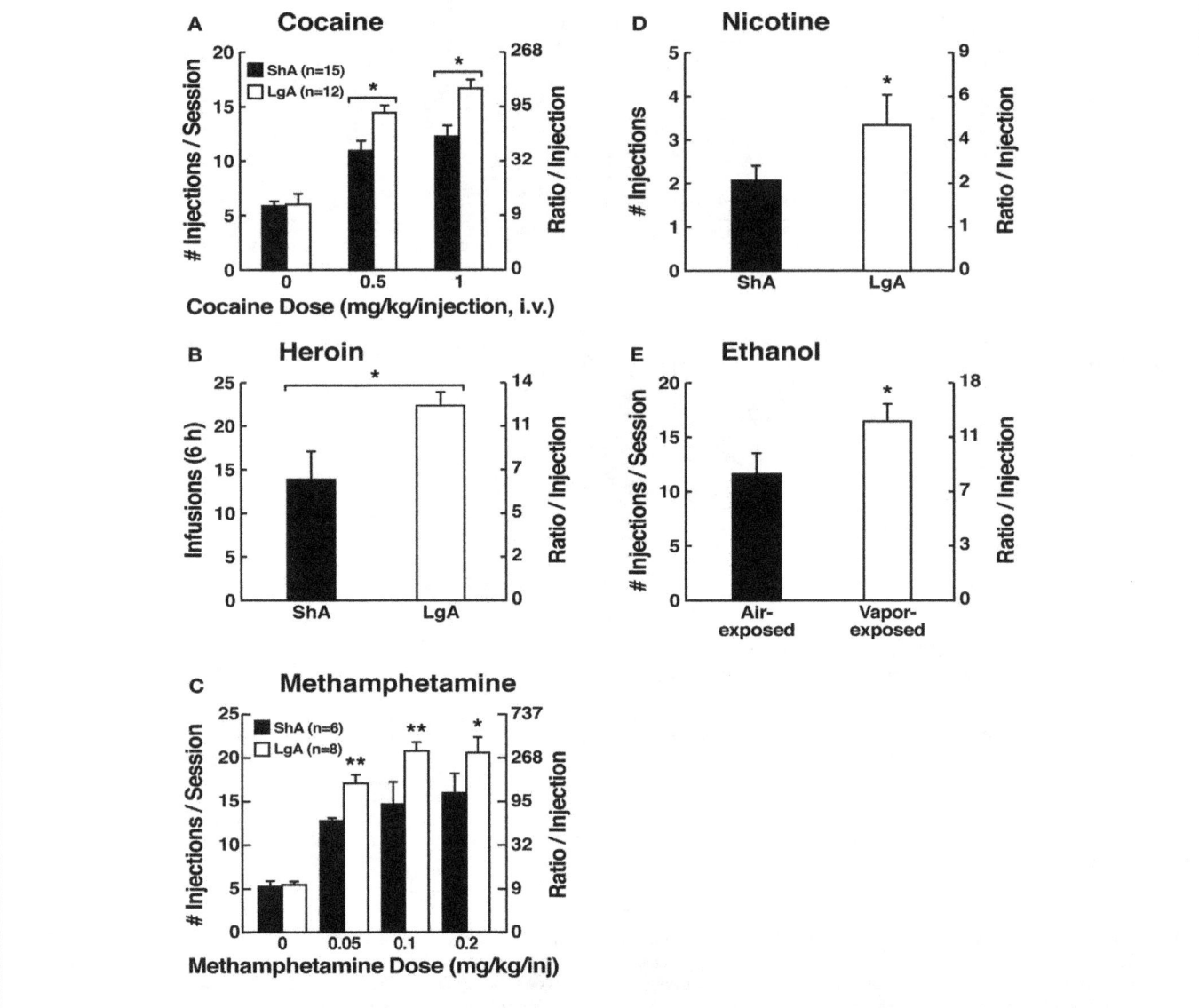

FIGURE 5 | (A) Dose-response function of cocaine by rats responding under a progressive-ratio schedule. Test sessions under a progressive-ratio schedule ended when rats did not achieve reinforcement within 1 h. The data are expressed as the number of injections per session on the left axis and ratio per injection on the right axis. *$p < 0.05$, compared with ShA rats at each dose of cocaine [taken with permission from Ref. (84)]. **(B)** Responding for heroin under a progressive-ratio schedule of reinforcement in ShA and LgA rats. *$p < 0.05$, LgA significantly different from LgA [Modified with permission from Ref. (187)]. **(C)** Dose-response for methamphetamine under a progressive-ratio schedule. Test sessions under a progressive-ratio schedule

ended when rats did not achieve reinforcement within 1 h. *$p < 0.05$, **$p < 0.01$, LgA significantly different from ShA [Modified from Ref. (188)]. **(D)** Breakpoints on a progressive-ratio schedule in long-access (LgA) rats that self-administered nicotine with 48 h abstinence between sessions. LgA rats on an intermittent schedule reached significantly higher breakpoints than LgA rats that self-administered nicotine daily. The data are expressed as mean ± SEM. *$p < 0.05$. $n = 9$ rats per group [taken with permission from Ref. (185)]. **(E)** Mean (±SEM) breakpoints for ethanol while in non-dependent and ethanol-dependent states. **$p < 0.01$, main effect of vapor exposure on ethanol self-administration [taken with permission from Ref. (85)].

chronic administration of all major drugs with dependence or abuse potential, with a common response of elevated adreno-corticotropic hormone, corticosterone, and amygdala CRF during acute withdrawal (24, 69, 111–116). Indeed, activation of the HPA response may be an early dysregulation associated with excessive drug taking that ultimately "sensitizes" the extrahypothalamic CRF systems (33, 92).

As noted above, the excessive release of dopamine and opioid peptides produces subsequent activation of dynorphin systems,

which has been hypothesized to feed back to decrease dopamine release and also contribute to the dysphoric syndrome associated with cocaine dependence (48). Dynorphins produce aversive dysphoric-like effects in animals and humans and have been hypothesized to mediate negative emotional states (42–45).

A common response to acute withdrawal and protracted abstinence from all major drugs of abuse is the manifestation of anxiety-like responses that are reversed by CRF antagonists. Withdrawal from repeated administration of cocaine produces an

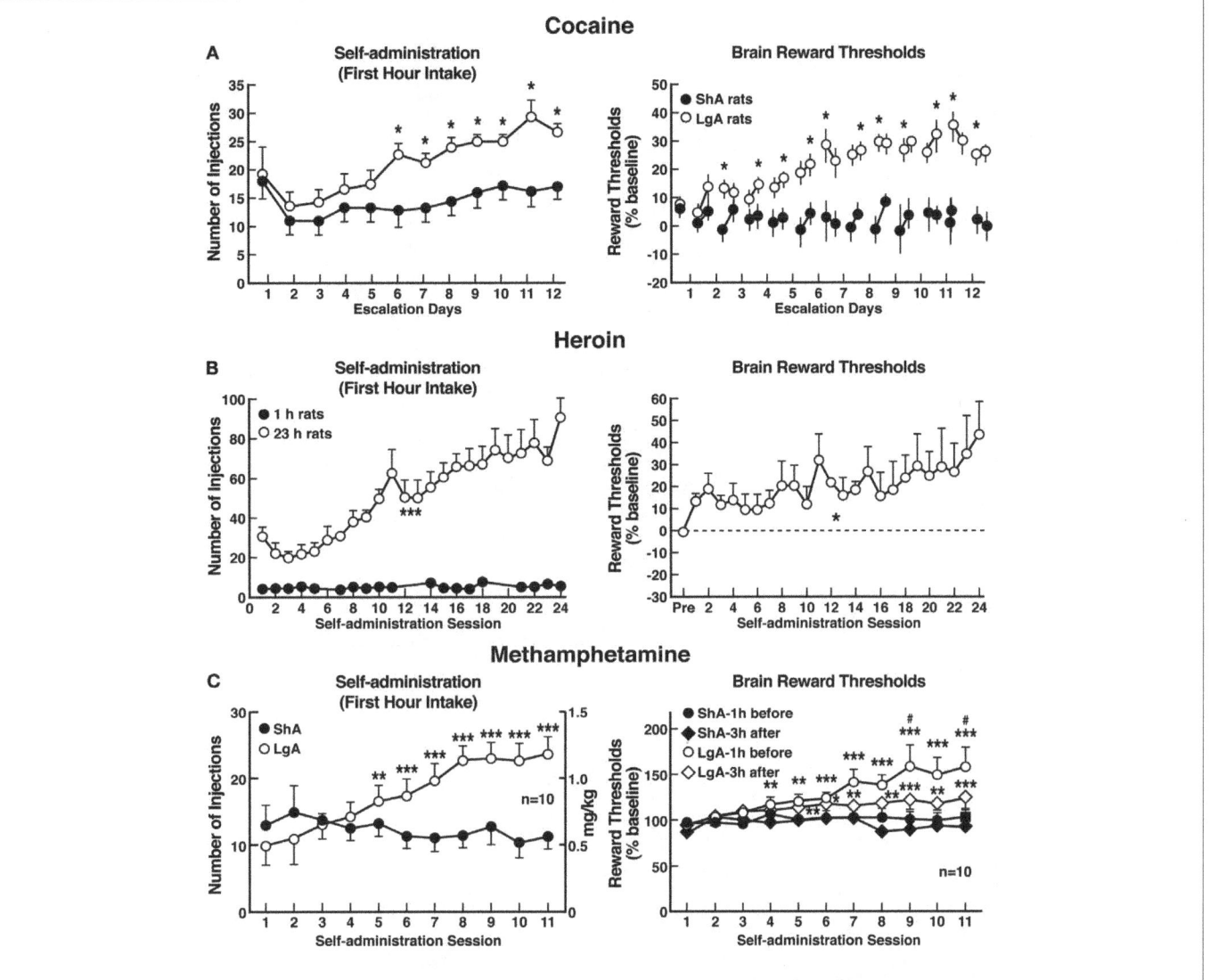

FIGURE 6 | (A) Relationship between elevation in ICSS reward thresholds and cocaine intake escalation (*Left*). Percent change from baseline response latencies (3 h and 17–22 h after each self-administration session; first data point indicates 1 h before the first session) (*Right*). Percent change from baseline ICSS thresholds. *$p < 0.05$, compared with drug-naive and/or ShA rats (tests for simple main effects) [taken with permission from Ref. (97)]. **(B)** Unlimited daily access to heroin escalated heroin intake and decreased the excitability of brain reward systems (*Left*). Heroin intake (±SEM; 20 μg per infusion) in rats during limited (1 h) or unlimited (23 h) self-administration sessions. ***$p < 0.001$, main effect of access (1 or 23 h) (*Right*). Percent change from baseline ICSS thresholds (±SEM) in 23 h rats. Reward thresholds, assessed immediately after each daily 23 h self-administration session, became progressively more elevated as exposure to self-administered heroin increased across sessions. *$p < 0.05$, main effect of heroin on reward thresholds [taken with permission from Ref. (99)]. **(C)** Escalation in methamphetamine self-administration and ICSS in rats. Rats were daily allowed to receive ICSS in the lateral hypothalamus 1 h before and 3 h after intravenous methamphetamine self-administration with either 1 or 6 h access (*Left*). Methamphetamine self-administration during the first hour of each session (*Right*). ICSS measured 1 h before and 3 h after methamphetamine self-administration. *$p < 0.05$, **$p < 0.01$, ***$p < 0.001$, compared with session 1. #$p < 0.05$, compared with LgA 3 h after [taken with permission from Ref. (98)].

anxiogenic-like response in the elevated plus maze and defensive burying test, both of which are reversed by administration of CRF receptor antagonists (117, 118). Opioid dependence also produces irritability-like effects that are reversed by CRF receptor antagonists (119, 120). Ethanol withdrawal produces anxiety-like behavior that is reversed by intracerebroventricular administration of CRF_1/CRF_2 peptidergic antagonists (121) and small-molecule CRF_1 antagonists (122–124) and intracerebral administration of a peptidergic CRF_1/CRF_2 antagonist into the amygdala (125). Thus,

some effects of CRF antagonists have been localized to the CeA (125). Precipitated withdrawal from nicotine produces anxiety-like responses that are also reversed by CRF antagonists (77, 126). CRF antagonists injected intracerebroventricularly or systemically also block the potentiated anxiety-like responses to stressors observed during protracted abstinence from chronic ethanol (127–131).

Another measure of negative emotional states during drug withdrawal in animals is conditioned place aversion, in which

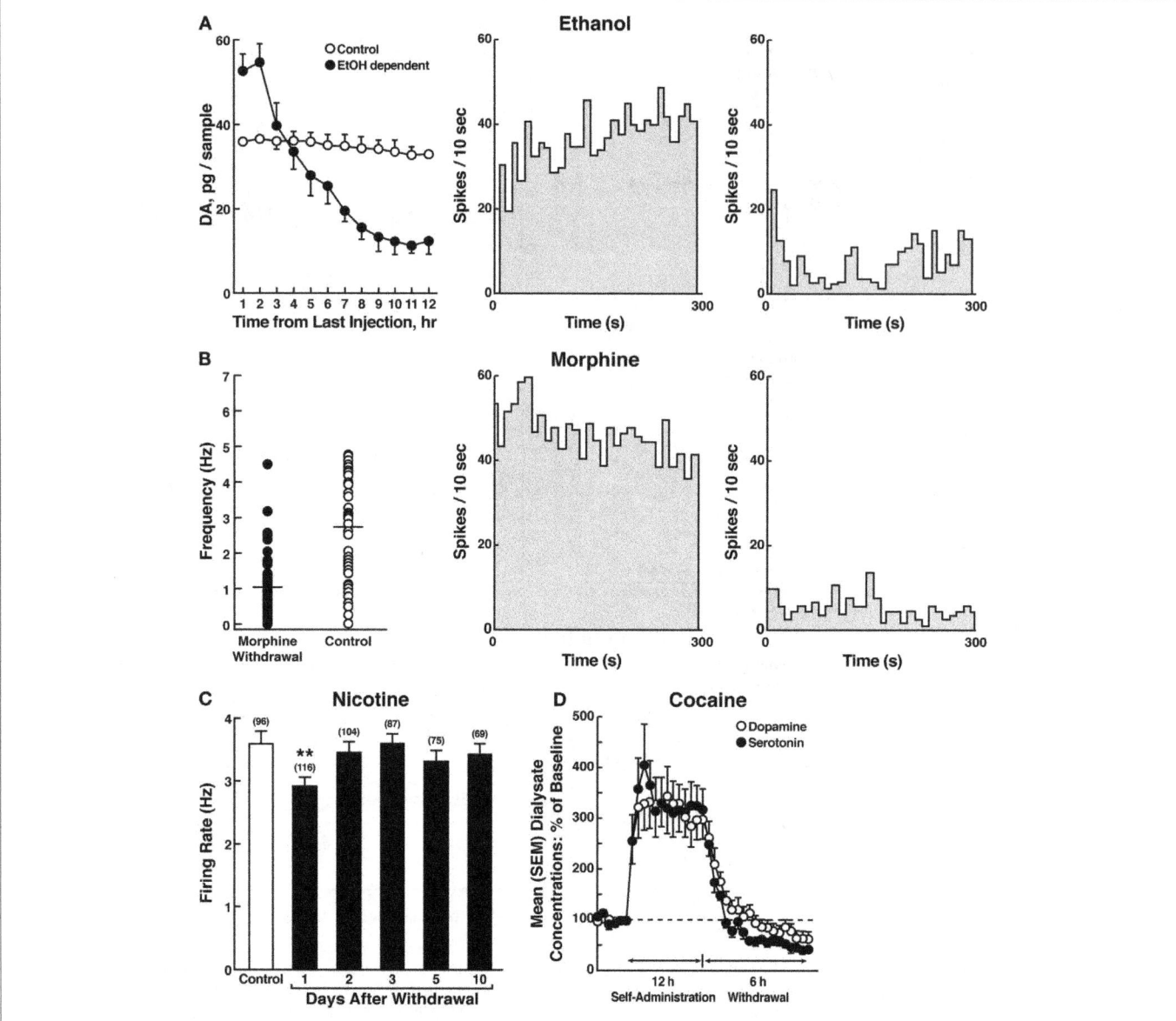

FIGURE 7 | (A) The left panel shows the effect of ethanol withdrawal on absolute extracellular dopamine concentrations in the nucleus accumbens in ethanol-withdrawn rats. The middle and right panels show the spontaneous activity of antidromically identified ventral tegmental area-nucleus accumbens dopamine neurons in control (*middle*) and ethanol-withdrawn (*right*) rats [taken with permission from Ref. (102)]. **(B)** The left panel shows individual firing rates of antidromically identified ventral tegmental area-nucleus accumbens dopamine neurons recorded from morphine-withdrawn and control rats. Each circle represents the mean firing of at least a 5-min recording. Horizontal lines indicate the mean activity. The middle and right panels show the spontaneous activity of a selected number (4) or antidromically identified ventral tegmental area-nucleus accumbens dopamine neurons in control (*middle*) and morphine-withdrawn (*right*) rats. Each panel represents the neuronal activity of a single cell. Recordings in both cases were obtained 24 h after the last morphine and saline administration, respectively [taken with permission from Ref. (103)]. **(C)** Firing rates of dopamine cells in the ventral tegmental area following 1–10 days of withdrawal from chronic nicotine treatment (6 mg/kg/day for 12 days). The data are expressed as mean ± SEM. The number of dopamine cells recorded is given in parentheses. *$p < 0.01$, compared with control group [taken with permission from Ref. (189)]. **(D)** Profile of dialysate serotonin and dopamine concentrations during a 12-h extended-access cocaine self-administration session. The mean ± SEM presession baseline dialysate concentrations of serotonin and dopamine were 0.98 ± 0.1 nM and 5.3 ± 0.5 nM, respectively ($n = 7$) [taken with permission from Ref. (104)].

animals avoid an environment previously paired with an aversive state. Such place aversions, when used to measure the aversive stimulus effects of withdrawal, have been observed largely in the context of opioids (132, 133). Systemic administration of a CRF$_1$ receptor antagonist and direct intracerebral administration of a peptide CRF$_1$/CRF$_2$ antagonist also decreased opioid withdrawal-induced place aversions (134–136). These effects have been hypothesized to be mediated by actions in the extended amygdala. The selective CRF$_1$ antagonist antalarmin blocked the place aversion produced by naloxone in morphine-dependent rats (134), and a CRF peptide antagonist injected into the CeA also reversed the place aversion produced by methylnaloxonium injected into the CeA (135). CRF₁ knockout mice failed to show conditioned place aversion to opioid withdrawal and failed to show an opioid-induced increase in dynorphin mRNA in the nucleus accumbens (136).

A compelling test of the hypothesis that CRF-induced increases in anxiety-like responses during drug withdrawal has motivational significance in contributing to negative emotional states is the observation that CRF antagonists can reverse the elevation in reward thresholds produced by drug withdrawal. Nicotine and alcohol withdrawal-induced elevations in reward thresholds were reversed by a CRF antagonist (137, 138). These effects have been localized to both the CeA and nucleus accumbens shell (139).

Enhanced dynorphin action is hypothesized to mediate the depression-like, aversive responses to stress, and dysphoric-like responses during withdrawal from drugs of abuse (49, 56, 57, 140–145). For example, pretreatment with a κ-opioid receptor antagonist blocked stress-induced analgesia and stress-induced immobility (57), decreased anxiety-like behavior in the elevated plus maze and open field, decreased conditioned fear in fear-potentiated startle (145), and blocked depressive-like behavior induced by cocaine withdrawal (140).

BRAIN STRESS SUBSTRATES THAT MEDIATE DRUG TAKING WITH EXTENDED ACCESS
CORTICOTROPIN-RELEASING FACTOR, COMPULSIVE-LIKE DRUG SEEKING, AND THE EXTENDED AMYGDALA
The ability of CRF antagonists to block the anxiogenic-like and aversive-like motivational effects of drug withdrawal predicted motivational effects of CRF antagonists in animal models of extended access to drugs. CRF antagonists selectively blocked the increased self-administration of drugs associated with extended access to intravenous self-administration of cocaine (146), nicotine (77), and heroin [(147); **Figure 8**]. For example, systemic administration of a CRF₁ antagonist blocked the increased self-administration of nicotine associated with withdrawal in extended-access (23 h) animals (77).

Corticotropin-releasing factor antagonists also blocked the increased self-administration of ethanol in dependent rats [(124); **Figure 8**]. For example, exposure to repeated cycles of chronic ethanol vapor produced substantial increases in ethanol intake in rats during both acute withdrawal and protracted abstinence [2 weeks post-acute withdrawal; 76, 148]. Intracerebroventricular administration of a CRF₁/CRF₂ antagonist blocked the dependence-induced increase in ethanol self-administration during both acute withdrawal and protracted abstinence (149). Systemic injections of small-molecule CRF₁ antagonists also blocked the increased ethanol intake associated with acute withdrawal (124) and protracted abstinence (150). When administered directly into the CeA, a CRF₁/CRF₂ antagonist blocked ethanol self-administration in ethanol-dependent rats (151). These effects appear to be mediated by the actions of CRF on GABAergic interneurons within the CeA, and a CRF antagonist administered chronically during the development of dependence blocked the development of compulsive-like responding for ethanol (116).

Altogether, these results suggest that CRF in the basal forebrain may also play an important role in the development of the aversive motivational effects that drive the increased drug-seeking associated with cocaine, heroin, nicotine, and alcohol dependence.

DYNORPHIN, COMPULSIVE-LIKE DRUG SEEKING, AND THE EXTENDED AMYGDALA
Recent evidence suggests that the dynorphin-κ opioid system also mediates compulsive-like drug responding (methamphetamine, heroin, and alcohol) with extended access and dependence. Evidence from our laboratory has shown a small-molecule κ antagonist selectively blocked responding on a progressive-ratio schedule for cocaine in rats with extended access (152). Even more compelling is that excessive drug self-administration can also be blocked by κ antagonists (152–155) and may be mediated by the shell of the nucleus accumbens (156). However, the neurobiological circuits involved in mediating the effects of activation of the dynorphin-κ opioid system on the escalation of methamphetamine intake with extended access, remain unknown.

NPY, COMPULSIVE DRUG SEEKING, AND THE EXTENDED AMGYDALA
Neuropeptide Y is a neuropeptide with dramatic anxiolytic-like properties localized to multiple brain regions but heavily innervating the amygdala. It is hypothesized to have effects opposite to CRF in the negative motivational state of withdrawal from drugs of abuse and as such increases in NPY function may act in opposition to the actions of increases in CRF (157). Significant evidence suggests that activation of NPY in the CeA can block the motivational aspects of dependence associated with chronic ethanol administration. NPY administered intracerebroventricularly blocked the increased drug intake associated with ethanol dependence (158, 159). NPY also decreased excessive alcohol intake in alcohol-preferring rats (160). Injection of NPY directly into the CeA (161) and viral vector-enhanced expression of NPY in the CeA also blocked the increased drug intake associated with ethanol dependence (162). At the cellular level, NPY, like CRF₁ antagonists, blocks the increase in GABA release in the CeA produced by ethanol and also when administered chronically blocks the transition to excessive drinking with the development of dependence (163). The role of NPY in the actions of other drugs of abuse is limited, particularly with regard to dependence and compulsive drug seeking. NPY₅ receptor knockout mice have a blunted response to the rewarding effects of cocaine (164, 165), and NPY knockout mice show hypersensitivity to cocaine self-administration (166). NPY itself injected intracerebroventricularly facilitated heroin and cocaine self-administration and induced reinstatement of heroin seeking in limited-access rats (167, 168). An NPY Y₂ antagonist, possibly acting presynaptically to release NPY, blocked social anxiety associated with nicotine withdrawal (169), and NPY injected intracerebroventricularly blocked the somatic signs but not reward deficits associated with nicotine withdrawal (170). However, the role of NPY in compulsive drug seeking with extended-access remains to be studied. The hypothesis here would be that NPY is a buffer or homeostatic response to between-system neuroadaptations that can return the brain emotional systems to homeostasis (157, 171).

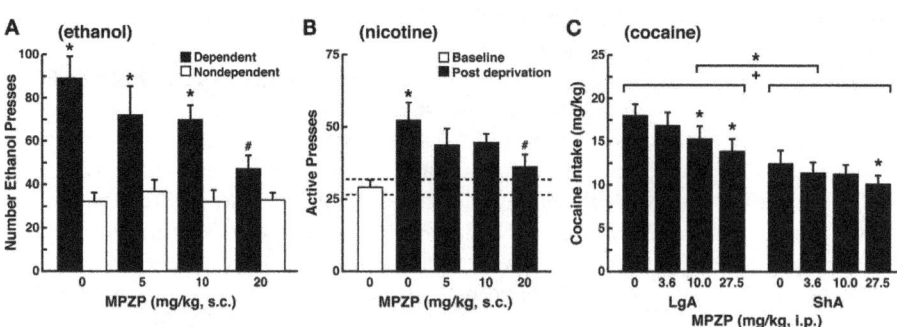

FIGURE 8 | Effects of CRF₁ antagonist on compulsive-like responding for drugs of abuse in rats with extended access to drug (A). The effect of the CRF₁ receptor antagonist MPZP on operant self-administration of alcohol in dependent and non-dependent rats. Testing was conducted when dependent animals were in acute withdrawal (6–8 h after removal from vapors). Dependent rats self-administered significantly more than non-dependent animals, and MPZP dose-dependently reduced alcohol self-administration only in dependent animals. The data are expressed as mean + SEM lever presses for alcohol [taken with permission from Ref. (190)].

(B) Abstinence-induced escalation of nicotine intake is blocked by a CRF₁ receptor antagonist. Effect of MPZP (s.c., −1 h) on nicotine self-administration during the active period in rats given extended access to nicotine. *$p < 0.05$, compared with baseline; #$p < 0.05$, compared with after-abstinence vehicle treatment; $n = 8$). The data are expressed as mean + SEM lever presses for nicotine [taken with permission from Ref. 77]. **(C)** MPZP reduces cocaine intake in ShA and LgA rats. The data are expressed as mean + SEM cocaine intake (mg/kg). *$p < 0.05$, **$p < 0.01$, compared with vehicle [taken with permission from Ref. (146)].

Corticotropin-releasing factor, stress, and the frontal cortex

Converging lines of evidence suggest that impairment of medial PFC (mPFC) cognitive function and overactivation of the CeA may be linked to the development of compulsive-like responding for drugs of abuse during extended access (172–174). Extended access to cocaine self-administration induced an escalated pattern of cocaine intake associated with an impairment of working memory and decrease in the density of dorsomedial PFC (dmPFC) neurons that lasted for months after cocaine cessation (172). Whereas LgA and ShA rats exhibited a high percentage of correct responses in the delayed non-matching-to-sample task under low cognitive demand (delay < 10 s), increasing the working memory load (i.e., close to the capacity limit of working memory) by increasing the delay from 10 to 70 and 130 s revealed a robust working memory deficit in LgA rats. Furthermore, the magnitude of escalation of cocaine intake was negatively correlated with working memory performance in ShA and LgA rats with the 70- and 130-s delays but not with the 10-s delay or with baseline performance during training, demonstrating that the relationship between the escalation of cocaine intake and behavioral performance in this task was restricted to working memory performance under high cognitive demand. The density of neurons and oligodendrocytes in the dmPFC was positively correlated with working memory performance. A lower density of neurons or oligodendrocytes in the dmPFC was associated with more severe working memory impairment. Working memory was also correlated with the density of oligodendrocytes in the orbitofrontal cortex (OFC), suggesting that OFC alterations after escalated drug intake may play a role in working memory deficits. However, no correlation was found between working memory performance and neuronal density in the OFC, suggesting that OFC neurons may be less vulnerable to the deleterious effects of chronic cocaine exposure than dmPFC neurons. Thus, PFC dysfunction may exacerbate the loss of control

associated with compulsive drug use and facilitate the progression to drug addiction.

Similar results have been observed in an animal model of binge alcohol consumption, even before the development of dependence. Using an animal model of escalation of alcohol intake with chronic intermittent access to alcohol, in which rats are given continuous (24 h per day, 7 days per week) or intermittent (3 days per week) access to alcohol (20% v/v) using a two-bottle choice paradigm, FBJ murine osteosarcoma viral oncogene homolog (Fos) expression in the mPFC, CeA, hippocampus, and nucleus accumbens were measured and correlated with working memory and anxiety-like behavior (175). Abstinence from alcohol in rats with a history of escalation of alcohol intake specifically recruited GABA and CRF neurons in the mPFC and produced working memory impairments associated with excessive alcohol drinking during acute (24–72 h) but not protracted (16–68 days) abstinence. The abstinence from alcohol was associated with a functional disconnection of the mPFC and CeA but not mPFC or nucleus accumbens. These results show that recruitment of a subset of GABA and CRF neurons in the mPFC during withdrawal and disconnection of the PFC CeA pathway may be critical for impaired executive control over motivated behavior, suggesting that dysregulation of mPFC interneurons may be an early index of neuroadaptation in alcohol dependence.

BRAIN STRESS SYSTEMS IN ADDICTION: AN ALLOSTATIC VIEW

More importantly for the present thesis, as dependence and withdrawal develop, brain anti-reward systems, such as CRF and dynorphin, are recruited in the extended amygdala. We hypothesize that this brain stress neurotransmitter that is known to be activated during the development of excessive drug taking

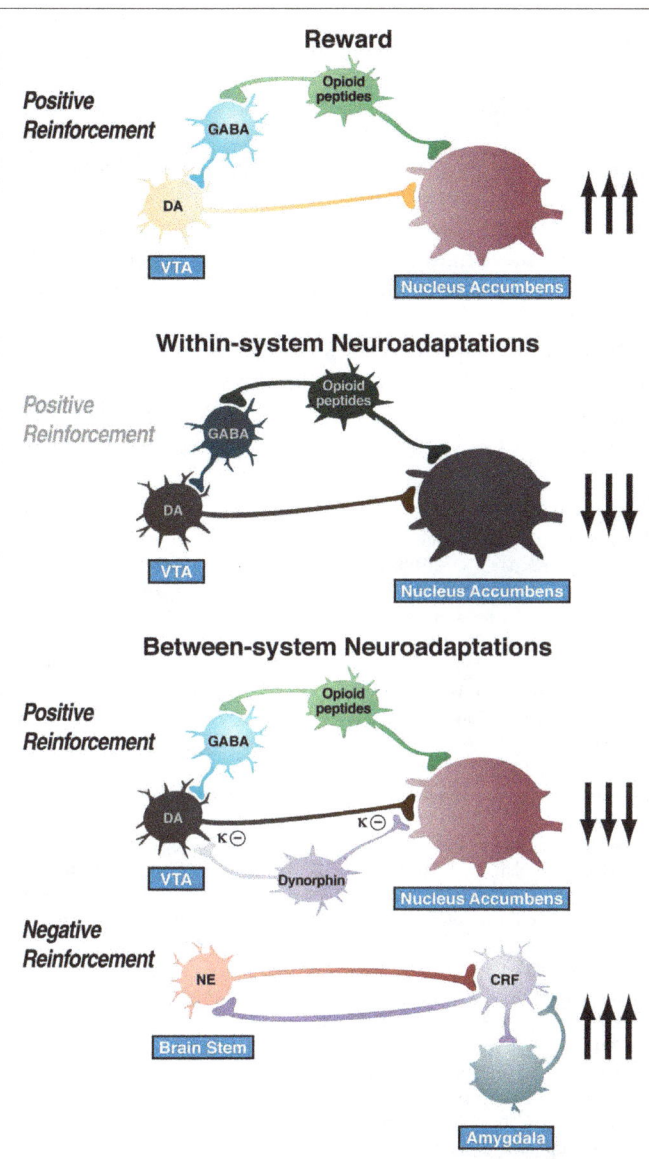

Reward

Within-system Neuroadaptations

Between-system Neuroadaptations

FIGURE 9 | Diagram of the hypothetical "within-system" and "between-system" changes that lead to the "darkness within". (Top) Circuitry for drug reward with major contributions from mesolimbic dopamine and opioid peptides that converge on the nucleus accumbens. During the *binge/intoxication* stage of the addiction cycle, the reward circuitry is excessively engaged, Middle. Such excessive activation of the reward system triggers "within-system" neurobiological adaptations during the *withdrawal/negative affect* stage, including activation of cyclic adenosine monophosphate (cAMP) and cAMP response element-binding protein (CREB), downregulation of dopamine D_2 receptors, and decreased firing of ventral tegmental area (VTA) dopaminergic neurons, Bottom. As dependence progresses and the *withdrawal/negative affect* stage is repeated, two major "between-system" neuroadaptations occur. One is activation of dynorphin feedback that further decreases dopaminergic activity. The other is recruitment of extrahypothalamic norepinephrine (NE)-corticotropin-releasing factor (CRF) systems in the extended amygdala. Facilitation of the brain stress system in the prefrontal cortex is hypothesized to exacerbate the between-system neuroadaptations while contributing to the persistence of the dark side into the *preoccupation/anticipation* stage of the addiction cycle [taken with permission from Ref. (191)].

comprises a between-system opponent process, and this activation is manifest when the drug in removed, producing anxiety, hyperkatifeia, and irritability symptoms associated with acute and protracted abstinence. Notably, however, there is evidence of CRF immunoreactivity in the ventral tegmental area, and a CRF_1 receptor antagonist injected directly into the ventral tegmental area blocked the social stress-induced escalation of cocaine self-administration (176). Altogether, these observations suggest between-system/within-system neuroadaptations that were originally hypothesized for dynorphin by Carlezon and Nestler (177), in which activation of CREB by excessive dopamine and opioid peptide receptor activation in the nucleus accumbens triggers the induction of dynorphin to feed back to suppress dopamine release. Thus, we hypothesize that anti-reward circuits are recruited as between-system neuroadaptations (178) during the development of addiction and produce aversive or stress-like states (179–181) via two mechanisms: direct activation of stress-like, fear-like states in the extended amygdala (CRF) and indirect activation of a depression-like state by suppressing dopamine (dynorphin).

A critical problem in drug addiction is chronic relapse, in which addicted individuals return to compulsive drug taking long after acute withdrawal. This corresponds to the *preoccupation/anticipation* stage of the addiction cycle outlined above. Koob and Le Moal also hypothesized that the dysregulations that comprise the "dark side" of drug addiction persist during protracted abstinence to set the tone for vulnerability to "craving" by activating drug-, cue-, and stress-induced reinstatement neurocircuits that are now driven by a reorganized and possibly hypofunctioning prefrontal system. The hypothesized allostatic, dysregulated reward, and sensitized stress state produces the motivational symptoms of acute withdrawal and protracted abstinence and provides the basis by which drug priming, drug cues, and acute stressors acquire even more power to elicit drug-seeking behavior (92). Thus, the combination of decreases in reward system function and recruitment of anti-reward systems provides a powerful source of negative reinforcement that contributes to compulsive drug-seeking behavior and addiction. A compelling argument can be made that the neuroplasticity that charges the CRF stress system may indeed begin much earlier that previously thought via stress actions in the PFC.

The overall conceptual theme argued here is that drug addiction represents an excessive and prolonged engagement of homeostatic brain regulatory mechanisms that regulate the response of the body to rewards and stressors. The dysregulation of the incentive salience systems may begin with the first administration of drug (182), and the dysregulation of the stress axis may begin with the binge and subsequent acute withdrawal, triggering a cascade of changes, from activation of the HPA axis to activation of CRF in the PFC to activation of CRF in the extended amygdala to activation of dynorphin in the ventral striatum (**Figure 9**). This cascade of overactivation of the stress axis represents more than simply a transient homeostatic dysregulation; it also represents the dynamic homeostatic dysregulation termed *allostasis*.

Repeated challenges, such as with drugs of abuse, lead to attempts of the brain stress systems at the molecular, cellular, and neurocircuitry levels to maintain stability but at a cost. For the drug addiction framework elaborated here, the residual decrease in the brain reward systems and activation of the brain stress systems to produce the consequent negative emotional state is termed an *allostatic state* (15). This state represents a combination of recruitment of anti-reward systems and consequent chronic decreased function of reward circuits, both of which lead to the compulsive drug seeking and loss of control over intake. How these systems are modulated by other known brain emotional systems localized to the basal forebrain, where the ventral striatum and extended amygdala project to convey emotional valence, how frontal cortex dysregulations in the cognitive domain are linked to impairments in executive function to contribute to the dysregulation of the extended amygdala, and how individuals differ at the molecular-genetic level of analysis to convey loading on these circuits remain challenges for future research.

ACKNOWLEDGMENTS

The author would like to thank Michael Arends and Mellany Santos for their assistance with the preparation of this manuscript. Research was supported by National Institutes of Health grants AA006420, AA020608, AA012602, and AA008459 from the National Institute on Alcohol Abuse and Alcoholism, DA010072, DA004043, DA023597, and DA004398 from the National Institute on Drug Abuse, and DK26741 from the National Institute of Diabetes and Digestive and Kidney Diseases. Research also was supported by the Pearson Center for Alcoholism and Addiction Research. This is publication number 24002 from The Scripps Research Institute.

REFERENCES

1. Koob GF, Le Moal M. Drug abuse: hedonic homeostatic dysregulation. *Science* (1997) **278**:52–8. doi:10.1126/science.278.5335.52

2. Olds J, Milner P. Positive reinforcement produced by electrical stimulation of septal area and other regions of rat brain. *J Comp Physiol Psychol* (1954) **47**:419–27. doi:10.1037/h0058775

3. Koob GF, Winger GD, Meyerhoff JL, Annau Z. Effects of D-amphetamine on concurrent self-stimulation of forebrain and brain stem loci. *Brain Res* (1977) **137**:109–26. doi:10.1016/0006-8993(77)91015-0

4. Simon H, Stinus L, Tassin JP, Lavielle S, Blanc G, Thierry AM, et al. Is the dopaminergic mesocorticolimbic system necessary for intracranial self-stimulation? Biochemical and behavioral studies from A10 cell bodies and terminals. *Behav Neural Biol* (1979) **27**:125–45. doi:10.1016/S0163-1047(79)91745-X

5. Kornetsky C, Esposito RU. Euphorigenic drugs: effects on the reward pathways of the brain. *Fed Proc* (1979) **38**:2473–6.

6. Hernandez G, Hamdani S, Rajabi H, Conover K, Stewart J, Arvanitogiannis A, et al. Prolonged rewarding stimulation of the rat medial forebrain bundle: neurochemical and behavioral consequences. *Behav Neurosci* (2006) **120**:888–904. doi:10.1037/0735-7044.120.4.888

7. Garris PA, Kilpatrick M, Bunin MA, Michael D, Walker QD, Wightman RM. Dissociation of dopamine release in the nucleus accumbens from intracranial self-stimulation. *Nature* (1999) **398**:67–9. doi:10.1038/18019

8. Miliaressis E, Emond C, Merali Z. Re-evaluation of the role of dopamine in intracranial self-stimulation using in vivo microdialysis. *Behav Brain Res* (1991) **46**:43–8. doi:10.1016/S0166-4328(05)80095-6

9. Robinson TE, Berridge KC. The neural basis of drug craving: an incentive-sensitization theory of addiction. *Brain Res Rev* (1993) **18**:247–91. doi:10.1016/0165-0173(93)90013-P

10. Robbins TW. Relationship between reward-enhancing and stereotypical effects of psychomotor stimulant drugs. *Nature* (1976) **264**:57–9. doi:10.1038/264057a0

11. Miliaressis E, Le Moal M. Stimulation of the medial forebrain bundle: behavioral dissociation of its rewarding and activating effects. *Neurosci Lett* (1976) **2**:295–300. doi:10.1016/0304-3940(76)90163-4

12. Salamone JD, Correa M, Farrar A, Mingote SM. Effort-related functions of nucleus accumbens dopamine and associated forebrain circuits. *Psychopharmacology (Berl)* (2007) **191**:461–82. doi:10.1007/s00213-006-0668-9

13. Le Moal M, Simon H. Mesocorticolimbic dopaminergic network: functional and regulatory roles. *Physiol Rev* (1991) **71**:155–234.

14. Robbins TW, Everitt BJ. A role for mesencephalic dopamine in activation: commentary on Berridge (2006). *Psychopharmacology (Berl)* (2007) **191**:433–7. doi:10.1007/s00213-006-0528-7

15. Koob GF, Le Moal M. Drug addiction, dysregulation of reward, and allostasis. *Neuropsychopharmacology* (2001) **24**:97–129. doi:10.1016/S0893-133X(00)00195-0

16. Koob GF. The neurobiology of addiction: a neuroadaptational view relevant for diagnosis. *Addiction* (2006) **101**:23–30. doi:10.1111/j.1360-0443.2006.01586.x

17. Nestler EJ. Is there a common molecular pathway for addiction? *Nat Neurosci* (2005) **8**:1445–9. doi:10.1038/nn1578

18. Koob GF. A role for brain stress systems in addiction. *Neuron* (2008) **59**:11–34. doi:10.1016/j.neuron.2008.06.012

19. Sidhpura N, Parsons LH. Endocannabinoid-mediated synaptic plasticity and addiction-related behavior. *Neuropharmacology* (2011) **61**:1070–87. doi:10.1016/j.neuropharm.2011.05.034

20. Heilig M. The NPY system in stress, anxiety and depression. *Neuropeptides* (2004) **38**:213–24. doi:10.1016/j.npep.2004.05.002

21. Rainnie DG, Bergeron R, Sajdyk TJ, Patil M, Gehlert DR, Shekhar A. Corticotrophin releasing factor-induced synaptic plasticity in the amygdala translates stress into emotional disorders. *J Neurosci* (2004) **24**:3471–9. doi:10.1523/JNEUROSCI.5740-03.2004

22. Lemos JC, Wanat MJ, Smith JS, Reyes BA, Hollon NG, Van Bockstaele EJ, et al. Severe stress switches CRF action in the nucleus accumbens from appetitive to aversive. *Nature* (2012) **490**:402–6. doi:10.1038/nature11436

23. Dunn AJ, Berridge CW. Physiological and behavioral responses to corticotropin-releasing factor administration: is CRF a mediator of anxiety or stress responses? *Brain Res Rev* (1990) **15**:71–100. doi:10.1016/0165-0173(90)90012-D

24. Koob GF, Heinrichs SC, Menzaghi F, Pich EM, Britton KT. Corticotropin releasing factor, stress and behavior. *Semin Neurosci* (1994) **6**:221–9. doi:10.1006/smns.1994.1029

25. Koob GF, Bartfai T, Roberts AJ. The use of molecular genetic approaches in the neuropharmacology of corticotropin-releasing factor. *Int J Comp Psychol* (2001) **14**:90–110.

26. Sarnyai Z, Shaham Y, Heinrichs SC. The role of corticotropin-releasing factor in drug addiction. *Pharmacol Rev* (2001) **53**:209–43.

27. Koob GF, Heinrichs SC. A role for corticotropin-releasing factor and urocortin in behavioral responses to stressors. *Brain Res* (1999) **848**:141–52. doi:10.1016/S0006-8993(99)01991-5

28. Spina M, Merlo-Pich E, Chan RKW, Basso AM, Rivier J, Vale W, et al. Appetite-suppressing effects of urocortin, a CRF-related neuropeptide. *Science* (1996) **273**:1561–4. doi:10.1126/science.273.5281.1561

29. Pelleymounter MA, Joppa M, Carmouche M, Cullen MJ, Brown B, Murphy B, et al. Role of corticotropin-releasing factor (CRF) receptors in the anorexic syndrome induced by CRF. *J Pharmacol Exp Ther* (2000) **293**:799–806.

30. Takahashi LK, Ho SP, Livanov V, Graciani N, Arneric SP. Antagonism of CRF₂ receptors produces anxiolytic behavior in animal models of anxiety. *Brain Res* (2001) **902**:135–42. doi:10.1016/S0006-8993(01)02405-2

31. Swanson LW, Sawchenko PE, Rivier J, Vale W. The organization of ovine corticotropin-releasing factor immunoreactive cells and fibers in the rat brain: an immunohistochemical study. *Neuroendocrinology* (1983) **36**:165–86. doi:10.1159/000123454

32. Turnbull AV, Rivier C. Corticotropin-releasing factor (CRF) and endocrine responses to stress: CRF receptors, binding protein, and related peptides. *Proc Natl Acad Sci U S A* (1997) **215**:1–10.

33. Koob GF, Kreek MJ. Stress, dysregulation of drug reward pathways, and the transition to drug dependence. *Am J Psychiatry* (2007) **164**:1149–59. doi:10.1176/appi.ajp.2007.05030503

34. Heimer L, Alheid G. Piecing together the puzzle of basal forebrain anatomy. In: Napier TC, Kalivas PW, Hanin I editors. *The Basal Forebrain: Anatomy to Function (series title: Advances in Experimental Medicine and Biology* (Vol. 295), New York: Plenum Press (1991). p. 1–42.

35. Alheid GF, De Olmos JS, Beltramino CA. Amygdala and extended amygdala. In: Paxinos G editor. *The Rat Nervous System.* San Diego, CA: Academic Press (1995). p. 495–578.

36. Maier SF, Watkins LR. Stressor controllability and learned helplessness: the roles of the dorsal raphe nucleus, serotonin, and corticotropin-releasing factor. *Neurosci Biobehav Rev* (2005) **29**:829–41. doi:10.1016/j.neubiorev.2005.03.021

37. Sink KS, Walker DL, Freeman SM, Flandreau EI, Ressler KJ, Davis M. Effects of continuously enhanced corticotropin releasing factor expression within the bed nucleus of the stria terminalis on conditioned and unconditioned anxiety. *Mol Psychiatry* (2013) **18**:308–19. doi:10.1038/mp.2011.188

38. Neugebauer V, Li W, Bird GC, Han JS. The amygdala and persistent pain. *Neuroscientist* (2004) **10**:221–34. doi:10.1177/1073858403261077

39. Chavkin C, James IF, Goldstein A. Dynorphin is a specific endogenous ligand of the κ opioid receptor. *Science* (1982) **215**:413–5. doi:10.1126/science.6120570

40. Watson SJ, Khachaturian H, Akil H, Coy DH, Goldstein A. Comparison of the distribution of dynorphin systems and enkephalin systems in brain. *Science* (1982) **218**:1134–6. doi:10.1126/science.6128790

41. Fallon JH, Leslie FM. Distribution of dynorphin and enkephalin peptides in the rat brain. *J Comp Neurol* (1986) **249**:293–336. doi:10.1002/cne.902490302

42. Shippenberg TS, Zapata A, Chefer VI. Dynorphin and the pathophysiology of drug addiction. *Pharmacol Ther* (2007) **116**:306–21. doi:10.1016/j.pharmthera.2007.06.011

43. Wee S, Koob GF. The role of the dynorphin-κ opioid system in the reinforcing effects of drugs of abuse. *Psychopharmacology (Berl)* (2010) **210**:121–35. doi:10.1007/s00213-010-1825-8

44. Mucha RF, Herz A. Motivational properties of kappa and mu opioid receptor agonists studied with place and taste preference conditioning. *Psychopharmacology (Berl)* (1985) **86**:274–80. doi:10.1007/BF00432213

45. Pfeiffer A, Brantl V, Herz A, Emrich HM. Psychotomimesis mediated by κ opiate receptors. *Science* (1986) **233**:774–6. doi:10.1126/science.3016896

46. Todtenkopf MS, Marcus JF, Portoghese PS, Carlezon WA Jr. Effects of κ-opioid receptor ligands on intracranial self-stimulation in rats. *Psychopharmacology (Berl)* (2004) **172**:463–70. doi:10.1007/s00213-003-1680-y

47. Pliakas AM, Carlson RR, Neve RL, Konradi C, Nestler EJ, Carlezon WA Jr. Altered responsiveness to cocaine and increased immobility in the forced swim test associated with elevated cAMP response element-binding protein expression in nucleus accumbens. *J Neurosci* (2001) **21**:7397–403.

48. Nestler EJ. Historical review: molecular and cellular mechanisms of opiate and cocaine addiction. *Trends Pharmacol Sci* (2004) **25**:210–8. doi:10.1016/j.tips.2004.02.005

49. Mague SD, Pliakas AM, Todtenkopf MS, Tomasiewicz HC, Zhang Y, Stevens WC Jr., et al. Antidepressant-like effects of κ-opioid receptor antagonists in the forced swim test in rats. *J Pharmacol Exp Ther* (2003) **305**:323–30. doi:10.1124/jpet.102.046433

50. Knoll AT, Carlezon WA Jr. Dynorphin, stress, and depression. *Brain Res* (2010) **1314**:56–73. doi:10.1016/j.brainres.2009.09.074

51. Hjelmstad GO, Fields HL. Kappa opioid receptor inhibition of glutamatergic transmission in the nucleus accumbens shell. *J Neurophysiol* (2001) **85**:1153–8.

52. Gray AM, Rawls SM, Shippenberg TS, McGinty JF. The kappa-opioid agonist, U-69593, decreases acute amphetamine-evoked behaviors and calcium-dependent

dialysate levels of dopamine and glutamate in the ventral striatum. *J Neurochem* (1999) **73**:1066–74. doi:10.1046/j.1471-4159.1999.0731066.x

53. Margolis EB, Lock H, Chefer VI, Shippenberg TS, Hjelmstad GO, Fields HL. Kappa opioids selectively control dopaminergic neurons projecting to the prefrontal cortex. *Proc Natl Acad Sci U S A* (2006) **103**:2938–42. doi:10.1073/pnas.0511159103

54. Tejeda HA. *Modulation of Extracellular Dopamine in the Prefrontal Cortex by Local and Ventral Tegmental Area Kappa-Opioid Receptors.* Society for Neuroscience Meeting, Chicago (2009). Abstract no: 751.7.

55. Valdez GR, Platt DM, Rowlett JK, Rüedi-Bettschen D, Spealman RD. κ Agonist-induced reinstatement of cocaine seeking in squirrel monkeys: a role for opioid and stress-related mechanisms. *J Pharmacol Exp Ther* (2007) **323**:525–33. doi:10.1124/jpet.107.125484

56. Land BB, Bruchas MR, Lemos JC, Xu M, Melief EJ, Chavkin C. The dysphoric component of stress is encoded by activation of the dynorphin kappa-opioid system. *J Neurosci* (2008) **28**:407–14. doi:10.1523/JNEUROSCI.4458-07.2008

57. McLaughlin JP, Marton-Popovici M, Chavkin C. κ Opioid receptor antagonism and prodynorphin gene disruption block stress-induced behavioral responses. *J Neurosci* (2003) **23**:5674–83.

58. Solomon RL, Corbit JD. An opponent-process theory of motivation: 1. Temporal dynamics of affect. *Psychol Rev* (1974) **81**:119–45.

59. McEwen BS. Allostasis and allostatic load: implications for neuropsychopharmacology. *Neuropsychopharmacology* (2000) **22**:108–24. doi:10.1016/S0893-133X(99)00129-3

60. American Psychiatric Association. *Diagnostic and Statistical Manual of Mental Disorders.* 4th ed. Washington DC: American Psychiatric Press (1994).

61. Koob GF. Theoretical frameworks and mechanistic aspects of alcohol addiction: alcohol addiction: alcohol addiction as a reward deficit disorder. In: Sommer WH, Spanagel R editors. *Behavioral Neurobiology of Alcohol Addiction (Series Title: Current Topics in Behavioral Neuroscience* (Vol. 13), Berlin: Springer-Verlag (2013). p. 3–30.

62. Khantzian EJ. The self-medication hypothesis of substance use disorders: a reconsideration and recent applications. *Harvard Rev Psychiatry* (1997) **4**:231–44. doi:10.3109/10673229709030550

63. Markou A, Koob GF. Post-cocaine anhedonia: an animal model of cocaine withdrawal. *Neuropsychopharmacology* (1991) **4**:17–26.

64. Paterson NE, Myers C, Markou A. Effects of repeated withdrawal from continuous amphetamine administration on brain reward function in rats. *Psychopharmacology (Berl)* (2000) **152**:440–6. doi:10.1007/s002130000559

65. Schulteis G, Markou A, Gold LH, Stinus L, Koob GF. Relative sensitivity to naloxone of multiple indices of opiate withdrawal: a quantitative dose-response analysis. *J Pharmacol Exp Ther* (1994) **271**:1391–8.

66. Gardner EL, Vorel SR. Cannabinoid transmission and reward-related events. *Neurobiol Dis* (1998) **5**:502–33. doi:10.1006/nbdi.1998.0219

67. Epping-Jordan MP, Watkins SS, Koob GF, Markou A. Dramatic decreases in brain reward function during nicotine withdrawal. *Nature* (1998) **393**:76–9. doi:10.1038/30001

68. Schulteis G, Markou A, Cole M, Koob GF. Decreased brain reward produced by ethanol withdrawal. *Proc Natl Acad Sci U S A* (1995) **92**:5880–4. doi:10.1073/pnas.92.13.5880

69. Koob GF. Neurobiological substrates for the dark side of compulsivity in addiction. *Neuropharmacology* (2009) **56**:18–31. doi:10.1016/j.neuropharm.2008.07.043

70. Kenny PJ, Polis I, Koob GF, Markou A. Low dose cocaine self-administration transiently increases but high dose cocaine persistently decreases brain reward function in rats. *Eur J Neurosci* (2003) **17**:191–5. doi:10.1046/j.1460-9568.2003.02443.x

71. Liu J, Schulteis G. Brain reward deficits accompany naloxone-precipitated withdrawal from acute opioid dependence. *Pharmacol Biochem Behav* (2004) **79**:101–8. doi:10.1016/j.pbb.2004.06.006

72. Schulteis G, Liu J. Brain reward deficits accompany withdrawal (hangover) from acute ethanol in rats. *Alcohol* (2006) **39**:21–8. doi:10.1016/j.alcohol.2006.06.008

73. Ahmed SH, Walker JR, Koob GF. Persistent increase in the motivation to take heroin in rats with a history of drug escalation. *Neuropsychopharmacology* (2000) **22**:413–21. doi:10.1016/S0893-133X(99)00133-5

74. Ahmed SH, Koob GF. Transition from moderate to excessive drug intake: change in hedonic set point. *Science* (1998) **282**:298–300. doi:10.1126/science.282.5387.298

75. Kitamura O, Wee S, Specio SE, Koob GF, Pulvirenti L. Escalation of methamphetamine self-administration in rats: a dose-effect function. *Psychopharmacology (Berl)* (2006) **186**:48–53. doi:10.1007/s00213-006-0353-z

76. O'Dell LE, Roberts AJ, Smith RT, Koob GF. Enhanced alcohol self-administration after intermittent versus continuous alcohol vapor exposure. *Alcohol Clin Exp Res* (2004) **28**:1676–82. doi:10.1097/01.ALC.0000145781.11923.4E

77. George O, Ghozland S, Azar MR, Cottone P, Zorrilla EP, Parsons LH, et al. CRF-CRF$_1$ system activation mediates withdrawal-induced increases in nicotine self-administration in nicotine-dependent rats. *Proc Natl Acad Sci U S A* (2007) **104**:17198–203. doi:10.1073/pnas.0707585104

78. Quadros IM, Miczek KA. Two modes of intense cocaine bingeing: increased persistence after social defeat stress and increased rate of intake due to extended access conditions in rats. *Psychopharmacology (Berl)* (2009) **206**:109–20. doi:10.1007/s00213-009-1584-6

79. Vendruscolo L, Schlosburg JE, Misra KK, Chen SA, Greenwell TN, Koob GF. Escalation patterns of varying periods of heroin access. *Pharmacol Biochem Behav* (2011) **98**:570–4. doi:10.1016/j.pbb.2011.03.004

80. Ahmed SH, Koob GF. Long-lasting increase in the set point for cocaine self-administration after escalation in rats. *Psychopharmacology (Berl)* (1999) **146**:303–12. doi:10.1007/s002130051121

81. Deroche V, Le Moal M, Piazza PV. Cocaine self-administration increases the incentive motivational properties of the drug in rats. *Eur J Neurosci* (1999) **11**:2731–6. doi:10.1046/j.1460-9568.1999.00696.x

82. Mantsch JR, Yuferov V, Mathieu-Kia AM, Ho A, Kreek MJ. Effects of extended access to high versus low cocaine doses on self-administration, cocaine-induced reinstatement and brain mRNA levels in rats. *Psychopharmacology (Berl)* (2004) **175**:26–36. doi:10.1007/s00213-004-1778-x

83. Paterson NE, Markou A. Increased motivation for self-administered cocaine after escalated cocaine intake. *Neuroreport* (2003) **14**:2229–32. doi:10.1097/00001756-200312020-00019

84. Wee S, Mandyam CD, Lekic DM, Koob GF. α$_1$-Noradrenergic system role in increased motivation for cocaine intake in rats with prolonged access. *Eur Neuropsychopharmacol* (2008) **18**:303–11. doi:10.1016/j.euroneuro.2007.08.003

85. Walker BM, Koob GF. The γ-aminobutyric acid-B receptor agonist baclofen attenuates responding for ethanol in ethanol-dependent rats. *Alcohol Clin Exp Res* (2007) **31**:11–8. doi:10.1111/j.1530-0277.2006.00259.x

86. Deroche V, Le Moal M, Piazza PV. Cocaine self-administration increases the incentive motivational properties of the drug in rats. *Eur J Neurosci* (1999) **11**:2731–6. doi:10.1046/j.1460-9568.1999.00696.x

87. Jonkman S, Pelloux Y, Everitt BJ. Drug intake is sufficient, but conditioning is not necessary for the emergence of compulsive cocaine seeking after extended self-administration. *Neuropsychopharmacology* (2012) **37**:1612–9. doi:10.1038/npp

88. Ben-Shahar O, Posthumus EJ, Waldroup SA, Ettenberg A. Heightened drug-seeking motivation following extended daily access to self-administered cocaine. *Prog Neuropsychopharmacol Biol Psychiatry* (2008) **32**:863–9. doi:10.1016/j.pnpbp.2008.01.002

89. Vanderschuren LJ, Everitt BJ. Drug seeking becomes compulsive after prolonged cocaine self-administration. *Science* (2004) **305**:1017–9. doi:10.1126/science.1098975

90. Deroche-Gamonet V, Belin D, Piazza PV. Evidence for addiction-like behavior in the rat. *Science* (2004) **305**:1014–7. doi:10.1126/science.1099020

91. Pelloux Y, Everitt BJ, Dickinson A. Compulsive drug seeking by rats under punishment: effects of drug taking history. *Psychopharmacology (Berl)* (2007) **194**:127–37. doi:10.1007/s00213-007-0805-0

92. Vendruscolo LF, Barbier E, Schlosburg JE, Misra KK, Whitfield T Jr., Logrip ML, et al. Corticosteroid-dependent plasticity mediates compulsive alcohol drinking in rats. *J Neurosci* (2012) **32**:7563–71. doi:10.1523/JNEUROSCI.0069-12.2012

93. Vezina P. Sensitization of midbrain dopamine neuron reactivity and the self-administration of psychomotor stimulant drugs. *Neurosci Biobehav Rev* (2004) **27**:827–39. doi:10.1016/j.neubiorev.2003.11.001

94. Ben-Shahar O, Ahmed SH, Koob GF, Ettenberg A. The transition from controlled to compulsive drug use is associated with a loss of sensitization. *Brain Res* (2004) **995**:46–54. doi:10.1016/j.brainres.2003.09.053

95. Knackstedt LA, Kalivas PW. Extended access to cocaine self-administration enhances drug-primed reinstatement but not behavioral sensitization. *J Pharmacol Exp Ther* (2007) **322**:1103–9. doi:10.1124/jpet.107.122861

96. Ahmed SH, Cador M. Dissociation of psychomotor sensitization from compulsive cocaine consumption. *Neuropsychopharmacology* (2006) **31**:563–71. doi:10.1038/sj.npp.1300834

97. Ahmed SH, Kenny PJ, Koob GF, Markou A. Neurobiological evidence for hedonic allostasis associated with escalating cocaine use. *Nat Neurosci* (2002) **5**:625–6.

98. Jang CG, Whitfield T, Schulteis G, Koob GF, Wee S. Sensitization of a negative emotional-like state during repeated withdrawal from extended access methamphetamine self-administration in rats. *Psychopharmacology (Berl)* (2013) **225**:753–63. doi:10.1007/s00213-012-2864-0

99. Kenny PJ, Chen SA, Kitamura O, Markou A, Koob GF. Conditioned withdrawal drives heroin consumption and decreases reward sensitivity. *J Neurosci* (2006) **26**:5894–900. doi:10.1523/JNEUROSCI.0740-06.2006

100. Harris AC, Pentel PR, Burroughs D, Staley MD, Lesage MG. A lack of association between severity of nicotine withdrawal and individual differences in compensatory nicotine self-administration in rats. *Psychopharmacology (Berl)* (2011) **217**:153–66. doi:10.1007/s00213-011-2273-9

101. Shurman J, Koob GF, Gutstein HB. Opioids, pain, the brain, and hyperkatifeia: a framework for the rational use of opioids for pain. *Pain Med* (2010) **11**:1092–8. doi:10.1111/j.1526-4637.2010.00881.x

102. Diana M, Pistis M, Carboni S, Gessa GL, Rossetti ZL. Profound decrement of mesolimbic dopaminergic neuronal activity during ethanol withdrawal syndrome in rats: electrophysiological and biochemical evidence. *Proc Natl Acad Sci U S A* (1993) **90**:7966–9. doi:10.1073/pnas.90.17.7966

103. Diana M, Pistis M, Muntoni A, Gessa G. Profound decrease of mesolimbic dopaminergic neuronal activity in morphine withdrawn rats. *J Phamacol Exp Ther* (1995) **272**:781–5.

104. Parsons LH, Koob GF, Weiss F. Serotonin dysfunction in the nucleus accumbens of rats during withdrawal after unlimited access to intravenous cocaine. *J Pharmacol Exp Ther* (1995) **274**:1182–91.

105. Volkow ND, Fowler JS, Wang GJ. The addicted human brain: insights from imaging studies. *J Clin Invest* (2003) **111**:1444–51. doi:10.1172/JCI18533

106. Mhatre MC, Pena G, Sieghart W, Ticku MK. Antibodies specific for GABAA receptor alpha subunits reveal that chronic alcohol treatment down-regulates (-subunit expression in rat brain regions. *J Neurochem* (1993) **61**:1620–5. doi:10.1111/j.1471-4159.1993.tb09795.x

107. Devaud LL, Fritschy JM, Sieghart W, Morrow AL. Bidirectional alterations of GABA$_A$ receptor subunit pepetide levels in rat cortex during chronic ethanol consumption and withdrawal. *J Neurochem* (1997) **69**:126–30. doi:10.1046/j.1471-4159.1997.69010126.x

108. Sapru MK, Diamond I, Gordon AS. Adenosine receptors mediate cellular adaptation to ethanol in NG108-15 cells. *J Pharmacol Exp Ther* (1994) **271**:542–8.

109. Chance WT, Sheriff S, Peng F, Balasubramaniam A. Antagonism of NPY-induced feeding by pretreatment with cyclic AMP response element binding protein antisense oligonucleotide. *Neuropeptides* (2000) **34**:167–72. doi:10.1054/npep.2000.0807

110. Pandey SC. The gene transcription factor cyclic AMP-responsive element binding protein: role in

positive and negative affective states of alcohol addiction. *Pharmacol Ther* (2004) **104**:47–58. doi: 10.1016/j.pharmthera.2004.08.002

111. Rivier C, Bruhn T, Vale W. Effect of ethanol on the hypothalamic-pituitary-adrenal axis in the rat: role of corticotropin-releasing factor (CRF). *J Pharmacol Exp Ther* (1984) **229**:127–31.

112. Merlo-Pich E, Lorang M, Yeganeh M, Rodriguez de Fonseca F, Raber J, Koob GF, et al. Increase of extracellular corticotropin-releasing factor-like immunoreactivity levels in the amygdala of awake rats during restraint stress and ethanol withdrawal as measured by microdialysis. *J Neurosci* (1995) **15**:5439–47.

113. Rasmussen DD, Boldt BM, Bryant CA, Mitton DR, Larsen SA, Wilkinson CW. Chronic daily ethanol and withdrawal: 1. Long-term changes in the hypothalamo-pituitary-adrenal axis. *Alcohol Clin Exp Res* (2000) **24**:1836–49. doi:10.1111/j.1530-0277.2000.tb01988.x

114. Olive MF, Koenig HN, Nannini MA, Hodge CW. Elevated extracellular CRF levels in the bed nucleus of the stria terminalis during ethanol withdrawal and reduction by subsequent ethanol intake. *Pharmacol Biochem Behav* (2002) **72**:213–20. doi:10.1016/S0091-3057(01)00748-1

115. Delfs JM, Zhu Y, Druhan JP, Aston-Jones G. Noradrenaline in the ventral forebrain is critical for opiate withdrawal-induced aversion. *Nature* (2000) **403**:430–4. doi:10.1038/35000212

116. Roberto M, Cruz MT, Gilpin NW, Sabino V, Schweitzer P, Bajo M, et al. Corticotropin releasing factor-induced amygdala gamma-aminobutyric acid release plays a key role in alcohol dependence. *Biol Psychiatry* (2010) **67**:831–9. doi:10.1016/j.biopsych.2009.11.007

117. Sarnyai Z, Biro E, Gardi J, Vecsernyes M, Julesz J, Telegdy G. Brain corticotropin-releasing factor mediates "anxiety-like" behavior induced by cocaine withdrawal in rats. *Brain Res* (1995) **675**:89–97. doi:10.1016/0006-8993(95)00043-P

118. Basso AM, Spina M, Rivier J, Vale W, Koob GF. Corticotropin-releasing factor antagonist attenuates the "anxiogenic-like" effect in the defensive burying paradigm

but not in the elevated plus-maze following chronic cocaine in rats. *Psychopharmacology (Berl)* (1999) **145**:21–30. doi:10.1007/s002130051028

119. Navarro-Zaragoza J, Núñez C, Laorden ML, Milanés MV. Effects of corticotropin-releasing factor receptor-1 antagonists on the brain stress system responses to morphine withdrawal. *Mol Pharmacol* (2010) **77**:864–73. doi:10.1124/mol.109.062463

120. Iredale PA, Alvaro JD, Lee Y, Terwilliger R, Chen YL, Duman RS. Role of corticotropin-releasing factor receptor-1 in opiate withdrawal. *J Neurochem* (2000) **74**:199–208. doi:10.1046/j.1471-4159.2000.0740199.x

121. Baldwin HA, Rassnick S, Rivier J, Koob GF, Britton KT. CRF antagonist reverses the "anxiogenic" response to ethanol withdrawal in the rat. *Psychopharmacology (Berl)* (1991) **103**:227–32. doi:10.1007/BF02244208

122. Knapp DJ, Overstreet DH, Moy SS, Breese GR. SB242084, flumazenil, and CRA1000 block ethanol withdrawal-induced anxiety in rats. *Alcohol* (2004) **32**:101–11. doi:10.1016/j.alcohol.2003.08.007

123. Overstreet DH, Knapp DJ, Breese GR. Modulation of multiple ethanol withdrawal-induced anxiety-like behavior by CRF and CRF$_1$ receptors. *Pharmacol Biochem Behav* (2004) **77**:405–13. doi:10.1016/j.pbb.2003.11.010

124. Funk CK, Zorrilla EP, Lee MJ, Rice KC, Koob GF. Corticotropin-releasing factor 1 antagonists selectively reduce ethanol self-administration in ethanol-dependent rats. *Biol Psychiatry* (2007) **61**:78–86. doi:10.1016/j.biopsych.2006.03.063

125. Rassnick S, Heinrichs SC, Britton KT, Koob GF. Microinjection of a corticotropin-releasing factor antagonist into the central nucleus of the amygdala reverses anxiogenic-like effects of ethanol withdrawal. *Brain Res* (1993) **605**:25–32. doi:10.1016/0006-8993(93)91352-S

126. Tucci S, Cheeta S, Seth P, File SE. Corticotropin releasing factor antagonist, α-helical CRF$_{9-41}$, reverses nicotine-induced conditioned, but not unconditioned, anxiety. *Psychopharmacology (Berl)* (2003) **167**:251–6.

127. Breese GR, Overstreet DH, Knapp DJ, Navarro M. Prior multiple ethanol withdrawals enhance stress-induced anxiety-like

behavior: inhibition by CRF$_1$- and benzodiazepine-receptor antagonists and a 5-HT$_{1a}$-receptor agonist. *Neuropsychopharmacology* (2005) **30**:1662–9. doi:10.1038/sj.npp.1300706

128. Valdez GR, Zorrilla EP, Roberts AJ, Koob GF. Antagonism of corticotropin-releasing factor attenuates the enhanced responsiveness to stress observed during protracted ethanol abstinence. *Alcohol* (2003) **29**:55–60. doi:10.1016/S0741-8329(03)00020-X

129. Huang MM, Overstreet DH, Knapp DJ, Angel R, Wills TA, Navarro M, et al. Corticotropin-releasing factor (CRF) sensitization of ethanol withdrawal-induced anxiety-like behavior is brain site specific and mediated by CRF-1 receptors: relation to stress-induced sensitization. *J Pharmacol Exp Ther* (2010) **332**:298–307. doi:10.1124/jpet.109.159186

130. Overstreet DH, Knapp DJ, Breese GR. Drug challenges reveal differences in mediation of stress facilitation of voluntary alcohol drinking and withdrawal-induced anxiety in alcohol-preferring P rats. *Alcohol Clin Exp Res* (2007) **31**:1473–81. doi:10.1111/j.1530-0277.2007.00445.x

131. Wills TA, Knapp DJ, Overstreet DH, Breese GR. Sensitization, duration, and pharmacological blockade of anxiety-like behavior following repeated ethanol withdrawal in adolescent and adult rats. *Alcohol Clin Exp Res* (2009) **33**:455–63. doi:10.1111/j.1530-0277.2008.00856.x

132. Hand TH, Koob GF, Stinus L, Le Moal M. Aversive properties of opiate receptor blockade: evidence for exclusively central mediation in naive and morphine-dependent rats. *Brain Res* (1988) **474**:364–8. doi:10.1016/0006-8993(88)90452-0

133. Stinus L, Le Moal M, Koob GF. Nucleus accumbens and amygdala are possible substrates for the aversive stimulus effects of opiate withdrawal. *Neuroscience* (1990) **37**:767–73. doi:10.1016/0306-4522(90)90106-E

134. Stinus L, Cador M, Zorrilla EP, Koob GF. Buprenorphine and a CRF1 antagonist block the acquisition of opiate withdrawal-induced conditioned place aversion in rats. *Neuropsychopharmacology* (2005) **30**:90–8. doi:10.1038/sj.npp.1300487

135. Heinrichs SC, Menzaghi F, Schulteis G, Koob GF, Stinus L. Suppression of corticotropin-releasing factor in the amygdala attenuates aversive consequences of morphine withdrawal. *Behav Pharmacol* (1995) **6**:74–80. doi:10.1097/00008877-199501000-00011

136. Contarino A, Papaleo F. The corticotropin-releasing factor receptor-1 pathway mediates the negative affective states of opiate withdrawal. *Proc Natl Acad Sci U S A* (2005) **102**:18649–54. doi:10.1073/pnas.0506999102

137. Bruijnzeel AW, Zislis G, Wilson C, Gold MS. Antagonism of CRF receptors prevents the deficit in brain reward function associated with precipitated nicotine withdrawal in rats. *Neuropsychopharmacology* (2007) **32**:955–63. doi:10.1038/sj.npp.1301192

138. Bruijnzeel AW, Small E, Pasek TM, Yamada H. Corticotropin-releasing factor mediates the dysphoria-like state associated with alcohol withdrawal in rats. *Behav Brain Res* (2010) **210**:288–91. doi:10.1016/j.bbr.2010.02.043

139. Marcinkiewcz CA, Prado MM, Isaac SK, Marshall A, Rylkova D, Bruijnzeel AW. Corticotropin-releasing factor within the central nucleus of the amygdala and the nucleus accumbens shell mediates the negative affective state of nicotine withdrawal in rats. *Neuropsychopharmacology* (2009) **34**:1743–52. doi:10.1038/npp.2008.231

140. Chartoff E, Sawyer A, Rachlin A, Potter D, Pliakas A, Carlezon WA. Blockade of kappa opioid receptors attenuates the development of depressive-like behaviors induced by cocaine withdrawal in rats. *Neuropharmacology* (2012) **62**:1167–76. doi:10.1016/j.neuropharm.2011.06.014

141. Schindler AG, Li S, Chavkin C. Behavioral stress may increase the rewarding valence of cocaine-associated cues through a dynorphin/kappa-opioid receptor-mediated mechanism without affecting associative learning or memory retrieval mechanisms. *Neuropsychopharmacology* (2010) **35**:1932–42. doi:10.1038/npp

142. Land BB, Bruchas MR, Schattauer S, Giardino WJ, Aita M, Messinger D, et al. Activation of the kappa opioid receptor in the dorsal raphe nucleus mediates the aversive

effects of stress and reinstates drug seeking. *Proc Natl Acad Sci U S A* (2009) **106**:19168–73. doi:10.1073/pnas.0910705106

143. Redila VA, Chavkin C. Stress-induced reinstatement of cocaine seeking is mediated by the kappa opioid system. *Psychopharmacology (Berl)* (2008) **200**:59–70. doi:10.1007/s00213-008-1122-y

144. McLaughlin JP, Li S, Valdez J, Chavkin TA, Chavkin C. Social defeat stress-induced behavioral responses are mediated by the endogenous kappa opioid system. *Neuropsychopharmacology* (2006) **31**:1241–8.

145. Knoll AT, Meloni EG, Thomas JB, Carroll FI, Carlezon WA Jr. Anxiolytic-like effects of kappa-opioid receptor antagonists in models of unlearned and learned fear in rats. *J Pharmacol Exp Ther* (2007) **323**:838–45. doi:10.1124/jpet.107.127415

146. Specio SE, Wee S, O'Dell LE, Boutrel B, Zorrilla EP, Koob GF. CRF₁ receptor antagonists attenuate escalated cocaine self-administration in rats. *Psychopharmacology (Berl)* (2008) **196**:473–82. doi:10.1007/s00213-007-0983-9

147. Greenwell TN, Funk CK, Cottone P, Richardson HN, Chen SA, Rice K, et al. Corticotropin-releasing factor-1 receptor antagonists decrease heroin self-administration in long-, but not short-access rats. *Addict Biol* (2009) **14**:130–43. doi:10.1111/j.1369-1600.2008.00142.x

148. Rimondini R, Arlinde C, Sommer W, Heilig M. Long-lasting increase in voluntary ethanol consumption and transcriptional regulation in the rat brain after intermittent exposure to alcohol. *FASEB J* (2002) **16**:27–35. doi:10.1096/fj.01-0593com

149. Valdez GR, Roberts AJ, Chan K, Davis H, Brennan M, Zorrilla EP, et al. Increased ethanol self-administration and anxiety-like behavior during acute withdrawal and protracted abstinence: regulation by corticotropin-releasing factor. *Alcohol Clin Exp Res* (2002) **26**:1494–501. doi:10.1111/j.1530-0277.2002.tb02448.x

150. Gehlert DR, Cippitelli A, Thorsell A, Le AD, Hipskind PA, Hamdouchi C, et al. 3-(4-Chloro-2-morpholin-4-yl-thiazol-5-yl)-8-(1-ethylpropyl)-2,6-dimethyl-imidazo[1,2-*b*]pyridazine: a novel brain-penetrant, orally available corticotropin-releasing factor receptor 1 antagonist with efficacy in animal models of alcoholism. *J Neurosci* (2007) **27**:2718–26. doi:10.1523/JNEUROSCI.4985-06.2007

151. Funk CK, O'Dell LE, Crawford EF, Koob GF. Corticotropin-releasing factor within the central nucleus of the amygdala mediates enhanced ethanol self-administration in withdrawn, ethanol-dependent rats. *J Neurosci* (2006) **26**:11324–32. doi:10.1523/JNEUROSCI.3096-06.2006

152. Wee S, Orio L, Ghirmai S, Cashman JR, Koob GF. Inhibition of kappa opioid receptors attenuated increased cocaine intake in rats with extended access to cocaine. *Psychopharmacology (Berl)* (2009) **205**:565–75. doi:10.1007/s00213-009-1563-y

153. Walker BM, Zorrilla EP, Koob GF. Systemic κ-opioid receptor antagonism by nor-binaltorphimine reduces dependence-induced excessive alcohol self-administration in rats. *Addict Biol* (2010) **16**:116–9. doi:10.1111/j.1369-1600.2010.00226.x

154. Whitfield TW Jr., Wee S, Gould A, Schlosburg J, Vendruscolo L, Koob GF. *Kappa Receptor Activation Underlies Compulsive Methamphetamine Intake.* Society for Neuroscience Meeting Abstracts, Washington DC (2011). Abstract no: 797.19.

155. Schlosburg JE, Vendruscolo LF, Park PE, Whitfield TW Jr., Koob GF. *Long-Term Antagonism of Kappa Opioid Receptors Prevents Escalation of, and Increased Motivation for, Heroin Intake.* Society for Neuroscience Meeting Abstracts, Washington DC (2011). Abstract no: 16.07.

156. Nealey KA, Smith AW, Davis SM, Smith DG, Walker BM. Kappa-opioid receptors are implicated in the increased potency of intra-accumbens nalmefene in ethanol-dependent rats. *Neuropharmacology* (2011) **61**:35–42. doi:10.1016/j.neuropharm.2011.02.012

157. Heilig M, Koob GF. A key role for corticotropin-releasing factor in alcohol dependence. *Trends Neurosci* (2007) **30**:399–406. doi:10.1016/j.tins.2007.06.006

158. Thorsell A, Slawecki CJ, Ehlers CL. Effects of neuropeptide Y and corticotropin-releasing factor on ethanol intake in Wistar rats: interaction with chronic ethanol exposure. *Behav Brain Res* (2005) **161**:133–40. doi:10.1016/j.bbr.2005.01.016

159. Thorsell A, Slawecki CJ, Ehlers CL. Effects of neuropeptide Y on appetitive and consummatory behaviors associated with alcohol drinking in wistar rats with a history of ethanol exposure. *Alcohol Clin Exp Res* (2005) **29**:584–90. doi:10.1097/01.ALC.0000160084.13148.02

160. Gilpin NW, Stewart RB, Murphy JM, Li TK, Badia-Elder NE. Neuropeptide Y reduces oral ethanol intake in alcohol-preferring (P) rats following a period of imposed ethanol abstinence. *Alcohol Clin Exp Res* (2003) **27**:787–94. doi:10.1097/01.ALC.0000065723.93234.1D

161. Gilpin NW, Misra K, Koob GF. Neuropeptide Y in the central nucleus of the amygdala suppresses dependence-induced increases in alcohol drinking. *Pharmacol Biochem Behav* (2008) **90**:475–80. doi:10.1016/j.pbb.2008.04.006

162. Thorsell A, Rapunte-Canonigo V, O'Dell L, Chen SA, King A, Lekic D, et al. Viral vector-induced amygdala NPY overexpression reverses increased alcohol intake caused by repeated deprivations in Wistar rats. *Brain* (2007) **130**:1330–7. doi:10.1093/brain/awm033

163. Gilpin NW, Misra K, Herman MA, Cruz MT, Koob GF, Roberto M. Neuropeptide Y opposes alcohol effects on gamma-aminobutyric acid release in amygdala and blocks the transition to alcohol dependence. *Biol Psychiatry* (2011) **69**:1091–9. doi:10.1016/j.biopsych.2011.02.004

164. Sørensen G, Wortwein G, Fink-Jensen A, Woldbye DPD. Neuropeptide Y Y5 receptor antagonism causes faster extinction and attenuates reinstatement in cocaine-induced place preference. *Pharmacol Biochem Behav* (2013) **105**:151–6. doi:10.1016/j.pbb.2013.02.010

165. Sørensen G, Jensen M, Weikop P, Dencker D, Christiansen SH, Loland CJ, et al. Neuropeptide Y Y5 receptor antagonism attenuates cocaine-induced effects in mice. *Psychopharmacology (Berl)* (2012) **222**:565–77. doi:10.1007/s00213-012-2651-y

166. Sørensen G, Woldbye DP. Mice lacking neuropeptide Y show increased sensitivity to cocaine. *Synapse* (2012) **66**:840–3. doi:10.1002/syn.21568

167. Maric T, Tobin S, Quinn T, Shalev U. Food deprivation-like effects of neuropeptide Y on heroin self-administration and reinstatement of heroin seeking in rats. *Behav Brain Res* (2008) **194**:39–43. doi:10.1016/j.bbr.2008.06.023

168. Maric T, Cantor A, Cuccioletta H, Tobin S, Shalev U. Neuropeptide Y augments cocaine self-administration and cocaine-induced hyperlocomotion in rats. *Peptides* (2009) **30**:721–6. doi:10.1016/j.peptides.2008.11.006

169. Aydin C, Oztan O, Isgor C. Effects of a selective Y2R antagonist, JNJ-31020028, on nicotine abstinence-related social anxiety-like behavior, neuropeptide Y and corticotropin releasing factor mRNA levels in the novelty-seeking phenotype. *Behav Brain Res* (2011) **222**:332–41. doi:10.1016/j.bbr.2011.03.067

170. Rylkova D, Boissoneault J, Isaac S, Prado M, Shah HP, Bruijnzeel AW. Effects of NPY and the specific Y1 receptor agonist [D-His²⁶]-NPY on the deficit in brain reward function and somatic signs associated with nicotine withdrawal in rats. *Neuropeptides* (2008) **42**:215–27. doi:10.1016/j.npep.2008.03.004

171. Valdez GR, Koob GF. Allostasis and dysregulation of corticotropin-releasing factor and Neuropeptide Y systems: implications for the development of alcoholism. *Pharmacol Biochem Behav* (2004) **79**:671–89. doi:10.1016/j.pbb.2004.09.020

172. George O, Mandyam CD, Wee S, Koob GF. Extended access to cocaine self-administration produces long-lasting prefrontal cortex-dependent working memory impairments. *Neuropsychopharmacology* (2008) **33**:2474–82. doi:10.1038/sj.npp.1301626

173. Briand LA, Flagel SB, Garcia-Fuster MJ, Watson SJ, Akil H, Sarter M, et al. Persistent alterations in cognitive function and prefrontal dopamine D2 receptors following extended, but not limited, access to self-administered cocaine. *Neuropsychopharmacology* (2008) **33**:2969–80. doi:10.1038/npp.2008.18

174. Briand LA, Gross JP, Robinson TE. Impaired object recognition following prolonged withdrawal from extended-access cocaine self-administration. *Neuroscience*

(2008) **155**:1–6. doi:10.1016/j.neuroscience.2008.06.004

175. George O, Sanders C, Freiling J, Grigoryan E, Vu S, Allen CD, et al. Recruitment of medial prefrontal cortex neurons during alcohol withdrawal predicts cognitive impairment and excessive alcohol drinking. *Proc Natl Acad Sci U S A* (2012) **109**:18156–61. doi:10.1073/pnas.1116523109

176. Boyson CO, Miguel TT, Quadros IM, Debold JF, Miczek KA. Prevention of social stress-escalated cocaine self-administration by CRF-R1 antagonist in the rat VTA. *Psychopharmacology (Berl)* (2011) **218**:257–69. doi:10.1007/s00213-011-2266-8

177. Carlezon WA Jr., Thome J, Olson VG, Lane-Ladd SB, Brodkin ES, Hiroi N, et al. Regulation of cocaine reward by CREB. *Science* (1998) **282**:2272–5. doi:10.1126/science.282.5397.2272

178. Koob GF, Bloom FE. Cellular and molecular mechanisms of drug dependence. *Science* (1988) **242**:715–23. doi:10.1126/science.2903550

179. Nestler EJ. Molecular basis of long-term plasticity underlying addiction. *Nat Rev Neurosci* (2001) **2**:119–28. doi:10.1038/35053570

180. Koob GF. Neuroadaptive mechanisms of addiction: studies on the extended amygdala. *Eur Neuropsychopharmacology* (2003) **13**:442–52. doi:10.1016/j.euroneuro.2003.08.005

181. Aston-Jones G, Delfs JM, Druhan J, Zhu Y. The bed nucleus of the stria terminalis: a target site for noradrenergic actions in opiate withdrawal. In: McGinty JF editor. *Advancing from the Ventral Striatum to the Extended Amygdala: Implications for Neuropsychiatry and Drug Abuse (series title: Annals of the New York Academy of Sciences* (Vol. 877), New York: New York Academy of Sciences (1999). p. 486–98.

182. Ungless MA, Whistler JL, Malenka RC, Bonci A. Single cocaine exposure *in vivo* induces long-term potentiation in dopamine neurons. *Nature* (2001) **411**:583–7. doi:10.1038/35079077

183. Edwards S, Koob GF. Neurobiology of dysregulated motivational systems in drug addiction. *Future Neurol* (2010) **5**:393–410. doi:10.2217/fnl.10.14

184. Solomon RL. The opponent-process theory of acquired motivation: the costs of pleasure and the benefits of pain. *Am Psychol* (1980) **35**:691–712. doi:10.1037/0003-066X.35.8.691

185. Cohen A, Koob GF, George O. Robust escalation of nicotine intake with extended access to nicotine self-administration and intermittent periods of abstinence. *Neuropsychopharmacology* (2012) **37**:2153–60. doi:10.1038/npp.2012.67

186. Edwards S, Guerrero M, Ghoneim OM, Roberts E, Koob GF. Evidence that vasopressin V_{1b} receptors mediate the transition to excessive drinking in ethanol-dependent rats. *Addict Biol* (2011) **17**:76–85. doi:10.1111/j.1369-1600.2010.00291.x

187. Barbier E, Vendruscolo LF, Schlosburg JE, Edwards S, Juergens N, Park PE, et al. The NK1 receptor antagonist L822429 reduces heroin reinforcement. *Neuropsychopharmacology* (2013). doi:10.1038/npp.2012.261 (in press)

188. Wee S, Wang Z, Woolverton WL, Pulvirenti L, Koob GF. Effect of aripiprazole, a partial D_2 receptor agonist, on increased rate of methamphetamine self-administration in rats with prolonged access. *Neuropsychopharmacology* (2007) **32**:2238–47. doi:10.1038/sj.npp.1301353

189. Liu ZH, Jin WQ. Decrease of ventral tegmental area dopamine neuronal activity in nicotine withdrawal rats. *Neuroreport* (2004) **15**:1479–81. doi:10.1097/01.wnr.0000126218.25235.b6

190. Richardson HN, Zhao Y, Fekete EM, Funk CK, Wirsching P, Janda KD, et al. MPZP: a novel small molecule corticotropin-releasing factor type 1 receptor (CRF_1) antagonist. *Pharmacol Biochem Behav* (2008) **88**:497–510. doi:10.1016/j.pbb.2007.10.008

191. Koob GF. Negative reinforcement in drug addiction: the darkness within. *Curr Opin Neurobiol* (2013). doi:10.1016/j.conb.2013.03.011 (in press)

9

The interplay between the hippocampus and amygdala in regulating aberrant hippocampal neurogenesis during protracted abstinence from alcohol dependence

Chitra D. Mandyam*

Committee on the Neurobiology of Addictive Disorders, The Scripps Research Institute, La Jolla, CA, USA

Edited by:
Nicholas W. Gilpin, LSUHSC-New
Orleans, USA

Reviewed by:
Kimberly Nixon, University of
Kentucky, USA
Scott E. Hemby, Wake Forest
University School of Medicine, USA

*Correspondence:
Chitra D. Mandyam, Committee on
the Neurobiology of Addictive
Disorders, The Scripps Research
Institute, 10550 North Torrey Pines
Road, SP30-2400, La Jolla, CA 92037,
USA
e-mail: cmandyam@scripps.edu

The development of alcohol dependence involves elevated anxiety, low mood, and increased sensitivity to stress, collectively labeled negative affect. Particularly interesting is the recent accumulating evidence that sensitized extrahypothalamic stress systems [e.g., hyperglutamatergic activity, blunted hypothalamic-pituitary-adrenal (HPA) hormonal levels, altered corticotropin-releasing factor signaling, and altered glucocorticoid receptor signaling in the extended amygdala] are evident in withdrawn dependent rats, supporting the hypothesis that pathological neuroadaptations in the extended amygdala contribute to the negative affective state. Notably, hippocampal neurotoxicity observed as aberrant dentate gyrus (DG) neurogenesis (neurogenesis is a process where neural stem cells in the adult hippocampal subgranular zone generate DG granule cell neurons) and DG neurodegeneration are observed in withdrawn dependent rats. These correlations between withdrawal and aberrant neurogenesis in dependent rats suggest that alterations in the DG could be hypothesized to be due to compromised HPA axis activity and associated hyperglutamatergic activity originating from the basolateral amygdala in withdrawn dependent rats. This review discusses a possible link between the neuroadaptations in the extended amygdala stress systems and the resulting pathological plasticity that could facilitate recruitment of new emotional memory circuits in the hippocampus as a function of aberrant DG neurogenesis.

Keywords: chronic ethanol, vapor induced dependence, self-administration, subgranular zone, hippocampus, BrdU

NEUROGENESIS IN THE ADULT DENTATE GYRUS

Accumulating evidence over the past four decades shows that forebrain neural stem cells populate two main areas, the subventricular zone of the lateral ventricles and subgranular zone (SGZ) of the hippocampal dentate gyrus (DG; **Figure 1**), where they give rise to neurons throughout adulthood. Adult neurogenesis is found in these forebrain regions in all mammalian species examined, including humans (Eriksson et al., 1998; Curtis et al., 2007), and may serve to replace cells damaged by brain disorders, such as addiction to drugs of abuse and alcohol. Whether they replace dying or diseased cells and if so to what extent are questions currently receiving intense research focus.

Adult neurogenesis in the hippocampal DG plays an important role in maintaining hippocampal plasticity. The process of neurogenesis involves stem-like precursor cells (type 1 cells) that proliferate into preneuronal progenitors (type 2 and type 3), which in turn differentiate into immature neurons and eventually mature into granule cell neurons (GCNs; Kempermann et al., 2004; Abrous et al., 2005; **Figure 1**). A large proportion (>80%) of hippocampal progenitors migrate a short distance to become GCNs in the DG (Kaplan and Hinds, 1977; Hastings et al., 2001), and there is evidence demonstrating functional incorporation of the newly born neurons in the DG (Gould et al., 1999; Shors et al., 2002; Aimone et al., 2006). For example, DG neurogenesis has been implicated in the maintenance of hippocampal networking (Aimone et al.,

2006; Clark et al., 2012; Lacefield et al., 2012) and assists with certain behaviors that depend on the hippocampus (Feng et al., 2001; Deisseroth et al., 2004; Schmidt-Hieber et al., 2004; Kim et al., 2012) and is critical for encoding new information by facilitating the formation of new memories that assist with hippocampus-dependent behaviors (McHugh et al., 2007; Bakker et al., 2008; Clelland et al., 2009; Aimone et al., 2011; Sahay et al., 2011).

Dentate gyrus neurogenesis is also strongly regulated by stress and glucocorticoids (Cameron and Gould, 1994; Mirescu and Gould, 2006; Oomen et al., 2007; Snyder et al., 2011). Conversely, DG neurogenesis regulates the secretion of glucocorticoids in response to stress (Snyder et al., 2011). This is important because the hippocampus provides negative control of the hypothalamic-pituitary-adrenal (HPA) axis, and DG neurogenesis regulates hippocampal regulation of the HPA axis (Snyder et al., 2011), although the circuitry mediating this effect is not well understood. Furthermore, the role of the glutamatergic system in the development and maintenance of DG neurogenesis is well documented (Cameron et al., 1995). For example, N-methyl-D-aspartate (NMDA) receptor activation reduces the proliferation of neural precursors in a normal state, and blockade of NMDA receptors increases the birth and survival of neural precursors in the DG, suggesting that neuronal inputs into the hippocampus regulate DG neurogenesis (**Figure 2**). Furthermore, recent evidence demonstrates compromised HPA axis activity (Richardson et al., 2008), altered

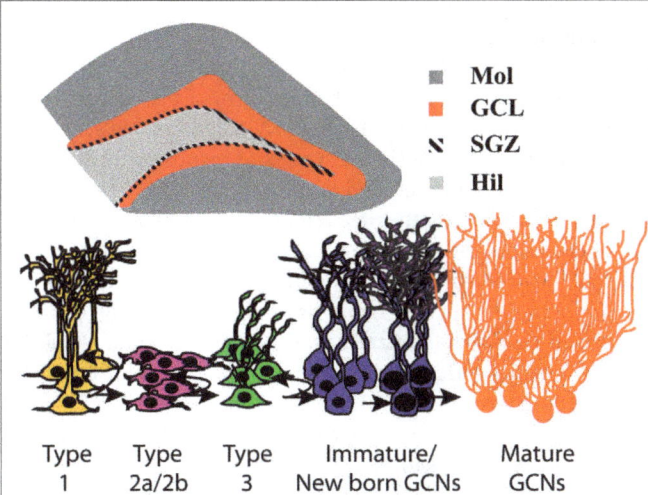

FIGURE 1 | Neurogenesis in the subgranular zone of the hippocampus. Schematic representation of the coronal view of the hippocampus region; magnification of the DG region in a coronal view −3.6 mm from bregma indicating the subregions of the DG and highlighting the neurogenic region; GCL in red and SGZ as the hatched area. DG, dentate gyrus; GCL, granule cell layer; Mol, molecular layer; SGZ, subgranular zone; Hil, hilus. Stages of adult hippocampal neurogenesis are indicated below the schematic of the coronal view of the hippocampus. In the DG, type 1 putative stem-like cells are slowly dividing and rarely label with the commonly used exogenous mitotic marker 5-bromo-2′-deoxyuridine (BrdU) but can be identified via morphology and staining for nestin/GFAP/Sox2. BrdU will label rapidly dividing type 2 and some type 3 cells. Type 3 cells mature and differentiate into immature granule cell neurons and migrate a short distance into the granule cell layer to become granule cell neurons and integrate into the hippocampal circuitry.

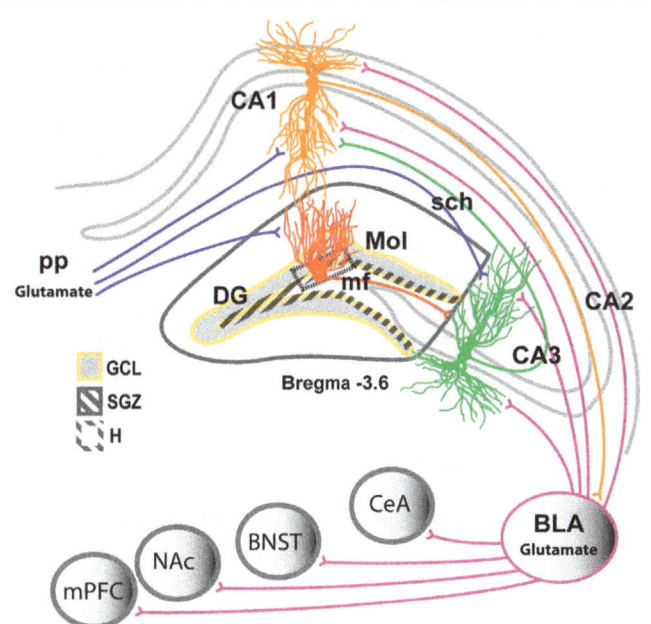

FIGURE 2 | Neuronal projections in the hippocampus. Schematic representation of the coronal view of the hippocampus region indicating the subregions of the hippocampus and their location within the hippocampus. CA, cornu ammonis; Trisynaptic circuitry in the hippocampus is indicated with axons from the entorhinal cortex projecting unidirectionally to the apical dendrites of the hippocampal DG, CA1, and CA3 neurons (perforant path projection). DG neurons project to the apical dendrites of the CA3 pyramidal neurons (mossy fiber projection). CA3 neurons project to the apical dendrites of the CA1 neurons (Schaffer collateral projection). The CA1 neurons have bidirectional projections to and from the BLA. The BLA also sends projections to the medial prefrontal cortex (mPFC), nucleus accumbens (NAc), bed nucleus of the stria terminalis (BNST), and central nucleus of the amygdala.

glucocorticoid signaling (Vendruscolo et al., 2012), increased sensitivity to NMDA-mediated function (Becker et al., 1998; Gonzalez et al., 2001), and significant reductions in the rate of DG neurogenesis (Nixon and Crews, 2002; Richardson et al., 2009; Hansson et al., 2010) in a preclinical models of alcohol addiction and dependence. These data suggest that the normalization of alcohol-impaired DG neurogenesis during withdrawal may help reverse altered hippocampal neuroplasticity during protracted abstinence and thus may help reduce the vulnerability to relapse and aid recovery.

ANIMAL MODELS OF CHRONIC ALCOHOL EXPOSURE AND ALCOHOL DEPENDENCE

There are several *in vitro* and *in vivo* preclinical model systems that represents various stages of alcohol intoxication, addiction, and dependence. Three models are highlighted in this review; *in vitro* organotypic hippocampal cell culture model, intragastric intubation model, and chronic ethanol vapor induced dependence (CEID) model. The incorporation of these models has allowed us to determine the toxic and neuromodulatory effects of ethanol in specific brain regions and reward systems. The *in vitro* organotypic hippocampal cell culture model is commonly used to study hippocampal excitotoxicity associated with alcoholism. The *in vitro* model harbors critical hippocampal heterogeneity that is necessary for neuron–neuron and neuron-glia interactions to occur, thus maintaining the structural and functional integrity of

hippocampal circuitry and pharmacology (Gutierrez and Heinemann, 1999; Martens and Wree, 2001). Notably, the *in vitro* model has been extensively used to study the effects of chronic ethanol and withdrawal from ethanol on hippocampal neurotoxicity and excitotoxicity (Gibson et al., 2003; Prendergast et al., 2004; Wilkins et al., 2006). Studies indicate that ethanol excitotoxicity is dependent on the concentration of ethanol and duration of withdrawal after ethanol exposure. The intragastric intubation model has been widely used to study hippocampal neurotoxicity associated with alcoholism. This model produces observable signs of prodromal detoxification and physiological dependence (Majchrowicz, 1975), and these extreme signs of ethanol intoxication and dependence have been correlated with reduced neuroplasticity and enhanced neurodegeneration (Nixon and Crews, 2002; Crews and Nixon, 2009).

The CEID model of alcohol dependence links chronic ethanol exposure regimens with self-administration procedures. This model is based on the idea that dependence and the experience of withdrawal during dependence drive excessive drinking during withdrawal through altered motivational processes (e.g., negative reinforcement; O'Dell et al., 2004; Lopez and Becker, 2005; Gehlert et al., 2007; Griffin et al., 2009). The CEID model has several advantages compared with the intragastric intubation model of alcohol dependence because it causes increases in ethanol self-administration and enhanced responsiveness to environmental stimuli that lead to excessive drinking in humans (Valdez et al., 2002; O'Dell et al., 2004). Importantly, CEID produces relatively high blood alcohol levels (BALs) during a short period of time, making this approach advantageous for studying the somatic aspects, motivational aspects, and neurobiological consequences of alcohol dependence (Macey et al., 1996; Liu and Weiss, 2002, 2003; Moore et al., 2004; Budygin et al., 2007; Miki et al., 2008; Gilpin et al., 2009; Richardson et al., 2009; Zahr et al., 2009). Altogether, investigating the neurobiological effects of chronic ethanol in CEID models has helped identify other vulnerability factors that contribute to the pathology of alcoholism in humans (Macey et al., 1996; Liu and Weiss, 2002, 2003; Moore et al., 2004; Budygin et al., 2007; Miki et al., 2008; Gilpin et al., 2009; Richardson et al., 2009; Zahr et al., 2009; Hansson et al., 2010).

ALCOHOL AND THE MORPHOLOGY AND PLASTICITY OF THE HIPPOCAMPUS

The hippocampus is involved in ethanol reward and relapse to ethanol seeking (Koob and Volkow, 2010; Zarrindast et al., 2010), suggesting that the hippocampus contributes to several aspects of alcohol dependence and can be implicated in the phenomena linked to alcohol use disorders. For example, alcohol dependence is linked to decreased hippocampus volume (Sullivan et al., 1995; Beresford et al., 2006), altered hippocampal morphology (Bengochea and Gonzalo, 1990; Durazzo et al., 2011), and deficits in hippocampus-dependent learning and memory (Brandt et al., 1983; Glenn and Parsons, 1991; Sullivan et al., 2000a,b, 2002). Alcohol exposure also alters the functional plasticity of hippocampal neurons. For instance, acute ethanol in hippocampal slices decreases hippocampal synaptic activity [i.e., decreases NMDA and α-amino-3-hydroxy-5-methyl-4-isoxazole-propionic acid (AMPA) receptor-mediated currents and increases γ-aminobutyric acid-A (GABA$_A$) receptor-mediated currents] and decreases hippocampal (CA1 and DG) long-term potentiation (LTP; Lovinger et al., 1989; Blitzer et al., 1990; Wayner et al., 1997; Weiner et al., 1999; Wright et al., 2003; Izumi et al., 2005; Fujii et al., 2008). Notably, chronic ethanol exposure also impairs hippocampal CA1 LTP through a presynaptic LTP mechanism (Durand and Carlen, 1984; Roberto et al., 2002) and produces tolerance to acute ethanol-mediated decreases in hippocampal LTP (Fujii et al., 2008), suggesting reorganization of hippocampal networking after chronic ethanol exposure. Furthermore, chronic ethanol exposure oppositely affects hippocampal synaptic activity compared with acute ethanol (increases in NMDA and decreases in GABA$_A$ receptor-mediated activity) and produces tolerance to acute ethanol-mediated impairment of NMDA activity and hippocampal-dependent behaviors (Sanna et al., 1993; Wu et al., 1993; Nelson et al., 2005; Sheela Rani and Ticku, 2006; Fujii et al., 2008). These findings indicate that the cellular mechanisms that maintain hippocampal plasticity are compensated in chronic ethanol-exposed animals. These maladaptive changes could contribute to the impairment of hippocampus-dependent behaviors in alcohol-dependent animals (Lukoyanov et al., 1999; Cippitelli et al., 2010; George et al., 2012). Chronic ethanol exposure produces dendritic retraction of CA1 pyramidal neurons (McMullen

et al., 1984), suggesting concomitant structural reorganization of hippocampal neurons compared with functional changes in hippocampal circuitry. Recent evidence demonstrated that ethanol exposure altered a new form of hippocampal plasticity, such as DG neurogenesis (reviewed in (Nixon, 2006; Mandyam and Koob, 2012). Ethanol exposure (i.e., intragastric intubation, two-bottle choice, ethanol liquid diet, and CEID) altered every stage of DG neurogenesis, including the proliferation, differentiation, maturation, and survival of neural stem cells (**Figure 1**). These effects varied by the dose, duration, and pattern of ethanol exposure and timing of ethanol exposure before labeling the neural progenitors (Nixon and Crews, 2002; Crews et al., 2004; Rice et al., 2004; He et al., 2005; Ieraci and Herrera, 2007; Richardson et al., 2009; Taffe et al., 2010; Contet et al., 2013). Therefore, the inhibitory effect of ethanol on the regenerative capacity of the adult hippocampus is now being considered a precursor for ethanol-induced neurodegeneration in the hippocampus (Nixon, 2006).

ALCOHOL EXPOSURE PRODUCES NEUROTOXICITY AND EXCITOTOXICITY IN THE HIPPOCAMPUS

Using the *in vitro* organotypic hippocampal cell culture model, it has been demonstrated that hippocampal CA1 excitotoxicity is evident after withdrawal from chronic ethanol exposure and not during ethanol exposure (Mulholland et al., 2003; Prendergast et al., 2004; Wilkins et al., 2006). Withdrawal-associated effects have been shown to be due to the release of excessive glutamate and polyamines and corresponding activation of NMDA-type receptors in the hippocampal region (Gibson et al., 2003). Importantly, ethanol studies that used the *in vitro* model indicate the importance of the glutamatergic system as a final common pathway mediating neurotoxicity and excitotoxicity. There are also *in vivo* studies that support the involvement of the glutamatergic system in ethanol-induced hippocampal neurotoxicity in chronic ethanol-exposed animals (Claus et al., 1982; Keller et al., 1983; Wilce et al., 1993; Snell et al., 1996; Wirkner et al., 1999). For example, glutamate release is increased in the hippocampus during ethanol withdrawal (Claus et al., 1982; Keller et al., 1983), and changes in glutamate levels are associated with enhanced polyamine levels in combination with an increased number of functional NMDA receptors (Davidson et al., 1993, 1995). These results suggest that increased glutamate levels may induce ethanol withdrawal hyperexcitability and lead to increased susceptibility to hippocampal excitotoxicity (Hoffman, 2003).

WITHDRAWAL AND PROTRACTED ABSTINENCE FROM ALCOHOL AND DG NEUROGENESIS

Very few studies have explored how forced withdrawal from drug exposure alters DG neurogenesis (Nixon and Crews, 2004; Nixon et al., 2008; Noonan et al., 2008; Barr et al., 2010; Hansson et al., 2010; Taffe et al., 2010; Garcia-Fuster et al., 2011; Deschaux et al., 2012; Recinto et al., 2012). Withdrawal from ethanol exposure in the intragastric intubation and CEID paradigms enhanced cell proliferation in the hippocampus (Nixon and Crews, 2004; Hansson et al., 2010), resulting in initial microglial proliferation (Nixon et al., 2008) followed by the production of immature neurons and eventual neurogenesis (Nixon and Crews, 2004). Aberrant neurogenesis during abstinence is thought to be attributable to central nervous system hyperexcitability associated with ethanol withdrawal symptomatology, such as whole-body tremors that result from the termination of ethanol exposure. However, the cellular mechanisms regulating ethanol withdrawal-induced aberrant neurogenesis in the DG have not been identified, and future mechanistic studies are needed to address the contribution of aberrant DG neurogenesis to brain changes associated with alcohol dependence.

WITHDRAWAL AND PROTRACTED ABSTINENCE FROM ALCOHOL AND EPILEPTOGENESIS AND NEUROADAPTATIONS IN THE HIPPOCAMPUS

As discussed earlier, both *in vitro* and *in vivo* evidence suggests that glutamatergic neurotransmission is a critical mediator of the experience-dependent synaptic plasticity that may underlie alcohol dependence. It is hypothesized that a hyperglutamatergic state in the basolateral amygdala (BLA) resulting from termination of ethanol exposure may be regulated by a variety of neuroadaptations in the extended amygdala. These alterations may regulate the plasticity in the hippocampus to produce the withdrawal hyperexcitability associated with dependence (Hoffman and Tabakoff, 1994; Tsai et al., 1995; Nixon and Crews, 2004; McCool et al., 2010; Prior and Galduroz, 2011). For example, withdrawal from ethanol, especially the termination of CEID, produces withdrawal symptomatology, manifested as increased acoustic startle reactivity and tremor activity that peaks 12–24 h post-withdrawal (Macey et al., 1996). These somatic symptoms of ethanol withdrawal seem to have an immediate effect on hippocampal plasticity. Withdrawal from CEID produces a rebound effect on the proliferation of neural progenitors that occurs 72 h after the termination of CEID. These cells propagate into aberrant immature GCNs during protracted abstinence (Hansson et al., 2010). Notably, pilocarpine-induced status epilepticus also produces abnormal proliferation of neural progenitors in the DG that is evident 72 h after seizure activity (Parent et al., 1997). This is a timeframe comparable to ethanol withdrawal-induced alterations. In addition to the alterations in DG neural progenitors, both epileptic activity and withdrawal from CEID have other common cellular and molecular neuroadaptations in the hippocampus. Particularly interesting is the increases in NMDA receptor 2B (NR2B) subunit expression in the hippocampus during CEID (Pian et al., 2010) and CRF levels in the hippocampus during withdrawal (Criado et al., 2011). These changes parallel the increased NR2B subunit and CRF expression in the hippocampus during epileptogenesis (Smith et al., 1997; Frasca et al., 2011). Altogether, it appears that the hyperactivity stemming from the neurocircuitry underlying ethanol withdrawal-induced kindling-like behaviors causes a hyperglutamatergic state and produces hippocampal excitotoxicity, which may be decisive factors for the maintenance of long-term dependence (Baram et al., 1992; Smith et al., 1997; Wilkins et al., 2006; Frasca et al., 2011; Prior and Galduroz, 2011).

WITHDRAWAL AND PROTRACTED ABSTINENCE FROM ALCOHOL ALTER HPA AXIS AND GLUCOCORTICOID RECEPTOR SIGNALING

Animals made dependent by CEID or liquid diet procedures have attenuated (opposing) basal stress hormone levels (adrenocorticotropic hormone and corticosterone) compared with non-dependent drinking animals (enhanced stress hormone levels). It has been demonstrated that the blunted stress response is a consequence of chronic ethanol exposure (Zorrilla et al., 2001; Richardson et al., 2008). Importantly, the findings from animal studies are consistent with clinical studies that link maladaptive HPA axis function with alcoholism, including a reduced ability to cope with stress and negative correlations between cortisol and craving and relapse in alcoholics (Lovallo et al., 2000; O'Malley et al., 2002). Although the precise mechanism underlying the attenuated stress response is unknown, several studies have implicated activation of CRF systems in the extended amygdala in the dysregulation of the stress system associated with dependence (Wand, 2005; Koob, 2008). Furthermore, enhanced glucocorticoid receptor (GR) levels in the extended amygdala during protracted abstinence have been demonstrated in dependent animals. Such associated changes in the GR system could play a mechanistic role in the sensitivity to stress/reward and relapse associated with alcohol dependence (Vendruscolo et al., 2012). However, the functional significance of altered GR system in mediating blunted stress responses in alcohol dependence is unknown.

RELATIONSHIP BETWEEN ETHANOL-INDUCED NEUROADAPTIVE CHANGES IN THE AMYGDALA AND ABERRANT DG NEUROGENESIS

The aberrant stimulation of cell proliferation in the DG during withdrawal from chronic ethanol exposure has been demonstrated in the *in vitro* organotypic hippocampal cell culture model (Wilkins et al., 2006), intragastric intubation model (Nixon and Crews, 2004; Nixon et al., 2008), and CEID model (Hansson et al., 2010). Further mechanistic experiments that used the intragastric intubation model demonstrated that observable withdrawal signs correlated with increases in cell proliferation. However, rescuing the observable withdrawal symptoms with diazepam did not normalize the cell proliferation effects (Nixon and Crews, 2004). This suggests that withdrawal-induced enhanced proliferation is not secondary to the physiological withdrawal experienced by the animal but may be related to the neuroadaptations linked to the negative affect symptoms associated with alcohol dependence.

Possible mechanisms underlying ethanol withdrawal-induced aberrant DG cell proliferation and neurogenesis can be postulated based on the available literature. For example, the increased synthesis of hippocampal CRF during withdrawal (Criado et al., 2011) might promote excitatory activity and lead to BLA hyperexcitability, which in turn may increase the level of CRF at critical hippocampal synapses (**Figure 2**). Such a mechanism would further enhance excitability in a positive-feedback manner in the hippocampus during ethanol withdrawal (Baram and Hatalski, 1998; Hollrigel et al., 1998; Chen et al., 2004). Increased CRF synthesis in the hippocampus could be due to decreased hippocampal inhibitory GABA activity seen during ethanol withdrawal (Frye et al., 1983; Fujii et al., 2008). The excitatory effect of CRF on DG neurons in the hippocampus may occur indirectly through CRF-induced activation of excitatory inputs into the hippocampus to cause DG hyperexcitability (Hollrigel et al., 1998). Epileptogenic studies suggest that excitatory glutamatergic projections from the

BLA are implicated in DG excitotoxicity and hyperexcitability (Baram et al., 1992; Freund and Buzsaki, 1996; Smith et al., 1997; Hollrigel et al., 1998; Yan et al., 1998; Wang et al., 2000). Notably, most of the projection neurons from the BLA to the hippocampus are glutamatergic and express CRF_1 receptors. Specific knockdown of CRF_1 in BLA glutamatergic neurons produces anxiolytic-like effects (Refojo et al., 2011). Furthermore, the CRF system in the BLA is hypothesized to be recruited by chronic kindling cycles of ethanol exposure/withdrawal (Baram et al., 1992; Rimondini et al., 2003; Breese et al., 2004; Knapp et al., 2004; Overstreet et al., 2004; O'Dell et al., 2004) and mediate the motivating, negative affective symptoms of both acute and protracted abstinence from ethanol. Protracted abstinence from CEID enhances BLA CRF_1 levels (Sommer et al., 2008), suggesting that BLA sensitivity to CRF increases in a kindling-like fashion during withdrawal (Sajdyk et al., 1999; Sajdyk and Gehlert, 2000; Rainnie et al., 2004). Recent functional studies demonstrated that DG neurogenesis is regulated by BLA neuronal activity (Kirby et al., 2012), and a kindling procedure specifically in the BLA produced aberrant DG neurogenesis, which resulted from the altered expression of cell differentiation factors in the DG neurogenic niche (Fournier et al., 2010). Therefore, increases in CRF in the extended amygdala could produce secondary effects on DG neurogenesis via the BLA. These alterations could be hypothesized to be regulated by corticosterone levels (Makino et al., 1994).

A related mechanism for ethanol withdrawal-induced increases in cell proliferation and DG neurogenesis could be ethanol withdrawal-induced blunting of corticosterone levels (Richardson et al., 2008) and corresponding increases in GR levels in the extended amygdala (Vendruscolo et al., 2012). The reduced levels of corticosterone could enhance DG proliferation and neurogenesis to assist with the hippocampal negative feedback regulation of HPA axis activity (Jankord and Herman, 2008; Snyder et al., 2011). Furthermore, it has been demonstrated that withdrawal is associated with upregulation of NMDA receptors, specifically in

the hippocampus (Hoffman, 2003), which is perhaps secondary to glucocorticoid-dependent excess release of endogenous glutamate and polyamines in the hippocampus and extended amygdala (Abraham et al., 2001; Gibson et al., 2003). Although NMDA receptor activation has been shown to reduce cell proliferation in a normal state (Cameron et al., 1995), this effect is reversed during cytotoxicity (e.g., ethanol withdrawal; Wilkins et al., 2006) and could be attributable to the altered expression of NMDA receptor subunits in chronic ethanol-exposed animals compared with ethanol-naive animals (Prendergast and Mulholland, 2012; Ren et al., 2013). Altogether, specific corticosteroid-mediated neuroadaptations in the CRF system in the extended amygdala following ethanol withdrawal could produce a hyperglutamatergic state in the hippocampus, which may regulate aberrant neurogenesis in the DG. The resulting pathological plasticity could facilitate the recruitment of new GCNs into emotional memory circuits and therefore contribute to the pathology of alcohol dependence (Farioli-Vecchioli et al., 2009; Fournier et al., 2013). Future studies should seek to understand the underlying mechanism of ethanol withdrawal-induced aberrant DG neurogenesis. Such studies may help determine whether hippocampal GCNs born during withdrawal perform improper functions to inhibit regeneration in the hippocampus (excitotoxicity) and aid with recruitment of new neurons into emotional memory circuitry (negative affect).

ACKNOWLEDGMENTS

Preparation of this review was supported by funds from the National Institute on Drug Abuse (DA022473). National Institute on Alcohol Abuse and Alcoholism (AA020098, AA006420), and the Alcoholic Beverage Medical Research Foundation. I would like to thank Dr. Leandro Vendruscolo for critically reading the manuscript and helpful discussions, Michael Arends for his editorial assistance and Janet Hightower for assistance with graphics. This is manuscript number 24035 from The Scripps Research Institute.

REFERENCES

Abraham, I. M., Harkany, T., Horvath, K. M., and Luiten, P. G. (2001). Action of glucocorticoids on survival of nerve cells: promoting neurodegeneration or neuroprotection? *J. Neuroendocrinol.* 13, 749–760. doi:10.1046/j.1365-2826.2001.00705.x

Abrous, D. N., Koehl, M., and Le Moal, M. (2005). Adult neurogenesis: from precursors to network and physiology. *Physiol. Rev.* 85, 523–569. doi:10.1152/physrev.00055.2003

Aimone, J. B., Deng, W., and Gage, F. H. (2011). Resolving new memories: a critical look at the dentate gyrus, adult neurogenesis, and pattern separation. *Neuron* 70, 589–596. doi:10.1016/j.neuron.2011.05.010

Aimone, J. B., Wiles, J., and Gage, F. H. (2006). Potential role for adult neurogenesis in the encoding of time in new memories. *Nat. Neurosci.* 9, 723–727. doi:10.1038/nn1707

Bakker, A., Kirwan, C. B., Miller, M., and Stark, C. E. (2008). Pattern separation in the human hippocampal CA3 and dentate gyrus. *Science* 319, 1640–1642. doi:10.1126/science.1152882

Baram, T. Z., and Hatalski, C. G. (1998). Neuropeptide-mediated excitability: a key triggering mechanism for seizure generation in the developing brain. *Trends Neurosci.* 21, 471–476. doi:10.1016/S0166-2236(98)01275-2

Baram, T. Z., Hirsch, E., Snead, O. C. 3rd, and Schultz, L. (1992). Corticotropin-releasing hormone-induced seizures in infant rats originate in the amygdala. *Ann. Neurol.* 31, 488–494. doi:10.1002/ana.410310505

Barr, J. L., Renner, K. J., and Forster, G. L. (2010). Withdrawal from chronic amphetamine produces persistent anxiety-like behavior but temporally-limited reductions in

monoamines and neurogenesis in the adult rat dentate gyrus. *Neuropharmacology* 59, 395–405. doi:10.1016/j.neuropharm.2010.05.011

Becker, H. C., Veatch, L. M., and Diaz-Granados, J. L. (1998). Repeated ethanol withdrawal experience selectively alters sensitivity to different chemoconvulsant drugs in mice. *Psychopharmacology (Berl.)* 139, 145–153. doi:10.1007/s002130050699

Bengochea, O., and Gonzalo, L. M. (1990). Effect of chronic alcoholism on the human hippocampus. *Histol. Histopathol.* 5, 349–357.

Beresford, T. P., Arciniegas, D. B., Alfers, J., Clapp, L., Martin, B., Du, Y., et al. (2006). Hippocampus volume loss due to chronic heavy drinking. *Alcohol. Clin. Exp. Res.* 30, 1866–1870. doi:10.1111/j.1530-0277.2006.00223.x

Blitzer, R. D., Gil, O., and Landau, E. M. (1990). Long-term potentiation in

rat hippocampus is inhibited by low concentrations of ethanol. *Brain Res.* 537, 203–208. doi:10.1016/0006-8993(90)90359-J

Brandt, J., Butters, N., Ryan, C., and Bayog, R. (1983). Cognitive loss and recovery in long-term alcohol abusers. *Arch. Gen. Psychiatry* 40, 435–442. doi:10.1001/archpsyc.1983.017900 40089012

Breese, G. R., Knapp, D. J., and Overstreet, D. H. (2004). Stress sensitization of ethanol withdrawal-induced reduction in social interaction: inhibition by CRF-1 and benzodiazepine receptor antagonists and a 5-HT1A-receptor agonist. *Neuropsychopharmacology* 29, 470–482. doi:10.1038/sj.npp.1300419

Budygin, E. A., Oleson, E. B., Mathews, T. A., Lack, A. K., Diaz, M. R., McCool, B. A., et al. (2007). Effects of chronic alcohol exposure on dopamine uptake in rat nucleus accumbens and caudate putamen. *Psychopharmacology (Berl.)* 193, 495–501. doi:10.1007/s00213-007-0812-1

Cameron, H. A., and Gould, E. (1994). Adult neurogenesis is regulated by adrenal steroids in the dentate gyrus. *Neuroscience* 61, 203–209. doi:10.1016/0306-4522(94)90224-0

Cameron, H. A., McEwen, B. S., and Gould, E. (1995). Regulation of adult neurogenesis by excitatory input and NMDA receptor activation in the dentate gyrus. *J. Neurosci.* 15, 4687–4692.

Chen, Y., Bender, R. A., Brunson, K. L., Pomper, J. K., Grigoriadis, D. E., Wurst, W., et al. (2004). Modulation of dendritic differentiation by corticotropin-releasing factor in the developing hippocampus. *Proc. Natl. Acad. Sci. U.S.A.* 101, 15782–15787. doi:10.1073/pnas.0403975101

Cippitelli, A., Zook, M., Bell, L., Damadzic, R., Eskay, R. L., Schwandt, M., et al. (2010). Reversibility of object recognition but not spatial memory impairment following binge-like alcohol exposure in rats. *Neurobiol. Learn. Mem.* 94, 538–546. doi:10.1016/j.nlm

Clark, P. J., Bhattacharya, T. K., Miller, D. S., Kohman, R. A., DeYoung, E. K., and Rhodes, J. S. (2012). New neurons generated from running are broadly recruited into neuronal activation associated with three different hippocampus-involved tasks. *Hippocampus* 22, 1860–1867. doi:10.1002/hipo.22020

Claus, D., Kim, J. S., Kornhuber, M. E., and Ahn, Y. S. (1982). Effect of ethanol on the neurotransmitters glutamate and GABA. *Arch. Psychiatr. Nervenkr.* 232, 183–189. doi:10.1007/BF00343699

Clelland, C. D., Choi, M., Romberg, C., Clemenson, G. D. Jr., Fragniere, A., Tyers, P., et al. (2009). A functional role for adult hippocampal neurogenesis in spatial pattern separation. *Science* 325, 210–213. doi:10.1126/science.1173215

Contet, C., Kim, A., Le, D., Iyengar, S. K., Kotzebue, R. W., Yuan, C. J., et al. (2013). mu-Opioid receptors mediate the effects of chronic ethanol binge drinking on the hippocampal neurogenic niche. *Addict. Biol.* doi:10.1111/adb.12040

Crews, F. T., and Nixon, K. (2009). Mechanisms of neurodegeneration and regeneration in alcoholism. *Alcohol Alcohol.* 44, 115–127. doi:10.1093/alcalc/agn079

Crews, F. T., Nixon, K., and Wilkie, M. E. (2004). Exercise reverses ethanol inhibition of neural stem cell proliferation. *Alcohol* 33, 63–71. doi:10.1016/S0741-8329(04)00081-3

Criado, J. R., Liu, T., Ehlers, C. L., and Mathe, A. A. (2011). Prolonged chronic ethanol exposure alters neuropeptide Y and corticotropin-releasing factor levels in the brain of adult Wistar rats. *Pharmacol. Biochem. Behav.* 99, 104–111. doi:10.1016/j.pbb.2011.04.005

Curtis, M. A., Kam, M., Nannmark, U., Anderson, M. F., Axell, M. Z., Wikkelso, C., et al. (2007). Human neuroblasts migrate to the olfactory bulb via a lateral ventricular extension. *Science* 315, 1243–1249. doi:10.1126/science.1136281

Davidson, M., Shanley, B., and Wilce, P. (1995). Increased NMDA-induced excitability during ethanol withdrawal: a behavioural and histological study. *Brain Res.* 674, 91–96. doi:10.1016/0006-8993(94)01440-S

Davidson, M. D., Wilce, P., and Shanley, B. C. (1993). Increased sensitivity of the hippocampus in ethanol-dependent rats to toxic effect of N-methyl-D-aspartic acid in vivo. *Brain Res.* 606, 5–9. doi:10.1016/0006-8993(93)91562-7

Deisseroth, K., Singla, S., Toda, H., Monje, M., Palmer, T. D., and Malenka, R. C. (2004). Excitation-neurogenesis coupling in adult neural stem/progenitor cells. *Neuron* 42, 535–552. doi:10.1016/S0896-6273(04)00266-1

Deschaux, O., Vendruscolo, L. F., Schlosburg, J. E., Diaz-Aguilar, L., Yuan, C. J., Sobieraj, J. C., et al. (2012). Hippocampal neurogenesis protects against cocaine-primed relapse. *Addict. Biol.* doi:10.1111/adb.12019

Durand, D., and Carlen, P. L. (1984). Impairment of long-term potentiation in rat hippocampus following chronic ethanol treatment. *Brain Res.* 308, 325–332. doi:10.1016/0006-8993(84)91072-2

Durazzo, T. C., Tosun, D., Buckley, S., Gazdzinski, S., Mon, A., Fryer, S. L., et al. (2011). Cortical thickness, surface area, and volume of the brain reward system in alcohol dependence: relationships to relapse and extended abstinence. *Alcohol. Clin. Exp. Res.* 35, 1187–1200. doi:10.1111/j.1530-0277.2011.01452.x

Eriksson, P. S., Perfilieva, E., Bjork-Eriksson, T., Alborn, A. M., Nordborg, C., Peterson, D. A., et al. (1998). Neurogenesis in the adult human hippocampus. *Nat. Med.* 4, 1313–1317. doi:10.1038/3305

Farioli-Vecchioli, S., Saraulli, D., Costanzi, M., Leonardi, L., Cina, I., Micheli, L., et al. (2009). Impaired terminal differentiation of hippocampal granule neurons and defective contextual memory in PC3/Tis21 knockout mice. *PLoS ONE* 4:e8339. doi:10.1371/journal.pone.0008339

Feng, R., Rampon, C., Tang, Y. P., Shrom, D., Jin, J., Kyin, M., et al. (2001). Deficient neurogenesis in forebrain-specific presenilin-1 knockout mice is associated with reduced clearance of hippocampal memory traces. *Neuron* 32, 911–926. doi:10.1016/S0896-6273(01)00523-2

Fournier, N. M., Andersen, D. R., Botterill, J. J., Sterner, E. Y., Lussier, A. L., Caruncho, H. J., et al. (2010). The effect of amygdala kindling on hippocampal neurogenesis coincides with decreased reelin and DISC1 expression in the adult dentate gyrus. *Hippocampus* 20, 659–671.

Fournier, N. M., Botterill, J. J., Marks, W. N., Guskjolen, A. J., and Kalynchuk, L. E. (2013). Impaired recruitment of seizure-generated neurons into functional memory networks of the adult dentate gyrus following long-term amygdala kindling. *Exp. Neurol.* 244, 96–104. doi:10.1016/j.expneurol.2012.11.031

Frasca, A., Aalbers, M., Frigerio, F., Fiordaliso, F., Salio, M., Gobbi, M., et al. (2011). Misplaced NMDA receptors in epileptogenesis contribute to excitotoxicity. *Neurobiol. Dis.* 43, 507–515. doi:10.1016/j.nbd.2011.04.024

Freund, T. F., and Buzsaki, G. (1996). Interneurons of the hippocampus. *Hippocampus* 6, 347–470. doi:10.1002/(SICI)1098-1063(1996)6:4<347::AID-HIPO1>3.0.CO;2-I

Frye, G. D., McCown, T. J., and Breese, G. R. (1983). Differential sensitivity of ethanol withdrawal signs in the rat to gamma-aminobutyric acid (GABA)mimetics: blockade of audiogenic seizures but not forelimb tremors. *J. Pharmacol. Exp. Ther.* 226, 720–725.

Fujii, S., Yamazaki, Y., Sugihara, T., and Wakabayashi, I. (2008). Acute and chronic ethanol exposure differentially affect induction of hippocampal LTP. *Brain Res.* 1211, 13–21. doi:10.1016/j.brainres.2008.02.052

Garcia-Fuster, M. J., Flagel, S. B., Mahmood, S. T., Mayo, L. M., Thompson, R. C., Watson, S. J., et al. (2011). Decreased proliferation of adult hippocampal stem cells during cocaine withdrawal: possible role of the cell fate regulator FADD. *Neuropsychopharmacology* 36, 2303–2317. doi:10.1038/npp.2011.119

Gehlert, D. R., Cippitelli, A., Thorsell, A., Le, A. D., Hipskind, P. A., Hamdouchi, C., et al. (2007). 3-(4-Chloro-2-morpholin-4-yl-thiazol-5-yl)-8-(1-ethylpropyl)-2,6-dimethyl-imidazo[1,2-b]pyridazine: a novel brain-penetrant, orally available corticotropin-releasing factor receptor 1 antagonist with efficacy in animal models of alcoholism. *J. Neurosci.* 27, 2718–2726. doi:10.1523/JNEUROSCI.4985-06.2007

George, O., Sanders, C., Freiling, J., Grigoryan, E., Vu, S., Allen, C. D., et al. (2012). Recruitment of medial prefrontal cortex neurons during alcohol withdrawal predicts cognitive impairment and excessive alcohol drinking. *Proc. Natl. Acad. Sci. U.S.A.* 109, 18156–18161. doi:10.1073/pnas.1116523109

Gibson, D. A., Harris, B. R., Prendergast, M. A., Hart, S. R., Blanchard, J. A. II, Holley, R. C., et al. (2003). Polyamines contribute to ethanol withdrawal-induced neurotoxicity in rat hippocampal slice cultures through interactions with the NMDA receptor. *Alcohol. Clin. Exp. Res.* 27, 1099–1106. doi:10.1097/01.ALC.0000075824.10502.DD

Gilpin, N. W., Smith, A. D., Cole, M., Weiss, F., Koob, G. F., and Richardson, H. N. (2009). Operant behavior and alcohol levels in blood and brain of alcohol-dependent rats. *Alcohol. Clin. Exp. Res.* 33, 2113–2123. doi:10.1111/j.1530-0277.2009.01051.x

Glenn, S. W., and Parsons, O. A. (1991). Impaired efficiency in female alcoholics' neuropsychological performance. *J. Clin. Exp. Neuropsychol.* 13, 895–908. doi:10.1080/01688639108405106

Gonzalez, L. P., Veatch, L. M., Ticku, M. K., and Becker, H. C. (2001). Alcohol withdrawal kindling: mechanisms and implications for treatment. *Alcohol. Clin. Exp. Res.* 25, 197S–201S. doi:10.1111/j.1530-0277.2001.tb02396.x

Gould, E., Beylin, A., Tanapat, P., Reeves, A., and Shors, T. J. (1999). Learning enhances adult neurogenesis in the hippocampal formation. *Nat. Neurosci.* 2, 260–265. doi:10.1038/6365

Griffin, W. C. 3rd, Lopez, M. F., and Becker, H. C. (2009). Intensity and duration of chronic ethanol exposure is critical for subsequent escalation of voluntary ethanol drinking in mice. *Alcohol. Clin. Exp. Res.* 33, 1893–1900. doi:10.1111/j.1530-0277.2009.01027.x

Gutierrez, R., and Heinemann, U. (1999). Synaptic reorganization in explanted cultures of rat hippocampus. *Brain Res.* 815, 304–316. doi:10.1016/S0006-8993(98)01101-9

Hansson, A. C., Nixon, K., Rimondini, R., Damadzic, R., Sommer, W. H., Eskay, R., et al. (2010). Long-term suppression of forebrain neurogenesis and loss of neuronal progenitor cells following prolonged alcohol dependence in rats. *Int. J. Neuropsychopharmacol.* 13, 583–593. doi:10.1017/S1461145710000246

Hastings, N. B., Tanapat, P., and Gould, E. (2001). Neurogenesis in the adult mammalian brain. *Clin. Neurosci. Res.* 1, 175–182. doi:10.1016/S1566-2772(01)00003-2

He, J., Nixon, K., Shetty, A. K., and Crews, F. T. (2005). Chronic alcohol exposure reduces hippocampal neurogenesis and dendritic growth of newborn neurons. *Eur. J. Neurosci.* 21, 2711–2720. doi:10.1111/j.1460-9568.2005.04120.x

Hoffman, P. L. (2003). NMDA receptors in alcoholism. *Int. Rev. Neurobiol.* 56, 35–82. doi:10.1016/S0074-7742(03)56002-0

Hoffman, P. L., and Tabakoff, B. (1994). The role of the NMDA receptor in ethanol withdrawal. *EXS* 71, 61–70.

Hollrigel, G. S., Chen, K., Baram, T. Z., and Soltesz, I. (1998). The pro-convulsant actions of corticotropin-releasing hormone in the hippocampus of infant rats. *Neuroscience* 84, 71–79. doi:10.1016/S0306-4522(97)00499-5

Ieraci, A., and Herrera, D. G. (2007). Single alcohol exposure in early life damages hippocampal stem/progenitor cells and reduces adult neurogenesis. *Neurobiol. Dis.* 26, 597–605. doi:10.1016/j.nbd.2007.02.011

Izumi, Y., Nagashima, K., Murayama, K., and Zorumski, C. F. (2005). Acute effects of ethanol on hippocampal long-term potentiation and long-term depression are mediated by different mechanisms. *Neuroscience* 136, 509–517. doi:10.1016/j.neuroscience.2005.08.002

Jankord, R., and Herman, J. P. (2008). Limbic regulation of hypothalamo-pituitary-adrenocortical function during acute and chronic stress. *Ann. N. Y. Acad. Sci.* 1148, 64–73. doi:10.1196/annals.1410.012

Kaplan, M. S., and Hinds, J. W. (1977). Neurogenesis in the adult rat: electron microscopic analysis of light radioautographs. *Science* 197, 1092–1094. doi:10.1126/science.887941

Keller, E., Cummins, J. T., and von Hungen, K. (1983). Regional effects of ethanol on glutamate levels, uptake and release in slice and synaptosome preparations from rat brain. *Subst. Alcohol Actions Misuse* 4, 383–392.

Kempermann, G., Jessberger, S., Steiner, B., and Kronenberg, G. (2004). Milestones of neuronal development in the adult hippocampus. *Trends Neurosci.* 27, 447–452. doi:10.1016/j.tins.2004.05.013

Kim, W. R., Christian, K., Ming, G. L., and Song, H. (2012). Time-dependent involvement of adult-born dentate granule cells in behavior. *Behav. Brain Res.* 227, 470–479. doi:10.1016/j.bbr.2011.07.012

Kirby, E. D., Friedman, A. R., Covarrubias, D., Ying, C., Sun, W. G., Goosens, K. A., et al. (2012). Basolateral amygdala regulation of adult hippocampal neurogenesis and fear-related activation of newborn neurons. *Mol. Psychiatry* 17, 527–536. doi:10.1038/mp.2011.71

Knapp, D. J., Overstreet, D. H., Moy, S. S., and Breese, G. R. (2004). SB242084, flumazenil, and CRA1000 block ethanol withdrawal-induced anxiety in rats. *Alcohol* 32, 101–111. doi:10.1016/j.alcohol.2003.08.007

Koob, G. F. (2008). A role for brain stress systems in addiction. *Neuron* 59, 11–34. doi:10.1016/j.neuron.2008.06.012

Koob, G. F., and Volkow, N. D. (2010). Neurocircuitry of addiction. *Neuropsychopharmacology* 35, 217–238. doi:10.1038/npp.2009.110

Lacefield, C. O., Itskov, V., Reardon, T., Hen, R., and Gordon, J. A. (2012). Effects of adult-generated granule cells on coordinated network activity in the dentate gyrus. *Hippocampus* 22, 106–116. doi:10.1002/hipo.20860

Liu, X., and Weiss, F. (2002). Additive effect of stress and drug cues on reinstatement of ethanol seeking: exacerbation by history of dependence and role of concurrent activation of corticotropin-releasing factor and opioid mechanisms. *J. Neurosci.* 22, 7856–7861.

Liu, X., and Weiss, F. (2003). Stimulus conditioned to foot-shock stress reinstates alcohol-seeking behavior in an animal model of relapse. *Psychopharmacology (Berl.)* 168, 184–191. doi:10.1007/s00213-002-1267-z

Lopez, M. F., and Becker, H. C. (2005). Effect of pattern and number of chronic ethanol exposures on subsequent voluntary ethanol intake in C57BL/6J mice. *Psychopharmacology (Berl.)* 181, 688–696. doi:10.1007/s00213-005-0026-3

Lovallo, W. R., Dickensheets, S. L., Myers, D. A., Thomas, T. L., and Nixon, S. J. (2000). Blunted stress cortisol response in abstinent alcoholic and polysubstance-abusing men. *Alcohol. Clin. Exp. Res.* 24, 651–658. doi:10.1111/j.1530-0277.2000.tb02036.x

Lovinger, D. M., White, G., and Weight, F. F. (1989). Ethanol inhibits NMDA-activated ion current in hippocampal neurons. *Science* 243, 1721–1724. doi:10.1126/science.2467382

Lukoyanov, N. V., Madeira, M. D., and Paula-Barbosa, M. M. (1999). Behavioral and neuroanatomical consequences of chronic ethanol intake and withdrawal. *Physiol. Behav.* 66, 337–346. doi:10.1016/S0031-9384(98)00301-1

Macey, D. J., Schulteis, G., Heinrichs, S. C., and Koob, G. F. (1996). Time-dependent quantifiable withdrawal from ethanol in the rat: effect of method of dependence induction. *Alcohol* 13, 163–170. doi:10.1016/0741-8329(95)02030-6

Majchrowicz, E. (1975). Induction of physical dependence upon ethanol and the associated behavioral changes in rats. *Psychopharmacologia* 43, 245–254. doi:10.1007/BF00429258

Makino, S., Gold, P. W., and Schulkin, J. (1994). Corticosterone effects on corticotropin-releasing hormone mRNA in the central nucleus of the amygdala and the parvocellular region of the paraventricular nucleus of the hypothalamus. *Brain Res.* 640, 105–112. doi:10.1016/0006-8993(94)91862-7

Mandyam, C. D., and Koob, G. F. (2012). The addicted brain craves new neurons: putative role for adult-born progenitors in promoting recovery. *Trends Neurosci.* 35, 250–260. doi:10.1016/j.tins.2011.12.005

Martens, U., and Wree, A. (2001). Distribution of [3H]MK-801, [3H]AMPA and [3H]Kainate binding sites in rat hippocampal long-term slice cultures isolated from external afferents. *Anat. Embryol.* 203, 491–500. doi:10.1007/s004290100174

McCool, B. A., Christian, D. T., Diaz, M. R., and Lack, A. K. (2010). Glutamate plasticity in the drunken amygdala: the making of an anxious synapse. *Int. Rev. Neurobiol.* 91, 205–233. doi:10.1016/S0074-7742(10)91007-6

McHugh, T. J., Jones, M. W., Quinn, J. J., Balthasar, N., Coppari, R., Elmquist, J. K., et al. (2007). Dentate gyrus NMDA receptors mediate rapid pattern separation in the hippocampal network. *Science* 317, 94–99. doi:10.1126/science.1140263

McMullen, P. A., Saint-Cyr, J. A., and Carlen, P. L. (1984). Morphological alterations in rat CA1 hippocampal pyramidal cell dendrites resulting from chronic ethanol consumption and withdrawal. *J. Comp. Neurol.* 225, 111–118. doi:10.1002/cne.902250112

Miki, T., Kuma, H., Yokoyama, T., Sumitani, K., Matsumoto, Y., Kusaka, T., et al. (2008). Early postnatal ethanol exposure induces fluctuation in the expression of BDNF mRNA in the developing rat hippocampus. *Acta Neurobiol. Exp. (Wars)* 68, 484–493.

Mirescu, C., and Gould, E. (2006). Stress and adult neurogenesis. *Hippocampus* 16, 233–238. doi:10.1002/hipo.20155

Moore, D. B., Madorsky, I., Paiva, M., and Barrow Heaton, M. (2004). Ethanol exposure alters neurotrophin receptor expression in the rat central nervous system: effects of neonatal exposure. *J. Neurobiol.* 60, 114–126. doi:10.1002/neu.20010

Mulholland, P. J., Harris, B. R., Wilkins, L. H., Self, R. L., Blanchard, J. A., Holley, R. C., et al. (2003). Opposing effects of ethanol and nicotine on hippocampal calbindin-D28k expression. *Alcohol* 31, 1–10. doi:10.1016/j.alcohol.2003.09.001

Nelson, T. E., Ur, C. L., and Gruol, D. L. (2005). Chronic intermittent ethanol exposure enhances NMDA-receptor-mediated synaptic responses and NMDA receptor expression in hippocampal CA1 region. *Brain Res.* 1048, 69–79. doi:10.1016/j.brainres.2005.04.041

Nixon, K. (2006). Alcohol and adult neurogenesis: roles in neurodegeneration and recovery in chronic alcoholism. *Hippocampus* 16, 287–295. doi:10.1002/hipo.20162

Nixon, K., and Crews, F. T. (2002). Binge ethanol exposure decreases neurogenesis in adult rat hippocampus. *J. Neurochem.* 83, 1087–1093. doi:10.1046/j.1471-4159.2002.01214.x

Nixon, K., and Crews, F. T. (2004). Temporally specific burst in cell proliferation increases hippocampal neurogenesis in protracted abstinence from alcohol. *J. Neurosci.* 24, 9714–9722. doi:10.1523/JNEUROSCI.3063-04.2004

Nixon, K., Kim, D. H., Potts, E. N., He, J., and Crews, F. T. (2008). Distinct cell proliferation events during abstinence after alcohol dependence: microglia proliferation precedes neurogenesis. *Neurobiol. Dis.* 31, 218–229. doi:10.1016/j.nbd.2008.04.009

Noonan, M. A., Choi, K. H., Self, D. W., and Eisch, A. J. (2008). Withdrawal from cocaine self-administration normalizes deficits in proliferation and enhances maturity of adult-generated hippocampal neurons. *J. Neurosci.* 28, 2516–2526. doi:10.1523/JNEUROSCI.4661-07.2008

O'Dell, L. E., Roberts, A. J., Smith, R. T., and Koob, G. F. (2004). Enhanced alcohol self-administration after intermittent versus continuous alcohol vapor exposure. *Alcohol. Clin. Exp. Res.* 28, 1676–1682. doi:10.1097/01.ALC.0000145781.11923.4E

O'Malley, S. S., Krishnan-Sarin, S., Farren, C., Sinha, R., and Kreek, M. J. (2002). Naltrexone decreases craving and alcohol self-administration in alcohol-dependent subjects and activates the hypothalamo-pituitary-adrenocortical axis. *Psychopharmacology (Berl.)* 160, 19–29. doi:10.1007/s002130100919

Oomen, C. A., Mayer, J. L., de Kloet, E. R., Joels, M., and Lucassen, P. J. (2007). Brief treatment with the glucocorticoid receptor antagonist mifepristone normalizes the reduction in neurogenesis after chronic stress. *Eur. J. Neurosci.* 26, 3395–3401. doi:10.1111/j.1460-9568.2007.05972.x

Overstreet, D. H., Knapp, D. J., and Breese, G. R. (2004). Modulation of multiple ethanol withdrawal-induced anxiety-like behavior by CRF and CRF1 receptors. *Pharmacol. Biochem. Behav.* 77, 405–413. doi:10.1016/j.pbb.2003.11.010

Parent, J. M., Yu, T. W., Leibowitz, R. T., Geschwind, D. H., Sloviter, R. S., and Lowenstein, D. H. (1997). Dentate granule cell neurogenesis is increased by seizures and contributes to aberrant network reorganization in the adult rat hippocampus. *J. Neurosci.* 17, 3727–3738.

Pian, J. P., Criado, J. R., Milner, R., and Ehlers, C. L. (2010). N-methyl-D-aspartate receptor subunit expression in adult and adolescent brain following chronic ethanol exposure. *Neuroscience* 170, 645–654. doi:10.1016/j.neuroscience.2010.06.065

Prendergast, M. A., Harris, B. R., Mullholland, P. J., Blanchard, J. A. II, Gibson, D. A., Holley, R. C., et al. (2004). Hippocampal CA1 region neurodegeneration produced by ethanol withdrawal requires activation of intrinsic polysynaptic hippocampal pathways and function of N-methyl-D-aspartate receptors. *Neuroscience* 124, 869–877. doi:10.1016/j.neuroscience.2003.12.013

Prendergast, M. A., and Mulholland, P. J. (2012). Glucocorticoid and polyamine interactions in the plasticity of glutamatergic synapses that contribute to ethanol-associated dependence and neuronal injury. *Addict. Biol.* 17, 209–223. doi:10.1111/j.1369-1600.2011.00375.x

Prior, P. L., and Galduroz, J. C. (2011). Glutamatergic hyperfunctioning during alcohol withdrawal syndrome: therapeutic perspective with zinc and magnesium. *Med. Hypotheses* 77, 368–370. doi:10.1016/j.mehy.2011.05.017

Rainnie, D. G., Bergeron, R., Sajdyk, T. J., Patil, M., Gehlert, D. R., and Shekhar, A. (2004). Corticotrophin releasing factor-induced synaptic plasticity in the amygdala translates stress into emotional disorders. *J. Neurosci.* 24, 3471–3479. doi:10.1523/JNEUROSCI.5740-03.2004

Recinto, P., Samant, A. R., Chavez, G., Kim, A., Yuan, C. J., Soleiman, M., et al. (2012). Levels of neural progenitors in the hippocampus predict memory impairment and relapse to drug seeking as a function of excessive methamphetamine self-administration. *Neuropsychopharmacology* 37, 1275–1287. doi:10.1038/npp.2011.315

Refojo, D., Schweizer, M., Kuehne, C., Ehrenberg, S., Thoeringer, C., Vogl, A. M., et al. (2011). Glutamatergic and dopaminergic neurons mediate anxiogenic and anxiolytic effects of CRHR1. *Science* 333, 1903–1907. doi:10.1126/science.1202107

Ren, J., Li, X., Zhang, X., Li, M., Wang, Y., and Ma, Y. (2013). The effects of intra-hippocampal microinfusion of d-cycloserine on fear extinction, and the expression of NMDA receptor subunit NR2B and neurogenesis in the hippocampus in rats. *Prog. Neuropsychopharmacol. Biol. Psychiatry* 44, 257–264. doi:10.1016/j.pnpbp.2013.02.017

Rice, A. C., Bullock, M. R., and Shelton, K. L. (2004). Chronic ethanol consumption transiently reduces adult neural progenitor cell proliferation. *Brain Res.* 1011, 94–98. doi:10.1016/j.brainres.2004.01.091

Richardson, H. N., Chan, S. H., Crawford, E. F., Lee, Y. K., Funk, C. K., Koob, G. F., et al. (2009). Permanent impairment of birth and survival of cortical and hippocampal proliferating cells following excessive drinking during alcohol dependence. *Neurobiol. Dis.* 36, 1–10. doi:10.1016/j.nbd.2009.05.021

Richardson, H. N., Lee, S. Y., O'Dell, L. E., Koob, G. F., and Rivier, C. L. (2008). Alcohol self-administration acutely stimulates the hypothalamic-pituitary-adrenal axis, but alcohol dependence leads to a dampened neuroendocrine state. *Eur. J. Neurosci.* 28, 1641–1653. doi:10.1111/j.1460-9568.2008.06455.x

Rimondini, R., Sommer, W., and Heilig, M. (2003). A temporal threshold for induction of persistent alcohol preference: behavioral evidence in a rat model of intermittent intoxication. *J. Stud. Alcohol* 64, 445–449.

Roberto, M., Nelson, T. E., Ur, C. L., and Gruol, D. L. (2002). Long-term potentiation in the rat hippocampus is reversibly depressed by chronic intermittent ethanol exposure. *J. Neurophysiol.* 87, 2385–2397.

Sahay, A., Scobie, K. N., Hill, A. S., O'Carroll, C. M., Kheirbek, M. A., Burghardt, N. S., et al. (2011). Increasing adult hippocampal neurogenesis is sufficient to improve pattern separation. *Nature* 472, 466–470. doi:10.1038/nature09817

Sajdyk, T. J., and Gehlert, D. R. (2000). Astressin, a corticotropin releasing factor antagonist, reverses the anxiogenic effects of urocortin when administered into the basolateral amygdala. *Brain Res.* 877, 226–234. doi:10.1016/S0006-8993(00)02638-X

Sajdyk, T. J., Schober, D. A., Gehlert, D. R., and Shekhar, A. (1999). Role of corticotropin-releasing factor and urocortin within the basolateral amygdala of rats in anxiety and panic responses. *Behav. Brain Res.* 100, 207–215. doi:10.1016/S0166-4328(98)00132-6

Sanna, E., Serra, M., Cossu, A., Colombo, G., Follesa, P., Cuccheddu, T., et al. (1993). Chronic ethanol intoxication induces differential effects on GABAA and NMDA receptor function in the rat brain. *Alcohol. Clin. Exp. Res.* 17, 115–123. doi:10.1111/j.1530-0277.1993.tb00735.x

Schmidt-Hieber, C., Jonas, P., and Bischofberger, J. (2004). Enhanced synaptic plasticity in newly generated granule cells of the adult hippocampus. *Nature* 429, 184–187. doi:10.1038/nature02553

Sheela Rani, C. S., and Ticku, M. K. (2006). Comparison of chronic ethanol and chronic intermittent ethanol treatments on the expression of GABA(A) and NMDA receptor subunits. *Alcohol* 38, 89–97. doi:10.1016/j.alcohol.2006.05.002

Shors, T. J., Townsend, D. A., Zhao, M., Kozorovitskiy, Y., and Gould, E. (2002). Neurogenesis may relate to some but not all types of hippocampal-dependent learning. *Hippocampus* 12, 578–584. doi:10.1002/hipo.10103

Smith, M. A., Weiss, S. R., Berry, R. L., Zhang, L. X., Clark, M., Massenburg, G., et al. (1997). Amygdala-kindled seizures increase the expression of corticotropin-releasing factor (CRF) and CRF-binding protein in GABAergic interneurons of the dentate hilus. *Brain Res.* 745, 248–256. doi:10.1016/S0006-8993(96)01157-2

Snell, L. D., Nunley, K. R., Lickteig, R. L., Browning, M. D., Tabakoff, B., and Hoffman, P. L. (1996). Regional and subunit specific changes in NMDA receptor mRNA and immunoreactivity in mouse brain following chronic ethanol ingestion. *Brain Res. Mol. Brain Res.* 40, 71–78. doi:10.1016/0169-328X(96)00038-1

Snyder, J. S., Soumier, A., Brewer, M., Pickel, J., and Cameron, H. A. (2011). Adult hippocampal neurogenesis buffers stress responses and depressive behaviour. *Nature* 476, 458–461. doi:10.1038/nature10287

Sommer, W. H., Rimondini, R., Hansson, A. C., Hipskind, P. A., Gehlert, D. R., Barr, C. S., et al. (2008). Upregulation of voluntary alcohol intake, behavioral sensitivity to stress, and amygdala crhr1 expression following a history of dependence. *Biol. Psychiatry* 63, 139–145. doi:10.1016/j.biopsych.2007.01.010

Sullivan, E. V., Fama, R., Rosenbloom, M. J., and Pfefferbaum, A. (2002). A profile of neuropsychological deficits in alcoholic women. *Neuropsychology* 16, 74–83. doi:10.1037/0894-4105.16.1.74

Sullivan, E. V., Marsh, L., Mathalon, D. H., Lim, K. O., and Pfefferbaum, A. (1995). Anterior hippocampal volume deficits in nonamnesic, aging chronic alcoholics. *Alcohol. Clin. Exp. Res.* 19, 110–122. doi:10.1111/j.1530-0277.1995.tb01478.x

Sullivan, E. V., Rosenbloom, M. J., and Pfefferbaum, A. (2000a). Pattern of motor and cognitive deficits in detoxified alcoholic men. *Alcohol. Clin. Exp. Res.* 24, 611–621. doi:10.1111/j.1530-0277.2000.tb02032.x

Sullivan, E. V., Rosenbloom, M. J., Lim, K. O., and Pfefferbaum, A. (2000b). Longitudinal changes in cognition, gait, and balance in abstinent and relapsed alcoholic men: relationships to changes in brain structure. *Neuropsychology* 14, 178–188. doi:10.1037/0894-4105.14.2.178

Taffe, M. A., Kotzebue, R. W., Crean, R. D., Crawford, E. F., Edwards, S., and Mandyam, C. D. (2010). Long-lasting reduction in hippocampal neurogenesis by alcohol consumption in adolescent nonhuman primates. *Proc. Natl. Acad. Sci. U.S.A.* 107, 11104–11109. doi:10.1073/pnas.0912810107

Tsai, G., Gastfriend, D. R., and Coyle, J. T. (1995). The glutamatergic basis of human alcoholism. *Am. J. Psychiatry* 152, 332–340.

Valdez, G. R., Roberts, A. J., Chan, K., Davis, H., Brennan, M., Zorrilla, E. P., et al. (2002). Increased ethanol self-administration and anxiety-like behavior during acute ethanol withdrawal and protracted abstinence: regulation by corticotropin-releasing factor. *Alcohol. Clin. Exp. Res.* 26, 1494–1501. doi:10.1111/j.1530-0277.2002.tb02448.x

Vendruscolo, L. F., Barbier, E., Schlosburg, J. E., Misra, K. K., Whitfield, T. W. Jr., Logrip, M. L., et al. (2012). Corticosteroid-dependent plasticity mediates compulsive alcohol drinking in rats. *J. Neurosci.* 32, 7563–7571. doi:10.1523/JNEUROSCI.0069-12.2012

Wand, G. (2005). The anxious amygdala: CREB signaling and predisposition to anxiety and alcoholism. *J. Clin. Invest.* 115, 2697–2699. doi:10.1172/JCI26436

Wang, H. L., Tsai, L. Y., and Lee, E. H. (2000). Corticotropin-releasing factor produces a protein synthesis – dependent long-lasting potentiation in dentate gyrus neurons. *J. Neurophysiol.* 83, 343–349.

Wayner, M. J., Chitwood, R., Armstrong, D. L., and Phelix, C. (1997). Ethanol affects hypothalamic neurons projecting to the hippocampus and inhibits dentate granule cell LTP. *Alcohol* 14, 1–7. doi:10.1016/S0741-8329(96)00077-8

Weiner, J. L., Dunwiddie, T. V., and Valenzuela, C. F. (1999). Ethanol inhibition of synaptically evoked kainate responses in rat hippocampal CA3 pyramidal neurons. *Mol. Pharmacol.* 56, 85–90.

Wilce, P. A., Le, F., Matsumoto, I., and Shanley, B. C. (1993). Ethanol inhibits NMDA-receptor mediated regulation of immediate early gene expression. *Alcohol. Alcohol Suppl.* 2, 359–363.

Wilkins, L. H. Jr., Prendergast, M. A., Blanchard, J., Holley, R. C., Chambers, E. R., and Littleton, J. M. (2006). Potential value of changes in cell markers in organotypic hippocampal cultures associated with chronic EtOH exposure and withdrawal: comparison with NMDA-induced changes. *Alcohol. Clin. Exp. Res.* 30, 1768–1780. doi:10.1111/j.1530-0277.2006.00210.x

Wirkner, K., Poelchen, W., Koles, L., Muhlberg, K., Scheibler, P., Allgaier, C., et al. (1999). Ethanol-induced inhibition of NMDA receptor channels. *Neurochem. Int.* 35, 153–162. doi:10.1016/S0197-0186(99)00057-1

Wright, J. W., Kramar, E. A., Myers, E. D., Davis, C. J., and Harding, J. W. (2003). Ethanol-induced suppression of LTP can be attenuated with an angiotensin IV analog. *Regul. Pept.* 113, 49–56. doi:10.1016/S0167-0115(02)00302-6

Wu, P. H., Mihic, S. J., Liu, J. F., Le, A. D., and Kalant, H. (1993). Blockade of chronic tolerance to ethanol by the NMDA antagonist, (+)-MK-801. *Eur. J. Pharmacol.* 231, 157–164. doi:10.1016/0014-2999(93)90444-M

Yan, X. X., Toth, Z., Schultz, L., Ribak, C. E., and Baram, T. Z. (1998). Corticotropin-releasing hormone (CRH)-containing neurons in the immature rat hippocampal formation: light and electron microscopic features and colocalization with glutamate decarboxylase and parvalbumin. *Hippocampus* 8, 231–243. doi:10.1002/(SICI)1098-1063(1998)8:3<231::AID-HIPO6>3.0.CO;2-M

Zahr, N. M., Mayer, D., Vinco, S., Orduna, J., Luong, R., Sullivan, E. V., et al. (2009). In vivo evidence for alcohol-induced neurochemical changes in rat brain without protracted withdrawal, pronounced thiamine deficiency, or severe liver damage. *Neuropsychopharmacology* 34, 1427–1442. doi:10.1038/npp.2008.119

Zarrindast, M. R., Meshkani, J., Rezayof, A., Beigzadeh, R., and Rostami, P. (2010). Nicotinic acetylcholine receptors of the dorsal hippocampus and the basolateral amygdala are involved in ethanol-induced conditioned place preference. *Neuroscience* 168, 505–513. doi:10.1016/j.neuroscience.2010.03.019

Zorrilla, E. P., Valdez, G. R., and Weiss, F. (2001). Changes in levels of regional CRF-like-immunoreactivity and plasma corticosterone during protracted drug withdrawal in dependent rats. *Psychopharmacology (Berl.)* 158, 374–381. doi:10.1007/s002130100773

10

Role of a genetic polymorphism in the corticotropin-releasing factor receptor 1 gene in alcohol drinking and seeking behaviors of Marchigian Sardinian alcohol-preferring rats

Lydia O. Ayanwuyi[1], Francisca Carvajal[1], Jose M. Lerma-Cabrera[1], Esi Domi[1], Karl Björk[2], Massimo Ubaldi[1], Markus Heilig[2], Marisa Roberto[3], Roberto Ciccocioppo[1]* and Andrea Cippitelli[1]

[1] Pharmacology Unit, School of Pharmacy, University of Camerino, Camerino, Italy
[2] Laboratory of Clinical and Translational Studies, National Institutes of Health, National Institute on Alcohol Abuse and Alcoholism, Bethesda, MD, USA
[3] Committee on the Neurobiology of Addictive Disorders, The Scripps Research Institute, La Jolla, CA, USA

Edited by:
Remi Martin-Fardon, The Scripps
Research Institute, USA

Reviewed by:
A. D. Lê, Centre for Addiction and
Mental Health, Canada
Andrey E. Ryabinin, Oregon Health
and Science University, USA

*Correspondence:
Roberto Ciccocioppo, Pharmacology
Unit, School of Pharmacy, University
of Camerino, Building of Experimental
Medicine, Via Madonna delle Carceri,
Camerino, Macerata 62032, Italy.
e-mail: roberto.ciccocioppo@unicam.it

Marchigian Sardinian alcohol-preferring (msP) rats exhibit innate preference for alcohol, are highly sensitive to stress and stress-induced alcohol seeking. Genetic analysis showed that over-expression of the corticotropin-releasing factor (CRF) system of msP rats is correlated with the presence of two single nucleotide polymorphisms (SNPs) occurring in the promoter region (position −1836 and −2097) of the CRF1 receptor (CRF1-R) gene. Here we examined whether these point mutations were associated to the innate alcohol preference, stress-induced drinking, and seeking. We have recently re-derived the msP rats to obtain two distinct lines carrying the wild type (GG) and the point mutations (AA), respectively. The phenotypic characteristics of these two lines were compared with those of unselected Wistar rats. Both AA and GG rats showed similar patterns of voluntary alcohol intake and preference. Similarly, the pharmacological stressor yohimbine (0.0, 0.625, 1.25, and 2.5 mg/kg) elicited increased operant alcohol self-administration under fixed and progressive ratio reinforcement schedules in all three lines. Following extinction, yohimbine (0.0, 0.625, 1.25, and 2.5 mg/kg) significantly reinstated alcohol seeking in the three groups. However, at the highest dose this effect was no longer evident in AA rats. Treatment with the CRF1-R antagonist antalarmin (0, 5, 10, and 20 mg/kg) significantly reduced alcohol-reinforced lever pressing in the AA line (10 and 20 mg/kg) while a weaker or no effect was observed in the Wistar and the GG group, respectively. Finally, antalarmin significantly reduced yohimbine-induced increase in alcohol drinking in all three groups. In conclusion, these specific SNPs in the CRF1-R gene do not seem to play a primary role in the expression of the msP excessive drinking phenotype or stress-induced drinking but may be associated with a decreased threshold for stress-induced alcohol seeking and an increased sensitivity to the effects of pharmacological blockade of CRF1-R on alcohol drinking.

Keywords: CRF, SNP, self-administration, msP, yohimbine, relapse

INTRODUCTION

Alcoholism is an etiologically and clinically heterogeneous disorder in which compulsive alcohol use and elevated vulnerability to relapse represent core symptoms (McLellan et al., 1992). Exposure to alcohol is a necessary precondition for development of alcoholism. However, environment and heritability factors play a dramatic role in controlling individual predisposition to developing alcohol abuse (Cloninger et al., 1981; Schuckit et al., 1985; Enoch and Goldman, 1999; Lovinger and Crabbe, 2005). Environmental stress has been recognized as one of the major factors for alcohol abuse and dependence (Pohorecky, 1991; Sarnyai et al., 2001; Sinha, 2001; Shaham et al., 2003; Breese et al., 2005b). However, the interaction between environmental stress and heritable factors in the development of alcoholism is still largely unexplored.

Understanding the nature of this interaction in regulating individual risk of becoming an alcohol abuser represents a major challenge in this research field and may provide invaluable help for the development of preventive strategies or pharmacotherapeutic remedies.

Studies conducted in our laboratory demonstrated that genetically selected Marchigian Sardinian alcohol-preferring (msP) rats show excessive daily alcohol drinking (6–8 g/kg body weight) in a binge-type pattern, leading to blood alcohol levels as high as 100–120 mg/dl (Ciccocioppo et al., 2006). This selected rat line is highly sensitive to stress and stress-induced alcohol seeking (Ciccocioppo et al., 2006), demonstrates an anxious phenotype (Hansson et al., 2006), and has depressive-like symptoms that recover following alcohol consumption (Ciccocioppo et al., 1999). Hence, these animals may represent a preclinical model of genetic predisposition to high alcohol drinking and relapse endowed with significant predictive validity. In addition, msP rats appear to share important common characteristics with the human disease that also confer to them important elements of face and construct validity (Ciccocioppo et al., 2006; Ciccocioppo, 2013).

The corticotropin-releasing factor (CRF) is a 41 amino acid peptide that integrates many of the endocrine, behavioral, and autonomic responses to stress (Sarnyai et al., 2001). CRF has been implicated in alcohol addiction because there is evidence that neuroadaptive changes triggered by a prolonged history of alcohol exposure lead to a chronically dysregulated CRF/CRF1 receptor (CRF1-R) system activity that, in turn may drive excessive and uncontrolled alcohol consumption motivated by relief of negative emotionality (Heilig and Koob, 2007; Koob, 2010; Breese et al., 2011). In particular, upregulation of the peptide has been observed in the extended amygdala during alcohol withdrawal (Merlo Pich et al., 1995; Zorrilla et al., 2001; Olive et al., 2002; Roberto et al., 2010) and long-term upregulation of CRF1-Rs has been also shown in these structures in animals with a previous history of alcohol dependence (Sommer et al., 2008). Similarly, msP animals show innate upregulation of CRF1-R expression and density in multiple corticolimbic regions, indicating hyperfunction of the CRF system (Hansson et al., 2006), which is attenuated by alcohol consumption (Hansson et al., 2007). In agreement with these findings, both alcohol-induced neuroadaptations leading to dysregulated CRF system and the innate hyperfunction of the system in msP rats have been shown to confer sensitivity to the treatment with CRF1-R antagonists. Core symptoms of alcohol dependence including excessive alcohol self-administration and stress-induced relapse to alcohol seeking were in fact attenuated at doses that had no effects in non-dependent unselected animals (Funk et al., 2006a; Hansson et al., 2006; Sabino et al., 2006; Gehlert et al., 2007; Ciccocioppo et al., 2009). All these similarities suggest that innate upregulation of CRF1-R expression mimics the post-dependent phenotype such that msP rats have been proposed as phenocopies of post-dependent animals (Heilig and Koob, 2007).

Further work done in msP rats provided evidence that excessive alcohol drinking and stress vulnerability may be associated with the occurrence of two single nucleotide polymorphisms (SNPs) in the promoter region (position −1836 and −2097) of the gene encoding the CRF1 receptor, an observation that closely correlated with innate upregulation of the CRF1-R transcript (Hansson et al., 2006). Genetic variation at the CRF1-R locus as a susceptibility factor for excessive alcohol drinking might have parallels in humans, where a similar association was reported (Treutlein et al., 2006). It is, however, unclear whether the −1836 and −2097 SNPs are causally related to escalated alcohol consumption. Of note, high alcohol preference is a complex trait, and may be driven by different genetic factors in different genetically selected preferring lines. These SNPs are unique to msP animals, and genetic screening in the Indiana alcohol-preferring [P (Li et al., 1991)] and the Sardinian alcohol-preferring [sP (Colombo et al., 1995)] indicates that these lines do not carry mutations at the CRF1-R locus (oral communication).

Here, we tested whether the occurrence of the SNPs is responsible for the high alcohol drinking and preference of msP rats and whether the occurrence of the point mutations may contribute to other behavioral differences including sensitivity to the treatment with CRF1-R antagonist and relapse susceptibility. To assess how environmental stress interacts with heritable factors, rats were rederived from the original msP line to obtain two distinct lines, one carrying the two point mutations (AA) and the wild type line (GG). The phenotypic characteristics of these two msP rat lines were assessed following stress exposure and compared with those of unselected Wistar rats.

MATERIALS AND METHODS
ANIMALS

Subjects were adult males from two distinct sub-lines derived from the original msP line (65th generation). Animals were bred at the animal facility of the University of Camerino, Italy. Breeding started following genetic screening of the promoter region encoding for CRF1-Rs. Sequence variation AA versus GG in position −1836 and −2097 respectively, of the CRF1-R transcript distinguished the two msP lines. Specifically, 80 msP rats were sequenced using Taqman-PCR analysis of tail DNA to identify animals carrying (AA) or not carrying (GG) both variants. The homozygous male and female AA and GG were then bred to obtain re-derived lines selectively carrying the AA and the GG types. They were bred for two more generations and then animals from the third and fourth generations were used for experiments. Male Wistar rats (Charles River, Calco, Italy) were employed as a behavioral control. All rats (350–450 g) at the time of the experiments were housed in groups of five or four except where otherwise specified, on a reverse 12 h light-dark cycle (lights off at 08:30 AM) at a constant temperature of $20 \pm 2°C$ and relative humidity of 45–55%, with free access to tap water and food pellets (4RF18, Mucedola, Settimo Milanese, Italy). Animals were handled three times before the onset of each experiment. All procedures followed the *EU Directive for Care and Use of Laboratory Animals*.

DRUGS

Alcohol solution (10% v/v) was prepared by diluting 95% alcohol (F.L. Carsetti s.n.c.-Camerino) in tap water. The selective CRF1-R antagonist antalarmin (N-butyl-N-ethyl-[2,5,6-trimethyl-7-(2,4,6-trimethylphenyl)-7H-pyrrolo[2,3-d]pyrimidin4-yl]-amine (Webster et al., 1996) was obtained from the National Institute on Alcohol Abuse and Alcoholism (NIAAA/NIH). Antalarmin was suspended in a vehicle composed of 10% Tween 80 and distilled water and given intraperitoneally (i.p.) in a 1 ml/kg volume injection. Yohimbine hydrochloride (17-hydroxyyohimban-16-carboxylic acid methyl ester hydrochloride) was purchased from Sigma (Sigma-Aldrich, Italy) and dissolved in distilled water. Yohimbine was administered i.p. in a 1 ml/kg volume injection. Physiological saline was injected three times prior to drug testing for habituation to the experimental procedures.

TWO-BOTTLE FREE CHOICE DRINKING PARADIGM

To ascertain the relation of CRF1-R promoter genotype to home cage alcohol intake, AA ($n = 8$) and GG ($n = 8$) msP rats were used and their intake measured daily. Rats were single-housed to provide accurate record of home cage drinking. Animals were provided *ad libitum* concurrent, continuous access to 10% alcohol solution, water, and food pellets. Fluids were presented in graduated plastic bottles equipped with a stainless-steel drinking spouts inserted through two grommets in front of the cage and were changed daily at 90–120 min into the dark period of the light/dark cycle. The placement of the alcohol bottle was alternated daily to control for side preference. This procedure was carried out for 15 days. Data are presented as daily alcohol intake (g/kg) and percentage of alcohol preference [100× alcohol intake (ml)/total fluid intake (ml)].

OPERANT SELF-ADMINISTRATION APPARATUS AND TRAINING

Training and testing were conducted in operant conditioning chambers housed in sound-attenuating cubicles (Med Associates Inc., Georgia, VT, USA). Each operant chamber was equipped with two retractable levers positioned laterally to a drinking reservoir. Visual stimuli were presented via a light located on the back panel. A microcomputer controlled the delivery of the fluids, presentation of visual stimuli, and recording of the behavioral data. Rats were trained to self-administer 10% alcohol (v/v) in 30 min daily sessions on a fixed ratio 1 (FR-1) schedule of reinforcement, in which each response on the active lever resulted in delivery of 0.1 ml of fluid. A response on the second lever had no programed consequences. For the first 3 days, rats were allowed to lever-press for a 0.2% (w/v) saccharin solution, and were then trained to self-administer 10% alcohol by gradually increasing the percentage of alcohol and fading out the saccharin (Cippitelli et al., 2008).

OPERANT ALCOHOL SELF-ADMINISTRATION ON A FIXED RATIO 3 SCHEDULE OF REINFORCEMENT FOLLOWING STRESS EXPOSURE

Rats ($n = 34$; 10 Wistars, 14 GG, and 10 AA msPs) were trained to self-administer 10% alcohol as described above. When all the rats reached the 10% alcohol stage, the schedule of reinforcement was changed from FR-1 to FR-3. Here, following three responses that delivered a reinforcer, a 5-s time-out period was in effect, during which responses were recorded but not reinforced. Once stable self-administration responding was obtained under this reinforcement schedule, the experiment was started. Stress exposure consisted of the challenge with the pharmacological stressor yohimbine at doses previously shown to increase alcohol-reinforced lever pressing in unselected Wistar animals (Marinelli et al., 2007). Yohimbine (0.0, 0.625, 1.25, and 2.5 mg/kg) was administered 30 min prior to the 30 min self-administration session. The experiment was conducted in parallel for the three rat lines using a Latin square counterbalanced within-subjects design. Test sessions were 4 days apart. Following each test session day, animals were allowed 1 day off, and a new baseline was then established over the following 2 days as previously reported (Cippitelli et al., 2010b). Results are described as number of rewards in 30 min.

OPERANT ALCOHOL SELF-ADMINISTRATION ON A PROGRESSIVE RATIO SCHEDULE OF REINFORCEMENT FOLLOWING STRESS EXPOSURE

Additional rats ($n = 30$; 10 Wistars, 10 GG and 10 AA msPs) were trained to self-administer 10% alcohol. When all the rats reached the 10% alcohol stage, the schedule of reinforcement was changed from FR-1 to FR-3. As described above, following three responses that delivered a reinforcer, a 5-s time-out period was in effect, during which responses were recorded but not reinforced. Once stable

self-administration responding was obtained under this reinforcement schedule, the three rat lines were tested under a progressive ratio (PR) schedule of reinforcement to measure the break point, defined as the last ratio completed by the animal (Cippitelli et al., 2007; Karlsson et al., 2012), to obtain 10% alcohol following stress exposure. For this purpose, the response requirement (i.e., the number of lever responses or the ratio required to receive one dose of 10% alcohol) was increased as follows: for each of the first four alcohol deliveries the ratio was increased by 1; for the next four deliveries the ratio was increased by 2 and for all of the following deliveries the ratio was increased by 4. Each alcohol-reinforced response resulted in the house light being turned on for 1 s, whereas sessions were terminated when more than 30 min had elapsed since the last reinforced response. The experiment was conducted in parallel for the three rat lines using a Latin square counterbalanced within-subjects design. The pharmacological stressor yohimbine at the dose of 0.625 mg/kg or its vehicle were administered 30 min prior to PR testing. Test sessions were 4 days apart. Following each test session day, animals were allowed 1 day off, and a new baseline was then established over the following 2 days.

OPERANT ALCOHOL SELF-ADMINISTRATION ON FR-3 SCHEDULE: EFFECT OF ANTALARMIN

Other rats ($n = 33$; 7 Wistars, 12 GG and 14 AA msPs) were trained to self-administer 10% alcohol as described above. Schedule of reinforcement was switched from FR-1 to FR-3. Following three responses that delivered a reinforcer, a 5-s time-out period was in effect, during which responses were recorded but not reinforced. Once stable self-administration was obtained under the FR-3 reinforcement schedule, treatment with the CRF1-R antagonist antalarmin was started. The experiment was conducted by using a Latin square counterbalanced design. Antalarmin at doses of 5, 10, and 20 mg/kg or its vehicle were administered 30 min prior to sessions. Test sessions were 4 days apart. Following each test session day, animals were allowed 1 day off, and a new baseline was then established over the following 2 days. Results are described as number of rewards in 30 min.

EFFECT OF ANTALARMIN ON YOHIMBINE-INDUCED INCREASE OF ALCOHOL-REINFORCED LEVER PRESSING (FR-3)

A new cohort of rats ($n = 33$; 8 Wistars, 10 GG and 15 AA msPs) was trained to self-administer 10% alcohol as described above. When stable baseline of responding was obtained under the FR-3 reinforcement schedule that included the 5 s time-out period, drug treatment started. In this experiment, we pre-treated the three rat lines either with the selective CRF1-R antagonist antalarmin or its vehicle prior to the injection of yohimbine (0.625 mg/kg) or yohimbine vehicle. Pre-treatments were given 30 min prior to treatments that in turn occurred 30 min prior to testing sessions. These testing sessions were conducted every fourth day using a Latin square counterbalanced design and occurred 4 days apart in which animals were allowed 1 day off, and a new baseline was then established over the following 2 days. Results are described as number of rewards in 30 min.

REINSTATEMENT INDUCED BY STRESS EXPOSURE

A new cohort of animals ($n = 24$; 7 Wistar rats, 8 GG and 9 AA msP rats) was trained at the same time to self-administer alcohol as described above. When 10% alcohol became available, the FR-1 schedule slightly changed such that each lever pressing was accompanied by the illumination of the house light for 5 s. During this time-out period response were recorded but not reinforced. 10% alcohol sessions lasted 30 min and were conducted for 15 days. Then, rats were subjected to 30 min daily extinction sessions for additional 15 consecutive days. During extinction the lever presses were no longer associated with alcohol delivery, but house light was still presented to allow for its concomitant extinction. Stress exposure consisted of the challenge with the pharmacological stressor yohimbine at doses previously shown to produce reinstatement to alcohol seeking in unselected Wistar rats (Le et al., 2005; Marinelli et al., 2007; Cippitelli et al., 2010a). Yohimbine (0.0, 0.625, 1.25, and 2.5 mg/kg) was administered 30 min prior to the 30 min reinstatement session that was conducted under identical condition of extinction sessions. A Latin square counterbalanced design was used. Test sessions were 4 days apart and conducted after three consecutive extinction sessions. Results are described as total number of responses in 30 min.

STATISTICAL ANALYSIS

All drug testing experiments were here analyzed by means of a two-way analysis of variance (ANOVA) with "drug treatment" as the within-subject factor and "rat line" as the between-subject factor. When appropriate, analyses were followed up by Fisher's least significant difference (LSD) *post hoc* tests. The same statistical approach was employed to analyze drinking patterns of intake and preference of GG versus AA msP rat lines with the exception that "rat line" was the between-subject factor and "day" was used as the within-subject factor.

RESULTS

MINIMAL CHANGES IN VOLUNTARY ALCOHOL INTAKE AND PREFERENCE OF GG AND AA msP RATS

The GG and AA msP animals show a similar pattern of alcohol intake and preference over a period of 15 days as shown in **Figure 1**. Overall ANOVA failed to revealed a main effect of "line" [$F(1,14) = 2.4$, NS]. However, there was a main effect of "day" [$F(14,196) = 24.4$, $p < 0.001$], accompanied by interaction "line × day" [$F(14,196) = 2.2$, $p < 0.01$] to suggest minimal changes in voluntary alcohol intake across the 15-day exposure. Indeed, *post hoc* analysis showed difference in alcohol drinking between the two msP lines only on day 6 and 13 ($p < 0.001$ and $p < 0.01$, respectively, **Figure 1A**).

Data analysis of alcohol preference only showed difference in the main effect of "day" [$F(14,196) = 24.4$, $p < 0.01$] while failing to reveal significant difference in the main effect of "line" [$F(1,14) = 2.4$, NS] and interaction "line × day" [$F(14,196) = 0.2$, NS]. However, a slight and non-significant trend to a higher alcohol preference of the AA line compared to the GG line was observed (**Figure 1B**).

In a separate experiment, a different batch of the two msP lines was subjected to a two-bottle free choice drinking across a 50 day exposure. Results generally paralleled those shown here, that is no major difference between lines on patterns of 10% voluntary alcohol drinking and preference was found.

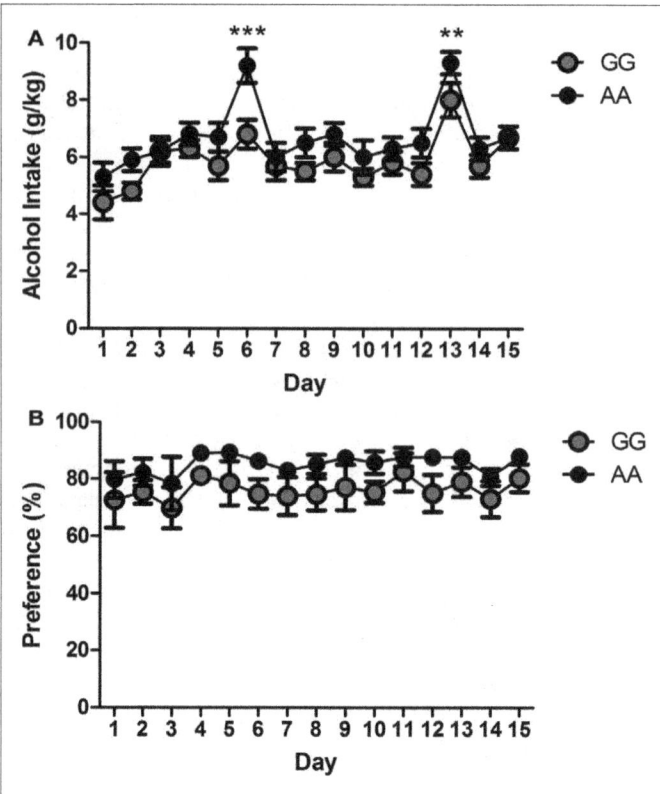

FIGURE 1 | Elevated alcohol drinking of the two msP lines GG ($n = 8$) and AA ($n = 8$) derived from the original msP line as assessed in the two-bottle free choice drinking paradigm. GG and AA msP rats show minimal changes in **(A)** drinking patterns and **(B)** alcohol preference across a period of 15 days. Values are presented as the daily mean g/kg of alcohol intake (±SEM) and percent (%) of alcohol preference (±SEM), respectively. **p < 0.01 and ***p < 0.001, significant difference between the two msP rat lines. GG: gray line; AA: black line. For detailed statistics, see "Results."

YOHIMBINE SIMILARLY INCREASES OPERANT ALCOHOL SELF-ADMINISTRATION UNDER A FIXED RATIO SCHEDULE OF REINFORCEMENT IN WISTAR, AS WELL AS GG, AND AA msP RATS

Although elevated level of alcohol consumption in msP rats is well known, overall ANOVA failed to show a main effect of "line" [$F(2,31) = 0.8$, NS], indicating that under the described experimental conditions alcohol-reinforced lever pressing was fairly equal between groups. A clear main effect of "treatment" [$F(3,93) = 18.2$, $p < 0.001$] that was not accompanied by a significant interaction "treatment × line" [$F(6,93) = 1.5$, NS] was also revealed to suggest that exposure to pharmacological stress similarly increased alcohol self-administration in all rat lines. On *post hoc* analysis of the collapsed variable of "treatment," yohimbine significantly increased the number of alcohol rewards at doses of 0.625 ($p < 0.001$) and 1.25 mg/kg [($p < 0.01$), **Figure 2A**].

YOHIMBINE SIMILARLY INCREASES BREAK POINT OF WISTAR, AS WELL AS GG, AND AA msP RATS UNDER A PROGRESSIVE SCHEDULE OF REINFORCEMENT

To further explore how stress exposure interacts with the genetic background of the two msP lines, yohimbine at the dose of 0.625 mg/kg was tested on motivation to earn alcohol rewards as

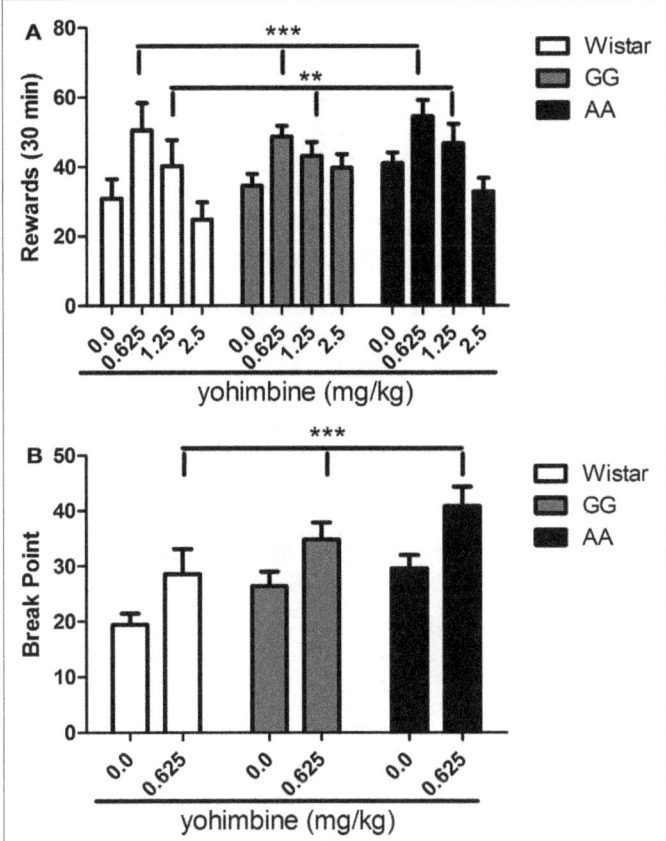

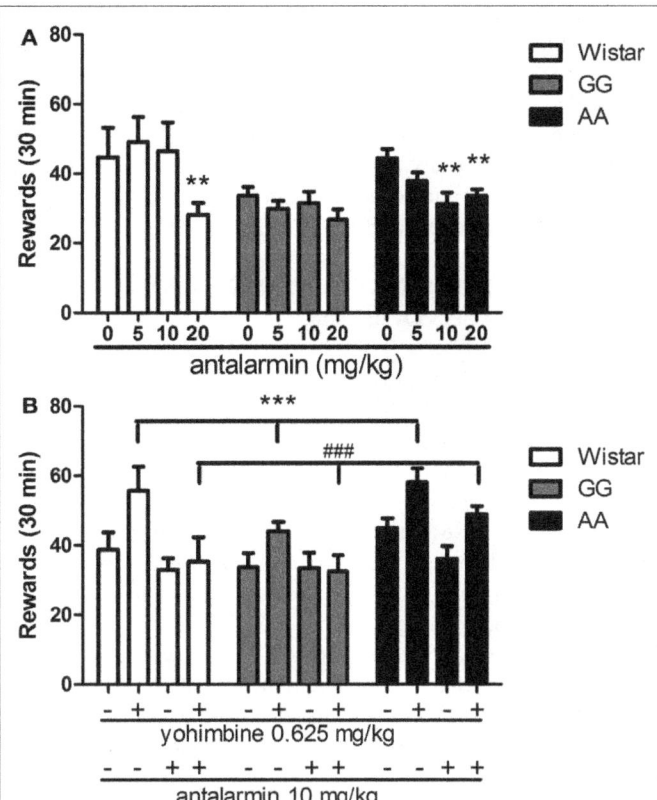

FIGURE 2 | (A) Operant alcohol self-administration in Wistar ($n = 10$), as well as GG ($n = 14$), and AA ($n = 10$) msP rats under a fixed ratio 3 (FR-3) schedule of reinforcement is significantly increased by the systemic (i.p.) administration of the pharmacological stressor yohimbine (0.0, 0.625, 1.25, 2.5 mg/kg) at the dose of 0.625 and 1.25 mg/kg. Values presented are the mean number of rewards earned in 30 min (±SEM). **(B)** Operant alcohol self-administration in Wistar ($n = 10$), as well as GG ($n = 10$), and AA ($n = 10$) msP rats under a progressive ratio (PR) schedule of reinforcement is significantly increased by the systemic (i.p.) administration of the pharmacological stressor yohimbine at the dose of 0.625 mg/kg. Values presented are the mean of break point measure (last ratio completed by the animal ±SEM). **$p < 0.01$, ***$p < 0.001$, significant difference from the collapsed means of vehicle-treated groups (0.0 mg/kg). Wistar: white bars; GG: gray bars; AA: black bars. For detailed statistics, see "Results."

FIGURE 3 | (A) Dose-response curve of antalarmin (0, 5, 10, 20 mg/kg) when systemically (i.p.) injected in Wistar ($n = 7$), as well as GG ($n = 12$), and AA ($n = 14$) msP rats as assessed on operant alcohol self-administration on a fixed ratio 3 (FR-3) schedule of reinforcement. The AA msP rat line shows increased sensitivity to antalarmin treatment compared to the other rat line examined. Data are the mean (±SEM) number of rewards earned in 30 min. **$p < 0.01$, difference from the vehicle-treated groups (0 mg/kg). **(B)** I.p. pre-treatment with antalarmin (10 mg/kg) fully blocks the escalation of alcohol self-administration (FR-3) elicited by systemic (i.p.) treatment with yohimbine at the dose of 0.625 mg/kg in all rat lines examined [Wistar ($n = 8$), as well as GG ($n = 10$) and AA ($n = 15$) msP rats]. Results are the mean (±SEM) number of rewards earned in 30 min. ***$p < 0.001$, difference from the groups receiving both vehicle-treatments of antalarmin and yohimbine (−/−); ###$p < 0.001$, difference from the groups receiving yohimbine 0.625 mg/kg (±). Wistar: white bars; GG: gray bars; AA: black bars. For detailed statistics, see "Results."

assessed by the PR schedule of reinforcement paradigm. Overall ANOVA showed a significant main effect of "line" [$F(2,27) = 4.7$, $p < 0.05$] accompanied by a significant main effect of treatment [$F(1,27) = 23.7$, $p < 0.001$] while interaction "treatment × line" was not significant [$F(2,27) = 0.18$, NS]. As revealed by *post hoc* analysis of the collapsed variable of "treatment," these results suggest that 0.625 mg/kg of yohimbine clearly increased the break point measure in all three rat lines examined [($p < 0.001$), **Figure 2B**].

THE AA LINE IS MORE SENSITIVE THAN OTHER RAT LINES TO THE EFFECT OF ANTALARMIN IN REDUCING ALCOHOL SELF-ADMINISTRATION

As shown in **Figure 3A**, treatment with the CRF1-R antagonist antalarmin differentially reduced alcohol-reinforced lever pressing

under FR-3 schedule. Overall ANOVA revealed a significant main effect of treatment [$F(3,90) = 7.1$, $p < 0.001$], significant main effect of "line" [$F(2,30) = 4.5$, $p < 0.05$] and significant interaction "treatment × line" [$F(6,90) = 2.5$, $p < 0.05$]. *Post hoc* analysis showed that antalarmin dose-dependently decreased lever pressing for alcohol in AA rats ($p < 0.01$ for doses of 10 and 20 mg/kg) while being ineffective in the GG line. Dose of 20 mg/kg antalarmin reduced the number of rewards in Wistar rats ($p < 0.01$).

YOHIMBINE INCREASES ALCOHOL SELF-ADMINISTRATION THROUGH A CRF-MEDIATED MECHANISM

As shown in **Figure 3B**, pre-treatment with antalarmin blocked the yohimbine-induced increase of alcohol self-administration in all rat lines examined. Overall ANOVA showed a main effect of "treatment" [$F(3,90) = 16.6$, $p < 0.001$] accompanied by a main effect of "line" [$F(2,30) = 3.8$, $p < 0.05$] with no interaction "treatment × line" [$F(6,90) = 1.4$, NS]. In agreement with the experiments described above, *post hoc* analysis clearly revealed that yohimbine (0.625 mg/kg) significantly increased the number of alcohol rewards as compared to the collapsed means of the control groups ($p < 0.001$), and administration of antalarmin (10 mg/kg) fully prevented the effect of yohimbine ($p < 0.001$).

YOHIMBINE AT HIGH DOSAGES FAILS TO PRODUCE REINSTATEMENT OF ALCOHOL SEEKING IN AA msP RATS

The administration of yohimbine (0.0, 0.625, 1.25, 2.5 mg/kg) robustly reinstated responding on the previously alcohol-associated lever as shown by the significant main effect of "treatment" [$F(3,63) = 11.6$, $p < 0.001$]. Overall ANOVA also revealed a barely significant main effect of "line" [$F(2,21) = 3.4$, $p = 0.05$] and lack of the interaction "treatment × line" [$F(6,63) = 0.8$, NS]. These results suggest that all three rat lines examined were sensitive to the challenge of the pharmacological stressor. This was confirmed by *post hoc* analysis on the collapsed variable of "treatment" (0.625 and 1.25 mg/kg, $p < 0.001$; 2.5 mg/kg, $p < 0.01$). However, *post hoc* analysis conducted on the collapsed variable of "line" revealed that relapse-like behavior of the AA line was different from that of both the GG msP ($p < 0.05$) and the Wistar line ($p = 0.05$) following yohimbine treatment. This effect was the result of the fact that the AA msP line failed to reinstate the operant response following administration of 2.5 mg/kg. In contrast, both Wistars and GG msPs showed similar vulnerability to the pharmacological stressor as observed with lower dosages (**Figure 4**).

DISCUSSION

We found that the two msP rat lines (GG and AA) showed similar patterns of alcohol intake and preference in the 24-h access two-bottle free choice drinking paradigm, which was comparable to the elevated levels of drinking previously shown by the original msP line (Ciccocioppo et al., 2006; Hansson et al., 2007; Stopponi et al., 2011). In addition, stress exposure elicited increased operant alcohol self-administration in FR-3 and PR reinforcement schedules in both lines through a CRF1-R mediated mechanism. However, the msP line carrying the point mutations at the CRF1-R promoter region (AA) showed higher sensitivity than the wild type line (GG) to the effects of the CRF1-R blockade by the selective CRF1-R antagonist antalarmin. Also, the AA line showed altered vulnerability to relapse-like behavior following pharmacological stress exposure when compared to the GG line or to an unselected strain such as Wistar rats.

The observation that the two derived lines showed minimal changes in voluntary alcohol intake and preference suggests that the occurrence of the SNPs in the CRF1-R promoter region is not a causal genetic factor behind high alcohol intake. In operant situations, where rats work for alcohol reinforcement under limited-access conditions, results paralleled those obtained under unlimited 24-h voluntary alcohol access. However, in the present study, voluntary alcohol consumption was different between sub-lines only in 2 out of 15 days (days 6 and 13) where higher intake was observed in the AA line. This transient increase in the amount

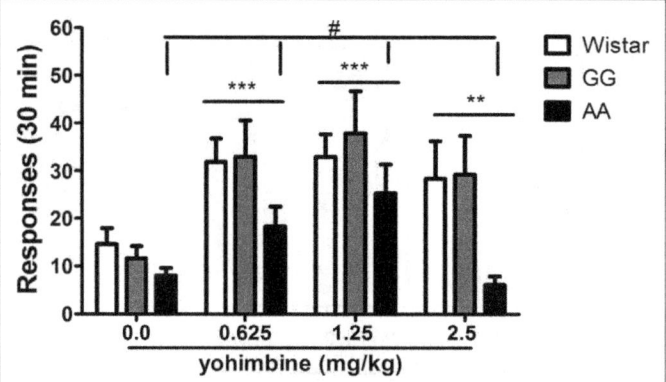

FIGURE 4 | Systemic (i.p.) administration of yohimbine (0.0, 0.625, 1.25, 2.5 mg/kg) elicits reinstatement of alcohol seeking in Wistar ($n = 7$), as well as GG ($n = 8$), and AA ($n = 9$) msP rats following extinction. The AA msP line shows decreased threshold for yohimbine-induced reinstatement due to different sensitivity on responding to the effects of 2.5 mg/kg yohimbine dose. Data are the mean (±SEM) of total number of responses in 30 min. **$p < 0.01$, ***$p < 0.001$, difference from the vehicle-treated groups (0.0 mg/kg); #$p \leq 0.05$, difference from the collapsed means of both the GG msP and the Wistar lines. Wistar: white bars; GG: gray bars; AA: black bars. For detailed statistics, see "Results."

of drinking was associated with weekly cleaning of the animal room or exchange of sawdust. Thus, either increased arousal or heightened anxiety behavior may account for these isolated over drinking episodes. Indeed, msP rats are known to couple elevated alcohol consumption with comorbid anxiety which is thought to drive excessive drinking due to self-medication and tension relief purposes (Ciccocioppo et al., 2006; Ciccocioppo, 2013).

To test the hypothesis that stress exposure may contribute to confer functional relevance to the polymorphism, both AA and GG lines were exposed to pharmacological stress before self-administering alcohol as previously shown (Le et al., 2005; Marinelli et al., 2007). Induction of stress consisted of the administration of yohimbine, an alpha-2 adrenoceptor antagonist that increases noradrenaline cell firing (Aghajanian and VanderMaelen, 1982) and enhances noradrenaline release in terminal areas (Abercrombie et al., 1988; Pacak et al., 1992). Yohimbine induces anxiety-like responses in both humans (Holmberg and Gershon, 1961; Bremner et al., 1996b) and laboratory animals (Bremner et al., 1996a), and induced craving in alcohol-dependent patients (Umhau et al., 2011). Results of the present study demonstrate that yohimbine similarly increased alcohol-reinforced lever pressing in both rat lines, indicating that the polymorphism does not seem to play a major role in stress-induced alcohol drinking. These data were completed by the evidence that unselected Wistar rats showed a similar outcome as the derived msP lines when challenged with yohimbine under identical experimental conditions, a finding that closely paralleled results shown in previous studies (Le et al., 2005; Marinelli et al., 2007). In addition, the dose of yohimbine that increased alcohol self-administration under FR-3 schedule (0.625 mg/kg) in all three rat lines also increased the break point measure in all lines examined under the PR schedule, a paradigm known to better assess motivation to obtain a drug

(Arnold and Roberts, 1997). This observation suggests that spontaneous occurrence of the polymorphism in msP animals does not appear to be associated with the exacerbated motivation to obtain alcohol following stress exposure.

The effect of yohimbine on increasing alcohol consumption shares some similarities with the effect of cycles of alcohol intoxication and withdrawal on inducing escalation of drinking (Rimondini et al., 2002; O'Dell et al., 2004; Gehlert et al., 2007; Walker and Koob, 2008; Gilpin and Koob, 2010), such that it has been hypothesized that yohimbine- and dependence-induced increases of operant alcohol self-administration may be mediated by similar neurobiological mechanisms (Marinelli et al., 2007). Firstly, both of these manipulations produce anxiety- and stress-like states (Breese et al., 2005a; Heilig and Koob, 2007). Secondly, both yohimbine treatment and alcohol dependence activate CRF system in structures of the extended amygdala (Merlo Pich et al., 1995; Zorrilla et al., 2001; Olive et al., 2002; Funk et al., 2006b; Sommer et al., 2008), brain areas thought to mediate the negative emotional state that leads to excessive alcohol use (Heilig and Koob, 2007; Koob, 2010; Breese et al., 2011). Lastly, antagonism at CRF1-R attenuates both yohimbine-induced (Marinelli et al., 2007) and dependence-induced increases of alcohol self-administration (Sabino et al., 2006; Chu et al., 2007; Funk et al., 2007; Gehlert et al., 2007). The observation that antalarmin prevented yohimbine-induced increase of alcohol operant responding in Wistar rats, as well as in the alcohol-preferring msP lines strongly supports a role of CRF-related mechanisms in the regulation of reinforcing effects of alcohol heightened by yohimbine treatment.

When antalarmin was tested under non-stressful conditions on the derived msP lines, the CRF1-R antagonist selectively reduced at doses of 10 and 20 mg/kg alcohol self-administration in the AA line, indicating that the polymorphism may confer sensitivity to this pharmacological manipulation. This observation parallels with what is previously shown in the original msP line where treatment with antalarmin reduced alcohol-reinforced lever pressing without altering that of unselected Wistar animals (Hansson et al., 2006). In that study, the differential effect of antalarmin on alcohol self-administration was associated with msP upregulation of CRF1-R expression and density, in turn linked to the occurrence of the point mutations in the CRF1-R gene. Thus, although data on CRF1-R expression or density of the AA versus GG line are not provided in the present study, it may be hypothesized that the selective reduction of operant responding for alcohol following antalarmin treatment in the AA line is due to upregulated CRF1-R function in these animals compared to the GG line. In addition, both the unique msP genetic profile and evidence showing that msP rats are, among other alcohol-preferring lines, the only one sensitive to CRF1-R antagonists (Ciccocioppo et al., 2006; Sabino et al., 2006; Gilpin et al., 2008) strongly supports the role of the polymorphism in eliciting increased sensitivity to the treatment with CRF1-R antagonists. Binding data on brain CRF1-R protein expression in AA and GG rats are needed to corroborate this hypothesis. Post-dependent animals were also shown to respond to this pharmacological treatment at doses that had no effects in non-dependent rats (Sabino et al., 2006; Chu et al., 2007; Funk et al., 2007; Gehlert et al., 2007) to suggest that the alcohol-dependent state recruits the CRF system. However, the CRF1-R signaling may be also be engaged when non-dependent animals escalate their levels of drinking (Sparta et al., 2008; Lowery et al., 2010; Cippitelli et al., 2012). Therefore, the reduction of alcohol self-administration observed in Wistar rats receiving the high dose of 20 mg/kg antalarmin is not surprising and may be due to abnormally elevated baseline of lever pressing of the cohort of animals employed in the present experiment. Of note, differences in operant alcohol drinking usually observed between msP and Wistar rats (Hansson et al., 2006; Gehlert et al., 2007) are not well reflected here probably due to different experimental conditions such as the use of an FR-3 reinforcement schedule. Previous studies employed an FR-1 schedule which may better reflect the rate of consumption as it delivers reinforcement after each response (Arnold and Roberts, 1997).

We have previously described that msP and unselected Wistar rats showed differential responses when exposed to increasing foot-shock stress intensities during extinction. Specifically, reinstatement of Wistar rats increased progressively with shock intensity while msPs reinstated responding on the previously alcohol-associated lever after low/medium but not high shock intensities which resulted in freezing behavior (Hansson et al., 2006). In the present study, a similar experiment that used different doses of yohimbine (0.625, 1.25, 2.5 mg/kg) instead of shock delivery was conducted to assess whether the polymorphism played a role on relapse-like behavior. Results showed that while yohimbine elicited reinstatement throughout the range of doses examined in both the GG line and the Wistar strain, animals carrying the polymorphism did not do so following injection of 2.5 mg/kg. This was likely due to highly stressed state of these rats and suggests that spontaneously occurring mutation at the CRF1-R gene may mediate an increased vulnerability to stress and possibly, mal-adaptive responses to intense stress exposure. MsP rats have anxiety and depression-like traits which are congruent to clinical alcoholism. Studies have shown that very high CRF1-R activation results in a passive behavior in anxiety models (Zhao et al., 2007; Tovote et al., 2010). As speculation, this inference could be extrapolated to our results where the AA rats, due to over-activated CRF signaling, were unable to reinstate responding at the highest yohimbine dose that may be able to further engage CRF system. However, by these data it is not possible to determine whether the polymorphism specifically regulates aspects of stress-induced alcohol seeking since CRF system has been shown to play a role in the reinstatement of various drugs of abuse (Shaham et al., 1997; Erb et al., 1998; Zislis et al., 2007) and natural rewards (Ghitza et al., 2006).

Alcoholism is a multi-genic disorder in which genetic predisposition combined with environmental factors may contribute to vulnerability to abuse. Studies have shown an association between alcoholism and several gene polymorphisms. For example, polymorphisms in the serotonin 2A receptor gene, dopamine transporter, μ-opioid, or GABA A receptor genes have been associated with alcohol dependence (Oslin et al., 2003; Edenberg and Kranzler, 2005; Ramchandani et al., 2011; Bhaskar et al., 2012; Wrzosek et al., 2012). In addition, recent clinical investigation has indicated the CRF1-R locus to mediate genetic susceptibility for excessive drinking (Treutlein et al., 2006). Polymorphisms in the CRF binding protein have also been associated with alcoholism (Enoch et al., 2008) and severity of stress-induced alcohol craving (Ray, 2011). Overall, these results suggest that incremental advances in treatment outcomes will result from an improved understanding of the genetic heterogeneity among patients with alcohol addiction that may ultimately lead to development of personalized treatments (Heilig et al., 2011). The present study may add to the field by providing evidence that spontaneously occurring mutations at the CRF1-R locus of msP animals acquire functional relevance leading to the expression of a particular phenotype which differs from that of animals with a normal genetic background.

CONCLUSION

Here we show that two previously identified point mutations at the CRF1-R gene locus do not seem to play a major role in the expression of the msP excessive drinking phenotype or stress-induced drinking. However, their occurrence appears to be associated to an increased sensitivity to the effects of the pharmacological blockade of CRF1-R and to the decreased threshold for stress-induced reinstatement of alcohol seeking behavior. Despite the fact that there is no evidence for a correspondence of the same polymorphisms in msP rats and human alcoholics, these findings may have important pharmacogenetic implications because they suggest that only a subpopulation of alcoholics, the one characterized by specific mutation at CRF1-R gene or possibly carrying over-expression of the CRF1-R system, may respond to CRF1-R antagonists. Nowadays, this consideration is particularly relevant since there are ongoing clinical trials in which the efficacy of CRF1-R antagonists on alcohol addiction are under exploration (Zorrilla et al., 2013). On one hand, results of the present study may provide important inputs to the analysis of the clinical data that will soon be available. On the other hand, as it has already been demonstrated for naltrexone, a drug approved for the treatment of alcohol addiction, our results suggest that pharmacogenetic considerations are critical for appropriate clinical use of the agents (Heilig et al., 2011).

ACKNOWLEDGMENTS

We are thankful to Rina Righi and Mariangela Fiorelli for animal care and Marino Cucculelli and Alfredo Fiorelli for technical support. This work was supported by the National Institutes of Health, grantRO1 AA017447, and RO1 AA014351 from the National Institute on Alcohol Abuse and Alcoholism.

REFERENCES

Abercrombie, E. D., Keller, R. W. Jr., and Zigmond, M. J. (1988). Characterization of hippocampal norepinephrine release as measured by microdialysis perfusion: pharmacological and behavioral studies. *Neuroscience* 27, 897–904.

Aghajanian, G. K., and VanderMaelen, C. P. (1982). Alpha 2-adrenoceptor-mediated hyperpolarization of locus coeruleus neurons: intracellular studies in vivo. *Science* 215, 1394–1396.

Arnold, J. M., and Roberts, D. C. (1997). A critique of fixed and progressive ratio schedules used to examine the neural substrates of drug reinforcement. *Pharmacol. Biochem. Behav.* 57, 441–447.

Bhaskar, L. V., Thangaraj, K., Wasnik, S., Singh, L., and Raghavendra Rao, V. (2012). Dopamine transporter (DAT1) VNTR polymorphism and alcoholism in two culturally different populations of south India. *Am. J. Addict.* 21, 343–347.

Breese, G. R., Overstreet, D. H., and Knapp, D. J. (2005a). Conceptual framework for the etiology of alcoholism: a "kindling"/stress hypothesis. *Psychopharmacology (Berl.)* 178, 367–380.

Breese, G. R., Overstreet, D. H., Knapp, D. J., and Navarro, M. (2005b). Prior multiple ethanol withdrawals enhance stress-induced anxiety-like behavior: inhibition by CRF1- and benzodiazepine-receptor antagonists and a 5-HT1a-receptor agonist. *Neuropsychopharmacology* 30, 1662–1669.

Breese, G. R., Sinha, R., and Heilig, M. (2011). Chronic alcohol neuroadaptation and stress contribute to susceptibility for alcohol craving and relapse. *Pharmacol. Ther.* 129, 149–171.

Bremner, J. D., Krystal, J. H., Southwick, S. M., and Charney, D. S. (1996a). Noradrenergic mechanisms in stress and anxiety: I. Preclinical studies. *Synapse* 23, 28–38.

Bremner, J. D., Krystal, J. H., Southwick, S. M., and Charney, D. S. (1996b). Noradrenergic mechanisms in stress and anxiety: II. Clinical studies. *Synapse* 23, 39–51.

Chu, K., Koob, G. F., Cole, M., Zorrilla, E. P., and Roberts, A. J. (2007). Dependence-induced increases in ethanol self-administration in mice are blocked by the CRF1 receptor antagonist antalarmin and by CRF1 receptor knockout. *Pharmacol. Biochem. Behav.* 86, 813–821.

Ciccocioppo, R. (2013). Genetically selected alcohol preferring rats to model human alcoholism. *Curr. Top. Behav. Neurosci.* 13, 251–269.

Ciccocioppo, R., Economidou, D., Cippitelli, A., Cucculelli, M., Ubaldi, M., Soverchia, L., et al. (2006). Genetically selected Marchigian Sardinian alcohol-preferring (msP) rats: an animal model to study the neurobiology of alcoholism. *Addict. Biol.* 11, 339–355.

Ciccocioppo, R., Gehlert, D. R., Ryabinin, A., Kaur, S., Cippitelli, A., Thorsell, A., et al. (2009). Stress-related neuropeptides and alcoholism: CRH, NPY, and beyond. *Alcohol* 43, 491–498.

Ciccocioppo, R., Panocka, I., Froldi, R., Colombo, G., Gessa, G. L., and Massi, M. (1999). Antidepressant-like effect of ethanol revealed in the forced swimming test in Sardinian alcohol-preferring rats. *Psychopharmacology (Berl.)* 144, 151–157.

Cippitelli, A., Bilbao, A., Gorriti, M. A., Navarro, M., Massi, M., Piomelli, D., et al. (2007). The anandamide transport inhibitor AM404 reduces ethanol self-administration. *Eur. J. Neurosci.* 26, 476–486.

Cippitelli, A., Cannella, N., Braconi, S., Duranti, A., Tontini, A., Bilbao, A., et al. (2008). Increase of brain endocannabinoid anandamide levels by FAAH inhibition and alcohol abuse behaviours in the rat. *Psychopharmacology (Berl.)* 198, 449–460.

Cippitelli, A., Damadzic, R., Hansson, A. C., Singley, E., Sommer, W. H., Eskay, R., et al. (2010a). Neuropeptide Y (NPY) suppresses yohimbine-induced reinstatement of alcohol seeking. *Psychopharmacology (Berl.)* 208, 417–426.

Cippitelli, A., Karlsson, C., Shaw, J. L., Thorsell, A., Gehlert, D. R., and Heilig, M. (2010b). Suppression of alcohol self-administration and reinstatement of alcohol seeking by melanin-concentrating hormone receptor 1 (MCH1-R) antagonism in Wistar rats. *Psychopharmacology (Berl.)* 211, 367–375.

Cippitelli, A., Damadzic, R., Singley, E., Thorsell, A., Ciccocioppo, R., Eskay, R. L., et al. (2012). Pharmacological blockade of corticotropin-releasing hormone receptor 1 (CRH1R) reduces voluntary consumption of high alcohol concentrations in nondependent Wistar rats. *Pharmacol. Biochem. Behav.* 100, 522–529.

Cloninger, C. R., Bohman, M., and Sigvardsson, S. (1981). Inheritance of alcohol abuse. Cross-fostering analysis of adopted men. *Arch. Gen. Psychiatry* 38, 861–868.

Colombo, G., Agabio, R., Lobina, C., Reali, R., Zocchi, A., Fadda, F., et al. (1995). Sardinian alcohol-preferring rats: a genetic animal model of anxiety. *Physiol. Behav.* 57, 1181–1185.

Edenberg, H. J., and Kranzler, H. R. (2005). The contribution of genetics to addiction therapy approaches. *Pharmacol. Ther.* 108, 86–93.

Enoch, M. A., and Goldman, D. (1999). Genetics of alcoholism and substance abuse. *Psychiatr. Clin. North Am.* 22, 289–299.

Enoch, M. A., Shen, P. H., Ducci, F., Yuan, Q., Liu, J., White, K. V., et al. (2008). Common genetic origins for EEG, alcoholism and anxiety: the role of CRH-BP. *PLoS ONE* 3:e3620. doi:10.1371/journal.pone.0003620

Erb, S., Shaham, Y., and Stewart, J. (1998). The role of corticotropin-releasing factor and corticosterone in stress- and cocaine-induced relapse to cocaine seeking in rats. *J. Neurosci.* 18, 5529–5536.

Funk, C. K., O'Dell, L. E., Crawford, E. F., and Koob, G. F. (2006a). Corticotropin-releasing factor within the central nucleus of the amygdala mediates enhanced ethanol self-administration in withdrawn, ethanol-dependent rats. *J. Neurosci.* 26, 11324–11332.

Funk, D., Li, Z., and Le, A. D. (2006b). Effects of environmental and pharmacological stressors on c-fos and corticotropin-releasing factor mRNA in rat brain: Relationship to the reinstatement of alcohol seeking. *Neuroscience* 138, 235–243.

Funk, C. K., Zorrilla, E. P., Lee, M. J., Rice, K. C., and Koob, G. F. (2007). Corticotropin-releasing factor 1 antagonists selectively reduce ethanol self-administration in ethanol-dependent rats. *Biol. Psychiatry* 61, 78–86.

Gehlert, D. R., Cippitelli, A., Thorsell, A., Le, A. D., Hipskind, P. A., Hamdouchi, C., et al. (2007). 3-(4-Chloro-2-morpholin-4-yl-thiazol-5-yl)-8-(1-ethylpropyl)-2,6-dimethyl-imidazo [1,2-b]pyridazine: a novel brain-penetrant, orally available corticotropin-releasing factor receptor 1 antagonist with efficacy in animal models of alcoholism. *J. Neurosci.* 27, 2718–2726.

Ghitza, U. E., Gray, S. M., Epstein, D. H., Rice, K. C., and Shaham, Y. (2006). The anxiogenic drug yohimbine reinstates palatable food seeking in a rat relapse model: a role of CRF1 receptors. *Neuropsychopharmacology* 31, 2188–2196.

Gilpin, N. W., and Koob, G. F. (2010). Effects of beta-adrenoceptor antagonists on alcohol drinking by alcohol-dependent rats. *Psychopharmacology (Berl.)* 212, 431–439.

Gilpin, N. W., Richardson, H. N., and Koob, G. F. (2008). Effects of CRF1-receptor and opioid-receptor antagonists on dependence-induced increases in alcohol drinking by alcohol-preferring (P) rats. *Alcohol. Clin. Exp. Res.* 32, 1535–1542.

Hansson, A. C., Cippitelli, A., Sommer, W. H., Ciccocioppo, R., and Heilig, M. (2007). Region-specific down-regulation of Crhr1 gene expression in alcohol-preferring msP rats following ad lib access to alcohol. *Addict. Biol.* 12, 30–34.

Hansson, A. C., Cippitelli, A., Sommer, W. H., Fedeli, A., Bjork, K., Soverchia, L., et al. (2006). Variation at the rat Crhr1 locus and sensitivity to relapse into alcohol seeking induced by environmental stress. *Proc. Natl. Acad. Sci. U.S.A.* 103, 15236–15241.

Heilig, M., Goldman, D., Berrettini, W., and O'Brien, C. P. (2011). Pharmacogenetic approaches to the treatment of alcohol addiction. *Nat. Rev. Neurosci.* 12, 670–684.

Heilig, M., and Koob, G. F. (2007). A key role for corticotropin-releasing factor in alcohol dependence. *Trends Neurosci.* 30, 399–406.

Holmberg, G., and Gershon, S. (1961). Autonomic and psychic effects of yohimbine hydrochloride. *Psychopharmacologia* 2, 93–106.

Karlsson, C., Zook, M., Ciccocioppo, R., Gehlert, D. R., Thorsell, A., Heilig, M., et al. (2012). Melanin-concentrating hormone receptor 1 (MCH1-R) antagonism: reduced appetite for calories and suppression of addictive-like behaviors. *Pharmacol. Biochem. Behav.* 102, 400–406.

Koob, G. F. (2010). The role of CRF and CRF-related peptides in the dark side of addiction. *Brain Res.* 1314, 3–14.

Le, A. D., Harding, S., Juzytsch, W., Funk, D., and Shaham, Y. (2005). Role of alpha-2 adrenoceptors in stress-induced reinstatement of alcohol seeking and alcohol self-administration in rats. *Psychopharmacology (Berl.)* 179, 366–373.

Li, T. K., Lumeng, L., Doolittle, D. P., and Carr, L. G. (1991). Molecular associations of alcohol-seeking behavior in rat lines selectively bred for high and low voluntary ethanol drinking. *Alcohol. Alcohol Suppl.* 1, 121–124.

Lovinger, D. M., and Crabbe, J. C. (2005). Laboratory models of alcoholism: treatment target identification and insight into mechanisms. *Nat. Neurosci.* 8, 1471–1480.

Lowery, E. G., Spanos, M., Navarro, M., Lyons, A. M., Hodge, C. W., and Thiele, T. E. (2010). CRF-1 antagonist and CRF-2 agonist decrease binge-like ethanol drinking in C57BL/6J mice independent of the HPA axis. *Neuropsychopharmacology* 35, 1241–1252.

Marinelli, P. W., Funk, D., Juzytsch, W., Harding, S., Rice, K. C., Shaham, Y., et al. (2007). The CRF1 receptor antagonist antalarmin attenuates yohimbine-induced increases in operant alcohol self-administration and reinstatement of alcohol seeking in rats. *Psychopharmacology (Berl.)* 195, 345–355.

McLellan, A. T., O'Brien, C. P., Metzger, D., Alterman, A. I., Cornish, J., and Urschel, H. (1992). How effective is substance abuse treatment – compared to what? *Res. Publ. Assoc. Res. Nerv. Ment. Dis.* 70, 231–252.

Merlo Pich, E., Lorang, M., Yeganeh, M., De Fonseca, F., Raber, J., Koob, G. F., et al. (1995). Increase of extracellular corticotropin-releasing factor-like immunoreactivity levels in the amygdala of awake rats during restraint stress and ethanol withdrawal as measured by microdialysis. *J. Neurosci.* 15, 5439–5447.

O'Dell, L. E., Roberts, A. J., Smith, R. T., and Koob, G. F. (2004). Enhanced alcohol self-administration after intermittent versus continuous alcohol vapor exposure. *Alcohol. Clin. Exp. Res.* 28, 1676–1682.

Olive, M. F., Koenig, H. N., Nannini, M. A., and Hodge, C. W. (2002). Elevated extracellular CRF levels in the bed nucleus of the stria terminalis during ethanol withdrawal and reduction by subsequent ethanol intake. *Pharmacol. Biochem. Behav.* 72, 213–220.

Oslin, D. W., Berrettini, W., Kranzler, H. R., Pettinati, H., Gelernter, J., Volpicelli, J. R., et al. (2003). A functional polymorphism of the mu-opioid receptor gene is associated with naltrexone response in alcohol-dependent patients. *Neuropsychopharmacology* 28, 1546–1552.

Pacak, K., Armando, I., Komoly, S., Fukuhara, K., Weise, V. K., Holmes, C., et al. (1992). Hypercortisolemia inhibits yohimbine-induced release of norepinephrine in the posterolateral hypothalamus of conscious rats. *Endocrinology* 131, 1369–1376.

Pohorecky, L. A. (1991). Stress and alcohol interaction: an update of human research. *Alcohol. Clin. Exp. Res.* 15, 438–459.

Ramchandani, V. A., Umhau, J., Pavon, F. J., Ruiz-Velasco, V., Margas, W., Sun, H., et al. (2011). A genetic determinant of the striatal dopamine response to alcohol in men. *Mol. Psychiatry* 16, 809–817.

Ray, L. A. (2011). Stress-induced and cue-induced craving for alcohol in heavy drinkers: preliminary evidence of genetic moderation by the OPRM1 and CRH-BP genes. *Alcohol. Clin. Exp. Res.* 35, 166–174.

Rimondini, R., Arlinde, C., Sommer, W., and Heilig, M. (2002). Long-lasting increase in voluntary ethanol consumption and transcriptional regulation in the rat brain after intermittent exposure to alcohol. *FASEB J.* 16, 27–35.

Roberto, M., Cruz, M. T., Gilpin, N. W., Sabino, V., Schweitzer, P., Bajo, M., et al. (2010). Corticotropin releasing factor-induced amygdala gamma-aminobutyric Acid release plays a key role in alcohol dependence. *Biol. Psychiatry* 67, 831–839.

Sabino, V., Cottone, P., Koob, G. F., Steardo, L., Lee, M. J., Rice, K. C., et al. (2006). Dissociation between opioid and CRF1 antagonist sensitive drinking in Sardinian alcohol-preferring rats. *Psychopharmacology (Berl.)* 189, 175–186.

Sarnyai, Z., Shaham, Y., and Heinrichs, S. C. (2001). The role of corticotropin-releasing factor in drug addiction. *Pharmacol. Rev.* 53, 209–243.

Schuckit, M. A., Li, T. K., Cloninger, C. R., and Deitrich, R. A. (1985). Genetics of alcoholism. *Alcohol. Clin. Exp. Res.* 9, 475–492.

Shaham, Y., Funk, D., Erb, S., Brown, T. J., Walker, C. D., and Stewart, J. (1997). Corticotropin-releasing factor, but not corticosterone, is involved in stress-induced relapse to heroin-seeking in rats. *J. Neurosci.* 17, 2605–2614.

Shaham, Y., Shalev, U., Lu, L., De Wit, H., and Stewart, J. (2003). The reinstatement model of drug relapse: history, methodology and major findings. *Psychopharmacology (Berl.)* 168, 3–20.

Sinha, R. (2001). How does stress increase risk of drug abuse and relapse? *Psychopharmacology (Berl.)* 158, 343–359.

Sommer, W. H., Rimondini, R., Hansson, A. C., Hipskind, P. A., Gehlert, D. R., Barr, C. S., et al. (2008). Upregulation of voluntary alcohol intake, behavioral sensitivity to stress, and amygdala crhr1 expression following a history of dependence. *Biol. Psychiatry* 63, 139–145.

Sparta, D. R., Sparrow, A. M., Lowery, E. G., Fee, J. R., Knapp, D. J., and Thiele, T. E. (2008). Blockade of the corticotropin releasing factor type 1 receptor attenuates elevated ethanol drinking associated with drinking in the dark procedures. *Alcohol. Clin. Exp. Res.* 32, 259–265.

Stopponi, S., Somaini, L., Cippitelli, A., Cannella, N., Braconi, S., Kallupi, M., et al. (2011). Activation of nuclear PPARgamma receptors by the antidiabetic agent pioglitazone suppresses alcohol drinking and relapse to alcohol seeking. *Biol. Psychiatry* 69, 642–649.

Tovote, P., Farrokhi, C. B., Gonzales, R. M., Schnitzbauer, U., Blanchard, D. C., Blanchard, R. J., et al. (2010). Activation of central CRF receptor 1 by cortagine results in enhanced passive coping with a naturalistic threat in mice. *Psychoneuroendocrinology* 35, 887–895.

Treutlein, J., Kissling, C., Frank, J., Wiemann, S., Dong, L., Depner, M., et al. (2006). Genetic association of the human corticotropin releasing hormone receptor 1 (CRHR1) with binge drinking and alcohol intake patterns in two independent samples. *Mol. Psychiatry* 11, 594–602.

Umhau, J. C., Schwandt, M. L., Usala, J., Geyer, C., Singley, E., George, D. T., et al. (2011). Pharmacologically induced alcohol craving in treatment seeking alcoholics correlates with alcoholism severity, but is insensitive to acamprosate. *Neuropsychopharmacology* 36, 1178–1186.

Walker, B. M., and Koob, G. F. (2008). Regarding "Dynorphin is a downstream effector of striatal BDNF regulation of ethanol intake." *FASEB J.* 22, 2113. author reply 2113-2114.

Webster, E. L., Lewis, D. B., Torpy, D. J., Zachman, E. K., Rice, K. C., and Chrousos, G. P. (1996). In vivo and in vitro characterization of antalarmin, a nonpeptide corticotropin-releasing hormone (CRH) receptor antagonist: suppression of pituitary ACTH release and peripheral inflammation. *Endocrinology* 137, 5747–5750.

Wrzosek, M., Jakubczyk, A., Matsumoto, H., Lukaszkiewicz, J., Brower, K. J., and Wojnar, M. (2012). Serotonin 2A receptor gene (HTR2A) polymorphism in alcohol-dependent patients. *Pharmacol. Rep.* 64, 449–453.

Zhao, Y., Valdez, G. R., Fekete, E. M., Rivier, J. E., Vale, W. W., Rice, K. C., et al. (2007). Subtype-selective corticotropin-releasing factor receptor agonists exert contrasting, but not opposite, effects on anxiety-related behavior in rats. *J. Pharmacol. Exp. Ther.* 323, 846–854.

Zislis, G., Desai, T. V., Prado, M., Shah, H. P., and Bruijnzeel, A. W. (2007). Effects of the CRF receptor antagonist D-Phe CRF(12-41) and the alpha2-adrenergic receptor agonist clonidine on stress-induced reinstatement of nicotine-seeking behavior in rats. *Neuropharmacology* 53, 958–966.

Zorrilla, E. P., Heilig, M., De Wit, H., and Shaham, Y. (2013). Behavioral, biological, and chemical perspectives on targeting CRF(1) receptor antagonists to treat alcoholism. *Drug Alcohol Depend.* 128, 175–186.

Zorrilla, E. P., Valdez, G. R., and Weiss, F. (2001). Changes in levels of regional CRF-like-immunoreactivity and plasma corticosterone during protracted drug withdrawal in dependent rats. *Psychopharmacology (Berl.)* 158, 374–381.

11

MicroRNAs and drug addiction

Purva Bali[1,2] *and Paul J. Kenny*[1,2]*

[1] Laboratory of Behavioral and Molecular Neuroscience, Department of Molecular Therapeutics, The Scripps Research Institute – Florida, Jupiter, FL, USA
[2] Laboratory of Behavioral and Molecular Neuroscience, Department of Neuroscience, The Scripps Research Institute – Florida, Jupiter, FL, USA

Edited by:
Andre Pietrzykowski, Rutgers University, USA

Reviewed by:
Marissa A. Ehringer, University of Colorado, USA
Hironori Kawahara, University of Pennsylvania School of Medicine, USA

Correspondence:
Paul J. Kenny, Laboratory of Behavioral and Molecular Neuroscience, Department of Molecular Therapeutics, The Scripps Research Institute – Florida, 130 Scripps Way, Jupiter, FL 33458, USA.
e-mail: pjkenny@scripps.edu

Drug addiction is considered a disorder of neuroplasticity in brain reward and cognition systems resulting from aberrant activation of gene expression programs in response to prolonged drug consumption. Non-coding RNAs (ncRNAs) are key regulators of almost all aspects of cellular physiology. MicroRNAs (miRNAs) are small (~21–23 nucleotides) ncRNAs transcripts that regulate gene expression at the post-transcriptional level. Recently, miRNAs were shown to play key roles in the drug-induced remodeling of brain reward systems that likely drives the emergence of addiction. Here, we review evidence suggesting that one particular miRNA, miR-212, plays a particularly prominent role in vulnerability to cocaine addiction. We review evidence showing that miR-212 expression is increased in the dorsal striatum of rats that show compulsive-like cocaine-taking behaviors. Increases in miR-212 expression appear to protect against cocaine addiction, as virus-mediated striatal miR-212 overexpression decreases cocaine consumption in rats. Conversely, disruption of striatal miR-212 signaling using an antisense oligonucleotide increases cocaine intake. We also review data that identify two mechanisms by which miR-212 may regulate cocaine intake. First, miR-212 has been shown to amplify striatal cAMP response element binding protein (CREB) signaling through a mechanism involving activation of Raf1 kinase. Second, miR-212 was also shown to regulate cocaine intake by repressing striatal expression of methyl CpG binding protein 2 (MeCP2), consequently decreasing protein levels of brain-derived neurotrophic factor (BDNF). The concerted actions of miR-212 on striatal CREB and MeCP2/BDNF activity greatly attenuate the motivational effects of cocaine. These findings highlight the unique role for miRNAs in simultaneously controlling multiple signaling cascades implicated in addiction.

Keywords: **miRNA, miR-212, MeCP2, cocaine**

INTRODUCTION

Non-coding RNAs (ncRNAs) can be defined as biologically functional RNAs that do not encode proteins. This class of transcripts is characterized by the presence of an increased density of stop codons and lack of extensive open reading frames (ORFs). For decades, work on ncRNAs focused almost exclusively on transport RNAs (tRNAs) and ribosomal RNAs (rRNAs), which are key regulators of mRNA translation into encoded proteins. However, recent advances in high throughput sequencing technologies have revealed tremendous diversity in ncRNAs. Moreover, ncRNAs are playing an increasingly more recognized role in key aspects of cellular function, including the regulation of gene expression, often through novel mechanisms of action. ncRNAs have also been implicated in key cellular process such as DNA imprinting, RNA splicing, editing, transcription, mRNA degradation, and translational repression. Interestingly, analysis of ncRNA complexity through evolution reveals that the proportion of non-coding sequences in eukaryotic genomes correlates closely with the complexity of the organism, even when proportion of the protein coding genes remains relatively static across organisms (Heimberg et al., 2008).

It is currently thought that only about 2% of the human genome codes for functional proteins, yet more than 80% of transcripts

encoded in the genome may have some biochemical activity. In a recent study, Djebali et al. (2012) used ultra-deep sequencing of RNAs from different cell lines and concluded that ~75% of the genome is transcribed at some point during the cellular life cycle. These extensive studies using sequencing and sophisticated ncRNA prediction algorithms have led to the identification of thousands of ncRNAs in the human genome, and perhaps many more remain to be discovered (Majer and Booth, 2010; Yang et al., 2010).

On the basis of their length and function this heterogeneous group of transcripts can be further categorized into short ncRNAs and long ncRNAs. The short ncRNAs include microRNAs (miRNAs) and short-interfering RNAs (siRNAs), which are generally 18–25 nucleotides in length. Small RNAs (smRNAs) such as the small nucleolar RNAs (snoRNAs), smRNAs, piwi-interacting RNA (piRNAs) are between 20 and 300 nucleotides in length. The long ncRNAs (>200 nucleotides) can further be grouped into different categories on the basis of their origin (Orom and Shiekhattar, 2011) and have a broader spectrum of functions including chromatin modulation, recruitment of transcription factors, and nuclear-cytoplasmic transport (Mattick and Makunin, 2006). Indeed, there is now compelling computational and experimental evidence that many previously uncharacterized ncRNAs of unknown function, considered largely "transcriptional noise," have key functional roles in almost all aspects of cellular physiology.

Using the high throughput *in situ* expression data from Allen Brain Atlas, Mercer et al. have recently shown that more than 800 different ncRNAs are widely expressed in the adult brain (Mercer et al., 2008). In another study, Landgraf et al. created a miRNA expression atlas by sequencing and analyzing multiple smRNAs libraries (Landgraf et al., 2007). Their data also reveals a tissue/cell specific expression of these RNAs, which correlates with *in situ* expression data. Hence, it is likely that ncRNAs play an important role in basic aspects of brain function and behavior.

MicroRNAs IN BRAIN

Amongst the different classes of ncRNAs, miRNAs are perhaps the best characterized. Since their discovery in *C. elegans* in 1993 (Lee et al., 1993), hundreds of miRNAs have been identified in different species. Initial studies demonstrated that these short (∼22 nucleotide) RNAs are mainly involved in binding to the 3′ untranslated region (3′UTR) of mRNA transcripts that share complementarity with nucleotides in their so-called seed sequence (nucleotides 2–7). Binding of miRNAs to mRNA transcripts results in post-transcription silencing of the target mRNA *via* RNA-induced silencing complex (RISC)-induced translational repression or sequestering them for storage or degradation (Bartel, 2004). However, emerging new evidence suggests that the non-seed region of miRNAs may bind to the 5′UTR or the coding sequence of target transcripts and thereby influence translation processes (Orom et al., 2008; Elcheva et al., 2009). To add further complexity, recent reports show that miRNAs can also positively regulate gene expression in some cellular contexts (Vasudevan et al., 2007; Place et al., 2008). Computational sequence analysis predicts that each miRNA can target 10–100s of mRNA transcripts (Esteller, 2011). In addition, each gene transcript can itself be targeted by potentially hundreds of miRNAs.

The brain may be a particularly prominent organ within which miRNAs play an important role in controlling gene expression and neuronal activity. In a study by Miska et al. it was established that there was considerable abundance of miRNAs in rodent and primate brain (Miska et al., 2004). Further, they developed a microarray-based method to monitor the spatiotemporal expression of miRNAs during mouse brain development and found that there was a dynamic change in miRNA expression levels during development. As a result of these new methodologies there have been more than 300 miRNAs identified in adult mouse brain. Of these brain-enriched miRNAs some are present ubiquitously whereas others are expressed in a cell specific manner (Bak et al., 2008).

Another powerful tool that improved our understanding of the functional relevance of miRNAs in neuronal tissues was the development of mice with genetic manipulations in the genes encoding Dicer and Arognaute2 (Ago2). Both of these proteins are important components of the miRNA biogenesis pathway. Dicer is an endoribonuclease that catalyzes the processing of precursor miRNA into its mature form. Characterization of Dicer1 mutants in *C. elegans* suggested that this protein plays a critical role in brain development (Grishok et al., 2001). To assess its role in mammalian brain development Bernstein et al. disrupted Dicer in mice

and observed embryonic lethality with depleted number of stem cells, suggesting that this enzyme is important for development in general (Bernstein et al., 2003). Subsequently a number of groups knocked down Dicer *via* conditional gene targeting, with the findings consistent in demonstrating that ablation of dicer results in decreased miRNA expression and defects in neuronal cell differentiation and survival (Kanellopoulou et al., 2005; Murchison et al., 2005; Schaefer et al., 2007). These phenotypes could be rescued by re-expression of the gene (Kanellopoulou et al., 2005), highlighting the importance for Dicer and the smRNAs species processed by this endoribonuclease in neuronal development and function. More recently, conditional deletion of Dicer established that miRNAs expressed during neurogenesis play a role in the maintenance of neural progenitor cells, with disruption in this action contributing to defects in neuronal migration and subsequently in cortical lamination (De Pietri Tonelli et al., 2008; Kawase-Koga et al., 2009; Clovis et al., 2012).

Arognaute2, a member of the argonaute family of proteins, is the catalytically active component of the RISC that not only facilitates miRNA processing but also their regulatory actions on target mRNA transcripts (Hock and Meister, 2008). In a study by Diederichs and Haber, it was shown that overexpression of Ago2 results in increased miRNA biogenesis (Diederichs and Haber, 2007). Similar to genetic disruption of Dicer, Ago2 deletion results in embryonic lethality in mice, but conditional knock down of Ago2 reveals defects in neural tube closure and mispatterning of the anterior structure of the brain. Mouse embryonic fibroblast (MEFs) isolated from these mutant mice have reduced miRNA expression, which can be reversed by Ago2 expression (Morita et al., 2007). These findings highlight the importance of Ago2 in neuronal differentiation, brain morphogenesis, and development (Liu et al., 2004; Morita et al., 2007).

Schratt et al. found that the brain-specific miRNA, miR-134, is localized to the synaptodendritic compartment and negatively regulates the size of dendritic spines (Schratt et al., 2006). This action of miR-134 occurs through its inhibitory action on lim1 kinase expression. Another brain-enriched miRNA, miR-124, has been shown to play a critical role in the transition of progenitor neuronal cells to adult neurons by inhibiting networks of non-neuronal genes, thereby facilitating the expression of the neuronal identity (Conaco et al., 2006; Makeyev et al., 2007). Aizawa and colleagues examined the effects of double deletion of miR-9-2 and miR-9-3 on brain development in mice (Shibata et al., 2008, 2011). They found that these miR-9 family members regulate the proliferation and differentiation of neural progenitor cells in telencephalon through inhibitory actions on regulator proteins important for neurogenesis, including the homeobox protein Meis2 and the transcription factor Forkhead box protein G1 (FOXG1) (Shibata et al., 2008, 2011). Other miRNAs shown to regulate neuronal lineage commitment include members of the let-7 family and miR-125b (Leucht et al., 2008; Rybak et al., 2008). More recently, hippocampus-expressed miRNAs such as miR-134 and miR-34 have been shown to target the deacetylase sirtuin-1 (SIRT1) and thereby influence learning and memory processes (Gao et al., 2010; Zovoilis et al., 2011). In addition to their role in neuronal development and function, miRNAs may also play key role in neuronal dysfunction associated neurodegenerative diseases. For example, miR-34c has been implicated in the cognitive impairment associated with dementia. As discussed below, miRNAs have also been implicated in drug addiction, considered by many to be an aberrant form of learning and memory.

DRUG ADDICTION AND MicroRNAs

Addiction can be defined as compulsive drug use despite negative consequences. During the last decade, multiple cellular and molecular studies have revealed significant convergence between the actions of drugs of abuse in the brain that drive the development of addiction and the molecular processes involved in learning and memory. Indeed, addiction is often conceptualized as a disorder of synaptic plasticity, and hence the cellular and molecular mechanisms involved in learning-associated synaptic plasticity and concomitant remodeling of neuronal circuits may provide an important heuristic framework to investigate the addiction process.

In a study by Schaefer et al. it was shown that cocaine-induced robust alterations in the expression of a wide-range of miRNAs in the striatum, a key brain site involved in addiction. Indeed, a subset of these miRNAs whose expression was impacted by cocaine were shown to regulate the expression levels of a wide-range of genes known to influence the motivational properties of cocaine, including *Bdnf*, *FosB* (*FBJ murine osteosarcoma viral oncogene homolog B*), and *Cdk5r1* (cyclin-dependent kinase 5 activator 1). In the same study, the effects on cocaine reinforcement of selectively ablating Ago2, the catalytic component of RISC involved in transducing the inhibitory actions of miRNAs on their target transcripts, was assessed. Specifically, Schaefer et al. investigated the effects knocking down Ago2 in medium spiny neurons (MSNs) of the striatum that express the dopamine D2 receptor (D2R) (Schaefer et al., 2010). Disruption of Ago2 in D2R MSNs resulted in dramatically reduced conditioned rewarding effects of cocaine in mice, reflected in attenuated cocaine-induced conditioned place preference (CPP). More importantly, the Ago2-D2R mutant mice also demonstrated reduced intravenous cocaine self-administration behavior across a wide-range of cocaine doses (Schaefer et al., 2010). Such downward shifts in the cocaine dose-response curve are interpreted as reduced motivation to consume the drug. Finally, Ago2 ablation in D2R MSNs dramatically decreased miRNA expression and activity in striatum. Hence, as cocaine self-administration behavior is considered the most direct measure of drug reinforcement in laboratory animals, these data provide compelling support for a key role for Ago2, and by extension miRNAs, in striatal MSNs in regulating the reinforcing properties of cocaine that drive the development of addiction (Schaefer et al., 2010).

Another interesting study performed by Eipper-Mains et al. (2011) links cocaine exposure to Ago2 induction (Eipper-Mains et al., 2011). Characterization of the subcellular fractions of the striatum shows that Ago2 is localized in synapses and is cocaine-responsive. Specifically, chronic cocaine exposure resulted in increased Ago2 mRNA and protein in the striatum, and concomitantly altered miRNA expression levels. This increase in Ago2 protein was associated with postsynaptic densities (PSDs) in striatum but not in medial prefrontal cortex (mPFC). Intriguingly, a large number of cocaine-responsive miRNAs identified so far (miR-8 family, miR-145, miR-451) can putatively target genes

implicated in addiction, including TrkB receptor, which transduces the actions of BDNF in brain and play a crucial role in activity-dependent synaptic plasticity.

Chandrasekar and Dreyer identified another set of miRNAs (miR-181a, let-7d, and miR-124) whose expression is sensitive to cocaine (Chandrasekar and Dreyer, 2009). They found that chronic cocaine administration suppressed the expression of miR-124 and let-7d, but induced miR-181a in the mesolimbic dopaminergic system. The critical role of the mesolimbic dopaminergic system in addiction is well established (Koob and Volkow, 2010). *In situ* hybridization confirmed that the alterations in the expression of these miRNAs occurred in brain regions related to reward and memory. Further, *in vitro* overexpression of these miRNAs modulated the expression levels of proteins like BDNF and the dopamine D3 receptor, which have been heavily implicated in drug addiction (Heidbreder et al., 2005; Ghitza et al., 2010). In a subsequent study the same group also showed that *in vivo* modulation of these miRNAs in ventral striatum (nucleus accumbens) affects cocaine-induced place conditioning (Chandrasekar and Dreyer, 2011). These data show that cocaine can impact the expression of a range of different miRNAs depending on treatment and testing context, and support an important role for such miRNAs and their targeted mRNA transcripts in the development of drug addiction.

Alterations in dopamine signaling can lead to long-lasting neuronal adaptations that result in decreased or increased propensity for drug use. One of the proposed mechanism by which this can occur is dopamine transmission-induced alterations in the expression and subunit composition of AMPA receptors (Wolf, 2010). AMPA receptors are postsynaptic glutamate gated ion channels that mediate excitatory neurotransmission in the central nervous system. As such, AMPA receptors are core regulators of synaptic plasticity and activity-dependent remodeling of brain circuitries (Du et al., 2004; Haas et al., 2006). In a recent study by Saba et al. it was found that miR-181a expression in nucleus accumbens was increased by dopamine-mediated transmission and by the psychomotor stimulant drugs cocaine and amphetamines (Saba et al., 2012). Moreover, miR-181a was shown to repress GluA2-AMPA receptor subunit expression, and thereby modulate the magnitude of AMPA receptor clustering. Hence, miR-181a may be a key miRNA involved in drug-induced remodeling of the nucleus accumbens and greater striatal complex in response to drug exposure, thereby driving regulating the emergence of addiction. Recent evidence suggests that miRNAs also play a key role in the actions of other classes of addictive drugs, including nicotine, alcohol, and opiates; for recent review and detailed table describing specific miRNAs see Im and Kenny (2012).

THE miR-212/132 CLUSTER

The miR-132/miR-212 family of miRNAs was first identified in a genome wide search for genes responsive to the transcription factor cAMP response element binding protein (CREB) using an approach termed Serial Analysis of chromatin occupancy (SACO) (Impey et al., 2004). This family of miRNAs is highly conserved in vertebrates, is transcribed as a polycistronic primary transcript, and is highly enriched in the mature neurons of the forebrain (Marson et al., 2008; Hansen et al., 2010). Analysis of the promoter for this miRNA gene cluster reveals the presence of multiple

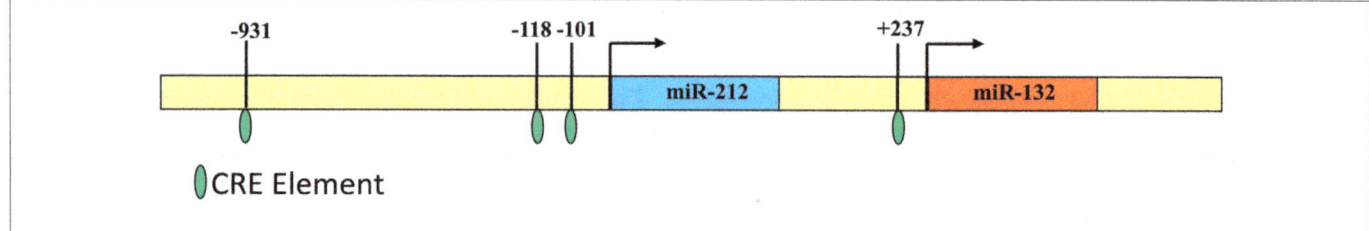

FIGURE 1 | The miR-212/132 gene cluster is located on chromosome 17 in humans, 10 in rats, and 11 in mouse. Shown are mouse/human miR-212 and miR-132 genes, with locations of CRE elements through which CREB can stimulate miR-212 and miR-132 transcription.

cAMP response element (CRE) sites and experimental evidence verifies that these miRNAs are indeed CREB inducible (Vo et al., 2005); (see **Figure 1**) Recent studies from Remenyi et al. have shown that this gene cluster in fact produces four mature miRNAs, namely miR-132, miR-132*, miR-212, and miR-212*, where miR-132* and miR-212* are encoded by the same primary transcript, but on the opposite strand, as the miR-132 and miR-212 miR-NAs, respectively (Remenyi et al., 2010). Moreover, each of these four miRNAs likely have their own unique set of target mRNA transcripts. Intriguingly, even though these four miRNAs are transcribed in equal measure (by virtue of all being encoded in the same primary transcript), their relative abundance varies dramatically within various cell types including neurons, with miR-132 being far more abundant than the other three transcripts (Remenyi et al., 2010). Hence, it is likely that as yet uncharacterized mechanisms are involved in preferentially stabilizing miR-132 levels, and/or destabilizing miR-132*, miR-212, and miR-212*.

A series of studies in the last few years have demonstrated the importance of miR-132 cluster in neuronal morphogenesis and in regulating synaptic plasticity. In particular, miR-132 has been shown to increase dendritic spine complexity in both immature cortical and hippocampal neurons in part by translational inhibition of p250GAP. As p250GAP is a Rho-Rac family GTPase activating protein, this finding highlights a role for Rho, and also transducers downstream of Rac-GTPases such as PAK, in the effects of miR-132 on activity-dependent neuronal remodeling (Wayman et al., 2008; Hansen et al., 2010; Magill et al., 2010).

COCAINE INTAKE AND miR-212

Two recent studies from our group have identified a key role for miR-212, also encoded by the miR-212/132 gene cluster, in regulating compulsive-like cocaine intake in rats (Hollander et al., 2010; Im et al., 2010). As described above, the striatum is a key brain region that regulates compulsive cocaine use. The first study showed that in rats with extended access to cocaine (6 h per day) there is a ~1.75-fold increase in both striatal miR-212 and miR-132 levels (Hollander et al., 2010). Similar increases in expression were not detected in rats that received non-contingent cocaine infusions time-locked to rats that volitionally consumed cocaine, or in rats with restricted access to cocaine (1 h per day). Further, lentivirus-mediated overexpression of miR-212 in the dorsal striatum resulted in a remarkable decrease in cocaine intake in the extended access rats compared to vector control, but overexpression did not alter cocaine intake in rats with restricted drug

access (**Figure 2**). The decreased cocaine intake is related to a profound decrease in the motivational properties of the drug, as reflected by a large downward shift in the cocaine dose-response curve in the same animals. Conversely, inhibition of miR-212 signaling in the striatum, achieved by infusion of an antisense oligonucleotide, dramatically increased the motivational properties of cocaine in rats with extended, but not restricted, access to the drug (**Figure 2**). These data suggest that intrinsic or drug-induce alterations in the expression or activity of striatal miR-212 may influence vulnerability to addiction in human cocaine users.

miR-212 REGULATES COCAINE INTAKE THROUGH STRIATAL CREB SIGNALING

As noted above, expression of miR-212 is regulated by CREB. In many cases, miRNAs have been shown to influence signaling cascades that increase their expression and further modify the activity those cascades through positive or negative feedback mechanisms (Tsang et al., 2007). As CREB overexpression in ventral striatum is known to diminish the motivational properties of cocaine (Carlezon et al., 1998), we tested the hypothesis that miR-212 may regulate cocaine intake in extended access rats by amplifying striatal CREB activity through positive feedback mechanisms. Consistent with a profound stimulatory effect of miR-212 on CREB in cultured cells *in vitro*, we found that levels of CREB that was phosphorylated at serine 133 (i.e., activated CREB) was significantly increased (Hollander et al., 2010). Furthermore, forskolin-stimulated expression of the CREB-responsive gene *fos* was also increased by miR-212, as was the activity of a luciferase-based CREB reporter construct (CRE-containing element from promoter of EVX-1). Dominant negative or phosphorylation-deficient mutant forms of CREB attenuated these stimulatory effects of miR-212 on CREB signaling. More importantly, we also found that miR-212 amplified CREB signaling in the striatum *in vivo*. Specifically, we found that rats with extended access to cocaine showed increased expression of the CREB-responsive gene *Nurr1*, and that expression levels were greatly increased by miR-212 overexpression in striatum (Hollander et al., 2010).

These findings identify miR-212 as a novel cocaine-responsive gene that is up regulated in the striatum in response to cocaine overconsumption that serves to promote CREB activity through positive feedback and thereby attenuate the motivational properties of the drug. Based on these findings, we next investigated the mechanisms by which miR-212 may amplify CREB signaling. We found that miR-212 increases activity-dependent production of cAMP by sensitizing adenylyl cyclase activity. This stimulatory

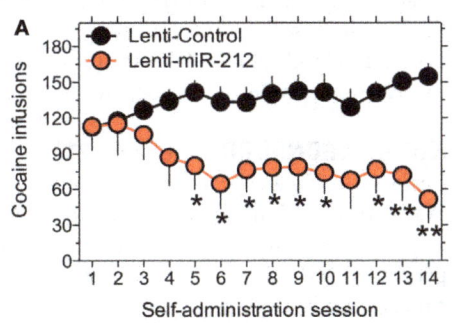

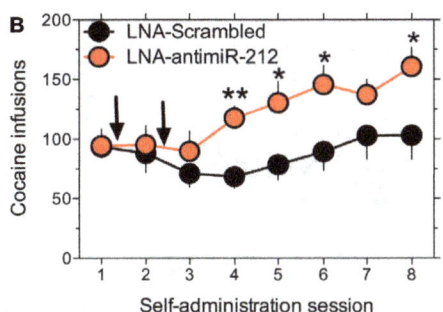

FIGURE 2 | Overexpression of miR-212 in striatum reverses the motivational properties of cocaine in rats with extended but not restricted access to cocaine. (A) Striatal miR-212 overexpression reverses the long-term trajectory of cocaine-taking behavior in rats with extended access. **(B)** Disruption of miR-212 signaling in striatum, achieved by local infusion of a locked nucleic acid (LNA) modified antisense oligonucleotide against miR-212 (LNA-antimiR-212) increases cocaine intake in extended access. Reproduced with permission from (Hollander et al., 2010).

action on adenylyl cyclase results in accumulation of phosphory-lated CREB and increased activity of the core CREB co-activators CREB-regulated transcription co-activator-1 and -2 (CRTC1 and CRTC2), also known as TORC1 and TORC2. Further investigation of the mechanism by which miR-212 enhances CREB signaling revealed that the kinase Raf1 was activated by miR-212, and was found to play a key role in sensitizing adenylyl cyclase activity. Finally, computational and biochemical analysis showed that Sprouty-related EVH1 domain-containing protein 1 (SPRED1), a known negative regulator of Raf1 signaling, is a miR-212 target mRNA transcript and SPRED1 repression by miR-212 contributes to its stimulatory effects on Raf1 and CREB activity (Hollander et al., 2010).

To investigate the functional relevance of miR-212-induced amplification of CREB activity *in vivo* on the suppressive effects of this miRNA on cocaine intake, we examined the effects of over-expressing the CREB co-activator CRTC1 (TORC1) on cocaine intake in rats with restricted or extended cocaine access. It is known that CRTC overexpression increases CREB activity and that miR-212 increases CRTC1 expression (Hollander et al., 2010). Consistent with an important role for striatal CREB signaling in attenuating the motivational properties of cocaine, we found that striatal TORC1 overexpression decreased cocaine intake in extended but not restricted access rats. These findings support the hypothesis that miR-212 controls cocaine intake at least in part by amplifying the CREB-TORC signaling axis in striatum. Moreover, these findings provide compelling support for a key role for miR-212 in regulating the development of compulsive drug taking in rats, and perhaps in influencing vulnerability to cocaine addiction in human drug users.

miR-212 ALSO REGULATES COCAINE INTAKE THROUGH STRIATAL MeCP2

Considering that miR-212 expression levels may play a key role in regulating vulnerability to cocaine addiction, we next inves-tigated the mechanisms by which baseline and cocaine-induced increases in striatal miR-212 levels are regulated. Interestingly, sequence analysis of the miR-212/132 gene cluster reveals that it is located in a CpG enriched region, which can serve as substrate

for DNA methylation and gene regulation. Methyl CpG binding protein 2 (MeCP2) is known to bind to methylated DNA and can act as a gene repressor by recruiting other chromatin remodeling proteins that combine to form the so-called repressor complex (Guy et al., 2011). Based on these observations, we hypothesized that MeCP2 may regulate baseline and cocaine-induced changes in miR-212 expression in striatum and thereby influence cocaine-taking behavior. Consistent with this hypothesis, *in vitro* stud-ies showed that knockdown of MeCP2 increased miR-212 (and miR-132) expression in cultured cells (Im et al., 2010). Similarly, pharmacologically induced disruption of DNA methyltransferase activity, which would be expected to attenuate the inhibitory activ-ity of MeCP2 on gene expression, also increased miR-212/132 levels. Furthermore, we found that knockdown of striatal MeCP2 expression, achieved by virus-mediated delivery of a short hairpin interfering RNA (shRNA) against MeCP2, resulted in profoundly decreased cocaine intake in rats with extended but not restricted access to cocaine (**Figure 3**). Knockdown of striatal MeCP2 dra-matically increased the stimulatory effects of self-administered cocaine on striatal miR-212 expression in rats with extended but not restricted access to the drug. More importantly, disruption of striatal miR-212 signaling, achieved by striatal infusion of an anti-sense oligonucleotide, reversed the inhibitory effects of MeCP2 knockdown on cocaine intake in extended access rats (Im et al., 2010). These findings are consistent with an inhibitory effect of MeCP2 on miR-212 expression, suggesting that MeCP2 acts as a pro-addiction transcriptional repressor that, by attenuating miR-212 expression in response to cocaine, increases vulnerability to addiction.

Intriguingly, miR-132 was previously shown to repress the expression of MeCP2 through direct interaction with the tran-script 3′UTR (Klein et al., 2007). Moreover, as miR-132 and miR-212 share the same seed region, this suggests that miR-212 may similarly repress MeCP2. Based on these observations, we hypothesized that in addition to the inhibitory effects of MeCP2 on miR-212 expression described above, MeCP2 levels in turn may be repressed by miR-212. In other words, miR-212 and MeCP2 may be locked in a homeostatic relationship that serves to control miR-212 expression level and thereby

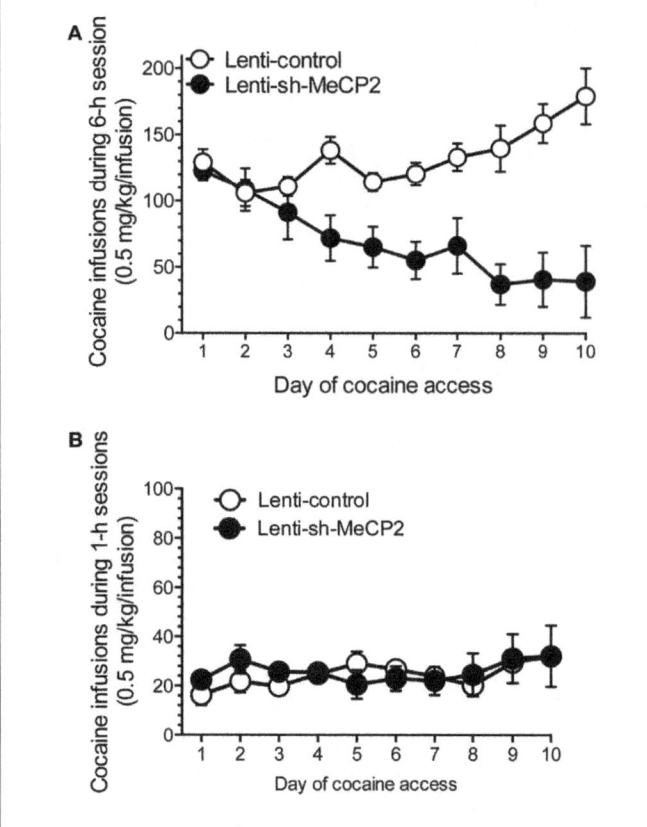

FIGURE 3 | Knockdown of MeCP2 in striatum reverses the motivational properties of cocaine in rats with extended but not restricted access to cocaine. (A) Lentivirus-mediated knockdown of MeCP2 in the striatum reverses the escalating cocaine intake typically seen in rats with extended access to cocaine. **(B)** In contract, MeCP2 knockdown does not alter cocaine intake in rats with restricted daily access to the drug. Reproduced with permission from (Im et al., 2010).

influence vulnerability to cocaine addiction. Consistent with this hypothesis, we found that miR-212 overexpression profoundly decreased MeCP2 expression in cultured cells and in the striatum *in vivo* (Im et al., 2010). Hence, homeostatic interactions between miR-212 and MeCP2 may determine vulnerability to cocaine addiction.

ROLE FOR BDNF IN REGULATING THE ACTIONS OF STRIATAL miR-212 ON COCAINE INTAKE

It has been reported that the levels of MeCP2 are closely related to those of, BDNF (Chang et al., 2006). However, the complex mechanisms by which MeCP2 regulates BDNF levels remain unclear. BDNF in the striatum is known to increase the motivational properties of cocaine (Horger et al., 1999; Schoenbaum et al., 2007). We therefore hypothesized that miR-212-MeCP2 interactions may regulate cocaine intake by influencing levels of BDNF in striatum. We observed that virus-mediated MeCP2 knockdown or miR-212 expression (which decreases MeCP2 levels) in striatum reduced BDNF expression. Moreover, virus-mediated increases in BDNF expression in striatum increased cocaine intake in rats with extended but not restricted access. Conversely, disruption of striatal BDNF signaling using a neutralizing antibody reduced cocaine

intake in extended but restricted access rats (Im et al., 2010). These findings suggest that miR-212-MeCP2 interactions may determine expression levels of BDNF in striatum, which in turn regulates the motivational properties of cocaine.

NON-NEURONAL ROLES OF miR-212

Besides playing a critical role in drug-induced neuroplasticity relevant to addiction, there is emerging evidence that miR-212 is also involved in a host of other biological and pathophysiological processes. Indeed, miR-212 expression is deregulated in various cancers and its expression has been correlated to disease progression. In pancreatic carcinomas it has been shown that miR-212 targets the tumor suppressor retinoblastoma (Rb1) (Park et al., 2011), whereas the methyl binding protein (MeCP2) seems to be the main target in some of the gastric tumors (Wada et al., 2010). Incoronato et al. showed that miR-212 targets phosphoprotein enriched in diabetes (PED), a wide spectrum anti-apoptotic protein, and thereby plays an important role in tumor suppression (Incoronato et al., 2010). In a follow up study the same group also demonstrated that the expression on miR-212 in lung carcinomas is regulated by histone modifications (Incoronato et al., 2011). This suggests that epigenetic mechanisms may play an important role in regulating miRNA expression in different cancers and other biological processes.

Besides cancer, miR-212 has also been implicated in regulating organogenesis by playing a key role in modulating epithelial stromal interactions (Ucar et al., 2010). In addition, miR-212 expression can be regulated by various hormones, adding another layer of complexity to their regulation and role in development and disease (Godoy et al., 2011). Studies from Turrini et al. reveal that miR-212 may mediate drug resistance by targeting the ABC efflux transporter (Turrini et al., 2012). Two recent reports implicate the importance of the miR-132/212 family in cardiovascular development and disorders. In the first study, smRNAs deep sequencing analysis in vascular smooth muscle cells show that the miR-132/miR-212 cluster is induced by the hormone angiotensin II and by targeting PTEN, increases the expression of the gene MCP1 (Monocyte chemotactic protein 1), a key regulator of cardiovascular disorders (Jin et al., 2012). In the other study, Ucar et al. demonstrate that these miRNAs activate calcineurin signaling in cardiomyocytes by targeting the transcription factor Foxo3, and thus play an important role in cardiac hypertrophy (Ucar et al., 2012).

CONCLUSION

Taken together, these studies highlight the fact that miR-212 plays a critical role in fine-tuning transcriptional and neuroplastic responses to drugs of abuse. Specifically, we found that miR-212 can control cocaine intake through two complementary mechanisms: amplifying CREB signaling and reducing MeCP2/BDNF transmission in striatum.

Since miR-212 and miR-132 share the same seed region it is widely believed that they target the same mRNAs. However, only a few putative miR-212/132 targets have been verified experimentally, which include MeCP2, Rb1and HB-EGF. There is increasing evidence available now showing that the 5′ and 3′ regions of the miRNAs can form the basis of differential target recognition despite having the identical seed region (Brennecke et al., 2005; Jalvy-Delvaille et al., 2012). There is also a possibility that differential expression or availability of these members can also regulate gene expression in a differential manner. Future studies in this respect could further help in improving our understanding of how miR-212 and miR-132 regulate different neuronal and non-neuronal functions or if these two miRNAs are functionally redundant? More generally, these findings highlight the novel role for miRNAs in addiction, and suggest that other ncRNAs may also play important roles in the disorder.

ACKNOWLEDGMENTS

Supported by a grant from the National Institute on Drug Abuse (DA025983 to Paul J. Kenny). This is manuscript number 21989 from The Scripps Research Institute.

REFERENCES

Bak, M., Silahtaroglu, A., Moller, M., Christensen, M., Rath, M. F., Skryabin, B., et al. (2008). MicroRNA expression in the adult mouse central nervous system. *RNA* 14, 432–444.

Bartel, D. P. (2004). MicroRNAs: genomics, biogenesis, mechanism, and function. *Cell* 116, 281–297.

Bernstein, E., Kim, S. Y., Carmell, M. A., Murchison, E. P., Alcorn, H., Li, M. Z., et al. (2003). Dicer is essential for mouse development. *Nat. Genet.* 35, 215–217.

Brennecke, J., Stark, A., Russell, R. B., and Cohen, S. M. (2005). Principles of microRNA-target recognition. *PLoS Biol.* 3:e85. doi:10.1371/journal.pbio.0030085

Carlezon, W. A. Jr., Thome, J., Olson, V. G., Lane-Ladd, S. B., Brodkin, E. S., Hiroi, N., et al. (1998). Regulation of cocaine reward by CREB. *Science* 282, 2272–2275.

Chandrasekar, V., and Dreyer, J. L. (2009). microRNAs miR-124, let-7d and miR-181a regulate cocaine-induced plasticity. *Mol. Cell. Neurosci.* 42, 350–362.

Chandrasekar, V., and Dreyer, J. L. (2011). Regulation of MiR-124, Let-7d, and MiR-181a in the accumbens affects the expression, extinction, and reinstatement of cocaine-induced conditioned place preference. *Neuropsychopharmacology* 36, 1149–1164.

Chang, Q., Khare, G., Dani, V., Nelson, S., and Jaenisch, R. (2006). The disease progression of Mecp2 mutant mice is affected by the level of BDNF expression. *Neuron* 49, 341–348.

Clovis, Y. M., Enard, W., Marinaro, F., Huttner, W. B., and De Pietri Tonelli, D. (2012). Convergent repression of Foxp2 3′UTR by miR-9 and miR-132 in embryonic mouse neocortex: implications for radial migration of neurons. *Development* 139, 3332–3342.

Conaco, C., Otto, S., Han, J. J., and Mandel, G. (2006). Reciprocal actions of REST and a microRNA promote neuronal identity. *Proc. Natl. Acad. Sci. U.S.A.* 103, 2422–2427.

De Pietri Tonelli, D., Pulvers, J. N., Haffner, C., Murchison, E. P., Hannon, G. J., and Huttner, W. B. (2008). miRNAs are essential for survival and differentiation of newborn neurons but not for expansion of neural progenitors during early neurogenesis in the mouse embryonic neocortex. *Development* 135, 3911–3921.

Diederichs, S., and Haber, D. A. (2007). Dual role for argonautes in microRNA processing and posttranscriptional regulation of microRNA expression. *Cell* 131, 1097–1108.

Djebali, S., Davis, C. A., Merkel, A., Dobin, A., Lassmann, T., Mortazavi, A., et al. (2012). Landscape of transcription in human cells. *Nature* 489, 101–108.

Du, J., Gray, N. A., Falke, C. A., Chen, W., Yuan, P., Szabo, S. T., et al. (2004). Modulation of synaptic plasticity by antimanic agents: the role of AMPA glutamate receptor subunit 1 synaptic expression. *J. Neurosci.* 24, 6578–6589.

Eipper-Mains, J. E., Kiraly, D. D., Palakodeti, D., Mains, R. E., Eipper, B. A., and Graveley, B. R. (2011). microRNA-Seq reveals cocaine-regulated expression of striatal microRNAs. *RNA* 17, 1529–1543.

Elcheva, I., Goswami, S., Noubissi, F. K., and Spiegelman, V. S. (2009). CRD-BP protects the coding region of betaTrCP1 mRNA from miR-183-mediated degradation. *Mol. Cell* 35, 240–246.

Esteller, M. (2011). Non-coding RNAs in human disease. *Nat. Rev. Genet.* 12, 861–874.

Gao, J., Wang, W. Y., Mao, Y. W., Graff, J., Guan, J. S., Pan, L., et al. (2010). A novel pathway regulates memory and plasticity via SIRT1 and miR-134. *Nature* 466, 1105–1109.

Ghitza, U. E., Zhai, H., Wu, P., Airavaara, M., Shaham, Y., and Lu, L. (2010). Role of BDNF and GDNF in drug reward and relapse: a review. *Neurosci. Biobehav. Rev.* 35, 157–171.

Godoy, J., Nishimura, M., and Webster, N. J. (2011). Gonadotropin-releasing hormone induces miR-132 and miR-212 to regulate cellular morphology and migration in immortalized LbetaT2 pituitary gonadotrope cells. *Mol. Endocrinol.* 25, 810–820.

Grishok, A., Pasquinelli, A. E., Conte, D., Li, N., Parrish, S., Ha, I., et al. (2001). Genes and mechanisms related to RNA interference regulate expression of the small temporal RNAs that control *C. elegans* developmental timing. *Cell* 106, 23–34.

Guy, J., Cheval, H., Selfridge, J., and Bird, A. (2011). The role of MeCP2 in the brain. *Annu. Rev. Cell Dev. Biol.* 27, 631–652.

Haas, K., Li, J., and Cline, H. T. (2006). AMPA receptors regulate experience-dependent dendritic arbor growth in vivo. *Proc. Natl. Acad. Sci. U.S.A.* 103, 12127–12131.

Hansen, K. F., Sakamoto, K., Wayman, G. A., Impey, S., and Obrietan, K. (2010). Transgenic miR132 alters neuronal spine density and impairs novel object recognition memory. *PLoS ONE* 5:e15497. doi:10.1371/journal.pone.0015497

Heidbreder, C. A., Gardner, E. L., Xi, Z. X., Thanos, P. K., Mugnaini, M., Hagan, J. J., et al. (2005). The role of central dopamine D3 receptors in drug addiction: a review of pharmacological evidence. *Brain Res. Brain Res. Rev.* 49, 77–105.

Heimberg, A. M., Sempere, L. F., Moy, V. N., Donoghue, P. C., and Peterson, K. J. (2008). MicroRNAs and the advent of vertebrate morphological complexity. *Proc. Natl. Acad. Sci. U.S.A.* 105, 2946–2950.

Hock, J., and Meister, G. (2008). The Argonaute protein family. *Genome Biol.* 9, 210.

Hollander, J. A., Im, H. I., Amelio, A. L., Kocerha, J., Bali, P., Lu, Q., et al. (2010). Striatal microRNA controls cocaine intake through CREB signalling. *Nature* 466, 197–202.

Horger, B. A., Iyasere, C. A., Berhow, M. T., Messer, C. J., Nestler, E. J., and Taylor, J. R. (1999). Enhancement of locomotor activity and conditioned reward to cocaine by brain-derived neurotrophic factor. *J. Neurosci.* 19, 4110–4122.

Im, H. I., Hollander, J. A., Bali, P., and Kenny, P. J. (2010). MeCP2 controls BDNF expression and cocaine intake through homeostatic interactions with microRNA-212. *Nat. Neurosci.* 13, 1120–1127.

Im, H. I., and Kenny, P. J. (2012). MicroRNAs in neuronal function and dysfunction. *Trends Neurosci.* 35, 325–334.

Impey, S., Mccorkle, S. R., Cha-Molstad, H., Dwyer, J. M., Yochum, G. S., Boss, J. M., et al. (2004). Defining the CREB regulon: a genome-wide analysis of transcription factor regulatory regions. *Cell* 119, 1041–1054.

Incoronato, M., Garofalo, M., Urso, L., Romano, G., Quintavalle, C., Zanca, C., et al. (2010). miR-212 increases tumor necrosis factor-related apoptosis-inducing ligand sensitivity in non-small cell lung cancer by targeting the antiapoptotic protein PED. *Cancer Res.* 70, 3638–3646.

Incoronato, M., Urso, L., Portela, A., Laukkanen, M. O., Soini, Y., Quintavalle, C., et al. (2011). Epigenetic regulation of miR-212 expression in lung cancer. *PLoS ONE* 6:e27722. doi:10.1371/journal.pone.0027722

Jalvy-Delvaille, S., Maurel, M., Majo, V., Pierre, N., Chabas, S., Combe, C., et al. (2012). Molecular basis of differential target regulation by miR-96 and miR-182: the Glypican-3 as a model. *Nucleic Acids Res.* 40, 1356–1365.

Jin, W., Reddy, M. A., Chen, Z., Putta, S., Lanting, L., Kato, M., et al. (2012). Small RNA sequencing reveals microRNAs that modulate angiotensin II effects in vascular smooth muscle cells. *J. Biol. Chem.* 287, 15672–15683.

Kanellopoulou, C., Muljo, S. A., Kung, A. L., Ganesan, S., Drapkin, R., Jenuwein, T., et al. (2005). Dicer-deficient mouse embryonic stem cells are defective in differentiation and centromeric silencing. *Genes Dev.* 19, 489–501.

Kawase-Koga, Y., Otaegi, G., and Sun, T. (2009). Different timings of Dicer deletion affect neurogenesis and gliogenesis in the developing mouse central nervous system. *Dev. Dyn.* 238, 2800–2812.

Klein, M. E., Lioy, D. T., Ma, L., Impey, S., Mandel, G., and Goodman, R. H. (2007). Homeostatic regulation of MeCP2 expression by a CREB-induced microRNA. *Nat. Neurosci.* 10, 1513–1514.

Koob, G. F., and Volkow, N. D. (2010). Neurocircuitry of addiction. *Neuropsychopharmacology* 35, 217–238.

Landgraf, P., Rusu, M., Sheridan, R., Sewer, A., Iovino, N., Aravin, A., et al. (2007). A mammalian microRNA expression atlas based on small RNA library sequencing. *Cell* 129, 1401–1414.

Lee, R. C., Feinbaum, R. L., and Ambros, V. (1993). The *C. elegans* heterochronic gene lin-4 encodes small RNAs with antisense complementarity to lin-14. *Cell* 75, 843–854.

Leucht, C., Stigloher, C., Wizenmann, A., Klafke, R., Folchert, A., and Bally-Cuif, L. (2008). MicroRNA-9 directs late organizer activity of the midbrain-hindbrain boundary. *Nat. Neurosci.* 11, 641–648.

Liu, J., Carmell, M. A., Rivas, F. V., Marsden, C. G., Thomson, J. M., Song, J. J., et al. (2004). Argonaute2 is the catalytic engine of mammalian RNAi. *Science* 305, 1437–1441.

Magill, S. T., Cambronne, X. A., Luikart, B. W., Lioy, D. T., Leighton, B. H., Westbrook, G. L., et al. (2010). microRNA-132 regulates dendritic growth and arborization of newborn neurons in the adult hippocampus. *Proc. Natl. Acad. Sci. U.S.A.* 107, 20382–20387.

Majer, A., and Booth, S. A. (2010). Computational methodologies for studying non-coding RNAs relevant to central nervous system function and dysfunction. *Brain Res.* 1338, 131–145.

Makeyev, E. V., Zhang, J., Carrasco, M. A., and Maniatis, T. (2007). The MicroRNA miR-124 promotes neuronal differentiation by triggering brain-specific alternative pre-mRNA splicing. *Mol. Cell* 27, 435–448.

Marson, A., Levine, S. S., Cole, M. F., Frampton, G. M., Brambrink, T., Johnstone, S., et al. (2008). Connecting microRNA genes to the core transcriptional regulatory circuitry of embryonic stem cells. *Cell* 134, 521–533.

Mattick, J. S., and Makunin, I. V. (2006). Non-coding RNA. *Hum. Mol. Genet.* 15, R17–R29.

Mercer, T. R., Dinger, M. E., Sunkin, S. M., Mehler, M. F., and Mattick, J. S. (2008). Specific expression of long noncoding RNAs in the mouse brain. *Proc. Natl. Acad. Sci. U.S.A.* 105, 716–721.

Miska, E. A., Alvarez-Saavedra, E., Townsend, M., Yoshii, A., Sestan, N., Rakic, P., et al. (2004). Microarray analysis of microRNA expression in the developing mammalian brain. *Genome Biol.* 5, R68.

Morita, S., Horii, T., Kimura, M., Goto, Y., Ochiya, T., and Hatada, I. (2007). One Argonaute family member, Eif2c2 (Ago2), is essential for development and appears not to be involved in DNA methylation. *Genomics* 89, 687–696.

Murchison, E. P., Partridge, J. F., Tam, O. H., Cheloufi, S., and Hannon, G. J. (2005). Characterization of Dicer-deficient murine embryonic stem cells. *Proc. Natl. Acad. Sci. U.S.A.* 102, 12135–12140.

Orom, U. A., Nielsen, F. C., and Lund, A. H. (2008). MicroRNA-10a binds the 5′UTR of ribosomal protein mRNAs and enhances their translation. *Mol. Cell* 30, 460–471.

Orom, U. A., and Shiekhattar, R. (2011). Long non-coding RNAs and enhancers. *Curr. Opin. Genet. Dev.* 21, 194–198.

Park, J. K., Henry, J. C., Jiang, J., Esau, C., Gusev, Y., Lerner, M. R., et al. (2011). miR-132 and miR-212 are increased in pancreatic cancer and target the retinoblastoma tumor suppressor. *Biochem. Biophys. Res. Commun.* 406, 518–523.

Place, R. F., Li, L. C., Pookot, D., Noonan, E. J., and Dahiya, R. (2008). MicroRNA-373 induces expression of genes with complementary promoter sequences. *Proc. Natl. Acad. Sci. U.S.A.* 105, 1608–1613.

Remenyi, J., Hunter, C. J., Cole, C., Ando, H., Impey, S., Monk, C. E., et al. (2010). Regulation of the miR-212/132 locus by MSK1 and CREB in response to neurotrophins. *Biochem. J.* 428, 281–291.

Rybak, A., Fuchs, H., Smirnova, L., Brandt, C., Pohl, E. E., Nitsch, R., et al. (2008). A feedback loop comprising lin-28 and let-7 controls pre-let-7 maturation during neural stem-cell commitment. *Nat. Cell Biol.* 10, 987–993.

Saba, R., Storchel, P. H., Aksoy-Aksel, A., Kepura, F., Lippi, G., Plant, T. D., et al. (2012). Dopamine-regulated microRNA MiR-181a controls GluA2 surface expression in hippocampal neurons. *Mol. Cell. Biol.* 32, 619–632.

Schaefer, A., Im, H. I., Veno, M. T., Fowler, C. D., Min, A., Intrator, A., et al. (2010). Argonaute 2 in dopamine 2 receptor-expressing neurons regulates cocaine addiction. *J. Exp. Med.* 207, 1843–1851.

Schaefer, A., O'Carroll, D., Tan, C. L., Hillman, D., Sugimori, M., Llinas, R., et al. (2007). Cerebellar neurodegeneration in the absence of microRNAs. *J. Exp. Med.* 204, 1553–1558.

Schoenbaum, G., Stalnaker, T. A., and Shaham, Y. (2007). A role for BDNF in cocaine reward and relapse. *Nat. Neurosci.* 10, 935–936.

Schratt, G. M., Tuebing, F., Nigh, E. A., Kane, C. G., Sabatini, M. E., Kiebler, M., et al. (2006). A brain-specific microRNA regulates dendritic spine development. *Nature* 439, 283–289.

Shibata, M., Kurokawa, D., Nakao, H., Ohmura, T., and Aizawa, S. (2008). MicroRNA-9 modulates Cajal-Retzius cell differentiation by suppressing Foxg1 expression in mouse medial pallium. *J. Neurosci.* 28, 10415–10421.

Shibata, M., Nakao, H., Kiyonari, H., Abe, T., and Aizawa, S. (2011). MicroRNA-9 regulates neurogenesis in mouse telencephalon by targeting multiple transcription factors. *J. Neurosci.* 31, 3407–3422.

Tsang, J., Zhu, J., and Van Oudenaarden, A. (2007). MicroRNA-mediated feedback and feedforward loops are recurrent network motifs in mammals. *Mol. Cell* 26, 753–767.

Turrini, E., Haenisch, S., Laechelt, S., Diewock, T., Bruhn, O., and Cascorbi, I. (2012). MicroRNA profiling in K-562 cells under imatinib treatment: influence of miR-212 and miR-328 on ABCG2 expression. *Pharmacogenet. Genomics* 22, 198–205.

Ucar, A., Gupta, S. K., Fiedler, J., Erikci, E., Kardasinski, M., Batkai, S., et al. (2012). The miRNA-212/132 family regulates both cardiac hypertrophy and cardiomyocyte autophagy. *Nat. Commun.* 3, 1078.

Ucar, A., Vafaizadeh, V., Jarry, H., Fiedler, J., Klemmt, P. A., Thum, T., et al. (2010). miR-212 and miR-132 are required for epithelial stromal interactions necessary for mouse mammary gland development. *Nat. Genet.* 42, 1101–1108.

Vasudevan, S., Tong, Y., and Steitz, J. A. (2007). Switching from repression to activation: microRNAs can up-regulate translation. *Science* 318, 1931–1934.

Vo, N., Klein, M. E., Varlamova, O., Keller, D. M., Yamamoto, T., Goodman, R. H., et al. (2005). A cAMP-response element binding protein-induced microRNA regulates neuronal morphogenesis. *Proc. Natl. Acad. Sci. U.S.A.* 102, 16426–16431.

Wada, R., Akiyama, Y., Hashimoto, Y., Fukamachi, H., and Yuasa, Y. (2010). miR-212 is downregulated and suppresses methyl-CpG-binding protein MeCP2 in human gastric cancer. *Int. J. Cancer* 127, 1106–1114.

Wayman, G. A., Davare, M., Ando, H., Fortin, D., Varlamova, O., Cheng, H. Y., et al. (2008). An activity-regulated microRNA controls dendritic plasticity by down-regulating p250GAP. *Proc. Natl. Acad. Sci. U.S.A.* 105, 9093–9098.

Wolf, M. E. (2010). The Bermuda Triangle of cocaine-induced neuroadaptations. *Trends Neurosci.* 33, 391–398.

Yang, J. H., Shao, P., Zhou, H., Chen, Y. Q., and Qu, L. H. (2010). deepBase: a database for deeply annotating and mining deep sequencing data. *Nucleic Acids Res.* 38, D123–D130.

Zovoilis, A., Agbemenyah, H. Y., Agis-Balboa, R. C., Stilling, R. M., Edbauer, D., Rao, P., et al. (2011). microRNA-34c is a novel target to treat dementias. *EMBO J.* 30, 4299–4308.

Conflict of Interest Statement: The authors declare that the research was conducted in the absence of any commercial or financial relationships that could be construed as a potential conflict of interest.

12

Behavioral, biochemical, and molecular indices of stress are enhanced in female versus male rats experiencing nicotine withdrawal

Oscar V. Torres[1], Luciana G. Gentil[2], Luis A. Natividad[1], Luis M. Carcoba[1] and Laura E. O'Dell[1]*

[1] Department of Psychology, The University of Texas at El Paso, El Paso, TX, USA
[2] Department of Biological Sciences, The University of Texas at El Paso, El Paso, TX, USA

Edited by:
Nicholas W. Gilpin, LSUHSC-New Orleans, USA

Reviewed by:
A. D. Lê, Centre for Addiction and Mental Health, Canada
Cynthia Kuhn, Duke University Medical Center, USA

*Correspondence:
Laura E. O'Dell, Department of Psychology, The University of Texas at El Paso, 500 West University Avenue, El Paso, TX 79968, USA.
e-mail: lodell@utep.edu

Stress is a major factor that promotes tobacco use and relapse during withdrawal. Although women are more vulnerable to tobacco use than men, the manner in which stress contributes to tobacco use in women versus men is unclear. Thus, the goal of this study was to compare behavioral and biological indices of stress in male and female rats during nicotine withdrawal. Since the effects of nicotine withdrawal are age-dependent, this study also included adolescent rats. An initial study was conducted to provide comparable nicotine doses across age and sex during nicotine exposure and withdrawal. Rats received sham surgery or an osmotic pump that delivered nicotine. After 14 days of nicotine, the pumps were removed and controls received a sham surgery. Twenty-four hours later, anxiety-like behavior and plasma corticosterone were assessed. The nucleus accumbens (NAcc), amygdala, and hypothalamus were examined for changes in corticotropin-releasing factor (CRF) gene expression. In order to differentiate the effects of nicotine withdrawal from exposure to nicotine, a cohort of rats did not have their pumps removed. The major finding is that during nicotine withdrawal, adult females display higher levels of anxiety-like behavior, plasma corticosterone, and CRF mRNA expression in the NAcc relative to adult males. However, during nicotine exposure, adult males exhibited higher levels of corticosterone and CRF mRNA in the amygdala relative to females. Adolescents displayed less nicotine withdrawal than adults. Moreover, adolescent males displayed an increase in anxiety-like behavior and an up-regulation of CRF mRNA in the amygdala during nicotine exposure and withdrawal. These findings are likely related to stress produced by the high doses of nicotine that were administered to adolescents to produce equivalent levels of cotinine as adults. In conclusion, these findings suggest that intense stress produced by nicotine withdrawal may contribute to tobacco use in women.

Keywords: sex difference, adolescent, adolescence, CRF, nucleus accumbens, tobacco

INTRODUCTION

Epidemiological reports have indicated that women are more susceptible to tobacco use as compared to men (Perkins, 2009; Lombardi et al., 2011; Rahmanian et al., 2011). For example, women consume more tobacco products relative to men (Hammond, 2009; Oh et al., 2010). Women also exhibit higher relapse rates and are less likely to benefit from nicotine replacement therapy (NRT) than men (Perkins, 2001; Cepeda-Benito et al., 2004; Schnoll et al., 2007; Perkins and Scott, 2008; Piper et al., 2010). During abstinence from tobacco, women also report more intense symptoms of withdrawal than men (Heishman et al., 2010; Nakajima and al'Absi, 2012; Perkins et al., 2013). There is also evidence to suggest that the enhanced susceptibility to tobacco use in women begins at a young age. For example, a recent survey revealed that the daily consumption of tobacco is higher in adolescent females than males [Centers for Disease Control and Prevention (CDC), 2012]. During abstinence from tobacco, adolescent females also report higher levels of stress and relapse rates as compared to adolescent males (Anderson and Burns, 2000; Colby et al., 2000; Dickmann

et al., 2009). Regardless of age, females are at a higher risk of developing tobacco-related diseases than males (Langhammer et al., 2000, 2003; Kiyohara and Ohno, 2010). Despite the magnitude of this problem, there is a critical knowledge gap regarding the factors that contribute to enhanced vulnerability to tobacco use among women.

Stress has emerged as a major factor that contributes to tobacco use in women. For example, women report more often than men that the anxiety-reducing effects of cigarettes are the main reason for smoking (Perkins and Scott, 2008; Piper et al., 2010; Perkins et al., 2012). Although tobacco is used to cope with anxiety, long-term tobacco use is also motivated by avoiding negative affective states, such as stress, that emerge during withdrawal (Aronson et al., 2008; Hughes and Callas, 2010; Parrott and Murphy, 2012; Perkins et al., 2012). Accordingly, women also report higher levels of stress during abstinence from tobacco than men (Schnoll et al., 2007; Perkins and Scott, 2008; Xu et al., 2008; Perkins et al., 2012; Saladin et al., 2012). In addition, women display higher levels of cortisol (a biological marker of stress in humans) during tobacco abstinence as compared to men (Hogle and Curtin, 2006). These studies suggest that stress is an important factor that contributes to tobacco use in women.

Pre-clinical evidence has established that the motivational properties of tobacco are due, in large part, to the presence of nicotine. A study comparing sex differences during withdrawal from nicotine demonstrated that female adult rats display more physical signs of nicotine withdrawal relative to males (Hamilton et al., 2009). Also, female adult mice display more anxiety-like behavior on the elevated plus maze during nicotine withdrawal as compared to males (Caldarone et al., 2008). Taken together, there is evidence at the clinical and pre-clinical levels to suggest that females experience higher levels of stress during nicotine withdrawal. However, there are several remaining questions with regard to the underlying neurobiology that modulates the contribution of stress to tobacco use in females.

The main neuroendocrine substrate of the stress response is the hypothalamic-pituitary-adrenal (HPA) axis (see Smith and Vale, 2006; Gallagher et al., 2008). When a stressor is experienced, corticotropin-releasing factor (CRF) is secreted from the hypothalamus that then stimulates adrenocorticotropic hormone (ACTH) release from the pituitary gland. ACTH then simulates the release of corticosterone and other glucocorticoids from the adrenal cortex. Corticosterone serves as a major negative feedback that terminates HPA axis activity. Within the hypothalamus, corticosterone binds to nuclear glucocorticoid receptor II subunits causing an inhibition of CRF mRNA synthesis. Studies comparing biological indices of stress produced by nicotine withdrawal have demonstrated that plasma levels of corticosterone and ACTH are increased in rats experiencing withdrawal from this drug (Rhodes et al., 2004; Semba et al., 2004; Lutfy et al., 2006). With regard to sex differences, female adult rats display elevated plasma levels of corticosterone and ACTH during nicotine withdrawal relative to males (Gentile et al., 2011; Skwara et al., 2012).

Recent theories of drug abuse have suggested that CRF plays a central role in the development of negative affective states that emerge during withdrawal (Koob and Volkow, 2010). Changes in CRF systems are hypothesized to occur within brain structures of the extended amygdala, including the central nucleus of the amygdala, and the nucleus accumbens (NAcc) (Koob, 2010; Bruijnzeel, 2012). Pre-clinical work with nicotine has supported this hypothesis, as CRF-like immunoreactivity is increased in the amygdala during nicotine withdrawal (George et al., 2007). Consistent with this, CRF mRNA levels are over-expressed in the central nucleus of the amygdala during nicotine withdrawal (Aydin et al., 2011). Also, administration of non-specific CRF-R1/R2 receptor antagonists into the amygdala or NAcc have been shown to reverse the deficits in brain reward function produced by nicotine withdrawal (Marcinkiewcz et al., 2009; Bruijnzeel et al., 2012). Collectively, these studies suggest that CRF systems within the NAcc and amygdala play an important role in mediating nicotine withdrawal. To our knowledge; however, no one has examined whether the influence of CRF systems on nicotine withdrawal is sex-dependent.

Thus, the goal of this study was to compare various biological and behavioral indices of stress during nicotine withdrawal in female and male rats. Anxiety-like behavior was examined on the elevated plus maze and open-field tests. Plasma corticosterone levels, and changes in CRF gene expression in the amygdala and NAcc were also explored. CRF gene expression was also examined in the hypothalamus given the primary role of this structure in initiating stress responses. A sub-goal of this study was to examine whether sex differences in adult rats occur during the adolescent period of development. Thus, the biological and behavioral indices of stress produced nicotine withdrawal were also compared in *adolescent* male and female rats. In order to differentiate the effects of withdrawal from those produced by nicotine exposure, a separate cohort of rats from both age and sex groups did not experience withdrawal and were assessed with nicotine circulating in their system. Another important factor to consider when comparing the effects of nicotine across age and sex is differences in metabolism of this drug. Given this potential confound, an initial study was conducted to determine equivalent plasma levels of nicotine in female and male rats of both ages.

MATERIALS AND METHODS
ANIMALS
Male and female adult ($n = 92$) and adolescent ($n = 98$) Wistar rats were used. Rats were bred in the Psychology Department from a stock of out bred Wistar rats from Harlan, Inc. (Indianapolis, IN, USA). All rats were housed in groups of two to three per cage in a humidity- and temperature-controlled (20–22°C) vivarium using a 12-/12-hour light/dark cycle with lights off at 8:00 a.m. The home cages consisted of a rectangular Plexiglas® hanging cage (41.5 cm long × 17 cm wide × 21 cm high) with pine bedding. Rats had *ad libitum* access to standard rodent chow and water at all times except during testing. Adults were postnatal day (PND) 60 and adolescents were PND 28 at the start of the experiment. All rats were handled for approximately 5 min/day for 3 days prior to the start of experimentation. All procedures were approved by the UTEP Animal Care and Use Committee and followed the guidelines of the National Institutes of Health Guide for the Care and Use of Laboratory Animals.

NICOTINE EXPOSURE AND WITHDRAWAL
Rats were anesthetized with an isoflurane/oxygen mixture (1–3% isoflurane) and received a sham surgery or were surgically prepared with subcutaneous pumps that delivered nicotine continuously for 14 days. After 14 days of nicotine exposure, the pumps were surgically removed and control rats received another sham surgery. After pump removal, rats were returned to their home cages. Twenty-four hours later, rats were tested for various behavioral and biological measures of anxiety.

STUDY 1: ASSESSING NICOTINE METABOLISM ACROSS EXPERIMENTAL CONDITIONS
Nicotine metabolism was assessed indirectly by comparing cotinine levels in plasma from adolescent and adult male and female rats during exposure and withdrawal from nicotine. Adult rats received pumps that were appropriately sized for larger animals (4.5 mm in length; Alzet model 2ml2), whereas adolescents received either one or two pumps that were approximately half as small (2.5 mm in length; Alzet model 2002). Different doses

of nicotine were delivered for 14 days, as described below. Plasma samples were collected from tail blood on days 7, 10, and 14 of nicotine exposure. After 14 days of nicotine exposure, the pumps were surgically removed and plasma samples were collected 6, 12, and 24 h later.

Separate groups of rats were used to determine equivalent doses in adolescent and adult male and female rats. One group of male and female adults was prepared with pumps (model 2ml2) that delivered a nicotine dose of 3.2 mg/kg/day (expressed as base form) that produces robust physical and affective signs of withdrawal in adult rats (O'Dell et al., 2004). Given the fast growth rates and drug metabolism during adolescence, three groups of adolescent rats received pumps with different nicotine doses and experimental procedures. First, a group of male and female adolescents was prepared with one small pump (model 2002) that delivered 4.7 mg/kg/day of nicotine for 14 days. This dose was selected from previous work showing that adolescents implanted with a large pump (model 2ml2) require 1.5-fold higher doses of nicotine to produce equivalent levels in adult rats (O'Dell et al., 2006). Second, a group of male and female adolescents was prepared with one small osmotic pump containing 4.7 mg/kg/day of nicotine. Seven days later, the pump was replaced with a new pump that was re-adjusted for the rats' rapid weight gain. Last, a third group of male and female adolescents was prepared with two small pumps that each delivered 4.7 mg/kg/day each of nicotine for 14 days. This group received a total of 9.4 mg/kg/day of nicotine. Plasma cotinine levels were analyzed using commercially available 96-well plate ELISA kits (OraSure Technologies, Inc., Bethlehem, PA, USA). Standard curves were used to estimate plasma cotinine levels using a Spectra Maxplus spectrophotometer (Molecular Devices Inc., Sunnyvale, CA, USA).

STUDY 2: ASSESSING BEHAVIORAL AND BIOLOGICAL INDICES OF STRESS DURING NICOTINE EXPOSURE AND WITHDRAWAL

Adolescent and adult male and female rats received a sham surgery or were implanted with nicotine pumps (Alzet model 2ml2 for adults and two Alzet models 2002 for adolescents). Adult rats received a nicotine dose of 3.2 mg/kg/day (expressed as base form) for 14 days and adolescent rats received a total nicotine dose of 9.4 mg/kg/day (expressed as base form) for 14 days. To minimize stress produced by repeated tail vein blood sampling from study 1, separate groups of rats were used in this study.

After 14 days of nicotine exposure, the pumps were removed to induce spontaneous withdrawal. Twenty-four hours after pump removal, behavioral tests were conducted to compare physical signs of withdrawal and anxiety-like behavior, using the elevated plus maze and open-field tests. After behavioral testing, the brains were removed and analyzed for CRF mRNA levels using qRT-PCR. Blood samples were also collected and analyzed for corticosterone levels. To examine anxiety-like behavior and biological markers of stress during nicotine exposure, separate cohorts of rats did not have their pumps removed and were tested with nicotine circulating in their system on the 14th day of nicotine exposure. At the time of testing, adult rats were PND 75 and adolescent rats were PND 43.

Rats were tested for anxiety-like behavior using the elevated plus maze procedure. The animals were first acclimated to the testing room in a rectangular Plexiglas® cage for 20 min. After 20 min, the rats were placed onto the elevated plus maze, which was in the middle of the testing room beneath a red light. The plus maze apparatus consisted of four arms (10 cm × 50 cm) that were elevated to a height of 50 cm above the ground. The closed arms had 40 cm high walls around them, and the open arms did not have walls that enclosed the open platforms. At the beginning of the test, the rats were placed into the maze facing the open arm and time spent in each arm was recorded for 5 min. The maze was thoroughly cleaned with 70% ethanol and then water between each individual test. Rats that fell off the maze were excluded from the study.

After elevated plus maze testing, the rats were returned to the isolation cage for 10 min. The open-field apparatus consisted of a clear Plexiglas® box (60 cm × 60 cm × 15 cm) that was positioned in the middle of an adjacent room beneath a red light. The walls of the maze were clear and the floor was divided into 25 equal squares (12 cm × 12 cm; 16 peripheral and 9 center squares). At the start of the test, rats were placed in the center of the open field, and time spent in the center versus corner areas was recorded for 5 min.

After the open-field test, the rats were returned to the isolation cage for somatic signs of withdrawal testing. Ten minutes later, the rats were moved to another testing room and placed in a clear Plexiglas® cylindrical container (30 cm × 29 cm) cage for 10 min. Rats were then monitored for physical signs of nicotine withdrawal for 10 min. The observed signs include blinks, writhes, body shakes, teeth chatters, gasps, and ptosis. If present, ptosis was counted only once. The total number of somatic signs was defined as the sum of individual occurrences of the aforementioned signs during the entire observation period. The duration of the entire test battery was approximately 70 min.

After behavioral testing, rats were sacrificed by rapid decapitation to ensure preservation of the neurochemical environment and minimize degradation during tissue dissection. The amygdala, hypothalamus, and NAcc from both hemispheres were collected and flash frozen at −80°C within an estimated time of 30 s from sacrifice. Total RNA was isolated from neuronal tissue samples using the All Prep DNA/RNA Mini kit (QIAGEN, Inc.) for small tissue sections. After isolation, RNA was quantified using a UV/V spectrophotometer (Beckman Coulter Inc.). The target ratio of 1.8–2.0 for A260/280 was used as an inclusion criterion for all RNA samples. The quality of the RNA was then visualized by MOPS 1% agarose gel (37% formaldehyde) using the Thermo Scientific easy cast electrophoresis system. The gels were verified for characteristic 18S and 28S ribosomal RNA bands using ethidium bromide and the Bio-Rad ChemiDoc XRS+ imaging system. Samples that had insufficient amounts of RNA were excluded from further analyses. One microgram of total RNA was then digested with DNaseI, Amp Grade (Invitrogen) prior to cDNA synthesis in order to remove any DNA contamination. The RNA was then reverse transcribed into cDNA with the Advantage® RT-for-PCR kit (Clontech) using Oligo(dT) primers, following the manufacturer's instructions. Once the cDNA was synthesized, the cDNA samples were diluted 1:10 in nuclease-free water, separated into aliquots and stored at −20°C. Specific primers for CRF and reference gene ribosomal protein L13A (RPL13A) were obtained from

Table 1 | Primer sequences.

Symbol	Forward primer	Reverse primer
CRF	5′ ATGCTGCTGGTGGCTCTGT 3′	5′ GGATCAGAATCGGCTGAGGT 3′
RPL13A	5′ GGATCCCTCCACCCTATGACA 3′	5′ CTGGTACTTCCACCCGACCTC 3′
GAPDH	5′ CAACTCCCTCAAGATTGTCAGCAA 3′	5′ GGCATGGACTGTGGTCATGA 3′
Pol2a	5′ CGTATCCGCATCATGAACAGTGA 3′	5′ TCATCCATCTTATCCACCACCTCTT 3′
Actb	5′ CTATGAGCTGCCTGACGGTC 3′	5′ AGTTTCATGGATGCCACAGG 3′

Integrated DNA Technologies, Inc., with amplicons between 71 and 142 base-pairs (see **Table 1**).

The rationale for using RPL13A as a reference gene is based upon an initial study examining tissue from a group of adult rats ($n = 27$) that was conducted before quantifying CRF gene expression across experimental groups. Four commonly used reference genes were tested as potential candidates for the normalizing gene, including: actin (Actb), glyceraldehyde-3-phosphate dehydrogenase (GAPDH), RNA polymerase II (Pol2a), and RPL13A. The findings revealed that the expression of RPL13A was the most stable and similar across male and female control and nicotine-treated rats. Based on our results, we believe that expression profiling of normalizing genes is important when employing qRT-PCR techniques involving male and female rats.

Commercially available SYBR® Fast qPCR fluorescent labeling kits (Kapa Biosystems, Inc.) were used to perform qRT-PCR using the Mastercycler ep Realplex2 System (Eppendorf, Inc.). All samples were analyzed in triplicates and amplified by the following protocol: initial denaturing at 95°C for 5 min, continued denaturing at 95°C for 15 s; annealing at 59°C for 15 s; extension at 68°C for 20 s, for a total of 40 cycles. CRF mRNA expression was normalized by RPl-13A mRNA expression using the comparative C_T method adopted from Schmittgen and Livak (2008). The amplification specificity for each primer was tested for a single-product, as shown by a single band via TAE 1% gel electrophoresis and visualized on the Bio-Rad ChemiDoc XRS+ system.

Corticosterone levels were assessed in blood samples that were collected from trunk blood during sacrifice. The samples were centrifuged for 15 min at $5,000 \times g$ at 4°C. The resultant plasma was then stored at −80°C until analyzed. Corticosterone levels were estimated using a 96-well plate ELISA kit (Assaypro Inc.) using a Spectra Maxplus spectrophotometer (Molecular Devices Inc.).

STATISTICAL APPROACH

For study 1, cotinine values during nicotine exposure were analyzed using a three-factor mixed model ANOVA with sex (male and female), and age (adult and adolescent) as between subject factors, and day of sampling (7, 10, and 14 days) as a repeated measures factor. Similarly, cotinine values during nicotine withdrawal were analyzed using a three-factor mixed model ANOVA with sex (male and female), and age (adult and adolescent) as between subject factors, and time of sampling (6, 12, and 24 h) as a repeated measures factor. For study 2, each measure was analyzed separately using three-factor ANOVAs with sex (male and female), age (adult and adolescent), and treatment (control, nicotine exposure, and nicotine withdrawal) as between subject

factors. In cases where three-way interaction effects were significant, individual group comparisons were reported. However, in cases where three-way interactions were not significant, two-way interactions were reported. All *post hoc* tests were conducted using Fisher's LSD tests where appropriate ($P < 0.05$). Given that the results revealed interaction effects, main effects were not reported. Thus, interaction effects were reported with *post hoc* tests, and main effects were not included given the interaction effects provide more information about group differences, which was the goal of the paper.

RESULTS

Figure 1 illustrates cotinine levels across adolescent and adult male and female rats during nicotine exposure and withdrawal. Regarding sex differences, the results revealed that there were no sex differences in cotinine levels during nicotine exposure [$F(1, 79) = 0.96$, $P > 0.05$] and withdrawal [$F(1, 84) = 0.19$, $P > 0.05$] regardless of the age of the animals. This suggests that sex differences can be appropriately compared across all of the nicotine pump conditions. Regarding age differences during nicotine exposure, adults displayed higher cotinine levels than adolescents prepared with one small pump and adolescents re-implanted with one small pump that was adjusted for weight gain (main effect of treatment) [$F(3, 79) = 8.96$, $P < 0.05$]. However, adult cotinine levels were similar to that of adolescents prepared with two small pumps that each delivered 4.7 mg/kg/day of nicotine for 14 days. A similar pattern was observed during nicotine withdrawal, such that similar levels of cotinine were observed in adults and adolescents that were implanted with two small pumps that each delivered a nicotine dose of 4.7 mg/kg/day. These data suggest that adolescents require two osmotic pumps delivering a total nicotine volume of 9.4 mg/kg/day to produce similar cotinine levels as adults with one pump that delivers 3.2 mg/kg/day.

Table 2 denotes total somatic signs of withdrawal (mean ± SEM) during nicotine exposure and withdrawal in adult and adolescent male and female rats. Somatic signs were analyzed using the total amount of signs elicited during the entire observation period. A three-way analysis of withdrawal signs revealed that there were no interaction effects between sex, age, and treatment [$F(2, 92) = 0.84$, $P > 0.05$]. However, a two-way analysis of withdrawal signs revealed a significant interaction between age and treatment [$F(2, 92) = 12.08$, $P < 0.05$]. Subsequent *post hoc* analyses revealed that adult rats that were tested during nicotine withdrawal displayed an increase in signs of withdrawal compared to their respective controls ($*P < 0.05$). There were no differences in the magnitude of withdrawal signs across male and female adolescent rats.

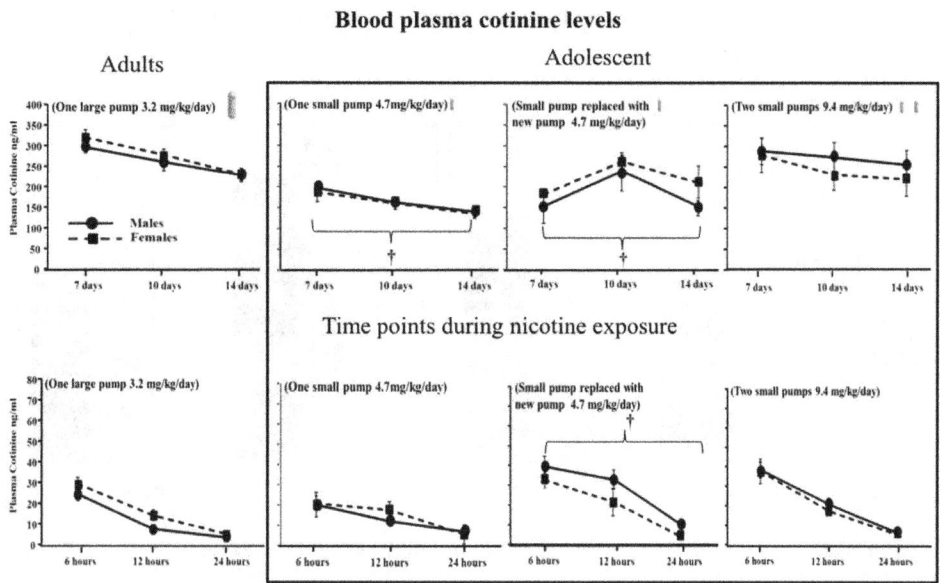

Blood plasma cotinine levels

Time points during nicotine exposure

Time points during nicotine withdrawal

FIGURE 1 | Blood plasma cotinine levels (ng/ml ± SEM) 7, 10, and 14 days during nicotine exposure (top row) and then 6, 12, and 24 h after pump removal (bottom row) in adult and adolescent male and female rats. Adult rats (n = 26) received a large pump (model 2ml2) that delivered nicotine 3.2 mg/kg for 14 days. Three separate groups of adolescent rats received a smaller model of pump (model 2002) that delivered: (1) a dose of 4.7 mg/kg/day for 14 days (n = 17), (2) a dose of 4.7 mg/kg/day that was replaced after 7 days with a new pump that also delivered 4.7 mg/kg/day (n = 17), and (3) a dose of 9.4 mg/kg/day that was divided in two small pumps (n = 32). The dagger (†) denotes a significant difference across all time points between nicotine-treated adolescents and adults (P < 0.05).

Figure 2 illustrates anxiety-like behavior as assessed by the elevated plus maze during nicotine exposure and withdrawal. Anxiety-like behavior was operationally defined as an increase in time spent in the closed arm as compared to controls. A three-way analysis of percent time spent in the closed arm revealed a significant interaction between sex, age, and treatment [$F(2, 96) = 8.85$, $P < 0.05$]. Subsequent *post hoc* analyses revealed that adult females that were tested during nicotine exposure displayed an increase in anxiety-like behavior relative to controls (*$P < 0.05$). However, adult females tested during nicotine withdrawal displayed an increase in anxiety-like behavior that was significantly higher than their respective controls (*$P < 0.05$), male counterparts (†$P < 0.05$), and adolescent counterparts (#$P < 0.05$). In adolescents, the males displayed the largest effects of nicotine exposure and withdrawal on anxiety-like behavior as compared to respective controls (*$P < 0.05$), female counterparts (†$P < 0.05$), and adolescent counterparts (#$P < 0.05$).

Figure 3 illustrates anxiety-like behavior as assessed by the open-field test during nicotine exposure and withdrawal. Anxiety-like behavior was operationally defined as an increase in time spent in the corners of the open field as compared to controls. A three-way analysis of percent corner time revealed a significant interaction between sex, age, and treatment [$F(2, 92) = 3.85$, $P < 0.05$]. Subsequent *post hoc* analyses revealed that adult females tested during nicotine exposure displayed an increase in anxiety-like behavior relative to controls (*$P < 0.05$). However, adult females tested during nicotine withdrawal displayed an increase in anxiety-like behavior that was higher than respective controls (*$P < 0.05$)

Table 2 | Physical signs of withdrawal.

Experimental group	Adult male	Adult female	Adolescent male	Adolescent female
Controls	7.6 ± 0.8	7.8 ± 0.9	5 ± 0.7	3.8 ± 0.3
Nicotine exposure	5.2 ± 0.4	4.3 ± 0.3	3.2 ± 0.3	4.3 ± 0.5
Nicotine withdrawal	*15.5 ± 1.8	*11.5 ± 1.4	3.8 ± 0.3	3.2 ± 0.6

The asterisks (*) denote a significant difference from respective controls (P < 0.05).

and their male counterparts (†$P < 0.05$). In adolescents, males tested during nicotine withdrawal displayed an increase in anxiety-like behavior relative to controls (*$P < 0.05$). Adolescent female controls displayed an increase in anxiety-like behavior relative to males (†$P < 0.05$) and their adult counterparts (#$P < 0.05$).

Figure 4 illustrates plasma corticosterone levels during nicotine exposure and withdrawal. A three-way analysis of corticosterone levels revealed a significant interaction between sex, age, and treatment [$F(2, 66) = 3.2$, $P < 0.05$]. Subsequent *post hoc* analyses revealed that adult males tested during nicotine exposure displayed an increase in corticosterone levels relative to controls (*$P < 0.05$). Adult females tested during nicotine withdrawal displayed an increase in corticosterone levels relative to controls (*$P < 0.05$), male counterparts (†$P < 0.05$), and adolescent counterparts (#$P < 0.05$). In adolescents, the male controls and males tested during nicotine withdrawal displayed an

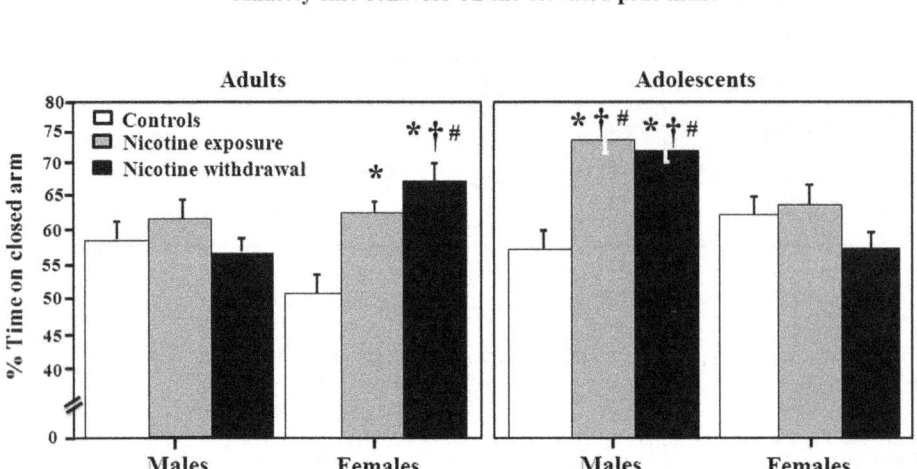

FIGURE 2 | Percent time spent in the closed arm of the elevated plus maze during nicotine exposure and withdrawal in adult male (control $n = 13$; nicotine exposure $n = 15$; nicotine withdrawal $n = 9$), adult female (control $n = 10$; nicotine exposure $n = 16$; nicotine withdrawal $n = 13$), adolescent male (control $n = 6$; nicotine exposure $n = 5$; nicotine withdrawal $n = 5$), and adolescent female (control $n = 6$; nicotine exposure $n = 5$; nicotine withdrawal $n = 5$) **rats**. The asterisks (*) denote a significant difference between nicotine-treated rats and their respective controls, the daggers (†) denote a significant difference between males and females, and the number signs (#) denote a significant difference between adults and adolescents ($P < 0.05$).

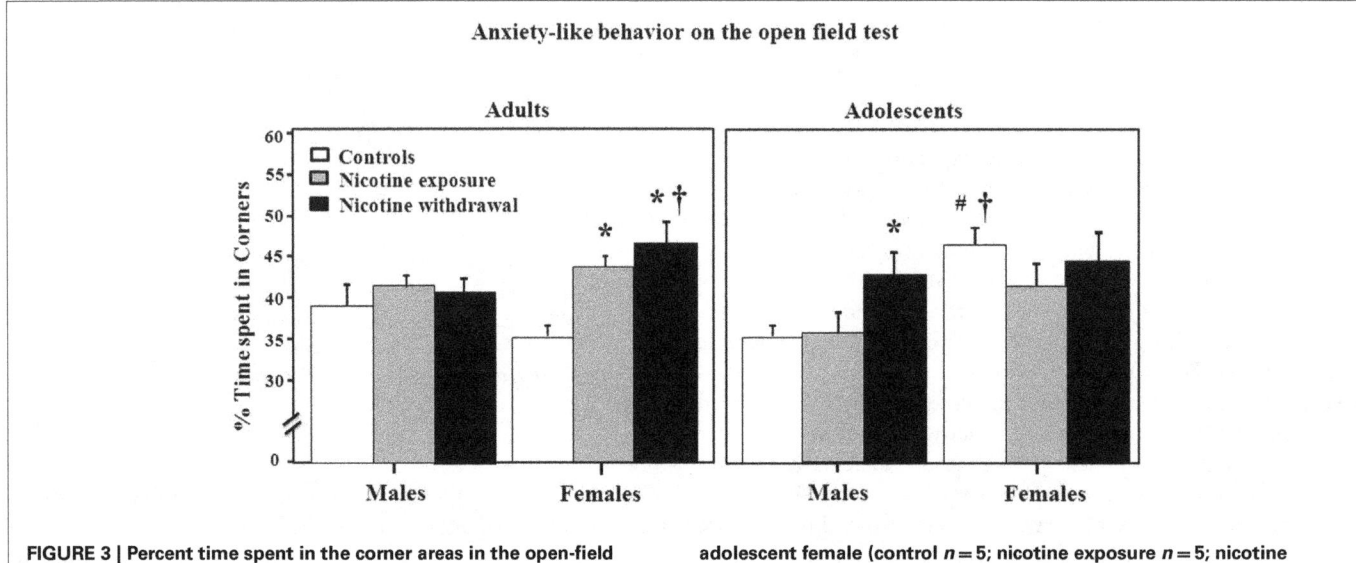

FIGURE 3 | Percent time spent in the corner areas in the open-field testing during nicotine exposure and withdrawal in adult male (control $n = 9$; nicotine exposure $n = 15$; nicotine withdrawal $n = 10$), adult female (control $n = 10$; nicotine exposure $n = 16$; nicotine withdrawal $n = 13$), adolescent male (control $n = 6$; nicotine exposure $n = 5$; nicotine withdrawal $n = 5$), and adolescent female (control $n = 5$; nicotine exposure $n = 5$; nicotine withdrawal $n = 5$) **rats**. The asterisks (*) denote a significant difference between nicotine-treated rats and their respective controls, the daggers (†) denote a significant difference between males and females, and the number sign (#) denotes a significant difference between adults and adolescents ($P < 0.05$).

increase in corticosterone levels relative to their adult counterparts (#$P < 0.05$).

Figure 5 illustrates CRF gene expression in the NAcc during nicotine exposure and withdrawal. A three-way analysis of CRF gene expression revealed a significant interaction between sex, age, and treatment in this brain region [$F(2, 42) = 4.34, P < 0.05$]. Subsequent *post hoc* analyses revealed that adult females tested during nicotine withdrawal displayed an increase in CRF gene expression relative to controls (*$P < 0.05$), male counterparts (†$P < 0.05$), and adolescent counterparts (#$P < 0.05$). In adolescents, females tested during nicotine withdrawal displayed a decrease in CRF gene expression relative to controls (*$P < 0.05$).

Figure 6 illustrates CRF gene expression in the amygdala during nicotine exposure and withdrawal. A three-way analysis

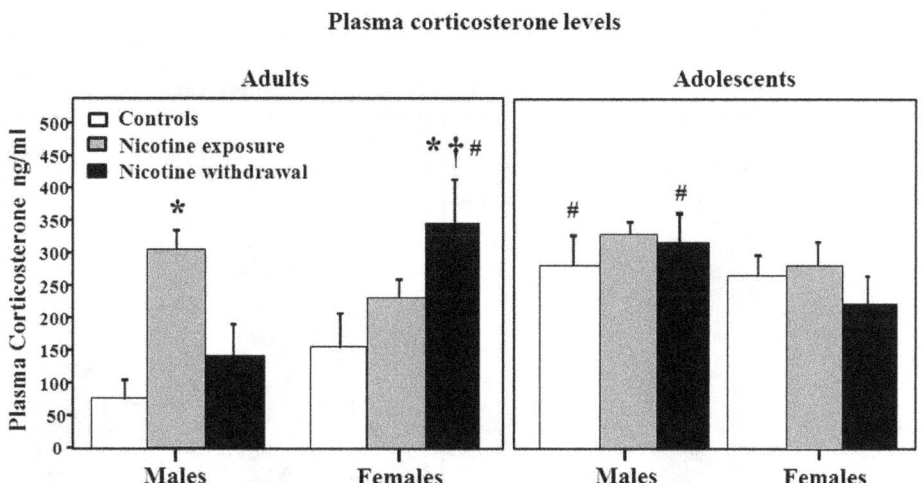

FIGURE 4 | Plasma corticosterone levels during nicotine exposure and withdrawal in adult male (control *n* = 7; nicotine exposure *n* = 9; nicotine withdrawal *n* = 6), adult female (control *n* = 8; nicotine exposure *n* = 8; nicotine withdrawal *n* = 8), adolescent male (control *n* = 6; nicotine exposure *n* = 5; nicotine withdrawal *n* = 5), and adolescent female (control *n* = 6; nicotine exposure *n* = 5; nicotine withdrawal *n* = 5) rats. The asterisks (*) denote a significant difference between nicotine-treated male and female adult rats and their respective controls, the dagger (†) denotes a significant difference between males and females, and the number signs (#) denote a significant difference between adolescents and adults (*P* < 0.05).

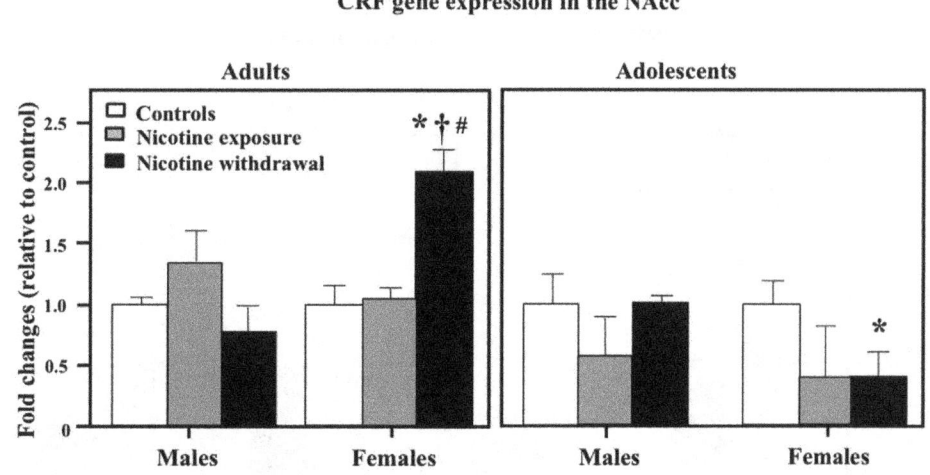

FIGURE 5 | CRF gene expression in the NAcc during nicotine exposure and withdrawal in adult male (control *n* = 4; nicotine exposure *n* = 4; nicotine withdrawal *n* = 4), adult female (control *n* = 4; nicotine exposure *n* = 4; nicotine withdrawal *n* = 4), adolescent male (control *n* = 6; nicotine exposure *n* = 5; nicotine withdrawal *n* = 5), and adolescent female (control *n* = 5; nicotine exposure *n* = 4; nicotine withdrawal *n* = 5) rats. The asterisks (*) denote a significant difference between nicotine-treated rats and their respective female controls, the dagger (†) denotes a significant difference between male and female rats, and the number sign (#) denotes a significant difference between adolescent and adult rats (*P* < 0.05).

of CRF gene expression revealed that there were no interaction effects between sex, age, and treatment in this brain region [$F(2, 52) = 0.21$, $P > 0.05$]. However, a two-way analysis of CRF gene expression in the amygdala revealed a significant interaction between sex and treatment [$F(2, 52) = 3.72$, $P < 0.05$]. Subsequent *post hoc* analyses revealed that adult and adolescent male rats tested during nicotine exposure displayed a significant increase in CRF gene expression as compared to controls (*$P < 0.05$) and female counterparts (†$P < 0.05$). In addition, adolescent males tested during nicotine withdrawal

displayed an increase in CRF gene expression relative to controls (*$P < 0.05$).

Figure 7 illustrates CRF gene expression in the hypothalamus during nicotine exposure and withdrawal. A three-way analysis of CRF gene expression revealed that there were no interaction effects between sex, age, and treatment in this brain region [$F(2, 68) = 0.02$, $P > 0.05$]. Also, a two-way analysis of CRF gene expression revealed that there were no interaction effects between sex and treatment [$F(2, 68) = 1.27$, $P > 0.05$] or age and treatment [$F(2, 68) = 0.41$, $P > 0.05$].

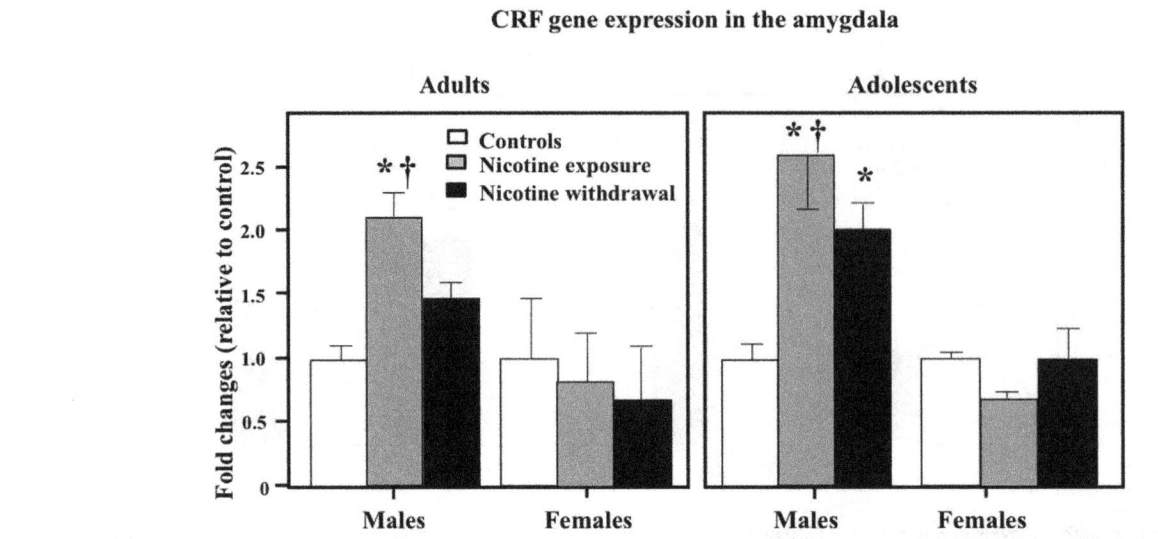

FIGURE 6 | CRF gene expression in the amygdala during nicotine exposure and withdrawal in adult male (control *n* = 10; nicotine exposure *n* = 5; nicotine withdrawal *n* = 5), adult female (control *n* = 7; nicotine exposure *n* = 7; nicotine withdrawal *n* = 4), adolescent male (control *n* = 4; nicotine exposure *n* = 6; nicotine withdrawal *n* = 4), and adolescent female (control *n* = 4; nicotine exposure *n* = 4; nicotine withdrawal *n* = 4) rats. The asterisks (*) denote a significant difference between nicotine-treated rats and their respective male controls ($P < 0.05$).

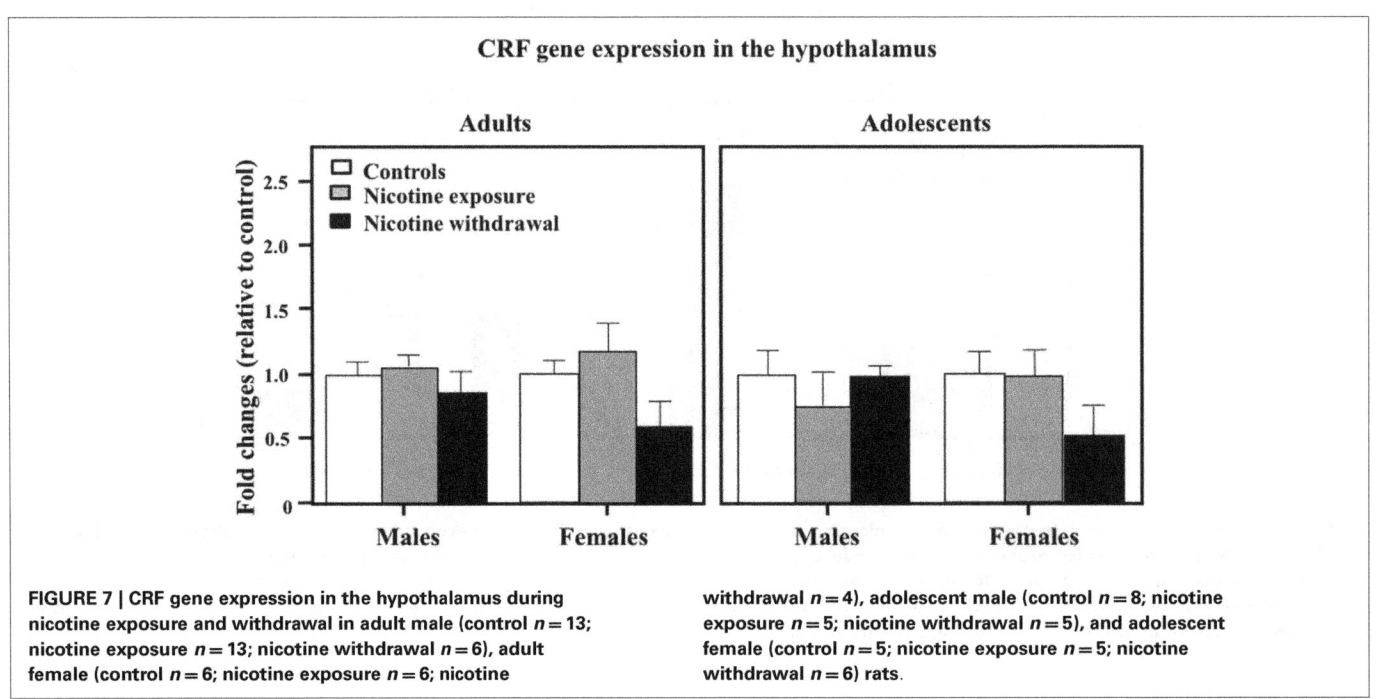

FIGURE 7 | CRF gene expression in the hypothalamus during nicotine exposure and withdrawal in adult male (control *n* = 13; nicotine exposure *n* = 13; nicotine withdrawal *n* = 6), adult female (control *n* = 6; nicotine exposure *n* = 6; nicotine withdrawal *n* = 4), adolescent male (control *n* = 8; nicotine exposure *n* = 5; nicotine withdrawal *n* = 5), and adolescent female (control *n* = 5; nicotine exposure *n* = 5; nicotine withdrawal *n* = 6) rats.

DISCUSSION

To summarize, during nicotine withdrawal, adult females displayed increases in anxiety-like behavior, increases in plasma corticosterone levels, and changes in CRF gene expression in the NAcc that were higher as compared to males. Control studies comparing sex differences during nicotine exposure, revealed that adult males displayed an increase in plasma corticosterone levels and increases in CRF gene expression in the amygdala. The sex differences in adults did not appear to be confounded by nicotine metabolism, since cotinine values were the same in male and female rats throughout our experimental procedures. Regarding age differences, adolescent males displayed some indices of stress during nicotine exposure that persisted into the withdrawal period. This may have been related to the high doses of nicotine that the adolescents required to produce comparable cotinine values as adults.

The major finding of this study is that adult females experience greater behavioral and biological indices of stress during nicotine withdrawal as compared to males. Adult females spent more time on the closed arm of the elevated plus maze during nicotine withdrawal as compared to males. Consistent with this, adult females also spent more time in the corner areas of the open field during nicotine withdrawal relative to males. Our behavioral results corroborate with our biological assessment of stress, as adult females also displayed increases in plasma corticosterone levels during nicotine withdrawal that were higher than males. Our results are consistent with previous reports demonstrating that female adult mice display more anxiety-like behavior on the elevated plus maze during nicotine withdrawal as compared to males (Kota et al., 2007, 2008; Caldarone et al., 2008). Two recent reports also showed that adult female rats display higher plasma corticosterone levels during nicotine withdrawal as compared to males (Gentile et al., 2011; Skwara et al., 2012).

The present study also revealed that adult females displayed an increase in CRF mRNA expression in the NAcc during nicotine withdrawal that was higher than males. Previous reports support the role of the NAcc in modulating stress. For example, intra-NAcc administration of CRF has been shown to produce anxiety-like behavior on the elevated plus maze (Chen et al., 2012). The NAcc is also strongly activated following presentation of a stressful stimulus (Noh et al., 2012). The latter report showed that the NAcc was activated to a greater extent following restraint stress as compared to cold-water submersion. Thus, the NAcc may be differentially responsive to various types of stressors. Our findings suggest that the NAcc is also involved in stress produced by nicotine withdrawal. Consistent with this hypothesis, the deficits in brain reward function produced by nicotine withdrawal are alleviated by blockade of CRF receptors in the NAcc (Marcinkiewcz et al., 2009). Our finding that the hypothalamus was not altered during withdrawal, is consistent with the finding that CRF mRNA was not altered in the hypothalamus of male rats experiencing spontaneous nicotine withdrawal (Semba et al., 2004). Thus, the hypothalamus may not play a central role in modulating negative affective states involving stress produced by nicotine withdrawal.

Our findings also suggest that the NAcc is a structure involved in sex-dependent differences to drug withdrawal. This is consistent with previous studies examining withdrawal from other drugs of abuse. For example, morphine withdrawal produced a decrease in μ-opioid receptors in the NAcc of female but not male mice (Diaz et al., 2006). Also, multiple withdrawal periods from ethanol produced an increase in proteins involved in vesicular packaging and exocytosis in the NAcc of female but not male rats (Bell et al., 2006, 2009). Following abstinence from cocaine self-administration, delta opioid receptors and dopamine phosphoproteins are increased to a greater extent in the NAcc of female versus male rats (Lynch et al., 2007; Ambrose-Lanci et al., 2008). Taken together with the present findings, there is strong evidence to suggest that the NAcc modulates sex differences produced by withdrawal from drugs of abuse.

There are several ways in which females may be more susceptible to stress produced by nicotine withdrawal. There is much evidence to suggest that CRF systems are enhanced in females versus males (Bangasser, 2013; Valentino et al., 2013). Females display hypersecretion of CRF and more CRF-1 receptors in the locus coeruleus, a brain region that coordinates arousal components of the stress response (Curtis et al., 2006; Bangasser et al., 2013). Females also display a higher ratio of CRF-1 receptors to coupling of G-proteins versus male rats, suggesting that the female CRF system has greater intracellular signaling capacity (Bangasser et al., 2010). The beta-arrestin2 protein is an intracellular protein that internalizes the CRF-1 receptor into the cell cytoplasm and prevents it from being activated by CRF (Aguilera et al., 2004; Holmes et al., 2006). Female rats display lower levels of beta-arrestin2 than male rats, suggesting that females are more responsive to CRF stimulation due to reduced internalization of the CRF-1 receptor as compared to males (Bangasser and Valentino, 2012). Females may also be more susceptible to stress produced by withdrawal via ovarian hormones. For example, direct activation of estrogen-beta receptors (ERβ) increase CRF mRNA expression *in vitro* (Chen et al., 2008; Lalmansingh and Uht, 2008; Zhu and Zhou, 2008). Furthermore, the estrogen gene sequence serves as a promoter of CRF gene transcription (Vamvakopoulos and Chrousos, 1993). Collectively, these studies suggest that females have a hypersensitive CRF system, and this may contribute to the enhanced stress produced by nicotine withdrawal in females versus males.

The present study also revealed a robust increase in CRF gene expression in the amygdala of male rats during nicotine exposure. A recent report showed that CRF levels were increased in the amygdala of adult male rats experiencing nicotine withdrawal (George et al., 2007). The rats in the latter study received a nicotine antagonist to precipitate withdrawal while nicotine was being delivered via an osmotic pump. The findings from the present study are consistent with those of George et al. (2007), given that the rats from both studies had circulating levels of nicotine in their system at the time of analysis. Thus, the possibility exists that nicotine directly activates CRF systems in the amygdala, especially given that the changes in CRF were not observed in the absence of nicotine in our study. Future studies are needed to fully understand the role of CRF systems in the amygdala in modulating the direct effects of nicotine and the long-term consequences of withdrawal from this drug. A unique challenge for this work is that nicotine exposure is an inherent part of studies that assess withdrawal, either by spontaneous or precipitated methods.

The present study also compared sex differences in the somatic signs of nicotine withdrawal. Our findings suggest that there were no differences in somatic signs of withdrawal between adult male and female rats. A report by Hamilton et al. (2009) showed that female rats display more somatic signs of withdrawal relative to males. The discrepancy between these reports may be related to differences in lighting conditions given that Hamilton et al. only reported sex differences in rats that were tested in dim, but not well-lit conditions. In the present study, the somatic signs data were collected in well-lit conditions whereas the anxiety-like behavior was collected in the dark under a red light. Perhaps different lighting conditions may be considered in future studies examining anxiety-like behavior produced by nicotine withdrawal, especially given the reported effects of lighting conditions on the somatic signs of withdrawal.

Another finding of this study is that male and female adolescents generally displayed fewer somatic signs of withdrawal as compared to adults. These findings are consistent with previous work in our laboratory and others demonstrating that the behavioral and neurochemical effects of withdrawal are diminished in adolescent versus adult rats (Smith et al., 2006; Wilmouth and Spear, 2006; Shram et al., 2008; O'Dell, 2009). This study extends this work by showing that adolescent females are also less sensitive to nicotine withdrawal as compared to adult females. An important caveat; however, is that adolescent males displayed anxiety-like behavior and biological markers of stress during nicotine exposure that persisted 24-h later into withdrawal. There are two possible explanations for this effect. First, adolescent males may not be impervious to all aspects of withdrawal, which may induce a stress response that contributes to tobacco use in adolescent males. Second, it is possible that nicotine elicited a stress response in adolescent males. This explanation is consistent with the finding that CRF gene expression was increased in the amygdala of adolescent males during nicotine exposure. We suggest that the ability of nicotine to induce a stress response was likely related to the three-fold higher doses of this drug that were used to produce equivalent plasma levels of cotinine as adults. The lack of stress effects in female adolescents was likely related to high tolerance to the aversive effects of nicotine, an effect that has been previously demonstrated (Torres et al., 2009). Future studies are needed to examine sex differences to stress produced by nicotine withdrawal, perhaps with a model such as nicotine vapor inhalation that circumvents the dosing issues that arose in the present study with osmotic pumps. Despite this, the present study provided important parametric information regarding equivalent doses of nicotine in adolescent and adult rats using different pump sizes. Our results raise an important issue for future studies comparing developmental differences to nicotine since high doses of nicotine may produce stress in adolescent males.

There are some limitations in the present study. In some cases, our behavioral and biochemical measures appear to contradict each other. For example, in adolescent males, we observed an increase in anxiety-like behavior in the plus maze but not the open field. This discrepancy is likely related to the sensitivity of these measures in assessing anxiety-like behavior. In adult females, during withdrawal, the pattern of changes was consistent (high anxiety-like behavior and corticosterone). However, during nicotine exposure the pattern of changes was not consistent (high anxiety-like behavior but no changes in corticosterone). The lack

of changes in corticosterone was likely due to a higher baseline value in adult females. In adult males, during withdrawal, the pattern of changes was consistent (no anxiety-like behavior and no changes in corticosterone). However, during nicotine exposure, the pattern of changes was not consistent (no changes in anxiety-like behavior and an increase in corticosterone). One might argue that the changes in corticosterone were aberrant; however, this group also showed an increase in CRF gene expression in the amygdala. Thus, it may be the case the nicotine exposure is more stress inducing in adult males as compared to withdrawal from this drug.

In conclusion, our results suggest that during nicotine withdrawal female rats display behavioral and biological markers of stress that are enhanced compared to males. These findings contribute to a body of literature showing that female rats display greater rewarding effects of nicotine as compared to males (Donny et al., 2000; Klein et al., 2004; Chaudhri et al., 2005; Torres et al., 2009). Taken together, there is pre-clinical evidence to suggest that enhanced rewarding effects of nicotine and intense stress produced by withdrawal both contribute to the greater vulnerability to tobacco use observed in women. In addition, our findings suggest that the most effective cessation treatments for women should also alleviate intense stress produced by nicotine withdrawal. For example, one approach might include CRF antagonists in combination with other tobacco cessation treatments, such as NRT or partial nicotinic agonists. Future studies are needed to understand the complex interactions in the brain that modulate sex differences to nicotine use. This work is important toward reducing health disparities related to tobacco use among women.

ACKNOWLEDGMENTS

The authors appreciate the insightful comments during the preparation of this manuscript from Drs. Eddie Castañeda, Christina Sobin, Kristin Gosselink, and Theodore Cooper. The authors would also like to thank Dr. James Orfila, Arturo Orona, Vanessa Valenzuela, Lorena De los Santos, and Adrian Muñiz for their technical assistance. This research was supported by The National Institute on Drug Abuse (R01-DA021274, R24-DA029989, and R25-DA033613) and The National Institute of Minority Health Disparities (G12MD007592). Student funding was also provided by the UTEP Dodson Doctoral Fellowship Program (Dr. Oscar Torres).

REFERENCES

Aguilera, G., Nikodemova, M., Wynn, P. C., and Catt, K. J. (2004). Corticotropin releasing hormone receptors: two decades later. *Peptides* 25, 319–329.

Ambrose-Lanci, L. M., Peiris, N. B., Unterwald, E. M., and Van Bockstaele, E. J. (2008). Cocaine withdrawal-induced trafficking of delta-opioid receptors in rat nucleus accumbens. *Brain Res.* 1210, 92–102.

Anderson, C., and Burns, D. M. (2000). Patterns of adolescent smoking initiation rates by ethnicity and sex. *Tob. Control.* 9, 4–8.

Aronson, K. R., Almeida, D. M., Stawski, R. S., Klein, L. C., and Kozlowski, L. T. (2008). Smoking is associated with worse mood on stressful days: results from a national diary study. *Ann. Behav. Med.* 36, 259–269.

Aydin, C., Oztan, O., and Isgor, C. (2011). Vulnerability to nicotine abstinence-related social anxiety-like behavior: molecular correlates in neuropeptide Y, Y2 receptor and corticotropin releasing factor. *Neurosci. Lett.* 490, 220–225.

Bangasser, D. A. (2013). Sex differences in stress-related receptors:

"micro" differences with "macro" implications for mood and anxiety disorders. *Biol. Sex Differ.* 4, 2.

Bangasser, D. A., Reyes, B. A., Piel, D., Garachh, V., Zhang, X. Y., Plona, Z. M., et al. (2013). Increased vulnerability of the brain norepinephrine system of females to corticotropin-releasing factor overexpression. *Mol. Psychiatry* 18, 166–173.

Bangasser, D. A., and Valentino, R. J. (2012). Sex differences in molecular and cellular substrates of stress. *Cell. Mol. Neurobiol.* 32, 709–723.

Bangasser, D. A., Curtis, A., Reyes, B. A., Bethea, T. T., Parastatidis, I.,

Ischiropoulos, H., et al. (2010). Sex differences in corticotropin-releasing factor receptor signaling and trafficking: potential role in female vulnerability to stress-related psychopathology. *Mol. Psychiatry* 15, 877, 896–904.

Bell, R. L., Kimpel, M. W., McClintick, J. N., Strother, W. N., Carr, L. G., Liang, T., et al. (2009). Gene expression changes in the nucleus accumbens of alcohol-preferring rats following chronic ethanol consumption. *Pharmacol. Biochem. Behav.* 94, 131–147.

Bell, R. L., Kimpel, M. W., Rodd, Z. A., Strother, W. N., Bai, F., Peper, C. L., et al. (2006). Protein expression changes in the nucleus accumbens and amygdala of inbred alcohol-preferring rats given either continuous or scheduled access to ethanol. *Alcohol* 40, 3–17.

Bruijnzeel, A. W. (2012). Tobacco addiction and the dysregulation of brain stress systems. *Neurosci. Biobehav. Rev.* 36, 1418–1441.

Bruijnzeel, A. W., Ford, J., Rogers, J. A., Scheick, S., Ji, Y., Bishnoi, M., et al. (2012). Blockade of CRF1 receptors in the central nucleus of the amygdala attenuates the dysphoria associated with nicotine withdrawal in rats. *Pharmacol. Biochem. Behav.* 101, 62–68.

Caldarone, B. J., King, S. L., and Picciotto, M. R. (2008). Sex differences in anxiety-like behavior and locomotor activity following chronic nicotine exposure in mice. *Neurosci. Lett.* 439, 187–191.

Centers for Disease Control and Prevention (CDC). (2012). Current tobacco use among middle and high school students – United States, 2011. *MMWR Morb. Mortal. Wkly. Rep.* 61, 581–585.

Cepeda-Benito, A., Reynoso, J. T., and Erath, S. (2004). Meta-analysis of the efficacy of nicotine replacement therapy for smoking cessation: differences between men and women. *J. Consult. Clin. Psychol.* 72, 712–722.

Chaudhri, N., Caggiula, A. R., Donny, E. C., Booth, S., Gharib, M. A., Craven, L. A., et al. (2005). Sex differences in the contribution of nicotine and nonpharmacological stimuli to nicotine self-administration in rats. *Psychopharmacology (Berl.)* 180, 258–266.

Chen, X. N., Zhu, H., Meng, Q. Y., and Zhou, J. N. (2008). Estrogen receptor-alpha and -beta regulate the human corticotropin-releasing hormone gene through similar pathways. *Brain Res.* 1223, 1–10.

Chen, Y. W., Rada, P. V., Butzler, B. P., Leibowitz, S. F., and Hoebel, B. G. (2012). Corticotropin-releasing factor in the nucleus accumbens shell induces swim depression, anxiety, and anhedonia along with changes in local dopamine/acetylcholine balance. *Neuroscience* 206, 155–166.

Colby, S. M., Tiffany, S. T., Shiffman, S., and Niaura, R. S. (2000). Are adolescent smokers dependent on nicotine? A review of the evidence. *Drug Alcohol Depend.* 59, 83–95.

Curtis, A. L., Bethea, T., and Valentino, R. J. (2006). Sexually dimorphic responses of the brain norepinephrine system to stress and corticotropin-releasing factor. *Neuropsychopharmacology* 31, 544–554.

Diaz, S. L., Barros, V. G., Antonelli, M. C., Rubio, M. C., and Balerio, G. N. (2006). Morphine withdrawal syndrome and its prevention with baclofen: autoradiographic study of mu-opioid receptors in prepubertal male and female mice. *Synapse* 60, 132–140.

Dickmann, P. J., Mooney, M. E., Allen, S. S., Hanson, K., and Hatsukami, D. K. (2009). Nicotine withdrawal and craving in adolescents: effects of sex and hormonal contraceptive use. *Addict. Behav.* 34, 620–623.

Donny, E. C., Caggiula, A. R., Rowell, P., Gharib, M. A., Maldovan, V., Booth, S., et al. (2000). Nicotine self-administration in rats: estrous cycle effects, sex differences and nicotinic receptor binding. *Psychopharmacology (Berl.)* 151, 392–405.

Gallagher, J. P., Orozco-Cabal, L. F., Liu, J., and Shinnick-Gallagher, P. (2008). Synaptic physiology of central CRF system. *Eur. J. Pharmacol.* 583, 215–225.

Gentile, N. E., Andrekanic, J. D., Karwoski, T. E., Czambel, R. K., Rubin, R. T., and Rhodes, M. E. (2011). Sexually diergic hypothalamic-pituitary-adrenal (HPA) responses to single-dose nicotine, continuous nicotine infusion, and nicotine withdrawal by mecamylamine in rats. *Brain Res. Bull.* 85, 145–152.

George, O., Ghozland, S., Azar, M. R., Cottone, P., Zorrilla, E. P., Parsons, L. H., et al. (2007). CRF–CRF 1 system activation mediates withdrawal-induced increases in nicotine self-administration in nicotine-dependent rats. *Proc. Natl. Acad. Sci. U.S.A.* 104, 17198–17203.

Hamilton, K. R., Berger, S. S., Perry, M. E., and Grunberg, N. E. (2009). Behavioral effects of nicotine withdrawal in adult male and female rats. *Pharmacol. Biochem. Behav.* 92, 51–59.

Hammond, S. K. (2009). Global patterns of nicotine and tobacco consumption. *Handb. Exp. Pharmacol.* 192, 3–28.

Heishman, S. J., Lee, D. C., Taylor, R. C., and Singleton, E. G. (2010). Prolonged duration of craving, mood, and autonomic responses elicited by cues and imagery in smokers: effects of tobacco deprivation and sex. *Exp. Clin. Psychopharmacol.* 18, 245–256.

Hogle, J. M., and Curtin, J. J. (2006). Sex differences in negative affective response during nicotine withdrawal. *Psychophysiology* 43, 344–356.

Holmes, K. D., Babwah, A. V., Dale, L. B., Poulter, M. O., and Ferguson, S. S. (2006). Differential regulation of corticotropin releasing factor 1alpha receptor endocytosis and trafficking by beta-arrestins and Rab GTPases. *J. Neurochem.* 96, 934–949.

Hughes, J. R., and Callas, P. W. (2010). Definition of a quit attempt: a replication test. *Nicotine Tob. Res.* 12, 1176–1179.

Kiyohara, C., and Ohno, Y. (2010). Sex differences in lung cancer susceptibility: a review. *Gend. Med.* 7, 381–401.

Klein, L. C., Stine, M. M., Vandenbergh, D. J., Whetzel, C. A., and Kamens, H. M. (2004). Sex differences in voluntary oral nicotine consumption by adolescent mice: a dose-response experiment. *Pharmacol. Biochem. Behav.* 78, 13–25.

Koob, G. F. (2010). The role of CRF and CRF-related peptides in the dark side of addiction. *Brain Res.* 1314, 3–14.

Koob, G. F., and Volkow, N. D. (2010). Neurocircuitry of addiction. *Neuropsychopharmacology* 35, 217–238.

Kota, D., Martin, B. R., and Damaj, M. (2008). Age-dependent differences in nicotine reward and withdrawal in female mice. *Psychopharmacology (Berl.)* 198, 201–210.

Kota, D., Martin, B. R., Robinson, S. E., and Damaj, M. I. (2007). Nicotine dependence and reward differ between adolescent and adult male mice. *J. Pharmacol. Exp. Ther.* 322, 399–407.

Lalmansingh, A. S., and Uht, R. M. (2008). Estradiol regulates corticotropin-releasing hormone gene (CRF) expression in a rapid and phasic manner that parallels estrogen receptor-alpha and -beta recruitment to a 3′,5′-cyclic adenosine 5′-monophosphate regulatory region of the proximal CRF promoter. *Endocrinology* 149, 346–357.

Langhammer, A., Johnsen, R., Gulsvik, A., Holmen, T. L., and Bjermer, L. (2003). Sex differences in lung vulnerability to tobacco smoking. *Eur. Respir. J.* 21, 1017–1023.

Langhammer, A., Johnsen, R., Holmen, J., Gulsvik, A., and Bjermer, L. (2000). Cigarette smoking gives more respiratory symptoms among women than among men. The Nord-Trondelag Health Study (HUNT). *J. Epidemiol. Community Health* 54, 917–922.

Lombardi, E. M., Prado, G. F., Santos Ude, P., and Fernandes, F. L. (2011). Women and smoking: risks, impacts, and challenges. *J. Bras. Pneumol.* 37, 118–128.

Lutfy, K., Brown, M. C., Nerio, N., Aimiuwu, O., Tran, B., Anghel, A., et al. (2006). Repeated stress alters the ability of nicotine to activate the hypothalamic-pituitary-adrenal axis. *J. Neurochem.* 99, 1321–1327.

Lynch, W. J., Kiraly, D. D., Caldarone, B. J., Picciotto, M. R., and Taylor, J. R. (2007). Effect of cocaine self-administration on striatal PKA-regulated signaling in male and female rats. *Psychopharmacology (Berl.)* 191, 263–271.

Marcinkiewcz, C. A., Prado, M. M., Isaac, S. K., Marshall, A., Rylkova, D., and Bruijnzeel, A. W. (2009). Corticotropin-releasing factor within the central nucleus of the amygdala and the nucleus accumbens shell mediates the negative affective state of nicotine withdrawal in rats. *Neuropsychopharmacology* 34, 1743–1752.

Nakajima, M., and al'Absi, M. (2012). Predictors of risk for smoking relapse in men and women: a prospective examination. *Psychol. Addict. Behav.* 26, 633–637.

Noh, S. J., Kang, D. W., Yoo, S. B., Lee, J. Y., Kim, J. Y., Kim, B. T., et al. (2012). Stress-responsive hypothalamic-nucleus accumbens regulation may vary depending on stressors. *Indian J. Exp. Biol.* 50, 447–454.

O'Dell, L. E. (2009). A psychobiological framework of the substrates that mediate nicotine use during adolescence. *Neuropharmacology* 56, 263–278.

O'Dell, L. E., Bruijnzeel, A. W., Ghozland, S., Markou, A., and Koob, G. F. (2004). Nicotine withdrawal in adolescent and adult rats. *Ann. N. Y. Acad. Sci.* 1021, 167–174.

O'Dell, L. E., Bruijnzeel, A. W., Smith, R. T., Parsons, L. H., Merves, M. L., Goldberger, B. A., et al. (2006). Diminished nicotine withdrawal in adolescent rats: implications for vulnerability to addiction. *Psychopharmacology (Berl.)* 186, 612–619.

Oh, D. L., Heck, J. E., Dresler, C., Allwright, S., Haglund, M., Del Mazo, S. S., et al. (2010). Determinants of smoking initiation among women in five European countries: a cross-sectional survey. *BMC Public Health* 10:74. doi:10.1186/1471-2458-10-74

Parrott, A. C., and Murphy, R. S. (2012). Explaining the stress-induced effects of nicotine to cigarette smokers. *Hum. Psychopharmacol.* 27, 150–155.

Perkins, K. A. (2001). Smoking cessation in women. Special considerations. *CNS Drugs* 15, 391–411.

Perkins, K. A. (2009). Sex differences in nicotine reinforcement and reward: influences on the persistence of tobacco smoking. *Nebr. Symp. Motiv.* 55, 143–169.

Perkins, K. A., Giedgowd, G. E., Karelitz, J. L., Conklin, C. A., and Lerman, C. (2012). Smoking in response to negative mood in men versus women as a function of distress tolerance. *Nicotine Tob. Res.* 14, 1418–1425.

Perkins, K. A., Karelitz, J. L., Giedgowd, G. E., and Conklin, C. A. (2013). Negative mood effects on craving to smoke in women versus men. *Addict. Behav.* 38, 1527–1531.

Perkins, K. A., and Scott, J. (2008). Sex differences in long-term smoking cessation rates due to nicotine patch. *Nicotine Tob. Res.* 10, 1245–1250.

Piper, M. E., Cook, J. W., Schlam, T. R., Jorenby, D. E., Smith, S. S., Bolt, D. M., et al. (2010). Gender, race, and education differences in abstinence rates among participants in two randomized smoking cessation trials. *Nicotine Tob. Res.* 12, 647–657.

Rahmanian, S. D., Diaz, P. T., and Wewers, M. E. (2011). Tobacco use and cessation among women: research and treatment-related issues. *J. Womens Health (Larchmt)* 20, 349–357.

Rhodes, M. E., Kennell, J. S., Belz, E. E., Czambel, R. K., and Rubin, R. T. (2004). Rat estrous cycle influences the sexual diergism of HPA axis stimulation by nicotine. *Brain Res. Bull.* 64, 205–213.

Saladin, M. E., Gray, K. M., Carpenter, M. J., LaRowe, S. D., DeSantis, S. M., and Upadhyaya, H. P. (2012). Gender differences in craving and cue reactivity to smoking and negative affect/stress cues. *Am. J. Addict.* 21, 210–220.

Schmittgen, T. D., and Livak, K. J. (2008). Analyzing real-time PCR data by the comparative C(T) method. *Nat. Protoc.* 3, 1101–1108.

Schnoll, R. A., Patterson, F., and Lerman, C. (2007). Treating tobacco dependence in women. *Womens Health* 16, 1211–1218.

Semba, J., Wakuta, M., Maeda, J., and Suhara, T. (2004). Nicotine withdrawal induces subsensitivity of hypothalamic-pituitary-adrenal axis to stress in rats: implications for precipitation of depression during smoking cessation. *Psychoneuroendocrinology* 29, 215–226.

Shram, M. J., Siu, E. C., Li, Z., Tyndale, R. F., and Lê, A. D. (2008). Interactions between age and the aversive effects of nicotine withdrawal under mecamylamine-precipitated and spontaneous conditions in male Wistar rats. *Psychopharmacology (Berl.)* 198, 181–190.

Skwara, A. J., Karwosk, T. E., Czambel, R. K., Rubin, R. T., and Rhodes, M. E. (2012). Influence of environmental enrichment on hypothalamic-pituitary-adrenal (HPA) responses to single-dose nicotine, continuous nicotine by osmotic minipumps, and nicotine withdrawal by mecamylamine in male and female rats. *Behav. Brain Res.* 234, 1–10.

Smith, L. N., McDonald, C. G., Bergstrom, H. C., Brielmaier, J. M., Eppolito, A. K., Wheeler, T. L., et al. (2006). Long-term changes in fear conditioning and anxiety-like behavior following nicotine exposure in adult versus adolescent rats. *Pharmacol. Biochem. Behav.* 85, 91–97.

Smith, S. M., and Vale, W. W. (2006). The role of the hypothalamic-pituitary-adrenal axis in neuroendocrine responses to stress. *Dialogues Clin. Neurosci.* 8, 383–395.

Torres, O. V., Natividad, L. A., Tejeda, H. A., Van Weelden, S. A., and O'Dell, L. E. (2009). Female rats display dose-dependent differences to the rewarding and aversive effects of nicotine in an age-, hormone-, and sex-dependent manner. *Psychopharmacology (Berl.)* 206, 303–312.

Valentino, R. J., Bangasser, D., and Van Bockstaele, E. J. (2013). Sex-biased stress signaling: the corticotropin-releasing factor receptor as a model. *Mol. Pharmacol.* 83, 737–745.

Vamvakopoulos, N. C., and Chrousos, G. P. (1993). Evidence of direct estrogenic regulation of human corticotropin-releasing hormone gene expression. Potential implications for the sexual dimorphism of the stress response and immune/inflammatory reaction. *J. Clin. Invest.* 92, 1896–1902.

Wilmouth, C. E., and Spear, L. P. (2006). Withdrawal from chronic nicotine in adolescent and adult rats. *Pharmacol. Biochem. Behav.* 85, 648–657.

Xu, J., Azizian, A., Monterosso, J., Domier, C. P., Brody, A. L., Fong, T. W., et al. (2008). Gender effects on mood and cigarette craving during early abstinence and resumption of smoking. *Nicotine Tob. Res.* 10, 1653–1661.

Zhu, H., and Zhou, J. N. (2008). SUMO1 enhances 17-beta estradiol's effect on CRF promoter activation through estrogen receptors. *Neuro Endocrinol. Lett.* 29, 230–234.

Animal models of nicotine exposure: relevance to second-hand smoking, electronic cigarette use, and compulsive smoking

Ami Cohen and Olivier George*

Committee on the Neurobiology of Addictive Disorders, The Scripps Research Institute, La Jolla, CA, USA

Edited by:
Nicholas W. Gilpin, Louisiana State University Health Sciences Center-New Orleans, USA

Reviewed by:
Angelo Giovanni Icro Maremmani, University of Pisa, Italy
M. I. Damaj, Virginia Commonwealth University, USA
Laura Elena O'Dell, The University of Texas at El Paso, USA

*Correspondence:
Olivier George, Committee on the Neurobiology of Addictive Disorders, The Scripps Research Institute, 10550 North Torrey Pines Road, SP30-2400, La Jolla, CA 92037, USA
e-mail: ogeorge@scripps.edu

Much evidence indicates that individuals use tobacco primarily to experience the psychopharmacological properties of nicotine and that a large proportion of smokers eventually become dependent on nicotine. In humans, nicotine acutely produces positive reinforcing effects, including mild euphoria, whereas a nicotine abstinence syndrome with both somatic and affective components is observed after chronic nicotine exposure. Animal models of nicotine self-administration and chronic exposure to nicotine have been critical in unveiling the neurobiological substrates that mediate the acute reinforcing effects of nicotine and emergence of a withdrawal syndrome during abstinence. However, important aspects of the transition from nicotine abuse to nicotine dependence, such as the emergence of increased motivation and compulsive nicotine intake following repeated exposure to the drug, have only recently begun to be modeled in animals. Thus, the neurobiological mechanisms that are involved in these important aspects of nicotine addiction remain largely unknown. In this review, we describe the different animal models available to date and discuss recent advances in animal models of nicotine exposure and nicotine dependence. This review demonstrates that novel animal models of nicotine vapor exposure and escalation of nicotine intake provide a unique opportunity to investigate the neurobiological effects of second-hand nicotine exposure, electronic cigarette use, and the mechanisms that underlie the transition from nicotine use to compulsive nicotine intake.

Keywords: addiction, tobacco, self-administration, vapor, dependence, escalation, abstinence, withdrawal

INTRODUCTION

Studies on the neurobiological substrates of tobacco addiction largely depend on the availability of suitable animal models. In this review, we first describe the features of tobacco smoking and nicotine abuse and dependence in humans. We then discuss the limits and advantages of the most used animal models of nicotine use and dependence and novel animal models of escalated nicotine intake and exposure to nicotine vapor. The last section discusses how these different animal models can be used to investigate the neurobiological mechanisms that mediate nicotine reinforcement and dependence.

FEATURES OF TOBACCO SMOKING, NICOTINE ABUSE, AND DEPENDENCE IN HUMANS

Tobacco use is the leading cause of preventable disease and premature death, leading to 440,000 deaths annually in the United States alone (Fellows et al., 2002). According to a recent review (Giovino et al., 2012), 24% of the United States population older than 15 years of age are cigarette smokers, and 1.8% are smokeless tobacco users. Cigarette smoking appears to be more central to the epidemiology of nicotine addiction compared with smokeless tobacco abuse. However, chewing tobacco, dry snuff, and moist snuff are a concern in certain countries (Bhattacharyya, 2012; Giovino et al., 2012). The rapid growth of electronic cigarette use worldwide (Caponnetto et al., 2012) is also an important health concern that requires the development of novel animal models of exposure to nicotine vapor.

ACUTE EFFECTS OF SMOKING

The primary psychoactive ingredient responsible for tobacco use is nicotine (Cummings and Mahoney, 2006), although tobacco smoke also contains more than 4,000 additional chemicals, many of which have psychoactive properties or may act in concert with nicotine to contribute to smoking dependence (Clemens et al., 2009; Hoffman and Evans, 2013). Cigarettes typically contain 10–14 mg of nicotine (Kozlowski et al., 1998), of which 1–1.5 mg is absorbed systemically in the lungs through inhalation (Armitage et al., 1975; Benowitz and Jacob, 1984). Nicotine rapidly enters the pulmonary venous circulation, reaches the brain within 10–20 s, and readily diffuses into brain tissue where it binds to nicotine acetylcholine receptors (nAChRs; Benowitz et al., 1988). The rate of absorption of smokeless tobacco products, with the exception of electronic cigarettes, is considerably slower (30 min to reach maximum blood levels), accounting for a lower abuse potential for these products (Benowitz et al., 1988). Acutely, cigarette smoking is reported to induce positive reinforcing effects, including mild euphoria, heightened arousal, reduced appetite, and reduced stress, anxiety, and pain (Pomerleau et al., 1984; Pomerleau and Pomerleau, 1992; Stolerman and Jarvis, 1995). However, the specific role for nicotine in these reinforcing effects is still unclear because of the difficulties performing intravenous nicotine self-administration in humans. However, smokers who self-administer nicotine report an overall profile of rewarding sensations, including mild euphoria, increased comfort, "drug liking," and reduced negative mood and pain sensation, accompanied by negative effects, such as tension and jitteriness (Henningfield and Goldberg, 1983; Perkins et al., 1994; Harvey et al., 2004; Sofuoglu et al., 2008; Rose et al., 2010). Thus, nicotine itself can serve as an effective reinforcer, at least among experienced smokers. However, the mixed subjective reports, early difficulties obtaining reliable intravenous nicotine self-administration in animals, and direct comparisons in animal models suggest that the reinforcing efficacy of nicotine is lower than other drugs of abuse (Risner and Goldberg, 1983; Manzardo et al., 2002; Le Foll and Goldberg, 2009). Non-nicotinic aspects of tobacco smoke, such as its other constituents (e.g., acetaldehyde, nornicotine, and harman) and sensory stimulation could substantially contribute to its abuse and addictive potential (Belluzzi et al., 2005; Rose, 2006; Rose et al., 2010; Kapelewski et al., 2011).

TOBACCO DEPENDENCE

Patterns of smoking among dependent smokers

Dependent smokers maintain relatively stable nicotine blood levels during waking hours (Benowitz and Jacob, 1984), with plasma levels ranging between 20 and 50 ng/ml. To maintain these relatively constant nicotine levels, smokers efficiently regulate the rate and intensity of cigarette smoking (Ashton and Watson, 1970; Benowitz, 1986). For example, smokers will compensate for reduced nicotine content when smoking cigarettes with lower nicotine yield than their usual brand (Russell et al., 1980; Maron and Fortmann, 1987).

Nicotine withdrawal and the escalation of nicotine intake

Discontinuation of smoking, even for only several hours, leads to withdrawal symptoms that peak within 1 week and may persist for up to 6 months (Hughes et al., 1991; Hughes, 2007; Markou, 2008). Nicotine withdrawal includes both somatic symptoms, such as bradycardia, gastrointestinal disturbances, and, increased appetite, and affective symptoms, such as nicotine craving, heightened anxiety, hyperalgesia, depressed mood, and irritability (Pomerleau et al., 1984; Hughes et al., 1991; Zaniewska et al., 2009; Rose et al., 2010). Converging evidence shows that avoidance of the affective symptoms of nicotine withdrawal, rather than somatic symptoms, plays a central role in the maintenance of nicotine dependence (Koob et al., 1993). It has been hypothesized that during the transition to dependence, the motivation to take drugs is caused by a shift from the positive reinforcing properties of the drug to its ability to attenuate the negative effects of abstinence. Thus, the negative affective states associated with abstinence potentiate the incentive value of nicotine to promote the escalation of compulsive drug intake through negative reinforcement mechanisms (Solomon and Corbit, 1973; Koob and Le Moal, 2001; Koob, 2010).

Adolescence and the escalation of tobacco smoking

Tobacco smoking typically begins in adolescence, with 14% of 15-year-olds and 22% of 17-year-olds reporting cigarette smoking (Substance Abuse and Mental Health Services Administration, 2003). Prospective studies report that ~30–50% of adolescents

and young adults who had initiated non-daily smoking showed an escalation in daily smoking within 4–5 years (U.S. Department of Health and Human Services, 1994, 2012; Tucker et al., 2003). For example, one 4-year prospective study reports that 53% of sixth-graders who experimented with smoking experience dependence symptoms, and 40% experience escalation to daily smoking (Doubeni et al., 2010). Some adolescents and young adults who experiment with smoking will eventually quit or remain light smokers (one to five cigarettes/day) or intermittent smokers ("chippers"; Shiffman, 1989; Shiffman et al., 1994), a subpopulation that encompasses up to 25–33% of all smokers (Coggins et al., 2009).

Various psychosocial factors, such as peer smoking and parenting style, have been suggested to contribute to the escalated smoking behavior of certain adolescents (Robinson et al., 2003; Kim et al., 2009; Dal Cin et al., 2012). Interestingly, studies suggest that, contrary to the common perception, symptoms of nicotine dependence, most commonly craving for tobacco and withdrawal symptoms (Gervais et al., 2007; Doubeni et al., 2010; Zhan et al., 2012), can develop at very early stages of initial intermittent smoking, even with as few as two cigarettes per week (DiFranza et al., 2002). According to Zhan et al. (2012), 20% of adolescents who smoke fewer than 100 cigarettes in their lifetime report experiencing "smoking to relieve restlessness" and "irritability." As expected, the early appearance of such symptoms of nicotine dependence predicts future escalation to daily chronic smoking (DiFranza et al., 2002, 2007; Dierker and Mermelstein, 2010; Doubeni et al., 2010). In contrast, people who engage in non-daily smoking without escalation ("chippers") have very few or no symptoms of dependence, and their smoking experience is primarily associated with positive rather than negative reinforcement (Coggins et al., 2009). Thus, intermittent tobacco use associated with withdrawal symptoms can promote the escalation of smoking behavior, which in turn accelerates the appearance of additional symptoms of dependence (Doubeni et al., 2010).

The importance of nicotine withdrawal as a negative reinforcer in the escalation of smoking is also suggested by the calming effects of nicotine when given after even a short period of abstinence, a primary reason given by both adults and adolescents for smoking (Dozois et al., 1995; Parrott, 1995). Although nicotine has anxiolytic properties under certain conditions (Pomerleau et al., 1984; Perkins and Grobe, 1992; Juliano and Brandon, 2002), it has also been argued that the calming effects of nicotine in dependent smokers represent the reversal of the negative affect induced by nicotine deprivation (Parrott, 1995, 1998, 2003). Thus, escalation may be more common among individuals with difficulties regulating negative affect, who are prone to develop withdrawal symptoms, and who have high expectancy of the calming effects of smoking (Heinz et al., 2010).

SECOND-HAND SMOKE

One generally overlooked factor that may contribute to the escalation of tobacco abuse, particularly among adolescents, is second-hand smoking. In the United States, it has been estimated that up to 60% of children are exposed to second-hand smoke (U.S. Department of Health and Human Services, 2006). Nicotine from moderate second-hand smoke exposure results in an increase in plasma nicotine concentration of approximately 0.2 ng/ml and to substantial brain $\alpha_4\beta_2^*$ nAChR occupancy (19%) in both smokers and non-smokers compared with 0.87 ng/ml and 50% $\alpha_4\beta_2^*$ nAChR occupancy from actively smoking one cigarette (Brody et al., 2006, 2011). Although second-hand smoking is clearly linked to serious illnesses among non-smokers (U.S. Department of Health and Human Services, 2006), including asthma, heart disease, sudden infant death syndrome, and cancer, it is currently unclear whether second-hand smoke can also contribute to the initiation and escalation of smoking. It is well documented that adolescents exposed to smoking by family members and peers are more likely to initiate and escalate smoking behavior (Brook et al., 2009; Leonardi-Bee et al., 2011; Wang et al., 2011). However, various psychological, psychosocial, and genetic factors may mediate this effect (Ajzen and Fishbein, 1980; O'Byrne et al., 2002; Audrain-McGovern et al., 2007). Nevertheless, escalated smoking can be observed in adolescent smokers with cotinine plasma levels comparable to levels of second-hand smoking in non-smokers (DiFranza et al., 2007). Moreover, adults and children who are non-smokers report symptoms of nicotine withdrawal after exposure to high levels of second-hand smoke (Okoli et al., 2007; Bélanger et al., 2008). Finally, prospective studies suggest that high levels of nicotine intake from second-hand smoking during childhood predict smoking behavior in teenage years, even when accounting for various social and environmental factors (Becklake et al., 2005). However, the controlled experimental conditions that are required to test the causal role of second-hand smoking in the escalation of smoking can only be employed in animal models and will be discussed below.

ELECTRONIC CIGARETTES

Electronic cigarettes deliver nicotine through the battery-powered vaporization of a nicotine/propylene-glycol solution. Electronic cigarettes (e-cigarettes) are thus generally less harmful than regular cigarettes because they deliver nicotine without the various toxic constituents of tobacco smoke (Cahn and Siegel, 2011; Etter and Bullen, 2011; O'Connor, 2012). According to a recent survey, 3.4% of the total population, including 11.4% of current smokers, 2.0% of former smokers, and 0.8% of never-smokers, use e-cigarettes (Pearson et al., 2012). Most smokers claim to use e-cigarettes for smoking cessation/reduction, and their use appears to enhance the motivation to quit (Etter and Bullen, 2011; Wagener et al., 2012). Indeed, two surveys reported that most smokers who used e-cigarettes decreased or completely quit smoking within 6 months (Polosa et al., 2011; Siegel et al., 2011). However, it is unclear the degree to which such reports coincide with the efficacy of e-cigarettes as nicotine delivery devices. Vansickel and Eissenberg (2013) report that experienced users who were allowed to use their own customized e-cigarettes reach blood nicotine concentrations similar to those obtained by regular cigarettes. However, other studies report that nicotine delivery greatly varies between brands but is generally lower than that of regular cigarettes, with certain brands delivering nicotine doses that are too low to be detected (Bullen et al., 2010; Vansickel et al., 2010; Goniewicz et al., 2013). These studies report that e-cigarette use reduces craving and partially alleviated withdrawal symptoms despite the low to moderate blood nicotine levels. The effect of e-cigarette use on

the brain stress and reward systems and vulnerability to become dependent or relapse is unknown and needs to be addressed using novel animal models. Another key question that needs to be investigated is the possible role of e-cigarettes as a gateway product to other drugs of abuse (Etter, 2012).

ANIMAL MODELS OF NICOTINE ABUSE AND DEPENDENCE
NON-CONTINGENT EXPOSURE TO NICOTINE

Most research on the behavioral and biological effects of nicotine involved experimenter-administered nicotine, given by subcutaneous (s.c.) or intraperitoneal (i.p.) injections (see **Figure 1**). Non-contingent nicotine injections were instrumental in identifying the effects of acute and chronic exposure to nicotine on a wide variety of phenomena, including locomotor activity (Clarke and Kumar, 1983), anxiety-like behavior (Irvine et al., 1999; Cheeta et al., 2001), feeding behavior (Clarke and Kumar, 1984), pain (Sahley and Berntson, 1979), the development of tolerance to such effects (Collins et al., 1988), and the brain systems involved (Rosecrans and Meltzer, 1981; Clarke et al., 1988; Niijima et al., 2001).

Conditioned place preference

In this model of drug reward, animals are tested for the development of conditioned preferences for distinct drug-paired environments (Carr et al., 1989). Achieving nicotine-induced conditioned place preference (CPP) in rodents has proven to be challenging compared with other drugs of abuse, and findings have been inconsistent. Nicotine-induced CPP is observed in some studies (Fudala et al., 1985; Horan et al., 1997; Ashby et al., 2002; Le Foll and Goldberg, 2005) but not in others (Clarke and Fibiger, 1987; Acquas et al., 1989; Jorenby et al., 1990; Parker, 1992). Nicotine can also induce conditioned place aversion (CPA; Horan et al., 1997; Laviolette and van der Kooy, 2003). The ability to achieve nicotine-induced CPP is facilitated by the use of a "biased" place preference procedure (i.e., pairing the drug with the initially non-preferred compartment of the CPP apparatus; Le Foll and Goldberg, 2005). The reasons for the difficulty obtaining CPP are unclear and may be related to the weak rewarding properties of nicotine and very narrow dose-response curve.

Dependence induction

Termination of repeated nicotine injections in rodents results in behavioral and physiological states consistent with drug withdrawal (see review by Malin, 2001), such as heightened stress responses (Benwell and Balfour, 1979), the disruption of appetitive operant responding (Ford and Balster, 1976; Carroll et al., 1989), and weight gain (Grunberg et al., 1986; Levin et al., 1987). The induction of nicotine dependence by subcutaneous nicotine delivery via osmotic minipumps has gained popularity since its first introduction by Malin et al. (1992). In this method, dependence is induced by ≥6 days of continuous subcutaneous nicotine infusion (commonly ≥3.16 mg/kg free base/day in rats and ≥12 mg/kg/day in mice). Withdrawal is subsequently induced by terminating the infusion (peaking within 18–22 h; Malin et al., 1992) or precipitated by injecting nAChR antagonists, such as mecamylamine (Malin et al., 1992; Isola et al., 1999; Damaj, 2000; Malin, 2001). The symptoms of withdrawal

	Acute non-contingent injections	Limited access self-administration	Chronic non-contingent exposure		Extended access self-administration	
			Exposure	Withdrawal	Exposure	Withdrawal
ICSS Brain reward threshold	↓0.1-1 mg/kg (1, 4, 6, 7, 14) ↑>1 mg/kg (1)	↓NSA<2h/d (8, 10, 12)	↓minipump (2, 7) →smoke (15)	↑minipump (3, 5, 7, 8, 11)	↓NSA: 2-12h/d(8, 10, 12)	↓NSA: 2-12h/day (8, 11, 12, 13) ↑NSA: 22h/day (16)
Anxiety-like behavior	↓<0.1 mg/kg s.c/i.p). ↑ >0.1 mg/kg (17-20)	↑NSA<2h/d (19)	Tolerance to anxiolytic and anxiogenic effects (19,21)	↑ (22, 23)	?	?
Conditioned place preference/aversion	CPP 0.1-1.4 mg/kg CPA >1.4 mg/kg (24)	?	?	CPA (25-29)	?	?
Pain	↓ (30-32)	?	↓With Tolerance (33,34) ↑(35)	↑(36-39)	?	?

FIGURE 1 | Effects of acute/chronic non-contingent nicotine exposure, limited/extended access to nicotine self-administration (NSA), and withdrawal from chronic nicotine on measures of reward threshold (ICSS), anxiety-like behavior, and reward (CPP) or aversion (CPA). Note that the effect of withdrawal from chronic nicotine on the reward thresholds differed depending on the type of nicotine delivery. 1. Huston-Lyons and Kornetsky (1992), 2. Bozarth et al. (1998a), 3. Bozarth et al. (1998b), 4. Bespalov et al. (1999), 5. Watkins et al. (2000a), 6. Harrison et al. (2002), 7. Cryan et al. (2003), 8. Kenny and Markou (2005), 9. Kenny and Markou (2006), 10. Kenny et al. (2009), 11. Johnson et al. (2008), 12. Paterson et al. (2008), 13. Bruijnzeel et al. (2009), 14. Spiller et al. (2009), 15. Yamada et al. (2010) 16. Harris et al. (2011); 17. Brioni et al. (1993); 18. Irvine et al. (1999), 19. Irvine et al. (2001), 20. Tucci et al. (2003); 21. Biala and Budzynska (2006), 22. Stoker et al. (2008), 23. Cippitelli et al. (2011), 24. Le Foll and Goldberg (2005), 25. Miyata et al. (2011), 26. Suzuki et al. (1996), 27. Shram et al. (2008), 28. Grieder et al. (2012), 29. Grieder et al. (2010), 30. Damaj et al. (1994), 31. Sahley and Berntson (1979), 32. Craft and Milholland (1998), 33. Yang et al. (1992), 34. Galeote et al. (2006), 35. Lough et al. (2007), 36. Grabus et al. (2005), 37. Jackson et al. (2008), 38. Schmidt et al. (2001), 39. Yang et al. (1992).

are commonly divided into "somatic" signs that resemble opiate withdrawal (e.g., teeth-chattering, chewing, writhing, tremors, and body shakes; Malin et al., 1992). Although a well-accepted marker for nicotine dependence, these somatic withdrawal signs do not appear to be similar to those in humans or strongly predict drug use or relapse compared with affective symptoms (Koob and Le Moal, 2001; Hughes, 2007). Affective symptoms can be measured using CPA to nicotine withdrawal (Shram et al., 2008; Jackson et al., 2009), anxiety-like behavior (Wilmouth and Spear, 2006), and increased reward thresholds in the intracranial self-stimulation (ICSS) paradigm. The increased reward thresholds are interpreted as reflecting a state of dysphoria or reduced ability to experience reward (Watkins et al., 2000a; Vlachou et al., 2011). Hyperalgesia, a withdrawal symptom that may be considered partly somatic and partly affective, is also observed in rodents following spontaneous or mecamylamine-induced withdrawal from chronic non-contingent nicotine delivery (Schmidt et al., 2001; Damaj et al., 2003; Jackson et al., 2009, 2010). Hyperalgesia in

such studies is operationally defined as increased sensitivity to nociceptive stimuli, usually in the form of tail-flick or hot-plate tests of latency to respond to noxious thermal stimuli.

Non-contingent exposure to nicotine is a simple and efficient way to induce nicotine dependence in animals and led to a great deal of findings regarding the possible neurobiological mechanisms of reward, dependence, and withdrawal (Malin, 2001; Malin and Goyarzu, 2009). However, the validity of this approach is limited when one wants to specifically investigate the neurobiological mechanisms that underlie the transition from occasional to compulsive use. Most importantly, contingent drug exposure (i.e., cigarette smoking and nicotine self-administration) and non-contingent exposure have very different psychological and physiological effects and recruit different brain systems (Dworkin et al., 1995; Markou et al., 1999). Nicotine absorption through subcutaneous or intraperitoneal administration is much slower than that achieved through inhalation, and the speed of administration has been shown to critically influence the reinforcing effects of drugs of abuse (Liu et al., 2005; Sorge and Clarke, 2009; but see Crombag et al., 2008). While minipumps deliver nicotine 24 h per day at a constant rate, humans smoke nicotine intermittently and not during sleep. Finally, the daily amount of nicotine typically delivered by minipumps (3.16 mg/kg) is similar to an average adult who smokes five packs of cigarettes, an amount consumed only by exceptionally heavy smokers (Armitage et al., 1975; Benowitz and Jacob, 1984). However, when differences between the metabolic rate of rats (nicotine half life = 45 min; Adir et al., 1976; Plowchalk et al., 1992) and humans (half life = 2 h) are taken into account, the actual disparity between the amounts absorbed is minimized (Malin, 2001), although comparisons remain difficult.

NICOTINE SELF-ADMINISTRATION

The self-administration method assesses an animal's propensity to self-administer a drug delivered (usually intravenously) contingently upon the emission of an operant response, usually a lever-press or nosepoke (Meisch and Lemaire, 1993). Since the early 1980s, an increasing number of laboratories have reported reliable rates of operant responding in nicotine self-administration studies with rodents (Corrigall and Coen, 1989; Donny et al., 1995; Watkins et al., 1999; Corrigall et al., 2000), but compared with other drugs of abuse, stable rates of nicotine self-administration remains difficult to establish and require careful control of a relatively high number of experimental parameters, such as the drug infusion duration, prior food training, restricted diets, and the need for cued infusions of nicotine (Henningfield and Goldberg, 1983; Collins et al., 1990; Stolerman and Jarvis, 1995; Le Foll and Goldberg, 2005; Chaudhri et al., 2006). At least some of the described difficulties obtaining nicotine self-administration may be related to the aversive properties of the drug (Benowitz, 1990). The difference between the rewarding and aversive doses of nicotine appears to be relatively small. Specifically, rats will intravenously self-administer nicotine at doses of 0.01–0.06 mg/kg (e.g., Corrigall and Coen, 1989; Donny et al., 1995; Shoaib et al., 1997), while an intravenous nicotine dose of 0.1 mg/kg has been reported to cause seizures (Hanson et al., 1979; Corrigall and Coen, 1989). Thus, when the behavioral criteria for demonstrating nicotine's reinforcing properties require that animals repeatedly self-administer the drug, the likelihood of an accumulating blood nicotine concentration that is no longer within the reinforcing dose range is greatly elevated (see Rose and Corrigall, 1997).

ESCALATION OF NICOTINE SELF-ADMINISTRATION

Rats allowed 1–3 h/day access to nicotine self-administration maintain stable and relatively low intake for weeks, exhibit very limited, if any, spontaneous withdrawal symptoms, and do not show increased motivation for nicotine after abstinence (Paterson and Markou, 2004; George et al., 2007; Cohen et al., 2012). The model of limited access to drug self-administration is highly relevant to the positive-reinforcement processes that account for the initiation and maintenance of occasional/recreational drug users but not for the transition to drug dependence, which is characterized in humans by escalated drug intake (Koob et al., 2004), robust somatic and affective withdrawal symptoms, and most importantly increased motivation for nicotine after protracted abstinence (Perkins et al., 2009). In contrast, rats exposed to

extended (6–23 h) daily opiate, cocaine, or methamphetamine self-administration sessions show escalation in drug intake (Ahmed and Koob, 1998, 1999; Ahmed et al., 2000; Ben-Shahar et al., 2004; Greenwell et al., 2009) that is characterized by an upward shift in the dose-effect function that could not be simply explained as the result of a change in the sensitivity to the drug (i.e., pharmacological tolerance or sensitization; Koob and Le Moal, 1997; Ahmed and Koob, 1998). It has been hypothesized that the escalation of drug intake reflects an allostatic increase in the hedonic set point as a result of downregulation of brain reward systems and recruitment of brain stress systems (Ahmed and Koob, 1998; Koob and Kreek, 2007). In line with this hypothesis, the escalation of opiate and cocaine intake is correlated with a progressive elevation in baseline reward thresholds (Ahmed et al., 2002; Kenny et al., 2006). Further supporting the validity of the escalation model for human addiction, the escalation of cocaine self-administration has also been shown to be accompanied by increased susceptibility to reinstatement (Mantsch et al., 2004; Wakabayashi et al., 2010) and increased stress reactivity (Aujla et al., 2008). However, the escalation of nicotine intake is not observed when rats are allowed daily extended access (6–24 h/day; 20–40 days) to nicotine (Cox et al., 1984; Valentine et al., 1997; DeNoble and Mele, 2006; Kenny and Markou, 2006; O'Dell et al., 2007), despite exhibiting levels of nicotine intake similar to human smokers (rats: 0.2–1.5 mg/kg/day; humans: 0.14–1.14 mg/kg/day; Benowitz and Jacob, 1984), and physical dependence as measured by spontaneous and mecamylamine-precipitated somatic signs (Paterson and Markou, 2004; O'Dell et al., 2007). Moreover, in contrast to the increased reward thresholds observed after extended access to cocaine, heroin, and methamphetamine, repeated exposure to nicotine self-administration (1–12 h/day for 20 days) has been shown to induce a long-lasting decrease in reward thresholds (Kenny and Markou, 2006), a result opposite to that observed after chronic exposure to osmotic minipumps (Epping-Jordan et al., 1998; Watkins et al., 2000a; see **Figure 1**). These results suggest either that nicotine dependence differs from dependence on the other drugs of abuse or that modeling the transition to escalation of compulsive nicotine intake requires revision of the existing model.

As discussed above, nicotine dependence commonly develops as adolescents and young adults who smoke intermittently escalate their drug intake. It has been repeatedly shown that intermittent access to alcohol leads to higher levels of alcohol intake than continuous access, suggesting that neurobiological changes that underlie dependence may be more readily triggered by repeated cycles of withdrawal followed by increased intake (Sinclair and Senter, 1967; O'Dell et al., 2004; Lopez and Becker, 2005; Becker and Baros, 2006). Thus, a model of dependence-induced excessive nicotine intake was developed in our laboratory, in which rats are allowed to self-administer nicotine 4 days per week for either 23 h/day (extended access) or 1 h/day (limited access), followed by 2–3 days of abstinence. Rats with extended access exhibit a pronounced increase in nicotine intake in the first post-abstinence session, with a gradual return to baseline intake levels within the remaining three daily sessions (George et al., 2007; O'Dell and Koob, 2007). This nicotine deprivation effect does not occur in rats with limited access to nicotine, suggesting that the extended-access model has better validity for studying the increased motivation for nicotine during abstinence. Moreover, 1–12 h/day of access to nicotine self-administration results in either decrease or no change in brain reward threshold during abstinence (Kenny and Markou, 2006; Patterson et al., 2008), while extending the access to 22 h/day produces an increase in brain reward threshold during the first 3 days of abstinence (measured during extinction of nicotine self-administration, Harris et al., 2011). This result is in accordance with the increase in brain reward threshold observed during withdrawal (Epping-Jordan et al., 1998) and conditioned withdrawal (Kenny and Markou, 2005) after chronic exposure to nicotine minipump, and with the increase dysphoria, depressed mood, anxiety, and frustration reported in humans during abstinence (Hughes et al., 1991).

Based on these results, we developed a novel animal model of the escalation of nicotine intake, in which rats have extended (21 h/day) but intermittent (every 24–48 h) access to nicotine self-administration (0.03 mg/kg). Escalation occur only when the rats are allowed extended but not limited access (Cohen et al., 2012), and is associated with increased motivation to take nicotine on a progressive-ratio schedule of reinforcement and with a more intense somatic signs following precipitated withdrawal. In line with the hypothesis that tobacco smoking is more reinforcing/addictive than pure nicotine because of non-nicotine compounds, such as monoamine oxidase inhibitors (MAOIs; Berlin and Anthenelli, 2001; Fowler et al., 2003; Guillem et al., 2005, 2006), the escalation is dramatically increased when rats are pretreated with the MAOI phenelzine (2 mg/kg, i.p.,) prior to each extended-access self-administration session.

As stated above, limited access (1–12 h/day) to nicotine self-administration does not produce escalation of nicotine intake, however, a recent report showed that rats with limited access to nicotine self-administration (2 h/day) escalate their nicotine intake if they are given access to nicotine 8–12 h into withdrawal from exposure to nicotine vapor (Gilpin et al., 2013). Considering that this exposure to nicotine vapor was sufficient to produce robust withdrawal symptoms (Gilpin et al., 2013), it suggests that emergence of a negative withdrawal syndrome is required for the development of escalation of nicotine intake (George et al., 2007; Gilpin et al., 2013), and suggest that exposure to nicotine vapor either passively (second-hand smoking) or actively (electronic cigarette) may have profound consequences on the acquisition and relapse of smoking behavior.

EFFECTS OF NICOTINE EXPOSURE AND WITHDRAWAL IN ADOLESCENCE

Converging lines of evidence suggest that adolescence is a vulnerable period in the development of tobacco addiction (O'Dell, 2009). Specifically, compared to adult, adolescent rats show increased sensitivity to the rewarding effects of nicotine as measured with both self-administration (Levin et al., 2003; Chen et al., 2007) and the CPP procedures (Belluzzi et al., 2004; Shram et al., 2006; Torres et al., 2008). On the other hand, adolescent rats demonstrate lower aversive responses to high nicotine doses measured with CPA and conditioned taste aversion (Shram et al., 2006; Torres et al., 2008). Interestingly, adolescent rats may be more sensitive also to the contribution of non-nicotinic tobacco smoke ingredients of tobacco

as acetaldehyde, a major component of tobacco smoke, appears to more readily enhance nicotine self-administration in adolescent but not adult rats (Belluzzi et al., 2005).

In addition to the increased rewarding effects and reduced aversive effect of nicotine in adolescents, studies using models of withdrawal from chronic passive nicotine delivery suggest that adolescent rats have a more benign nicotine withdrawal syndrome, as reflected by lower levels of somatic signs (O'Dell et al., 2004; Shram et al., 2008), withdrawal thresholds (O'Dell et al., 2006), CPA (O'Dell et al., 2007), and anxiety-like behavior in the elevated plus maze (Wilmouth and Spear, 2006).

Importantly, the human data on adolescence as a critical period in the establishment of smoking behavior in adulthood is supported by the finding that exposure to nicotine during adolescence is associated with enhanced rewarding effects of nicotine. For example, adult rats that initiated nicotine self-administration during adolescence, show higher levels of nicotine intake than rats that initiated nicotine self-administration during adulthood (Adriani et al., 2003) and rats that received nicotine during adolescence show in adulthood greater nicotine-induced place preference (Adriani et al., 2006) and increased anxiety induced withdrawal (Slawecki et al., 2003). However, the transition from nicotine use to nicotine addiction (i.e., escalation) has not yet been examined in adolescent rats.

EXPOSURE TO CIGARETTE SMOKE AND NICOTINE VAPOR

Animal models that utilize inhalation as the route of administering cigarette smoke or nicotine have exceptional face validity because they best simulate the unique pharmacokinetic characteristics (i.e., rate of absorption and brain delivery) that are associated with smoking, which may have implications for its addictive properties (Benowitz, 1990). Moreover, the stimulation of the respiratory tract by tobacco smoke (e.g., by local nicotinic receptors; Ginzel and Eldred, 1977) may play a role in nicotine dependence (Rose and Corrigall, 1997). Another advantage of inhalation-based models is that they are non-invasive and much less labor-intensive than those that involve osmotic minipumps. Although current inhalation technology allows only for non-contingent passive exposure and not for self-administration, it is particularly suitable for the study of the detrimental effects of second hand smoke and their contribution to addiction in particular.

Automated smoke machines that deliver cigarette smoke to animals in exposure chambers have been used extensively to study the toxic effects of mainstream and sidestream ("second hand") tobacco smoke (Hecht, 2005; Farkas et al., 2006; Coggins, 2007). Particularly, chronic exposure to sidestream smoke simulating environmental tobacco smoke has been recently shown to induce behavioral and neurobiological changes in laboratory animals. In primates, prenatal and postnatal environmental smoke exposure induces neuronal damage to the cortex and midbrain (Slotkin et al., 2006) and impaired memory (Golub et al., 2007). In rats, chronic exposure during postnatal days 8–23 leads to perturbed mitochondrial processes in the cerebellum that is associated with a heightened locomotor response in a novel environment (Fuller et al., 2012). Similar chronic exposure during adulthood results in biochemical changes in several brain regions (hippocampus, cerebellum, frontal cortex) indicative of enhanced inflammatory processes and cell death (Fuller et al., 2010) as well as in learning and memory impairments (Jaques et al., 2012).

Repeated exposure to mainstream cigarette smoke (modeling exposure of active smokers) induces effects similar to those of nicotine injections, including nAChR-dependent analgesia in rats, with the development of tolerance following repeated exposures (Anderson et al., 2004; Simons et al., 2005), sensitization to the effects of nicotine on locomotion (Suemaru et al., 1992; Bruijnzeel et al., 2009), and dependence as indicated by mecamylamine-precipitated somatic withdrawal signs and elevated reward thresholds (Small et al., 2010; Yamada et al., 2010). Small et al. (2010) reports that despite induction of a dependent state, nicotine self-administration is decreased 24 h after the termination of 28 consecutive tobacco smoke exposure sessions (4 h/day) and returns to control levels 5 days later. However, these results need to be interpreted with caution because the levels of nicotine and carbon monoxide to which the rats were exposed were very high in most of these studies. For example, average plasma nicotine levels in dependent smokers are 10–50 ng/ml (Russell et al., 1980; Benowitz and Jacob, 1984; Henningfield and Keenan, 1993), and average blood carboxyhemoglobin (COHgb) saturation, resulting from carbon monoxide exposure, is 4–10% (Benowitz et al., 1982; Turner et al., 1986; Law et al., 1997). Plasma nicotine concentrations in the cigarette smoke exposure studies described above ranged from 38.5 (Bruijnzeel et al., 2009) to 95.4–188 ng/ml (Anderson et al., 2004; Small et al., 2010; Yamada et al., 2010). Although COHgb levels were not reported, carbon monoxide levels in the chambers [150–402 parts per million (PPM)] were 40–400% higher than the level needed to induce COHgb saturation of 10.5% (Harris et al., 2010). These are especially high compared with the values in non-smokers exposed to second-hand smoke (5.9 ng/ml of serum nicotine; Pacifici et al., 1995) and carbon monoxide levels of 5–20 PPM (Office of Technology Assessment, 1986), leading to COHgb levels of 4.43% (Yee et al., 2010). In addition to nicotine, tobacco smoke contains at least 4,000 additional substances, many of which are toxic or psychoactive, further complicating data interpretation. For example, rats exposed to high levels of carbon monoxide and other toxins may develop adverse effects that will hinder their motivation to take nicotine. Alternatively, some components of tobacco smoke may negate certain effects of nicotine. This could explain the finding that although daily nicotine (0.125 mg/kg, s.c.) reverses the elevated reward thresholds induced by withdrawal from chronic nicotine, cigarette smoke exposure that induces the same serum nicotine levels (25–55 ng/ml) did not (Harris et al., 2010). Thus, although cigarette smoke exposure uniquely allows the determination of the net effect of tobacco smoke, isolating the specific effects of different components of tobacco smoke is difficult.

The recently developed model of nicotine vapor (George et al., 2010; Gilpin et al., 2013) addresses this shortcoming. The vaporization of nicotine is achieved without the use of heat by constantly bubbling nicotine with air and allowing for the reliable induction of air-nicotine concentrations that induce blood nicotine levels comparable to those of different tobacco exposure levels (heavy smokers, moderate smokers, and second-hand smoking). Intermittent exposure to nicotine vapor (0.2 mg/m^3 for 8 h/day

for 7 days) produces a concentration of nicotine in the blood of 22 ng/m, which is in the range of moderate smokers, and induces significant somatic withdrawal signs precipitated by mecamylamine (George et al., 2010). The concentration of nicotine in vapor chamber air can be adjusted to produce blood nicotine levels that are relevant to heavy, regular, or second-hand smoking and e-cigarette use. Moreover, as stated above, rats exposed to nicotine vapor (7.5 mg/m^3 over a 12-h period) to the point of dependence produce an escalation of nicotine self-administration relative to both their own baseline (200% increase) and non-dependent controls.

Thus, models based on the inhalation of tobacco smoke or pure nicotine have the potential to reliably detect the biological mechanisms that are unique to the consumption of tobacco via smoking and determine the possible contribution of constituents in second-hand smoke, particularly nicotine, in the transition to nicotine dependence, reflected by the escalation of nicotine intake. Future studies will need to address this issue using relatively low levels of nicotine/smoke exposure and examine the effects of exposure to a combination of nicotine and certain other selected constituents of tobacco smoke (e.g., acetaldehyde and harman) on different aspects of tobacco dependence. Finally, nicotine vapor is the only model available to date that can be used to investigate the neurobiological effects of nicotine delivery by e-cigarettes on the vulnerability to develop nicotine dependence and relapse.

NEUROBIOLOGICAL MECHANISMS OF NICOTINE ADDICTION

The different animal models of nicotine abuse and dependence have been widely used to unveil the neurobiological mechanisms that mediate the acute and chronic effects of nicotine. Models of the acute reinforcing effects of nicotine were established more than two decades ago, and the biological processes involved are well-characterized. In contrast, the neurobiological mechanisms that mediate the increased motivation for nicotine associated with drug dependence are poorly known.

ACUTE EFFECTS OF NICOTINE
Nicotine acetylcholine receptors
Nicotine acetylcholine receptors are distributed throughout the central nervous system (Paterson and Nordberg, 2000), and their activation increases the release of various neurotransmitters (Wilkie et al., 1993; McGehee et al., 1995; Clarke and Reuben, 1996; Pontieri et al., 1996; Yang et al., 1996). The acute reinforcing and rewarding effects of nicotine are mediated by the activation of nAChRs, which are composed of five subunits that can either be homomeric or heteromeric (Millar and Gotti, 2009). Twelve different neuronal nAChR subunits ($\alpha2$–$\alpha10$ and $\beta2$–$\beta4$) have been identified (Dani and Bertrand, 2007). Inactivation of $\alpha7$-, $\alpha4$-, $\alpha6$-, and $\beta2$-containing nAChRs by pharmacological or genetic manipulations decrease nicotine self-administration in rodents (Picciotto et al., 1988; Dwoskin et al., 1999; Markou and Paterson, 2001). These subunits likely mediate the acute reinforcing effects of nicotine. In contrast, $\alpha5$ knockout mice show increased nicotine self-administration at a high unit dose, suggesting the involvement of this subunit in mediating the aversive effects of high nicotine doses (Fowler et al., 2011).

Mesocorticolimbic system: dopamine

The acute reinforcing effects of nicotine and other drugs of abuse are in part mediated by activation of the mesocorticolimbic dopamine system (Koob and Le Moal, 2008). The mesocorticolimbic dopamine system includes dopaminergic neurons that originate in the ventral tegmental area (VTA) and project to the nucleus accumbens (NAc), hippocampus, amygdala, and prefrontal cortex (PFC). Indeed, nicotine exposure increases dopamine release in mesolimbic terminal fields (Di Chiara, 2000). Rats will self-administer nicotine directly into the VTA (Ikemoto et al., 2006), and intra-VTA infusion of a nicotine antagonist decreases nicotine self-administration (Corrigall et al., 1994). In addition, disruption of dopamine transmission either systemically or in the VTA attenuates nicotine self-administration (Corrigall and Coen, 1991) and prevents the reduction of brain reward thresholds induced by nicotine (Huston-Lyons et al., 1993). In the place preference procedure, dopamine antagonists block nicotine-induced CPP (Acquas et al., 1989), but in a study by Laviolette and van der Kooy (2003), nicotine infusion into the VTA dose-dependently induced CPA at low dose and CPP at high doses, and systemic infusion of a dopamine antagonist potentiated the rewarding effects of mid-range nicotine doses and switched the motivational effects of a low concentration from aversive to rewarding. These results appear to be contradictory to those obtained with the self-administration model (Ikemoto et al., 2006) and may suggest different roles for dopamine in mediating specific functions of reward and reinforcement that may be dose-dependent.

Glutamate, GABA, and acetylcholine

Nicotine increases dopamine neurotransmission in the mesocorticolimbic system by activating nAChRs, particularly α4β2, on dopaminergic neurons in the VTA (Nisell et al., 1994; Mansvelder and McGehee, 2003) and nAChRs, particularly α7-containing glutamatergic neurons that originate in the VTA, NAc, amygdala, hippocampus, and PFC (Fu et al., 2000; Mansvelder and McGehee, 2003) and project to dopaminergic neurons in the VTA (Grillner and Svensson, 2000). Consequently, antagonists of various glutamate receptors, including NMDA, AMPA, and mGluR5, decrease nicotine self-administration, whether delivered systemically or into the VTA (Kenny et al., 2003, 2009; Patterson et al., 2003; Liechti and Markou, 2008), and NMDA and AMPA receptor antagonists block nicotine-induced dopamine release in the NAc (Kosowski et al., 2004). Moreover, lesions of glutamatergic inputs from the pedunculopontine tegmental nucleus (PPT) to VTA inhibit nicotine self-administration and CPP (Lança et al., 2000; Laviolette et al., 2002; Picciotto and Corrigall, 2002). The PPT also contains cholinergic neurons that are activated by nicotine and project to dopaminergic neurons in the VTA. Indeed, delivery of an antagonist of non-α7 nAChRs to the PPT or lesions of cholinergic neurons in the PPT reduced nicotine self-administration (Lança et al., 2000; Corrigall et al., 2001, 2002; Alderson et al., 2006). Finally, intra-VTA GABAergic neurons are activated by nicotine and inhibit dopamine neurons. However nAChR on GABAergic neurons desensitize faster than nAChRs on dopamine neurons, leading to a facilitation of dopamine neuron firing (Laviolette and van der Kooy, 2004). Accordingly, enhanced activation of GABA_B receptors inhibits nicotine self-administration

and CPP in rats (Patterson et al., 2004, 2008; Le Foll et al., 2008).

Endogenous opioids

The endogenous opioid system may also play an important role in the rewarding and reinforcing effects of nicotine (for review, see Berrendero et al., 2010). Briefly, endogenous opioid systems include three main receptors, μ (MOR), δ (DOR), and κ (KOR; Kieffer and Evans, 2009). Of the opioid peptides in the brain, β-endorphin binds with a higher affinity to MORs than DORs or KORs, and it is a main endogenous ligand for MORs. Dynorphins are the main endogenous ligands for KORs (Roth-Deri et al., 2008). Nicotine enhances the release of endogenous opioid peptides and modifies the expression of their receptors. For example, acute nicotine induces increases in met-enkephalin, dynorphin, and prodynorphin mRNA in the striatum of mice after acute nicotine injection (Dhatt et al., 1995; Isola et al., 2009). Nicotine-induced dopamine increase in the NAc can be blocked by the administration of MOR antagonists or KOR agonists (Maisonneuve and Glick, 1999). However, although systemic inhibition of β-endorphin-MORs by pharmacological or genetic manipulations generally reduces the rewarding effects of nicotine in animal models (Berrendero et al., 2002; Göktalay et al., 2006; Trigo et al., 2009), the blockade of opioid receptors in the VTA and NAc does not interfere with nicotine self-administration in rats (Corrigall and Coen, 1991; Corrigall et al., 2000). Interestingly, prodynorphin knockout mice show enhanced acquisition of nicotine self-administration (Galeote et al., 2009), suggesting that the prodynorphin-KOR system may mediate the aversive effects of nicotine, particularly at high doses, as was demonstrated with other drugs of abuse (Mendizábal et al., 2006; Shippenberg et al., 2007).

Serotonergic system

Serotonin [5-hydroxytryptamine (5-HT)] neurons in the median and dorsal raphe nuclei provide the majority of 5-HT innervation to the forebrain and are associated with appetitive behavior and affect regulation (Steinbusch, 1984). Their involvement in nicotine reinforcement is suggested by nicotine-induced increases in dorsal raphe neuron firing and 5-HT release (Ribeiro et al., 1993; Li et al., 1998; Mihailescu et al., 1998, 2002; Martinez-Gonzalez et al., 2002). Agonists of 5-HT_{2C} receptors reduce nicotine self-administration (Grottick et al., 2001) but not nicotine-induced CPP (Hayes et al., 2009).

Endocannabinoids

Endocannabinoid systems may also be involved in the rewarding and reinforcing effects of nicotine. CB_1 receptor antagonists decrease nicotine self-administration and CPP in rodents (Cohen et al., 2002; Le Foll and Goldberg, 2004; Merritt et al., 2008) and the nicotine-induced enhancement of dopamine levels in the NAc (Cohen et al., 2002).

CHRONIC NICOTINE AND WITHDRAWAL

The pathological motivational state that characterizes dependence on nicotine involves the appearance of negative affective states when nicotine exposure is discontinued (i.e., nicotine withdrawal).

These may involve disruptions of the same neurobiological mechanisms that are involved in the positive reinforcing effects of the drug (i.e., within-system neuroadaptations) and recruitment of stress systems (e.g., between-system neuroadaptations). This negative affective state may represent a negative reinforcer that will enhance the incentive value of nicotine, leading to increased nicotine intake in an attempt to alleviate the negative emotional state (Solomon and Corbit, 1973; Koob and Le Moal, 2001, 2008; Koob, 2008, 2010).

Spontaneous or precipitated withdrawal from chronic nicotine produces anxiety-like behavior, CPA, and elevations of brain reward thresholds (Balerio et al., 2004; Jackson et al., 2008; Johnson et al., 2008). These affective and reward deficits likely involve downregulation of dopaminergic neurotransmission in the mesocorticolimbic system. Withdrawal from chronic nicotine results in decreased tonic firing of dopamine neurons in the VTA (Grieder et al., 2012) and decreases dopamine levels in the NAc (Fung et al., 1996; Hildebrand et al., 1998). Chronic exposure to nicotine produces a desensitization of nAChRs (Dani and Heinemann, 1996; Fenster et al., 1999; Picciotto et al., 2008) and an upregulation of nAChRs (Marks et al., 1983, 1992; Changeux et al., 1984; Dani and Heinemann, 1996; Koob and Le Moal, 2005). However, differences exist between nAChRs. For example, brain nicotine concentrations in an average smoker reach levels sufficient to desensitize $\alpha4\beta2$ nAChRs without affecting $\alpha7$ nAChRs, which requires much higher concentrations (Wooltorton et al., 2003). Glutamate release is regulated by $\alpha7$ nAChRs located presynaptically (Marchi et al., 2002). Thus, during nicotine exposure, desensitization of $\alpha4\beta2$ nAChRs on GABAergic neurons will suppress GABA release and inhibit dopamine neurons in the VTA, whereas $\alpha7$ nAChRs on glutamatergic afferents will remain active and increase glutamate release on dopamine neurons in this region, facilitating dopamine secretion in the NAc (Dani, 2001; Wooltorton et al., 2003). However, nicotine withdrawal produces an opposite effect, with decreases in VTA glutamate levels and increases in VTA GABA levels (Natividad et al., 2012). Consequently, antagonism of presynaptic mGluR2/3 antagonists, known to negatively modulate glutamate release (Schoepp et al., 2003), attenuates reward deficits associated with nicotine withdrawal in rodents and alleviates the depressive-like symptoms related to nicotine abstinence in humans (Kenny et al., 2003; Liechti and Markou, 2008). Inhibition of glutamate transmission by the delivery of mGluR5 antagonists in rats and knocking out mGluR5 in mice further elevates reward thresholds during nicotine withdrawal (Harrison et al., 2002; Liechti and Markou, 2007; Stoker et al., 2012).

Endogenous opioids may play an important role in the development of nicotine dependence, reflected by the resemblance between the somatic signs induced by the cessation of nicotine exposure and those of opiate withdrawal (Malin et al., 1993; Watkins et al., 2000a) and the ability of the opioid receptor naloxone to induce somatic signs of withdrawal in heavy smokers (Sutherland et al., 1995; Krishnan-Sarin et al., 1999). Naloxone administration in rodents chronically treated with nicotine induces somatic signs of withdrawal (Malin et al., 1993; Balerio et al., 2004; Biala et al., 2005), CPA, and elevations in reward thresholds (Watkins et al., 2000a,b). MOR (Berrendero et al., 2002) and proenkephalin (Berrendero et al., 2005) knockout mice chronically

exposed to nicotine show reduced somatic signs of withdrawal. Interestingly, knockout of the prodynorphin gene does not impact the somatic signs of nicotine withdrawal (Galeote et al., 2009). Moreover, nicotine withdrawal is associated with increased prodynorphin expression in the NAc (Isola et al., 2008). Thus, it can be hypothesized that during chronic nicotine exposure, there is a release of opioid peptides, which leads to downregulation of MORs and upregulation of prodynorphin-KOR systems. These opposing effects may combine to participate in the mediation of the somatic and affective aspects of nicotine withdrawal.

There is also evidence that 5-HT neurotransmission is involved in the mediation of nicotine dependence. Chronic nicotine treatment decreases the concentration of 5-HT in the hippocampus and increases the number of hippocampal 5-HT$_{1A}$ receptors (Benwell and Balfour, 1979). This receptor upregulation may reflect reduced levels of 5-HT input from the median raphe nucleus, which is the main source of brain 5-HT and projects to various brain areas, including the hippocampus and amygdala (Benwell et al., 1990). During nicotine abstinence, decreased 5-HT, combined with upregulated 5HT$_1$ receptors, may contribute to symptoms of depression and anxiety that are associated with 5-HT deficits (Coppen, 1967; Young et al., 1985; Markou et al., 1998) and nicotine withdrawal (Hughes et al., 1991). Indeed, antagonism of 5-HT receptors attenuates withdrawal-induced CPA in animals (Suzuki et al., 1997) and anxiety in withdrawn human smokers (West et al., 1991; Hilleman et al., 1992, 1994). Interestingly, a recent study suggests that acute nicotine activates 5-HT neurons in the dorsal raphe that are regionally distinct from those involved in nicotine withdrawal (Sperling and Commons, 2011).

STRESS IN NICOTINE DEPENDENCE

Convergent lines of evidence (Koob and Le Moal, 2001, 2005) suggest that stress [e.g., corticotropin-releasing factor (CRF) and orexin] and anti-stress [e.g., neuropeptide Y (NPY)] systems are involved in the emotional and motivational aspects of drug dependence (see Bruijnzeel, 2012, for an extensive review) and are largely localized to the extended amygdala, a forebrain macrostructure composed of the bed nucleus of he stria terminalis (BNST), central nucleus of the amygdala (CeA), and NAc shell (Heimer and Alheid, 1991; Smith and Aston-Jones, 2008).

Corticotropin-releasing factor

Nicotine self-administration increases the release of adrenocorticotropic hormone (ACTH) and cortisol/corticosterone (CORT; Donny et al., 2000; Chen et al., 2008). Evidence suggests that while CORT facilitates the reinforcing effects of drugs in nondependent subjects, high circulating levels of CORT, as a result of repeated drug use, can feed back to shut off the hypothalamic-pituitary adrenal (HPA) axis and sensitize extrahypothalamic CRF systems, contributing to escalated and compulsive drug intake (Vendruscolo et al., 2012). CRF is a neuropeptide that has three paralogs – Ucn 1, 2, and 3 – and is involved in regulating the neuroendocrine autonomic and behavioral responses to stress (Vale et al., 1981, 1983; Dunn and Berridge, 1990; Koob, 1999). Two G-protein-coupled CRF receptors have been identified: CRF$_1$ and CRF$_2$. Notably, although CRF and Ucn 1 have high selectively for the CRF$_1$ receptor, Ucn 2 and Ucn 3 have high selectivity for the CRF$_2$ receptor (Bale and Vale, 2004). While activation of the CRF$_1$ receptor leads to increases in anxiety-like behavior, activation of the CRF$_2$ receptor generally triggers a compensatory anti-stress response. For example, selective CRF$_1$ antagonists have been shown to reduce anxiety-like behavior in animals (Griebel et al., 1998; Deak et al., 1999; Zorrilla et al., 2002), whereas the CRF$_2$ receptor agonist Ucn 3 decreases behavioral stress responses (Valdez et al., 2002, 2003). Various findings suggest that recruitment of CRF–CRF$_1$ systems, particularly in regions of the extended amygdala, may be involved in producing the negative emotional states during withdrawal or protracted abstinence from chronic nicotine. First, precipitated nicotine withdrawal increases Fos expression (i.e., neuronal activation) in the CeA. Second, CRF levels in the basal forebrain (Matta et al., 2007) and CeA (George et al., 2007) are elevated during nicotine withdrawal. Third, the elevation of reward thresholds induced by nicotine withdrawal is attenuated by intracerebroventricular or intra-CeA infusion of the CRF$_1$ antagonist D-Phe CRF$_{12-41}$ and non-specific CRF antagonist α-helical CRF$_{9-41}$ (Bruijnzeel et al., 2009; Marcinkiewcz et al., 2009; Bruijnzeel, 2012) but not a CRF$_2$ antagonist (Bruijnzeel et al., 2009). Infusion of D-Phe CRF$_{12-41}$ into the NAc shell, another region of the extended amygdala, also blocks the withdrawal-induced elevation in reward thresholds (Marcinkiewcz et al., 2009). Fourth, a CRF$_1$ antagonist (MPZP) administered systemically attenuates the abstinence-induced increases in nicotine intake and nicotine withdrawal-induced anxiety-like behavior (George et al., 2007). Finally, CRF$_1$ antagonists administered systemically attenuate the escalated intake of heroin and cocaine in rats with extended access to the drug (Specio et al., 2008; Greenwell et al., 2009).

Neuropeptide Y

Neuropeptide Y is a 36-amino-acid polypeptide with powerful anxiolytic-like properties in various animal models of anxiety and stress (Heilig and Murison, 1987; Broqua et al., 1995; Sajdyk et al., 1999; Tovote et al., 2004). The involvement of NPY in addiction was mainly studied with regard to alcohol dependence, with alcohol-preferring rats having lower basal levels of NPY in the CeA that correlate with greater levels of anxiety-like behavior compared with alcohol non-preferring rats (Suzuki et al., 2004; Pandey et al., 2005). Moreover, viral vector-induced overexpression of NPY in the CeA decreases alcohol intake in alcohol-dependent rats (Thorsell et al., 2007). These results suggest that downregulation of the NPY system in the CeA may mediate the transition from non-dependent to dependent alcohol intake. The role of NPY in nicotine dependence has been less studied. Rylkova et al. (2008) report that NPY prevents the somatic signs of withdrawal but not elevation in brain reward thresholds that result from precipitated nicotine withdrawal in rats. Yet, abstinence from nicotine induced anxiety-like behavior that was associated with a decreased ratio of NPY to CRF in the amygdala, suggesting an allostatic change in both stress and anti-stress neuropeptide systems (Slawecki et al., 2005; Aydin et al., 2011).

Norepinephrine

Several lines of evidence suggest that norepinephrine (NE) signaling from the nucleus tractus solitarius (NTS) to extended amygdala

mediates the aversive effects of opiate and cocaine withdrawal (e.g., anxiety-like behavior; Smith and Aston-Jones, 2008). Moreover, morphine withdrawal enhances subsequent morphine-induced CPP, which is reduced by delivery of the α$_2$-adrenoceptor agonist clonidine (Nader and van der Kooy, 1996). The role of NE in nicotine dependence has been less explored, but clonidine appears to decrease anxiety and irritation associated with smoking cessation and promote abstinence (Prochazka et al., 1992; Gourlay et al., 2004). The few animal studies conducted have yielded conflicting results. Deficits in brain reward function during nicotine withdrawal were attenuated by antagonism of α$_1$-adrenoceptors (Bruijnzeel et al., 2010) and antagonism of α$_2$-adrenoceptors in another study (Semenova and Markou, 2010). This is puzzling given the positive effect of clonidine, a α$_2$ agonist, in human abstinent smokers. More studies are needed to clarify the role of NE in nicotine dependence.

Orexin/hypocretin

Orexin A (hypocretin-1) and orexin B (hypocretin-2) are neuropeptides that have two known receptors, Hcrt-r1 and Hcrt-r2, and regulate several processes, including arousal (Sutcliffe and de Lecea, 2002; Taheri et al., 2002) and stress responses (Baldo et al., 2003; Winsky-Sommerer et al., 2004). Orexin/hypocretin neurons are especially abundant in the lateral hypothalamus and project to various brain regions, including the extended amygdala (Peyron et al., 1998; Baldo et al., 2003). Interestingly, intracerebroventricular infusion of orexin A induces Fos activation in approximately half of the CRF-containing neurons in the CeA (Sakamoto et al., 2004). Orexin neurons also receive inputs from the amygdala (Sakurai et al., 2005), and a possible positive feedback circuit between hypothalamic orexin neurons and amygdala CRF neurons has been suggested (Corrigall, 2009). Indeed, dependent smokers during early withdrawal show a significant negative correlation between hypocretin plasma concentration and nicotine craving (von der Goltz et al., 2010). A recent study reports that nicotine withdrawal increases hypocretin cell activity in the hypothalamus and that the hypocretin-1 receptor antagonist SB334867 as well as preprohypocretin knockout attenuate somatic nicotine withdrawal signs in mice (Plaza-Zabala et al., 2012). This study also revealed that the hypothalamic paraventricular nucleus (PVN) is strongly involved in this effect. Infusion of SB334867 into this region attenuates the somatic signs of withdrawal.

Nociceptin/orphanin FQ

Nociceptin/orphanin FQ is a 17-amino-acid peptide that shows structural homology with the dynorphin A peptide (Reinscheid et al., 1995) and binds to the nociceptin/orphanin peptide (NOP) receptor. Nociceptin/orphanin FQ and NOP receptors are distributed throughout the central nervous system, with relatively high densities in the extended amygdala, PFC, and VTA (Neal et al., 1999). Nociceptin/orphanin FQ generally inhibits stress responses by functionally antagonizing CRF activity (Ciccocioppo et al., 2003). Chronic exposure to alcohol decreases the levels of brain nociceptin/orphanin FQ (Lindholm et al., 2002), and activation of the nociceptin/orphanin FQ system attenuates alcohol withdrawal symptoms and reverses increased anxiety-like behavior associated with ethanol dependence (Economidou et al.,

2011; Aujla et al., 2013). Nociceptin/orphanin FQ might be similarly involved in nicotine dependence. NOP receptor knockout mice, unlike wildtype mice, show a significant mecamylamine-induced CPA to nicotine withdrawal (Sakoori and Murphy, 2009).

ESCALATION OF NICOTINE INTAKE

Unlike cocaine and opiates, daily extended self-administration sessions do not induce escalation of nicotine intake but rather a reduction in intake following the first daily session and stable intake afterward (Valentine et al., 1997; Kenny and Markou, 2006; O'Dell et al., 2007; Cohen et al., 2012). However, humans typically do not have continuous access to smoking but instead alternate between periods of access (daytime) and no access (nighttime). The escalation of nicotine intake only occurs when 24–48 h of abstinence are given between extended-access (21 h) sessions (Cohen et al., 2012). It is possible that escalation does not take place when given continuous access because of nAChR desensitization (see above), which requires a period ranging from a few hours to a few days to recover (Collins et al., 1990, 1994; Girod and Role, 2001). Additionally, the escalated intake of nicotine could reflect the increased incentive value of nicotine that results from experiencing a negative affective state because of recruitment of stress systems and downregulation of anti-stress systems (Koob and Le Moal, 2001; Koob, 2010). Supporting such a hypothesis, CRF levels in the CeA are increased during precipitated withdrawal. Moreover, blocking CRF_1 receptors systemically with MPZP attenuates both the increase in anxiety-like behavior during precipitated withdrawal and increase in nicotine intake following 72 h of abstinence (George et al., 2007). In accordance with the hypothesis that emergence of a negative emotional state is required in order to observe escalation of nicotine intake is the fact that rats with limited access to nicotine self-administration (2 h/day) escalate their nicotine intake only if they are tested under withdrawal from daily exposure to nicotine vapor that is sufficient to produce a robust withdrawal syndrome (Gilpin et al., 2013).

To further support the hypothesis that negative affective symptoms drive the escalation of nicotine self-administration, possible associations between anxiety-like behavior (among other negative affective symptoms) and the escalation of nicotine self-administration will need to be explored, and the possibility that manipulation of CRF and other stress and anti-stress systems can block the escalation of nicotine intake should be examined.

SUMMARY AND CONCLUSION

Animal models of the acute effects of nicotine have provided us with ample evidence regarding the reinforcing and affective effects of nicotine and neurobiological processes that mediate them. These studies support a central role for the mesocorticolimbic dopamine system and neuronal circuits that interact with it in the acute reinforcing effects of nicotine. Studies using chronic passive delivery of nicotine via intracranial or intraperitoneal routes of administration have provided evidence that chronic nicotine dysregulates nAChRs and downregulates the same neurobiological mechanisms that are involved in the positive reinforcing effects of the drug. However, most of these studies did not examine the relationships between these neurobiological alterations and motivation to consume nicotine after dependence developed. Human smokers tend to begin smoking intermittently, especially at early ages, and quickly develop initial aversive symptoms of abstinence. Their smoking behavior escalates until daily smoking reaches a stable high level that is considered compulsive. Novel models of escalated nicotine intake will allow investigation of the mechanisms that underlie the development of compulsive nicotine intake in rats. Initial evidence suggests that recruitment of brain stress systems is a key factor in this process, but further research is needed. Novel models of nicotine exposure that utilize inhalation also provide a unique opportunity to evaluate the effects of e-cigarette use and second-hand smoking exposure on the vulnerability to dependence and relapse.

ACKNOWLEDGMENTS

This is publication number 23025 from The Scripps Research Institute. This work was supported by National Institutes of Health Grant DA023597 from the National Institute on Drug Abuse and the Pearson Center for Alcoholism and Addiction Research. The authors would like to thank Michael Arends for his help with manuscript preparation.

REFERENCES

Acquas, E., Carboni, E., Leone, P., and Di Chiara, G. (1989). SCH 23390 blocks drug-conditioned place-preference and place-aversion: anhedonia (lack of reward) or apathy (lack of motivation) after dopamine-receptor blockade? *Psychopharmacology (Berl.)* 99, 151–155. doi:10.1007/BF00442800

Adir, J., Miller, R. P., and Rotenberg, K. S. (1976). Disposition of nicotine in the rat after intravenous administration. *Res. Commun. Chem. Pathol. Pharmacol.* 13, 173–183.

Adriani, W., Deroche-Gamonet, V., Le Moal, M., Laviola, G., and Piazza, P. V. (2006). Preexposure during or following adolescence differently affects nicotine-rewarding properties in adult rats. *Psychopharmacology (Berl.)* 184, 382–390. doi:10.1007/s00213-005-0125-1

Adriani, W., Spijker, S., Deroche-Gamonet, V., Laviola, G., Le Moal, M., Smit, A. B., et al. (2003). Evidence for enhanced neurobehavioral vulnerability to nicotine during periadolescence in rats. *J. Neurosci.* 23, 4712–4716.

Ahmed, S. H., Kenny, P. J., Koob, G. F., and Markou, A. (2002). Neurobiological evidence for hedonic allostasis associated with escalating cocaine use. *Nat. Neurosci.* 5, 625–626.

Ahmed, S. H., and Koob, G. F. (1998). Transition from moderate to excessive drug intake: change in hedonic set point. *Science* 282, 298–300. doi:10.1126/science.282.5 387.298

Ahmed, S. H., and Koob, G. F. (1999). Long-lasting increase in the set point for cocaine self-administration after escalation in rats. *Psychopharmacology (Berl.)* 146, 303–312. doi:10.1007/s002130051121

Ahmed, S. H., Walker, J. R., and Koob, G. F. (2000). Persistent increase in the motivation to take heroin in rats with a history of drug escalation. *Neuropsychopharmacology* 22, 413–421. doi:10.1016/S0893-133X(99)00133-5

Ajzen, I., and Fishbein, M. (1980). *Understanding Attitudes and Predicting Social Behavior.* Englewood Cliffs, NJ: Prentice Hall.

Alderson, H. L., Latimer, M. P., and Winn, P. (2006). Intravenous self-administration of nicotine is altered by lesions of the posterior, but not anterior, pedunculopontine tegmental nucleus. *Eur. J. Neurosci.* 23, 2169–2175. doi:10.1111/j.1460-9568.2006.04737.x

Anderson, K. L., Pinkerton, K. E., Uyeminami, D., Simons, C. T., Carstens, M. I., and Carstens, E. (2004). Antinociception induced by chronic exposure of rats to cigarette smoke. *Neurosci. Lett.* 366, 86–91. doi:10.1016/j.neulet.2004. 05.020

Armitage, A. K., Dollery, C. T., George, C. F., Houseman, T. H., Lewis, P. J., and Turner, D. M. (1975). Absorption and metabolism of nicotine from cigarettes. *Br. Med. J.* 4, 313–316. doi:10.1136/bmj.4.5992.313

Ashby, C. R. Jr., Paul, M., Gardner, E. L., Gerasimov, M. R., Dewey, S. L., Lennon, I. C., et al. (2002). Systemic administration of 1R,4S- 4-amino-cyclopent-2-ene-carboxylic acid, a reversible inhibitor of GABA transaminase, blocks expression of conditioned place preference to cocaine and nicotine in rats. *Synapse* 44, 61–63. doi:10.1002/syn.10052

Ashton, H., and Watson, D. W. (1970). Puffing frequency and nicotine intake in cigarette smokers. *Br. Med. J.* 3, 679–681. doi:10.1136/bmj.3.5724.679

Audrain-McGovern, J., Al Koudsi, N., Rodriguez, D., Wileyto, E. P., Shields, P. G., and Tyndale, R. F. (2007). The Role of CYP2A6 in the emergence of nicotine dependence in adolescents. *Pediatrics* 119, 264–274. doi:10.1542/peds.2006-1583

Aujla, H., Cannarsa, R., Romualdi, P., Ciccocioppo, R., Martin-Fardon, R., and Weiss, F. (2013). Modification of anxiety-like behaviors by nociceptin/orphanin FQ (N/OFQ) and time-dependent changes in N/OFQ-NOP gene expression following ethanol withdrawal. *Addict. Biol.* 18, 467–479. doi:10.1111/j.1369-1600.2012.00466.x

Aujla, H., Martin-Fardon, R., and Weiss, F. (2008). Rats with extended access to cocaine exhibit increased stress reactivity and sensitivity to the anxiolytic-like effects of the mGluR 2/3 agonist LY379268 during abstinence. *Neuropsychopharmacology* 33, 1818–1826. doi:10.1038/sj.npp.1301588

Aydin, C., Oztan, O., and Isgor, C. (2011). Vulnerability to nicotine abstinence-related social anxiety-like behavior: molecular correlates in neuropeptide Y, Y2. *Neurosci. Lett.* 490, 220–225. doi:10.1016/j.neulet.2010.12.056

Baldo, B. A., Daniel, R. A., Berridge, C. W., and Kelley, A. E. (2003). Overlapping distributions of orexin/hypocretin and dopamine-beta-hydroxylase immunoreactive fibers in rat brain regions mediating arousal, motivation, and stress. *J. Comp. Neurol.* 464, 220–237. doi:10.1002/cne.10783

Bale, T. L., and Vale, W. W. (2004). CRF and CRF receptors: role in stress responsivity and other

behaviors. *Annu. Rev. Pharmacol. Toxicol.* 44, 525–557. doi:10.1146/annurev.pharmtox.44.101802.121410

Balerio, G. N., Aso, E., Berrendero, F., Murtra, P., and Maldonado, R. (2004). Delta9-tetrahydrocannabinol decreases somatic and motivational manifestations of nicotine withdrawal in mice. *Eur. J. Neurosci.* 20, 2737–2748. doi:10.1111/j.1460-9568.2004.03714.x

Becker, H. C., and Baros, A. M. (2006). Effect of duration and pattern of chronic ethanol exposure on tolerance to the discriminative stimulus effects of ethanol in C57BL/6J mice. *J. Pharmacol. Exp. Ther.* 319, 871–878. doi:10.1124/jpet.106.108795

Becklake, M. R., Ghezzo, H., and Ernst, P. (2005). Childhood predictors of smoking in adolescence: a follow-up study of Montréal schoolchildren. *Can. Med. Assoc. J.* 173, 377–379. doi:10.1503/cmaj.1041428

Bélanger, M., O'Loughlin, J., Okoli, C. T., McGrath, J. J., Setia, M., and Guyon, L. (2008). Nicotine dependence symptoms among young never-smokers exposed to secondhand tobacco smoke. *Addict. Behav.* 33, 1557–1563. doi:10.1016/j.addbeh.2008.07.011

Belluzzi, J. D., Lee, A. G., Oliff, H. S., and Leslie, F. M. (2004). Age-dependent effects of nicotine on locomotor activity and conditioned place preference in rats. *Psychopharmacology (Berl.)* 174, 389–395. doi:10.1007/s00213-003-1758-6

Belluzzi, J. D., Wang, R., and Leslie, F. M. (2005). Acetaldehyde enhances acquisition of nicotine self-administration in adolescent rats. *Neuropsychopharmacology* 30, 705–712. doi:10.1038/sj.npp.1300586

Benowitz, N. L. (1986). Clinical pharmacology of nicotine. *Annu. Rev. Med.* 37, 21–32. doi:10.1146/annurev.me.37.020186.000321

Benowitz, N. L. (1990). Pharmacokinetic considerations in understanding nicotine dependence. *Ciba Found. Symp.* 152, 186–200.

Benowitz, N. L., and Jacob, P. III. (1984). Daily intake of nicotine during cigarette smoking. *Clin. Pharmacol. Ther.* 35, 499–504. doi:10.1038/clpt.1984.67

Benowitz, N. L., Kuyt, F., and Jacob, P. III. (1982). Circadian blood nicotine concentrations during cigarette smoking. *Clin. Pharmacol. Ther.* 32, 758–764. doi:10.1038/clpt.1982.233

Benowitz, N. L., Porchet, H., Sheiner, L., and Jacob, P. III. (1988). Nicotine absorption and cardiovascular effects with smokeless tobacco use: comparison with cigarettes and nicotine gum. *Clin. Pharmacol. Ther.* 44, 23–28. doi:10.1038/clpt.1988.107

Ben-Shahar, O., Ahmed, S. H., Koob, G. F., and Ettenberg, A. (2004). The transition from controlled to compulsive drug use is associated with a loss of sensitization. *Brain Res.* 995, 46–54. doi:10.1016/j.brainres.2003.09.053

Benwell, M. E., and Balfour, D. J. (1979). Effects of nicotine administration and its withdrawal on plasma corticosterone and brain 5-hydroxyindoles. *Psychopharmacology (Berl.)* 63, 7–11. doi:10.1007/BF00426913

Benwell, M. E., Balfour, D. J., and Anderson, J. M. (1990). Smoking-associated changes in the serotonergic systems of discrete regions of human brain. *Psychopharmacology (Berl.)* 102, 68–72. doi:10.1007/BF02245746

Berlin, I., and Anthenelli, R. M. (2001). Monoamine oxidases and tobacco smoking. *Int. J. Neuropsychopharmacol.* 4, 33–42.

Berrendero, F., Kieffer, B. L., and Maldonado, R. (2002). Attenuation of nicotine-induced antinociception, rewarding effects, and dependence in mu-opioid receptor knock-out mice. *J. Neurosci.* 22, 10935–10940.

Berrendero, F., Mendizabal, V., Robledo, P., Galeote, L., Bilkei-Gorzo, A., Zimmer, A., et al. (2005). Nicotine-induced antinociception, rewarding effects, and physical dependence are decreased in mice lacking the preproenkephalin gene. *J. Neurosci.* 25, 1103–1112. doi:10.1523/JNEUROSCI.3008-04.2005

Berrendero, F., Robledo, P., Trigo, J. M., Martín-García, E., and Maldonado, R. (2010). Neurobiological mechanisms involved in nicotine dependence and reward: participation of the endogenous opioid system. *Neurosci. Biobehav. Rev.* 35, 220–231. doi:10.1016/j.neubiorev.2010.02.006

Bespalov, A., Lebedev, A., Panchenko, G., and Zvartau, E. (1999). Effects of abused drugs on thresholds and breaking points of intracranial self-stimulation in rats. *Eur. Neuropsychopharmacol.* 9, 377–383. doi:10.1016/S0924-977X(99)00008-5

Bhattacharyya, N. (2012). Trends in the use of smokeless tobacco in United

States, 2000-2010. *Laryngoscope* 122, 2175–2178. doi:10.1002/lary.23448

Biala, G., and Budzynska, B. (2006). Effects of acute and chronic nicotine on elevated plus maze in mice: involvement of calcium channels. *Life Sci.* 30, 81–88. doi:10.1016/j.lfs.2005.12.043

Biala, G., Budzynska, B., and Kruk, M. (2005). Naloxone precipitates nicotine abstinence syndrome and attenuates nicotine-induced antinociception in mice. *Pharmacol. Rep.* 57, 755–760.

Bozarth, M. A., Pudiak, C. M., and KuoLee, R. (1998a). Effect of chronic nicotine on brain stimulation reward. II. An escalating dose regimen. *Behav. Brain Res.* 96, 189–194. doi:10.1016/S0166-4328(98)00050-3

Bozarth, M. A., Pudiak, C. M., and KuoLee, R. (1998b). Effect of chronic nicotine on brain stimulation reward. I. Effect of daily injections. *Behav. Brain Res.* 96, 185–188. doi:10.1016/S0166-4328(98)00050-3

O'Dell, L. E., Torres, O. V., Natividad, L. A., and Tejeda, H. A. (2007). Adolescent nicotine exposure produces less affective measures of withdrawal relative to adult nicotine exposure in male rats. *Neurotoxicol. Teratol.* 29, 17–22. doi:10.1016/j.ntt.2006.11.003

Brioni, J. D., O'Neill, A. B., Kim, D. J. B., and Decker, M. W. (1993). Nicotinic receptor agonists exhibit anxiolytic-like effects on the elevated plus-maze test. *Eur. J. Pharmacol.* 283, 1–8. doi:10.1016/0014-2999(93)90498-7

Brody, A. L., Mandelkern, M. A., London, E. D., Khan, A., Kozman, D., Costello, M. R., et al. (2011). Effect of secondhand smoke on occupancy of nicotinic acetylcholine receptors in brain. *Arch. Gen. Psychiatry* 68, 953–960. doi:10.1001/archgenpsychiatry.2011.51

Brody, A. L., Mandelkern, M. A., London, E. D., Olmstead, R. E., Farahi, J., Scheibal, D., et al. (2006). Cigarette smoking saturates brain alpha 4 beta 2 nicotinic acetylcholine receptors. *Arch. Gen. Psychiatry* 63, 907–915. doi:10.1001/archpsyc.63.8.907

Brook, J. S., Saar, N. S., Zhang, C., and Brook, D. W. (2009). Familial and non-familial smoking: effects on smoking and nicotine dependence. *Drug Alcohol Depend.* 101, 62–68. doi:10.1016/j.drugalcdep.2008.11.003

Broqua, P., Wettstein, J. G., Rocher, M. N., Gauthier-Martin, B., and Junien, J. L. (1995). Behavioral effects of neuropeptide Y receptor agonists in the elevated plus-maze and fear-potentiated startle procedures. *Behav. Pharmacol.* 6, 215–222. doi:10.1097/00008877-199504000-00001

Bruijnzeel, A. W. (2012). Tobacco addiction and the dysregulation of brain stress systems. *Neurosci. Biobehav. Rev.* 36, 1418–1441. doi:10.1016/j.neubiorev.2012.02.015

Bruijnzeel, A. W., Bishnoi, M., Van Tuijl, I. A., Keijzers, K. F., Yavarovich, K. R., Pasek, T. M., et al. (2010). Effects of prazosin, clonidine, and propranolol on the elevations in brain reward thresholds and somatic signs associated with nicotine withdrawal in rats. *Psychopharmacology (Berl.)* 212, 485–499. doi:10.1007/s00213-010-1970-0

Bruijnzeel, A. W., Prado, M., and Isaac, S. (2009). Corticotropin-releasing factor-1 receptor activation mediates nicotine withdrawal-induced deficit in brain reward function and stress-induced relapse. *Biol. Psychiatry* 66, 110–117. doi:10.1016/j.biopsych.2009.01.010

Bullen, C., McRobbie, H., Thornley, S., Glover, M., Lin, R., and Laugesen, M. (2010). Effect of an electronic nicotine delivery device (e cigarette) on desire to smoke and withdrawal, user preferences and nicotine delivery: randomised crossover trial. *Tob. Control* 19, 98–103. doi:10.1136/tc.2009.031567

Cahn, Z., and Siegel, M. (2011). Electronic cigarettes as a harm reduction strategy for tobacco control: a step forward or a repeat of past mistakes? *J. Public Health Policy* 32, 16–31. doi:10.1057/jphp.2010.41

Caponnetto, P., Campagna, D., Papale, G., Russo, C., and Polosa, R. (2012). The emerging phenomenon of electronic cigarettes. *Expert. Rev. Respir. Med.* 6, 63–74. doi:10.1586/ers.11.92

Carr, G. D., Fibiger, H. C., and Phillips, A. G. (1989). "Conditioned place preference as a measure of drug reward," in *Neuropharmacological Basis of Reward*, eds J. M. Liebman and S. J. Cooper (New York: Oxford University Press), 264–319.

Carroll, M. E., Lac, S. T., Asencio, M., and Keenan, R. M. (1989). Nicotine dependence in rats. *Life Sci.* 45, 1381–1388. doi:10.1016/0024-3205(89)90025-8

Changeux, J. P., Devillers-Thiery, A., and Chemouilli, P. (1984). Acetylcholine receptor: an allosteric protein. *Science* 225, 1335–1345. doi:10.1126/science.6382611

Chaudhri, N., Caggiula, A. R., Donny, E. C., Palmatier, M. I., Liu, X., and Sved,

A. F. (2006). Complex interactions between nicotine and nonpharmacological stimuli reveal multiple roles for nicotine in reinforcement. *Psychopharmacology (Berl.)* 184, 353–366. doi:10.1007/s00213-005-0178-1

Cheeta, S., Irvine, E., and File, S. E. (2001). Social isolation modifies nicotine's effects in animal tests of anxiety. *Br. J. Pharmacol.* 132, 1389–1395. doi:10.1038/sj.bjp.0703991

Chen, H., Fu, Y., and Sharp, B. M. (2008). Chronic nicotine self-administration augments hypothalamic–pituitary–adrenal responses to mild acute stress. *Neuropsychopharmacology* 33, 721–730. doi:10.1038/sj.npp.1301466

Chen, H., Matta, S. G., and Sharp, B. M. (2007). Acquisition of nicotine self-administration in adolescent rats given prolonged access to the drug. *Neuropsychopharmacology* 32, 700–709. doi:10.1038/sj.npp.1301135

Ciccocioppo, R., Fedeli, A., Economidou, D., Policani, F., Weiss, F., and Massi, M. (2003). corticotropin-releasing factor and its reversal by nociceptin/orphanin FQ. *J. Neurosci.* 23, 9445–9451.

Cippitelli, A., Astarita, G., Duranti, A., Caprioli, G., Ubaldi, M., Stopponi, S., et al. (2011). Endocannabinoid regulation of acute and protracted nicotine withdrawal: effect of FAAH inhibition. *PLoS ONE* 6:e28142. doi:10.1371/journal.pone.0028142

Clarke, P. B., and Fibiger, H. C. (1987). Apparent absence of nicotine-induced conditioned place preference in rats. *Psychopharmacology (Berl.)* 92, 84–88. doi:10.1007/BF00215484

Clarke, P. B., Fu, D. S., Jakubovic, A., and Fibiger, H. C. (1988). Evidence that mesolimbic dopaminergic activation underlies the locomotor stimulant action of nicotine in rats. *J. Pharmacol. Exp. Ther.* 246, 701–708.

Clarke, P. B., and Kumar, R. (1983). The effects of nicotine on locomotor activity in non-tolerant and tolerant rats. *Br. J. Pharmacol.* 78, 329–337. doi:10.1111/j.1476-5381.1983.tb09398.x

Clarke, P. B., and Kumar, R. (1984). Some effects of nicotine on food and water intake in undeprived rats. *Br. J. Pharmacol.* 82, 233–239. doi:10.1111/j.1476-5381.1984.tb16463.x

Clarke, P. B. S., and Reuben, M. (1996). Release of [3H]-noradrenaline from rat hippocampal synaptosomes

by nicotine: mediation by different nicotinic receptor subtypes from striatal [3H]-dopamine release. *Br. J. Pharmacol.* 117, 595–606. doi:10.1111/j.1476-5381.1996.tb15232.x

Clemens, K. J., Caillé, S., Stinus, L., and Cador, M. (2009). The addition of five minor tobacco alkaloids increases nicotine-induced hyperactivity, sensitization and intravenous self-administration in rats. *Int. J. Neuropsychopharmacol.* 12, 1355–1366. doi:10.1017/S1461145709000273

Coggins, C. R. (2007). An updated review of inhalation studies with cigarette smoke in laboratory animals. *Int. J. Toxicol.* 26, 331–338. doi:10.1080/10915810701490190

Coggins, C. R., Murrelle, E. L., Carchman, R. A., and Heidbreder, C. (2009). Light and intermittent cigarette smokers: a review (1989–2009). *Psychopharmacology (Berl.)* 207, 343–363. doi:10.1007/s00213-009-1675-4

Cohen, A., Koob, G. F., and George, O. (2012). Robust escalation of nicotine intake with extended access to nicotine self-administration and intermittent periods of abstinence. *Neuropsychopharmacology* 37, 2153–2160. doi:10.1038/npp.2012.67

Cohen, C., Perrault, G., Voltz, C., Steinberg, R., and Soubrie, P. (2002). SR141716, a central cannabinoid (CB(1)) receptor antagonist, blocks the motivational and dopamine-releasing effects of nicotine in rats. *Behav. Pharmacol.* 13, 451–463. doi:10.1097/00008877-200209000-00018

Collins, A. C., Bhat, R. V., Pauly, J. R., and Marks, M. J. (1990). Modulation of nicotine receptors by chronic exposure to nicotinic agonists and antagonists. *Ciba Found. Symp.* 152, 68–82.

Collins, A. C., Luo, Y., Selvaag, S., and Marks, M. J. (1994). Sensitivity to nicotine and brain nicotinic receptors are altered by chronic nicotine and mecamylamine infusion. *J. Pharmacol. Exp. Ther.* 271, 125–133.

Collins, A. C., Romm, E., and Wehner, J. M. (1988). Nicotine tolerance: an analysis of the time course of its development and loss in the rat. *Psychopharmacology (Berl.)* 96, 7–14. doi:10.1007/BF02431526

Coppen, A. (1967). The biochemistry of affective disorders. *Br. J. Psychiatry* 113, 1237–1264. doi:10.1192/bjp.113.504.1237

Corrigall, W. A. (2009). Hypocretin mechanisms in nicotine addiction:

evidence and speculation. *Psychopharmacology (Berl.)* 206, 23–37. doi:10.1007/s00213-009-1588-2

Corrigall, W. A., and Coen, K. M. (1989). Nicotine maintains robust self-administration in rats on a limited-access schedule. *Psychopharmacology (Berl.)* 99, 473–478. doi:10.1007/BF00589894

Corrigall, W. A., and Coen, K. M. (1991). Opiate antagonists reduce cocaine but not nicotine self-administration. *Psychopharmacology (Berl.)* 104, 167–170. doi:10.1007/BF02244174

Corrigall, W. A., Coen, K. M., and Adamson, K. L. (1994). Self-administered nicotine activates the mesolimbic dopamine system through the ventral tegmental area. *Brain Res.* 653, 278–284. doi:10.1016/0006-8993(94)90401-4

Corrigall, W. A., Coen, K. M., Adamson, K. L., Chow, B. L., and Zhang, J. (2000). Response of nicotine self-administration in the rat to manipulations of mu-opioid and gamma-aminobutyric acid receptors in the ventral tegmental area. *Psychopharmacology (Berl.)* 149, 107–114. doi:10.1007/s002139900355

Corrigall, W. A., Coen, K. M., Zhang, J., and Adamson, K. L. (2001). GABA mechanisms in the pedunculopontine tegmental nucleus influence particular aspects of nicotine self-administration selectively in the rat. *Psychopharmacology (Berl.)* 158, 190–197. doi:10.1007/s002130100869

Corrigall, W. A., Coen, K. M., Zhang, J., and Adamson, L. (2002). Pharmacological manipulations of the pedunculopontine tegmental nucleus in the rat reduce self-administration of both nicotine and cocaine. *Psychopharmacology (Berl.)* 160, 198–205. doi:10.1007/s00213-001-0965-2

Cox, B. M., Goldstein, A., and Nelson, W. T. (1984). Nicotine self-administration in rats. *Br. J. Pharmacol.* 83, 49–55. doi:10.1111/j.1476-5381.1984.tb10118.x

Craft, R. M., and Milholland, R. B. (1998). Sex differences in cocaine- and nicotine-induced antinociception in the rat. *Brain Res.* 809, 137–140. doi:10.1016/S0006-8993(98)00841-5

Crombag, H. S., Ferrario, C. R., and Robinson, T. E. (2008). The rate of intravenous cocaine or amphetamine delivery does not influence drug-taking and drug-seeking behavior in rats. *Pharmacol. Biochem. Behav.* 90, 797–804. doi:10.1016/j.pbb

Cryan, J. F., Bruijnzeel, A. W., Skjei, K. L., and Markou, A. (2003). Bupropion enhances brain reward function and reverses the affective and somatic aspects of nicotine withdrawal in the rat. *Psychopharmacology (Berl.)* 168, 347–358. doi:10.1007/s00213-003-1445-7

Cummings, K. M., and Mahoney, M. (2006). Current and emerging treatment approaches for tobacco dependence. *Curr. Oncol. Rep.* 8, 475–483. doi:10.1007/s11912-006-0077-6

Dal Cin, S., Stoolmiller, M., and Sargent, J. D. (2012). When movies matter: exposure to smoking in movies and changes in smoking behavior. *J. Health Commun.* 17, 76–89. doi:10.1080/10810730.2011.585697

Damaj, M. I. (2000). The involvement of spinal Ca2+/calmodulin-protein kinase II in nicotine-induced antinociception in mice. *Eur. J. Pharmacol.* 404, 103–110. doi:10.1016/S0014-2999(00)00579-3

Damaj, M. I., Kao, W., and Martin, B. R. (2003). Characterization of spontaneous and precipitated nicotine withdrawal in the mouse. *J. Pharmacol. Exp. Ther.* 307, 526–534. doi:10.1124/jpet.103.054908

Damaj, M. I., Welch, S. P., and Martin, B. R. (1994). Nicotine-induced antinociception in mice: role of G-proteins and adenylate cyclase. *Pharmacol. Biochem. Behav.* 48, 37–42. doi:10.1016/0091-3057(94)90494-4

Dani, J. A. (2001). Nicotinic receptor activity alters synaptic plasticity. *ScientificWorldJournal* 1, 393–395. doi:10.1100/tsw.2001.74

Dani, J. A., and Bertrand, D. (2007). Nicotinic acetylcholine receptors and nicotinic cholinergic mechanisms of the central nervous system. *Annu. Rev. Pharmacol. Toxicol.* 47, 699–729. doi:10.1146/annurev.pharmtox.47.120505.105214

Dani, J. A., and Heinemann, S. (1996). Molecular and cellular aspects of nicotine abuse. *Neuron* 16, 905–908. doi:10.1016/S0896-6273(00)80112-9

Deak, T., Nguyen, T., Ehrlich, A. L., Watkins, L. R., Spencer, R. L., Maier, S. F., et al. (1999). The impact of the nonpeptide corticotropin-releasing hormone antagonist antalarmin on behavioral and endocrine responses to stress. *Endocrinology* 140, 79–86. doi:10.1210/en.140.1.79

DeNoble, V. J., and Mele, P. C. (2006). Intravenous nicotine self-administration in rats: effects of mecamylamine, hexamethonium and naloxone. *Psychopharmacology (Berl.)* 184, 266–272. doi:10.1007/s00213-005-0054-z

von der Goltz, C., Koopmann, A., Dinter, C., Richter, A., Rockenbach, C., Grosshans, M., et al. (2010). Orexin and leptin are associated with nicotine craving: a link between smoking, appetite and reward. *Psychoneuroendocrinology* 35, 570–577. doi:10.1016/j.psyneuen.2009.09.005

Dhatt, R. K., Gudehithlu, K. P., Wemlinger, T. A., Tejwani, G. A., Neff, N. H., and Hadjiconstantinou, M. (1995). Preproenkephalin mRNA and methionine-enkephalin content are increased in mouse striatum after treatment with nicotine. *J. Neurochem.* 64, 1878–1883. doi:10.1046/j.1471-4159.1995.64041878.x

Di Chiara, G. (2000). Role of dopamine in the behavioural actions of nicotine related to addiction. *Eur. J. Pharmacol.* 393, 295–314. doi:10.1016/S0014-2999(00)00122-9

Dierker, L., and Mermelstein, R. (2010). Early emerging nicotine-dependence symptoms: a signal of propensity for chronic smoking behavior in adolescents. *J. Pediatr.* 156, 818–822. doi:10.1016/j.jpeds.2009.11.044

DiFranza, J. R., Savageau, J. A., Fletcher, K., O'Loughlin, J., Pbert, L., Ockene, J. K., et al. (2007). Symptoms of tobacco dependence after brief intermittent use. The development and assessment of nicotine dependence in youth-2 study. *Arch. Pediatr. Adolesc. Med.* 161, 704–710. doi:10.1001/archpedi.161.7.704

DiFranza, J. R., Savageau, J. A., Rigotti, N. A., Fletcher, K., Ockene, J. K., McNeill, A. D., et al. (2002). Development of symptoms of tobacco dependence in youths: 30 month follow up data from the DANDY study. *Tob. Control* 11, 228–235. doi:10.1136/tc.11.3.228

Donny, E. C., Caggiula, A. R., Knopf, S., and Brown, C. (1995). Nicotine self-administration in rats. *Psychopharmacology (Berl.)* 122, 390–394. doi:10.1007/BF02246272

Donny, E. C., Caggiula, A. R., Rowell, P. P., Gharib, M. A., Maldovan, V., Booth, S., et al. (2000). Nicotine self-administration in rats: estrous cycle effects, sex differences and nicotinic receptor binding. *Psychopharmacology (Berl.)* 151, 392–405. doi:10.1007/s002130000497

Doubeni, C. A., Reed, G., and Difranza, J. R. (2010). Early course of nicotine dependence in adolescent smokers. *Pediatrics* 125, 1127–1133. doi:10.1542/peds.2009-0238

Dozois, D. N., Farrow, J. A., and Miser, A. (1995). Smoking patterns

and cessation motivations during adolescence. *Int. J. Addict.* 30, 1485–1498.

Dunn, A. J., and Berridge, C. W. (1990). Physiological and behavioral responses to corticotropin-releasing factor administration: is CRF a mediator of anxiety or stress responses? *Brain Res. Rev.* 15, 71–100. doi:10.1016/0165-0173(90)90012-D

Dworkin, S. I., Mirkis, S., and Smith, J. E. (1995). Response-dependent versus response-independent presentation of cocaine: differences in the lethal effects of the drug. *Psychopharmacology (Berl.)* 117, 262–266. doi:10.1007/BF02246100

Dwoskin, L. P., Crooks, P. A., Teng, L., Green, T. A., and Bardo, M. T. (1999). Acute and chronic effects of nornicotine on locomotor activity in rats: altered response to nicotine. *Psychopharmacology (Berl.)* 145, 442–451. doi:10.1007/s002130051079

Economidou, D., Cippitelli, A., Stopponi, S., Braconi, S., Clementi, S., Ubaldi, M., et al. (2011). Activation of brain NOP receptors attenuates acute and protracted alcohol withdrawal symptoms in the rat. *Alcohol. Clin. Exp. Res.* 35, 747–755. doi:10.1111/j.1530-0277.2010.01392.x

Epping-Jordan, M. P., Watkins, S. S., Koob, G. F., and Markou, A. (1998). Dramatic decreases in brain reward function during nicotine withdrawal. *Nature* 393, 76–79. doi:10.1038/30001

Etter, J. F. (2012). Commentary on Wagener et al. (2012): electronic cigarettes – the Holy Grail of nicotine replacement? *Addiction* 107, 1550–1552. doi:10.1111/j.1360-0443.2012.03909.x

Etter, J. F., and Bullen, C. (2011). Electronic cigarette: users profile, utilization, satisfaction and perceived efficacy. *Addiction* 106, 2017–2028. doi:10.1111/j.1360-0443.2011.03505.x

Farkas, S., Hussein, J., Ariano, R. E., Sitar, D. S., and Hasan, S. U. (2006). Prenatal cigarette smoke exposure: pregnancy outcome and gestational changes in plasma nicotine concentration, hematocrit, and carboxyhemoglobin in a newly standardized rat model. *Toxicol. Appl. Pharmacol.* 214, 118–125. doi:10.1016/j.taap.2005.12.010

Fellows, J. L., Trosclair, A., and Adams, E. K. (2002). Annual smoking-attributable mortality, years of potential life lost, and economic costs: United States, 1995-1999.

MMWR Morb. Mortal. Wkly. Rep. 51, 300–303.

Fenster, C. P., Whitworth, T. L., Sheffield, E. B., Quick, M. W., and Lester, R. A. (1999). Upregulation of surface alpha4beta2 nicotinic receptors is initiated by receptor desensitization after chronic exposure to nicotine. *J. Neurosci.* 19, 4804–4814.

Ford, R. D., and Balster, R. (1976). Schedule-controlled behavior in the morphine-dependent rat. *Pharmacol. Biochem. Behav.* 4, 569–573. doi:10.1016/0091-3057(76)90199-4

Fowler, C. D., Lu, Q., Johnson, P. M., Marks, M. J., and Kenny, P. J. (2011). Habenular α5 nicotinic receptor subunit signalling controls nicotine intake. *Nature* 471, 597–601. doi:10.1038/nature09797

Fowler, J. S., Logan, J., Wang, G. J., Volkow, N. D., Telang, F., Zhu, W., et al. (2003). Low monoamine oxidase B in peripheral organs in smokers. *Proc. Natl. Acad. Sci. U.S.A.* 100, 11600–11605. doi:10.1073/pnas.1833106100

Fu, Y., Matta, S. G., Gao, W., Brower, V. G., and Sharp, B. M. (2000). Systemic nicotine stimulates dopamine release in nucleus accumbens: re-evaluation of the role of N-methyl-D-aspartate receptors in the ventral tegmental area. *J. Pharmacol. Exp. Ther.* 294, 458–465.

Fudala, P. J., Teoh, K. W., and Iwamoto, E. T. (1985). Pharmacologic characterization of nicotine-induced conditioned place preference. *Pharmacol. Biochem. Behav.* 22, 237–241. doi:10.1016/0091-3057(85)90384-3

Fuller, B. F., Cortes, D. F., Landis, M. K., Yohannes, H., Griffin, H. E., Stafflinger, J. E., et al. (2012). Exposure of rats to environmental tobacco smoke during cerebellar development alters behavior and perturbs mitochondrial energetics. *Environ. Health Perspect.* 120, 1684–1691. doi:10.1289/ehp.1104857

Fuller, B. F., Gold, M. S., Wang, K. K., and Ottens, A. K. (2010). Effects of environmental tobacco smoke on adult rat brain biochemistry. *J. Mol. Neurosci.* 41, 165–171. doi:10.1007/s12031-009-9316-2

Fung, Y. K., Schmid, M. J., Anderson, T. M., and Lau, Y. S. (1996). Effects of nicotine withdrawal on central dopaminergic systems. *Pharmacol. Biochem. Behav.* 53, 635–640. doi:10.1016/0091-3057(95)02063-2

Galeote, L., Berrendero, F., Bura, S. A., Zimmer, A., and Maldonado, R. (2009). Prodynorphin gene disruption increases the sensitivity to nicotine self-administration in mice. *Int. J. Neuropsychopharmacol.* 12, 615–625. doi:10.1017/S1461145708009450

Galeote, L., Kieffer, B. L., Maldonado, R., and Berrendero, F. (2006). Mu-opioid receptors are involved in the tolerance to nicotine antinociception. *J. Neurochem.* 97, 416–423. doi:10.1111/j.1471-4159.2006.03751.x

George, O., Ghozland, S., Azar, M. R., Cottone, P., Zorrilla, E. P., Parsons, L. H., et al. (2007). CRF-CRF1 system activation mediates withdrawal-induced increases in nicotine self-administration in nicotine-dependent rats. *Proc. Natl. Acad. Sci. U.S.A.* 104, 17198–17203. doi:10.1073/pnas.0707585104

George, O., Grieder, T. E., Cole, M., and Koob, G. F. (2010). Exposure to chronic intermittent nicotine vapor induces nicotine dependence. *Pharmacol. Biochem. Behav.* 96, 104–107. doi:10.1016/j.pbb.2010.04.013

Gervais, A., O'Loughlin, J., Dugas, E., Eisenberg, M. J., Wellman, R. J., and DiFranza, J. R. (2007). A systematic review of randomized controlled trials of youth smoking cessation interventions. *Drogues, santé et société* 6(Suppl. 2):ii1–ii26.

Gilpin, N. W., Whitaker, A. M., Baynes, B., Abdel, A. Y., Weil, M. T., and George, O. (2013). Nicotine vapor inhalation escalates nicotine self-administration. *Addict. Biol.* doi:10.1111/adb.12021. [Epub ahead of print].

Ginzel, K. H., and Eldred, E. (1977). "Reflex depression of somatic motor activity from heart, lungs and carotid sinus," in *Krogh Centenary Symposium on Respiratory Adaptation, Capillary Exchange and Reflex Mechanisms*, eds A. S. Paintal and P. Gill-Kumar (Delhi: Vallabhbhai Patel Chest Institute, University of Delhi), 358–395.

Giovino, G. A., Mirza, S. A., Samet, J. M., Gupta, P. C., Jarvis, M. J., Bhala, N., et al. (2012). GATS Collaborative Group. Tobacco use in 3 billion individuals from 16 countries: an analysis of nationally representative cross-sectional household surveys. *Lancet* 380, 668–679. doi:10.1016/S0140-6736(12)61085-X

Girod, R., and Role, L. W. (2001). Long-lasting enhancement of glutamatergic synaptic transmission by acetylcholine contrasts with response adaptation after exposure to low-level nicotine. *J. Neurosci.* 21, 5182–5190.

Göktalay, G., Cavun, S., Levendusky, M. C., Hamilton, J. R., and

Millington, W. R. (2006). Glycyl-glutamine inhibits nicotine conditioned place preference and withdrawal. *Eur. J. Pharmacol.* 530, 95–102. doi:10.1016/j.ejphar.2005.11.034

Golub, M. S., Slotkin, T. A., Tarantal, A. F., and Pinkerton, K. E. (2007). Visual recognition memory and auditory brainstem response in infant rhesus monkeys exposed perinatally to environmental tobacco smoke. *Brain Res.* 2, 102–106.

Goniewicz, M. L., Kuma, T., Gawron, M., Knysak, J., and Kosmider, L. (2013). Nicotine levels in electronic cigarettes. *Nicotine Tob. Res.* 15, 158–166. doi:10.1093/ntr/nts103

Gourlay, S. G., Stead, L. F., and Benowitz, N. L. (2004). Clonidine for smoking cessation. *Cochrane Database Syst. Rev.* 2004:CD000058. doi:10.1002/14651858.CD000058.pub2

Grabus, S. D., Martin, B. R., Batman, A. M., Tyndale, R. F., Sellers, E., and Damaj, M. I. (2005). Nicotine physical dependence and tolerance in the mouse following chronic oral administration. *Psychopharmacology (Berl.)* 178, 183–192. doi:10.1007/s00213-004-2007-3

Greenwell, T. N., Funk, C. K., Cottone, P., Richardson, H. N., Chen, S. A., Rice, K. C., et al. (2009). Corticotropin-releasing factor-1 receptor antagonists decrease heroin self-administration in long-but not short-access rats. *Addict. Biol.* 14, 130–143. doi:10.1111/j.1369-1600.2008.00142.x

Griebel, G., Perrault, G., and Sanger, D. J. (1998). Characterization of the behavioral profile of the non-peptide CRF receptor antagonist CP-154,526 in anxiety models in rodents. Comparison with diazepam and buspirone. *Psychopharmacology (Berl.)* 138, 55–66. doi:10.1007/s002130050645

Grieder, T. E., George, O., Tan, H., George, S. R., Le Foll, B., Laviolette, S. R., et al. (2012). Phasic D1 and tonic D2 dopamine receptor signaling double dissociate the motivational effects of acute nicotine and chronic nicotine withdrawal. *Proc. Natl. Acad. Sci. U.S.A.* 109, 3101–3106. doi:10.1073/pnas.1114422109

Grieder, T. E., Sellings, L. H., Vargas-Perez, H., Ting-A-Kee, R., Siu, E. C., Tyndale, R. F., et al. (2010). Dopaminergic signaling mediates the motivational response underlying the opponent process to chronic but not acute nicotine. *Neuropsychopharmacology* 35, 943–954. doi:10.1038/npp.2009.198

Grillner, P., and Svensson, T. H. (2000). Nicotine-induced excitation of midbrain dopamine neurons in vitro involves ionotropic glutamate receptor activation. *Synapse* 38, 1–9. doi:10.1002/1098-2396(200010)38:1<1::AID-SYN1>3.0.CO;2-A

Grottick, A. J., Corrigall, W. A., and Higgins, G. A. (2001). Activation of 5-HT(2C) receptors reduces the locomotor and rewarding effects of nicotine. *Psychopharmacology (Berl.)* 157, 292–298. doi:10.1007/s002130100801

Grunberg, N. E., Bowen, D. J., and Winders, S. E. (1986). Effects of nicotine on body weight and food consumption in female rats. *Psychopharmacology (Berl.)* 90, 101–105. doi:10.1007/BF00172879

Guillem, K., Vouillac, C., Azar, M. R., Parsons, L. H., Koob, G. F., Cador, M., et al. (2005). Monoamine oxidase inhibition dramatically increases the motivation to self-administer nicotine in rats. *J. Neurosci.* 25, 8593–8600. doi:10.1523/JNEUROSCI.2139-05.2005

Guillem, K., Vouillac, C., Azar, M. R., Parsons, L. H., Koob, G. F., Cador, M., et al. (2006). Monoamine oxidase A rather than monoamine oxidase B inhibition increases nicotine reinforcement in rats. *Eur. J. Neurosci.* 24, 3532–3540. doi:10.1111/j.1460-9568.2006.05217.x

Hanson, H. M., Ivester, C. A., and Morton, B. R. (1979). "Nicotine self-administration in rats," in *Cigarette Smoking as a Dependence Process*, ed. N. A. Kraznegor (Rockville, MD: NIDA Res Monogr 23. Alcohol, Drug Abuse and Mental Health Administration), 70–90.

Harris, A. C., Mattson, C., Lesage, M. G., Keyler, D. E., and Pentel, P. R. (2010). Comparison of the behavioral effects of cigarette smoke and pure nicotine in rats. *Pharmacol. Biochem. Behav.* 96, 217–227. doi:10.1016/j.pbb.2010.05.008

Harris, A. C., Pentel, P. R., Burroughs, D., Staley, M. D., and Lesage, M. G. (2011). A lack of association between severity of nicotine withdrawal and individual differences in compensatory nicotine self-administration in rats. *Psychopharmacology (Berl.)* 217, 153–166. doi:10.1007/s00213-011-2273-9

Harrison, A. A., Gasparini, F., and Markou, A. (2002). Nicotine potentiation of brain stimulation reward reversed by DH beta E and SCH

23390, but not by eticlopride, LY 314582 or MPEP in rats. *Psychopharmacology (Berl.)* 160, 56–66. doi:10.1007/s00213-001-0953-6

Harvey, D. M., Yasar, S., Heishman, S. J., Panlilio, L. V., Henningfield, J. E., and Goldberg, S. R. (2004). Nicotine serves as an effective reinforcer of intravenous drug-taking behavior in human cigarette smokers. *Psychopharmacology (Berl.)* 175, 134–142. doi:10.1007/s00213-004-1818-6

Hayes, D. J., Mosher, T. M., and Greenshaw, A. J. (2009). Differential effects of 5-HT2C receptor activation by WAY 161503 on nicotine-induced place conditioning and locomotor activity in rats. *Behav. Brain Res.* 197, 323–330. doi:10.1016/j.bbr.2008.08.034

Hecht, S. S. (2005). Carcinogenicity studies of inhaled cigarette smoke in laboratory animals: old and new. *Carcinogenesis* 26, 1488–1492. doi:10.1093/carcin/bgi148

Heilig, M., and Murison, R. (1987). Intracerebroventricular neuropeptide Y protects against stress-induced gastric erosion in the rat. *Eur. J. Pharmacol.* 137, 127–129. doi:10.1016/0014-2999(87)90191-9

Heimer, L., and Alheid, G. (1991). "Piecing together the puzzle of basal forebrain anatomy," in *The Basal Forebrain: Anatomy to Function (Series Title: Advances in Experimental Medicine and Biology*, Vol. 295), eds T. C. Napier, P. W. Kalivas, and I. Hanin (New York: Plenum Press), 1–42.

Heinz, A. J., Kassel, J. D., Berbaum, M., and Mermelstein, R. (2010). Adolescents' expectancies for smoking to regulate affect predict smoking behavior and nicotine dependence over time. *Drug Alcohol Depend.* 111, 128–135. doi:10.1016/j.drugalcdep.2010.04.001

Henningfield, J. E., and Goldberg, S. R. (1983). Nicotine as a reinforcer in human subjects and laboratory animals. *Pharmacol. Biochem. Behav.* 19, 989–992. doi:10.1016/0091-3057(83)90405-7

Henningfield, J. E., and Keenan, R. M. (1993). Nicotine delivery kinetics and abuse liability. *J. Consult. Clin. Psychol.* 61, 743–750. doi:10.1037/0022-006X.61.5.743

Hildebrand, B. E., Nomikos, G. G., Hertel, P., Schilström, B., and Svensson, T. H. (1998). Reduced dopamine output in the nucleus accumbens but not in the medial prefrontal cortex in rats displaying a mecamylamine-precipitated nicotine withdrawal syndrome. *Brain Res.* 779, 214–225. doi:10. 1016/S0006-8993(97)01135-9

Hilleman, D. E., Mohiuddin, S. M., Del Core, M. G., and Sketch, M. H. Sr. (1992). Effect of buspirone on withdrawal symptoms associated with smoking cessation. *Arch. Intern. Med.* 152, 350–352. doi:10.1001/archinte.152.2.350

Hilleman, D. E., Mohiuddin, S. M., and Delcore, M. G. (1994). Comparison of fixed-dose transdermal nicotine, tapered-dose transdermal nicotine, and buspirone in smoking cessation. *J. Clin. Pharmacol.* 34, 222–224. doi:10.1002/j.1552-4604.1994.tb03989.x

Hoffman, A. C., and Evans, S. E. (2013). Abuse potential of non-nicotine tobacco smoke components: acetaldehyde, nornicotine, cotinine, and anabasine. *Nicotine Tob. Res.* 15, 622–632. doi:10.1093/ntr/nts192

Horan, B., Smith, M., Gardner, E. L., Lepore, M., and Ashby, C. R. Jr. (1997). Nicotine produces conditioned place preference in Lewis, but not Fischer 344 rats. *Synapse* 26, 93–94. doi:10.1002/(SICI)1098-2396(199705)26:1<93::AID-SYN10>3.0.CO;2-W

Hughes, J. R. (2007). Effects of abstinence from tobacco: valid symptoms and time course. *Nicotine Tob. Res.* 9, 315–327. doi:10.1080/14622200701188919

Hughes, J. R., Gust, S. W., Skoog, K., Keenan, R. M., and Fenwick, J. W. (1991). Symptoms of tobacco withdrawal. A replication and extension. *Arch. Gen. Psychiatry* 48, 52–59. doi:10.1001/archpsyc.1991.01810250054007

Huston-Lyons, D., and Kornetsky, C. (1992). Effects of nicotine on the threshold for rewarding brain stimulation in rats. *Pharmacol. Biochem. Behav.* 41, 755–759. doi:10.1016/0091-3057(92)90223-3

Huston-Lyons, D., Sarkar, M., and Kornetsky, C. (1993). Nicotine and brain-stimulation reward: interactions with morphine, amphetamine and pimozide. *Pharmacol. Biochem. Behav.* 46, 453–457. doi:10.1016/0091-3057(93)90378-7

Ikemoto, S., Qin, M., and Liu, Z. H. (2006). Primary reinforcing effects of nicotine are triggered from multiple regions both inside and outside the ventral tegmental area. *J. Neurosci.* 18, 723–730. doi:10. 1523/JNEUROSCI.4542-05.2006

Irvine, E. E., Cheeta, S., and File, S. E. (1999). Time-course of changes in the social interaction test of anxiety following acute and chronic administration of nicotine. *Behav. Pharmacol.* 10, 691–697. doi:10.1097/00008877-199911000-00016

Irvine, E. E., Cheeta, S., Marshall, M., and File, S. E. (2001). Different treatment regimens and the development of tolerance to nicotine's anxiogenic effects. *Pharmacol. Biochem. Behav.* 68, 769–776. doi:10.1016/S0091-3057(01)00469-5

Isola, R., Vogelsberg, V., Wemlinger, T. A., Neff, N. H., and Hadjiconstantinou, M. (1999). Nicotine abstinence in the mouse. *Brain Res.* 850, 189–196. doi:10.1016/S0006-8993(99)02131-9

Isola, R., Zhang, H., Tejwani, G. A., Neff, N. H., and Hadjiconstantinou, M. (2008). Dynorphin and prodynorphin mRNA changes in the striatum during nicotine withdrawal. *Synapse* 62, 448–455. doi:10.1002/syn.20515

Isola, R., Zhang, H., Tejwani, G. A., Neff, N. H., and Hadjiconstantinou, M. (2009). Acute nicotine changes dynorphin and prodynorphin mRNA in the striatum. *Psychopharmacology (Berl.)* 201, 507–516. doi:10.1007/s00213-008-1315-4

Jackson, K. J., Carroll, F. I., Nequs, S. S., and Damaj, M. I. (2010). Effect of the selective kappa-opioid receptor antagonist JDTic on nicotine antinociception, reward, and withdrawal in the mouse. *Psychopharmacology (Berl.)* 210, 285–294. doi:10.1007/s00213-010-1803-1

Jackson, K. J., Martin, B. R., Changeux, J. P., and Damaj, M. I. (2008). Differential role of nicotinic acetylcholine receptor subunits in physical and affective nicotine withdrawal signs. *J. Pharmacol. Exp. Ther.* 325, 302–312. doi:10.1124/jpet.107.132977

Jackson, K. J., McIntosh, J. M., Brunzell, D. H., Sanjakdar, S. S., and Damaj, M. I. (2009). The role of alpha6-containing nicotinic acetylcholine receptors in nicotine reward and withdrawal. *J. Pharmacol. Exp. Ther.* 331, 547–554. doi:10.1124/jpet.109.155457

Jaques, J. A., Rezer, J. F., Carvalho, F. B., da Rosa, M. M., Gutierres, J. M., Gonçalves, J. F., et al. (2012). Curcumin protects against cigarette smoke-induced cognitive impairment and increased acetylcholinesterase activity in rats. *Physiol. Behav.* 106, 664–669. doi:10.1016/j.physbeh.2012.05.001

Johnson, P. M., Hollander, J. A., and Kenny, P. J. (2008). Decreased brain reward function during nicotine withdrawal in C57BL6 mice: evidence from intracranial self-stimulation (ICSS) studies. *Pharmacol. Biochem. Behav.* 90, 409–415. doi:10.1016/j.pbb

Jorenby, D. E., Steinpreis, R. E., Sherman, J. E., and Baker, T. B. (1990). Aversion instead of preference learning indicated by nicotine place conditioning in rats. *Psychopharmacology (Berl.)* 101, 533–538. doi:10.1007/BF02244233

Juliano, L. M., and Brandon, T. H. (2002). Effects of nicotine dose, instructional set, and outcome expectancies on the subjective effects of smoking in the presence of a stressor. *J. Abnorm. Psychol.* 111, 88–97. doi:10.1037/0021-843X.111.1.88

Kapelewski, C. H., Vandenbergh, D. J., and Klein, L. C. (2011). Effect of the monoamine oxidase inhibition on rewarding effects of nicotine in rodents. *Curr. Drug Abuse Rev.* 4, 110–121. doi:10.2174/1874473711104020110

Kenny, P. J., Chartoff, E., Roberto, M., Carlezon, W. A. Jr., and Markou, A. (2009). NMDA receptors regulate nicotine-enhanced brain reward function and intravenous nicotine self-administration: role of the ventral tegmental area and central nucleus of the amygdala. *Neuropsychopharmacology* 34, 266–281. doi:10.1038/npp.2008.58

Kenny, P. J., Chen, S. A., Kitamura, O., Markou, A., and Koob, G. F. (2006). Conditioned withdrawal drives heroin consumption and decreases reward sensitivity. *J. Neurosci.* 26, 5894–5900. doi:10.1523/JNEUROSCI.0740-06.2006

Kenny, P. J., and Markou, A. (2005). Conditioned nicotine withdrawal profoundly decreases the activity of brain reward systems. *J. Neurosci.* 25, 6208–6212. doi:10.1523/JNEUROSCI.4785-04.2005

Kenny, P. J., and Markou, A. (2006). Nicotine self-administration acutely activates brain reward systems and induces a long-lasting increase in reward sensitivity. *Neuropsychopharmacology* 31, 1203–1211.

Kenny, P. J., Paterson, N. E., Boutrel, B., Semenova, S., Harrison, A. A., Gasparini, F., et al. (2003). Metabotropic glutamate 5 receptor antagonist MPEP decreased nicotine and cocaine self-administration but not nicotine and cocaine-induced facilitation of brain reward function in rats. *Ann. N. Y. Acad. Sci.* 1003, 415–418. doi:10.1196/annals.1300.040

Kieffer, B. L., and Evans, C. J. (2009). Opioid receptors: from binding sites to visible molecules in vivo. Opioid receptors: from binding sites to visible molecules in vivo. *Neuropharmacology* 56(Suppl. 1), 205–212. doi:10.1016/j.neuropharm.2008.07.033

Kim, M. J., Fleming, C. B., and Catalano, R. F. (2009). Individual and social influences on progression to daily smoking during adolescence. *Pediatrics* 124, 895–902. doi:10.1542/peds.2008-2015

Koob, G. F. (1999). Stress, corticotropin-releasing factor, and drug addiction. *Ann. N. Y. Acad. Sci.* 897, 27–45. doi:10.1111/j.1749-6632.1999.tb07876.x

Koob, G. F. (2008). A role for brain stress systems in addiction. *Neuron* 59, 11–34. doi:10.1016/j.neuron.2008.06.012

Koob, G. F. (2010). The role of CRF and CRF-related peptides in the dark side of addiction. *Brain Res.* 1314, 3–14. doi:10.1016/j.brainres.2009.11.008

Koob, G. F., Ahmed, S. H., Boutrel, B., Chen, S. A., Kenny, P. J., Markou, A., et al. (2004). Neurobiological mechanisms in the transition from drug use to drug dependence. *Neurosci. Biobehav. Rev.* 27, 739–749. doi:10.1016/j.neubiorev.2003.11.007

Koob, G. F., Heinrichs, S. C., Pich, E. M., Menzaghi, F., Baldwin, H., Miczek, K., et al. (1993). The role of corticotropin-releasing factor in behavioural responses to stress. *Ciba Found. Symp.* 172, 277–289.

Koob, G. F., and Kreek, M. J. (2007). Stress, dysregulation of drug reward pathways, and the transition to drug dependence. *Am. J. Psychiatry* 164, 1149–1159. doi:10.1176/appi.ajp.2007.05030503

Koob, G. F., and Le Moal, M. (1997). Drug abuse: hedonic homeostatic dysregulation. *Science* 278, 52–58. doi:10.1126/science.278.5335.52

Koob, G. F., and Le Moal, M. (2001). Drug addiction, dysregulation of reward, and allostasis. *Neuropsychopharmacology* 24, 97–129. doi:10.1016/S0893-133X(00)00195-0

Koob, G. F., and Le Moal, M. (2005). Plasticity of reward neurocircuitry and the 'dark side' of drug addiction. *Nat. Neurosci.* 8, 1442–1444. doi:10.1038/nn1105-1442

Koob, G. F., and Le Moal, M. (2008). Addiction and the brain antireward system. *Annu. Rev. Psychol.* 59, 29–53. doi:10.1146/annurev.psych.59.103006.093548

Kosowski, A. R., Cebers, G., Cebere, A., Swanhagen, A. C., and Liljequist, S. (2004). Nicotine-induced dopamine release in the nucleus accumbens is inhibited by the novel AMPA antagonist ZK200775 and the NMDA antagonist CGP39551. *Psychopharmacology (Berl.)* 175, 114–123. doi:10.1007/s00213-004-1797-7

Kozlowski, L. T., Mehta, N. Y., Sweeney, C. T., Schwartz, S. S., Vogler, G. P., Jarvis, M. J., et al. (1998). Filter ventilation and nicotine content of tobacco in cigarettes from Canada, the United Kingdom, and the United States. *Tob. Control* 7, 369–375. doi:10.1136/tc.7.4.369

Krishnan-Sarin, S., Rosen, M. I., and O'Malley, S. S. (1999). Naloxone challenge in smokers. Preliminary evidence of an opioid component in nicotine dependence. *Arch. Gen. Psychiatry* 56, 663–668. doi:10.1001/archpsyc.56.7.663

Lança, A. J., Adamson, K. L., Coen, K. M., Chow, B. L., and Corrigall, W. A. (2000). The pedunculopontine tegmental nucleus and the role of cholinergic neurons in nicotine self-administration in the rat: a correlative neuroanatomical and behavioral study. *Neuroscience* 96, 735–742. doi:10.1016/S0306-4522(99)00607-7

Laviolette, S. R., Alexson, T. O., and van der Kooy, D. (2002). Lesions of the tegmental pedunculopontine nucleus block the rewarding effects and reveal the aversive effects of nicotine in the ventral tegmental area. *J. Neurosci.* 22, 8653–8660.

Laviolette, S. R., and van der Kooy, D. (2003). The motivational valence of nicotine in the rat ventral tegmental area is switched from rewarding to aversive following blockade of the alpha7-subunit-containing nicotinic acetylcholine receptor. *Psychopharmacology (Berl.)* 166, 306–313.

Laviolette, S. R., and van der Kooy, D. (2004). The neurobiology of nicotine addiction: bridging the gap from molecules to behaviour. *Nat. Rev. Neurosci.* 5, 55–65. doi:10.1038/nrn1298

Law, M. R., Morris, J. K., and Wald, N. J. (1997). Environmental tobacco smoke exposure and ischaemic heart disease: an evaluation of the evidence. *Br. Med. J.* 315, 973–980. doi:10.1136/bmj.315.7114.973

Le Foll, B., and Goldberg, S. R. (2004). Rimonabant, a CB1 antagonist, blocks nicotine-conditioned place preferences. *Neuroreport* 15,

2139–2143. doi:10.1097/00001756-200409150-00028

Le Foll, B., and Goldberg, S. R. (2005). Nicotine induces conditioned place preferences over a large range of doses in rats. *Psychopharmacology (Berl.)* 178, 481–492. doi:10.1007/s00213-004-2021-5

Le Foll, B., and Goldberg, S. R. (2009). Effects of nicotine in experimental animals and humans: an update on addictive properties. *Handb. Exp. Pharmacol.* 192, 335–367. doi:10.1007/978-3-540-69248-5_12

Le Foll, B., Wertheim, C. E., and Goldberg, S. R. (2008). Effects of baclofen on conditioned rewarding and discriminative stimulus effects of nicotine in rats. *Neurosci. Lett.* 443, 236–240. doi:10.1016/j.neulet.2008.07.074

Leonardi-Bee, J., Jere, M. L., and Britton, J. (2011). Exposure to parental and sibling smoking and the risk of smoking uptake in childhood and adolescence: a systematic review and meta-analysis. *Thorax* 66, 847–855. doi:10.1136/thx.2010.153379

Levin, E. D., Morgan, M. M., Galvez, C., and Ellison, G. D. (1987). Chronic nicotine and withdrawal effects on body weight and food and water consumption in female rats. *Physiol. Behav.* 39, 441–444. doi:10.1016/0031-9384(87)90370-2

Levin, E. D., Rezvani, A. H., Montoya, D., Rose, J. E., and Swartzwelder, H. S. (2003). Adolescent-onset nicotine self-administration modeled in female rats. *Psychopharmacology (Berl.)* 169, 141–149. doi:10.1007/s00213-003-1486-y

Li, X., Rainnie, D. G., McCarley, R. W., and Greene, R. W. (1998). Presynaptic nicotinic receptors facilitate monoaminergic transmission. *J. Neurosci.* 18, 1904–1912.

Liechti, M. E., and Markou, A. (2007). Interactive effects of the mGlu5 receptor antagonist MPEP and the mGlu2/3 receptor antagonist LY341495 on nicotine self-administration and reward deficits associated with nicotine withdrawal in rats. *Eur. J. Pharmacol.* 554, 164–174. doi:10.1016/j.ejphar.2006.10.011

Liechti, M. E., and Markou, A. (2008). Role of the glutamatergic system in nicotine dependence: implications for the discovery and development of new pharmacological smoking cessation therapies. *CNS Drugs* 22, 705–724. doi:10.2165/00023210-200822090-00001

Lindholm, S., Ploj, K., Franck, J., and Nylander, I. (2002). The bed nucleus is a neuroanatomical

substrate for the anorectic effect of Nociceptin/orphanin FQ tissue concentration in the rat brain. Effects of repeated ethanol administration at various post-treatment intervals. *Prog. Neuropsychopharmacol. Biol. Psychiatry* 26, 303–306. doi:10.1016/S0278-5846(01)00270-6

Liu, Y., Roberts, D. C., and Morgan, D. (2005). Sensitization of the reinforcing effects of self-administered cocaine in rats: effects of dose and intravenous injection speed. *Eur. J. Neurosci.* 22, 195–200. doi:10.1111/j.1460-9568.2005.04195.x

Lopez, M. F., and Becker, H. C. (2005). Effect of pattern and number of chronic ethanol exposures on subsequent voluntary ethanol intake in C57BL/6J mice. *Psychopharmacology (Berl.)* 181, 688–696. doi:10.1007/s00213-005-0026-3

Lough, C., Young, T., Parker, R., Wittenauer, S., and Vincler, M. (2007). Increased spinal dynorphin contributes to chronic nicotine-induced mechanical hypersensitivity in the rat. *Neurosci. Lett.* 422, 54–58. doi:10.1016/j.neulet.2007.06.002

Maisonneuve, I. M., and Glick, S. D. (1999). (±)Cyclazocine blocks the dopamine response to nicotine. *Neuroreport* 10, 693–696. doi:10.1097/00001756-199903170-00006

Malin, D. H. (2001). Nicotine dependence: studies with a laboratory model. *Pharmacol. Biochem. Behav.* 70, 551–559. doi:10.1016/S0091-3057(01)00699-2

Malin, D. H., and Goyarzu, P. (2009). Rodent models of nicotine withdrawal syndrome. *Handb. Exp. Pharmacol.* 192, 401–434. doi:10.1007/978-3-540-69248-5_14

Malin, D. H., Lake, J. R., Carter, V. A., Cunningham, J. S., and Wilson, O. B. (1993). Naloxone precipitates nicotine abstinence syndrome in the rat. *Psychopharmacology (Berl.)* 112, 339–342. doi:10.1007/BF02244930

Malin, D. H., Lake, J. R., Newlin-Maultsby, P., Roberts, L. K., Lanier, J. G., Carter, V. A., et al. (1992). Rodent model of nicotine abstinence syndrome. *Pharmacol. Biochem. Behav.* 43, 779–784. doi:10.1016/0091-3057(92)90408-8

Mansvelder, H. D., and McGehee, D. S. (2003). Cellular and synaptic mechanisms of nicotine addiction. *J. Neurobiol.* 53, 606–617. doi:10.1002/neu.10148

Mantsch, J. R., Yuferov, V., Mathieu-Kia, A. M., Ho, A., and Kreek, M. J. (2004). Effects of extended access to high versus low cocaine doses on self-administration, cocaine-induced reinstatement and brain mRNA levels in rats. *Psychopharmacology (Berl.)* 175, 26–36. doi:10.1007/s00213-004-1778-x

Manzardo, A. M., Stein, L., and Belluzzi, J. D. (2002). Rats prefer cocaine over nicotine in a two-lever self-administration choice test. *Brain Res.* 924, 10–19. doi:10.1016/S0006-8993(01)03215-2

Marchi, M., Risso, F., Viola, C., Cavazzani, P., and Raiteri, M. (2002). Direct evidencethatrelease-stimulatingalpha7* nicotinic cholinergic receptors are localized on human and rat brain glutamatergic axon terminals. *J. Neurochem.* 80, 1071–1078. doi:10.1046/j.0022-3042.2002.00805.x

Marcinkiewcz, C. A., Prado, M. M., Isaac, S. K., Marshall, A., Rylkova, D., and Bruijnzeel, A. W. (2009). Corticotropin-releasing factor within the central nucleus of the amygdala and the nucleus accumbens shell mediates the negative affective state of nicotine withdrawal in rats. *Neuropsychopharmacology* 34, 1743–1752. doi:10.1038/npp.2008.231

Markou, A. (2008). Review. Neurobiology of nicotine dependence. *Philos. Trans. R. Soc. Lond. B Biol. Sci.* 363, 3159–3168. doi:10.1098/rstb.2008.0095

Markou, A., Arroyo, M., and Everitt, B. J. (1999). Effects of contingent and non-contingent cocaine on drug-seeking behavior measured using a second-order schedule of cocaine reinforcement in rats. *Neuropsychopharmacology* 20, 542–555. doi:10.1016/S0893-133X(98)00080-3

Markou, A., Kosten, T. R., and Koob, G. F. (1998). Neurobiological similarities in depression and drug dependence: a self-medication hypothesis. *Neuropsychopharmacology* 18, 135–174. doi:10.1016/S0893-133X(97)00113-9

Markou, A., and Paterson, N. E. (2001). The nicotinic antagonist methyllycaconitine has differential effects on nicotine self-administration and nicotine withdrawal in the rat. *Nicotine Tob. Res.* 3, 361–373. doi:10.1080/14622200110073380

Marks, M. J., Burch, J. B., and Collins, A. C. (1983). Effects of chronic nicotine infusion on tolerance development and cholinergic receptors. *J. Pharmacol. Exp. Ther.* 226, 806–816.

Marks, M. J., Pauly, J. R., Gross, S. D., Deneris, E. S., Hermans-Borgmeyer, I., Heinemann, S. F., et al. (1992). Nicotine binding and nicotinic receptor subunit RNA after chronic nicotine treatment. *J. Neurosci.* 12, 2765–2784.

Maron, D. J., and Fortmann, S. P. (1987). Nicotine yield and measures of cigarette smoke exposure in a large population: are lower-yield cigarettes safer? *Am. J. Public Health* 77, 546–549. doi:10.2105/AJPH.77.5.546

Martinez-Gonzalez, D., Prospero-Garcia, O., Mihailescu, S., and Drucker-Colin, R. (2002). Effects of nicotine on alcohol intake in a rat model of depression. *Pharmacol. Biochem. Behav.* 72, 355–364. doi:10.1016/S0091-3057(01)00772-9

Matta, S. G., Balfour, D. J., Benowitz, N. L., Boyd, R. T., Buccafusco, J. J., Caggiula, A. R., et al. (2007). Guidelines on nicotine dose selection for in vivo research. *Psychopharmacology (Berl.)* 190, 269–319. doi:10.1007/s00213-006-0441-0

McGehee, D. S., Heath, M. J., Gelber, S., Devay, P., and Role, L. W. (1995). Nicotine enhancement of fast excitatory synaptic transmission in CNS by presynaptic receptors. *Science* 269, 1692–1696. doi:10.1126/science.7569895

Meisch, R. A., and Lemaire, G. A. (1993). "Drug self-administration," in *Methods in Behavioral Pharmacology*, ed. F. van Harren (Amsterdam: Elsevier), 257.

Mendizábal, V., Zimmer, A., and Maldonado, R. (2006). Involvement of kappa/dynorphin system in WIN 55,212-2 self-administration in mice. *Neuropsychopharmacology* 31, 1957–1966. doi:10.1038/sj.npp.1300957

Merritt, L. L., Martin, B. R., Walters, C., Lichtman, A. H., and Damaj, M. I. (2008). The endogenous cannabinoid system modulates nicotine reward and dependence. *J. Pharmacol. Exp. Ther.* 326, 483–492. doi:10.1124/jpet.108.138321

Mihailescu, S., Guzman-Marin, R., Dominguez, M., and Drucker-Colin, R. (2002). Mechanisms of nicotine actions on dorsal raphe serotoninergic neurons. *Eur. J. Pharmacol.* 452, 77–82. doi:10.1016/S0014-2999(02)02244-6

Mihailescu, S., Palomero-Rivero, M., Meade-Huerta, P., Maza-Flores, A., and Drucker-Colin, R. (1998). Effects of nicotine and mecamylamine on rat dorsal raphe neurons.

Eur. J. Pharmacol. 360, 31–36. doi:10.1016/S0014-2999(98)00658-X

Millar, N. S., and Gotti, C. (2009). Diversity of vertebrate nicotinic acetylcholine receptors. *Neuropharmacology* 56, 237–246. doi:10.1016/j.neuropharm.2008.07.041

Miyata, H., Itasaka, M., Kimura, N., and Nakayama, K. (2011). Decreases in brain reward function reflect nicotine- and methamphetamine-withdrawal aversion in rats. *Curr. Neuropharmacol.* 9, 63–67. doi:10.2174/157015911795017218

Nader, K., and van der Kooy, D. (1996). Clonidine antagonizes the aversive effects of opiate withdrawal and the rewarding effects of morphine only in opiate withdrawn rats. *Behav. Neurosci.* 110, 389–400. doi:10.1037/0735-7044.110.2.389

Natividad, L. A., Buczynski, M. W., Parsons, L. H., Torres, O. V., and O'Dell, L. E. (2012). Adolescent rats are resistant to adaptations in excitatory and inhibitory mechanisms that modulate mesolimbic dopamine during nicotine withdrawal. *J. Neurochem.* 123, 578–588. doi:10.1111/j.1471-4159.2012.07926.x

Neal, C. R. Jr., Mansour, A., Reinscheid, R., Nothacker, H. P., Civelli, O., Akil, H., et al. (1999). Opioid receptor-like (ORL1) receptor distribution in the rat central nervous system: comparison of ORL1 receptor mRNA expression with (125)I-[(14)Tyr]-orphanin FQ binding. *J. Comp. Neurol.* 412, 563–605. doi:10.1002/(SICI)1096-9861(19991004)412:4<563::AID-CNE2>3.3.CO;2-Q

Niijima, A., Miyata, G., Sato, T., and Meguid, M. M. (2001). Hepatovagal pathway associated with nicotine's anorectic effect in the rat. *Auton. Neurosci.* 93, 48–55. doi:10.1016/S1566-0702(01)00328-9

Nisell, M., Nomikos, G. G., and Svensson, T. H. (1994). Systemic nicotine-induced dopamine release in the rat nucleus accumbens is regulated by nicotinic receptors in the ventral tegmental area. *Synapse* 16, 36–44. doi:10.1002/syn.890160105

O'Byrne, K. K., Haddock, C. K., and Poston, W. S. (2002). Parenting style and adolescent smoking. *J. Adolesc. Health* 30, 418–425. doi:10.1016/S1054-139X(02)00370-1

O'Connor, R. J. (2012). Non-cigarette tobacco products: what have we learnt and where are we headed? *Tob. Control* 21, 181–190. doi:10.1136/tobaccocontrol-2011-050281

O'Dell, L. E. (2009). A psychobiological framework of the substrates that mediate nicotine use during adolescence. *Neuropharmacology* 56(Suppl. 1), 263–278. doi:10.1016/j.neuropharm.2008.07.039

O'Dell, L. E., Bruijnzeel, A. W., Ghozland, S., Markou, A., and Koob, G. F. (2004). Nicotine withdrawal in adolescent and adult rats. *Ann. N. Y. Acad. Sci.* 1021, 167–174. doi:10.1196/annals.1308.022

O'Dell, L. E., Bruijnzeel, A. W., Smith, R. T., Parsons, L. H., Merves, M. L., Goldberger, B. A., et al. (2006). Diminished nicotine withdrawal in adolescent rats: Implications for vulnerability to addiction. *Psychopharmacology (Berl.)* 186, 612–619. doi:10.1007/s00213-006-0383-6

O'Dell, L. E., and Koob, G. F. (2007). 'Nicotine deprivation effect' in rats with intermittent 23-hour access to intravenous nicotine self-administration. *Pharmacol. Biochem. Behav.* 86, 346–353. doi:10.1016/j.pbb.2007.01.004

Office of Technology Assessment. (1986). *Passive Smoking in the Workplace: U.S. Congress.* Washington: The Special Projects Office.

Okoli, C. T., Kelly, T., and Hahn, E. J. (2007). Secondhand smoke and nicotine exposure: a brief review. *Addict. Behav.* 32, 1977–1988. doi:10.1016/j.addbeh.2006.12.024

Pacifici, R., Altieri, I., Gandini, L., Lenzi, A., Passa, A. R., Pichini, S., et al. (1995). Environmental tobacco smoke: nicotine and cotinine concentration in semen. *Environ. Res.* 68, 69–72. doi:10.1006/enrs.1995.1009

Pandey, S. C., Zhang, H., Roy, A., and Xu, T. (2005). Deficits in amygdaloid cAMP-responsive element-binding protein signaling play a role in genetic predisposition to anxiety and alcoholism. *J. Clin. Invest.* 115, 2762–2773. doi:10.1172/JCI24381

Parker, L. A. (1992). Place conditioning in a three- or four-choice apparatus: role of stimulus novelty in drug-induced place conditioning. *Behav. Neurosci.* 106, 294–306. doi:10.1037/0735-7044.106.2.294

Parrott, A. C. (1995). Smoking cessation leads to reduced stress, but why? *Int. J. Addict.* 30, 1509–1516.

Parrott, A. C. (1998). Nesbitt's paradox resolved? Stress and arousal modulation during cigarette smoking. *Addiction* 93, 27–39. doi:10.1046/j.1360-0443.1998.931274.x

Parrott, A. C. (2003). Cigarette-derived nicotine is not a medicine.

World J. Biol. Psychiatry 4, 49–55. doi:10.3109/15622970309167951

Paterson, D., and Nordberg, A. (2000). Neuronal nicotinic receptors in the human brain. *Prog. Neurobiol.* 61, 75–111. doi:10.1016/S0301-0082(99)00045-3

Paterson, N. E., Balfour, D. J., and Markou, A. (2008). Chronic bupropion differentially alters the reinforcing, reward-enhancing and conditioned motivational properties of nicotine in rats. *Nicotine Tob. Res.* 10, 995–1008. doi:10.1080/14622200802097571

Paterson, N. E., and Markou, A. (2004). Prolonged nicotine dependence associated with extended access to nicotine self-administration in rats. *Psychopharmacology (Berl.)* 173, 64–72. doi:10.1007/s00213-003-1692-7

Patterson, F., Benowitz, N., Shields, P., Kaufmann, V., Jepson, C., Wileyto, P., et al. (2003). Individual differences in nicotine intake per cigarette. *Cancer Epidemiol. Biomarkers Prev.* 12, 468–471.

Patterson, F., Lerman, C., Kaufmann, V. G., Neuner, G. A., and Audrain-McGovern, J. (2004). Cigarette smoking practices among American college students: review and future directions. *J. Am. Coll. Health* 52, 203–212. doi:10.3200/JACH.52.5.203-212

Patterson, F., Schnoll, R., Wileyto, E., Pinto, A., Epstein, L., Shields, P., et al. (2008). Toward personalized therapy for smoking cessation: a randomized placebo-controlled trial of bupropion. *Clin. Pharmacol. Ther.* 84, 320–325. doi:10.1038/clpt.2008.57

Pearson, J. L., Richardson, A., Niaura, R. S., Vallone, D. M., and Abrams, D. B. (2012). e-Cigarette awareness, use, and harm perceptions in US adults. *Am. J. Public Health* 102, 1758–1766. doi:10.2105/AJPH.2011.300526

Perkins, K. A., Briski, J., Fonte, C., Scott, J., and Lerman, C. (2009). Severity of tobacco abstinence symptoms varies by time of day. *Nicotine. Tob. Res.* 11, 84–91. doi:10.1093/ntr/ntn003

Perkins, K. A., and Grobe, J. E. (1992). Increased desire to smoke during acute stress. *Br. J. Addict.* 87, 1037–1040. doi:10.1111/j.1360-0443.1992.tb03121.x

Perkins, K. A., Sexton, J. E., Reynolds, W. A., Grobe, J. E., Fonte, C., and Stiller, R. L. (1994). Comparison of acute subjective and heart rate effects of nicotine intake via tobacco smoking versus nasal spray. *Pharmacol. Biochem. Behav.* 47, 295–299. doi:10.1016/0091-3057(94)90013-2

Peyron, C., Tighe, D. K., van den Pol, A. N., de Lecea, L., Heller, H. C., Sutcliffe, J. G., et al. (1998). Neurons containing hypocretin (orexin) project to multiple neuronal systems. *J. Neurosci.* 18, 9996–10015.

Picciotto, M. R., Addy, N. A., Mineur, Y. S., and Brunzell, D. H. (2008). It is not "either/or": activation and desensitization of nicotinic acetylcholine receptors both contribute to behaviors related to nicotine addiction and mood. *Prog. Neurobiol.* 84, 329–342. doi:10.1016/j.pneurobio.2007.12.005

Picciotto, M. R., and Corrigall, W. A. (2002). Neuronal systems underlying behaviors related to nicotine addiction: neural circuits and molecular genetics. *J. Neurosci.* 22, 3338–3341.

Picciotto, M. R., Zoli, M., Rimondini, R., Léna, C., Marubio, L. M., Pich, E. M., et al. (1988). Acetylcholine receptors containing the beta2 subunit are involved in the reinforcing properties of nicotine. *Nature* 391, 173–177.

Plaza-Zabala, A., Flores, Á., Maldonado, R., and Berrendero, F. (2012). Hypocretin/orexin signaling in the hypothalamic paraventricular nucleus is essential for the expression of nicotine withdrawal. *Biol. Psychiatry* 71, 214–223. doi:10.1016/j.biopsych.2011.06.025

Plowchalk, D. R., Andersen, M. E., and deBethizy, J. D. (1992). A physiologically based pharmacokinetic model for nicotine disposition in the Sprague-Dawley rat. *Toxicol. Appl. Pharmacol.* 116, 177–188. doi:10.1016/0041-008X(92)90297-6

Polosa, R., Caponnetto, P., Morjaria, J. B., Papale, G., Campagna, D., and Russo, C. (2011). Effect of an electronic nicotine delivery device (e-Cigarette) on smoking reduction and cessation: a prospective 6-month pilot study. *BMC Public Health* 11:786. doi:10.1186/1471-2458-11-786

Pomerleau, C. S., and Pomerleau, O. F. (1992). Euphoriant effects of nicotine in smokers. *Psychopharmacology (Berl.)* 108, 460–465. doi:10.1007/BF02247422

Pomerleau, O. F., Turk, D. C., and Fertig, J. B. (1984). The effects of cigarette smoking on pain and anxiety. *Addict. Behav.* 9, 265–271. doi:10.1016/0306-4603(84)90018-2

Pontieri, F. E., Tanda, G., Orzi, F., and Di Chiara, G. (1996). Effects of nicotine on the nucleus accumbens and similarity to those of addictive drugs. *Nature* 382, 255–257. doi:10.1038/382255a0

Prochazka, A. V., Petty, T. L., Nett, L., Silvers, G. W., Sachs, D. P., Rennard, S. I., et al. (1992). Transdermal clonidine reduced some withdrawal symptoms but did not increase smoking cessation. *Arch. Intern. Med.* 152, 2065–2069. doi:10.1001/archinte.1992.0040022 0083015

Reinscheid, R. K., Nothacker, H. P., Bourson, A., Ardati, A., Henningsen, R. A., Bunzow, J. R., et al. (1995). Orphanin FQ: a neuropeptide that activates an opioid like G protein-coupled receptor. *Science* 270, 792–794. doi:10.1126/science.270.5237.792

Ribeiro, E. B., Bettiker, R. L., Bogdanov, M., and Wurtman, R. J. (1993). Effects of systemic nicotine on serotonin release in rat brain. *Brain Res.* 621, 311–318. doi:10.1016/0006-8993(93)90121-3

Risner, M. E., and Goldberg, S. R. (1983). A comparison of nicotine and cocaine self-administration in the dog: fixed-ratio and progressive-ratio schedules of intravenous drug infusion. *J. Pharmacol. Exp. Ther.* 224, 319–326.

Robinson, L. A., Vander Weg, M. W., Riedel, B. W., Klesges, R. C., and McLain-Allen, B. (2003). Start to stop: results of a randomized controlled trial of a smoking cessation program for teens. *Tob. Control* 12(Suppl. 4), iv26–iv33. doi:10.1136/tc.12.suppl_4.iv26

Rose, J. E. (2006). Nicotine and non-nicotine factors in cigarette addiction. *Psychopharmacology (Berl.)* 184, 274–285. doi:10.1007/s00213-005-0250-x

Rose, J. E., and Corrigall, W. A. (1997). Nicotine self-administration in animals and humans: similarities and differences. *Psychopharmacology (Berl.)* 130, 28–40. doi:10.1007/s002130050209

Rose, J. E., Salley, A., Behm, F. M., Bates, J. E., and Westman, E. C. (2010). Reinforcing effects of nicotine and non-nicotine components of cigarette smoke. *Psychopharmacology (Berl.)* 210, 1–12. doi:10.1007/s00213-010-1810-2

Rosecrans, J. A., and Meltzer, L. T. (1981). Central sites and mechanisms of action of nicotine. *Neurosci. Biobehav. Rev.* 5, 497–501. doi:10.1016/0149-7634(81)90020-8

Roth-Deri, I., Green-Sadan, T., and Yadid, G. (2008). Beta-endorphin and drug-induced reward and reinforcement. *Prog. Neurobiol.* 86, 1–21. doi:10.1016/j.pneurobio.2008.06.003

Russell, M. A., Jarvis, M., Iyer, R., and Feyerabend, C. (1980). Relation of nicotine yield of cigarettes to blood nicotine concentrations in smokers. *Br. Med. J.* 280, 972–976. doi:10.1136/bmj.280.6219.972

Rylkova, D., Boissoneault, J., Isaac, S., Prado, M., Shah, H. P., and Bruijnzeel, A. W. (2008). Effects of NPY and the specific Y1 receptor agonist [D-His(26)]-NPY on the deficit in brain reward function and somatic signs associated with nicotine withdrawal in rats. *Neuropeptides* 42, 215–227. doi:10.1016/j.npep.2008.03.004

Sahley, T. L., and Berntson, G. G. (1979). Antinociceptive effects of central and systemic administrations of nicotine in the rat. *Psychopharmacology (Berl.)* 65, 279–283. doi:10.1007/BF00492216

Sajdyk, T. J., Vandergriff, M. G., and Gehlert, D. R. (1999). Amygdalar neuropeptide Y Y1 receptors mediate the anxiolytic-like actions of neuropeptide Y in the social interaction test. *Eur. J. Pharmacol.* 368, 143–147. doi:10.1016/S0014-2999(99)00018-7

Sakamoto, F., Yamada, S., and Ueta, Y. (2004). Centrally administered orexin-A activates corticotropin-releasing factor-containing neurons in the hypothalamic paraventricular nucleus and central amygdaloid nucleus of rats: possible involvement of central orexins on stress-activated central CRF neurons. *Regul. Pept.* 118, 183–191. doi:10.1016/j.regpep.2003.12.014

Sakoori, K., and Murphy, N. P. (2009). Enhanced nicotine sensitivity in nociceptin/orphanin FQ receptor knockout mice. *Neuropharmacology* 56, 896–904. doi:10.1016/j.neuropharm.2009.01.016

Sakurai, T., Nagata, R., Yamanaka, A., Kawamura, H., Tsujino, N., Muraki, Y., et al. (2005). Input of orexin/hypocretin neurons revealed by a genetically encoded tracer in mice. *Neuron* 46, 297–308. doi:10.1016/j.neuron.2005.03.010

Schmidt, B. L., Tambeli, C. H., Gear, R. W., and Levine, J. D. (2001). Nicotine withdrawal hyperalgesia and opioid-mediated analgesia depend on nicotine receptors in nucleus accumbens. *Neuroscience* 106, 129–136. doi:10.1016/S0306-4522(01)00264-0

Schoepp, D. D., Wright, R. A., Levine, L. R., Gaydos, B., and Potter, W. Z. (2003). LY354740, an mGlu2/3 receptor agonist as a novel approach to treat anxiety/stress. *Stress* 6, 189–197. doi:10.1080/1025389031000146773

Semenova, S., and Markou, A. (2010). The alpha2 adrenergic receptor antagonist idazoxan, but not the serotonin-2A receptor antagonist M100907, partially attenuated reward deficits associated with nicotine, but not amphetamine, withdrawal in rats. *Eur. Neuropsychopharmacol.* 20, 731–746. doi:10.1016/j.euroneuro.2010.05.003

Shiffman, S. (1989). Tobacco bchippersQ – individual differences in tobacco dependence. *Psychopharmacology (Berl.)* 97, 539–547. doi:10.1007/BF00439561

Shiffman, S., Paty, J. A., Kassel, J. D., Gnys, M., and Zettler-Segal, M. (1994). Smoking behavior and smoking history of tobacco chippers. *Exp. Clin. Psychopharmacol.* 2, 126–142. doi:10.1037/1064-1297.2.2.126

Shippenberg, T. S., Zapata, A., and Chefer, V. I. (2007). Dynorphin and the pathophysiology of drug addiction. *Pharmacol. Ther.* 116, 306–321. doi:10.1016/j.pharmthera.2007.06.011

Shoaib, M., Schindler, C. W., and Goldberg, S. R. (1997). Nicotine self-administration in rats: strain and nicotine pre-exposure effects on acquisition. *Psychopharmacology (Berl.)* 129, 35–43. doi:10.1007/s002130050159

Shram, M. J., Funk, D., Li, Z., and Le, A. D. (2006). Periadolescent and adult rats respond differently in tests measuring the rewarding and aversive effects of nicotine. *Psychopharmacology (Berl.)* 186, 201–208. doi:10.1007/s00213-006-0373-8

Shram, M. J., Siu, E. C., Li, Z., Tyndale, R. F., and Lê, A. D. (2008). Interactions between age and the aversive effects of nicotine withdrawal under mecamylamine-precipitated and spontaneous conditions in male Wistar rats. *Psychopharmacology (Berl.)* 198, 181–190. doi:10.1007/s00213-008-1115-x

Siegel, M. B., Tanwar, K. L., and Wood, K. S. (2011). Electronic cigarettes as a smoking-cessation: tool results from an online survey. *Am. J. Prev. Med.* 40, 472–475. doi:10.1016/j.amepre.2010.12.006

Simons, C. T., Cuellar, J. M., Moore, J. A., Pinkerton, K. E., Uyeminami, D., Carstens, M. I., et al. (2005). Nicotinic receptor involvement in antinociception induced by exposure to cigarette smoke. *Neurosci. Lett.* 389, 71–76. doi:10.1016/j.neulet.2005.07.025

Sinclair, J. D., and Senter, R. J. (1967). Increased preference for ethanol in rats following alcohol deprivation. *Psychonom. Sci.* 8, 11–12.

Slawecki, C. J., Gilder, A., Roth, J., and Ehlers, C. L. (2003). Increased anxiety-like behavior in adult rats exposed to nicotine as adolescents. *Pharmacol. Biochem. Behav.* 75, 355–361. doi:10.1016/S0091-3057(03)00093-5

Slawecki, C. J., Thorsell, A. K., Khoury, A. E., Mathe, A. A., and Ehlers, C. L. (2005). Increased CRF-like and NPY-like immunoreactivity in adult rats exposed to nicotine during adolescence: relation to anxiety-like and depressive-like behavior. *Neuropeptides* 39, 369–377. doi:10.1016/j.npep.2005.06.002

Slotkin, T. A., Pinkerton, K. E., and Seidler, F. J. (2006). Perinatal environmental tobacco smoke exposure in rhesus monkeys: critical periods and regional selectivity for effects on brain cell development and lipid peroxidation. *Environ. Health Perspect.* 114, 34–39.

Small, E., Shah, H. P., Davenport, J. J., Geier, J. E., Yamada, H., Sabarinath, S. N., et al. (2010). Tobacco smoke exposure induces nicotine dependence in rats. *Psychopharmacology (Berl.)* 208, 143–158. doi:10.1007/s00213-009-1716-z

Smith, R. J., and Aston-Jones, G. (2008). Noradrenergic transmission in the extended amygdala: role in increased drug-seeking and relapse during protracted drug abstinence. *Brain Struct. Funct.* 213, 43–61. doi:10.1007/s00429-008-0191-3

Sofuoglu, M., Yoo, S., Hill, K. P., and Mooney, M. (2008). Self-administration of intravenous nicotine in male and female cigarette smokers. *Neuropsychopharmacology* 33, 715–720. doi:10.1038/sj.npp.1301460

Solomon, R. L., and Corbit, J. D. (1973). An opponent-process theory of motivation: II. Cigarette addiction. *J. Abnorm. Psychol.* 81, 158–171. doi:10.1037/h0034534

Sorge, R. E., and Clarke, P. B. (2009). Rats self-administer intravenous nicotine delivered in a novel smoking-relevant procedure: effects of dopamine antagonists. *J. Pharmacol. Exp. Ther.* 330, 633–640. doi:10.1124/jpet.109.154641

Specio, S. E., Wee, S., O'Dell, L. E., Boutrel, B., Zorrilla, E. P., and Koob, G. F. (2008). CRF1 receptor antagonists attenuate escalated cocaine self-administration in rats. *Psychopharmacology (Berl.)* 196, 473–482. doi:10.1007/s00213-007-0983-9

Sperling, R., and Commons, K. G. (2011). Shifting topographic

activation and 5-HT1A receptor-mediated inhibition of dorsal raphe serotonin neurons produced by nicotine exposure and withdrawal. *Eur. J. Neurosci.* 33, 1866–1875. doi:10.1111/j.1460-9568.2011.07677.x

Spiller, K., Xi, Z. X., Li, X., Ashby, C. R., Callahan, P. M., Tehim, A., et al. (2009). Varenicline attenuates nicotine-enhanced brain-stimulation reward by activation of alpha4beta2 nicotinic receptors in rats. *Neuropharmacology* 57, 60–66. doi:10.1016/j.neuropharm.2009.04.006

Steinbusch, H. (1984). "Serotonin-immunoreactive neurons and their projections in the CNS," in *Handbook of Chemical Neuroanatomy*, eds A. Bjorklund, T. Hokfelt, and M. Kuhar (Amsterdam: Elsevier Science Publishers), 68–121.

Stoker, A. K., Olivier, B., and Markou, A. (2012). Involvement of metabotropic glutamate receptor 5 in brain reward deficits associated with cocaine and nicotine withdrawal and somatic signs of nicotine withdrawal. *Psychopharmacology (Berl.)* 221, 317–327. doi:10.1007/s00213-011-2578-8

Stoker, A. K., Semenova, S., and Markou, A. (2008). Affective and somatic aspects of spontaneous and precipitated nicotine withdrawal in C57BL/6J and BALB/cByJ mice. *Neuropharmacology* 54, 1223–1232. doi:10.1016/j.neuropharm.2008.03.013

Stolerman, I. P., and Jarvis, M. J. (1995). The scientific case that nicotine is addictive. *Psychopharmacology (Berl.)* 117, 2–10; discussion, 14–20.

Substance Abuse and Mental Health Services Administration. (2003). *Results from the 2002 National Survey on Drug Use and Health: National Findings.* Rockville: U.S. Office of Applied Studies.

Suemaru, K., Oishi, R., Gomita, Y., Saeki, K., and Araki, Y. (1992). Effect of long-term cigarette smoke exposure on locomotor activity and brain monoamine levels in rats. *Pharmacol. Biochem. Behav.* 41, 655–658. doi:10.1016/0091-3057(92)90388-V

Sutcliffe, J. G., and de Lecea, L. (2002). The hypocretins: setting the arousal threshold. *Nat. Rev. Neurosci.* 3, 339–349. doi:10.1038/nrn808

Sutherland, G., Stapleton, J. A., Russell, M. A., and Feyerabend, C. (1995). Naltrexone, smoking behaviour and cigarette withdrawal. *Psychopharmacology (Berl.)* 120, 418–425. doi:10.1007/BF02245813

Suzuki, R., Lumeng, L., McBride, W. J., Li, T. K., and Hwang, B. H. (2004). Reduced neuropeptide Y mRNA expression in the central nucleus of amygdala of alcohol preferring (P) rats: its potential involvement in alcohol preference and anxiety. *Brain Res.* 1014, 251–254. doi:10.1016/j.brainres.2004.04.037

Suzuki, T., Ise, Y., Mori, T., and Misawa, M. (1997). Attenuation of mecamylamine-precipitated nicotine-withdrawal aversion by the 5-HT3 receptor antagonist ondansetron. *Life Sci.* 61, L249–254. doi:10.1016/S0024-3205(97)00745-5

Suzuki, T., Ise, Y., Tsuda, M., Maeda, J., and Misawa, M. (1996). Mecamylamine-precipitated nicotine-withdrawal aversion in rats. *Eur. J. Pharmacol.* 314, 281–284. doi:10.1016/S0014-2999(96)00723-6

Taheri, S., Zeitzer, J. M., and Mignot, E. (2002). The role of hypocretins (orexins) in sleep regulation and narcolepsy. *Annu. Rev. Neurosci.* 25, 283–313. doi:10.1146/annurev.neuro.25.112701.142826

Thorsell, A., Repunte-Canonigo, V., O'Dell, L. E., Chen, S. A., King, A. R., Lekic, D., et al. (2007). Viral vector-induced amygdala NPY over expression reverses increased alcohol intake caused by repeated deprivations in Wistar rats. *Brain* 130, 1330–1337. doi:10.1093/brain/awm033

Torres, O. V., Tejeda, H. A., Natividad, L. A., and O'Dell, L. E. (2008). Enhanced vulnerability to the rewarding effects of nicotine during the adolescent period of development. *Pharmacol. Biochem. Behav.* 90, 658–663. doi:10.1016/j.pbb.2008.05.009

Tovote, P., Meyer, M., Beck-Sickinger, A. G., von Hörsten, S., Ove Ogren, S., Spiess, J., et al. (2004). Central NPY receptor-mediated alteration of heart rate dynamics in mice during expression of fear conditioned to an auditory cue. *Regul. Pept.* 120, 205–214. doi:10.1016/j.regpep.2004.03.011

Trigo, J. M., Zimmer, A., and Maldonado, R. (2009). Nicotine anxiogenic and rewarding effects are decreased in mice lacking beta-endorphin. *Neuropharmacology* 56, 1147–1153. doi:10.1016/j.neuropharm.2009.03.013

Tucci, S., Cheeta, S., Seth, P., and File, S. E. (2003). Corticotropin releasing factor antagonist, -helical CRF9-41, reverses nicotine-induced

conditioned, but not unconditioned, anxiety. *Psychopharmacology (Berl.)* 167, 251–256.

Tucker, J. S., Ellickson, P. L., and Klein, D. J. (2003). Predictors of the transition to regular smoking during adolescence and young adulthood. *J. Adolesc. Health* 32, 314–324. doi:10.1016/S1054-139X(02)00709-7

Turner, J. A., McNicol, M. W., and Sillett, R. W. (1986). Distribution of carboxyhaemoglobin concentrations in smokers and non-smokers. *Thorax* 41, 25–27.

U.S. Department of Health and Human Services. (1994). *Preventing Tobacco Use Among Youth and Young Adults: A Report of the Surgeon General.* Atlanta, GA: Centers for Disease Control and Prevention, Office on Smoking and Health.

U.S. Department of Health and Human Services. (2006). *The Health Consequences of Involuntary Exposure to Tobacco Smoke: A Report of the Surgeon General.* Atlanta, GA: Centers for Disease Control and Prevention, Office on Smoking and Health.

U.S. Department of Health and Human Services. (2012). *Preventing Tobacco Use Among Young People: A Report of the Surgeon General.* Atlanta, GA: Centers for Disease Control and Prevention, Office on Smoking and Health.

Valdez, G. R., Inoue, K., Koob, G. F., Rivier, J., Vale, W. W., and Zorrilla, E. P. (2002). Human urocortin II: mild locomotor suppressive and delayed anxiolytic-like effects of a novel corticotropin-releasing factor related peptide. *Brain Res.* 943, 142–150. doi:10.1016/S0006-8993(02)02707-5

Valdez, G. R., Zorrilla, E. P., Rivier, J., Vale, W. W., and Koob, G. F. (2003). Locomotor suppressive and anxiolytic-like effects of urocortin 3, a highly selective type 2 corticotropin-releasing factor agonist. *Brain Res.* 980, 206–212. doi:10.1016/S0006-8993(03)02971-8

Vale, W., Rivier, C., Brown, M. R., Spiess, J., Koob, G., Swanson, L., et al. (1983). Chemical and biological characterization of corticotropin releasing factor. *Recent Prog. Horm. Res.* 39, 245–270.

Vale, W., Spiess, J., Rivier, C., and Rivier, J. (1981). Characterization of a 41-residue ovine hypothalamic peptide that stimulates secretion of corticotropin and beta-endorphin. *Science* 213, 1394–1397. doi:10.1126/science.6267699

Valentine, J. D., Hokanson, J. S., Matta, S. G., and Sharp, B. M.

(1997). Self-administration in rats allowed unlimited access to nicotine. *Psychopharmacology (Berl.)* 133, 300–304. doi:10.1007/s002130050405

Vansickel, A. R., Cobb, C. O., Weaver, M. F., and Eissenberg, T. E. (2010). A clinical laboratory model for evaluating the acute effects of electronic "cigarettes": nicotine delivery profile and cardiovascular and subjective effects. *Cancer Epidemiol. Biomarkers Prev.* 19, 1945–1953. doi:10.1158/1055-9965.EPI-10-0288

Vansickel, A. R., and Eissenberg, T. (2013). Electronic cigarettes: effective nicotine delivery after acute administration. *Nicotine Tob. Res.* 15, 267–270. doi:10.1093/ntr/ntr316

Vendruscolo, L. F., Barbier, E., Schlosburg, J. E., Misra, K. K., Whitfield, T. W., Logrip, M. L., et al. (2012). Corticosteroid-dependent plasticity mediates compulsive alcohol drinking in rats. *J. Neurosci.* 32, 7563–7571. doi:10.1523/JNEUROSCI.0069-12.2012

Vlachou, P. A., Khalili, K., Jang, H. J., Fischer, S., Hirschfield, G. M., and Kim, T. K. (2011). IgG4-related sclerosing disease: autoimmune pancreatitis and extrapancreatic manifestations. *Radiographics* 31, 1379–1402. doi:10.1148/rg.315105735

Wagener, T. L., Siegel, M., and Borrelli, B. (2012). Electronic cigarettes: achieving a balanced perspective. *Addiction* 107, 1545–1548. doi:10.1111/j.1360-0443.2012.03826.x

Wakabayashi, K. T., Weiss, M. J., Pickup, K. N., and Robinson, T. E. (2010). Rats markedly escalate their intake and show a persistent susceptibility to reinstatement only when cocaine is injected rapidly. *J. Neurosci.* 30, 11346–11355. doi:10.1523/JNEUROSCI.2524-10.2010

Wang, M. P., Ho, S. Y., and Lam, T. H. (2011). Parental smoking, exposure to secondhand smoke at home, and smoking initiation among young children. *Nicotine Tob. Res.* 13, 827–832. doi:10.1093/ntr/ntr083

Watkins, S. S., Epping-Jordan, M. P., Koob, G. F., and Markou, A. (1999). Blockade of nicotine self-administration with nicotinic antagonists in rats. *Pharmacol. Biochem. Behav.* 62, 743–751. doi:10.1016/S0091-3057(98)00226-3

Watkins, S. S., Stinus, L., Koob, G. F., and Markou, A. (2000a). Reward and somatic changes during precipitated nicotine withdrawal in rats: centrally and peripherally mediated effects. *J. Pharmacol. Exp. Ther.* 292, 1053–1064.

Watkins, S. S., Koob, G. F., and Markou, A. (2000b). Neural mechanisms underlying nicotine addiction: acute positive reinforcement and withdrawal. *Nicotine Tob. Res.* 2, 19–37. doi:10.1080/14622200050011277

West, R., Hajek, P., and McNeill, A. (1991). Effect of buspirone on cigarette withdrawal symptoms and short-term abstinence rates in a smokers clinic. *Psychopharmacology (Berl.)* 104, 91–96. doi:10.1007/BF02244560

Wilkie, G. I., Hutson, P. H., Stephens, M. W., Whiting, P., and Wonnacott, S. (1993). Hippocampal nicotinic autoreceptors modulate acetylcholine release. *Biochem. Soc. Trans.* 21, 429–431.

Wilmouth, C. E., and Spear, L. P. (2006). Withdrawal from chronic nicotine in adolescent and adult rats. *Psychol. Addict. Behav.* 21, 127–137.

Winsky-Sommerer, R., Yamanaka, A., Diano, S., Borok, E., Roberts, A. J., Sakurai, T., et al. (2004). Interaction between the corticotropin-releasing factor system and hypocretins (orexins): a novel circuit mediating stress response. *J. Neurosci.* 24, 11439–11448. doi:10.1523/JNEUROSCI.3459-04.2004

Wooltorton, J. R., Pidoplichko, V. I., Broide, R. S., and Dani, J. A. (2003). Differential desensitization and distribution of nicotinic acetylcholine receptor subtypes in midbrain dopamine areas. *J. Neurosci.* 23, 3176–3185.

Yamada, H., Bishnoi, M., Keijzers, K. F., van Tuijl, I. A., Small, E., Shah, H. P., et al. (2010). Preadolescent tobacco smoke exposure leads to acute nicotine dependence but does not affect the rewarding effects of nicotine or nicotine withdrawal in adulthood in rats. *Pharmacol. Biochem. Behav.* 95, 401–409. doi:10.1016/j.pbb.2010.02.018

Yang, C. Y., Wu, W. H., and Zbuzek, V. K. (1992). Antinociceptive effect of chronic nicotine and nociceptive effect of its withdrawal measured by hot-plate and tail-flick in rats. *Psychopharmacology (Berl.)* 106, 417–420. doi:10.1007/BF02245428

Yang, X., Criswell, H. E., and Breese, G. R. (1996). Nicotine-induced inhibition in medial septum involves activation of presynaptic nicotinic cholinergic receptors on gamma-aminobutyric acid-containing neurons. *J. Pharmacol. Exp. Ther.* 276, 482–489.

Yee, B. E., Ahmed, M. I., Brugge, D., Farrell, M., Lozada, G., Idupaganthi, R., et al. (2010). Second-hand smoking and carboxyhemoglobin levels in children: a prospective observational study. *Paediatr. Anaesth.* 20, 82–89. doi:10.1111/j.1460-9592.2009.03192.x

Young, S. N., Smith, S. E., Pihl, R. O., and Ervin, F. R. (1985). Tryptophan depletion causes a rapid lowering of mood in normal males. *Psychopharmacology (Berl.)* 87, 173–177. doi:10.1007/BF00431803

Zaniewska, M., Przegalinski, E., and Filip, M. (2009). Nicotine dependence – human and animal studies, current pharmacotherapies and future perspectives. *Pharmacol. Rep.* 61, 957–965.

Zhan, W., Dierker, L. C., Rose, J. S., Selya, A., and Mermelstein, R. J. (2012). The natural course of nicotine dependence symptoms among adolescent smokers. *Nicotine Tob. Res.* 14, 1445–1452. doi:10.1093/ntr/nts031

Zorrilla, E. P., Valdez, G. R., Nozulak, J., Koob, G. F., and Markou, A. (2002). Effects of antalarmin, a CRF type 1 receptor antagonist, on anxiety-like behavior and motor activation in the rat. *Brain Res.* 952, 188–199. doi:10.1016/S0006-8993(02)03189-X

14

The plasticity of extinction: contribution of the prefrontal cortex in treating addiction through inhibitory learning

J. T. Gass and L. J. Chandler*

Department of Neurosciences, Medical University of South Carolina, Charleston, SC, USA

Edited by:
Nicholas W. Gilpin, Louisiana State University Health Sciences Center New Orleans, USA

Reviewed by:
Nicholas J. Grahame, Indiana University, USA
Ryan LaLumiere, University of Iowa, USA

*Correspondence:
L. J. Chandler, Department of Neurosciences, Medical University of South Carolina, 67 President Street MSC 861, Charleston, SC 29425, USA
e-mail: chandj@musc.edu

Theories of drug addiction that incorporate various concepts from the fields of learning and memory have led to the idea that classical and operant conditioning principles underlie the compulsiveness of addictive behaviors. Relapse often results from exposure to drug-associated cues, and the ability to extinguish these conditioned behaviors through inhibitory learning could serve as a potential therapeutic approach for those who suffer from addiction. This review will examine the evidence that extinction learning alters neuronal plasticity in specific brain regions and pathways. In particular, subregions of the prefrontal cortex (PFC) and their projections to other brain regions have been shown to differentially modulate drug-seeking and extinction behavior. Additionally, there is a growing body of research demonstrating that manipulation of neuronal plasticity can alter extinction learning. Therefore, the ability to alter plasticity within areas of the PFC through pharmacological manipulation could facilitate the acquisition of extinction and provide a novel intervention to aid in the extinction of drug-related memories.

Keywords: extinction learning, prelimbic, infralimbic, prefrontal cortex, addiction

Once believed to result from an immoral personality or lack of will power, it is now clear that drug addiction is a disease of the nervous system that involves uncontrollable drug intake and compulsive drug-seeking behavior. As such, addiction is characterized by periods of repeated drug use followed by unsuccessful attempts to maintain abstinence. As a chronic relapsing disorder, addiction is associated with numerous brain changes that include signaling pathways, neurotransmitters, and cell mechanisms that overlap with those that mediate normal learning and memory processes. Thus, there have been numerous theories that incorporate mechanisms of learning and memory as a basis for drug addiction (O'Brien et al., 1992; Di Chiara, 1999; Volkow et al., 2002; Kelley, 2004; Wise, 2004; Hyman, 2005; Weiss, 2005). These theories suggest that through basic conditioning principles, certain behaviors and drug-environment associations become "overlearned" and thus contribute to the compulsive behavior of addicts.

In classical Pavlovian conditioning, also referred to as stimulus-outcome conditioning, the presentation of a conditioned stimulus (CS) paired with presentation of an unconditioned stimulus (US) after repeated pairings comes to elicit a conditional response (CR). In a drug context, the repeated pairing of the CS (e.g., environmental cues) with the reinforcing properties of a drug (US) results in the ability of the CS alone to elicit drug-seeking behaviors. Conversely, instrumental conditioning, also referred to as response-outcome conditioning, involves learning through consequences (either positive or negative) that are contingent upon a particular behavior. In a drug context, behaviors that lead to the reinforcing effects of a drug are more likely to be repeated in the future. It is believed that drug-taking behaviors become compulsive and automatic (instrumental conditioning) with repeated drug exposure, and the associations between drugs and specific environmental cues and context become overly salient (classical conditioning). Conditioning processes also play a role in the influence of environments that predict drug availability to induce craving and promote relapse (Childress et al., 1988, 1999; Kalivas and Volkow, 2005).

The ability to suppress drug-seeking behaviors that are heavily influenced by drug memories is a logical therapeutic approach in the prevention of relapse. Extinction is the gradual reduction of a CR when the CS is no longer paired with the US. Functionally, it is observed as a decrease in responding from higher levels observed prior to extinction to lower levels following extinction training. Theoretically, this type of inhibitory training could reduce the occurrence of behaviors that are trademarks of addiction including drug-seeking and relapse. However, current implementations of extinction-based techniques, such as exposure therapy, have a poor record of efficacy (Childress et al., 1993; Conklin and Tiffany, 2002a,b). Therefore, there is a need to better understand the neural mechanisms that underlie extinction learning and develop therapeutic interventions that increase the success rates of cue exposure therapies. This could lead to treatments involving a combination of behavioral training and pharmacological interventions that create a more robust and persistent decrease in cue-induced affective responses to drug memories (Davis et al., 2006). A substantial amount of research has focused on the neurobiological processes that underlie the extinction of conditioned fear and non-drug reinforcers (e.g., food). While the majority of previous work has focused on understanding the mechanisms involved in fear/non-drug extinction, there is an increasing interest in understanding how these principles apply to addiction related behaviors. Results from the fear and non-drug extinction field have greatly informed and helped guide studies in addiction. Therefore, while the focus of this review is on the extinction of drug-seeking behavior, observations from the fear/non-drug extinction field will be incorporated where appropriate.

WHAT IS EXTINCTION LEARNING?

At first glance, the phenomenon of extinction may appear to simply represent a process that involves the unlearning, forgetting, and/or erasure of a previously formed memory (Rescorla and Wagner, 1972). However, a large body of evidence gained over the past several decades provides strong support for the idea originally suggested by Pavlov (1927) that extinction is "new" and "active" learning and is not simply the "unlearning" or erasure of previously formed associations. Many of these studies have been carried out in rodents and involve the extinction of responding for a natural reinforcer such as food. In contrast, studies of extinction learning in addiction typically involve extinction of self-administration of a drug of abuse such as cocaine. These experimental procedures incorporate aspects of both instrumental and classical conditioning to train animals to perform a behavior (e.g., lever pressing) to receive access to a drug and associate discrete cues (e.g., auditory and/or visual) with the drug's reinforcing effects. Regardless of the type of reinforcer used (e.g., food or drug), extinction is defined in this review as the omission of a previously delivered unconditioned stimuli/reinforcers or the absence of a contingency between a response and reinforcer (Lattal and Lattal, 2012). In addition, while extinction behavior can be observed in both classical and instrumental conditioning paradigms, this review will not attempt to define the neural mechanisms associated with each form of learning.

The idea that extinction involves new learning has great implications for not only understanding how drug memories can have a lasting influence on relapse but also for the development of pharmacological treatments for addiction. The following lines of evidence from studies examining the extinction of drug-related behaviors support the idea that extinction is indeed new learning:

(1) After extinction training, drug-seeking behavior can be reactivated with a single stimulus without the need for additional behavioral training (Sinha et al., 2000; Stewart, 2000, 2003; Sinha, 2001; Shalev et al., 2002; See, 2005; Epstein et al., 2006; Kalivas et al., 2006; Olmstead, 2006).

(2) Drug-seeking can resume after lengthy periods of abstinence or extinction training indicating that the original drug-memory remains and has not simply been deleted (Hammersley, 1992; Tobena et al., 1993; Corty and Coon, 1995; Di Ciano and Everitt, 2004).

(3) Extinction is context-specific (Bouton, 2000, 2002, 2004; Chaudhri et al., 2008; Wells et al., 2011), which suggests that original memory of drug reinforcement is still present even after extinction training.

(4) The retraining of self-administration after extinction is considerably less compared to original training (Carroll, 1998; Grasing et al., 2005).

(5) Extinction learning has been shown to involve classic cellular hallmarks of learning and memory (Crombag and Shaham, 2002; Sutton et al., 2003; Self and Choi, 2004; Self et al., 2004; Knackstedt et al., 2010).

Thus, findings from the literature on addiction support the idea that extinction training is not the removal of a previously formed association but instead involves the generation of a new memory that competes with the initial memory for control of behavior. As such, the original associative and instrumental conditioning that occurs during the early stages of addiction remains intact. Based on similar findings from the fear extinction literature, Quirk et al. (2006) presented a schematic model to illustrate the idea that even though fear behavior decreases, the original fear memory remains. As depicted in **Figure 1** the same concept can be mapped onto the processes of addiction such that drug-seeking behavior declines during extinction training, but the drug-memory remains and competes with the newly formed extinction memory for the control of behavior. The formation of new memories during extinction training likely utilizes neural circuitry involved in basic learning and memory process. In the following sections we review studies that have highlighted specific brain regions and mechanisms involved in extinction learning.

NEUROCIRCUITRY OF THE EXTINCTION LEARNING

While the neurocircuitry of extinction is likely diffuse and involves a distributed network, there is evidence for the involvement of several key brain regions in drug-seeking, fear expression, and extinction behavior that could constitute differential circuits associated with each of these behaviors.

THE PREFRONTAL CORTEX

Increasing evidence has implicated the prefrontal cortex (PFC) in the extinction of both fear and drug-seeking behaviors. Anatomically, the rodent PFC is located in the anterior pole of the frontal cortex and is loosely defined as the anterior cingulate (ACC), medial PFC (mPFC), and orbital frontal cortex (OFC). As illustrated in **Figure 2**, the rodent mPFC can be further subdivided into a dorsal region called the prelimbic (PrL) cortex and a ventral region called the infralimbic (IfL) cortex. These subregions do not have well demarcated structural boundaries that can often make it difficult to clearly delineate these subregions, especially given the small size of the rodent brain. For this reason, investigators often simply divide this area into a dorsomedial PFC that includes the dorsal region of the PrL cortex and much of the overlying ACC, and a ventromedial PFC that includes the IfL cortex and the ventral portions of the PrL cortex (**Figure 2**). Defining analogous subregions of the PFC of rodents and human brain is also difficult due to the evolutionary expansion of the PFC. Therefore definitions are based not only upon common anatomical circuitry but also upon function. Based upon similarities in thalamic inputs, the rodent PrL region is considered to be equivalent to Brodmann area 32 (pregenual anterior cortex) and the IfL cortex is equivalent to Brodmann area 25 (subgenual anterior cortex) in the human (**Figure 2**). It should also be noted that the dorsolateral PFC of humans (conservatively defined as areas 9 and 46) is also considered to be equivalent to the rodent mPFC using a functional definition as both regions are involved in working-memory processes.

While complex behaviors such as working memory, impulsivity, motivation, and decision-making have often been linked to

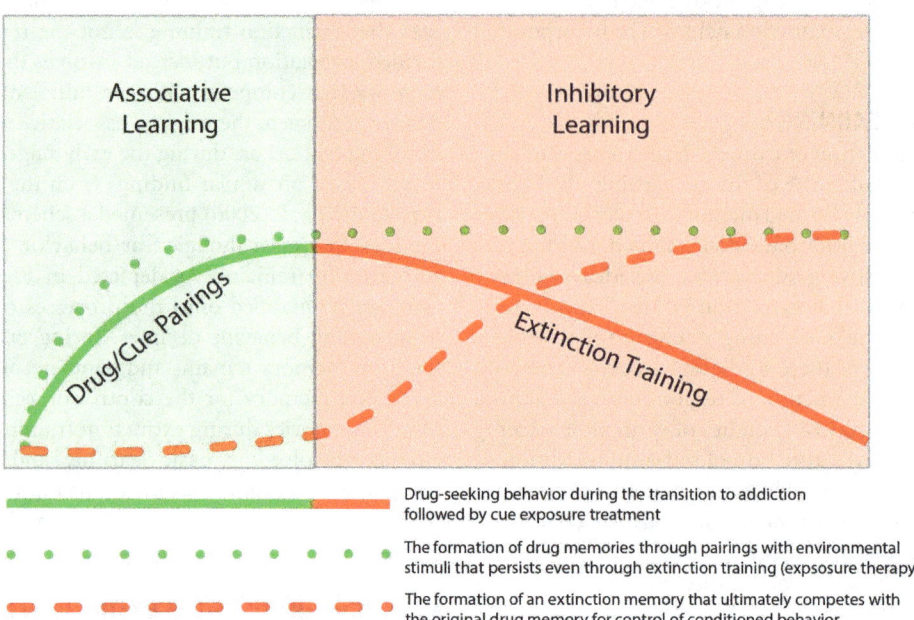

FIGURE 1 | Depiction of the temporal relationship of associative learning of drug-seeking behavior with inhibitory learning during subsequent extinction of the drug-seeking behavior. The initial phase of addiction involves associative learning processes in which drug-taking becomes linked through classic Pavlovian conditioning with drug-related cues (e.g., drug paraphernalia or drug-taking environment). With repeated pairing, this association results in formation of a persistent "drug memory." This memory trace remains long after discontinuation of drug-taking. The extinction of drug-seeking by pairing unreinforced exposure of drug-related cues, does not result in the deletion of the original drug memory, but instead involves the formation of a new inhibitory "extinction memory." While this new memory provides inhibitory drive over drug-seeking behavior in the short term, the original drug-memory remains, which may explain the high rate of relapse following behavioral extinction therapies.

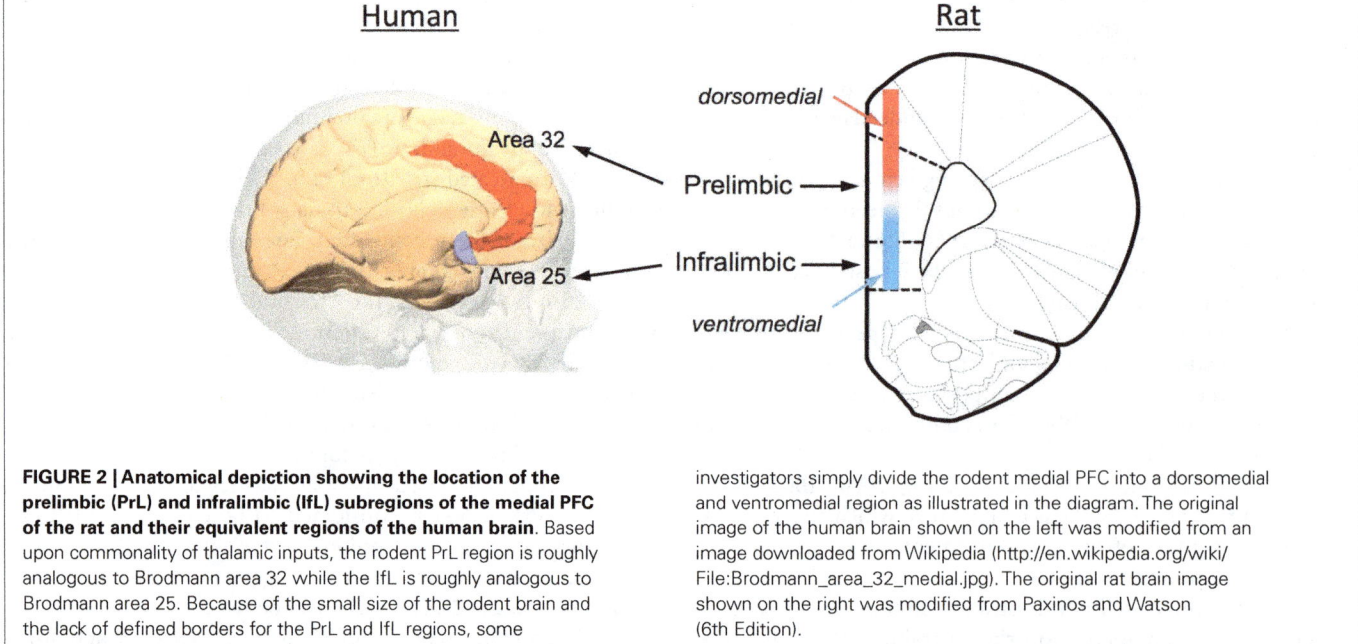

FIGURE 2 | Anatomical depiction showing the location of the prelimbic (PrL) and infralimbic (IfL) subregions of the medial PFC of the rat and their equivalent regions of the human brain. Based upon commonality of thalamic inputs, the rodent PrL region is roughly analogous to Brodmann area 32 while the IfL is roughly analogous to Brodmann area 25. Because of the small size of the rodent brain and the lack of defined borders for the PrL and IfL regions, some investigators simply divide the rodent medial PFC into a dorsomedial and ventromedial region as illustrated in the diagram. The original image of the human brain shown on the left was modified from an image downloaded from Wikipedia (http://en.wikipedia.org/wiki/File:Brodmann_area_32_medial.jpg). The original rat brain image shown on the right was modified from Paxinos and Watson (6th Edition).

the cognitive function of the PFC, a number of recent studies have implicated PFC subregions in extinction behavior. In particular, lesion studies have shown that the PrL cortex is necessary for the expression of conditioned fear while the IfL cortex is critical for the expression of extinction behavior (for reviews, see Quirk et al., 2010; Sierra-Mercado et al., 2011; Milad and Quirk, 2012).

Drug-seeking behavior has been studied extensively in humans where it has been shown that presentation of drug stimuli significantly increase activation in specific regions of the PFC (for a review, see Goldstein and Volkow, 2011). Several inactivation studies have also implicated the PrL cortex of the rat as a critical component in the circuitry for drug-seeking behavior including cocaine (McFarland and Kalivas, 2001; Capriles et al., 2003; McLaughlin and See, 2003; McFarland et al., 2004; See, 2005; Di Pietro et al., 2006) and heroin (LaLumiere and Kalivas, 2008; Rogers et al., 2008). Additionally, the IfL cortex, which has been studied extensively in fear extinction, has also been implicated in the extinction of drug-seeking behavior (Ovari and Leri, 2008; Peters et al., 2008a,b). As depicted in **Figure 3**, converging lines of evidence from both the fear- and drug-conditioning fields suggest that the PrL cortex serves as an "on-switch" for conditioned fear expression and drug-seeking, while the IfL cortex functions as an "off-switch" for the expression of extinction behavior (LaLumiere and Kalivas, 2008; Peters et al., 2008a; Quirk and Mueller, 2008; LaLumiere et al., 2010). These subregions of the PFC could thus serve as candidate regions for plasticity-related changes associated with extinction behavior.

DORSAL AND VENTRAL STRIATUM

Different subregions of the striatum are important for mediating components of reward. The rodent striatum is divided into the dorsal and ventral striatum, and each of these regions can be further subdivided. Due to its involvement in habit learning, the dorsal striatum has been implicated in various aspects of the transition from voluntary behavior to uncontrolled habitual behavior that characterizes drug abuse (Robbins and Everitt, 2002; Weiss, 2005; Izquierdo et al., 2006). In particular, the dorsomedial subregion has been shown to modulate goal-direction actions that transitions to the dorsolateral striatum as these actions become habitual. The ventral striatum or nucleus accumbens (NAc) can be further divided into a lateral "core" and medial "shell" subregion. Through its connections with the PFC, amygdala, hippocampus, and motor regions, the NAc plays a role in guiding emotionally relevant behavioral responses related to the reinforcing properties of drugs and drug-related stimuli (Bonci et al., 2003; Di Chiara and Bassareo, 2007).

Recent studies have also implicated the NAc in extinction of drug-seeking behavior. Cocaine self-administration causes a decrease in tyrosine hydroxylase in the NAc shell which is reversed

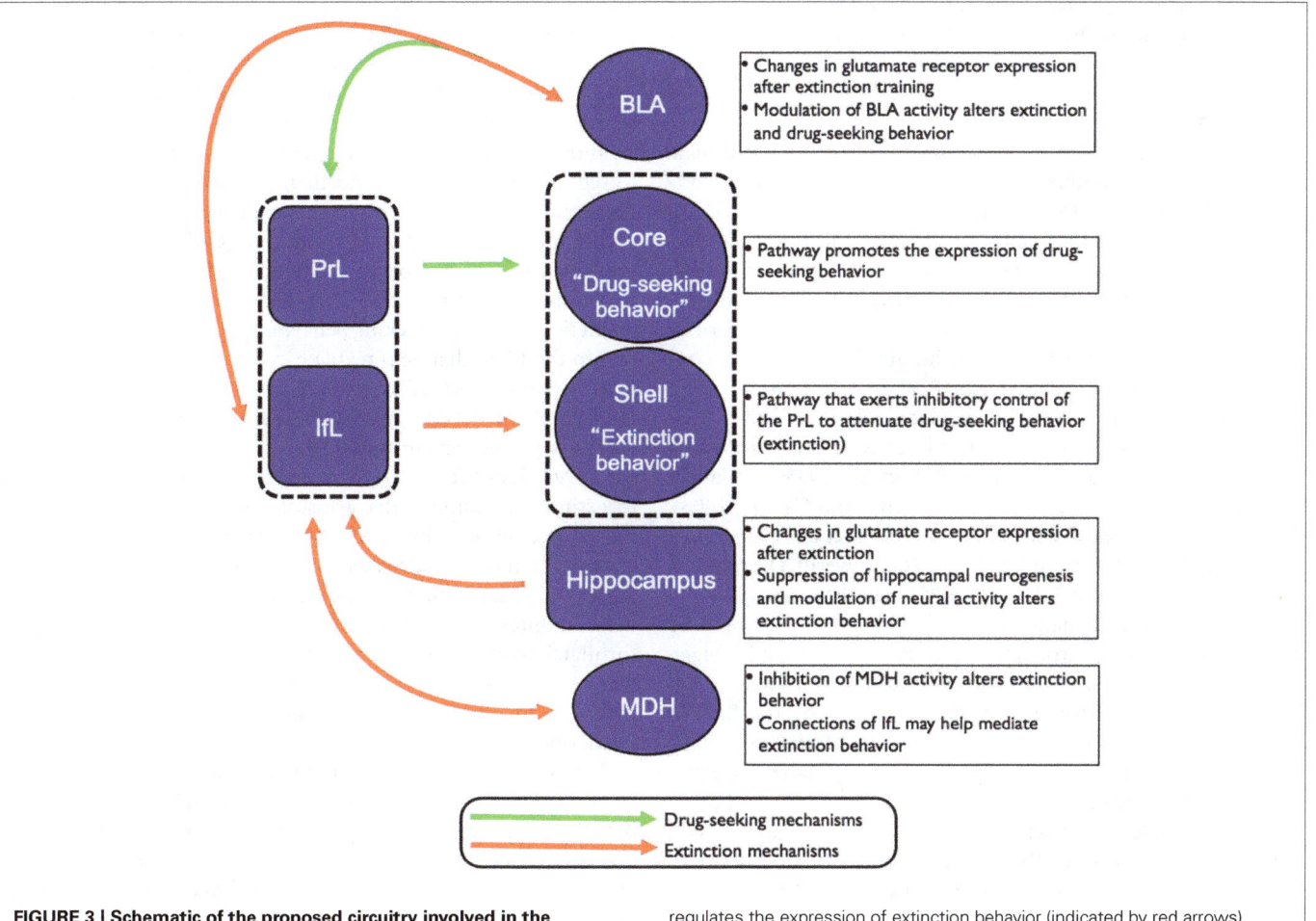

FIGURE 3 | Schematic of the proposed circuitry involved in the drug-seeking and extinction behavior. Projections from the PrL cortex to the NAc core regulates the expression of cocaine-seeking behavior (indicated by green arrows) while projections from the IfL cortex to the NAc shell regulates the expression of extinction behavior (indicated by red arrows). Recent studies have also implicated the involvement of other brain regions such as the hippocampus, MDH, and BLA in the neurocircuitry of extinction of drug-seeking behavior.

with extinction training during withdrawal from cocaine (Schmidt et al., 2001). Extinction training also induces an upregulation in the expression of AMPA receptor subunits within the NAc shell (Sutton et al., 2003; Self et al., 2004). More recently, it was shown that inactivation for the NAc shell resulted in the expression of cocaine-seeking behavior, possibly through an interaction with the IfL cortex (Peters et al., 2008a). Similarly, activation of IfL glutamatergic projections with an AMPA receptor positive allosteric modulator reduced cocaine-seeking behavior, and blockade of AMPA activity in the NAc shell attenuated this effect (LaLumiere et al., 2012). Similar findings have been observed with the extinction of ethanol-seeking behavior. For instance, the NAc shell, possibly through interactions with the hypothalamus or the amygdala, helps mediate the expression of extinction behavior (Millan et al., 2010; Millan and McNally, 2011). With regards to the NAc core, extinction training also normalizes cocaine-induced deficits in levels of the GluN1 subunit of the NMDA receptor (Self et al., 2004). Consistent with its role in goal-directed and habitual actions, the dorsal striatum has also been implicated in the extinction of habitual cocaine-seeking behavior (Fuchs et al., 2006). These lines of evidence suggest that there is a significant amount of plasticity that occurs within the dorsal striatum and NAc during extinction learning, and that these regions are central in the neurocircuitry of extinction of drug-seeking behavior.

AMYGDALA

As is the case with the PFC and the striatum, the amygdala is made up of a complex of different substructures that differentially contribute to extinction of fear- and drug-seeking behavior. The amydaloid complex includes the basal and lateral subregions (collectively known as the basolateral amygdala, BLA), medial amygdala (MeA), central amygdala (CeA), and cortical amygdala (CoA). The amygdala is involved with various learning and memory processes including formation and consolidation of emotional memories (Cahill et al., 2001; LaBar, 2003). The BLA also has an established role in synaptic plasticity associated with emotion-related behaviors, the processing of emotionally relevant stimuli (Cahill et al., 1995; McGaugh, 2004; Phelps et al., 2004; Maren, 2005; LaBar and Cabeza, 2006), and in stimulus-reward associations (Hatfield et al., 1996; Blundell et al., 2001; Baxter and Murray, 2002; Everitt et al., 2003; See, 2005; Balleine and Killcross, 2006). The BLA also plays an integral role in the formation of associations between drugs and environmental cues (Hiroi and White, 1991; Brown and Fibiger, 1993; Whitelaw et al., 1996; Rizos et al., 2005). While there has been a substantial amount of research implicating the BLA in the extinction of fear conditioning (Myers and Davis, 2002, 2007; Quirk et al., 2010; Sierra-Mercado et al., 2011), studies have also implicated this region in the extinction of drug-seeking behavior. For example, enhancement of glutamatergic transmission within the BLA facilities the extinction of a drug-paired conditioned place preference (CPP) (Shidara and Richmond, 2002; Schroeder and Packard, 2004), and given the essential role of the BLA in drug-seeking (See et al., 2003), it is logical to assume that plasticity within this structure may also influence extinction learning.

HIPPOCAMPUS

The hippocampus is known to play an important role in various forms of learning and spatial/contextual memory and in memory consolidation/retrieval (Neves et al., 2008). The hippocampus is also involved in extinction behavior as evidenced by impairments in context-dependent extinction of fear conditioning that results from inactivation of this brain region (Corcoran and Maren, 2001; Corcoran et al., 2005; Ji and Maren, 2005) and cellular substrate inhibition (Szapiro et al., 2003; Vianna et al., 2003; Power et al., 2006). Similarly, studies have also implicated the hippocampus in the extinction of drug-related behaviors. Electrical stimulation of the ventral subiculum of the hippocampus reinstates cocaine-seeking (Vorel et al., 2001), and inactivation of this region abolishes cocaine drug-seeking (Sun et al., 2005). Neuronal activity within the CA1 and dentate gyrus (DG) has also been shown to change with extinction training of cocaine-associated cues providing further evidence that plasticity within this structure is associated with extinction behavior (Neisewander et al., 2000).

HYPOTHALAMUS

A less investigated structure that has recently been implicated in extinction behavior is the hypothalamus. This structure has traditionally been shown to be involved in reward and feeding but its influence on drug-seeking behavior is becoming better understood (for reviews, see Millan et al., 2011; Marchant et al., 2012). The medial dorsal hypothalamus (MDH) is associated with the termination of motivated behaviors and, therefore, is a logical candidate for involvement in extinction learning. In rats trained to self-administer alcohol and then exposed to extinction training, infusion of the inhibitory neuropeptide known as cocaine and amphetamine-regulated transcript (CART) into the MDH prevented the expression of extinction (Marchant et al., 2010). It is important to note that a similar effect was found with the extinction of sucrose-seeking behavior suggesting the mechanisms within the LDH that help regulate extinction may not be unique to drug reinforcers (Millan et al., 2011). To add further support for the role of the MDH in extinction behavior, this region receives extensive projections from the IfL cortex (Thompson and Swanson, 1998; Heidbreder and Groenewegen, 2003). In rats exposed to extinction training after a history of alcohol administration, the expression of extinction is associated with induction of c-Fos expression in retrograde labeled IfL cortical neurons projecting to the MDH (Marchant et al., 2010; Millan et al., 2011). Together, these findings suggest plasticity-related changes in the MDH, and through its connections with the IfL cortex, can mediate the extinction of reward-seeking behavior. These results also identify a brain region to investigate as a novel candidate for the facilitation of extinction behavior.

Based on findings detailed in the preceding sections, there are several key brain regions involved in extinction behavior. The exact details of how these structures interact to form a neurocircuitry that mediates extinction behavior have yet to be fully established. However, converging lines of evidence indicate that subregions of the PFC (and their corresponding projections to subcortical structures) play a major role in the extinction of drug and fear behaviors. Peters et al. (2009) proposed that extinction of drug memories comprises overlapping neural circuitry with that of fear memories. According to the model of the neurocircuitry of fear conditioning, the PrL cortex sends excitatory projections to the BLA that, in turn, promote the expression of conditioned fear via excitation of the CeA. In contrast, the IfL cortex sends excitatory projections to GABAergic inhibitory neurons in the intercalated (ITC) cell masses in the amygdala. This leads to inhibition of the CeA and attenuation of the expression of conditioned fear, and promotes the expression of extinction behavior. In the neurocircuitry of the extinction of drug memories, the PrL cortex also sends excitatory projections to the core region of the NAc where it has been shown to regulate the expression of cocaine-seeking behavior. In contrast, excitatory projections from the IfL cortex to the shell region of the NAc promote the extinction of cocaine-seeking behavior. This proposed circuitry for the extinction of drug behaviors is depicted in **Figure 3**. What is currently unknown is how structures such as the BLA, hippocampus, and MDH contribute to the established role of the PFC subregions in extinction behavior.

GLUTAMATERGIC MECHANISMS IN EXTINCTION

In recent years, a number of studies have provided a more detailed analysis of the plasticity-related mechanisms that may mediate extinction behavior. Pathways connecting the various brain regions involved in extinction may differentially modulate the expression of drug-seeking and extinction of drug-seeking behavior. For instance, it was observed that there is increased activity of ventromedial PFC neurons in response to presentation of cocaine-related cues during extinction training. Interestingly, when activity in this region was inhibited, there was a corresponding decrease in extinction responding (Koya et al., 2009). Additionally, it has been shown that prefrontal regions have the ability to influence activity in other extinction-related brain structures. For instance, stimulation of IfL cortical output results in an inhibition of pyramidal neurons in the PrL cortex through a feed-forward mechanism (Ferrante et al., 2009). Similar results were found in a study that utilized optogenetic procedures to activate or inhibit specific cell types in isolated brain regions in combination with single-unit recordings of neuronal activity. It was revealed that optogenetic stimulation of viral vector encoding channel rhodopsin 2 (ChR2) excitatory neurons in the IfL cortex produced excitation of IfL cortical pyramidal neurons and also increased their responsiveness to excitatory input from multisensory brain regions (Ji and Neugebauer, 2012). It was further observed that activation of the IfL cortex inhibits PrL output, supporting the suggestion that IfL cortex mediated extinction mechanisms may involve inhibition of PrL cortex output that would ultimately mediate fear expression and possibly drug-seeking. Previous research has also shown that stimulation of the PrL region results in excitation of BLA neurons (Likhtik et al., 2005) and stimulation of the IfL region reduced the responsiveness of CeA neurons to inputs from the insula and BLA (Quirk et al., 2003). While these studies did not directly address extinction of fear expression or drug-seeking behavior, they provide support for how the IfL region of the PFC-through its direct projections to subcortical regions (e.g., amygdala, NAc, and hippocampus)-can mediate extinction behavior. Additionally, the ability of IfL cortical activation to exert inhibitory control over output from pyramidal neurons in the PrL

cortex may also impact the expression of fear and drug-seeking behaviors.

The highly persistent nature of drug- and fear-related cues to induce relapse and the ineffectiveness of behavioral therapies to reduce the impact of these cues has led to a focus on understanding the neural mechanisms involved in relapse with the goal that they may be targeted as a means to enhance extinction learning. Studies have pharmacologically manipulated cellular process and substrates in specific brain regions in an attempt to "strengthen" inhibitory learning formed during extinction training. Using various behavioral paradigms such as fear-conditioning procedures and drug-self administration, investigators have begun to uncover plasticity-related mechanisms that facilitate extinction learning. Given the importance of glutamatergic transmission in learning and memory processes, a strong focus has been placed on targeting glutamate-related processes in extinction learning. Manipulation of both ionotropic and metabotropic receptors facilitates the extinction of fear-conditioning and drug-seeking behavior (for reviews, see Cleva et al., 2010; Myers et al., 2011). While blockade of NMDA receptors impairs extinction learning, enhancement of these receptors with the NMDA partial agonist D-cycloserine (DCS) facilitates the acquisition of extinction of conditioned fear and drug-seeking behavior (Myers and Carlezon, 2012). Similarly, modulation of AMPA receptor activity, which like NMDA receptors is also critically involved in synaptic plasticity, can also facilitate extinction learning (Kaplan and Moore, 2011; Myers et al., 2011).

In addition to targeting ionotropic glutamate receptors, activation of mGluR5 have been shown to facilitate extinction learning through a process that may involve enhanced NMDA receptor function. Systemic administration of the mGluR5 positive allosteric modulator CDPPB facilitates extinction of cocaine-seeking behavior in CPP (Gass and Olive, 2009) and self-administration (Cleva et al., 2011) paradigms, but does not alter the extinction of methamphetamine self-administration (Widholm et al., 2011). Further implicating mGluR5 in extinction, studies in mGluR5 knockout mice revealed marked deficits in both contextual and auditory fear extinction (Xu et al., 2009). Additionally, inhibition of mGluR5 prior to extinction learning prevented the recall of extinction learning while localized infusion of a mGluR5 antagonist in the IfL cortex produced a similar effect (Fontanez-Nuin et al., 2011). A recent study also highlighted the importance of group 1 mGluRs in the ventromedial PFC in the extinction of cocaine-seeking behavior. In rats trained to self-administer cocaine, infusion of a mGluR1/5 antagonist into the dorsomedial PFC failed to alter the rate of extinction. In contrast, infusion of a mGluR1/5 agonist had a facilitating effect on extinction of cocaine-seeking behavior (Ben-Shahar et al., 2013). This study also revealed that animals displaying deficits in extinction learning also had a significant reduction in group 1 mGluR function in the ventromedial PFC. Together these intriguing findings provide further support for glutamate-related plasticity in the IfL cortex in extinction learning.

Studies of conditioned fear have shown that inactivation of the rostral BLA (rBLA) slows cocaine cue extinction learning, and it has been suggested that simultaneous activity in the rBLA and hippocampus might be required for the acquisition of cocaine cue extinction learning (Szalay et al., 2011). Another study has shown that inactivation of the BLA not only resulted in a delay in extinction recall of an opiate reward memory, but also caused an increase in the spontaneous firing of neurons in the PrL cortex (Sun and Laviolette, 2012). This suggests that a functional link between the PrL cortex and BLA might modulate the processing of an opiate-related memory. An influence of AMPA receptor activity in the BLA during the extinction of cocaine-seeking behavior has also been reported. It was observed that expression of AMPA receptor subunit GluA1 decreased in the BLA but increased in the ventromedial PFC in response to extinction training (Nic Dhonnchadha et al., 2013), adding further support for a functional connection between the mPFC and amygdala in the extinction of drug-seeking behavior. In the hippocampus, extinction of a morphine-conditioned context was associated with changes in the phosphorylation of AMPA receptors at hippocampal synapses while no changes were observed in animals that were not exposed to extinction training (Billa et al., 2009). Furthermore, suppression of neurogenesis in the adult hippocampus after the acquisition of cocaine self-administration significantly enhanced resistance to extinction (Noonan et al., 2010). Similar to the effects observed in the rBLA, inactivation of the dorsal hippocampus slowed the rate of extinction of a cocaine memory (Szalay et al., 2011). Furthermore, cocaine self-administration training reduces neurogenesis in the DG, an effect that was normalized by extinction training (Deschaux et al., 2012). It was also observed that low frequency stimulation of the hippocampus prevented this extinction-induced normalization of DG neurogenesis. Together, these studies indicate a critical role of plasticity-related changes within the amygdala and hippocampus in the extinction of drug-seeking behavior. Although it has yet to be explored, it is possible that pharmacological manipulation of plasticity within these brain regions could serve to facilitate extinction of conditioned drug-seeking behavior.

NORADRENERGIC MECHANISMS IN EXTINCTION

While glutamate-related neurochemical processes have received the most attention in extinction behavior, an emerging area of interest is the role that noradrenergic mechanisms play in extinction learning (for an extensive review, see Mueller and Cahill, 2010). Norepinephrine has been shown to be involved in various aspects of memory, most notably the strengthening of memory formation (McGaugh, 2004). While there has been a renewed interest in the ability of noradrenergic mechanisms to mediate fear extinction, the results have been inconsistent. For example, it has been shown that systemic administration of the beta-adrenergic antagonist propranolol prior to extinction training impaired subsequent retrieval of contextual fear extinction (Ouyang and Thomas, 2005). However, direct infusions of norepinephrine into the amygdala after extinction training facilitated the extinction of contextual fear (Berlau and McGaugh, 2006), suggesting that noradrenergic mechanisms may help mediate the consolidation of extinction learning. It has also been shown that arousal-related norepinephrine release in the IfL cortex is important for the formation of fear extinction memory (Mueller et al., 2008).

There have been several interesting observations regarding the influence of noradrenergic mechanisms on the extinction of drug-seeking behavior. Yohimbine, an alpha2-receptor antagonist that promotes the release of norepinephrine, impairs the extinction of cocaine CPP (Davis et al., 2008) and slows the rate of extinction of cocaine self-administration (Kupferschmidt et al., 2009). Furthermore, infusion of the beta-receptor agonist clenbuterol into the IfL cortex facilitates extinction of cocaine-seeking behavior (LaLumiere et al., 2010). These studies add support to the growing body of evidence that areas of the PFC are heavily involved in extinction behavior, and one possible mechanism could be noradrenergic-related changes in this region. Norepinephrine release alters the cellular properties of target neurons that may enhance excitability and synaptic plasticity and thus promote the formation of an extinction memory (Mueller and Cahill, 2010). Support for this comes from studies showing that norepinephrine enhances intrinsic excitability in the IfL cortex (Barth et al., 2007; Mueller et al., 2008), amygdala (Tully et al., 2007), and hippocampus (Pedreira and Maldonado, 2003).

EPIGENETICS AND EXTINCTION

Epigenetic mechanisms associated with extinction learning have received substantial attention over the pass several years and are providing unique insight into plasticity-related mechanisms of extinction. Epigenetic modification refers to the structural adaptation of chromosomes that results in altered activity states (Bird, 2007; Graff and Tsai, 2013). Epigenetic mechanisms exert lasting control over gene expression without altering the genetic code and may mediate stable changes in brain function (Tsankova et al., 2007). Investigation into the epigenetic regulation of neurobiological adaptations that are associated with psychiatric disorders, including addiction and PTSD, could provide novel approaches to the mechanisms underlying extinction learning.

The formation of long-term memories is thought to correlate with changes in gene expression. Research suggests that epigenetic-related mechanisms, such as histone acetylation/deacytylation and DNA methylation/demethylation, may mediate some of these processes (for a review, see Tsankova et al., 2007). For example, memory deficits in rodents can be recovered with administration of a histone deacetylase (HDAC) inhibitor, while conditioning in rodents is associated with histone protein H3 phosphoacetylation and chromatin remodeling (Levenson and Sweatt, 2005). Furthermore, synaptic plasticity is associated with epigenetic changes and can be promoted with HDAC inhibitors (Levenson et al., 2004). While these data indicate that epigenetic mechanisms are involved during the acquisition of conditioning, evidence also indicates that these same mechanisms may play a role in extinction learning.

In fear conditioning, it has been shown that acetylation and deacetylation of histones can enhance memories formed during conditioning and extinction behavior (Levenson et al., 2004; Bredy et al., 2007; Lattal et al., 2007). The non-selective HDAC inhibitor valproic acid can facilitate not only the acquisition and extinction of conditioned fear, but also the reconsolidation of this memory (Bredy and Barad, 2008). Similar results have been obtained with the HDAC inhibitor vorinostat (Fujita et al., 2012). It has also been shown that deficits in the extinction learning of conditioned fear in isogenic 129S1 (S1) mice can be recovered by administration of an HDAC inhibitor (Whittle et al., 2013). Administration of another non-selective HDAC inhibitor sodium butyrate (NaB) has a facilitating effect on the extinction of a fear memory in mice (Itzhak et al., 2012), which might be due, at least in part, to epigenetic-related mechanisms in the hippocampus and IfL cortex (Stafford et al., 2012). Furthermore, overexpression of HDAC1 in the hippocampus has also been shown to facilitate the extinction of contextual fear memories, and this effect can be prevented by inhibition of HDAC1 (Bahari-Javan et al., 2012). Finally, inhibition of p300 (a histone acetyltransferase) in the IfL cortex can enhance extinction of fear conditioning in mice, which was suggested to result from the influence of p300 on LTP in this brain region (Marek et al., 2011).

While there have been substantially fewer studies examining the epigenetic changes that accompany the extinction of drug-seeking behavior, similar results to the fear-conditioning literature have been observed. Malvaez et al. (2010) examined the effect of HDAC inhibition on the extinction of a cocaine-induced CPP. They found that systemic administration of NaB facilitated the extinction of the cocaine memory and attenuated reinstatement of cocaine-seeking behavior. Importantly, these behavioral effects correlated with enhanced acetylation of histone H3 in the NAc. Systemic administration of the HDAC3 inhibitor RGFP966 also facilitates the extinction of a cocaine-related memory, and it was suggested that this effect was mediated by enhancement of memory consolidation during extinction learning (Malvaez et al., 2013). These effects were also associated with histone acetylation linked to gene expression in the IfL cortex, hippocampus, and NAc. Taken together, observations from the fear and addiction fields have provided intriguing insights into the possible therapeutic targets related to epigenetics that could potentially be utilized to facilitate the extinction of emotionally salient memories. While further research is needed to fully clarify the roles of these mechanisms in the extinction of drug-related memories, this is a promising area of investigation for the extinction of drug cues given the established role of epigenetic mechanisms in memory.

EXTINCTION VERSUS RECONSOLIDATION

The widely held belief that extinction learning involves the acquisition of new memories has been challenged recently with the idea that behavior typically interpreted as extinction learning may actually represent *reconsolidation* of previously formed memories (for reviews on this topic, see Dudai and Eisenberg, 2004; Nader and Einarsson, 2010; Sorg, 2012). During the initial coding of events, memories are labile, but subsequently consolidate into long-term storage through protein synthesis-dependent mechanisms (Quirk et al., 2010). Thus, extinction training may serve to reverse or update previously formed contingencies (Sorg, 2012). As such, exposure to extinction training shortly after reactivation of a fear memory attenuates recovery, renewal, and reinstatement of conditioned fear (Monfils et al., 2009; Quirk et al., 2010). Importantly, studies have shown that timing of the CS presentation is critical in order to temporarily activate the labile state in which updates to the CS-US association can occur. Reconsolidation typically requires short presentations of the CS (Nader and Hardt, 2009), and presentation of the CS alone within 6 h after memory reactivation results in behavioral effects that reflect unlearning as opposed to the inhibition of fear (Nader et al., 2000; Quirk et al., 2010). Theoretically, the ability to modify existing memories, as opposed to creating

new inhibitory associations through the facilitation of extinction learning, could be advantageous over extinction-based exposure therapies. Studies show that while extinction learning can be facilitated pharmacologically, these effects can be context-dependent (Bouton, 2000, 2002, 2004; Milad et al., 2005; Woods and Bouton, 2006). Modification of the original memory, rather than the creation of competitive memories, might manifest a behavior that is more resistant to the influence of context (Quirk et al., 2010), an idea that has clinical support. For instance, administration of a beta-adrenergic receptor antagonist during reconsolidation removes the fear-arousing aspects of the conditioned memory (Soeter and Kindt, 2011). This effect was not specific to the initial stimuli used in the fear-conditioning paradigm and generalized to related stimuli. While there is excitement in the field that revolves around the influence of reconsolidation on extinction behavior, more research is clearly needed to fully elucidate the contributions of both processes in the inhibition of behavior.

CONCLUSION

In this review, we focused on studies that incorporate learning principles in extinction training with the goal of lessening the influence of these cues on addictive behavior. It has been widely recognized that drug use and relapse are strongly cue specific (Drummond and Glautier, 1994) and one of the most important factors that contributes to relapse is the impact of drug cues on drug-seeking behavior. In recent years, there has been increasing attention on the neural mechanisms that underlie extinction learning in an effort to manipulate and possibly enhance learning that occurs during inhibitory conditioning. Clinically, extinction-based behavioral therapies have generally proven ineffective for suppression of relapse to drug taking. This lack of efficacy may relate to the fact that extinction learning does not erase the original drug memory but instead involves formation of a new extinction memory that acts in competition for control of behavior with the drug memory. However, the intransigent nature of the drug-memory appears to promote subsequent relapse to drug-taking. The temporal relationship of extinction and relapse are depicted in **Figure 4**. While extinction training alone can initially reduce drug-seeking behavior, these effects are likely context-specific. Thus, when the addict is exposed to drug cues outside of the treatment environment, the drug memory that was suppressed but not erased during extinction training, can reinitiate drug-seeking and drug use. Although speculative, pharmacological facilitation of extinction learning may enhance formation of an inhibitory memory that is much "stronger" than the initial drug memory and may help protect against cue-induced relapse. Recent research has shed light on pharmacologically targeting glutamatergic, adrenergic, and epigenetic mechanisms to enhance inhibitory learning during extinction training. Furthermore, while the neurocircuitry of extinction likely involves a distributed network of different brain regions that include the mPFC, NAc, amygdala, hippocampus, and hypothalamus, recent studies have implicated opposing roles of the PrL and IfL subregions of the PFC in the control of drug-related behavior. A model has emerged in which drug-seeking is likely a PrL cortex driven behavior while extinction learning and the resulting inhibition of drug-seeking is a IfL cortex driven behavior. One aim of future research is to elucidate the contribution

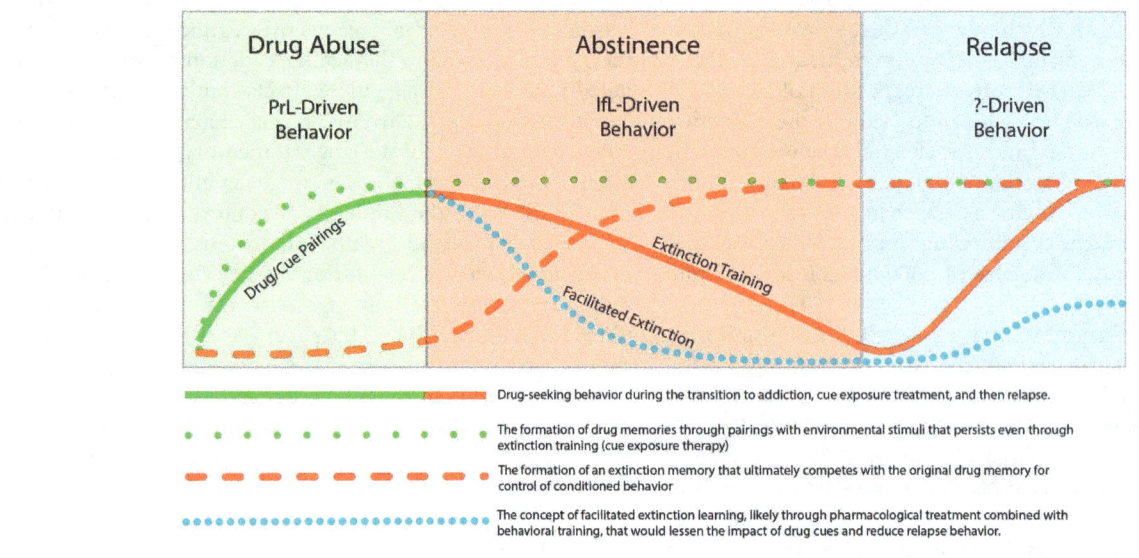

FIGURE 4 | Illustration showing that while behavioral extinction training can reduce drug-seeking behavior, the persistence of the original drug memory can promote subsequent relapse. However, pharmacological facilitation of the extinction process may promote a stronger and more persistent extinction memory that may lead to reductions in the rate of relapse.

of these different neural regions and mechanisms to the facilitation of extinction learning to ultimately develop more effective treatments for addiction.

Although there have been substantial advances in our understanding of the neural mechanisms involved in the extinction of drug-related memories, a number of important issues need to be addressed by additional studies in the field of drug addiction. For example, while the neural circuits that mediate extinction of fear behavior do not overlap directly with those in drug-seeking behaviors, are the mechanisms that mediate extinction the same for all drugs of abuse? There is strong evidence for involvement of the PrL cortex in cocaine-seeking and IfL cortex in cocaine extinction behavior. However, there are few and sometimes conflicting findings with other drugs of abuse, such as heroin (Rogers et al., 2008), methamphetamine (Rocha and Kalivas, 2010), and alcohol (Millan et al., 2010). In addition, as recent research begins to highlight the importance of other structures in the extinction of drug memories, how do they interact with the established role of the PFC in mediating extinction behavior? The identification of the specific roles of the hippocampus, amygdala, and hypothalamus and their influence on a "final common pathway" through the PFC could provide insight into possible therapeutic targets to enhance extinction learning.

The standard procedure for extinction training is repeated presentations of the CS in absence of the US. While this method has permeated the literature since the days of Pavlov, it is not clear whether this is the most effective approach. It is of interest that several studies have examined the "retrieval-extinction" approach that combines extinction training with brief drug-memory retrieval (to activate the labile state of the memory) that have produced encouraging results (Hutton-Bedbrook and McNally, 2013).

With an increased focus on the importance of consolidation in promotion of extinction learning, a particularly interesting area of future research will be to understand the effect of sleep and sleep insomnia in extinction learning. Coordinated activity in the PFC and hippocampus during sleep is critical for the consolidation of memories (Euston et al., 2007). Sleep has been shown to promote retention of fear extinction memory (Pace-Schott et al., 2009, 2012). Interestingly, while extinction training can attenuate sleep disturbances (Wellman et al., 2008), the bidirectional relationship between these two processes and how they contribute to the extinction of drug memories is largely unexplored.

Lastly, there are multiple studies showing that context is a major hurdle in using extinction-based treatment approaches, and another important area of research will be to determine whether context specificity of extinction can be prevented. Context is not limited to common environmental stimuli associated with drug use and can include factors such as drug states and the passage of time (Bouton et al., 2012). Thus, there are many types of stimuli that serve as contextual cues to promote relapse, and future research is needed in order to understand how pharmacological manipulation of extinction training could be used to minimize the influence of context.

REFERENCES

Bahari-Javan, S., Maddalena, A., Kerimoglu, C., Wittnam, J., Held, T., Bahr, M., et al. (2012). HDAC1 regulates fear extinction in mice. *J. Neurosci.* 32, 5062–5073. doi:10.1523/JNEUROSCI.0079-12.2012

Balleine, B. W., and Killcross, S. (2006). Parallel incentive processing: an integrated view of amygdala function. *Trends Neurosci.* 29, 272–279. doi:10.1016/j.tins.2006.03.002

Barth, A. M., Vizi, E. S., and Lendvai, B. (2007). Noradrenergic enhancement of Ca2(responses of basal dendrites in layer 5 pyramidal neurons of the prefrontal cortex. *Neurochem. Int.* 51, 323–327. doi:10.1016/j.neuint.2007.05.008

Baxter, M. G., and Murray, E. A. (2002). The amygdala and reward.

Nat. Rev. Neurosci. 3, 563–573. doi:10.1038/nrn875

Ben-Shahar, O., Sacramento, A. D., Miller, B. W., Webb, S. M., Wroten, M. G., Silva, H. E., et al. (2013). Deficits in ventromedial prefrontal cortex group 1 metabotropic glutamate receptor function mediate resistance to extinction during protracted withdrawal from an extensive history of cocaine self-administration. *J. Neurosci.* 33, 495–506a. doi:10.1523/JNEUROSCI.3710-12.2013

Berlau, D. J., and McGaugh, J. L. (2006). Enhancement of extinction memory consolidation: the role of the noradrenergic and GABAergic systems within the basolateral amygdala. *Neurobiol. Learn. Mem.* 86, 123–132. doi:10.1016/j.nlm.2005.12.008

Billa, S. K., Sinha, N., Rudrabhatla, S. R., and Moron, J. A. (2009). Extinction of morphine-dependent conditioned behavior is associated with increased phosphorylation of the GluR1 subunit of AMPA receptors at hippocampal synapses. *Eur. J. Neurosci.* 29, 55–64. doi:10.1111/j.1460-9568.2008.06560.x

Bird, A. (2007). Perceptions of epigenetics. *Nature* 447, 396–398. doi:10.1038/nature05913

Blundell, P., Hall, G., and Killcross, S. (2001). Lesions of the basolateral amygdala disrupt selective aspects of reinforcer representation in rats. *J. Neurosci.* 21, 9018–9026.

Bonci, A., Bernardi, G., Grillner, P., and Mercuri, N. B. (2003). The dopamine-containing neuron: maestro or simple musician in the orchestra of addiction? *Trends Pharmacol. Sci.* 24, 172–177. doi:10.1016/S0165-6147(03)00068-3

Bouton, M. E. (2000). A learning theory perspective on lapse, relapse, and the maintenance of behavior change. *Health Psychol.* 19, 57–63. doi:10.1037/0278-6133.19.Suppl1.57

Bouton, M. E. (2002). Context, ambiguity, and unlearning: sources of relapse after behavioral extinction. *Biol. Psychiatry* 52, 976–986. doi:10.1016/S0006-3223(02)01546-9

Bouton, M. E. (2004). Context and behavioral processes in extinction. *Learn. Mem.* 11, 485–494. doi:10.1101/lm.78804

Bouton, M. E., Winterbauer, N. E., and Todd, T. P. (2012). Relapse processes after the extinction of instrumental learning: renewal, resurgence, and reacquisition. *Behav. Processes* 90, 130–141. doi:10.1016/j.beproc.2012.03.004

Bredy, T. W., and Barad, M. (2008). The histone deacetylase inhibitor valproic acid enhances acquisition, extinction, and reconsolidation of conditioned fear. *Learn. Mem.* 15, 39–45. doi:10.1101/lm.801108

Bredy, T. W., Wu, H., Crego, C., Zellhoefer, J., Sun, Y. E., and Barad, M. (2007). Histone modifications around individual BDNF gene promoters in prefrontal cortex are associated with extinction of conditioned fear. *Learn. Mem.* 14, 268–276. doi:10.1101/lm.500907

Brown, E. E., and Fibiger, H. C. (1993). Differential effects of excitotoxic lesions of the amygdala on cocaine-induced conditioned locomotion and conditioned place preference. *Psychopharmacology (Berl.)* 113, 123–130. doi:10.1007/BF02244344

Cahill, L., Babinsky, R., Markowitsch, H. J., and McGaugh, J. L. (1995). The amygdala and emotional memory. *Nature* 377, 295–296. doi:10.1038/377295a0

Cahill, L., McGaugh, J. L., and Weinberger, N. M. (2001). The neurobiology of learning and memory: some reminders to remember. *Trends Neurosci.* 24, 578–581. doi:10.1016/S0166-2236(00)01885-3

Capriles, N., Rodaros, D., Sorge, R. E., and Stewart, J. (2003). A role for the prefrontal cortex in stress- and cocaine-induced reinstatement of cocaine seeking in rats. *Psychopharmacology (Berl.)* 168, 66–74. doi:10.1007/s00213-002-1283-z

Carroll, M. E. (1998). Acquisition and reacquisition (relapse) of drug abuse: modulation by alternative reinforcers. *NIDA Res. Monogr.* 169, 6–25.

Chaudhri, N., Sahuque, L. L., Cone, J. J., and Janak, P. H. (2008). Reinstated ethanol-seeking in rats is modulated by environmental context and requires the nucleus accumbens core. *Eur. J. Neurosci.* 28, 2288–2298. doi:10.1111/j.1460-9568.2008.06517.x

Childress, A. R., Hole, A. V., Ehrman, R. N., Robbins, S. J., McLellan, A. T., and O'Brien, C. P. (1993). Cue reactivity and cue reactivity interventions in drug dependence. *NIDA Res. Monogr.* 137, 73–95.

Childress, A. R., McLellan, A. T., Ehrman, R., and O'Brien, C. P. (1988). Classically conditioned responses in opioid and cocaine dependence: a role in relapse? *NIDA Res. Monogr.* 84, 25–43.

Childress, A. R., Mozley, P. D., McElgin, W., Fitzgerald, J., Reivich, M., and O'Brien, C. P. (1999). Limbic activation during cue-induced cocaine craving. *Am. J. Psychiatry* 156, 11–18.

Cleva, R. M., Gass, J. T., Widholm, J. J., and Olive, M. F. (2010). Glutamatergic targets for enhancing extinction learning in drug addiction. *Curr. Neuropharmacol.* 8, 394–408. doi:10.2174/157015910793358169

Cleva, R. M., Hicks, M. P., Gass, J. T., Wischerath, K. C., Plasters, E. T., Widholm, J. J., et al. (2011). mGluR5 positive allosteric modulation enhances extinction learning following cocaine self-administration. *Behav. Neurosci.* 125, 10–19. doi:10.1037/a0022339

Conklin, C. A., and Tiffany, S. T. (2002a). Applying extinction research and theory to cue-exposure addiction treatments. *Addiction* 97, 155–167. doi:10.1046/j.1360-0443.2002.00014.x

Conklin, C. A., and Tiffany, S. T. (2002b). Cue-exposure treatment: time for change. *Addiction* 97, 1219–1221. doi:10.1046/j.1360-0443.2002.00205.x

Corcoran, K. A., Desmond, T. J., Frey, K. A., and Maren, S. (2005). Hippocampal inactivation disrupts the acquisition and contextual encoding of fear extinction. *J. Neurosci.* 25, 8978–8987. doi:10.1523/JNEUROSCI.2246-05.2005

Corcoran, K. A., and Maren, S. (2001). Hippocampal inactivation disrupts contextual retrieval of fear memory after extinction. *J. Neurosci.* 21, 1720–1726.

Corty, E. W., and Coon, B. (1995). The extinction of naturally occurring conditioned reactions in psychoactive substance users: analog studies. *Addict. Behav.* 20, 605–618. doi:10.1016/0306-4603(95)00020-D

Crombag, H. S., and Shaham, Y. (2002). Renewal of drug seeking by contextual cues after prolonged extinction in rats. *Behav. Neurosci.* 116, 169–173. doi:10.1037/0735-7044.116.1.169

Davis, A. R., Shields, A. D., Brigman, J. L., Norcross, M., McElligott, Z. A., Holmes, A., et al. (2008). Yohimbine impairs extinction of cocaine-conditioned place preference in an alpha2-adrenergic receptor independent process. *Learn. Mem.* 15, 667–676. doi:10.1101/lm.1079308

Davis, M., Barad, M., Otto, M., and Southwick, S. (2006). Combining pharmacotherapy with cognitive behavioral therapy: traditional and new approaches. *J. Trauma. Stress* 19, 571–581. doi:10.1002/jts.20149

Deschaux, O., Vendruscolo, L. F., Schlosburg, J. E., Diaz-Aguilar, L., Yuan, C. J., Sobieraj, J. C., et al. (2012). Hippocampal neurogenesis protects against cocaine-primed relapse. *Addict. Biol.* doi:10.1111/adb.12019. [Epub ahead of print].

Di Chiara, G. (1999). Drug addiction as dopamine-dependent associative learning disorder. *Eur. J. Pharmacol.* 375, 13–30. doi:10.1016/S0014-2999(99)00372-6

Di Chiara, G., and Bassareo, V. (2007). Reward system and addiction: what dopamine does and doesn't do. *Curr. Opin. Pharmacol.* 7, 69–76. doi:10.1016/j.coph.2006.11.003

Di Ciano, P., and Everitt, B. J. (2004). Direct interactions between the basolateral amygdala and nucleus accumbens core underlie cocaine-seeking behavior by rats. *J. Neurosci.* 24, 7167–7173. doi:10.1523/JNEUROSCI.1581-04.2004

Di Pietro, N. C., Black, Y. D., and Kantak, K. M. (2006). Context-dependent prefrontal cortex regulation of cocaine self-administration and reinstatement behaviors in rats. *Eur. J. Neurosci.* 24, 3285–3298. doi:10.1111/j.1460-9568.2006.05193.x

Drummond, D. C., and Glautier, S. (1994). A controlled trial of cue exposure treatment in alcohol dependence. *J. Consult. Clin. Psychol.* 62, 809–817. doi:10.1037/0022-006X.62.4.809

Dudai, Y., and Eisenberg, M. (2004). Rites of passage of the engram: reconsolidation and the lingering consolidation hypothesis. *Neuron* 44, 93–100. doi:10.1016/j.neuron.2004.09.003

Epstein, D. H., Preston, K. L., Stewart, J., and Shaham, Y. (2006). Toward a model of drug relapse: an assessment of the validity of the reinstatement procedure. *Psychopharmacology (Berl.)* 189, 1–16. doi:10.1007/s00213-006-0529-6

Euston, D. R., Tatsuno, M., and McNaughton, B. L. (2007). Fast-forward playback of recent memory sequences in prefrontal cortex during sleep. *Science* 318, 1147–1150. doi:10.1126/science.1148979

Everitt, B. J., Cardinal, R. N., Parkinson, J. A., and Robbins, T. W. (2003). Appetitive behavior: impact of amygdala-dependent mechanisms of emotional learning. *Ann. N. Y. Acad. Sci.* 985, 233–250. doi:10.1111/j.1749-6632.2003.tb07085.x

Ferrante, M., Migliore, M., and Ascoli, G. A. (2009). Feed-forward inhibition as a buffer of the neuronal input-output relation. *Proc. Natl.*

Acad. Sci. U.S.A. 106, 18004–18009. doi:10.1073/pnas.0904784106

Fontanez-Nuin, D. E., Santini, E., Quirk, G. J., and Porter, J. T. (2011). Memory for fear extinction requires mGluR5-mediated activation of infralimbic neurons. Cereb. Cortex 21, 727–735. doi:10.1093/cercor/bhq147

Fuchs, R. A., Branham, R. K., and See, R. E. (2006). Different neural substrates mediate cocaine seeking after abstinence versus extinction training: a critical role for the dorsolateral caudate-putamen. J. Neurosci. 26, 3584–3588. doi:10.1523/JNEUROSCI.5146-05.2006

Fujita, Y., Morinobu, S., Takei, S., Fuchikami, M., Matsumoto, T., Yamamoto, S., et al. (2012). Vorinostat, a histone deacetylase inhibitor, facilitates fear extinction and enhances expression of the hippocampal NR2B-containing NMDA receptor gene. J. Psychiatr. Res. 46, 635–643. doi:10.1016/j.jpsychires.2012.01.026

Gass, J. T., and Olive, M. F. (2009). Positive allosteric modulation of mGluR5 receptors facilitates extinction of a cocaine contextual memory. Biol. Psychiatry 65, 717–720. doi:10.1016/j.biopsych.2008.11.001

Goldstein, R. Z., and Volkow, N. D. (2011). Dysfunction of the prefrontal cortex in addiction: neuroimaging findings and clinical implications. Nat. Rev. Neurosci. 12, 652–669. doi:10.1038/nrn3119

Graff, J., and Tsai, L. H. (2013). The potential of HDAC inhibitors as cognitive enhancers. Annu. Rev. Pharmacol. Toxicol. 53, 311–330. doi:10.1146/annurev-pharmtox-011112-140216

Grasing, K., He, S., and Li, N. (2005). Selegiline modifies the extinction of responding following morphine self-administration, but does not alter cue-induced reinstatement, reacquisition of morphine reinforcement, or precipitated withdrawal. Pharmacol. Res. 51, 69–78. doi:10.1016/j.phrs.2004.07.004

Hammersley, R. (1992). Cue exposure and learning theory. Addict. Behav. 17, 297–300. doi:10.1016/0306-4603(92)90035-T

Hatfield, T., Han, J. S., Conley, M., Gallagher, M., and Holland, P. (1996). Neurotoxic lesions of basolateral, but not central, amygdala interfere with Pavlovian second-order conditioning and reinforcer devaluation effects. J. Neurosci. 16, 5256–5265.

Heidbreder, C. A., and Groenewegen, H. J. (2003). The medial

prefrontal cortex in the rat: evidence for a dorso-ventral distinction based upon functional and anatomical characteristics. Neurosci. Biobehav. Rev. 27, 555–579. doi:10.1016/j.neubiorev.2003.09.003

Hiroi, N., and White, N. M. (1991). The lateral nucleus of the amygdala mediates expression of the amphetamine-produced conditioned place preference. J. Neurosci. 11, 2107–2116.

Hutton-Bedbrook, K., and McNally, G. P. (2013). The promises and pitfalls of retrieval-extinction procedures in preventing relapse to drug seeking. Front. Psychiatry 4:14. doi:10.3389/fpsyt.2013.00014

Hyman, S. E. (2005). Addiction: a disease of learning and memory. Am. J. Psychiatry 162, 1414–1422. doi:10.1176/appi.ajp.162.8.1414

Itzhak, Y., Anderson, K. L., Kelley, J. B., and Petkov, M. (2012). Histone acetylation rescues contextual fear conditioning in nNOS KO mice and accelerates extinction of cued fear conditioning in wild type mice. Neurobiol. Learn. Mem. 97, 409–417. doi:10.1016/j.nlm.2012.03.005

Izquierdo, I., Bevilaqua, L. R., Rossato, J. I., Bonini, J. S., Medina, J. H., and Cammarota, M. (2006). Different molecular cascades in different sites of the brain control memory consolidation. Trends Neurosci. 29, 496–505. doi:10.1016/j.tins.2006.07.005

Ji, G., and Neugebauer, V. (2012). Modulation of medial prefrontal cortical activity using in vivo recordings and optogenetics. Mol Brain 5, 36. doi:10.1186/1756-6606-5-36

Ji, J., and Maren, S. (2005). Electrolytic lesions of the dorsal hippocampus disrupt renewal of conditional fear after extinction. Learn. Mem. 12, 270–276. doi:10.1101/lm.91705

Kalivas, P. W., Peters, J., and Knackstedt, L. (2006). Animal models and brain circuits in drug addiction. Mol. Interv. 6, 339–344. doi:10.1124/mi.6.6.7

Kalivas, P. W., and Volkow, N. D. (2005). The neural basis of addiction: a pathology of motivation and choice. Am. J. Psychiatry 162, 1403–1413. doi:10.1176/appi.ajp.162.8.1403

Kaplan, G. B., and Moore, K. A. (2011). The use of cognitive enhancers in animal models of fear extinction. Pharmacol. Biochem. Behav. 99, 217–228. doi:10.1016/j.pbb.2011.01.009

Kelley, A. E. (2004). Memory and addiction: shared neural circuitry and molecular

mechanisms. Neuron 44, 161–179. doi:10.1016/j.neuron.2004.09.016

Knackstedt, L. A., Moussawi, K., LaLumiere, R., Schwendt, M., Klugmann, M., and Kalivas, P. W. (2010). Extinction training after cocaine self-administration induces glutamatergic plasticity to inhibit cocaine seeking. J. Neurosci. 30, 7984–7992. doi:10.1523/JNEUROSCI.1244-10.2010

Koya, E., Uejima, J. L., Wihbey, K. A., Bossert, J. M., Hope, B. T., and Shaham, Y. (2009). Role of ventral medial prefrontal cortex in incubation of cocaine craving. Neuropharmacology 56(Suppl. 1), 177–185. doi:10.1016/j.neuropharm.2008.04.022

Kupferschmidt, D. A., Tribe, E., and Erb, S. (2009). Effects of repeated yohimbine on the extinction and reinstatement of cocaine seeking. Pharmacol. Biochem. Behav. 91, 473–480. doi:10.1016/j.pbb.2008.08.026

LaBar, K. S. (2003). Emotional memory functions of the human amygdala. Curr. Neurol. Neurosci. Rep. 3, 363–364. doi:10.1007/s11910-003-0015-z

LaBar, K. S., and Cabeza, R. (2006). Cognitive neuroscience of emotional memory. Nat. Rev. Neurosci. 7, 54–64. doi:10.1038/nrn1825

LaLumiere, R. T., and Kalivas, P. W. (2008). Glutamate release in the nucleus accumbens core is necessary for heroin seeking. J. Neurosci. 28, 3170–3177. doi:10.1523/JNEUROSCI.5129-07.2008

LaLumiere, R. T., Niehoff, K. E., and Kalivas, P. W. (2010). The infralimbic cortex regulates the consolidation of extinction after cocaine self-administration. Learn. Mem. 17, 168–175. doi:10.1101/lm.1576810

LaLumiere, R. T., Smith, K. C., and Kalivas, P. W. (2012). Neural circuit competition in cocaine-seeking: roles of the infralimbic cortex and nucleus accumbens shell. Eur. J. Neurosci. 35, 614–622. doi:10.1111/j.1460-9568.2012.07991.x

Lattal, K. M., Barrett, R. M., and Wood, M. A. (2007). Systemic or intrahippocampal delivery of histone deacetylase inhibitors facilitates fear extinction. Behav. Neurosci. 121, 1125–1131. doi:10.1037/0735-7044.121.5.1125

Lattal, K. M., and Lattal, K. A. (2012). Facets of Pavlovian and operant extinction. Behav. Processes 90, 1–8. doi:10.1016/j.beproc.2012.03.009

Levenson, J. M., O'Riordan, K. J., Brown, K. D., Trinh, M. A., Molfese, D. L., and Sweatt, J. D. (2004). Regulation

of histone acetylation during memory formation in the hippocampus. J. Biol. Chem. 279, 40545–40559. doi:10.1074/jbc.M402229200

Levenson, J. M., and Sweatt, J. D. (2005). Epigenetic mechanisms in memory formation. Nat. Rev. Neurosci. 6, 108–118. doi:10.1038/nrn1604

Likhtik, E., Pelletier, J. G., Paz, R., and Pare, D. (2005). Prefrontal control of the amygdala. J. Neurosci. 25, 7429–7437. doi:10.1523/JNEUROSCI.2314-05.2005

Malvaez, M., McQuown, S. C., Rogge, G. A., Astarabadi, M., Jacques, V., Carreiro, S., et al. (2013). HDAC3-selective inhibitor enhances extinction of cocaine-seeking behavior in a persistent manner. Proc. Natl. Acad. Sci. U.S.A. 110, 2647–2652. doi:10.1073/pnas.1213364110

Malvaez, M., Sanchis-Segura, C., Vo, D., Lattal, K. M., and Wood, M. A. (2010). Modulation of chromatin modification facilitates extinction of cocaine-induced conditioned place preference. Biol. Psychiatry 67, 36–43. doi:10.1016/j.biopsych.2009.07.032

Marchant, N. J., Furlong, T. M., and McNally, G. P. (2010). Medial dorsal hypothalamus mediates the inhibition of reward seeking after extinction. J. Neurosci. 30, 14102–14115. doi:10.1523/JNEUROSCI.4079-10.2010

Marchant, N. J., Millan, E. Z., and McNally, G. P. (2012). The hypothalamus and the neurobiology of drug seeking. Cell. Mol. Life Sci. 69, 581–597. doi:10.1007/s00018-011-0817-0

Marek, R., Coelho, C. M., Sullivan, R. K., Baker-Andresen, D., Li, X., Ratnu, V., et al. (2011). Paradoxical enhancement of fear extinction memory and synaptic plasticity by inhibition of the histone acetyltransferase p300. J. Neurosci. 31, 7486–7491. doi:10.1523/JNEUROSCI.0133-11.2011

Maren, S. (2005). Building and burying fear memories in the brain. Neuroscientist 11, 89–99. doi:10.1177/1073858404269232

McFarland, K., Davidge, S. B., Lapish, C. C., and Kalivas, P. W. (2004). Limbic and motor circuitry underlying footshock-induced reinstatement of cocaine-seeking behavior. J. Neurosci. 24, 1551–1560. doi:10.1523/JNEUROSCI.4177-03.2004

McFarland, K., and Kalivas, P. W. (2001). The circuitry mediating cocaine-induced reinstatement of drug-seeking behavior. *J. Neurosci.* 21, 8655–8663.

McGaugh, J. L. (2004). The amygdala modulates the consolidation of memories of emotionally arousing experiences. *Annu. Rev. Neurosci.* 27, 1–28. doi:10.1146/annurev.neuro.27.070203.144157

McLaughlin, J., and See, R. E. (2003). Selective inactivation of the dorsomedial prefrontal cortex and the basolateral amygdala attenuates conditioned-cued reinstatement of extinguished cocaine-seeking behavior in rats. *Psychopharmacology (Berl.)* 168, 57–65. doi:10.1007/s00213-002-1196-x

Milad, M. R., Orr, S. P., Pitman, R. K., and Rauch, S. L. (2005). Context modulation of memory for fear extinction in humans. *Psychophysiology* 42, 456–464. doi:10.1111/j.1469-8986.2005.00302.x

Milad, M. R., and Quirk, G. J. (2012). Fear extinction as a model for translational neuroscience: ten years of progress. *Annu. Rev. Psychol.* 63, 129–151. doi:10.1146/annurev.psych.121208.131631

Millan, E. Z., Furlong, T. M., and McNally, G. P. (2010). Accumbens shell-hypothalamus interactions mediate extinction of alcohol seeking. *J. Neurosci.* 30, 4626–4635. doi:10.1523/JNEUROSCI.4933-09.2010

Millan, E. Z., Marchant, N. J., and McNally, G. P. (2011). Extinction of drug seeking. *Behav. Brain Res.* 217, 454–462. doi:10.1016/j.bbr.2010.10.037

Millan, E. Z., and McNally, G. P. (2011). Accumbens shell AMPA receptors mediate expression of extinguished reward seeking through interactions with basolateral amygdala. *Learn. Mem.* 18, 414–421. doi:10.1101/lm.2144411

Monfils, M. H., Cowansage, K. K., Klann, E., and Ledoux, J. E. (2009). Extinction-reconsolidation boundaries: key to persistent attenuation of fear memories. *Science* 324, 951–955. doi:10.1126/science.1167975

Mueller, D., and Cahill, S. P. (2010). Noradrenergic modulation of extinction learning and exposure therapy. *Behav. Brain Res.* 208, 1–11. doi:10.1016/j.bbr.2009.11.025

Mueller, D., Porter, J. T., and Quirk, G. J. (2008). Noradrenergic signaling in infralimbic cortex increases cell excitability and strengthens memory for fear extinction. *J. Neurosci.* 28, 369–375.

doi:10.1523/JNEUROSCI.3248-07.2008

Myers, K. M., and Carlezon, W. A. Jr. (2012). D-cycloserine effects on extinction of conditioned responses to drug-related cues. *Biol. Psychiatry* 71, 947–955. doi:10.1016/j.biopsych.2012.02.030

Myers, K. M., Carlezon, W. A. Jr., and Davis, M. (2011). Glutamate receptors in extinction and extinction-based therapies for psychiatric illness. *Neuropsychopharmacology* 36, 274–293. doi:10.1038/npp.2010.88

Myers, K. M., and Davis, M. (2002). Behavioral and neural analysis of extinction. *Neuron* 36, 567–584. doi:10.1016/S0896-6273(02)01064-4

Myers, K. M., and Davis, M. (2007). Mechanisms of fear extinction. *Mol. Psychiatry* 12, 120–150. doi:10.1038/sj.mp.4001939

Nader, K., and Einarsson, E. O. (2010). Memory reconsolidation: an update. *Ann. N. Y. Acad. Sci.* 1191, 27–41. doi:10.1111/j.1749-6632

Nader, K., and Hardt, O. (2009). A single standard for memory: the case for reconsolidation. *Nat. Rev. Neurosci.* 10, 224–234. doi:10.1038/nrn2590

Nader, K., Schafe, G. E., and Le Doux, J. E. (2000). Fear memories require protein synthesis in the amygdala for reconsolidation after retrieval. *Nature* 406, 722–726. doi:10.1038/35021052

Neisewander, J. L., Baker, D. A., Fuchs, R. A., Tran-Nguyen, L. T., Palmer, A., and Marshall, J. F. (2000). Fos protein expression and cocaine-seeking behavior in rats after exposure to a cocaine self-administration environment. *J. Neurosci.* 20, 798–805.

Neves, G., Cooke, S. F., and Bliss, T. V. (2008). Synaptic plasticity, memory and the hippocampus: a neural network approach to causality. *Nat. Rev. Neurosci.* 9, 65–75. doi:10.1038/nrn2303

Nic Dhonnchadha, B. A., Lin, A., Leite-Morris, K. A., Kaplan, G. B., Man, H. Y., and Kantak, K. M. (2013). Alterations in expression and phosphorylation of GluA1 receptors following cocaine-cue extinction learning. *Behav. Brain Res.* 238, 119–123. doi:10.1016/j.bbr.2012.10.012

Noonan, M. A., Bulin, S. E., Fuller, D. C., and Eisch, A. J. (2010). Reduction of adult hippocampal neurogenesis confers vulnerability in an animal model of cocaine addiction. *J. Neurosci.* 30, 304–315. doi:10.1523/JNEUROSCI.4256-09.2010

O'Brien, C. P., Childress, A. R., McLellan, A. T., and Ehrman, R. (1992).

A learning model of addiction. *Res. Publ. Assoc. Res. Nerv. Ment. Dis.* 70, 157–177.

Olmstead, M. C. (2006). Animal models of drug addiction: where do we go from here? *Q. J. Exp. Psychol. (Hove)* 59, 625–653. doi:10.1080/17470210500356308

Ouyang, M., and Thomas, S. A. (2005). A requirement for memory retrieval during and after long-term extinction learning. *Proc. Natl. Acad. Sci. U.S.A.* 102, 9347–9352. doi:10.1073/pnas.0502315102

Ovari, J., and Leri, F. (2008). Inactivation of the ventromedial prefrontal cortex mimics re-emergence of heroin seeking caused by heroin reconditioning. *Neurosci. Lett.* 444, 52–55. doi:10.1016/j.neulet.2008.08.015

Pace-Schott, E. F., Milad, M. R., Orr, S. P., Rauch, S. L., Stickgold, R., and Pitman, R. K. (2009). Sleep promotes generalization of extinction of conditioned fear. *Sleep* 32, 19–26.

Pace-Schott, E. F., Verga, P. W., Bennett, T. S., and Spencer, R. M. (2012). Sleep promotes consolidation and generalization of extinction learning in simulated exposure therapy for spider fear. *J. Psychiatr. Res.* 46, 1036–1044. doi:10.1016/j.jpsychires.2012.04.015

Pavlov, I. P. (1927). *Conditioned Reflexes.* Oxford: Oxford University Press.

Pedreira, M. E., and Maldonado, H. (2003). Protein synthesis subserves reconsolidation or extinction depending on reminder duration. *Neuron* 38, 863–869. doi:10.1016/S0896-6273(03)00352-0

Peters, J., Kalivas, P. W., and Quirk, G. J. (2009). Extinction circuits for fear and addiction overlap in prefrontal cortex. *Learn. Mem.* 16, 279–288. doi:10.1101/lm.1041309

Peters, J., LaLumiere, R. T., and Kalivas, P. W. (2008a). Infralimbic prefrontal cortex is responsible for inhibiting cocaine seeking in extinguished rats. *J. Neurosci.* 28, 6046–6053. doi:10.1523/JNEUROSCI.1045-08.2008

Peters, J., Vallone, J., Laurendi, K., and Kalivas, P. W. (2008b). Opposing roles for the ventral prefrontal cortex and the basolateral amygdala on the spontaneous recovery of cocaine-seeking in rats. *Psychopharmacology (Berl.)* 197, 319–326. doi:10.1007/s00213-007-1034-2

Phelps, E. A., Delgado, M. R., Nearing, K. I., and Ledoux, J. E. (2004). Extinction learning in humans: role of the amygdala and vmPFC. *Neuron* 43, 897–905. doi:10.1016/j.neuron.2004.08.042

Power, A. E., Berlau, D. J., McGaugh, J. L., and Steward, O. (2006). Anisomycin infused into the hippocampus fails to block "reconsolidation" but impairs extinction: the role of re-exposure duration. *Learn. Mem.* 13, 27–34. doi:10.1101/lm.91206

Quirk, G. J., Garcia, R., and Gonzalez-Lima, F. (2006). Prefrontal mechanisms in extinction of conditioned fear. *Biol. Psychiatry* 60, 337–343. doi:10.1016/j.biopsych.2006.03.010

Quirk, G. J., Likhtik, E., Pelletier, J. G., and Pare, D. (2003). Stimulation of medial prefrontal cortex decreases the responsiveness of central amygdala output neurons. *J. Neurosci.* 23, 8800–8807.

Quirk, G. J., and Mueller, D. (2008). Neural mechanisms of extinction learning and retrieval. *Neuropsychopharmacology* 33, 56–72. doi:10.1038/sj.npp.1301555

Quirk, G. J., Pare, D., Richardson, R., Herry, C., Monfils, M. H., Schiller, D., et al. (2010). Erasing fear memories with extinction training. *J. Neurosci.* 30, 14993–14997. doi:10.1523/JNEUROSCI.4268-10.2010

Rescorla, R. A., and Wagner, A. R. (1972). "A theory of Pavlovian conditioning: variations in the effectiveness of reinforcement and nonreinforcement," in *Classical Conditioning II: Current Research and Theory*, eds A. H. Black and W. K. Prokasy (New York: Appleton-Century-Crofts), 64–99.

Rizos, Z., Ovari, J., and Leri, F. (2005). Reconditioning of heroin place preference requires the basolateral amygdala. *Pharmacol. Biochem. Behav.* 82, 300–305. doi:10.1016/j.pbb.2005.08.019

Robbins, T. W., and Everitt, B. J. (2002). Limbic-striatal memory systems and drug addiction. *Neurobiol. Learn. Mem.* 78, 625–636. doi:10.1006/nlme.2002.4103

Rocha, A., and Kalivas, P. W. (2010). Role of the prefrontal cortex and nucleus accumbens in reinstating methamphetamine seeking. *Eur. J. Neurosci.* 31, 903–909. doi:10.1111/j.1460-9568.2010.07134.x

Rogers, J. L., Ghee, S., and See, R. E. (2008). The neural circuitry underlying reinstatement of heroin-seeking behavior in an animal model of relapse. *Neuroscience* 151, 579–588. doi:10.1016/j.neuroscience.2007.10.012

Schmidt, E. F., Sutton, M. A., Schad, C. A., Karanian, D. A., Brodkin, E. S., and Self, D. W. (2001).

Extinction training regulates tyrosine hydroxylase during withdrawal from cocaine self-administration. *J. Neurosci.* 21, RC137.

Schroeder, J. P., and Packard, M. G. (2004). Facilitation of memory for extinction of drug-induced conditioned reward: role of amygdala and acetylcholine. *Learn. Mem.* 11, 641–647. doi:10.1101/lm.78504

See, R. E. (2005). Neural substrates of cocaine-cue associations that trigger relapse. *Eur. J. Pharmacol.* 526, 140–146. doi:10.1016/j.ejphar.2005.09.034

See, R. E., Fuchs, R. A., Ledford, C. C., and McLaughlin, J. (2003). Drug addiction, relapse, and the amygdala. *Ann. N. Y. Acad. Sci.* 985, 294–307. doi:10.1111/j.1749-6632.2003.tb07089.x

Self, D. W., and Choi, K. H. (2004). Extinction-induced neuroplasticity attenuates stress-induced cocaine seeking: a state-dependent learning hypothesis. *Stress* 7, 145–155. doi:10.1080/10253890400012677

Self, D. W., Choi, K. H., Simmons, D., Walker, J. R., and Smagula, C. S. (2004). Extinction training regulates neuroadaptive responses to withdrawal from chronic cocaine self-administration. *Learn. Mem.* 11, 648–657. doi:10.1101/lm.81404

Shalev, U., Grimm, J. W., and Shaham, Y. (2002). Neurobiology of relapse to heroin and cocaine seeking: a review. *Pharmacol. Rev.* 54, 1–42. doi:10.1124/pr.54.1.1

Shidara, M., and Richmond, B. J. (2002). Anterior cingulate: single neuronal signals related to degree of reward expectancy. *Science* 296, 1709–1711. doi:10.1126/science.1069504

Sierra-Mercado, D., Padilla-Coreano, N., and Quirk, G. J. (2011). Dissociable roles of prelimbic and infralimbic cortices, ventral hippocampus, and basolateral amygdala in the expression and extinction of conditioned fear. *Neuropsychopharmacology* 36, 529–538. doi:10.1038/npp.2010.184

Sinha, R. (2001). How does stress increase risk of drug abuse and relapse? *Psychopharmacology (Berl.)* 158, 343–359. doi:10.1007/s002130100917

Sinha, R., Fuse, T., Aubin, L. R., and O'Malley, S. S. (2000). Psychological stress, drug-related cues and cocaine craving. *Psychopharmacology (Berl.)* 152, 140–148. doi:10.1007/s002130000499

Soeter, M., and Kindt, M. (2011). Disrupting reconsolidation: pharmacological and behavioral manipulations. *Learn. Mem.* 18, 357–366. doi:10.1101/lm.2148511

Sorg, B. A. (2012). Reconsolidation of drug memories. *Neurosci. Biobehav. Rev.* 36, 1400–1417. doi:10.1016/j.neubiorev.2012.02.004

Stafford, J. M., Raybuck, J. D., Ryabinin, A. E., and Lattal, K. M. (2012). Increasing histone acetylation in the hippocampus-infralimbic network enhances fear extinction. *Biol. Psychiatry* 72, 25–33. doi:10.1016/j.biopsych.2011.12.012

Stewart, J. (2000). Pathways to relapse: the neurobiology of drug- and stress-induced relapse to drug-taking. *J. Psychiatry Neurosci.* 25, 125–136.

Stewart, J. (2003). Stress and relapse to drug seeking: studies in laboratory animals shed light on mechanisms and sources of long-term vulnerability. *Am. J. Addict.* 12, 1–17. doi:10.1111/j.1521-0391.2003.tb00535.x

Sun, N., and Laviolette, S. R. (2012). Inactivation of the basolateral amygdala during opiate reward learning disinhibits prelimbic cortical neurons and modulates associative memory extinction. *Psychopharmacology (Berl.)* 222, 645–661. doi:10.1007/s00213-012-2665-5

Sun, W., Akins, C. K., Mattingly, A. E., and Rebec, G. V. (2005). Ionotropic glutamate receptors in the ventral tegmental area regulate cocaine-seeking behavior in rats. *Neuropsychopharmacology* 30, 2073–2081. doi:10.1038/sj.npp.1300744

Sutton, M. A., Schmidt, E. F., Choi, K. H., Schad, C. A., Whisler, K., Simmons, D., et al. (2003). Extinction-induced upregulation in AMPA receptors reduces cocaine-seeking behaviour. *Nature* 421, 70–75. doi:10.1038/nature01249

Szalay, J. J., Morin, N. D., and Kantak, K. M. (2011). Involvement of the dorsal subiculum and rostral basolateral amygdala in cocaine cue extinction learning in rats. *Eur. J. Neurosci.* 33, 1299–1307. doi:10.1111/j.1460-9568.2010.07581.x

Szapiro, G., Vianna, M. R., McGaugh, J. L., Medina, J. H., and Izquierdo, I. (2003). The role of NMDA glutamate receptors, PKA, MAPK, and CAMKII in the hippocampus in extinction of conditioned fear. *Hippocampus* 13, 53–58. doi:10.1002/hipo.10043

Thompson, R. H., and Swanson, L. W. (1998). Organization of inputs to the dorsomedial nucleus of the hypothalamus: a reexamination with Fluorogold and PHAL in the rat. *Brain Res. Brain Res.*

Rev. 27, 89–118. doi:10.1016/S0165-0173(98)00010-1

Tobena, A., Fernandez-Teruel, A., Escorihuela, R. M., Nunez, J. F., Zapata, A., Ferre, P., et al. (1993). Limits of habituation and extinction: implications for relapse prevention programs in addictions. *Drug Alcohol Depend.* 32, 209–217. doi:10.1016/0376-8716(93)90085-5

Tsankova, N., Renthal, W., Kumar, A., and Nestler, E. J. (2007). Epigenetic regulation in psychiatric disorders. *Nat. Rev. Neurosci.* 8, 355–367. doi:10.1038/nrn2132

Tully, K., Li, Y., Tsvetkov, E., and Bolshakov, V. Y. (2007). Norepinephrine enables the induction of associative long-term potentiation at thalamo-amygdala synapses. *Proc. Natl. Acad. Sci. U.S.A.* 104, 14146–14150. doi:10.1073/pnas.0704621104

Vianna, M. R., Igaz, L. M., Coitinho, A. S., Medina, J. H., and Izquierdo, I. (2003). Memory extinction requires gene expression in rat hippocampus. *Neurobiol. Learn. Mem.* 79, 199–203. doi:10.1016/S1074-7427(03)00003-0

Volkow, N. D., Fowler, J. S., Wang, G. J., and Goldstein, R. Z. (2002). Role of dopamine, the frontal cortex and memory circuits in drug addiction: insight from imaging studies. *Neurobiol. Learn. Mem.* 78, 610–624. doi:10.1006/nlme.2002.4099

Vorel, S. R., Liu, X., Hayes, R. J., Spector, J. A., and Gardner, E. L. (2001). Relapse to cocaine-seeking after hippocampal theta burst stimulation. *Science* 292, 1175–1178. doi:10.1126/science.1058043

Weiss, F. (2005). Neurobiology of craving, conditioned reward and relapse. *Curr. Opin. Pharmacol.* 5, 9–19. doi:10.1016/j.coph.2004.11.001

Wellman, L. L., Yang, L., Tang, X., and Sanford, L. D. (2008). Contextual fear extinction ameliorates sleep disturbances found following fear conditioning in rats. *Sleep* 31, 1035–1042.

Wells, A. M., Lasseter, H. C., Xie, X., Cowhey, K. E., Reittinger, A. M., and Fuchs, R. A. (2011). Interaction between the basolateral amygdala and dorsal hippocampus is critical for cocaine memory reconsolidation and subsequent drug context-induced cocaine-seeking behavior in rats. *Learn. Mem.* 18, 693–702. doi:10.1101/lm.2273111

Whitelaw, R. B., Markou, A., Robbins, T. W., and Everitt, B. J. (1996). Excitotoxic lesions of the basolateral amygdala impair the acquisition of cocaine-seeking behaviour under a second-order schedule

of reinforcement. *Psychopharmacology (Berl.)* 127, 213–224. doi:10.1007/BF02246129

Whittle, N., Schmuckermair, C., Gunduz Cinar, O., Hauschild, M., Ferraguti, F., Holmes, A., et al. (2013). Deep brain stimulation, histone deacetylase inhibitors and glutamatergic drugs rescue resistance to fear extinction in a genetic mouse model. *Neuropharmacology* 64, 414–423. doi:10.1016/j.neuropharm.2012.06.001

Widholm, J. J., Gass, J. T., Cleva, R. M., and Olive, M. F. (2011). The mGluR5 positive allosteric modulator CDPPB does not alter extinction or contextual reinstatement of methamphetamine-seeking behavior in rats. *J. Addict. Res. Ther.* S1, ii:004.

Wise, R. A. (2004). Dopamine, learning and motivation. *Nat. Rev. Neurosci.* 5, 483–494. doi:10.1038/nrn1406

Woods, A. M., and Bouton, M. E. (2006). D-cycloserine facilitates extinction but does not eliminate renewal of the conditioned emotional response. *Behav. Neurosci.* 120, 1159–1162. doi:10.1037/0735-7044.120.5.1159

Xu, J., Zhu, Y., Contractor, A., and Heinemann, S. F. (2009). mGluR5 has a critical role in inhibitory learning. *J. Neurosci.* 29, 3676–3684. doi:10.1523/JNEUROSCI.5716-08.2009

15

Chronic exposure to a gambling-like schedule of reward predictive stimuli can promote sensitization to amphetamine in rats

Martin Zack[1]*, Robert E. Featherstone[2], Sarah Mathewson[3] and Paul J. Fletcher[3]

[1] Cognitive Psychopharmacology Laboratory, Neuroscience Department, Centre for Addiction and Mental Health, Toronto, ON, Canada
[2] Translational Neuroscience Program, Department of Psychiatry, School of Medicine, University of Pennsylvania, Philadelphia, PA, USA
[3] Biopsychology Section, Neuroscience Department, Centre for Addiction and Mental Health, Toronto, ON, Canada

Edited by:
Bryan F. Singer, University of Michigan, USA

Reviewed by:
Louk Vanderschuren, University of Utrecht, Netherlands
Ruud Van Den Bos, Radboud University Nijmegen, Netherlands
Patrick Anselme, University of Liège, Belgium

*Correspondence:
Martin Zack, Cognitive Psychopharmacology Laboratory, Neuroscience Department, Centre for Addiction and Mental Health, 33 Russell Street, Toronto, ON M5S 2S1, Canada
e-mail: martin.zack@camh.ca

Addiction is considered to be a brain disease caused by chronic exposure to drugs. Sensitization of brain dopamine (DA) systems partly mediates this effect. Pathological gambling (PG) is considered to be a behavioral addiction. Therefore, PG may be caused by chronic exposure to gambling. Identifying a gambling-induced sensitization of DA systems would support this possibility. Gambling rewards evoke DA release. One episode of slot machine play shifts the DA response from reward delivery to onset of cues (spinning reels) for reward, in line with temporal difference learning principles. Thus, conditioned stimuli (CS) play a key role in DA responses to gambling. In primates, DA response to a CS is strongest when reward probability is 50%. Under this schedule the CS elicits an expectancy of reward but provides no information about whether it will occur on a given trial. During gambling, a 50% schedule should elicit maximal DA release. This closely matches reward frequency (46%) on a commercial slot machine. DA release can contribute to sensitization, especially for amphetamine. Chronic exposure to a CS that predicts reward 50% of the time could mimic this effect. We tested this hypothesis in three studies with rats. Animals received 15 × 45-min exposures to a CS that predicted reward with a probability of 0, 25, 50, 75, or 100%. The CS was a light; the reward was a 10% sucrose solution. After training, rats received a sensitizing regimen of five separate doses (1 mg/kg) of d-amphetamine. Lastly they received a 0.5 or 1 mg/kg amphetamine challenge prior to a 90-min locomotor activity test. In all three studies the 50% group displayed greater activity than the other groups in response to both challenge doses. Effect sizes were modest but consistent, as reflected by a significant group × rank association ($\phi = 0.986$, $p = 0.025$). Chronic exposure to a gambling-like schedule of reward predictive stimuli can promote sensitization to amphetamine much like exposure to amphetamine itself.

Keywords: pathological gambling, sensitization, amphetamine, dopamine, uncertainty

INTRODUCTION

Addiction has been characterized as a brain disease caused by chronic exposure to drugs of abuse (Leshner, 1997). Neuroplasticity is thought to mediate the effects of such exposure (Nestler, 2001). Sensitization of brain dopamine (DA) systems is a form of neuroplasticity implicated in hyper-reactivity to conditioned stimuli (CS) for drugs, and compulsive drug seeking (Robinson and Berridge, 2001). Sensitization has been operationally defined by increased DA release in response to a CS for reward and by increased locomotor response to pharmacological DA challenge (Robinson and Berridge, 1993; Pierce and Kalivas, 1997; Vanderschuren and Kalivas, 2000). Although sensitization is only one of many brain changes linked with addiction (cf. Robbins and Everitt, 1999; Koob and Le Moal, 2008), changes in presynaptic dopamine release have been suggested to represent common neuroadaptations involved in addiction-based drug-seeking (e.g., relapse), in that drugs that induce

locomotor sensitization to opiate (e.g., morphine) or stimulant challenge (e.g., amphetamine), also cause reinstatement of extinguished operant responses for heroin or cocaine self-administration—an animal model of relapse (Vanderschuren et al., 1999). Evidence that incentive sensitization (increased value of drug reward) is most pronounced after initial exposure to addictive drugs further suggests that sensitization may be involved in the early stages of addiction as well (Vanderschuren and Pierce, 2010).

Pathological gambling (PG) has been described as a behavioral addiction and recently reclassified to the same category as substance dependence disorders in the 5th edition of the Diagnostic and Statistical Manual of Mental Disorders (Frascella et al., 2010; A.P.A., 2013). This implies that PG may be caused by chronic exposure to gambling-like activity, that common mechanisms may mediate the effects of gambling and drug exposure (Zack and Poulos, 2009; Leeman and Potenza, 2012); and that sensitization of brain DA pathways may be one important element of this process.

Clinical evidence indirectly supports this possibility: Using positron emission tomography (PET) Boileau and colleagues found that male PG subjects exhibit significantly greater striatal DA release in response to amphetamine (0.4 mg/kg) than healthy male controls (Boileau et al., 2013). Overall group differences were significant in the associative and somatosensory striatum. In the limbic striatum, which includes the nucleus accumbens, the groups did not differ. However, in PG subjects, DA release in the limbic striatum correlated directly with the severity of PG symptoms. These findings are consistent with sensitization of brain DA pathways in PG, but also suggest some important differences with human substance dependent individuals and with the classic animal model of amphetamine sensitization. Unlike PG subjects and animals exposed to low doses of amphetamine (cf. Robinson et al., 1982), humans with substance dependence consistently exhibit decreased DA release to a stimulant challenge (Volkow et al., 1997; Martinez et al., 2007), and evidence from animals suggests that this may reflect deficits in DA function during the initial stages of abstinence following binge patterns of substance abuse (Mateo et al., 2005). In studies where stimulant sensitization is demonstrated in animals, enhanced DA release is usually observed in the limbic striatum rather than the dorsal (associative, somatosensory) striatum (Vezina, 2004). However, cue-induced (i.e., conditioned) drug-seeking in animals repeatedly exposed to cocaine has been linked with enhanced DA release in the dorsal striatum, a result thought to indicate a more habitual form of motivated behavior (Ito et al., 2002). Thus, the overall elevation in DA release in dorsal regions in PG subjects may be related to habit-based (inflexible, routinized) reward seeking involving "a progression from ventral to more dorsal domains of the striatum" (Everitt and Robbins, 2005, p. 1481), whereas the severity-dependent DA release in limbic striatum in these subjects may correspond more closely to incentive sensitization as typically modeled in animals. The PET findings cannot reveal whether DA hyper-reactivity was a pre-existing feature of these PG subjects, a consequence of gambling exposure, or a result of some other process entirely. To address this question, it is necessary to demonstrate induction of sensitization by chronic gambling exposure in subjects that are normal prior to exposure. This raises questions as to what features of gambling are most likely to induce sensitization.

Skinner noted that the variable schedule of reinforcement was fundamental to gambling's allure (or at least its persistence) (Skinner, 1953). Betting behavior in a slot machine game conforms well to the basic principles of instrumental conditioning, as reflected by a prospective correlation between monetary payoff and bet size on consecutive spins (Tremblay et al., 2011). Thus, variable ratio operant responding appears to provide an externally valid model of slot machine gambling.

Recent research with animals provides strong initial support for a causal effect of gambling exposure on sensitization. Singer and colleagues examined the effects of 55 1–h daily sessions of fixed (FR20) or variable (VR20) saccharin reinforcement in an operant lever-press paradigm on subsequent locomotor response to low dose (0.5 mg/kg) amphetamine in healthy male (Sprague Dawley) rats (Singer et al., 2012). They hypothesized that, if gambling leads to sensitization, rats exposed to the variable schedule, which mimics gambling, should exhibit greater response to amphetamine than rats exposed to the fixed schedule. As predicted, the VR20 group displayed 50% greater locomotor response to amphetamine than the FR20 group. In contrast, the groups displayed equivalent locomotion following a saline injection. These findings confirm that chronic exposure to variable reinforcement is sufficient to induce hyper-reactivity to a DA challenge in healthy animals randomized to the respective schedules.

A number of questions arise from this result: First, to what extent does the perceived contingency—or lack thereof—between the operant response and its outcome mediate these effects? In learning terms, does this effect involve a "response-outcome expectancy," or might a similar effect be seen in the absence of an operant response, i.e., "a stimulus-outcome expectancy" in a Pavlovian paradigm (cf. Bolles, 1972)? Second, does the degree of contingency between the antecedent event (response or stimulus) and its outcome influence the degree of sensitization?

The second question concerns the role of uncertainty in sensitization. For example, do games whose outcome is truly random—completely unpredictable—have greater potential to induce sensitization than games where the odds of winning are clearly defined but not random, even if the absolute rate of reward is low? The present research addressed these questions.

The experimental design was informed by a seminal study on reward expectancy and DA neuron response in monkeys (Fiorillo et al., 2003). The animals in that study received a juice reward (US) under 0, 25, 50, 75, or 100% variable ratio schedules. The schedules were designated by 1 of 4 different CS (icons). The 0% schedule delivered reward as often as the 100% schedule, but omitted the CS. Firing rate of DA neurons during the interval between CS onset and US delivery or omission was the key dependent measure. The study found that DA response increased as a function of the uncertainty of reward delivery. Thus, under the 100% schedule the CS evoked little activity, under the 25 and 75% schedules, the CS evoked moderate and similar levels of activity, and under the 50% schedule the CS evoked maximal activity. In each case, firing rate escalated over the course of the CS-US interval, i.e., as the expectancy approached fruition.

These findings indicate that DA activity not only varies with whether or not reward is certain (Fixed Ratio) or uncertain (Variable Ratio), but also varies in inverse proportion to the amount of information about reward delivery conveyed by the CS. In the 100% condition, the CS evokes the reward expectancy and also perfectly predicts its delivery. In the 25 and 75% conditions, the CS evokes the expectancy and predicts reward delivery three out of four times. In the 50% condition the CS evokes the expectancy but provides no information about reward delivery beyond chance alone. Based on their findings, Fiorillo et al. concluded: "This uncertainty-induced increase in dopamine could contribute to the rewarding properties of gambling" (p. 1901).

The effects of 50% variable reward in a single session should not change over the course of multiple sessions because the likelihood of reward remains entirely unpredictable on every trial. Thus, when considering the conditions that would maximize chronic activation of DA neurons over repeated episodes of gambling the 50% schedule should engender the most enduring as well as the most robust effect. This is noteworthy given that the long run rate of reward (payoff > 0) observed over thousands of spins on a commercial slot machine was 45.8% (Tremblay et al., 2011). Thus, 50% variable reward appears to accurately reflect the payoff schedule administered by actual gambling devices.

The present study used the same conditioning schedules as Fiorillo et al. in a chronic exposure, between-groups' design with rats. Animals underwent ~3 weeks of daily conditioning sessions, where a CS (light) was paired with a US (small amount of sucrose). After the training phase, animals rested prior to assessment of sensitization indexed by locomotor response to amphetamine. Based on the literature, it was predicted that rats exposed to different reward schedules would not differ in their drug free locomotor behavior but would exhibit significantly different levels of locomotion following amphetamine, with the 50% group displaying a greater locomotor response to the drug relative to the other groups over the course of doses, a pattern that would be expected if the 50% animals had been previously exposed to additional doses of amphetamine itself (i.e., cross-sensitization).

EXPERIMENT 1
MATERIALS AND METHODS
Subjects
Four groups ($n = 8$/group) of adult (300–350 g) male Sprague-Dawley rats (Charles River, St. Constant, Quebec, Canada) were housed individually in clear polycarbonate boxes (20 × 43 × 22 cm) under a reverse 12:12 light-dark cycle. They received *ad libitum* access to food and water, and daily handling by an experimenter for 2 weeks prior to the study. Each group was conditioned under one of four variable reward schedules: 0, 25, 50, or 100%. The 75% group was omitted in this initial study, as Fiorillo et al. (2003) found equivalent post-CS DA release under 25 and 75% reward schedules, such that both conditions led to greater DA release than did the 100% CS-US condition, but less than the 50% condition.

Apparatus
Access to sucrose presentations and to the CS was provided individually in operant conditioning boxes (33 × 31 × 29 cm). Each box was equipped with a reinforcer magazine, located on the front wall. A light in the top of the magazine served as the CS. A motorized, solenoid-controlled liquid dipper could be elevated to the floor of the magazine. Events in the box were controlled by Med Associates equipment and software, using an in-house program written in MED-PC. Locomotor testing was conducted individually in Plexiglas cages (27 × 48 × 20 cm). Each cage was equipped with a monitoring system consisting of six photo-beam cells to detect horizontal movement.

Procedure
Training. The study was conducted in compliance with the ethical guidelines set out by the Canadian Council on Animal Care. Rats were food-restricted to 90% of their body weight for the duration of the study and housed individually. Each rat received 15 days of sucrose reward training (10% water solution at 0.06 ml per reward): 5 consecutive days × 3 weeks, with weekends off. Animals were maintained on standard chow before and after the training phase; sucrose exposure was restricted to the fifteen ~40-min training sessions. Each daily session consisted of 15 stimulus presentations (a light; CS), each separated by an inter-trial interval of 120 s. The light was located in the top panel of the magazine, and remained on for 25 s, with sucrose made available during the last 5 s. In the case of group 0 the sucrose dipper was raised every 140 s (for 5 s) but the stimulus light was not illuminated. This equated the interval between presentations of the dipper in group 0 and the other groups (120 + 25 s). Each treatment session lasted ~40 min. On average, group 25 received sucrose once for every four CS presentations; group 50 received sucrose once for every two CS presentations, and group 100 received sucrose after every CS presentation.

Testing. Two weeks after the last sucrose access (or "conditioning") session, the locomotor response to d-amphetamine (AMPH; i.p.) was assessed. Rats were given three 2-h sessions to habituate to the locomotor boxes, followed by six AMPH test sessions. AMPH test days occurred at 1-wk intervals. On test days, rats were given 30 min to habituate to boxes then received a single 0.5 mg/kg dose of AMPH followed, on separate weekly sessions, by five 1.0 mg/kg doses (one dose per day) on test days 1 through 5. Post-AMPH locomotion was assessed for 90 min on each session.

Data analytic approach
Statistical analyses were conducted with SPSS (v. 16 and v. 21; SPSS Inc., Chicago IL). Immediate behavioral response to the CS was assessed in terms of nose pokes into the aperture where the sucrose was dispensed. The mean number of nose pokes during this interval (5 s per trial) was then compared to the mean number of nose pokes for the same duration (5 s) averaged over the time when the CS was absent. Group × Session ANOVAs of nose-pokes with CS present and absent tracked the acquisition of discriminative responding to the cue and indiscriminate nose poke responses under the different schedules over the course of the 15 sucrose training sessions.

Effects of treatment on locomotor responses were assessed with Group × Session ANOVAs for the drug-free habituation phase (three sessions), pre-sensitization 0.5 mg/kg AMPH challenge (one session), and during the five-session 1 mg/kg AMPH sensitization regimen, when groups were expected to differ in response to repeated doses of AMPH. Group × Session ANOVAs also assessed drug-free locomotor responses during the 30-min pre-injection habituation phase from each AMPH test session. Planned comparisons assessed the difference in mean performance for group 50 vs. group 0 (no expectancy control) and group 100 (no uncertainty control), by means of t-tests (Howell, 1992), using the MS error and df error terms for the relevant effect (i.e., group or group × session interaction) from the ANOVA (Winer, 1971). Polynomial trend analyses tested the profile of changes over the course of sessions.

To determine if approach responses in the presence and absence of the CS during the 15 sucrose training sessions contributed to variation in locomotor response to AMPH, or mediated group differences in AMPH response, follow-up analyses of covariance (ANCOVAs) were performed on the AMPH locomotor data, including total nose pokes (sum for 15 sessions) when the CS was absent as the covariate. A significant effect of the covariate would indicate that drug-free approach responses moderated (influenced the strength of) the effects of group or session. A decline in the significance of the effects of group or session in the presence of a significant covariate would indicate that approach responses mediated (accounted for) the effects of group or session. A decline in the significance of group or session effects in the absence of a significant covariate effect would simply reflect a loss of statistical power due to the reallocation of df from the error term to the covariate, and would not have bearing on the interpretation of the effects of group or session.

RESULTS

Nose pokes during sucrose conditioning sessions

CS present. **Figure 1A** shows the mean nose pokes for groups 25, 50, and 100 while the CS was present on the 15 sucrose conditioning sessions (nose pokes were not coded for group 0, which received no CS). A 3 Group × 15 Session ANOVA yielded significant main effects of Group, $F_{(2, 21)} = 5.63$, $p = 0.011$, and Session, $F_{(14, 294)} = 14.00$, $p < 0.001$, along with a significant Group × Session interaction, $F_{(28, 294)} = 2.93$, $p < 0.001$. **Figure 1A** indicates that the main effect of Session reflected an increase in nose pokes across sessions in all three groups, and the main effect of Group reflected generally higher overall scores in group 100 vs. group 25 with intermediate scores in group 50. A significant Group × Session interaction for the cubic trend, $F_{(2, 21)} = 4.42$, $p = 0.030$, indicated a rapid rise, dip, and leveling off in nose pokes over sessions in group 100, as against a linear increase over sessions in group 50, and a shallower linear increase over sessions in group 25.

CS absent. **Figure 1B** shows the mean nose pokes for all four groups for an equivalent duration (5 s × 15 trials) averaged over the time when the CS was absent. A 4 Group × 15 Session ANOVA yielded significant main effects of Group, $F_{(3, 28)} = 7.06$, $p = 0.001$, and Session $F_{(14, 392)} = 2.84$, $p < 0.001$, along with a significant Group × Session interaction, $F_{(42, 392)} = 3.93$, $p < 0.001$. A significant Group × Session interaction for the quadratic trend, $F_{(3, 28)} = 3.91$, $p = 0.019$, along with no interaction for the cubic trend, $F_{(3, 28)} < 0.93$, $p > 0.44$, reflected an "inverted-U" profile of nose pokes over sessions in group 0, as against a generally stable profile over sessions in the other groups.

Habituation to locomotor chambers

A 4 Group × 3 Session ANOVA yielded a main effect of Session, $F_{(2, 56)} = 5.67$, $p = 0.006$, and no other significant effects, $F_{(3, 28)} < 1.60$, $p > 0.21$. Mean (SE) beam breaks per 2 h in the locomotor boxes were 1681 (123) on session 1, 1525 (140) on session 2, and 1269 (96) on session 3. Planned comparisons found no significant differences between group 50 and group 0 or group 100 on the first or final habituation session, $t_{(84)} < 1.69$, $p > 0.05$. Thus, in the absence of AMPH, repeated exposure to the test boxes was associated with a consistent decline in spontaneous locomotor activity in the four groups (i.e., Session effect), and

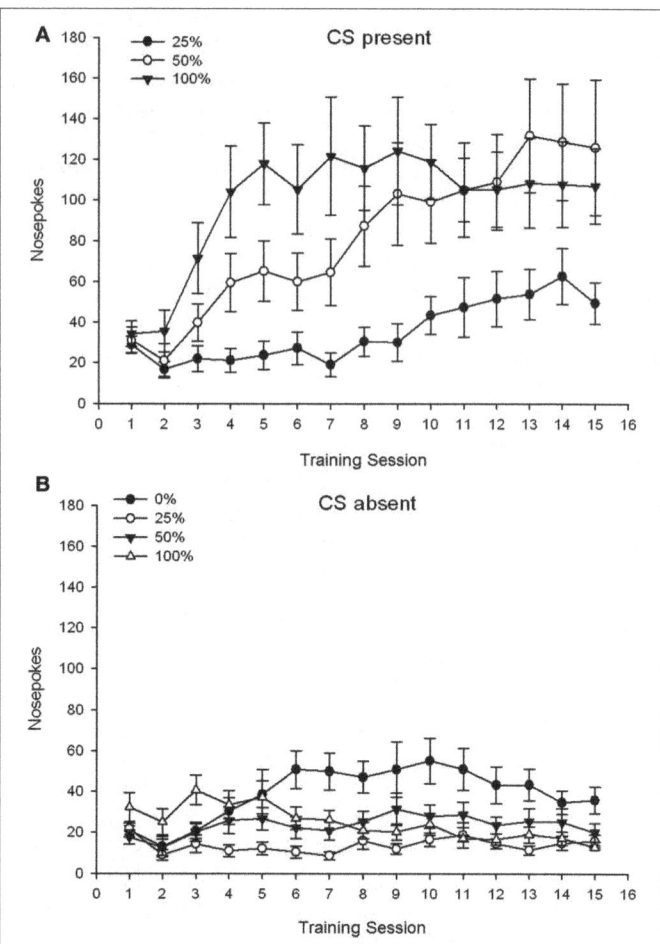

FIGURE 1 | Mean (SE) approach responses (nose pokes) on 15 sucrose training sessions in groups of Sprague Dawley rats (*n* = 8/group) exposed to sucrose reward (10% solution) delivered under 0, 25, 50, or 100% variable schedules. The conditioned stimulus was a light (120 s). Group 0 received the same number of rewards as group 100 in the absence of conditioned stimuli. **(A)** Scores when CS was present (5 s × 15 trials). **(B)** Scores when CS was absent (average for 5 × 15 s while light was off).

no differential response as a function of sucrose training schedule (no interaction).

Test sessions

Effects of pre-sensitization 0.5 mg/kg AMPH challenge.

Pre-injection locomotion. A 4 Group one-way ANOVA of locomotor response during the 30-min pre-injection habituation phase yielded no significant effects, $F_{(3, 28)} < 1.05$, $p > 0.38$. Planned comparisons found no significant difference between group 50 and group 0 or group 100, $t_{(32)} < 0.87$, $p > 0.40$. Therefore, baseline differences in pre-injection locomotion did not account for group differences in locomotor response to AMPH. Mean (SE) beam breaks for the sample were 559 (77).

Post-injection locomotion vs. final drug-free habituation session. A 4 Group × 2 Session ANOVA compared the groups' locomotor responses on the final habituation session, and immediately after the pre-sensitization 0.5 mg/kg AMPH challenge. Scores for the habituation session (120 min) were scaled to correspond with the duration of the AMPH test session (90 min) (raw habituation score × 90/120). The analysis yielded a significant main effect of Session, $F_{(1, 28)} = 34.16$, $p < 0.001$, and no other significant effects, $F_{(3, 28)} < 2.26$, $p > 0.10$. The Session effect reflected an increase in mean (SE) beam breaks in response to the dose, from 952 (72) to 1859 (151). Planned comparisons found no significant differences between group 50 and group 0 or group 100 in response to the dose, $t_{(56)} < 1.72$, $p > 0.10$. However, the rank order of beam break scores (M; SE) aligned with the hypothesis: group 50 (2205; 264) > group 0 (2025; 203) > group 100 (1909; 407) > group 25 (1296; 299).

Effects of 1 mg/kg AMPH.

Pre-injection locomotion. A 4 Group × 5 Session ANOVA of locomotor response during the 30-min pre-injection habituation phase on 1 mg/kg AMPH test sessions yielded a main effect of Session, $F_{(4, 112)} = 43.64$, $p < 0.0001$, and no other significant effects, $F_{(3, 28)} < 0.97$, $p > 0.42$. Planned comparisons found no significant difference between group 50 and group 0 or group 100 on the first or final test session, $t_{(140)} < 0.84$, $p > 0.30$. Therefore, baseline differences in locomotion did not account for group differences in locomotor response to AMPH. Mean (SE) beam break scores for the pre-dose habituation phase on sessions 1–5 were: 454 (30), 809 (53), 760 (36), 505 (35), 756 (39).

Post-injection locomotion. **Figure 2** shows the effects of five injections of 1 mg/kg AMPH (one per week) on locomotor activity scores in the four groups. A 4 Group × 5 Session ANOVA yielded a main effect of Session, $F_{(4, 112)} = 8.21$, $p < 0.001$, a marginal main effect of Group, $F_{(2, 45)} = 3.28$, $p = 0.085$, and no significant interaction, $F_{(12, 122)} < 0.77$, $p > 0.68$.

Planned comparisons revealed that group 50 scores differed significantly from group 0, $t_{(14)} = 2.19$, $p = 0.037$, and group 100, $t_{(14)} = 2.36$, $p = 0.025$ [and differed marginally from group 25, $t_{(14)} = 2.03$, $p = 0.051$]. Thus, in group 50, locomotor response to 1 mg/kg AMPH reliably exceeded that of the other three groups across all five test sessions. Polynomial trend analysis detected a significant quadratic trend across sessions, $F_{(1, 28)} = 32.47$, $p < 0.0001$, and no other significant trends, $F_{(1, 28)} < 1.78$, $p > 0.19$. **Figure 2** shows that this result reflected an "inverted U" pattern across sessions.

Control for variation in nose poke responding during sucrose training

The follow-up ANCOVA of locomotor responses to 1 mg/kg AMPH, with nose pokes (CS present) as the covariate, in the three groups that received the CS, yielded a marginal main effect of Group, $F_{(2, 20)} = 3.07$, $p = 0.069$, and no significant covariate-related effects, $F_{(4, 80)} < 0.05$, $p > 0.85$. Thus, cued approach responding during training did not explain significant variation in the locomotor response to 1 mg/kg AMPH in groups 25, 50, or 100.

The follow-up ANCOVA of locomotor responses to 1 mg/kg AMPH, with nose pokes (CS absent) as a covariate, yielded a significant effect of the covariate, $F_{(1, 27)} = 6.17$, $p = 0.020$, a significant main effect of Group, $F_{(3, 27)} = 4.13$, $p = 0.016$, a marginal Session × Covariate interaction, $p = 0.080$, and no

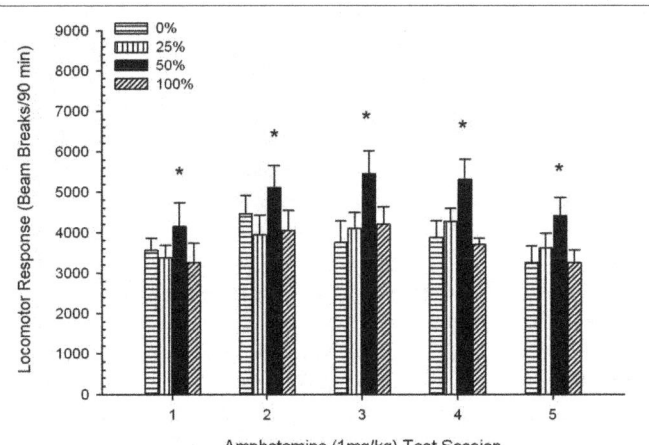

FIGURE 2 | Mean (SE) locomotor response (number of beam breaks in an electronic array per 90 min) to 1 mg/kg d-amphetamine (i.p.) on 5 weekly sessions in groups of Sprague Dawley rats (n = 8/group) previously exposed to 15 daily conditioning sessions with sucrose reward (10% solution) delivered under 0, 25, 50, or 100% variable schedules. The conditioned stimulus was a light (120 s). Group 0 received the same number of rewards as group 100 in the absence of conditioned stimuli. *$p < 0.05$ for mean difference between group 50 and group 0 as well as group 100, based on planned comparisons.

other significant effects, $F_{(4, 108)} < 1.48$, $p > 0.21$. Thus, un-cued (indiscriminate) approach responding during training explained significant variation in locomotor response to 1 mg/kg AMPH. However, this variation was non-overlapping with group-related variance, because inclusion of the covariate in the analysis increased rather than decreased the significance of the group effect.

DISCUSSION

The nose poke data while the CS was present show that groups acquired the association between CS and sucrose delivery as reflected by an increase in cued responses over training sessions. The profile of responding over sessions while the CS was present suggested that 100 and 50% CS-US schedules were equally effective in eliciting approach, whereas the 25% schedule elicited a more modest increase in cue-induced approach. The nose poke data while the CS was absent suggest that groups that received any of the three CS-sucrose training schedules (group 25, 50, 100) rapidly learned to reduce their nose pokes in the absence of the CS, whereas animals in group 0, which received no CS, only learned to decrease their approach behavior to a limited degree after extensive training.

The habituation data show that the groups did not differ prior to AMPH and that repeated exposure to the test boxes was associated with decreased drug-free locomotor response. Therefore, between-group differences and increased responding over repeated doses of AMPH cannot be attributed to pre-existing differences in locomotor behavior.

Results of the pre-sensitization challenge with 0.5 mg/kg AMPH confirmed that the drug increased locomotor activity relative to the final drug-free habituation day. In line with the hypothesis, group 50 ranked higher than groups 0 or 100 (as well as group 25) in terms of mean response to the dose, although the mean differences between groups were not significant.

For the sensitization sessions, the between-groups' planned comparisons showed that prior exposure to 50% conditioned sucrose reward led to a significant increase in locomotor response to a 1.0 mg/kg dose of amphetamine relative to the other three schedules. This effect was evident from the first dose and did not change appreciably over repeated doses. The trend analysis indicated a biphasic response (for the full sample) to repeated doses of AMPH, increasing up to the third dose and decreasing thereafter. The results of the follow-up ANCOVA with nose-pokes (CS absent) as the covariate confirmed that differences in the four groups' locomotor responses to 1 mg/kg AMPH were not mediated by un-cued approach responding during the sucrose training sessions.

The group effect during the sensitization sessions is consistent with our hypothesis. The bi-phasic session effect is not consistent with the expected continued escalation in locomotor responses with repeated AMPH doses. This may be related to the dosing interval. To address this issue, a procedure (alternate daily doses) shown to induce consistent escalation in locomotor response to 1.0 mg/kg doses of AMPH (i.e., behavioral sensitization) should be employed. The impact of a sensitizing regimen of AMPH on subsequent response to a second 0.5 mg/kg challenge would further support the generality of this effect. Inclusion of a saline challenge prior to AMPH would determine the role of expectancy or injection-related (e.g., stress) effects on the locomotor response to AMPH. Inclusion of a 75% conditioned sucrose group would help to clarify the role of reward uncertainty vs. reward infrequency on the pattern of responses for groups 50 and group 25. In addition, to permit assessment (by ANCOVA) of the contribution of drug-free cued approach responses to locomotion under AMPH (using nose pokes with CS present as the covariate), nose pokes were also coded for group 0 during the interval when the CS was present in the other four groups (i.e., so that nose pokes from all five groups—including group 0 which received no CS—could be included in the analysis of covariance with CS present as the covariate). These refinements were incorporated in experiment 2.

EXPERIMENT 2
MATERIALS AND METHODS

The methodology of experiment 2 was similar to that of experiment 1 but revised to better approximate a regimen found to reliably induce AMPH sensitization (Fletcher et al., 2005). Changes were as follows: (a) The 75% CS-sucrose group ($n = 8$) was included; (b) During sucrose training, rats (except for group 0) received 20 CS (light) presentations (as opposed to 15 in experiment 1); (c) CS presentations were each separated by an average inter-trial interval of 90 s; range: 30–180 s (vs. 120 s in experiment 1), which offset the increase in training trials to equate the duration of each training session to that of experiment 1; (d) the duration of each of the three habituation sessions was decreased from 120 to 90 min to correspond with the duration of the test sessions; (e) A saline (i.p., 1 ml/kg) challenge (90 min) was added

(post-sucrose training day 8), to assess the locomotor effects of injection *per se* (e.g., expectation, stress); (f) The 1 mg/kg sensitization sessions were held on alternate weekdays (post-training days 12–21) rather than at weekly intervals as in experiment 1; (g) Along with the pre-sensitization 0.5 mg/kg AMPH challenge (post-training day 9) a second post-sensitization 0.5 mg/kg AMPH challenge was added (post-sucrose training day 28), to test the generality of the sensitization effect across doses; (h) nose pokes while CS was present were coded for all groups (including group 0); (i) nose pokes while CS was absent were recorded specifically from the 5-s interval immediately prior to the onset of the CS to index premature approach responding.

RESULTS
Nose pokes during sucrose conditioning sessions

A 5 Group × 15 Session × 2 Phase (CS present, CS absent) ANOVA of nose pokes yielded significant main effects of Group, $F_{(4, 19)} = 2.89$, $p = 0.050$, Session $F_{(14, 266)} = 2.28$, $p = 0.006$, and Phase, $F_{(1, 19)} = 14.72$, $p = 0.001$, as well as a significant three-way interaction, $F_{(56, 266)} = 1.38$, $p = 0.050$. Panels (**A,B**) of **Figure 3** plot the groups' mean nose poke scores for the CS present and CS absent phases, respectively. Comparison of the two panels reveals that the main effect of Phase reflected more overall nose poke responses when the CS was present vs. absent. Therefore, cued responses occurred significantly more often than did premature un-cued responses. The main effects of Group and Session were not readily interpreted due to the higher order interaction. This latter result reflected a convergence of scores for the five groups at a relatively stable low level across sessions when the CS was absent (**Figure 3B**), together with a divergence of scores into high (group 75, group 100), intermediate (group 50), and low (group 0, group 25) levels of nose poke responding over sessions when the CS was present (**Figure 3A**). Of the lower order polynomial trends (linear, quadratic, cubic) only the three-way interaction for the linear trend approached significance, $F_{(4, 19)} = 2.32$, $p = 0.094$, reflecting the generally monotonic increase in nose pokes over sessions in group 75 and relatively more rapid stabilization at high, intermediate, and low levels of responding in the other groups when the CS was present.

Habituation to locomotor boxes

A 5 Group × 3 Session ANOVA of drug-free locomotor responses yielded a significant main effect of Session, $F_{(2, 70)} = 60.01$, $p < 0.0001$, and no other significant effects, $F_{(4, 35)} < 0.70$, $p > 0.60$. Planned comparisons of group 50 with group 0 and with group 100 on the first and final habituation sessions yielded no significant effects, t's < 0.84, $p > 0.40$. Therefore, mean drug-free locomotor response in the key groups did not differ prior to testing. Mean (SE) number of beam breaks per 90 min were 2162 (118) on session 1, 1470 (116) on session 2, and 1250 (98) on session 3.

Test sessions

Saline. A 5 Group × 2 Session ANOVA compared locomotor response on the final habituation session and saline challenge session. The ANOVA yielded a main effect of Session, $F_{(1, 35)} = 62.46$, $p < 0.0001$, and no other significant effects,

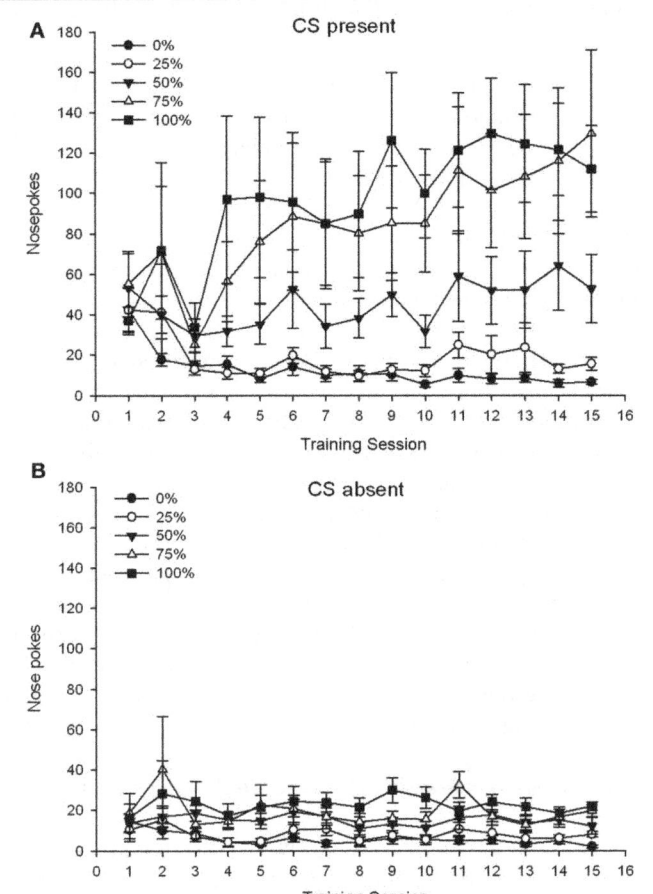

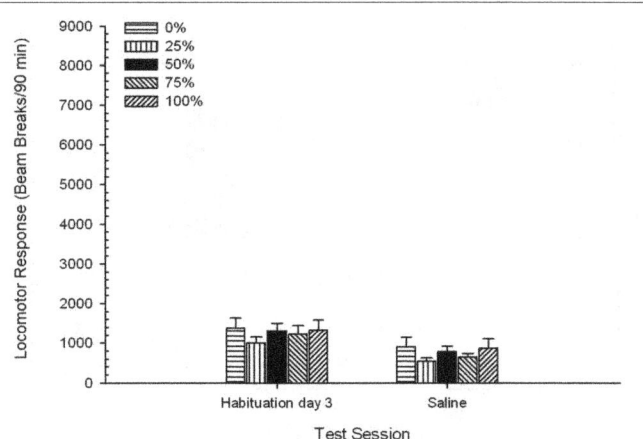

FIGURE 4 | Mean (SE) locomotor response (number of beam breaks in an electronic array per 90 min) on the last of 3 drug-free habituation sessions and on a subsequent session after saline injection (i.p., 1 ml/kg) in groups of Sprague Dawley rats (*n* = 8/group) previously exposed to 15 daily conditioning sessions with sucrose reward (10% solution) delivered under 0, 25, 50, 75, or 100% variable schedules. The conditioned stimulus was a light (120 s). Group 0 received the same number of rewards as group 100 in the absence of conditioned stimuli.

FIGURE 3 | Mean (SE) approach responses (nose pokes) on 15 sucrose training sessions in groups of Sprague Dawley rats (*n* = 8/group) exposed to sucrose reward (10% solution) delivered under 0, 25, 50, 75, or 100% variable schedules. The conditioned stimulus was a light (120 s). Group 0 received the same number of rewards as group 100 in the absence of conditioned stimuli. **(A)** Scores when CS was present (5 s × 20 trials). **(B)** Scores when CS was absent (average for 5 × 20 s while light was off).

$F_{(4, 35)} < 0.65, p > 0.64$. **Figure 4** plots the group means and shows that the Session effect reflected an overall decrease in locomotor response from the final drug-free habituation session to the saline session, which did not vary by group. Thus, the decline in locomotor response seen over the three habituations sessions continued on the fourth drug-free exposure to the test boxes.

Effects of 0.5 mg/kg AMPH.

Pre-injection locomotion. A 5 Group × 2 Session ANOVA of pre-injection locomotion (30-min) on the pre- and post-sensitization 0.5 mg/kg AMPH test days yielded a significant main effect of Session, $F_{(1, 35)} = 13.39, p = 0.001$, and no other significant effects, $F_{(4, 35)} < 1.79, p > 0.15$. Planned comparisons found no significant differences between group 50 and group 0 or group 100 on the first session, $t_{(70)} < 1.00, p > 0.30$. However, on the second (post-sensitization) session group 50 (1203; 121) displayed significantly more pre-injection beam breaks (M; SE) than

did group 100 (756; 103), $t_{(70)} = 5.11, p < 0.001$, but did not differ from group 0 (1126; 211), $t_{(7)} < 0.88, p > 0.40$. Therefore, baseline differences in locomotion did not account for group differences in locomotor response to the first 0.5 mg/kg dose of AMPH but may have contributed to differences between group 50 and group 100 in locomotor response to the second 0.5 mg/kg dose of AMPH. Mean (SE) beam breaks for the pre-injection phase on the first and second 0.5 mg/kg AMPH test sessions were 757 (41) and 974 (59).

Post-injection locomotion. A 5 Group × 2 Session ANOVA of locomotor response to 0.5 mg/kg AMPH before and after the 5-dose sensitizing regimen yielded a main effect of Session, $F_{(1, 35)} = 76.05, p < 0.0001$, and no other significant effects, $F_{(4, 35)} < 1.10, p > 0.37$. **Figure 5** shows the mean scores for each group and session.

The figure shows that the Session effect involved a significant increase in overall mean (SE) beam breaks per 90 min from 0.5 mg/kg dose 1, 3674 (216) to 0.5 mg/kg dose 2, 6123 (275). The lack of interaction or group effect suggested that sensitization to AMPH did not vary reliably across groups. Despite the lack of significant group-related effects in the ANOVA, inspection of the figure reveals that group 50 displayed the greatest response to both the first and second 0.5 mg/kg doses. Planned comparisons of response to the first 0.5 mg/kg dose revealed no significant difference between group 50 and group 0 or group 100, t's$_{(35)} < 0.48, p > 0.50$. However, in response to the second (post-sensitization) 0.5 mg/kg dose, group 50 displayed significantly greater locomotion than group 0, $t_{(35)} = 2.00, p < 0.05$, as well as group 100, $t_{(35)} = 3.29, p < 0.01$.

In light of the significant group difference in pre-injection locomotion on the second 0.5 mg/kg AMPH session reported above, a follow-up 5 Group × 2 Session ANCOVA of locomotor

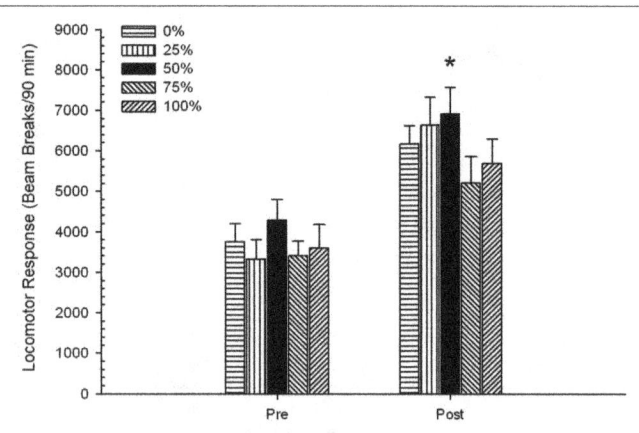

FIGURE 5 | Mean (SE) locomotor response (number of beam breaks in an electronic array per 90 min) to 0.5 mg/kg d-amphetamine on separate sessions before and after a 5-session sensitizing regimen of d-amphetamine (1.0 mg/kg; i.p. per session) in groups of Sprague Dawley rats (*n* = 8/group) previously exposed to 15 daily conditioning sessions with sucrose reward (10% solution) delivered under 0, 25, 50, 75, or 100% variable schedules. The conditioned stimulus was a light (120 s). Group 0 received the same number of rewards as group 100 in the absence of conditioned stimuli. *$p < 0.05$ for mean difference between group 50 and group 0 as well as group 100, based on planned comparisons.

response to 0.5 mg/kg AMPH was conducted, controlling for pre-injection locomotion on the second session. This analysis yielded a significant effect of the covariate, $F_{(1, 34)} = 8.65$, $p = 0.006$, a main effect of Session $F_{(1, 34)} = 10.83$, $p = 0.002$, and no other significant effects, $F_{(4, 34)} < 0.85$, $p > 0.50$. Importantly, planned comparisons based on the MS error and df error from the ANCOVA confirmed that mean locomotor response to the second 0.5 mg/kg dose of AMPH remained significantly greater in group 50 than group 100, $t_{(34)} = 3.09$, $p < 0.01$, and group 0, $t_{(34)} = 1.88$, $p < 0.05$ (one-tailed), when pre-injection variation from session 2 was controlled. Thus, group 50 displayed significantly greater post-sensitization locomotor response to 0.5 mg/kg AMPH than did group 100 or group 0, and these group differences were not mediated by pre-injection locomotion on test days.

Effects of 1.0 mg/kg AMPH.

Pre-injection locomotion. A 5 Group × 5 Session ANOVA of 30-min pre-injection scores for the 1 mg/kg AMPH sensitization sessions yielded a main effect of Session, $F_{(4, 140)} = 16.70$, $p < 0.0001$, and no other significant effects, $F_{(4, 35)} < 0.94$, $p > 0.45$. Planned comparisons found no significant difference in pre-injection locomotion between group 50 and group 0 or group 100 on the first session, $t_{(175)} < 1.66$, $p > 0.10$. However, on the final session, group 50 (1167; 140) displayed significantly more beam breaks (M; SE) than did group 100 (1000; 99), $t_{(175)} = 2.35$, $p < 0.05$, but did not differ from group 0 (1085, 120), $t_{(175)} < 1.16$, $p > 0.20$. Therefore, differences in pre-injection locomotion contributed to differences between groups 50 and 100 in locomotor response to the final 1 mg/kg AMPH dose. Mean (SE) overall beam breaks for the sample during the pre-injection phase for

Sessions 1 through 5 were: 810 (46), 784 (52), 760 (53), 726 (46), 1009 (51).

Post-injection locomotion. A 5 Group × 5 Session ANOVA of responses to 1 mg/kg AMPH yielded a significant main effect of Session, $F_{(4, 140)} = 6.72$, $p < 0.001$, a marginal Group × Session interaction, $F_{(16, 140)} = 1.57$, $p = 0.085$, and no main effect of Group, $F_{(4, 35)} < 0.44$, $p > 0.77$. Polynomial trend analyses revealed a significant linear trend, $F_{(1, 35)} = 9.19$, $p = 0.005$, and cubic trend, $F_{(1, 35)} = 21.63$, $p < 0.001$, over sessions 1 through 5. **Figure 6** shows the mean locomotor scores for each group and session.

The figure shows that the Session effect reflected a significant increase in overall mean (SE) beam breaks for the full sample from session 1, 4624 (213) to session 5, 5736 (272), confirming the emergence of sensitization to AMPH. The cubic trend denoted relative maxima on sessions 1, 3, and 5, with dips on sessions 2 and 4, particularly for groups 0 and 50. The figure also reveals that, despite the lack of significant interaction, group 25 displayed progressively greater locomotor response over sessions and differed considerably from the other groups on sessions 4 and 5 (9 and 22% greater respectively, than next highest group). Planned comparisons found that group 50 did not differ significantly from groups 0 or 100, $t_{(175)} < 0.89$, $p > 0.40$ on the first or final 1 mg/kg AMPH test session.

Control for variation in nose poke responding during sucrose training

Two 5 Group × 2 Session ANCOVAs of locomotor response to 0.5 mg/kg AMPH before and after the sensitization regimen, including total nose pokes during sucrose training with CS present and with CS absent as separate covariates, found no significant effects for either covariate, $F_{(1, 18)} < 1.03$, $p > 0.31$. Therefore, approach responding during training did not mediate group differences in response to 0.5 mg/kg AMPH.

Two 5 Group × 5 Session ANCOVAs of locomotor response to 1 mg/kg during the sensitization sessions with total nose pokes (CS present, CS absent) as separate covariates yielded no significant effects of the covariate while the CS was present, $F_{(4, 104)} < 1.04$, $p > 0.38$, and a marginal main effect of the covariate while the CS was absent, $F_{(1, 18)} = 3.32$, $p = 0.085$.

DISCUSSION

The results of this study did not consistently support the hypothesis that group 50 would demonstrate higher locomotor response over sessions compared to the other groups. The 1 mg/kg AMPH data confirmed the emergence of sensitization with the alternate-day dosing regimen. The pattern across groups indicated a trend for greater sensitization during the latter sessions in group 25, with no such evidence for group 50. In contrast, the 0.5 mg/kg dose results indicated a trend for greater sensitization in group 50, while at the same time confirming a significant overall increase in locomotor response across groups to the second vs. the first 0.5 mg/kg AMPH dose. The null effect of saline injection confirmed that expectancy or injection-related stress did not contribute to the AMPH effects.

The nose poke data again revealed an overall increase in approach responding over the course of training sessions when

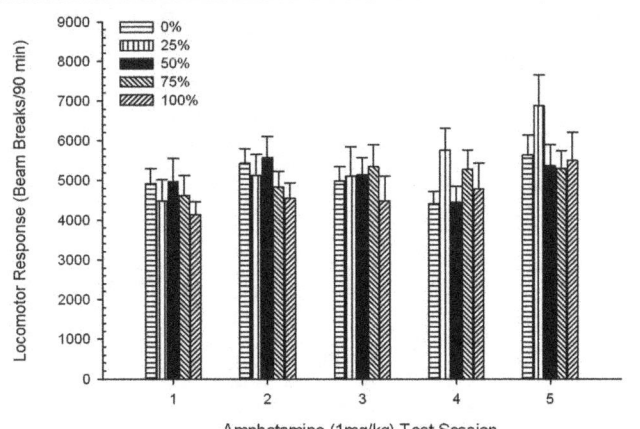

FIGURE 6 | Mean (SE) locomotor response (number of beam breaks in an electronic array per 90 min) to 1 mg/kg d-amphetamine (i.p.) on 5 weekly sessions in groups of Sprague Dawley rats (n = 8/ group) previously exposed to 15 daily conditioning sessions with sucrose reward (10% solution) delivered under 0, 25, 50, 75, or 100% variable schedules. The conditioned stimulus was a light (120 s). Group 0 received the same number of rewards as group 100 in the absence of conditioned stimuli.

the CS was present, with no corresponding increase when the CS was absent. Therefore, the animals appeared to acquire the association between the CS and the prospect of sucrose reward. Group differences in the frequency of nose pokes when the CS was present conformed roughly to the frequency of reward delivery under the respective schedules, with groups 75 and 100 displaying the most nose pokes, group 50 displaying intermediate numbers of nose pokes, and groups 0 and 25 displaying the fewest nose pokes. These results suggest that the CS came to control approach responding in a manner consistent with the overall probability of reward. Although speculative, one possible explanation for the lower nose poke rates with CS present in group 50 in experiment 2 vs. experiment 1 may be the shortening of the inter-trial interval, as longer inter-trial intervals (experiment 1) appear to encourage impulsive tendencies and this is associated with increased turnover of DA in anterior cingulate, prelimbic and infralimbic cortices (Dalley et al., 2002). Therefore, the 30% reduction in inter-trial interval in experiment 2 (and 3) may have altered cortical DA levels and promoted more selective (i.e., guided by the relative frequency of reward) vs. impulsive (not guided by reward frequency) approach responding in group 50 during training trials in experiment 2 as compared with experiment 1.

The lack of significant covariate-related effects for nose pokes in the CS present condition in the ANCOVAs indicates that approach responding during sucrose training did not mediate the effects of the different CS-sucrose schedules on responses to AMPH. The marginally significant effect of the covariate for the CS absent condition in the ANCOVA of locomotor responses to 1 mg/kg AMPH suggests that the tendency toward premature drug-free responding explained some of the variability in locomotor effects of AMPH during the sensitization sessions.

Together, the evidence suggests that the effects of conditioning history may be more discernible with 0.5 AMPH than with

1 mg/kg AMPH, and that a protocol that generates sensitization in the absence of any other manipulation may obscure or render redundant the effects of a putative sensitization-promoting behavioral manipulation (i.e., chronic variable reward).

Behavioral sensitization to AMPH is a robust effect in the laboratory. However, outside the laboratory, only a minority of individuals who gamble chronically escalate to pathological levels. Although risk for sensitization is related to risk for addiction (or drug seeking), especially for psychostimulants (Vezina, 2004; Flagel et al., 2008), many factors aside from sensitization risk may predispose one to addiction (e.g., Verdejo-Garcia et al., 2008; Conversano et al., 2012; Volkow et al., 2012). Nevertheless, trait factors that confer vulnerability to sensitization may interact with conditioning history to accentuate the effects of unpredictable reward (i.e., 50% CS-US schedule) on DA system reactivity. To investigate this possibility, experiment 3 employed the same procedure as experiment 2 but used Lewis strain instead of Sprague Dawley strain rats.

Sprague Dawley rats display intermediate levels of DA transporters, with lower levels than Wistar strain rats (Zamudio et al., 2005), but higher levels than Wistar-Kyoto rats (a "depressive"-like strain) in the nucleus accumbens, amygdala, ventral tegmental area and substantia nigra (Jiao et al., 2003). This profile may render Sprague Dawley rats only moderately sensitive to environmental or pharmacological manipulations of DA function. In contrast, Lewis rats exhibit low levels of DA transporters as well as D2 and D3 DA receptors in the nucleus accumbens and dorsal striatum compared to other strains (e.g., F344) (Flores et al., 1998). These morphological differences may contribute to Lewis rats' differential response to DA manipulations. Lewis rats also exhibit a range of accentuated responses to experimental drug manipulations compared to other strains (e.g., F344). Most importantly, Lewis rats display greater sensitization to methamphetamine, characterized by low response to initial doses but higher response to later doses (Camp et al., 1994). Lewis rats also exhibit greater locomotor sensitization to a range of doses of cocaine (Kosten et al., 1994; Haile et al., 2001). Based on this pattern of effects, we surmised that Lewis rats would enable us to investigate whether susceptibility to sensitization amplifies the effects of conditioning schedule on subsequent response to AMPH.

EXPERIMENT 3
MATERIALS AND METHODS
The methodology was the same as in experiment 2, aside from the use of Lewis rats (200–225 g on arrival, Charles River, Quebec, Canada).

RESULTS
Nose pokes during sucrose conditioning sessions
A 5 Group × 15 Session × 2 Phase (CS present, CS absent) ANOVA of nose pokes yielded significant main effects of Group, $F_{(4, 34)} = 6.12$, $p = 0.001$, Session, $F_{(14, 476)} = 3.42$, $p < 0.001$, and Phase, $F_{(1, 34)} = 20.83$, $p < 0.001$, as well as a significant three-way interaction, $F_{(56, 476)} = 1.56$, $p = 0.008$. Panels **(A,B)** of **Figure 7** plot the groups' mean nose poke scores for the CS present and CS absent phases, respectively. Comparison of

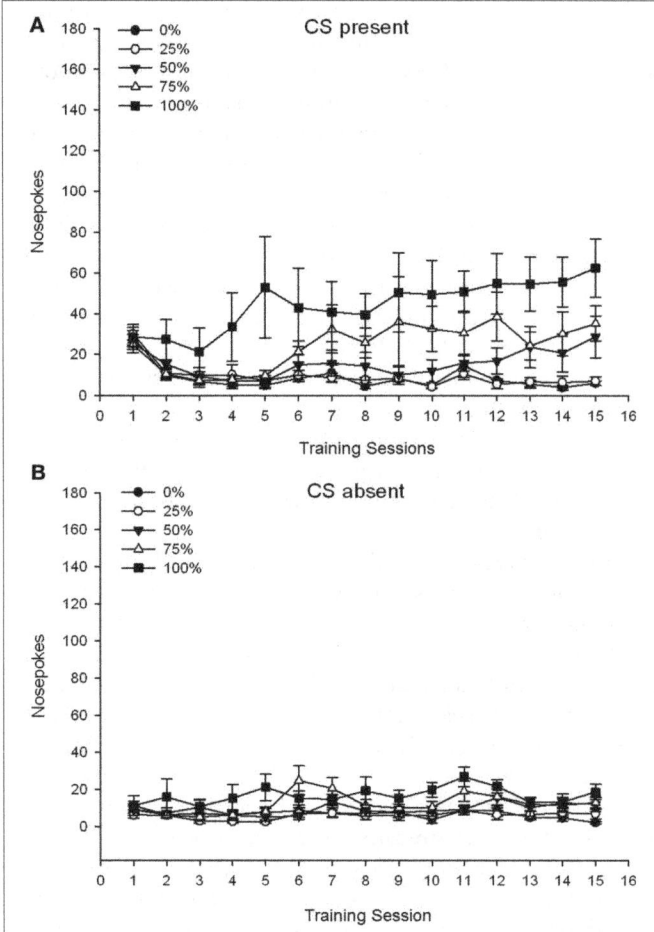

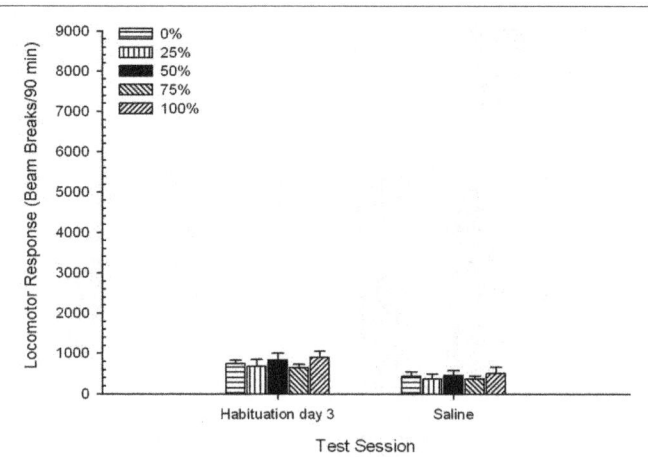

FIGURE 8 | Mean (SE) locomotor response (number of beam breaks in an electronic array per 90 min) on the last of 3 drug-free habituation sessions and on a subsequent session after saline injection (i.p., 1 ml/kg) in groups of Lewis rats ($n = 8$/group) previously exposed to 15 daily conditioning sessions with sucrose reward (10% solution) delivered under 0, 25, 50, 75, or 100% variable schedules. The conditioned stimulus was a light (120 s). Group 0 received the same number of rewards as group 100 in the absence of conditioned stimuli.

FIGURE 7 | Mean (SE) approach responses (nose pokes) on 15 sucrose training sessions in groups of Lewis rats ($n = 8$/group) exposed to sucrose reward (10% solution) delivered under 0, 25, 50, 75, or 100% variable schedules. The conditioned stimulus was a light (120 s). Group 0 received the same number of rewards as group 100 in the absence of conditioned stimuli. **(A)** Scores when CS was present (5 s × 20 trials). **(B)** Scores when CS was absent (average for 5 × 20 s while light was off).

the two panels reveals that the main effect of Phase reflected more overall nose poke responses when the CS was present vs. absent. Therefore, cued responses occurred significantly more often than did pre-mature responses. The main effects of Group and Session were not readily interpreted due to the higher order interaction. The three-way interaction reflected a convergence of scores for the five groups at a relatively stable low level across sessions when the CS was absent [Panel (**B**)], together with a divergence of scores when the CS was present into relatively discrete profiles for each group that paralleled their rank order of reward frequency: from highest (group 100) to lowest (group 25) [Panel (**A**)]. Only the linear trend for the interaction was significant, $F_{(4, 34)} = 4.03$, $p = 0.009$, reflecting the generally consistent increase in nose pokes over sessions in group 100 when the CS was present as against the relatively inconsistent profile of increase in nose pokes across sessions in the other groups during this phase.

Habituation to locomotor boxes

A 5 Group × 3 Session ANOVA yielded a main effect of Session, $F_{(2, 70)} = 23.07$, $p < 0.0001$, and no other significant effects, $F_{(8, 70)} < 1.47$, $p > 0.18$. A curvilinear pattern of mean (SE) locomotor scores emerged from session 1, 1076 (74), through session 2, 644 (48), to session 3, 762 (59). Planned comparisons of group 50 with group 0 and with group 100 on the first and final habituation sessions revealed significantly fewer beam breaks in group 50 ($M = 911$; $SE = 109$) vs. group 0 ($M = 1103$; $SE = 176$) on habituation session 1, $t_{(105)} = 2.02$, $p < 0.05$, but no difference between group 50 and group 100 ($M = 1066$; $SE = 150$), $t_{(105)} < 1.20$, $p > 0.20$, on this session. Group 50 did not differ significantly from either group 0 or group 100 on the final habituation session, $t_{(105)} < 0.93$, $p > 0.30$. Therefore, mean drug-free locomotor response in the key groups did not differ consistently prior to testing.

Test sessions

Saline. A 5 Group × 2 Session ANOVA of locomotor responses on the final habituation session and the saline test session yielded a significant main effect of Session, $F_{(1, 35)} = 50.12$, $p < 0.0001$, and no other significant effects, $F_{(4, 35)} < 0.57$, $p > 0.68$. **Figure 8** shows the group mean scores for the two sessions and indicates that the Session effect reflected a significant decline from habituation to saline test. Thus, receipt of the injection *per se* (e.g., expectancy, stress) did not enhance locomotor responding.

Effects of 0.5 mg/kg AMPH.

Pre-injection locomotion. A 5 Group × 2 Session ANOVA of pre-injection locomotion yielded a significant main effect of Session, $F_{(1, 35)} = 15.04$, $p < 0.001$, and no other significant effects, $F_{(4, 35)} < 1.19$, $p > 0.33$. Planned comparisons found no significant difference between group 50 and group 0 or group 100 on either test session, $t_{(70)} < 0.99, p > 0.30$. Therefore, baseline differences in pre-injection locomotion did not account for group differences in locomotor response to 0.5 mg/kg AMPH. Mean (SE) beam breaks for the pre-injection phase for the first and second (post-sensitization) 0.5 mg/kg sessions were 325 (25) and 473 (36).

Post-injection locomotion. A 5 Group × 2 Session ANOVA of locomotor response to 0.5 mg/kg doses delivered before and after chronic 1 mg/kg AMPH yielded a main effect of Session, $F_{(1, 34)} = 87.44$, $p < 0.0001$, and no other significant effects, $F_{(4, 34)} < 0.94$, $p > 0.45$. **Figure 9** plots the mean locomotor scores for each group and session and shows that the Session effect reflected an increased overall response to the second 0.5 mg/kg dose, consistent with sensitization. The figure also shows that the groups performed very similarly on session 1, but that group 50 displayed more locomotor activity than the other groups on session 2. Planned comparisons in response to the first 0.5 mg/kg dose revealed no significant differences between group 50 and group 0 or group 100, $t_{(35)} < 1.28$, $p > 0.20$. However, group 50 displayed significantly greater locomotor response to the second 0.5 mg/kg dose than did group 0, $t_{(35)} = 4.32$, $p < 0.001$, or group 100, $t_{(35)} = 2.24$, $p < 0.05$.

Effects of 1 mg/kg AMPH.

Pre-injection locomotion. A 5 Group × 5 Session ANOVA of 30-min pre-injection scores for the sensitization sessions yielded a main effect of Session, $F_{(4, 140)} = 4.10$, $p = 0.004$, and no other significant effects, $F_{(4, 35)} = 1.25$, $p > 0.31$. Planned comparisons found that beam breaks during the pre-injection phase

(M; SE) were significantly lower in group 50 (395; 62) than in group 100 (508; 62), $t_{(175)} = 2.58$, $p < 0.01$, but not group 0, $t_{(175)} < 1.83, p > 0.10$, on 1 mg/kg AMPH session 1. On the final 1 mg/kg AMPH session, planned comparisons also found that pre-injection locomotion in group 50 (378; 60) was significantly lower than in group 100 (650; 75), $t_{(175)} = 6.17$, $p < 0.001$, but not in group 0, $t_{(175)} < 1.84, p > 0.10$. As the direction of these group differences (control group = group 50) was opposite to the hypothesized pattern, group differences in post-injection locomotion that align with the hypothesis cannot be attributed to pre-injection baseline differences. Mean (SE) overall beam breaks during the pre-injection phase for Sessions 1 through 5 were: 442 (34), 452 (32), 542 (40), 411 (26), 504 (37).

Post-injection locomotion. A 5 Group × 5 Sessions ANOVA of responses to the 1 mg/kg doses yielded a significant main effect of Session, $F_{(4, 140)} = 6.15$, $p < 0.001$, and no other significant effects, $F_{(4, 35)} < 0.57$, $p > 0.68$. Polynomial trend analyses revealed a significant linear trend, $F_{(1, 35)} = 9.34, p = 0.004$, and cubic trend, $F_{(1, 35)} = 5.08$, $p = 0.031$, the latter result denoting relative maxima on sessions 3 and 5. **Figure 10** plots these scores and shows that, despite the lack of significant interaction in the ANOVA, group 50 exhibited substantially greater locomotion than the other four groups in response to the final 1 mg/kg dose. Accordingly, planned comparisons revealed significantly greater mean scores on session 5 in group 50 than in all other groups, $t_{(35)} > 3.68, p < 0.001$.

Control for variation in nose poke responding during sucrose training

Two 5 Group × 2 Session ANCOVAs of locomotor response to 0.5 mg/kg AMPH before and after the sensitization regimen, including total nose pokes during sucrose training with CS

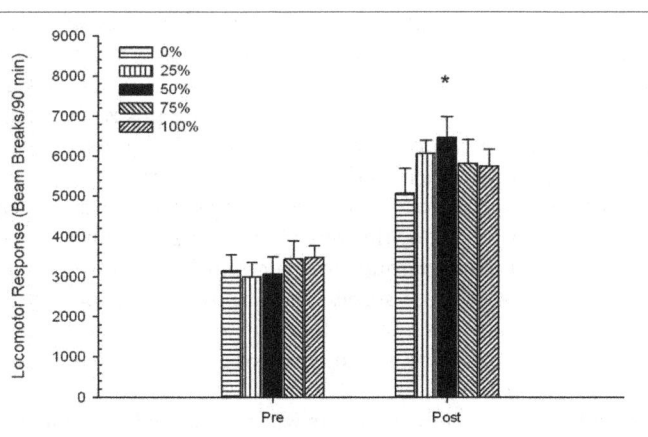

FIGURE 9 | Mean (SE) locomotor response (number of beam breaks in an electronic array per 90 min) to 0.5 mg/kg d-amphetamine on separate sessions before and after a 5-session sensitizing regimen of d-amphetamine (1.0 mg/kg; i.p. per session) in groups of Lewis rats (*n* = 8/group) previously exposed to 15 daily conditioning sessions with sucrose reward (10% solution) delivered under 0, 25, 50, 75, or 100% variable schedules. The conditioned stimulus was a light (120 s). Group 0 received the same number of rewards as group 100 in the absence of conditioned stimuli. *p < 0.05 for mean difference between group 50 and group 0 as well as group 100, based on planned comparisons.

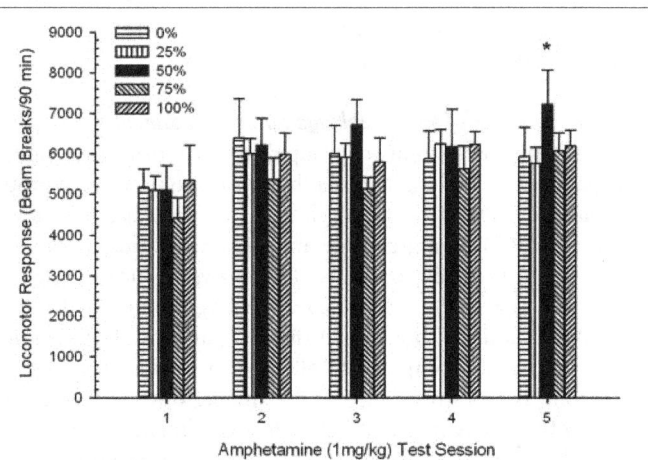

FIGURE 10 | Mean (SE) locomotor response (number of beam breaks in an electronic array per 90 min) to 1 mg/kg d-amphetamine (i.p.) on 5 weekly sessions in groups of Lewis rats (*n* = 8/group) previously exposed to 15 daily conditioning sessions with sucrose reward (10% solution) delivered under 0, 25, 50, 75, or 100% variable schedules. The conditioned stimulus was a light (120 s). Group 0 received the same number of rewards as group 100 in the absence of conditioned stimuli. *p < 0.05 for mean difference between group 50 and group 0 as well as group 100, based on planned comparisons.

present and with CS absent as separate covariates, found no significant effects for either covariate, $F_{(1, 32)} < 0.44\ p > 0.51$. Two 5 Group × 5 Session ANCOVAs of locomotor response to 1 mg/kg AMPH during the sensitization sessions with total nose pokes (CS present, CS absent) as separate covariates yielded no significant effects of the covariate while the CS was present or absent, $F_{(1, 33)} < 0.14, p > 0.71$. Therefore, drug-free approach responding did not account for group differences in locomotor responses to either dose of AMPH.

DISCUSSION

Sensitization developed to the effects of repeated 1.0 mg/kg amphetamine. The habituation and saline data confirm that this effect was not due to pre-existing differences, expectancy, or stress-related responses to the injection. The ANCOVAs with nose pokes confirm that these effects were not due to drug-free approach behavior. The nose poke data themselves indicated that the groups acquired the association between the CS and prospect of sucrose reward. The groups' rank level of nose-poke responding at the end of training matched the overall frequency of reward under the different schedules from highest (group 100) to lowest (group 0), as it did in experiment 2. The relatively lower overall mean nose poke levels in this experiment compared to experiments 1 and 2 may reflect more selective approach responding to cues for reward in Lewis rats (Kosten et al., 2007).

The 0.5 mg/kg dose data showed that initial locomotor response to AMPH in Lewis rats (**Figure 9**) was somewhat suppressed compared to Sprague Dawley rats (experiment 2; **Figure 5**), but the within-group increase in response to the second dose in Lewis rats was considerable (nearly double the response to the first 0.5 mg/kg dose) following the 5-session AMPH regimen Most notably, group 50 displayed a greater locomotor response than all groups except group 25 to the second (i.e., post-sensitization) 0.5 mg/kg AMPH dose and a greater locomotor response than all other groups, including group 25, to the final 1 mg/kg AMPH dose (final sensitization session).

Summary analysis of group rankings across experiments

To determine the reliability of group differences in sensitization, a non-parametric analysis assessed the contingency between group and rank of mean locomotor response to the second (post-chronic AMPH) 0.5 mg/kg dose and the final 1.0 mg/kg dose of AMPH from the 3 experiments. The analysis yielded a significant effect, $\varphi = 0.986$, $p = 0.025$, reflecting the fact that group 50 ranked first in all but one of the comparisons. The superior rank of group 50 compared to all other groups in response to the second (post-chronic AMPH) 0.5 mg/kg dose is depicted in **Figure 5** (experiment 2) and **Figure 9** (experiment 3). The superior rank of group 50 relative to other groups in response to the final 1.0 mg/kg dose is depicted in **Figure 2** (experiment 1) and **Figure 10** (experiment 3). The only exception to this pattern was the response to the final 1.0 mg/kg dose in Sprague-Dawley rats in experiment 2.

GENERAL DISCUSSION

The present series of experiments tested the hypothesis that chronic exposure to a gambling-like schedule of reward can sensitize brain DA pathways much like chronic exposure to drugs of abuse. Evidence for such an effect would suggest that neuroplasticity, of the same kind thought to contribute to drug addiction, can be induced by chronic exposure to unpredictable reward schedules. In line with the literature on drug addiction, locomotor response to 0.5 and 1.0 mg/kg doses of AMPH indexed DA system reactivity, with greater locomotion in response to later doses operationally defining sensitization (cf. Robinson and Berridge, 1993; Pierce and Kalivas, 1997; Vanderschuren and Kalivas, 2000).

Overall, the results are in line with our hypothesis. However, they also indicate considerable variability in experimental effects due to procedural factors. The effects of conditioning schedule were modest but consistent, with group 50 demonstrating greater response than the other four groups to both doses following the five dose-regimen. Although overall F-values for group-related effects in the variance analyses were often non-significant, key group differences were confirmed with pairwise planned comparisons. In this regard it should be noted that, "Current thinking, however, is that overall significance [for F in the ANOVA] is not necessary. First of all, the hypotheses tested by the overall test and a multiple-comparison test are quite different, with quite different levels of power. For example, the overall F actually distributes differences among groups across the number of degrees of freedom for groups. This has the effect of diluting the overall F in the situation where several group means are equal to each other but different from some other mean" (Howell, 1992, p. 338). This is the precisely the situation that applied in the present experiments, where group 50 was expected to differ from group 0 and group 100 controls but no difference between these control groups was predicted for group 25 or group 75.

The nose poke data confirmed that, in every experiment, the animals acquired the association between the CS and the prospect of sucrose reward. The correspondence between nose poke frequency for the different groups and overall frequency of reward under their respective training schedules suggests that the average rate of sucrose reward guided drug-free approach responding. However, the lack of mediating effect of nose pokes on group-related locomotor responses to AMPH in the ANCOVAs indicated that separate processes underlie the two behaviors.

In some cases, the effect of conditioning schedule was evident in response to the first AMPH dose; in other cases it only emerged after repeated doses. Group differences in locomotor response to the first AMPH dose suggest that exposure to gambling-like reward schedules is sufficient by itself to induce sensitization. Group differences in locomotion following multiple AMPH doses indicate a more subtle effect that could be characterized as "susceptibility," which only manifests when combined with ongoing exposure to the primary sensitizing agent (i.e., amphetamine).

Differences in the pattern of response across experiments suggest that a longer interval between training and initial AMPH challenge may maximize the opportunity to detect the inherent sensitizing effect of the conditioning treatment. This in turn suggests that effects of conditioned reward exposure may incubate over time, a phenomenon also seen with stimulant sensitization (Grimm et al., 2006). The pattern of response to the two doses of amphetamine suggests that the 0.5 mg/kg dose may be more effective in revealing the effects of conditioning history. This in turn suggests that conditioning effects under the current training protocol are somewhat subtle and may be camouflaged by ceiling effects under doses of AMPH and conditions that generate *de novo* sensitization.

In experiment 3, the biphasic pattern of response to the 0.5 mg/kg doses and progressive emergence of superiority in group 50 is consistent with the expected profile for Lewis rats in response to methamphetamine (Camp et al., 1994). This lends support to the validity of the present findings and suggests overlap between the factors that moderate vulnerability to psychostimulant sensitization and to gambling-like schedules of reward.

Across experiments, the post-sensitization locomotor response of group 50 generally exceeded that of the other groups under different doses of amphetamine and in different strains of animals. However, the high within-group variability and modest between-group effect sizes indicate a role for other factors in DA system reactivity to amphetamine following exposure to varying schedules of conditioned sucrose reward. Although responses of DA neurons to reward signals may provide a coarse model of gambling (Fiorillo et al., 2003), like all models, there is a loss of information for the sake of parsimony—i.e., to demonstrate a key process. As a result, the pattern of effects across CS-US conditions in the original Fiorillo et al. study does not fully generalize to locomotor response to amphetamine. Further refinements of the model are called for to fully capture the aspects of gambling that impact on DA system function.

Taken together, the results of this series of experiments provide provisional support for the hypothesis that chronic exposure to gambling-like schedules of reward enhances the reactivity of the brain DA system to psychostimulant challenge. As such, they extend the findings of Singer et al. (2012) who demonstrated that, relative to a fixed schedule, prior exposure to a variable reinforcement schedule in an operant paradigm enhances subsequent locomotor response to amphetamine. More specifically, the present findings point to uncertainty of reward delivery as the critical factor underlying the effects of variable reward. The magnitude of effects in the operant paradigm was substantially greater than the effects found in the present experiments. This may reflect greater chronic exposure to the gambling-like activity (55 vs. 15 days); it may reflect the effects of requiring an operant response to elicit the reward (i.e., a role for agency) rather than passive exposure, as in the present study. Increasing the duration of training in the present paradigm would help to resolve these questions.

The validity of variable reward and reinforcement schedules as models of gambling cannot be gleaned from these experiments. Future research that examines the impact of conditioning history on risk-taking behavior in rodent gambling tasks could address this issue. Similarly, the correspondence between the behavioral sensitization found here and the elevated striatal DA response to amphetamine recently found in pathological gamblers must await further investigation (Boileau et al., 2013). Micro-dialysis could address this question, and the prediction based on the human data would be that greater DA release in the group 50 "gambling phenotype" would be most clearly observed in the dorsal (sensorimotor) striatum rather than the ventral (limbic) striatum. Validation of 50% variable CS + reward exposure in these other paradigms would support its utility as a bona fide experimental model of PG.

Whereas some forms of gambling clearly entail an instrumental response (e.g., slot machines), in other forms of gambling (e.g., lottery) the link between the action (purchasing the ticket, i.e., placing the bet), the cues for reward (i.e., lottery numbers) and the reward itself (the winning number and monetary payoff) is much more diffuse. Nevertheless, activation of DA during the CS-US interval may well occur. This may explain why, when the "winning number" is announced, attention is riveted as each individual lottery ball drops in succession to compose the specific sequence of digits in the winning number. Although the probability of a specific digit occurring is mathematically defined, the outcome for each individual lottery ball is binary—hit (matches the player's number) or miss (does not match the player's number)—and the outcome on any given trial is unknown. Such a scenario may better characterize the experience of group 50 in the present experiments, where reward was provided non-contingently but also unpredictably and the CS merely indicated the potential for reward without revealing whether it would occur on a given trial. Slot machines are more strongly linked with PG than are lottery tickets (Cox et al., 2000; Bakken et al., 2009), indicating an important role for instrumental factors (and immediacy) in the rewarding aspects of gambling for this population (Loba et al., 2001). Nonetheless, the Pavlovian process modeled in the present experiments (CS + uncertain reward) appears to be a necessary if not sufficient element of the gambling experience.

Along with the lack of a clear instrumental requirement, a number of other design features may have contributed to the relatively modest and variable pattern of experimental effects. The groups differed in overall sucrose exposure as well as the contingency between CS and sucrose reward. Although this may have contributed to inter-group variability, it cannot readily explain why animals with the greatest sucrose exposure (group 100) displayed less sensitization than group 50. In addition, group 0 received no stimulus before sucrose exposure on every trial. Although this precluded a cue-induced expectation of reward, it did not control for the presence of a stimulus before reward delivery, which existed in all other groups. To address this issue, future research should include a condition where animals receive reward on every trial following random exposure to a neutral stimulus (i.e., whose presence does not signal the potential for reward).

Another design limitation is the potential emergence of adjunctive behavior that could influence the effects of training schedule. In the face of uncertainty, animals may develop superstitious behaviors designed to enhance perceived control and reduce uncertainty-induced DA activation (cf. Harris et al., 2013). It is therefore possible that uncontrolled aspects of the experimental design enabled the animals to offset the effects of conditioning schedule. Such an effect could contribute to the relatively modest and variable response to amphetamine in group 50 following CS + sucrose training. Future research should record spontaneous behavior, aside from nose pokes, during training sessions to test this possibility, and control for it statistically should it emerge. Because such behavior would be expected to counteract or dampen the effects of schedule-induced uncertainty, locomotor response to amphetamine in group 50 should be enhanced when it is controlled (procedurally or statistically). Therefore, the present (uncontrolled) design provides a conservative test of the effects of 50% CS + reward on amphetamine sensitization.

In terms of external validity, the use of male rats also limits the generalizability of the results. The lack of a clear "punishment" condition also differs from gambling, where large monetary losses are common and exert important motivational effects (Nieuwenhuis et al., 2005; Singh and Khan, 2012). The ability to accumulate reward is also absent from the present paradigm and cumulative winnings in a slot machine game have been found to interact with DA manipulations in humans (Tremblay et al., 2011; Smart et al., 2013). Similarly, the opportunity for a jackpot is an important difference between the present model and actual gambling.

Despite these limitations, the present results suggest that 50% variable CS + reward can engage DA pathways implicated in the reinforcing effects of gambling (Fiorillo et al., 2003; Anselme, 2013). Cross-sensitization of response to AMPH following this gambling-like schedule is consistent with a pivotal role for DA in gambling and psychostimulant drug effects (Zack and Poulos, 2009), and extends earlier studies on cross-priming of motivation to gamble by AMPH in pathological gamblers (Zack and Poulos, 2004). The present results also indirectly suggest that modest doses of AMPH, which do not cause supra-physiological DA release, may better model brain activity in response to intermittent reward signals (i.e., during gambling) than exposure to high (i.e., binge-like) doses of stimulant drugs (cf. Vanderschuren and Pierce, 2010). Direct support for this correspondence could be derived by assessing DA release in response to the 50% variable CS-US schedule and different doses of AMPH using microdialysis.

From an experimental standpoint, the present Pavlovian model and the previous operant model of variable reinforcement both appear to engender a phenotype resembling the human pathological gambler. As such, they provide a valuable complement to rodent gambling tasks which model gambling behavior (as a dependent measure) but have, until now, only employed healthy animals, the equivalent of human social gamblers. Based on the literature, the animals chronically exposed to variable reward may well differ in these tasks, particularly in response to DA-ergic drugs. Combining the rat gambling phenotype with gambling tasks may permit systematic development of medications for the treatment of PG, which might not be fully accomplished with healthy animals alone. Further refinements in the experimental design and training regimen, as described above, should improve the correspondence between animals trained in this paradigm and actual pathological gamblers.

From the clinical-sociological standpoint, the finding that exposure to 50% variable CS + reward, which closely matches the reward schedule on a commercial slot machine (Tremblay et al., 2011), changes the brain DA system in reliable and enduring ways suggests that, in some cases, gambling activity, like drugs of abuse, may be a "pathogen" capable of causing addiction. However, the modest effect size and high variability in response to 50% CS + reward suggest that, like drugs of abuse, the tendency for gambling-like reward schedules to promote addiction will depend greatly on the pre-existing risk profile of the gambler. Nevertheless, to spare high risk individuals exposure to potential adverse gambling-related effects, it seems reasonable that policies applied to deter use and minimize harm from drugs of abuse could be extended to gambling as well.

ACKNOWLEDGMENTS

This research was funded by grants from The Natural Sciences and Engineering Research Council of Canada to Paul J. Fletcher. We sincerely thank Ms. Djurdja Djordjevic for preparing the figures.

REFERENCES

Anselme, P. (2013). Dopamine, motivation, and the evolutionary significance of gambling-like behaviour. *Behav. Brain Res.* 256, 1–4. doi: 10.1016/j.bbr.2013.07.039

A.P.A. (2013). *Diagnostic and Statistical Manual of Mental Disorders, 5th Edn*. Arlington, VA: American Psychiatric Publishing.

Bakken, I. J., Gotestam, K. G., Grawe, R. W., Wenzel, H. G., and Oren, A. (2009). Gambling behavior and gambling problems in Norway 2007. *Scand. J. Psychol.* 50, 333–339. doi: 10.1111/j.1467-9450.2009.00713.x

Boileau, I., Payer, D., Chugani, B., Lobo, D. S., Houle, S., Wilson, A. A., et al. (2013). *In vivo* evidence for greater amphetamine-induced dopamine release in pathological gambling: a positron emission tomography study with [C]-(+)-PHNO. *Mol. Psychiatry* doi: 10.1038/mp.2013.163. [Epub ahead of print].

Bolles, R. C. (1972). Reinforcement, expectancy, and learning. *Psychol. Rev.* 79, 394–409. doi: 10.1037/h0033120

Camp, D. M., Browman, K. E., and Robinson, T. E. (1994). The effects of metham- phetamine and cocaine on motor behavior and extracellular dopamine in the ventral striatum of Lewis versus Fischer 344 rats. *Brain Res.* 668, 180–193. doi: 10.1016/0006-8993(94)90523-1

Conversano, C., Marazziti, D., Carmassi, C., Baldini, S., Barnabei, G., and Dell'Osso, L. (2012). Pathological gambling: a systematic review of biochemical, neuroimaging, and neuropsychological findings. *Harv. Rev. Psychiatry* 20, 130–148. doi: 10.3109/10673229.2012.694318

Cox, B. J., Kwong, J., Michaud, V., and Enns, M. W. (2000). Problem and probable pathological gambling: considerations from a community survey. *Can. J. Psychiatry* 45, 548–553.

Dalley, J. W., Theobald, D. E., Eagle, D. M., Passetti, F., and Robbins, T. W. (2002). Deficits in impulse control associated with tonically-elevated seroton- ergic function in rat prefrontal cortex. *Neuropsychopharmacology* 26, 716–728. doi: 10.1016/S0893-133X(01)00412-2

Everitt, B. J., and Robbins, T. W. (2005). Neural systems of reinforcement for drug addiction: from actions to habits to compulsion. *Nat. Neurosci.* 8, 1481–1489. doi: 10.1038/nn1579

Fiorillo, C. D., Tobler, P. N., and Schultz, W. (2003). Discrete coding of reward probability and uncertainty by dopamine neurons. *Science* 299, 1898–1902. doi: 10.1126/science.1077349

Flagel, S. B., Watson, S. J., Akil, H., and Robinson, T. E. (2008). Individual differences in the attribution of incentive salience to a reward-related cue: influence on cocaine sensitization. *Behav. Brain Res.* 186, 48–56. doi: 10.1016/j.bbr.2007.07.022

Fletcher, P. J., Tenn, C. C., Rizos, Z., Lovic, V., and Kapur, S. (2005). Sensitization to amphetamine, but not PCP, impairs attentional set shifting: reversal by a D1 receptor agonist injected into the medial prefrontal cortex. *Psychopharmacology (Berl.)* 183, 190–200. doi: 10.1007/s00213-005-0157-6

Flores, G., Wood, G. K., Barbeau, D., Quirion, R., and Srivastava, L. K., (1998).Lewis and Fischer rats: a comparison of dopamine transporter and receptors levels. *Brain Res.* 814, 34–40. doi: 10.1016/S0006-8993(98)01011-7

Frascella, J., Potenza, M. N., Brown, L. L., and Childress, A. R. (2010). Shared brain vulnerabilities open the way for nonsubstance addictions: carving addiction at a new joint? *Ann. N.Y. Acad. Sci.* 1187, 294–315. doi: 10.1111/j.1749-6632.2009.05420.x

Grimm, J. W., Buse, C., Manaois, M., Osincup, D., Fyall, A., and Wells, (2006). Time-dependent dissociation of cocaine dose-response effects on sucrose craving and locomotion. *Behav. Pharmacol.* 17, 143–149. doi: 10.1097/01.fbp.0000190686.23103.f8

Haile, C. N., Hiroi, N., Nestler, E. J., and Kosten, T. A. (2001). Differential behavioral responses to cocaine are associated with dynamics of mesolimbic dopamine proteins in Lewis and Fischer 344 rats. *Synapse* 41, 179–190. doi: 10.1002/syn.1073

Harris, J. A., Andrew, B. J., and Kwok, D. W. (2013). Magazine approach during a signal for food depends on Pavlovian, not instrumental, conditioning. *J. Exp. Psychol. Anim. Behav. Process.* 39, 107–116. doi: 10.1037/a0031315

Howell, D. C. (1992). *Statistical Methods for Psychology.* Boston, MA: Duxbury.

Ito, R., Dalley, J. W., Robbins, T. W., and Everitt, B. J. (2002). Dopamine release in the dorsal striatum during cocaine-seeking behavior under the control of a drug-associated cue. *J. Neurosci.* 22, 6247–6253.

Jiao, X., Pare, W. P., and Tejani-Butt, S. (2003). Strain differences in the distribution of dopamine transporter sites in rat brain. *Prog. Neuropsychopharmacol. Biol. Psychiatry* 27, 913–919. doi: 10.1016/S0278-5846(03)00150-7

Koob, G. F., and Le Moal, M. (2008). Review. Neurobiological mechanisms for opponent motivational processes in addiction. *Philos. Trans. R. Soc.* Lond. B Biol. Sci. 363, 3113–3123. doi: 10.1098/rstb.2008.0094

Kosten, T. A., Miserendino, M. J., Chi, S., and Nestler, E. J. (1994). Fischer and Lewis rat strains show differential cocaine effects in conditioned place preference and behavioral sensitization but not in locomotor activity or conditioned taste aversion. *J. Pharmacol. Exp. Ther.* 269, 137–144.

Kosten, T. A., Zhang, X. Y., and Haile, C. N. (2007). Strain differences in maintenance of cocaine self-administration and their relationship to novelty activity responses. *Behav. Neurosci.* 121, 380–388. doi: 10.1037/0735-7044.121.2.380

Leeman, R. F., and Potenza, M. N. (2012). Similarities and differences between pathological gambling and substance use disorders: a focus on impulsivity and compulsivity. *Psychopharmacology (Berl.)* 219, 469–490. doi: 10.1007/s00213-011-2550-7

Leshner, A. I. (1997). Addiction is a brain disease, and it matters. *Science* 278, 45–47. doi: 10.1126/science.278.5335.45

Loba, P., Stewart, S. H., Klein, R. M., and Blackburn, J. R. (2001). Manipulations of the features of standard video lottery terminal (VLT) games: effects in pathological and non-pathological gamblers. *J. Gambl. Stud.* 17, 297–320. doi: 10.1023/A:1013639729908

Martinez, D., Narendran, R., Foltin, R. W., Slifstein, M., Hwang, D. R., Broft, A., et al. (2007). Amphetamine-induced dopamine release: markedly blunted in cocaine dependence and predictive of the choice to self-administer cocaine. *Am. J. Psychiatry* 164, 622–629. doi: 10.1176/appi.ajp.164.4.622

Mateo, Y., Lack, C. M., Morgan, D., Roberts, D. C., and Jones, S. R. (2005). Reduced dopamine terminal function and insensitivity to cocaine following cocaine binge self-administration and deprivation. *Neuropsychopharmacology* 30, 1455–1463. doi: 10.1038/sj.npp.1300687

Nestler, E. J. (2001). Molecular basis of long-term plasticity underlying addiction. *Nat. Rev. Neurosci.* 2, 119–128. doi: 10.1038/35053570

Nieuwenhuis, S., Heslenfeld, D. J., von Geusau, N. J., Mars, R. B., Holroyd, B., and Yeung, N. (2005). Activity in human reward-sensitive brain areas is strongly context dependent. *Neuroimage* 25, 1302–1309. doi: 10.1016/j.neuroimage.2004.12.043

Pierce, R. C., and Kalivas, P. W. (1997). A circuitry model of the expression of behavioral sensitization to amphetamine-like psychostimulants. *Brain Res. Brain Res. Rev.* 25, 192. doi: 10.1016/S0165-0173(97)00021-0

Robbins, T. W., and Everitt, B. J. (1999). Drug addiction: bad habits add up. *Nature* 398, 567–570. doi: 10.1038/19208

Robinson, T. E., Becker, J. B., and Presty, S. K. (1982). Long-term facilitation of amphetamine-induced rotational behavior and striatal dopamine release produced by a single exposure to amphetamine: sex differences. *Brain Res.* 253, 231–241. doi: 10.1016/0006-8993(82)90690-4

Robinson, T. E., and Berridge, K. C. (1993). The neural basis of drug craving: an incentive-sensitization theory of addiction. *Brain Res. Brain Res. Rev.* 18, 247–291. doi: 10.1016/0165-0173(93)90013-P

Robinson, T. E., and Berridge, K. C. (2001). Incentive-sensitization and addiction. *Addiction* 96, 103–114. doi: 10.1046/j.1360-0443.2001.9611038.x

Singer, B. F., Scott-Railton, J., and Vezina, P. (2012). Unpredictable saccharin reinforcement enhances locomotor responding to amphetamine. *Behav. Brain Res.* 226, 340–344. doi: 10.1016/j.bbr.2011.09.003

Singh, V., and Khan, A. (2012). Decision making in the reward and punishment variants of the iowa gambling task: evidence of "foresight" or "framing"? *Front. Neurosci.* 6:107. doi: 10.3389/fnins.2012.00107

Skinner, B. F. (1953). *Science and Human Behavior.* New York, NY: Free Press.

Smart, K., Desmond, R. C., Poulos, C. X., and Zack, M. (2013). Modafinil increases reward salience in a slot machine game in low and high impulsivity pathological gamblers. *Neuropharmacology* 73, 66–74. doi: 10.1016/j. neuropharm.2013.05.015

Tremblay, A. M., Desmond, R. C., Poulos, C. X., and Zack, M. (2011). Haloperidol modifies instrumental aspects of slot machine gambling in pathological gamblers and healthy controls. *Addict. Biol.* 16, 467–484. doi: 10.1111/j.1369-1600.2010.00208.x

Vanderschuren, L. J., and Kalivas, P. W. (2000). Alterations in dopaminergic and glutamatergic transmission in the induction and expression of behavioral sensitization: a critical review of preclinical studies. *Psychopharmacology (Berl.)* 151, 99–120. doi: 10.1007/s002130000493

Vanderschuren, L. J., and Pierce, R. C. (2010). Sensitization processes in drug addiction. *Curr. Top. Behav. Neurosci.* 3, 179–195. doi: 10.1007/7854_2009_21

Vanderschuren, L. J., Schoffelmeer, A. N., Mulder, A. H., and De Vries, T. J. (1999). Dopaminergic mechanisms mediating the long-term expression of locomotor sensitization following pre-exposure to morphine or amphetamine. *Psychopharmacology (Berl.)* 143, 244–253. doi: 10.1007/s002130050943

Verdejo-Garcia, A., Lawrence, A. J., and Clark, L. (2008). Impulsivity as a vulnerability marker for substance-use disorders: review of findings from high-risk research, problem gamblers and genetic association studies. *Neurosci. Biobehav. Rev.* 32, 777–810. doi: 10.1016/j.neubiorev.2007.11.003

Vezina, P. (2004). Sensitization of midbrain dopamine neuron reactivity and the self-administration of psychomotor stimulant drugs. *Neurosci. Biobehav. Rev.* 27, 827–839. doi: 10.1016/j.neubiorev.2003.11.001

Volkow, N. D., Wang, G. J., Fowler, J. S., Logan, J., Gatley, S. J., Hitzemann, R.,et al. (1997). Decreased striatal dopaminergic responsiveness in detoxified cocaine-dependent subjects. *Nature* 386, 830–833. doi: 10.1038/386830a0

Volkow, N. D., Wang, G. J., Fowler, J. S., and Tomasi, D., (2012). Addiction circuitry in the human brain. *Annu. Rev. Pharmacol. Toxicol.* 52, 321–336. doi: 10.1146/annurev-pharmtox-010611-134625

Winer, B. (ed.). (1971). *Statistical Principles in Experimental Design*. New York, NY: McGraw-Hill.

Zack, M., and Poulos, C. X. (2004). Amphetamine primes motivation to gamble and gambling-related semantic networks in problem gamblers. *Neuropsychopharmacology* 29, 195–207. doi: 10.1038/sj.npp.1300333

Zack, M., and Poulos, C. X. (2009). Parallel roles for dopamine in pathological gambling and psychostimulant addiction. *Curr. Drug Abuse Rev.* 2, 11–25. doi: 10.2174/1874473710902010011

Zamudio, S., Fregoso, T., Miranda, A., De La Cruz, F., and Flores, G. (2005). Strain differences of dopamine receptor levels and dopamine related behaviors in rats. *Brain Res. Bull.* 65, 339–347. doi: 10.1016/j.brainresbull.2005.01.009

16

Neuronal nicotinic acetylcholine receptors: common molecular substrates of nicotine and alcohol dependence

*Linzy M. Hendrickson, Melissa J. Guildford and Andrew R. Tapper ***

Department of Psychiatry, Brudnick Neuropsychiatric Research Institute, University of Massachusetts Medical School, Worcester, MA, USA

Edited by:
Nicholas W. Gilpin, Louisiana State University Health Sciences Center New Orleans, USA

Reviewed by:
Shaolin Wang, University of Virginia, USA
Darlene H. Brunzell, Virginia Commonwealth University, USA
Shafiqur Rahman, South Dakota State University, USA

*Correspondence:
Andrew R. Tapper, Department of Psychiatry, Brudnick Neuropsychiatric Research Institute, University of Massachusetts Medical School, 303 Belmont Street, Worcester, MA 01604, USA.
e-mail: andrew.tapper@ umassmed.edu

Alcohol and nicotine are often co-abused. As many as 80–95% of alcoholics are also smokers, suggesting that ethanol and nicotine, the primary addictive component of tobacco smoke, may functionally interact in the central nervous system and/or share a common mechanism of action. While nicotine initiates dependence by binding to and activating neuronal nicotinic acetylcholine receptors (nAChRs), ligand-gated cation channels normally activated by endogenous acetylcholine (ACh), ethanol is much less specific with the ability to modulate multiple gene products including those encoding voltage-gated ion channels, and excitatory/inhibitory neurotransmitter receptors. However, emerging data indicate that ethanol interacts with nAChRs, both directly and indirectly, in the mesocorticolimbic dopaminergic (DAergic) reward circuitry to affect brain reward systems. Like nicotine, ethanol activates DAergic neurons of the ventral tegmental area (VTA) which project to the nucleus accumbens (NAc). Blockade of VTA nAChRs reduces ethanol-mediated activation of DAergic neurons, NAc DA release, consumption, and operant responding for ethanol in rodents. Thus, ethanol may increase ACh release into the VTA driving activation of DAergic neurons through nAChRs. In addition, ethanol potentiates distinct nAChR subtype responses to ACh and nicotine *in vitro* and in DAergic neurons. The smoking cessation therapeutic and nAChR partial agonist, varenicline, reduces alcohol consumption in heavy drinking smokers and rodent models of alcohol consumption. Finally, single nucleotide polymorphisms in nAChR subunit genes are associated with alcohol dependence phenotypes and smoking behaviors in human populations. Together, results from pre-clinical, clinical, and genetic studies indicate that nAChRs may have an inherent role in the abusive properties of ethanol, as well as in nicotine and alcohol co-dependence.

Keywords: **nicotine, alcoholism, acetylcholine, nicotinic receptors, mesolimbic dopamine system**

INTRODUCTION

Alcoholism is the third leading cause of preventable mortality in the world (Mokdad et al., 2004). Worldwide, about 2 billion people consume alcohol, with 76.3 million who have diagnosable alcohol use disorders (AUDs). Additionally, when analyzing the global burden of this disease, alcohol causes 2.5 million deaths per year (4% of the worldwide total) (World Health Organization, 2011). The estimated economic cost of alcoholism in the US alone, due to health care costs as well as productivity impacts such as lost wages, was $220 billion in 2005, which was significantly higher than cancer ($196 billion) or obesity ($133 billion) (CASA, 2000).

Interestingly, several reports from the 1980s to 1990s have estimated that 80% of alcohol-dependent people are also smokers (Bobo, 1992; Miller and Gold, 1998) and that smokers have an increased risk of developing AUDs (DiFranza and Guerrera, 1990; Grant et al., 2004). In addition, while the smoking rates in the general population of the U.S. have dramatically decreased over the past two decades, smoking has remained high in alcoholic individuals (Meyerhoff et al., 2006), with current estimates still between 70 and 75% (Bobo and Husten, 2000). These high rates of co-abuse of nicotine and alcohol have led some researchers to define this population as "alcoholic smokers" as compared to "smokers" (Littleton et al., 2007). Many hypotheses have been proposed as to the

basis of the high rates of nicotine and alcohol co-abuse. For example, it is possible that alcohol use leads to nicotine use or vice versa (Tyndale, 2003), or that because alcohol and nicotine are legal and readily available, the likelihood of their co-use is increased (Funk et al., 2006). However, mounting genetic, pre-clinical, and clinical evidence indicates that neuronal nicotinic acetylcholine receptors (nAChRs), the molecular targets of nicotine that initiate dependence in smokers, may also contribute to alcohol's abusive properties. In addition, neuronal nAChRs may represent common molecular targets where nicotine and ethanol functionally interact, potentially explaining the widespread co-morbidity between smoking and alcohol consumption. The focus of this review is to highlight this evidence, summarize recent findings, and identify gaps in knowledge regarding the role of nAChRs in alcohol dependence and nicotine and alcohol co-abuse.

NEURONAL nAChRs

Neuronal nAChRs are ligand-gated cation channels that are activated by the endogenous neurotransmitter acetylcholine (ACh) and the exogenous tertiary alkaloid nicotine (Albuquerque et al., 2009). They belong to the superfamily of Cys-loop ligand-gated ion channels that include receptors for γ-amino butyric acid (GABA, the $GABA_A$, and $GABA_C$ receptor), glycine, and

5-hydroxytryptamine (5-HT$_3$) (Le Novere and Changeux, 1995; Changeux and Edelstein, 1998). These ligand-gated ion channels have similar structural and functional features. All subunits in this family contain a pair of disulfide-bonded cysteines separated by 13 residues (Cys-loop) in their extracellular amino terminus (Karlin, 2002).

Neuronal nAChRs, like all members of the cys-loop family of ligand-gated ion channels are formed by the arrangement of five subunits to create a central pore (Albuquerque et al., 2009). The structure of neuronal nAChRs is homologous to muscle nAChRs (Karlin, 2002), for which the atomic structure has been determined from electron microscopy studies from the fish electric organ (*Torpedo* nAChRs) (Miyazawa et al., 2003; Unwin, 2005). Each nAChR gene encodes a protein subunit consisting of a large amino-terminal extracellular domain composed of β-strands, four trans-membrane α-helices segments (M1-M4), a variable intracellular loop between M3 and M4, and an extracellular carboxy-terminus (Corringer et al., 2000) (**Figure 1A**). The extracellular N-terminus contains the ACh binding domain that forms a hydrophobic pocket located between adjacent subunits in an assembled receptor (Sine, 2002). The M2 segment of all five subunits forms the conducting pore of the channel, and regions in the M2 intracellular loop contribute to cation selectivity and channel conductivity (Corringer et al., 2000) (**Figure 1B**).

In vertebrates, 12 genes encoding 12 distinct neuronal nAChR subunits have been identified (Cholinergic Receptor Nicotinic Alpha: CHRNA2-10 and Cholinergic Receptor Nicotinic Beta: CHRNB2-4 encoding α2-α10 and β2-β4 nAChR subunits, respectively all of which can be found in humans and other mammals, except for α8 which has only been identified in avian species (Millar and Gotti, 2009). Subunits are classified as either α-, by the presence of a Cys-Cys pair near the start of TM1, or non-α (β)

when the Cys pair is missing (Le Novere and Changeux, 1995; Changeux and Edelstein, 1998).

Five subunits combine to form two classes of receptors: homomeric receptors containing only α subunits (α7-α9) or heteromeric receptors that contain α and β subunits (α2- α6 and β2-β4) (Dani and Bertrand, 2007) (**Figures 1C,D**). The most abundant subtypes in the brain are the low affinity α7 homomeric and high affinity α4β2* heteromeric nAChRs. An asterisk in nAChR nomenclature (i.e., α4*, α4β2*) indicates that other unidentified nAChR subunits may also be present and can be read as "α4 subunit containing nAChRs." Importantly, heteromeric nAChRs are incredibly complex as they can contain two or three alpha subunits co-assembled with two or three beta subunits. For example, α4β2 nAChRs can be formed by either two α and three β subunits [(α4)$_2$(β2)$_3$] or three α and two β subunits [(α4)$_3$(β2)$_2$] (Zwart and Vijverberg, 1998; Nelson et al., 2003; Moroni et al., 2006). Each stoichiometry of the nAChR exhibits distinct sensitivity to agonist: [(α4)$_2$(β2)$_3$] nAChRs have a higher sensitivity to agonist (EC$_{50}$ = ~1 μM ACh); whereas [(α4)$_3$(β2)$_2$] nAChRs have a lower sensitivity to agonist (EC$_{50}$ = ~100 μM ACh) (Buisson and Bertrand, 2001; Nelson et al., 2003; Moroni et al., 2006). In addition, more than one type of alpha and/or beta subunit may be present in a functional receptor. For example, a subtype identified in midbrain dopaminergic (DAergic) neurons contains α4 and β2 subunits co-assembled with α6 and β3 subunits to form the α4α6β2β3* nAChR (Salminen et al., 2004, 2007; Zhao-Shea et al., 2011; Liu et al., 2012). This subunit diversity allows for a vast array of nAChR subtypes each with distinct pharmacological and biophysical properties (McGehee and Role, 1995; Gotti et al., 2007).

Neuronal nAChRs can exist in three conformational states and are regulated by exposure to agonist: closed at rest, when the receptor has low affinity for agonist and the channel is closed; the active

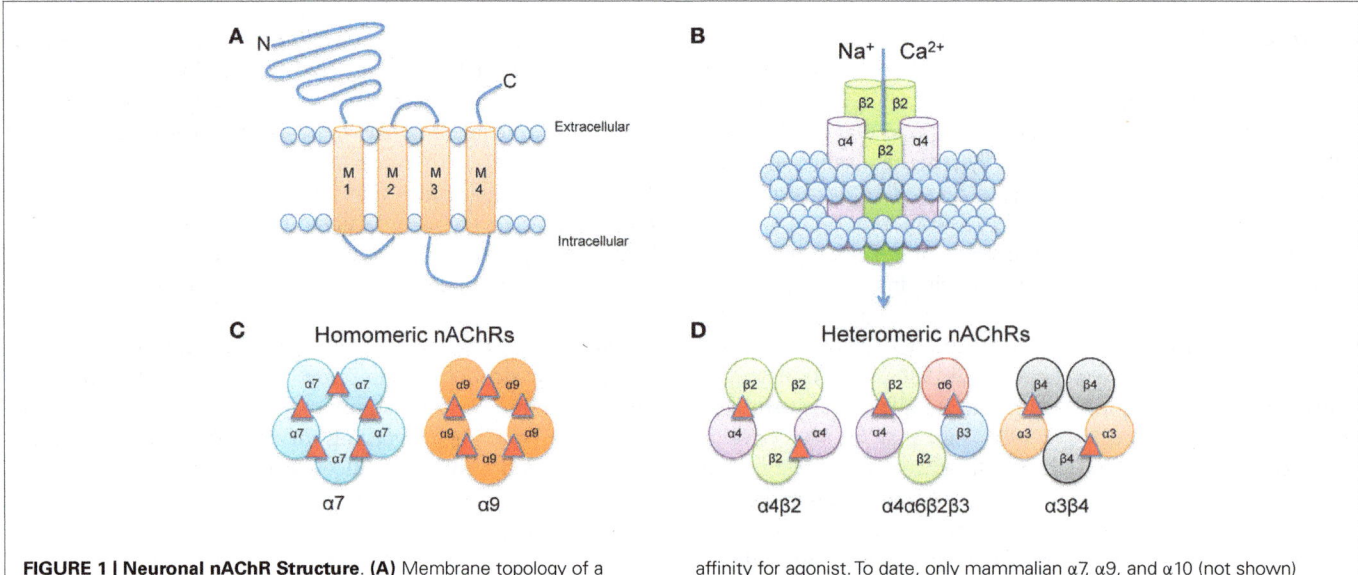

FIGURE 1 | Neuronal nAChR Structure. (A) Membrane topology of a neuronal nAChR subunit. Each nAChR subunit contains four transmembrane domains (M1-M4), an extracellular amino- and carboxy-terminus, and a prominent M3-M4 intracellular loop of variable length. **(B)** Five subunits coassemble to form a functional subunit. **(C)** Homomeric receptors consist of α subunits only and usually have low

affinity for agonist. To date, only mammalian α7, α9, and α10 (not shown) subunits may form functional homomers. **(D)** The majority of high affinity nAChRs are heteromeric and consist of a combination of α and β subunits. Importantly, multiple α subunits may coassemble with multiple β subunits in the pentameric nAChR complex (illustrated here by α4α6β3β2). ACh binding sites are depicted as red triangles.

state, when agonist occupies the ligand binding site and the channel is open allowing cations to flow down their electrochemical gradient; and the desensitized state, when the channel is occluded and the receptor is unresponsive to ligand (Dani and Bertrand, 2007; Albuquerque et al., 2009).

Interestingly, while nAChRs mediate fast, direct synaptic transmission at neuromuscular junctions and autonomic ganglia, there are very few examples of fast nicotinic transmission in the mammalian brain (Dani and Bertrand, 2007). However, neuronal nAChRs are expressed at the soma in neurons where they presumably modulate excitability directly. In addition, a significant proportion of nAChRs are located on presynaptic terminals (Role and Berg, 1996) where they facilitate Ca^{2+} dependent release of neurotransmitters (McGehee et al., 1995; Wonnacott, 1997). This may occur indirectly as a result of Na^+ influx causing membrane depolarization and activation of voltage-gated Ca^{2+} channels or directly through Ca^{2+} influx through the channel itself (Albuquerque et al., 2009).

ETHANOL MODULATION OF NEURONAL nAChRs: *IN VITRO* STUDIES

While ethanol modulates several ligand-gated ion channels including $GABA_A$, NMDA, and $5-HT_3$ receptors (For a review see Spanagel, 2009), ethanol also potently modulates nAChRs at low concentrations of ethanol ($100\,\mu M$–$10\,mM$), identifying nAChRs as potential targets for ethanol action (Nagata et al., 1996). In heterologous expression systems, the effect of ethanol on nAChRs depends on the subunit composition of the nAChR. Expression of different combinations of human neuronal nAChR alpha and beta subunits in *Xenopus* oocytes, indicate acute ethanol ($75\,mM$) potentiates ACh-induced current of $\alpha2\beta4$, $\alpha4\beta4$, $\alpha2\beta2$, and $\alpha4\beta2$ nAChRs while lower concentrations of ethanol (20–$50\,mM$) inhibits nicotine-induced current of $\alpha7$ nAChRs and all concentrations of ethanol tested have no effect on $\alpha3\beta2$ or $\alpha3\beta4$ nAChRs (Cardoso et al., 1999). Similar ethanol effects on heterologous expression of rat nAChRs in *Xenopus* oocytes have been observed except that ethanol could potentiate or inhibit $\alpha3\beta4$ nAChRs at all ethanol concentrations tested likely reflecting oocyte batch to batch variability. In cultured rat cortical neurons, ACh-evoked nAChR currents insensitive to α-bungarotoxin (α-Bgtx), which blocks $\alpha7$ nAChRs (i.e., heteromeric nAChRs) are significantly enhanced by physiologically relevant concentrations of ethanol while nAChRs sensitive to α-Bgtx (i.e., $\alpha7$ homomeric nAChRs) are inhibited (Aistrup et al., 1999). Although not tested directly the α-Bgtx insensitive current profile was most similar to native $\alpha4\beta2^*$ nAChRs (Marszalec et al., 1999).

Similar to other ligand-gated ion channels, ethanol potentiation of nAChRs is hypothesized to be a result of the ethanol-induced stabilization of the open channel state of the receptor (Wu et al., 1994; Forman and Zhou, 1999; Zuo et al., 2004). Site directed cysteine mutagenesis and covalent labeling with sulfhydryl reagents indicate that amino acid residues in the pore forming M2 region of neuronal nAChR at least partly contribute to the ethanol binding pocket (Borghese et al., 2002, 2003a,b). While individual amino acid residues forming the ethanol binding pocket may be distinct from other cys-loop receptors, the overall motif, the extracellular domain of M2, is critical for ethanol actions on nAChRs as well

as $GABA_A$ and glycine receptors (Borghese et al., 2003a). Additionally, it is possible that the ethanol-induced inhibitory effect seen with $\alpha7$ nAChRs is due to the inherently fast desensitization rate of these receptors, implying that ethanol inhibition results in enhanced desensitization (Dopico and Lovinger, 2009). Thus, these and *in vivo* studies discussed below, suggest that ethanol modulation of nAChRs, either by enhancing or inhibiting function, may contribute to (1) the inherent mechanism of action of ethanol reward and (2) the common co-abuse of nicotine and alcohol.

NEURONAL nAChR EXPRESSION IN THE MESOCORTICOLIMBIC DA PATHWAY

Although neuronal nAChRs are expressed throughout the CNS, most studies focusing on the role of nAChRs in addiction have examined the mesocorticolimbic "reward" circuitry. Indeed, it is widely accepted that the mesocorticolimbic dopamine system plays a central role in modulating the rewarding effects of drugs of abuse (Wise and Bozarth, 1987; Koob, 1992).

The ventral tegmental area (VTA) is located in the ventral midbrain, medial to the substantia nigra, and ventral to the red nucleus. It is referred to as an "area" and not considered to be a "nucleus" because the cryoarchitecture of the region is not well defined such that the boundaries of the VTA are determined by its neighboring structures (Fields et al., 2007; Ikemoto, 2007). Within the VTA are two main cell populations, DAergic projection neurons, which comprise ~60% of cells in this region (Swanson, 1982), as well as local GABAergic interneurons and projection neurons (Carr and Sesack, 2000; Margolis et al., 2006a). The VTA receives inputs from regions throughout the CNS (Geisler and Zahm, 2005) including glutamatergic projections from the prefrontal cortex (PFC) (Sesack and Pickel, 1992), as well as glutamatergic, cholinergic, and GABAergic projections from two groups of mesopontine tegmental area neurons, the pedunculopontine tegmental nucleus (PPTg) and the laterodorsal tegmental nucleus (LDT; **Figure 2A**) (Cornwall et al., 1990; Semba and Fibiger, 1992; Oakman et al., 1995). Other regions projecting to the VTA include the nucleus accumbens (NAc), amygdala, ventral pallidum, superior colliculus, and lateral hypothalamus (For a review see Fields et al., 2007). Additionally, the lateral habenula (LH), a small nucleus that is a part of the epithalamus, has been shown to project to midbrain areas, and modulate the release of DA from the VTA and substantia nigra pars compacta (Herkenham and Nauta, 1979; Ji and Shepard, 2007; Matsumoto and Hikosaka, 2007).

Neurons in the VTA primarily project to the ventromedial striatum including the NAc shell and core as well as smaller projections to the PFC, hippocampus, entorhinal cortex, and lateral septal areas (Fields et al., 2007). Furthermore, studies using retrograde markers have shown that distinct groups of neurons originating in the VTA project to specific forebrain regions (Fallon et al., 1984; Margolis et al., 2006b). Projections to the NAc contain the largest proportion of DA neurons, with 65–85% being DAergic, while the PFC projections are only 30–40% DAergic (Swanson, 1982; Fallon et al., 1984). The remaining component of VTA afferents to the NAc and PFC contain GABAergic neurons (Carr and Sesack, 2000). The VTA is not a homogeneous region and can be divided

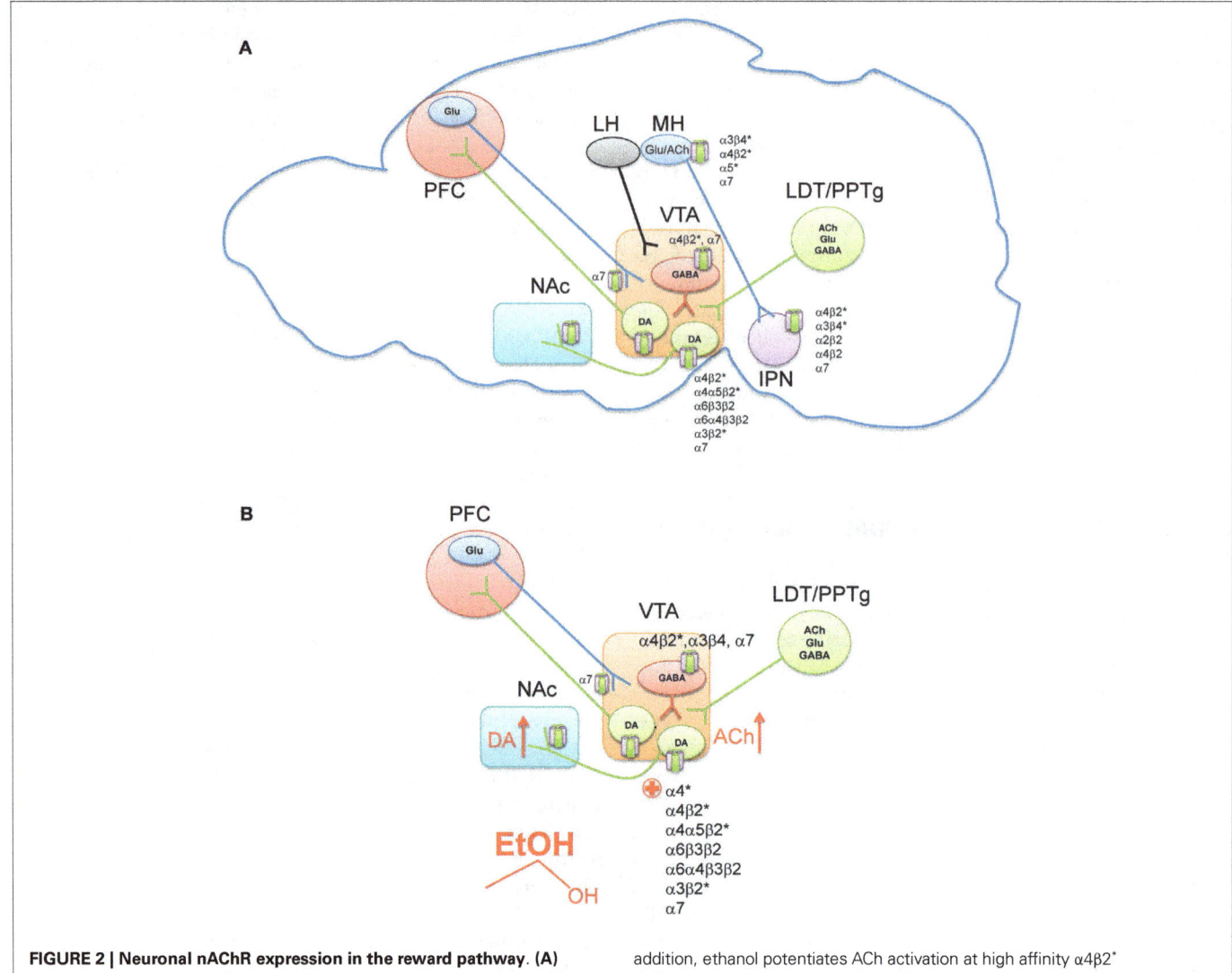

FIGURE 2 | Neuronal nAChR expression in the reward pathway. (A) Sagittal rodent section illustrating the simplified mesocorticolimbic and habenulo-peduncular circuitry. Known neuronal nAChR subtypes expressed in different nuclei are indicated [for a review see (Millar and Gotti, 2009)]. **(B)** In the VTA, alcohol stimulates DAergic neurons at least, in part, via nAChR activation. Ethanol increases ACh release (red arrow, presumably through cholinergic projection from the LDT/PPTg) which in turn activates nAChRs on DAergic neurons driving activity. In addition, ethanol potentiates ACh activation at high affinity α4β2* nAChRs (red plus sign). The effect of alcohol on additional nAChRs in the VTA is unknown. This confluence of events in combination with other effects of alcohol in the VTA ultimately increases DA release in NAc (red arrow). VTA, Ventral tegmental area; NAc, Nucleus accumbens; PFC, Prefrontal cortex; LH, Lateral habenula; MH, Medial habenula; IPN, Interpeduncular nucleus; LDT, Lateral dorsal tegmentum; PPTg, Pedunculopontine tegmentum.

into three sub-regions, the anterior VTA, posterior VTA, and the tail VTA. Additionally, evidence indicates that each region may project to distinct regions of the striatum and may also respond differently to drugs of abuse including nicotine and ethanol (Rodd et al., 2004a, 2010; Ikemoto, 2007; Shabat-Simon et al., 2008; Zhao-Shea et al., 2011). Importantly, nAChRs are robustly expressed in the VTA. DAergic neurons contain several nAChR subtypes including α4β2*, α4α5β2*, α4α6β2*, α6β2*, α3β2*, and α7 (Picciotto et al., 1998; Champtiaux et al., 2002; Marubio et al., 2003; Grady et al., 2007; Gotti et al., 2010; Zhao-Shea et al., 2011; Liu et al., 2012); whereas GABAergic VTA neurons express α4β2, α7, and α3β4 nAChRs (**Figure 2A**) (Klink et al., 2001; Mansvelder et al., 2002; Pidoplichko et al., 2004; Nashmi et al., 2007; Tolu et al., 2012).

NEURONAL nAChRs AND ETHANOL: *IN VIVO* STUDIES

The rewarding or reinforcing properties of ethanol and nicotine, as with most drugs of abuse, are associated with an increase in DA release in the NAc (Di Chiara and Imperato, 1988; Lewis and June, 1990; Benwell and Balfour, 1992; Samson et al., 1992; Diana et al., 1993; Weiss et al., 1993; Lanca, 1994; Pontieri et al., 1996). Both drugs increase the baseline firing frequency of VTA DAergic neurons and also increase the firing pattern from phasic to bursting, facilitating NAc DA release (Mereu et al., 1984; Gessa et al., 1985; Foddai et al., 2004; Exley et al., 2011; Li et al., 2011). Although the precise role of NAc DA release in reward is still under debate (Schultz, 2004; Salamone and Correa, 2012), ethanol- and nicotine-induced release of DA is critical for the onset and maintenance of dependence. Pharmacological blockade of DA receptors, destruction of DA neurons or lesioning of the NAc reduces ethanol and nicotine self-administration (Kiianmaa, 1978; Koob and Weiss, 1990; Corrigall and Coen, 1991; Corrigall et al., 1992, 1994; Rassnick et al., 1993; Ikemoto et al., 1997). In addition, rats will self-administer ethanol or nicotine directly into the VTA (Gatto et al., 1994; Ikemoto et al., 2006), and more specifically, the posterior VTA (Rodd et al., 2004b).

It is becoming increasingly clear that nicotine dependence is initiated by activation of DAergic neurons via nAChRs containing $\alpha 4$ and $\beta 2$ subunits with some contribution of $\alpha 6^*$ nAChRs (Picciotto et al., 1998; Tapper et al., 2004; Maskos et al., 2005; Pons et al., 2008; Exley et al., 2011; Tolu et al., 2012). In the context of this review, we will not focus further on the mechanistic bases of nicotine dependence; rather we direct readers to a recent review article (De Biasi and Dani, 2011). In contrast to nicotine, multiple mechanisms underlying ethanol-mediated activation of VTA DAergic neurons have been proposed including modulation of intrinsic ion channels within these neurons, as well as ethanol-mediated alterations in synaptic input, both excitatory and inhibitory (Okamoto et al., 2006; Job et al., 2007; Xiao and Ye, 2008; Xiao et al., 2009; Rodd et al., 2010; Theile et al., 2011; Guan et al., 2012). However, cholinergic signaling through nAChRs also contributes to NAc DA release and ethanol reinforcement (Blomqvist et al., 1992, 1993, 1996; Ericson et al., 1998; Nadal et al., 1998; Dyr et al., 1999; Le et al., 2000; Soderpalm et al., 2000; Farook et al., 2009a; Kuzmin et al., 2009). One of the most consistent findings implicating nAChRs in ethanol behaviors associated with reward/reinforcement is that the non-specific nAChR antagonist, mecamylamine, reduces ethanol consumption and blocks ethanol-induced DA release in the NAc. Originally discovered by pioneering work of Soderpalm and Engel, systemic mecamylamine significantly reduces ethanol-mediated extracellular DA release in the NAc (Blomqvist et al., 1993), and reduces ethanol consumption in rats (Blomqvist et al., 1996). The effect of mecamylamine is localized to the VTA, as local infusion of the antagonist in rat midbrain but not NAc reduces NAc DA release elicited by ethanol (Blomqvist et al., 1997). VTA infusion of mecamylamine also reduces rat operant responding for ethanol and ethanol-associated cues, as well as consumption during relapse (Lof et al., 2007; Kuzmin et al., 2009). In mice, mecamylamine delivered systemically reduces ethanol consumption in C57Bl/6J mice in the restricted access ethanol consumption "drinking in the dark" (DID) paradigm (Hendrickson et al., 2009), a model of binge drinking (Rhodes et al., 2005, 2007), as well as in the two-bottle choice consumption assay (Farook et al., 2009a). What is mecamylamine's mechanism of action in reducing ethanol consumption? In mice, mecamylamine apparently blocks activation of VTA DAergic neurons by ethanol as measured by c-Fos induction after challenge with an intraperitoneal injection (i.p.) of ethanol (Hendrickson et al., 2009). More recently, it has been demonstrated that mecamylamine blocks ethanol-mediated activation of VTA DAergic neurons in mouse midbrain slices (Liu et al., 2013). Mecamylamine also blocks the ability of ethanol to condition a place preference in mice (Bhutada et al., 2012). Thus, these data suggest that nAChR expressed in the VTA contribute to ethanol activation of DAergic neurons and ethanol reward. The effects of mecamylamine in these pre-clinical models may have predictive

validity as patients administered mecamylamine report reduced pleasurable effects of alcoholic beverages (Chi and de Wit, 2003). As discussed above, ethanol is not a direct agonist at nAChRs; rather it potentiates or inhibits nAChRs depending on subtype. Thus, nAChR involvement in ethanol reward implies that ethanol must increase ACh concentrations in brain regions involved in reward/reinforcement. To date, one study has measured extracellular concentrations of ACh in the VTA of rats that voluntarily consumed ethanol and found that ACh levels were increased after ethanol consumption and shortly thereafter, DA concentrations were elevated in the NAc as well (Larsson et al., 2005). These data indicate that the increase in VTA ACh could drive activation of DAergic neurons through nAChRs (**Figure 2B**). While the predominant VTA cholinergic afferents project from the PPTg and LDT area (Oakman et al., 1995), brain regions that have also been implicated in mediating natural as well as drug-reward behavior (Yeomans et al., 1993), additional experiments will be needed to verify that these inputs mediate ethanol-induced increases in VTA ACh. In addition, the mechanism by which ethanol could elicit an increase in ACh release into the VTA is unknown and warrants further study.

NEURONAL nAChRs AND ALCOHOL: IDENTIFYING RELEVANT SUBTYPES: PHARMACOLOGY

Because mecamylamine blocks virtually all subtypes of nAChRs, it provides little insight into the subunit composition of key nAChRs involved in ethanol activation of DAergic neurons or ethanol behaviors associated with the VTA such as consumption. Thus, several studies have used additional, more selective nAChR antagonists, in an effort to uncover the nAChR subtype(s) that may be involved in ethanol's mechanism of action (**Table 1**). Studies in VTA responses to *nicotine* indicate that DAergic neurons contain several nAChR subtypes including $\alpha 4\beta 2^*$, $\alpha 4\alpha 5\beta 2^*$, $\alpha 4\alpha 6\beta 2^*$, $\alpha 6\beta 2^*$, $\alpha 3\beta 2^*$, and $\alpha 7$ (Picciotto et al., 1998; Champtiaux et al., 2002; Marubio et al., 2003; Grady et al., 2007; Gotti et al., 2010; Zhao-Shea et al., 2011; Liu et al., 2012). Identifying the precise subunit composition of nAChRs involved in ethanol consumption and activation of VTA DAergic neurons is challenging due to the sheer number of potential subunit combinations that may be expressed in the VTA. However, identifying one or more nAChR subtypes involved in ethanol activation of VTA and/or reward may lead to novel targets to reduce consumption. Systemic injection or VTA infusion of the competitive $\alpha 4\beta 2$ nAChR antagonist, dihydro-β-erythroidine (DHβE), in rats, fails to reduce ethanol-mediated DA release in the NAc and ethanol intake (Ericson et al., 2003; Chatterjee et al., 2011). In addition, low doses of DHβE also have little effect on operant responding for ethanol in rats, although a higher dose can reduce responding (Kuzmin et al., 2009). Systemic injection of DHβE does not reduce consumption in mice as measured in the DID assay nor ethanol-induced NAc DA release (Larsson et al., 2002; Hendrickson et al., 2009). Together these data suggest that $\alpha 4\beta 2$ nAChRs may not be critical for ethanol reward and consumption behavior. However, sensitivity of $\alpha 4\beta 2^*$ nAChR blockade by DHβE is dependent on the stoichiometry of the receptor and the expression of other non-$\alpha 4\beta 2$ subunits that may also be present in an $\alpha 4\beta 2^*$ nAChR complex (Harvey and Luetje, 1996; Harvey et al., 1996; Le et al., 2000; Larsson et al., 2002; Ericson

Table 1 | Neuronal nAChR ligands that modulate alcohol behaviors.

Drug	nAChR subtype target	Route of delivery	Effect on ethanol behavior (in rodents)
Mecamylamine	Non-selective antagonist	i.p.	Decreased ethanol intake in rats (Blomqvist et al., 1996)
		i.p.	Decreased ethanol intake in mice (Hendrickson et al., 2009)
		i.p.	Blocked ethanol-induced DA release in NAc in rats (Blomqvist et al., 1993)
		i.p.	Partially counteracted ethanol-induced enhancements of locomotor activity and brain DA turnover in mice (Blomqvist et al., 1992)
		i.p.	Blocked ethanol-induced activation of DA neurons in mice (Hendrickson et al., 2009)
		i.p.	Reduced operant self-administration and blocked deprivation-induced increase in alcohol consumption in rats (Kuzmin et al., 2009)
		VTA	Reduced ethanol-induced accumbal DA release in rats (Ericson et al., 1998)
		i.p.	Reduced ethanol intake in rats (Le et al., 2000)
Nicotine	Agonist	s.c. (chronic)	Increased ethanol intake in rats (Potthoff et al., 1983; Le et al., 2000)
		s.c. (subchronic/acute)	Increased ethanol intake in rats (Blomqvist et al., 1996; Le et al., 2000)
		s.c. (subchronic)	Increased ethanol preference in rats (Blomqvist et al., 1996)
		s.c. (acute)	Enhanced ethanol-induced locomotor stimulation in mice (Blomqvist et al., 1992)
		s.c. (subchronic)	Enhanced ethanol-induced locomotor stimulation in rats (Blomqvist et al., 1996)
		s.c. (subchronic)	Enhanced DA turnover-increasing effect of ethanol in rats (Johnson et al., 1995)
		s.c. (chronic)	Decreased ethanol intake in rats (Sharpe and Samson, 2002)
		s.c. (chronic)	Decreased ethanol seeking in rats (Sharpe and Samson, 2002)
		i.p. (acute)	Decreased ethanol intake in mice (Hendrickson et al., 2011)
Varenicline	α4β2 Partial agonist high affinity α3β2, α3β4, α6*, α7 low affinity binding	i.p. and VTA	Decreased ethanol intake in mice (Hendrickson et al., 2010; Kamens et al., 2010; Santos et al., 2012)
		i.p.	Decreased ethanol intake in rats (Steensland et al., 2007)
		i.p.	Reduced ethanol seeking and consumption with no rebound increase in ethanol after cessation in rats (Steensland et al., 2007)
		i.p.	Reduced operant ethanol self-administration and blocked deprivation-induced relapse-like consumption in rats (Kuzmin et al., 2009)
		s.c.	Blocks increase in extracellular DA in NAc following acute ethanol injection in rats (Ericson et al., 2009)
α-Conotoxin MII	α6*, α3β2* Antagonist	VTA	Reduced alcohol-induced DA release in mice (Larsson et al., 2004)
		VTA	Reduced locomotor stimulation in mice (Larsson et al., 2004)
		VTA	Decreased self-administration of ethanol in rats (Kuzmin et al., 2009)
		VTA	Blocked deprivation-induced relapse-like ethanol consumption in rats (Kuzmin et al., 2009)
DHβE	α4β2* antagonist	s.c.	No effect on ethanol consumption in rats (Le et al., 2000)
		s.c.	No effect on DA-enhancing effect of ethanol in mice (Larsson et al., 2002)
		i.p.	Inhibited ethanol intake at 4mg/kg in rats (Kuzmin et al., 2009)
		s.c.	No effect on ethanol consumption in rats (Chatterjee et al., 2011)
MLA	α7* antagonist	i.p.	No effect on DA-enhancing effect of ethanol in mice (Larsson et al., 2002)
		i.p.	No effect on self-administration of ethanol or deprivation-induced relapse-like drinking in rats (Kuzmin et al., 2009)
		i.p.	No effect on ethanol consumption in DID in mice (Hendrickson et al., 2009)
α-Conotoxin PIA	α6* antagonist	VTA	No effect on ethanol-induced locomotor stimulation or enhanced DA release in mice (Jerlhag et al., 2006)

(Continued)

Table 1 | Continued

Drug	nAChR subtype target	Route of delivery	Effect on ethanol behavior (in rodents)
CP-601932	α3β4 and α4β2 high affinity partial agonist	s.c.	Decreased ethanol consumption and operant self-administration in rats (Chatterjee et al., 2011)
PF-4575180	α3β4 high affinity partial agonist	s.c.	Decreased ethanol consumption and operant self-administration in rats (Chatterjee et al., 2011)
Lobeline	Non-selective antagonist, particularly at β2* nAChRs	s.c.	Reduced ethanol consumption in DID and during continuous ethanol access in mice (Farook et al., 2009b; Sajja and Rahman, 2011)
		s.c.	Reduced ethanol-induced DA and its metabolite levels in ventral striatum in mice (Sajja et al., 2010)
Cytisine	Low-efficacy partial agonist with high affinity for α4β2* nAChRs. Full agonist at β4* and α7* nAChRs	s.c.	Reduced ethanol consumption in DID in mice and during continuous ethanol access in mice (Hendrickson et al., 2009; Sajja and Rahman, 2011)
		s.c.	Reduced ethanol-induced DA and its metabolite in mice (Sajja et al., 2010)
Sazetidine-A	Highly selective α4β2 desensitizer	s.c.	Reduces alcohol intake in rats (Rezvani et al., 2010)

et al., 2003; Moroni et al., 2006; Lof et al., 2007; Kamens and Phillips, 2008). The α7 selective antagonist, methyllycaconitine (MLA), does not affect ethanol-mediated behaviors including consumption, ethanol-induced DA release in NAc and ethanol operant responding in rats, as well as, consumption in mice. While caution with interpretation of these results is warranted due to data indicating higher concentrations of MLA may also antagonize non-α7 nAChRs (of an unknown nAChR subtype that may include α6 and/or α3 subunits (Mogg et al., 2002)), homomeric α7 nAChRs may not be involved in ethanol reinforcement (Larsson et al., 2002; Hendrickson et al., 2009; Kuzmin et al., 2009). On the other hand, the α3β2*, β3*, and α6* subtype-selective antagonist, α-conotoxin MII (Cartier et al., 1996), when infused into the VTA does inhibit ethanol consumption, operant responding, and DA release in the NAc of rats (Larsson et al., 2004, 2005; Kuzmin et al., 2009) and reduce ethanol-induced locomotor stimulation and increases in NAc DA release in mice (Larsson et al., 2004; Jerlhag et al., 2006). Importantly, recent data indicate that approximately half of α-conotoxin MII-sensitive nAChRs in the striatum also contain the α4 subunit (Grady et al., 2007; Salminen et al., 2007) and deletion of β2* nAChRs nearly abolishes α-conotoxin MII binding in the VTA (Marubio et al., 2003). However, infusion of α-conotoxin PIA, which may have more selectivity for α6* nAChRs than α3* nAChRs (Dowell et al., 2003), failed to reduce ethanol-induced DA release in NAc when infused in the VTA suggesting that α3* nAChRs may be more critical for ethanol reward. Finally, systemic injection of the α3β4* nAChR-selective antagonist 18-methoxycoranaridine (18-MC) reduces ethanol consumption in alcohol-preferring rats (Rezvani et al., 1997). However, direct infusion of 18-MC into the VTA fails to reduce alcohol consumption (Carnicella et al., 2010) in rats consistent with data indicating low expression of β4* nAChRs in VTA DAergic neurons (Gotti et al., 2010; Zhao-Shea et al., 2011).

NEURONAL nAChRs AND ALCOHOL: IDENTIFYING RELEVANT SUBTYPES: MOUSE GENETICS

Behavioral studies in genetically engineered mice have also been used to glean information on nAChR subtypes that may be involved in alcohol consumption and reward. Mice that do not express chrnb2, the gene encoding the nAChR β2 subunit (β2 KO) consume and prefer ethanol in a 24 h access two-bottle choice paradigm similar to wild-type (WT) littermates indicating that β2* nAChR may not play a role in baseline ethanol consumption in this assay (Kamens et al., 2010). Similarly, α6 KO and β3 KO mice consume ethanol similar to WT in a 24 h access two-bottle choice consumption assay (Kamens et al., 2012). Female α7 KO mice consume significantly less ethanol in this paradigm compared to female WT littermates; whereas male α7 KO and WT mice consume similar amounts of ethanol indicating a potential gender effect of α7 nAChRs on ethanol consumption (Kamens et al., 2010). α5 KO mice do not differ in acute ethanol consumption, as measured by the DID assay, compared to WT (Santos et al., 2012). Together, these data indicate that nAChRs containing α5, α6, β2, or β3 subunits may not be critical for ethanol consumption *per se*. However, as nAChRs are robustly expressed in a variety of brain regions, subunit compensation may occur in a KO mouse background (Drago et al., 2003). Thus, these results will need to be verified using shRNAs to knock-down nAChR subunits in discreet brain regions. Interestingly, sleep time elicited by high doses of ethanol is increased in α6 and α5, but not β3 KO mice compared to their WT littermates indicating a role for α6* and α5* nAChR in alcohol-induced sedation (Kamens et al., 2012; Santos et al., 2012).

In contrast to the majority of KO models discussed above, acute ethanol consumption in the DID paradigm is significantly less in α4 KO mice compared to WT for high (20%) but not low (2%) concentrations of ethanol implicating a role for α4* nAChR in ethanol consumption (Hendrickson et al., 2010, 2011). In addition, the ability of ethanol to condition a place preference in α4 KO mice is reduced compared to WT. Conversely, in mice harboring a point mutation in α4* nAChRs that renders receptors hypersensitive to agonist [the Leu9′Ala α4 knock-in line (Tapper et al., 2004; Fonck et al., 2005)], a sub-threshold dose of ethanol is sufficient to condition a place preference indicating that α4* nAChRs modulate alcohol reward (Liu et al., 2013). Consistent with behavioral data, ethanol activation of VTA DAergic neurons is reduced in α4 KO midbrain slices and more robust in Leu9′Ala midbrain slices. Finally, ethanol potentiates the response to bath applied ACh in midbrain DAergic neurons and potentiation is abolished in DAergic neurons of α4 KO mice (Liu et al., 2013). Together, these data indicate that α4* nAChRs in VTA DAergic neurons may contribute to ethanol activation of the VTA and alcohol reward although additional experiments are needed to confirm that the observed difference in ethanol-mediated behaviors in these mouse models are due to α4* nAChRs in the VTA as these receptors are expressed throughout the CNS (Baddick and Marks, 2011).

NICOTINE AND ALCOHOL INTERACTIONS: *IN VIVO* STUDIES

Human studies have shown that individuals dependent on alcohol have higher rates of nicotine dependence (Room, 2004), and smokers tend to consume more ethanol than non-smoking alcohol users (York and Hirsch, 1995). Unlike the majority of clinical studies, nicotine administration can either increase ethanol intake (Potthoff et al., 1983; Blomqvist et al., 1996; Smith et al., 1999; Le et al., 2000; Clark et al., 2001; Ericson et al., 2003), or decrease ethanol intake (Nadal et al., 1998; Dyr et al., 1999; Sharpe and Samson, 2002) in rats. These conflicting results have led to a complex and interesting questions: under what conditions (i.e., time delay between nicotine and ethanol, dose of nicotine, length of ethanol presentation, acute versus chronic nicotine/ethanol etc.) does nicotine increase ethanol intake, and what conditions cause a decrease in ethanol intake?

Blomqvist et al. (1996) demonstrated that daily nicotine during ethanol deprivation and ethanol reinstatement increases ethanol intake and preference in rats shown to have a medium baseline preference (25–65%) for ethanol over water. Similarly, Le et al. (2003) demonstrated that rats increased lever presses for ethanol during the course of daily nicotine injection paired 15 min prior to an operant session. These data are in agreement with various other experiments in which nicotine was given either constantly or repeatedly (Potthoff et al., 1983; Smith et al., 1999; Ericson et al., 2000; Olausson et al., 2001). In rats, nicotine can also reinstate alcohol seeking after extinction and increase ethanol self-administration when administered during an ethanol deprivation period (Lopez-Moreno et al., 2004). Interestingly, rats given nicotine only during the relapse period, once self-administration has resumed after a deprivation period, consume less ethanol, and rats given nicotine during both abstinence and relapse increased ethanol intake compared to control (Alen et al., 2009).

In contrast, Sharpe and Samson demonstrated that ethanol intake and lever pressing during operant ethanol self-administration are both decreased after a high dose of nicotine (0.7 mg/kg, subcutaneous injection (s.c.), expressed as free base nicotine) 30 min prior to ethanol self-administration, and with a lower dose of nicotine (0.35 mg/kg, s.c.). While locomotor

depression by nicotine could potentially confound the interpretation of decreased ethanol self-administration, this is unlikely as nicotine injections did not decrease sucrose self-administration. Thus, Sharpe and Samson (2002) propose that nicotine could be acting as a reinforcer of ethanol, decreasing the amount of ethanol necessary to achieve satiety. This is in agreement with other studies in which nicotine is administered either immediately prior to, or within 30 min of, ethanol presentation or self-administration (Nadal et al., 1998; Damaj, 2001).

To reconcile differences in nicotine effects on ethanol consumption and self-administration, Hauser et al. demonstrated that acute nicotine administration affects ethanol seeking and relapse in a time-dependent manner. Nicotine injection immediately prior to an ethanol operant self-administration session in ethanol preferring rats elicits reduced responding for ethanol compared to a saline injection; whereas nicotine exposure 4 h prior will increase responses (Hauser et al., 2012). These data indicate that acute nicotine may initially act as a substitute for ethanol at the immediate time-point causing a reduction in craving for ethanol and, at the later time-point, nicotine may lead to desensitization of nAChRs in the brain, enhancing ethanol seeking.

As in rats, acute nicotine immediately prior to presentation of ethanol in the DID paradigm reduces consumption in mice (Hendrickson et al., 2009); whereas chronic nicotine treatment increases consumption (Sajja and Rahman, 2012). The reduction of ethanol consumption is mediated by nAChRs containing the α4 subunit: nicotine fails to reduce consumption in α4 KO mice; whereas acute sub-threshold nicotine doses are sufficient to reduce consumption in Leu9′Ala mice (Hendrickson et al., 2011). The effect of acute nicotine activates the posterior VTA as measured by increased c-Fos in mouse VTA DAergic neurons while an additional injection of ethanol does not further activate these neurons, consistent with nicotine substituting for ethanol during this treatment schedule (Hendrickson et al., 2009).

The mechanistic basis of chronic nicotine on ethanol consumption is unclear. However, nicotine potentiates the response to ethanol in VTA DAergic neurons (Clark and Little, 2004) and repeated nicotine infusion into the posterior VTA increases the stimulatory effects of ethanol (Ding et al., 2012). These data indicate that chronic nicotine treatment may actually increase the reinforcing/rewarding properties of alcohol. Interestingly, chronic nicotine upregulates midbrain nAChRs which may lead to increased DAergic neuron activation by ethanol (Nashmi et al., 2007).

NEURONAL nAChR LIGANDS FOR REDUCING ETHANOL CONSUMPTION

While several areas of alcoholism research exist, the end goal of the majority of research is to identify new and improved treatment options for those suffering from alcoholism. Currently, there are three FDA approved medications for treating alcoholism. The first, disulfiram, was approved in 1954, and is classified as an anti-relapse medication (Christensen et al., 1991). It is an acetaldehyde dehydrogenase inhibitor, which after drinking alcohol allows the buildup of acetaldehyde in the blood, causing symptoms including headache, nausea, vomiting, weakness, mental confusion, or anxiety (Christensen et al., 1991). However, in recent years, many physicians have stopped prescribing this drug because of the severe symptoms it causes and the fact that if a patient wished to drink again, they could simply not take their medication. Naltrexone, available since 1994, is a competitive opioid receptor antagonist that works by decreasing the euphoric effects produced by alcohol. It is considered to be an anti-relapsing drug because it decreases heavy drinking in patients with alcoholism and prevents relapse to heaving drinking (O'Malley et al., 1992; Volpicelli et al., 1992). The third drug, acamprosate, is a partial agonist of NMDA glutamate receptors and an antagonist of metabotropic glutamate receptors and is thought to act as an anti-craving medication by inhibiting glutamate signaling (Mason, 2003; Mason et al., 2006). While European studies have reported modest benefits with acamprosate, these studies have not been reproducible in the US (Pettinati et al., 2006).

Unfortunately, while these medications have been effective for some, only 20–30% of treated patients respond to the anti-craving and anti-relapsing compounds (Spanagel, 2009). Interestingly, new studies have shown that people with different genetic profiles may drink for different reasons, and also that they may respond better to one type of medication versus another. For example, populations with a specific type of mu opioid receptor respond to naltrexone better than others, and this group has been described as "feel good drinkers" (Oslin et al., 2006; Anton et al., 2008). Another population of alcoholics report that they drink to relieve feelings of stress and anxiety (Kuehn, 2009) for which new medications are currently being tested (George et al., 2008). This large variability in patient response is a driving force in identifying new molecular targets for improved pharmacotherapeutic drugs. Consequently, the main focus of alcoholism treatments has been to restore the balance to the different biochemical pathways in the brain that are disrupted during alcohol dependence.

Varenicline, an α4β2 partial agonist clinically approved as a smoking cessation therapeutic (Coe et al., 2005; Gonzales et al., 2006; Jorenby et al., 2006; Tonstad et al., 2006; Steensland et al., 2007), can reduce ethanol intake, ethanol seeking, and cue-induced ethanol reinstatement in rats (Steensland et al., 2007; Wouda et al., 2011) and ethanol consumption in mice (Hendrickson et al., 2010; Kamens et al., 2010; Santos et al., 2012). In addition, varenicline can also reduce the enhancing effect of chronic nicotine on ethanol self-administration in rats (Bito-Onon et al., 2011). Coupled with clinical data indicating that varenicline reduces ethanol consumption in heavy drinking smokers (McKee et al., 2009; Fucito et al., 2011; Mitchell et al., 2012), uncovering the mechanism of action of varenicline could lead to more refined nAChR partial agonists for the treatment of alcoholism. In mice, systemic injection of lower doses of varenicline immediately prior to ethanol bottle presentation reduces ethanol consumption in the DID paradigm (Hendrickson et al., 2010). In addition, this effect of varenicline is reduced in α4 KO mice and enhanced in mice that express α4* nAChR that are hypersensitive to agonist indicating that activation of α4* nAChR may underlie varenicline effects on binge drinking. However, while varenicline was designed to be selective for α4β2* nAChRs at low doses, at high concentrations, varenicline is also a partial agonist at α6β2* nAChRs, a full agonist at α3β4 and α7 nAChRs, as well as at 5-HT$_3$ receptors (Mihalak et al., 2006; Papke et al., 2010; Lummis et al., 2011; Bordia et al., 2012), which may

also explain some of its effects on ethanol consumption especially in response to high doses used to reduce ethanol preference and seeking in most studies using the two-bottle choice 24 h access paradigm of ethanol consumption. Indeed, varenicline still reduces ethanol consumption in β2 and α7 KO mice (Kamens et al., 2010). Varenicline also reduces ethanol consumption in the DID paradigm in α5 KO mice (Santos et al., 2012). Thus, the mechanism of varenicline induced reduction in ethanol consumption and the nAChR subtype responsible for this effect is still unclear. However, acutely, varenicline reduces ethanol-mediated DA release in NAc of rats, an effect that diminishes with repeated exposure of the partial agonist (Ericson et al., 2009), consistent with varenicline reducing the rewarding properties of ethanol. In contrast, a recent clinical study found that varenicline potentiated aversion to ethanol in social drinkers (Childs et al., 2012), suggesting the agonist may reduce consumption through an anti-reward pathway.

In addition to varenicline, pre-clinical data are emerging regarding other nAChR ligands that may prove effective in reducing ethanol consumption. Sazetidine-A, an α4β2* nAChR-selective "desensitizer" and partial agonist can reduces ethanol consumption in rats (Rezvani et al., 2010). Lobeline, an antagonist with high affinity for α4β2* and α3β2* nAChRs reduces ethanol consumption in mice in the DID and two-bottle choice paradigm (Farook et al., 2009b). Cytisine, a partial agonist that preferentially activates high affinity β2* nAChRs at low doses but also is a full β4* nAChR agonist at high doses also reduces ethanol consumption (Bell et al., 2009; Hendrickson et al., 2009; Sajja and Rahman, 2011, 2012). Both lobeline and cytisine reduced ethanol-mediated DA release in ventral striatum of mice consistent with blocking of ethanol reward/reinforcement (Sajja et al., 2010). In addition, lobeline and cytisine also reduce the increase in alcohol consumption that occurs with chronic nicotine exposure in the DID paradigm (Sajja and Rahman, 2012). Finally, novel partial agonists targeting α3β4* nAChRs reduce ethanol consumption and seeking in rats (Chatterjee et al., 2011).

NEURONAL nAChR SUBUNIT GENES AND ALCOHOL: HUMAN GENETIC ASSOCIATION STUDIES

There is growing evidence that suggests that common genes may influence the development of alcohol and nicotine behaviors individually as well as contribute to both disorders in humans (True et al., 1999; Bierut et al., 2000; Madden and Heath, 2002). Using twin studies, it was determined that identical twins are two times as likely to be dependent on alcohol and/or nicotine if the other twin is dependent, compared to fraternal twins (Heath et al., 1997).

Recent genome wide association studies have identified several polymorphisms within genetic loci that includes the nAChR subunit genes CHRNA5/A3/B4 (which encode the nAChR α5, α3, β4 subunit, respectively), that are associated with nicotine dependence, COPD, and lung cancer (Amos et al., 2008; Berrettini et al., 2008; Bierut et al., 2008; Hung et al., 2008; Saccone et al., 2010). Interestingly, genetic variation in these genes has also been associated with age of initiation of smoking and alcohol use and level of response of alcohol use (Joslyn et al., 2008; Schlaepfer et al., 2008). Two SNPs associated with nicotine dependence and lung cancer have been found to also be associated with a low level of response to alcohol, a phenotype considered a risk factor for likelihood of developing an AUD (Joslyn et al., 2008). Thus, common SNPs may confer susceptibility to both nicotine dependence and alcoholism. In addition, genetic variation in CHRNA5, distinct from those associated with nicotine dependence, are also associated with alcohol dependence (Wang et al., 2009). The mechanistic bases for how polymorphisms in CHRNA5/A3/B4 modulate nicotine and alcohol phenotypes are unclear although distinct SNPs in CHRNA5 have been shown to affect $\alpha4\beta2$ nAChR function in vitro and mRNA expression in human brain (Bierut et al., 2008; Wang et al., 2009). It is also unclear if genetic variation in CHRNA5/A3/B4 is specific for modulation of nicotine and alcohol dependence as SNPs are also associated with cocaine and opioid dependence, as well as substance use initiation (Grucza et al., 2008; Sherva et al., 2010; Lubke et al., 2012; but see Chen et al., 2012). Thus, SNPs in this region may affect aspects of addiction common to all drugs of abuse, such as reward, tolerance, or withdrawal. Alternatively, CHRNA5/A3/B4 may play a role in general risk taking behavior or impulsivity which may significantly predispose one to drug addiction (Stephens et al., 2012).

Additional genes encoding nAChR subunits have been linked to alcohol phenotype. SNPs in CHRNB2, have been associated with the subjective responses to both alcohol and nicotine (Ehringer et al., 2007); whereas only a modest association of alcohol responses with CHRNA4 SNPs were reported. An additional study identified a CHRNA4 SNP associated with alcoholism in a small Korean population (Kim et al., 2004). Finally, SNPs within CHRNA6 and CHRNB3 are associated with heavy alcohol consumption (Hoft et al., 2009; Landgren et al., 2009), as well as smoking behavior (Thorgeirsson et al., 2010).

Together these human genetic studies indicate that heritable polymorphisms within nAChR subunit genes may predispose distinct populations to increased risk for AUDs and, perhaps nicotine and alcohol co-dependence.

FUTURE DIRECTIONS

Emerging evidence indicates that SNPs within genes encoding nAChR subunits are associated with alcohol dependence phenotypes. Additional research is needed to understand how SNPs in these subunits modulate the effects of ethanol on nAChRs directly and in animal models of ethanol dependence. It will also be critical to expand the focus of nAChRs and ethanol effects on circuits outside of the mesocorticolimbic pathway. Indeed, recent data indicate that nicotine intake is controlled by the habenulo-peduncular axis. This circuit consists of a small, epithalamic structure, the habenula (Hb) which can be divided into medial (MH) and lateral (LH) sub-regions (Hikosaka, 2010). The Hb projects

to its target brain regions through a conspicuous bundle of axons that make up the fasciculus retroflexus. The LH projects to the rostromedial tegmental nucleus that is involved in the modulation of DA release from the susbstantia nigra pars compacta and VTA (Kaufling et al., 2009; Bromberg-Martin et al., 2010a,b; Balcita-Pedicino et al., 2011; Hong et al., 2011; Lecca et al., 2011). The MH projects to the interpeduncular nucleus (IPN) which, in turn, projects to the median and dorsal raphe nuclei in addition to other brain regions (**Figure 2A**) (Morley, 1986). Recent data indicate that expression of nAChRs containing the $\alpha5$ and/or $\beta4$ subunits within the MH control nicotine intake such that genetic deletion of $\alpha5$ nAChRs increases acute intake; whereas overexpression of the $\beta4$ nAChR subunit reduces intake and increases sensitivity to nicotine's aversive properties (Fowler et al., 2011; Frahm et al., 2011). Thus, while the mesocorticolimbic pathway confers acute nicotine reward/reinforcement, the MH-IPN pathway may signal nicotine aversion (but see Laviolette et al., 2008). In addition, the Hb-IPN is a critical circuit for the expression of physical signs of nicotine withdrawal (Salas et al., 2009). Because (1) SNPs in nAChR subunit genes CHRNA3/A5/B4 are associated with alcohol dependence phenotypes, (2) these genes are robustly expressed in the Hb-IPN circuitry, and (3) $\alpha3\beta4$ ligands modulate ethanol consumption in rodent models, future studies should explore the role of MH-IPN nAChRs in ethanol consumption and withdrawal behaviors.

SUMMARY

Neuronal nAChR represent novel therapeutic targets to not only treat nicotine dependence, but also alcohol dependence. The reinforcing properties of acute ethanol, are mediated, in part, by $\alpha4^*$ nAChRs, likely expressed in DAergic neurons of the mesocorticolimbic pathway. Ethanol potentiates the response of high affinity heteromeric nAChRs to both ACh and nicotine. Thus, if ethanol increases ACh release in the VTA, DAergic neurons will be activated via nAChRs and ethanol will further potentiate this effect (**Figure 2B**). Chronic nicotine may upregulate these receptors and increase the reinforcing properties of ethanol. Future studies should focus on identifying additional nAChR subunits critical for ethanol effects within and outside the mesocorticolimbic circuitry.

ACKNOWLEDGMENTS

This study was supported by the National Institute on Alcohol Abuse and Alcoholism award number R01AA017656 (Andrew R. Tapper) and F31AA018915 (Linzy M. Hendrickson). The content is solely the responsibility of the authors and does not necessarily represent the official views of the National Institutes of Health.

REFERENCES

Aistrup, G. L., Marszalec, W., and Narahashi, T. (1999). Ethanol modulation of nicotinic acetylcholine receptor currents in cultured cortical neurons. *Mol. Pharmacol.* 55, 39–49.

Albuquerque, E. X., Pereira, E. F., Alkondon, M., and Rogers, S. W. (2009). Mammalian nicotinic acetylcholine receptors: from structure to function. *Physiol. Rev.* 89, 73–120.

Alen, F., Gomez, R., Gonzalez-Cuevas, G., Navarro, M., and Lopez-Moreno, J. A. (2009). Nicotine causes opposite effects on alcohol intake: evidence in an animal experimental model of abstinence and relapse from alcohol. *Nicotine Tob. Res.* 11, 1304–1311.

Amos, C. I., Wu, X., Broderick, P. I., Gorlov, P., Gu, J., Eisen, T., et al. (2008). Genome-wide association scan of tag SNPs identifies a

susceptibility locus for lung cancer at 15q25.1. *Nat. Genet.* 40, 616–622.

Anton, R. F., Oroszi, G., O'Malley, S., Couper, D., Swift, R., Pettinati, H., et al. (2008). An evaluation of mu-opioid receptor (OPRM1) as a predictor of naltrexone response in the treatment of alcohol dependence: results from the combined pharmacotherapies and behavioral interventions for alcohol dependence

(COMBINE) study. *Arch. Gen. Psychiatry* 65, 135–144.

Baddick, C. G., and Marks, M. J. (2011). An autoradiographic survey of mouse brain nicotinic acetylcholine receptors defined by null mutants. *Biochem. Pharmacol.* 82, 828–841.

Balcita-Pedicino, J. J., Omelchenko, N., Bell, R., and Sesack, S. R. (2011). The inhibitory influence of the lateral habenula on midbrain dopamine cells: ultrastructural evidence for indirect mediation via the rostromedial mesopontine tegmental nucleus. *J. Comp. Neurol.* 519, 1143–1164.

Bell, R. L., Eiler, B. J. II, Cook, J. B., and Rahman, S. (2009). Nicotinic receptor ligands reduce ethanol intake by high alcohol-drinking HAD-2 rats. *Alcohol* 43, 581–592.

Benwell, M. E., and Balfour, D. J. (1992). The effects of acute and repeated nicotine treatment on nucleus accumbens dopamine and locomotor activity. *Br. J. Pharmacol.* 105, 849–856.

Berrettini, W., Yuan, X., Tozzi, F., Song, K., Francks, C., Chilcoat, H., et al. (2008). Alpha-5/alpha-3 nicotinic receptor subunit alleles increase risk for heavy smoking. *Mol. Psychiatry* 13, 368–373.

Bhutada, P., Mundhada, Y., Ghodki, Y., Dixit, P., Umathe, S., and Jain, K. (2012). Acquisition, expression, and reinstatement of ethanol-induced conditioned place preference in mice: effects of exposure to stress and modulation by mecamylamine. *J. Psychopharmacol.* 26, 315–323.

Bierut, L. J., Schuckit, M. A., Hesselbrock, V., and Reich, T. (2000). Co-occurring risk factors for alcohol dependence and habitual smoking. *Alcohol Res. Health* 24, 233–241.

Bierut, L. J., Stitzel, J. A., Wang, J. C., Hinrichs, A. L., Grucza, R. A., Xuei, X., et al. (2008). Variants in nicotinic receptors and risk for nicotine dependence. *Am. J. Psychiatry* 165, 1163–1171.

Bito-Onon, J. J., Simms, J. A., Chatterjee, S., Holgate, J., and Bartlett, S. E. (2011). Varenicline, a partial agonist at neuronal nicotinic acetylcholine receptors, reduces nicotine-induced increases in 20% ethanol operant self-administration in Sprague-Dawley rats. *Addict. Biol.* 16, 440–449.

Blomqvist, O., Engel, J. A., Nissbrandt, H., and Soderpalm, B. (1993). The mesolimbic dopamine-activating properties of ethanol are antagonized by mecamylamine. *Eur. J. Pharmacol.* 249, 207–213.

Blomqvist, O., Ericson, M., Engel, J. A., and Soderpalm, B. (1997). Accumbal dopamine overflow after ethanol: localization of the antagonizing effect of mecamylamine. *Eur. J. Pharmacol.* 334, 149–156.

Blomqvist, O., Ericson, M., Johnson, D. H., Engel, J. A., and Soderpalm, B. (1996). Voluntary ethanol intake in the rat: effects of nicotinic acetylcholine receptor blockade or subchronic nicotine treatment. *Eur. J. Pharmacol.* 314, 257–267.

Blomqvist, O., Soderpalm, B., and Engel, J. A. (1992). Ethanol-induced locomotor activity: involvement of central nicotinic acetylcholine receptors? *Brain Res. Bull.* 29, 173–178.

Bobo, J. K. (1992). Nicotine dependence and alcoholism epidemiology and treatment. *J. Psychoactive Drugs* 24, 123–129.

Bobo, J. K., and Husten, C. (2000). Sociocultural influences on smoking and drinking. *Alcohol Res. Health* 24, 225–232.

Bordia, T., Hrachova, M., Chin, M., McIntosh, J. M., and Quik, M. (2012). Varenicline is a potent partial agonist at α6β2* nicotinic acetylcholine receptors in rat and monkey striatum. *J. Pharmacol. Exp. Ther.* 342, 327–334.

Borghese, C. M., Ali, D. N., Bleck, V., and Harris, R. A. (2002). Acetylcholine and alcohol sensitivity of neuronal nicotinic acetylcholine receptors: mutations in transmembrane domains. *Alcohol. Clin. Exp. Res.* 26, 1764–1772.

Borghese, C. M., Henderson, L. A., Bleck, V., Trudell, J. R., and Harris, R. A. (2003a). Sites of excitatory and inhibitory actions of alcohols on neuronal alpha2beta4 nicotinic acetylcholine receptors. *J. Pharmacol. Exp. Ther.* 307, 42–52.

Borghese, C. M., Wang, L., Bleck, V., and Harris, R. A. (2003b). Mutation in neuronal nicotinic acetylcholine receptors expressed in Xenopus oocytes blocks ethanol action. *Addict. Biol.* 8, 313–318.

Bromberg-Martin, E. S., Matsumoto, M., Nakahara, H., and Hikosaka, O. (2010a). Multiple timescales of memory in lateral habenula and dopamine neurons. *Neuron* 67, 499–510.

Bromberg-Martin, E. S., Matsumoto, M., and Hikosaka, O. (2010b). Distinct tonic and phasic anticipatory activity in lateral habenula and dopamine neurons. *Neuron* 67, 144–155.

Buisson, B., and Bertrand, D. (2001). Chronic exposure to nicotine upregulates the human (alpha)4((beta)2 nicotinic acetylcholine receptor function. *J. Neurosci.* 21, 1819–1829.

Cardoso, R. A., Brozowski, S. J., Chavez-Noriega, L. E., Harpold, M., Valenzuela, C. F., and Harris, R. A. (1999). Effects of ethanol on recombinant human neuronal nicotinic acetylcholine receptors expressed in Xenopus oocytes. *J. Pharmacol. Exp. Ther.* 289, 774–780.

Carnicella, S., He, D. Y., Yowell, Q. V., Glick, S. D., and Ron, D. (2010). Noribogaine, but not 18-MC, exhibits similar actions as ibogaine on GDNF expression and ethanol self-administration. *Addict. Biol.* 15, 424–433.

Carr, D. B., and Sesack, S. R. (2000). GABA-containing neurons in the rat ventral tegmental area project to the prefrontal cortex. *Synapse* 38, 114–123.

Cartier, G. E., Yoshikami, D., Gray, W. R., Luo, S., Olivera, B. M., and McIntosh, J. M. (1996). A new alpha-conotoxin which targets alpha3beta2 nicotinic acetylcholine receptors. *J. Biol. Chem.* 271, 7522–7528.

CASA. (2000). CASA's cost of living adjustment, using the Bureau of Labor Statistics Inflation Calculator, of 1998 data by Harwood, H. *Updating Estimates of the Economic Costs of Alcohol Abuse in the United States: Estimates, Update Methods, and Data.* Report prepared by The Lewin Group for the National Institute on Alcohol Abuse and Alcoholism, 2000. Based on estimates, analyses, and data reported in Harwood, H., Fountain, D., and Livermore, G. (1992). *The Economic Costs of Alcohol and Drug Abuse in the United States.* Report prepared for the National Institute on Drug Abuse and the National Institute on Alcohol Abuse and Alcoholism National Institutes of Health, U.S. Department of Health and Human Services. NIH Publication No 98-4327. Rockville, MD. (2005).

Champtiaux, N., Han, Z. Y., Bessis, A., Rossi, F. M., Zoli, M., Marubio, L., et al. (2002). Distribution and pharmacology of alpha 6-containing nicotinic acetylcholine receptors analyzed with mutant mice. *J. Neurosci.* 22, 1208–1217.

Changeux, J. P., and Edelstein, S. J. (1998). Allosteric receptors after 30 years. *Neuron* 21, 959–980.

Chatterjee, S., Steensland, P., Simms, J. A., Holgate, J., Coe, J. W., Hurst, R. S., et al. (2011). Partial agonists of the alpha3beta4* neuronal nicotinic acetylcholine receptor reduce ethanol consumption and seeking in rats. *Neuropsychopharmacology* 36, 603–615.

Chen, L. S., Xian, H., Grucza, R. A., Saccone, N. L., Wang, J. C., Johnson, E. O., et al. (2012). Nicotine dependence and comorbid psychiatric disorders: examination of specific genetic variants in the CHRNA5-A3-B4 nicotinic receptor genes. *Drug Alcohol Depend.* 123(Suppl. 1), S42–51.

Chi, H., and de Wit, H. (2003). Mecamylamine attenuates the subjective stimulant-like effects of alcohol in social drinkers. *Alcohol. Clin. Exp. Res.* 27, 780–786.

Childs, E., Roche, D. J., King, A. C., and de Wit, H. (2012). Varenicline potentiates alcohol-induced negative subjective responses and offsets impaired eye movements. *Alcohol. Clin. Exp. Res.* 36, 906–914.

Christensen, J. K., Moller, I. W., Ronsted, P., and Johansson, B. (1991). Dose-effect relationship of disulfiram in human volunteers. I: clinical studies. *Pharmacol. Toxicol.* 68, 163–165.

Clark, A., Lindgren, S., Brooks, S. P., Watson, W. P., and Little, H. J. (2001). Chronic infusion of nicotine can increase operant self-administration of alcohol. *Neuropharmacology* 41, 108–117.

Clark, A., and Little, H. J. (2004). Interactions between low concentrations of ethanol and nicotine on firing rate of ventral tegmental dopamine neurones. *Drug Alcohol Depend.* 75, 199–206.

Coe, J. W., Brooks, P. R., Vetelino, M. G., Wirtz, M. C., Arnold, E. P., Huang, J., et al. (2005). Varenicline: an alpha4beta2 nicotinic receptor partial agonist for smoking cessation. *J. Med. Chem.* 48, 3474–3477.

Cornwall, J., Cooper, J. D., and Phillipson, O. T. (1990). Afferent and efferent connections of the laterodorsal tegmental nucleus in the rat. *Brain Res. Bull.* 25, 271–284.

Corrigall, W. A., and Coen, K. M. (1991). Selective dopamine antagonists reduce nicotine self-administration. *Psychopharmacology (Berl.)* 104, 171–176.

Corrigall, W. A., Coen, K. M., and Adamson, K. L. (1994). Self-administered nicotine activates the mesolimbic dopamine system through the ventral tegmental area. *Brain Res.* 653, 278–284.

Corrigall, W. A., Franklin, K. B., Coen, K. M., and Clarke, P. B. (1992). The mesolimbic dopaminergic system is implicated in the reinforcing effects of nicotine. *Psychopharmacology (Berl.)* 107, 285–259.

Corringer, P. J., Le Novere, N., and Changeux, J. P. (2000). Nicotinic receptors at the amino acid level. *Annu. Rev. Pharmacol. Toxicol.* 40, 431–458.

Damaj, M. I. (2001). Influence of gender and sex hormones on nicotine acute pharmacological effects in mice. *J. Pharmacol. Exp. Ther.* 296, 132–140.

Dani, J. A., and Bertrand, D. (2007). Nicotinic acetylcholine receptors and nicotinic cholinergic mechanisms of the central nervous system. *Annu. Rev. Pharmacol. Toxicol.* 47, 699–729.

De Biasi, M., and Dani, J. A. (2011). Reward, addiction, withdrawal to nicotine. *Annu. Rev. Neurosci.* 34, 105–130.

Di Chiara, G., and Imperato, A. (1988). Drugs abused by humans preferentially increase synaptic dopamine concentrations in the mesolimbic system of freely moving rats. *Proc. Natl. Acad. Sci. U.S.A.* 85, 5274–5278.

Diana, M., Rossetti, Z. L., and Gessa, G. (1993). Rewarding and aversive effects of ethanol: interplay of GABA, glutamate and dopamine. *Alcohol. Alcohol Suppl.* 2, 315–319.

DiFranza, J. R., and Guerrera, M. P. (1990). Alcoholism and smoking. *J. Stud. Alcohol* 51, 130–135.

Ding, Z. M., Katner, S. N., Rodd, Z. A., Truitt, W., Hauser, S. R., Deehan, G. A. Jr., et al. (2012). Repeated exposure of the posterior ventral tegmental area to nicotine increases the sensitivity of local dopamine neurons to the stimulating effects of ethanol. *Alcohol* 46, 217–223.

Dopico, A. M., and Lovinger, D. M. (2009). Acute alcohol action and desensitization of ligand-gated ion channels. *Pharmacol. Rev.* 61, 98–114.

Dowell, C., Olivera, B. M., Garrett, J. E., Staheli, S. T., Watkins, M., Kuryatov, A., et al. (2003). Alpha-conotoxin PIA is selective for alpha6 subunit-containing nicotinic acetylcholine receptors. *J. Neurosci.* 23, 8445–8452.

Drago, J., McColl, C. D., Horne, M. K., Finkelstein, D. I., and Ross, S. A. (2003). Neuronal nicotinic receptors: insights gained from gene knockout and knockin mutant mice. *Cell. Mol. Life Sci.* 60, 1267–1280.

Dyr, W., Koros, E., Bienkowski, P., and Kostowski, W. (1999). Involvement of nicotinic acetylcholine receptors in the regulation of alcohol drinking in Wistar rats. *Alcohol Alcohol.* 34, 43–47.

Ehringer, M. A., Clegg, H. V., Collins, A. C., Corley, R. P., Crowley, T., Hewitt, J. K., et al. (2007). Association of the neuronal nicotinic receptor beta2 subunit gene (CHRNB2) with subjective responses to alcohol and nicotine. *Am. J. Med. Genet. B Neuropsychiatr. Genet.* 144B, 596–604.

Ericson, M., Blomqvist, O., Engel, J. A., and Soderpalm, B. (1998). Voluntary ethanol intake in the rat and the associated accumbal dopamine overflow are blocked by ventral tegmental mecamylamine. *Eur. J. Pharmacol.* 358, 189–196.

Ericson, M., Engel, J. A., and Soderpalm, B. (2000). Peripheral involvement in nicotine-induced enhancement of ethanol intake. *Alcohol* 21, 37–47.

Ericson, M., Lof, E., Stomberg, R., and Soderpalm, B. (2009). The smoking cessation medication varenicline attenuates alcohol and nicotine interactions in the rat mesolimbic dopamine system. *J. Pharmacol. Exp. Ther.* 329, 225–230.

Ericson, M., Molander, A., Lof, E., Engel, J. A., and Soderpalm, B. (2003). Ethanol elevates accumbal dopamine levels via indirect activation of ventral tegmental nicotinic acetylcholine receptors. *Eur. J. Pharmacol.* 467, 85–93.

Exley, R., Maubourguet, N., David, V., Eddine, R., Evrard, A., Pons, S., et al. (2011). Distinct contributions of nicotinic acetylcholine receptor subunit alpha4 and subunit alpha6 to the reinforcing effects of nicotine. *Proc. Natl. Acad. Sci. U.S.A.* 108, 7577–7582.

Fallon, J. H., Schmued, L. C., Wang, C., Miller, R., and Banales, G. (1984). Neurons in the ventral tegmentum have separate populations projecting to telencephalon and inferior olive, are histochemically different, and may receive direct visual input. *Brain Res.* 321, 332–336.

Farook, J. M., Lewis, B., Gaddis, J. G., Littleton, J. M., and Barron, S. (2009a). Effects of mecamylamine on alcohol consumption and preference in male C57BL/6J mice. *Pharmacology* 83, 379–384.

Farook, J. M., Lewis, B., Gaddis, J. G., Littleton, J. M., and Barron, S. (2009b). Lobeline, a nicotinic partial agonist attenuates alcohol consumption and preference in male C57BL/6J mice. *Physiol. Behav.* 97, 503–506.

Fields, H. L., Hjelmstad, G. O., Margolis, E. B., and Nicola, S. M. (2007). Ventral tegmental area neurons in learned appetitive behavior and positive reinforcement. *Annu. Rev. Neurosci.* 30, 289–316.

Foddai, M., Dosia, G., Spiga, S., and Diana, M. (2004). Acetaldehyde increases dopaminergic neuronal activity in the VTA. *Neuropsychopharmacology* 29, 530–536.

Fonck, C., Cohen, B. N., Nashmi, R., Whiteaker, P., Wagenaar, D. A., Rodrigues-Pinguet, N., et al. (2005). Novel seizure phenotype and sleep disruptions in knock-in mice with hypersensitive alpha 4* nicotinic receptors. *J. Neurosci.* 25, 11396–11411.

Forman, S. A., and Zhou, Q. (1999). Novel modulation of a nicotinic receptor channel mutant reveals that the open state is stabilized by ethanol. *Mol. Pharmacol.* 55, 102–108.

Fowler, C. D., Lu, Q., Johnson, P. M., Marks, M. J., and Kenny, P. J. (2011). Habenular alpha5 nicotinic receptor subunit signalling controls nicotine intake. *Nature* 471, 597–601.

Frahm, S., Slimak, M. A., Ferrarese, L., Santos-Torres, J., Antolin-Fontes, B., Auer, S., et al. (2011). Aversion to nicotine is regulated by the balanced activity of beta4 and alpha5 nicotinic receptor subunits in the medial habenula. *Neuron* 70, 522–535.

Fucito, L. M., Toll, B. A., Wu, R., Romano, D. M., Tek, E., and O'Malley, S. S. (2011). A preliminary investigation of varenicline for heavy drinking smokers. *Psychopharmacology (Berl.)* 215, 655–663.

Funk, D., Marinelli, P. W., and Le, A. D. (2006). Biological processes underlying co-use of alcohol and nicotine: neuronal mechanisms, cross-tolerance, and genetic factors. *Alcohol Res. Health* 29, 186–192.

Gatto, G. J., McBride, W. J., Murphy, J. M., Lumeng, L., and Li, T. K. (1994). Ethanol self-infusion into the ventral tegmental area by alcohol-preferring rats. *Alcohol* 11, 557–564.

Geisler, S., and Zahm, D. S. (2005). Afferents of the ventral tegmental area in the rat-anatomical substratum for integrative functions. *J. Comp. Neurol.* 490, 270–294.

George, D. T., Gilman, J., Hersh, J., Thorsell, A., Herion, D., Geyer, C., et al. (2008). Neurokinin 1 receptor antagonism as a possible therapy for alcoholism. *Science* 319, 1536–1539.

Gessa, G. L., Muntoni, F., Collu, M., Vargiu, L., and Mereu, G. (1985). Low doses of ethanol activate dopaminergic neurons in the ventral tegmental area. *Brain Res.* 348, 201–203.

Gonzales, D., Rennard, S. I., Nides, M., Oncken, C., Azoulay, S., Billing, C. B., et al. (2006). Varenicline, an alpha4beta2 nicotinic acetylcholine receptor partial agonist, vs sustained-release bupropion and placebo for smoking cessation: a randomized controlled trial. *JAMA* 296, 47–55.

Gotti, C., Guiducci, S., Tedesco, V., Corbioli, S., Zanetti, L., Moretti, M., et al. (2010). Nicotinic acetylcholine receptors in the mesolimbic pathway: primary role of ventral tegmental area alpha6beta2* receptors in mediating systemic nicotine effects on dopamine release, locomotion, and reinforcement. *J. Neurosci.* 30, 5311–5325.

Gotti, C., Moretti, M., Gaimarri, A., Zanardi, A., Clementi, F., and Zoli, M. (2007). Heterogeneity and complexity of native brain nicotinic receptors. *Biochem. Pharmacol.* 74, 1102–1111.

Grady, S. R., Salminen, O., Laverty, D. C., Whiteaker, P., McIntosh, J. M., Collins, A. C., et al. (2007). The subtypes of nicotinic acetylcholine receptors on dopaminergic terminals of mouse striatum. *Biochem. Pharmacol.* 74, 1235–1246.

Grant, B. F., Hasin, D. S., Chou, S. P., Stinson, F. S., and Dawson, D. A. (2004). Nicotine dependence and psychiatric disorders in the United States: results from the national epidemiologic survey on alcohol and related conditions. *Arch. Gen. Psychiatry* 61, 1107–1115.

Grucza, R. A., Wang, J. C., Stitzel, J. A., Hinrichs, A. L., Saccone, S. F., Saccone, N. L., et al. (2008). A risk allele for nicotine dependence in CHRNA5 is a protective allele for cocaine dependence. *Biol. Psychiatry* 64, 922–929.

Guan, Y., Xiao, C., Krnjevic, K., Xie, G., Zuo, W., and Ye, J. H. (2012). GABAergic actions mediate opposite ethanol effects on dopaminergic neurons in the anterior and posterior ventral tegmental area. *J. Pharmacol. Exp. Ther.* 341, 33–42.

Harvey, S. C., and Luetje, C. W. (1996). Determinants of competitive antagonist sensitivity on neuronal nicotinic receptor beta subunits. *J. Neurosci.* 16, 3798–3806.

Harvey, S. C., Maddox, F. N., and Luetje, C. W. (1996). Multiple determinants of dihydro-beta-erythroidine sensitivity on rat neuronal nicotinic receptor alpha subunits. *J. Neurochem.* 67, 1953–1959.

Hauser, S. R., Getachew, B., Oster, S. M., Dhaher, R., Ding, Z. M., Bell, R. L., et al. (2012). Nicotine modulates alcohol-seeking and relapse by alcohol-preferring (P) rats in a time-dependent manner. *Alcohol. Clin. Exp. Res.* 36, 43–54.

Heath, A. C., Bucholz, K. K., Madden, P. A., Dinwiddie, S. H., Slutske, W. S., Bierut, L. J., et al. (1997). Genetic and environmental contributions to alcohol dependence risk in a national twin sample: consistency of findings in women and men. *Psychol. Med.* 27, 1381–1396.

Hendrickson, L. M., Gardner, P., and Tapper, A. R. (2011). Nicotinic acetylcholine receptors containing the alpha4 subunit are critical for the nicotine-induced reduction of acute voluntary ethanol consumption. *Channels (Austin)* 5, 124–127.

Hendrickson, L. M., Zhao-Shea, R., Pang, X., Gardner, P. D., and Tapper, A. R. (2010). Activation of alpha4* nAChRs is necessary and sufficient for varenicline-induced reduction of alcohol consumption. *J. Neurosci.* 30, 10169–10176.

Hendrickson, L. M., Zhao-Shea, R., and Tapper, A. R. (2009). Modulation of ethanol drinking-in-the-dark by mecamylamine and nicotinic acetylcholine receptor agonists in C57BL/6J mice. *Psychopharmacology (Berl.)* 204, 563–572.

Herkenham, M., and Nauta, W. J. (1979). Efferent connections of the habenular nuclei in the rat. *J. Comp. Neurol.* 187, 19–47.

Hikosaka, O. (2010). The habenula: from stress evasion to value-based decision-making. *Nat. Rev. Neurosci.* 11, 503–513.

Hoft, N. R., Corley, R. P., McQueen, M. B., Huizinga, D., Menard, S., and Ehringer, M. A. (2009). SNPs in CHRNA6 and CHRNB3 are associated with alcohol consumption in a nationally representative sample. *Genes Brain Behav.* 8, 631–637.

Hong, S., Jhou, T. C., Smith, M., Saleem, K. S., and Hikosaka, O. (2011). Negative reward signals from the lateral habenula to dopamine neurons are mediated by rostromedial tegmental nucleus in primates. *J. Neurosci.* 31, 11457–11471.

Hung, R. J., McKay, J. D., Gaborieau, V., Boffetta, P., Hashibe, M., Zaridze, D., et al. (2008). A susceptibility locus for lung cancer maps to nicotinic acetylcholine receptor subunit genes on 15q25. *Nature* 452, 633–637.

Ikemoto, S. (2007). Dopamine reward circuitry: two projection systems from the ventral midbrain to the nucleus accumbens-olfactory tubercle complex. *Brain Res. Rev.* 56, 27–78.

Ikemoto, S., McBride, W. J., Murphy, J. M., Lumeng, L., and Li, T. K. (1997). 6-OHDA-lesions of the nucleus accumbens disrupt the acquisition but not the maintenance of ethanol consumption in the alcohol-preferring P line of rats. *Alcohol. Clin. Exp. Res.* 21, 1042–1046.

Ikemoto, S., Qin, M., and Liu, Z. H. (2006). Primary reinforcing effects of nicotine are triggered from multiple regions both inside and outside the ventral tegmental area. *J. Neurosci.* 26, 723–730.

Jerlhag, E., Grotli, M., Luthman, K., Svensson, L., and Engel, J. A. (2006). Role of the subunit composition of central nicotinic acetylcholine receptors for the stimulatory and dopamine-enhancing effects of ethanol. *Alcohol Alcohol.* 41, 486–493.

Ji, H., and Shepard, P. D. (2007). Lateral habenula stimulation inhibits rat midbrain dopamine neurons through a GABA(A) receptor-mediated mechanism. *J. Neurosci.* 27, 6923–6930.

Job, M. O., Tang, A., Hall, F. S., Sora, I., Uhl, G. R., Bergeson, S. E., et al. (2007). Mu (mu) opioid receptor regulation of ethanol-induced dopamine response in the ventral striatum: evidence of genotype specific sexual dimorphic epistasis. *Biol. Psychiatry* 62, 627–634.

Johnson, D. H., Blomqvist, O., Engel, J. A., and Soderpalm, B. (1995). Subchronic intermittent nicotine treatment enhances ethanol-induced locomotor stimulation and dopamine turnover in mice. *Behav. Pharmacol.* 6, 203–207.

Jorenby, D. E., Hays, J. T., Rigotti, N. A., Azoulay, S., Watsky, E. J., Williams, K. E., et al. (2006). Efficacy of varenicline, an alpha4beta2 nicotinic acetylcholine receptor partial agonist, vs placebo or sustained-release bupropion for smoking cessation: a randomized controlled trial. *JAMA* 296, 56–63.

Joslyn, G., Brush, G., Robertson, M., Smith, T. L., Kalmijn, J., Schuckit, M., et al. (2008). Chromosome 15q25.1 genetic markers associated with level of response to alcohol in humans. *Proc. Natl. Acad. Sci. U.S.A.* 105, 20368–20373.

Kamens, H. M., Andersen, J., and Picciotto, M. R. (2010). Modulation of ethanol consumption by genetic and pharmacological manipulation of nicotinic acetylcholine receptors in mice. *Psychopharmacology (Berl.)* 208, 613–626.

Kamens, H. M., Hoft, N. R., Cox, R. J., Miyamoto, J. H., and Ehringer, M. A. (2012). The alpha6 nicotinic acetylcholine receptor subunit influences ethanol-induced sedation. *Alcohol* 46, 463–471.

Kamens, H. M., and Phillips, T. J. (2008). A role for neuronal nicotinic acetylcholine receptors in ethanol-induced stimulation, but not cocaine- or methamphetamine-induced stimulation. *Psychopharmacology (Berl.)* 196, 377–387.

Karlin, A. (2002). Emerging structure of the nicotinic acetylcholine receptors. *Nat. Rev. Neurosci.* 3, 102–114.

Kaufling, J., Veinante, P., Pawlowski, S. A., Freund-Mercier, M. J., and Barrot, M. (2009). Afferents to the GABAergic tail of the ventral tegmental area in the rat. *J. Comp. Neurol.* 513, 597–621.

Kiianmaa, K. (1978). Decreased intoxicating effect of ethanol in rats after 6-hydroxydopamine-induced degeneration of ascending dopamine pathways. *Pharmacol. Biochem. Behav.* 9, 391–393.

Kim, S. A., Kim, J. W., Song, J. Y., Park, S., Lee, H. J., and Chung, J. H. (2004). Association of polymorphisms in nicotinic acetylcholine receptor alpha 4 subunit gene (CHRNA4), mu-opioid receptor gene (OPRM1), and ethanol-metabolizing enzyme genes with alcoholism in Korean patients. *Alcohol* 34, 115–120.

Klink, R., de Kerchove d'Exaerde, A., Zoli, M., and Changeux, J. P. (2001). Molecular and physiological diversity of nicotinic acetylcholine receptors in the midbrain dopaminergic nuclei. *J. Neurosci.* 21, 1452–1463.

Koob, G. F. (1992). Drugs of abuse: anatomy, pharmacology and function of reward pathways. *Trends Pharmacol. Sci.* 13, 177–184.

Koob, G. F., and Weiss, F. (1990). Pharmacology of drug self-administration. *Alcohol* 7, 193–197.

Kuehn, B. M. (2009). Findings on alcohol dependence point to promising avenues for targeted therapies. *JAMA* 301, 1643–1645.

Kuzmin, A., Jerlhag, E., Liljequist, S., and Engel, J. (2009). Effects of subunit selective nACh receptors on operant ethanol self-administration and relapse-like ethanol-drinking behavior. *Psychopharmacology (Berl.)* 203, 99–108.

Lanca, A. J. (1994). Reduction of voluntary alcohol intake in the rat by modulation of the dopaminergic mesolimbic system: transplantation of ventral mesencephalic cell suspensions. *Neuroscience* 58, 359–369.

Landgren, S., Engel, J. A., Andersson, M. E., Gonzalez-Quintela, A., Campos, J., Nilsson, S., et al. (2009). Association of nAChR gene haplotypes with heavy alcohol use and body mass. *Brain Res.* 1305(Suppl.), S72–9.

Larsson, A., Edstrom, L., Svensson, L., Soderpalm, B., and Engel, J. A. (2005). Voluntary ethanol intake increases extracellular acetylcholine levels in the ventral tegmental area in the rat. *Alcohol Alcohol.* 40, 349–358.

Larsson, A., Jerlhag, E., Svensson, L., Soderpalm, B., and Engel, J. A. (2004). Is an alpha-conotoxin MII-sensitive mechanism involved in the neurochemical, stimulatory, and rewarding effects of ethanol? *Alcohol* 34, 239–250.

Larsson, A., Svensson, L., Soderpalm, B., and Engel, J. A. (2002). Role of different nicotinic acetylcholine receptors in mediating behavioral and neurochemical effects of ethanol in mice. *Alcohol* 28, 157–167.

Laviolette, S. R., Lauzon, N. M., Bishop, S. F., Sun, N., and Tan, H. (2008). Dopamine signaling through D1-like versus D2-like receptors in the nucleus accumbens core versus shell differentially modulates nicotine reward sensitivity. *J. Neurosci.* 28, 8025–8033.

Le, A. D., Corrigall, W. A., Harding, J. W., Juzytsch, W., and Li, T. K. (2000). Involvement of nicotinic receptors in alcohol self-administration. *Alcohol. Clin. Exp. Res.* 24, 155–163.

Le, A. D., Wang, A., Harding, S., Juzytsch, W., and Shaham, Y. (2003). Nicotine increases alcohol self-administration and reinstates alcohol seeking in rats. *Psychopharmacology (Berl.)* 168, 216–221.

Le Novere, N., and Changeux, J. P. (1995). Molecular evolution of the nicotinic acetylcholine receptor: an example of multigene family in excitable cells. *J. Mol. Evol.* 40, 155–172.

Lecca, S., Melis, M., Luchicchi, A., Ennas, M. G., Castelli, M. P., Muntoni, A. L., et al. (2011). Effects of drugs of abuse on putative rostromedial tegmental neurons, inhibitory afferents to midbrain dopamine cells. *Neuropsychopharmacology* 36, 589–602.

Lewis, M. J., and June, H. L. (1990). Neurobehavioral studies of ethanol reward and activation. *Alcohol* 7, 213–219.

Li, W., Doyon, W. M., and Dani, J. A. (2011). Acute in vivo nicotine administration enhances synchrony among dopamine neurons. *Biochem. Pharmacol.* 82, 977–983.

Littleton, J., Barron, S., Prendergast, M., and Nixon, S. J. (2007). Smoking kills (alcoholics)! shouldn't we do something about it? *Alcohol Alcohol.* 42, 167–173.

Liu, L., Hendrickson, L. M., Guildford, M., Zhao-Shea, R., Gardner, P. D., and Tapper, A. R. (2013). Nicotinic acetylcholine receptors containing the alpha4 subunit modulate alcohol reward. *Biol. Psychiatry.* 73, 738–746.

Liu, L., Zhao-Shea, R., McIntosh, J. M., Gardner, P. D., and Tapper,

A. R. (2012). Nicotine persistently activates ventral tegmental area dopaminergic neurons via nicotinic acetylcholine receptors containing alpha4 and alpha6 subunits. *Mol. Pharmacol.* 81, 541–548.

Lof, E., Olausson, P., deBejczy, A., Stomberg, R., McIntosh, J. M., Taylor, J. R., et al. (2007). Nicotinic acetylcholine receptors in the ventral tegmental area mediate the dopamine activating and reinforcing properties of ethanol cues. *Psychopharmacology (Berl.)* 195, 333–343.

Lopez-Moreno, J. A., Trigo-Diaz, J. M., Rodriguez de Fonseca, F., Gonzalez Cuevas, G., Gomez de Heras, R., Crespo Galan, I., et al. (2004). Nicotine in alcohol deprivation increases alcohol operant self-administration during reinstatement. *Neuropharmacology* 47, 1036–1044.

Lubke, G. H., Stephens, S. H., Lessem, J. M., Hewitt, J. K., and Ehringer, M. A. (2012). The CHRNA5/A3/B4 gene cluster and tobacco, alcohol, cannabis, inhalants and other substance use initiation: replication and new findings using mixture analyses. *Behav. Genet.* 42, 636–646.

Lummis, S. C., Thompson, A. J., Bencherif, M., and Lester, H. A. (2011). Varenicline is a potent agonist of the human 5-hydroxytryptamine3 receptor. *J. Pharmacol. Exp. Ther.* 339, 125–131.

Madden, P. A., and Heath, A. C. (2002). Shared genetic vulnerability in alcohol and cigarette use and dependence. *Alcohol. Clin. Exp. Res.* 26, 1919–1921.

Mansvelder, H. D., Keath, J. R., and McGehee, D. S. (2002). Synaptic mechanisms underlie nicotine-induced excitability of brain reward areas. *Neuron* 33, 905–919.

Margolis, E. B., Lock, H., Hjelmstad, G. O., and Fields, H. L. (2006a). The ventral tegmental area revisited: is there an electrophysiological marker for dopaminergic neurons? *J. Physiol. (Lond.)* 577, 907–924.

Margolis, E. B., Lock, H., Chefer, V. I., Shippenberg, T. S., Hjelmstad, G. O., and Fields, H. L. (2006b). Kappa opioids selectively control dopaminergic neurons projecting to the prefrontal cortex. *Proc. Natl. Acad. Sci. U.S.A.* 103, 2938–2942.

Marszalec, W., Aistrup, G. L., and Narahashi, T. (1999). Ethanol-nicotine interactions at alpha-bungarotoxin-insensitive nicotinic acetylcholine receptors in rat cortical neurons. *Alcohol. Clin. Exp. Res.* 23, 439–445.

Marubio, L. M., Gardier, A. M., Durier, S., David, D., Klink, R., Arroyo-Jimenez, M. M., et al. (2003). Effects of nicotine in the dopaminergic system of mice lacking the alpha4 subunit of neuronal nicotinic acetylcholine receptors. *Eur. J. Neurosci.* 17, 1329–1337.

Maskos, U., Molles, B. E., Pons, S., Besson, M., Guiard, B. P., Guilloux, J. P., et al. (2005). Nicotine reinforcement and cognition restored by targeted expression of nicotinic receptors. *Nature* 436, 103–107.

Mason, B. J. (2003). Acamprosate and naltrexone treatment for alcohol dependence: an evidence-based risk-benefits assessment. *Eur. Neuropsychopharmacol.* 13, 469–475.

Mason, B. J., Goodman, A. M., Chabac, S., and Lehert, P. (2006). Effect of oral acamprosate on abstinence in patients with alcohol dependence in a double-blind, placebo-controlled trial: the role of patient motivation. *J. Psychiatr. Res.* 40, 383–393.

Matsumoto, M., and Hikosaka, O. (2007). Lateral habenula as a source of negative reward signals in dopamine neurons. *Nature* 447, 1111–1115.

McGehee, D. S., Heath, M. J., Gelber, S., Devay, P., and Role, L. W. (1995). Nicotine enhancement of fast excitatory synaptic transmission in CNS by presynaptic receptors. *Science* 269, 1692–1696.

McGehee, D. S., and Role, L. W. (1995). Physiological diversity of nicotinic acetylcholine receptors expressed by vertebrate neurons. *Annu. Rev. Physiol.* 57, 521–546.

McKee, S. A., Harrison, E. L., O'Malley, S. S., Krishnan-Sarin, S., Shi, J., Tetrault, J. M., et al. (2009). Varenicline reduces alcohol self-administration in heavy-drinking smokers. *Biol. Psychiatry* 66, 185–190.

Mereu, G., Fadda, F., and Gessa, G. L. (1984). Ethanol stimulates the firing rate of nigral dopaminergic neurons in unanesthetized rats. *Brain Res.* 292, 63–69.

Meyerhoff, D. J., Tizabi, Y., Staley, J. K., Durazzo, T. C., Glass, J. M., and Nixon, S. J. (2006). Smoking comorbidity in alcoholism: neurobiological and neurocognitive consequences. *Alcohol. Clin. Exp. Res.* 30, 253–264.

Mihalak, K. B., Carroll, F. I., and Luetje, C. W. (2006). Varenicline is a partial agonist at alpha4beta2 and a full agonist at alpha7 neuronal nicotinic receptors. *Mol. Pharmacol.* 70, 801–805.

Millar, N. S., and Gotti, C. (2009). Diversity of vertebrate nicotinic acetylcholine receptors. *Neuropharmacology* 56, 237–246.

Miller, N. S., and Gold, M. S. (1998). Comorbid cigarette and alcohol addiction: epidemiology and treatment. *J. Addict. Dis.* 17, 55–66.

Mitchell, J. M., Teague, C. H., Kayser, A. S., Bartlett, S. E., and Fields, H. L. (2012). Varenicline decreases alcohol consumption in heavy-drinking smokers. *Psychopharmacology (Berl.)* 223, 299–306.

Miyazawa, A., Fujiyoshi, Y., and Unwin, N. (2003). Structure and gating mechanism of the acetylcholine receptor pore. *Nature* 423, 949–955.

Mogg, A. J., Whiteaker, P., McIntosh, J. M., Marks, M., Collins, A. C., and Wonnacott, S. (2002). Methyllycaconitine is a potent antagonist of alpha-conotoxin-MII-sensitive presynaptic nicotinic acetylcholine receptors in rat striatum. *J. Pharmacol. Exp. Ther.* 302, 197–204.

Mokdad, A. H., Marks, J. S., Stroup, D. F., and Gerberding, J. L. (2004). Actual causes of death in the United States, 2000. *JAMA* 291, 1238–1245.

Morley, B. J. (1986). The interpeduncular nucleus. *Int. Rev. Neurobiol.* 28, 157–182.

Moroni, M., Zwart, R., Sher, E., Cassels, B. K., and Bermudez, I. (2006). alpha4beta2 nicotinic receptors with high and low acetylcholine sensitivity: pharmacology, stoichiometry, and sensitivity to long-term exposure to nicotine. *Mol. Pharmacol.* 70, 755–768.

Nadal, R., Chappell, A. M., and Samson, H. H. (1998). Effects of nicotine and mecamylamine microinjections into the nucleus accumbens on ethanol and sucrose self-administration. *Alcohol. Clin. Exp. Res.* 22, 1190–1198.

Nagata, K., Aistrup, G. L., Huang, C. S., Marszalec, W., Song, J. H., Yeh, J. Z., et al. (1996). Potent modulation of neuronal nicotinic acetylcholine receptor-channel by ethanol. *Neurosci. Lett.* 217, 189–193.

Nashmi, R., Xiao, C., Deshpande, P., McKinney, S., Grady, S. R., Whiteaker, P., et al. (2007). Chronic nicotine cell specifically upregulates functional alpha 4* nicotinic receptors: basis for both tolerance in midbrain and enhanced long-term potentiation in perforant path. *J. Neurosci.* 27, 8202–8218.

Nelson, M. E., Kuryatov, A., Choi, C. H., Zhou, Y., and Lindstrom, J. (2003). Alternate stoichiometries of alpha4beta2 nicotinic acetylcholine receptors. *Mol. Pharmacol.* 63, 332–341.

Oakman, S. A., Faris, P. L., Kerr, P. E., Cozzari, C., and Hartman, B. K. (1995). Distribution of pontomes-encephalic cholinergic neurons projecting to substantia nigra differs significantly from those projecting to ventral tegmental area. *J. Neurosci.* 15, 5859–5869.

Okamoto, T., Harnett, M. T., and Morikawa, H. (2006). Hyperpolarization-activated cation current (Ih) is an ethanol target in midbrain dopamine neurons of mice. *J. Neurophysiol.* 95, 619–626.

Olausson, P., Ericson, M., Lof, E., Engel, J. A., and Soderpalm, B. (2001). Nicotine-induced behavioral disinhibition and ethanol preference correlate after repeated nicotine treatment. *Eur. J. Pharmacol.* 417, 117–123.

O'Malley, S. S., Jaffe, A. J., Chang, G., Schottenfeld, R. S., Meyer, R. E., and Rounsaville, B. (1992). Naltrexone and coping skills therapy for alcohol dependence. A controlled study. *Arch. Gen. Psychiatry* 49, 881–887.

Oslin, D. W., Berrettini, W. H., and O'Brien, C. P. (2006). Targeting treatments for alcohol dependence: the pharmacogenetics of naltrexone. *Addict. Biol.* 11, 397–403.

Papke, R. L., Wecker, L., and Stitzel, J. A. (2010). Activation and inhibition of mouse muscle and neuronal nicotinic acetylcholine receptors expressed in Xenopus oocytes. *J. Pharmacol. Exp. Ther.* 333, 501–518.

Pettinati, H. M., Anton, R. F., and Willenbring, M. L. (2006). The combine study-: an overview of the largest pharmacotherapy study to date for treating alcohol dependence. *Psychiatry (Edgmont)* 3, 36–39.

Picciotto, M. R., Zoli, M., Rimondini, R., Lena, C., Marubio, L. M., Pich, E. M., et al. (1998). Acetylcholine receptors containing the beta2 subunit are involved in the reinforcing properties of nicotine. *Nature* 391, 173–177.

Pidoplichko, V. I., Noguchi, J., Areola, O. O., Liang, Y., Peterson, J., Zhang, T., et al. (2004). Nicotinic cholinergic synaptic mechanisms in the ventral tegmental area contribute to nicotine addiction. *Learn. Mem.* 11, 60–69.

Pons, S., Fattore, L., Cossu, G., Tolu, S., Porcu, E., McIntosh, J. M., et al. (2008). Crucial role of alpha4 and alpha6 nicotinic acetylcholine receptor subunits from ventral tegmental area in systemic nicotine self-administration. *J. Neurosci.* 28, 12318–12327.

Pontieri, F. E., Tanda, G., Orzi, F., and Di Chiara, G. (1996). Effects of nicotine on the nucleus accumbens and similarity to those of addictive drugs. *Nature* 382, 255–257.

Potthoff, A. D., Ellison, G., and Nelson, L. (1983). Ethanol intake increases during continuous administration of amphetamine and nicotine, but not several other drugs. *Pharmacol. Biochem. Behav.* 18, 489–493.

Rassnick, S., Stinus, L., and Koob, G. F. (1993). The effects of 6-hydroxydopamine lesions of the nucleus accumbens and the mesolimbic dopamine system on oral self-administration of ethanol in the rat. *Brain Res.* 623, 16–24.

Rezvani, A. H., Overstreet, D. H., Yang, Y., Maisonneuve, I. M., Bandarage, U. K., Kuehne, M. E., et al. (1997). Attenuation of alcohol consumption by a novel nontoxic ibogaine analogue (18-methoxycoronaridine) in alcohol-preferring rats. *Pharmacol. Biochem. Behav.* 58, 615–619.

Rezvani, A. H., Slade, S., Wells, C., Petro, A., Lumeng, L., Li, T. K., et al. (2010). Effects of sazetidine-A, a selective alpha4beta2 nicotinic acetylcholine receptor desensitizing agent on alcohol and nicotine self-administration in selectively bred alcohol-preferring (P) rats. *Psychopharmacology (Berl.)* 211, 161–174.

Rhodes, J. S., Best, K., Belknap, J. K., Finn, D. A., and Crabbe, J. C. (2005). Evaluation of a simple model of ethanol drinking to intoxication in C57BL/6J mice. *Physiol. Behav.* 84, 53–63.

Rhodes, J. S., Ford, M. M., Yu, C. H., Brown, L. L., Finn, D. A., Garland, T. Jr., et al. (2007). Mouse inbred strain differences in ethanol drinking to intoxication. *Genes Brain Behav.* 6, 1–18.

Rodd, Z. A., Bell, R. L., Melendez, R. I., Kuc, K. A., Lumeng, L., Li, T. K., et al. (2004a). Comparison of intracranial self-administration of ethanol within the posterior ventral tegmental area between alcohol-preferring and Wistar rats. *Alcohol. Clin. Exp. Res.* 28, 1212–1219.

Rodd, Z. A., Melendez, R. I., Bell, R. L., Kuc, K. A., Zhang, Y., Murphy, J. M., et al. (2004b). Intracranial self-administration of ethanol within the ventral tegmental area of male Wistar rats: evidence for involvement of dopamine neurons. *J. Neurosci.* 24, 1050–1057.

Rodd, Z. A., Bell, R. L., Oster, S. M., Toalston, J. E., Pommer, T. J., McBride, W. J., et al. (2010). Serotonin-3 receptors in the posterior ventral tegmental area regulate ethanol self-administration of alcohol-preferring (P) rats. *Alcohol* 44, 245–255.

Role, L. W., and Berg, D. K. (1996). Nicotinic receptors in the development and modulation of CNS synapses. *Neuron* 16, 1077–1085.

Room, R. (2004). Smoking and drinking as complementary behaviours. *Biomed. Pharmacother.* 58, 111–115.

Saccone, N. L., Culverhouse, R. C., Schwantes-An, T. H., Cannon, D. S., Chen, X., and Cichon, S. (2010). Giegling multiple independent loci at chromosome 15q25.1 affect smoking quantity: a meta-analysis and comparison with lung cancer and COPD. *PLoS Genet.* 6:ii:e1001053. doi:10.1371/journal.pgen.1001053

Sajja, R. K., Dwivedi, C., and Rahman, S. (2010). Nicotinic ligands modulate ethanol-induced dopamine function in mice. *Pharmacology* 86, 168–173.

Sajja, R. K., and Rahman, S. (2011). Lobeline and cytisine reduce voluntary ethanol drinking behavior in male C57BL/6J mice. *Prog. Neuropsychopharmacol. Biol. Psychiatry* 35, 257–264.

Sajja, R. K., and Rahman, S. (2012). Neuronal nicotinic receptor ligands modulate chronic nicotine-induced ethanol consumption in C57BL/6J mice. *Pharmacol. Biochem. Behav.* 102, 36–43.

Salamone, J. D., and Correa, M. (2012). The mysterious motivational functions of mesolimbic dopamine. *Neuron* 76, 470–485.

Salas, R., Sturm, R., Boulter, J., and De Biasi, M. (2009). Nicotinic receptors in the habenulo-interpeduncular system are necessary for nicotine withdrawal in mice. *J. Neurosci.* 29, 3014–3018.

Salminen, O., Drapeau, J. A., McIntosh, J. M., Collins, A. C., Marks, M. J., and Grady, S. R. (2007). Pharmacology of alpha-conotoxin MII-sensitive subtypes of nicotinic acetylcholine receptors isolated by breeding of null mutant mice. *Mol. Pharmacol.* 71, 1563–1571.

Salminen, O., Murphy, K. L., McIntosh, J. M., Drago, J., Marks, M. J., Collins, A. C., et al. (2004). Subunit composition and pharmacology of two classes of striatal presynaptic nicotinic acetylcholine receptors mediating dopamine release in mice. *Mol. Pharmacol.* 65, 1526–1535.

Samson, H. H., Tolliver, G. A., Haraguchi, M., and Hodge, C. W. (1992). Alcohol self-administration: role of mesolimbic dopamine. *Ann. N. Y. Acad. Sci.* 654, 242–253.

Santos, N., Chatterjee, S., Henry, A., Holgate, J., and Bartlett, S. E. (2012). The alpha5 neuronal nicotinic acetylcholine receptor subunit plays an important role in the sedative effects of ethanol but does not modulate consumption in mice. *Alcohol. Clin. Exp. Res.* 37, 655–662.

Schlaepfer, I. R., Hoft, N. R., Collins, A. C., Corley, R. P., Hewitt, J. K., Hopfer, C. J., et al. (2008). The CHRNA5/A3/B4 gene cluster variability as an important determinant of early alcohol and tobacco initiation in young adults. *Biol. Psychiatry* 63, 1039–1046.

Schultz, W. (2004). Neural coding of basic reward terms of animal learning theory, game theory, microeconomics and behavioural ecology. *Curr. Opin. Neurobiol.* 14, 139–147.

Semba, K., and Fibiger, H. C. (1992). Afferent connections of the laterodorsal and the pedunculopontine tegmental nuclei in the rat: a retro- and antero-grade transport and immunohistochemical study. *J. Comp. Neurol.* 323, 387–410.

Sesack, S. R., and Pickel, V. M. (1992). Prefrontal cortical efferents in the rat synapse on unlabeled neuronal targets of catecholamine terminals in the nucleus accumbens septi and on dopamine neurons in the ventral tegmental area. *J. Comp. Neurol.* 320, 145–160.

Shabat-Simon, M., Levy, D., Amir, A., Rehavi, M., and Zangen, A. (2008). Dissociation between rewarding and psychomotor effects of opiates: differential roles for glutamate receptors within anterior and posterior portions of the ventral tegmental area. *J. Neurosci.* 28, 8406–8416.

Sharpe, A. L., and Samson, H. H. (2002). Repeated nicotine injections decrease operant ethanol self-administration. *Alcohol* 28, 1–7.

Sherva, R., Kranzler, H. R., Yu, Y., Logue, M. W., Poling, J., Arias, A. J., et al. (2010). Variation in nicotinic acetylcholine receptor genes is associated with multiple substance dependence phenotypes. *Neuropsychopharmacology* 35, 1921–1931.

Sine, S. M. (2002). The nicotinic receptor ligand binding domain. *J. Neurobiol.* 53, 431–446.

Smith, B. R., Horan, J. T., Gaskin, S., and Amit, Z. (1999). Exposure to nicotine enhances acquisition of ethanol drinking by laboratory rats in a limited access paradigm. *Psychopharmacology (Berl.)* 142, 408–412.

Soderpalm, B., Ericson, M., Olausson, P., Blomqvist, O., and Engel, J. A. (2000). Nicotinic mechanisms involved in the dopamine activating and reinforcing properties of ethanol. *Behav. Brain Res.* 113, 85–96.

Spanagel, R. (2009). Alcoholism: a systems approach from molecular physiology to addictive behavior. *Physiol. Rev.* 89, 649–705.

Steensland, P., Simms, J. A., Holgate, J., Richards, J. K., and Bartlett, S. E. (2007). Varenicline, an alpha4beta2 nicotinic acetylcholine receptor partial agonist, selectively decreases ethanol consumption and seeking. *Proc. Natl. Acad. Sci. U.S.A.* 104, 12518–12523.

Stephens, S. H., Hoft, N. R. I., Schlaepfer, R., Young, S. E., Corley, R. C., McQueen, M. B., et al. (2012). Externalizing behaviors are associated with SNPs in the CHRNA5/CHRNA3/CHRNB4 gene cluster. *Behav. Genet.* 42, 402–414.

Swanson, L. W. (1982). The projections of the ventral tegmental area and adjacent regions: a combined fluorescent retrograde tracer and immunofluorescence study in the rat. *Brain Res. Bull.* 9, 321–353.

Tapper, A. R., McKinney, S. L., Nashmi, R., Schwarz, J., Deshpande, P., Labarca, C., et al. (2004). Nicotine activation of alpha4* receptors: sufficient for reward, tolerance, and sensitization. *Science* 306, 1029–1032.

Theile, J. W., Morikawa, H., Gonzales, R. A., and Morrisett, R. A. (2011). GABAergic transmission modulates ethanol excitation of ventral tegmental area dopamine neurons. *Neuroscience* 172, 94–103.

Thorgeirsson, T. E., Gudbjartsson, D. F., Surakka, I., Vink, J. M., Amin, N., Geller, F., et al. (2010). Sequence variants at CHRNB3-CHRNA6 and CYP2A6 affect smoking behavior. *Nat. Genet.* 42, 448–453.

Tolu, S., Eddine, R., Marti, F., David, V., Graupner, M., Pons, S., et al. (2012). Co-activation of VTA DA and GABA neurons mediates nicotine reinforcement. *Mol. Psychiatry* 18, 382–393.

Tonstad, S., Tonnesen, P., Hajek, P., Williams, K. E., Billing, C. B., and Reeves, K. R. (2006). Effect of maintenance therapy with varenicline on smoking cessation: a randomized controlled trial. *JAMA* 296, 64–71.

True, W. R., Xian, H., Scherrer, J. F., Madden, P. A., Bucholz, K. K., Heath, A. C., et al. (1999). Common genetic vulnerability for nicotine and alcohol dependence in men. *Arch. Gen. Psychiatry* 56, 655–661.

Tyndale, R. F. (2003). Genetics of alcohol and tobacco use in humans. *Ann. Med.* 35, 94–121.

Unwin, N. (2005). Refined structure of the nicotinic acetylcholine receptor at 4A resolution. *J. Mol. Biol.* 346, 967–989.

Volpicelli, J. R., Alterman, A. I., Hayashida, M., and O'Brien, C. P. (1992). Naltrexone in the treatment of alcohol dependence. *Arch. Gen. Psychiatry* 49, 876–880.

Wang, J. C., Grucza, R., Cruchaga, C., Hinrichs, A. L., Bertelsen, S., Budde, J. P., et al. (2009). Genetic variation in the CHRNA5 gene affects mRNA levels and is associated with risk for alcohol dependence. *Mol. Psychiatry* 14, 501–510.

Weiss, F., Lorang, M. T., Bloom, F. E., and Koob, G. F. (1993). Oral alcohol self-administration stimulates dopamine release in the rat nucleus accumbens: genetic and motivational determinants. *J. Pharmacol. Exp. Ther.* 267, 250–258.

Wise, R. A., and Bozarth, M. A. (1987). A psychomotor stimulant theory of addiction. *Psychol. Rev.* 94, 469–492.

Wonnacott, S. (1997). Presynaptic nicotinic ACh receptors. *Trends Neurosci.* 20, 92–98.

World Health Organization. (2011). *Department of Mental Health and Substance Abuse, Global Status Report on Alcohol 2011*, World Health Organization, Department of Mental Health and Substance Abuse, Geneva.

Wouda, J. A., Riga, D., De Vries, W., Stegeman, M., van Mourik, Y., Schetters, D., et al. (2011). Varenicline attenuates cue-induced relapse to alcohol, but not nicotine seeking, while reducing inhibitory response control. *Psychopharmacology (Berl.)* 216, 267–277.

Wu, G., Tonner, P. H., and Miller, K. W. (1994). Ethanol stabilizes the open channel state of the Torpedo nicotinic acetylcholine receptor. *Mol. Pharmacol.* 45, 102–108.

Xiao, C., Shao, X. M., Olive, M. F., Griffin, W. C. III, Li, K. Y., Krnjevic, K., et al. (2009). Ethanol facilitates glutamatergic transmission to dopamine neurons in the ventral tegmental area. *Neuropsychopharmacology* 34, 307–318.

Xiao, C., and Ye, J. H. (2008). Ethanol dually modulates GABAergic synaptic transmission onto dopaminergic neurons in ventral tegmental area: role of mu-opioid receptors. *Neuroscience* 153, 240–248.

Yeomans, J. S., Mathur, A., and Tampakeras, M. (1993). Rewarding brain stimulation: role of tegmental cholinergic neurons that activate dopamine neurons. *Behav. Neurosci.* 107, 1077–1087.

York, J. L., and Hirsch, J. A. (1995). Drinking patterns and health status in smoking and nonsmoking alcoholics. *Alcohol. Clin. Exp. Res.* 19, 666–673.

Zhao-Shea, R., Liu, L., Soll, L. G., Improgo, M. R., Meyers, E. E., McIntosh, J. M., et al. (2011). Nicotine-mediated activation of dopaminergic neurons in distinct regions of the ventral tegmental area. *Neuropsychopharmacology* 36, 1021–1032.

Zuo, Y., Nagata, K., Yeh, J. Z., and Narahashi, T. (2004). Single-channel analyses of ethanol modulation of neuronal nicotinic acetylcholine receptors. *Alcohol. Clin. Exp. Res.* 28, 688–696.

Zwart, R., and Vijverberg, H. P. (1998). Four pharmacologically distinct subtypes of alpha4beta2 nicotinic acetylcholine receptor expressed in *Xenopus laevis* oocytes. *Mol. Pharmacol.* 54, 1124–1131.

17

The effects of maternal separation on adult methamphetamine self-administration, extinction, reinstatement, and MeCP2 immunoreactivity in the nucleus accumbens

Candace R. Lewis*, Kelsey Staudinger, Lena Scheck and M. Foster Olive

Department of Psychology, Arizona State University, Tempe, AZ, USA

Edited by:
Remi Martin-Fardon, The Scripps Research Institute, USA

Reviewed by:
Paul J. Kenny, The Scripps Research Institute, USA
Zachary A. Rodd, Indiana University School of Medicine, USA

*Correspondence:
Candace R. Lewis, Department of Psychology, Arizona State University, PO Box 871104, Tempe, AZ 85287, USA
e-mail: candace.lewis@asu.edu

The maternal separation (MS) paradigm is an animal model of early life stress. Animals subjected to MS during the first 2 weeks of life display altered behavioral and neuroendocrinological stress responses as adults. MS also produces altered responsiveness to and self-administration (SA) of various drugs of abuse including cocaine, ethanol, and amphetamine. However, no studies have yet examined the effects of MS on methamphetamine (METH) SA. This study was performed to examine the effects of MS on the acquisition of METH SA, extinction, and reinstatement of METH-seeking behavior in adulthood. Given the known influence of early life stress and drug exposure on epigenetic processes, we also investigated group differences in levels of the epigenetic marker methyl CpG binding protein 2 (MeCP2) in the nucleus accumbens (NAc) core. Long–Evans pups and dams were separated on postnatal days (PND) 2–14 for either 180 (MS180) or 15 min (MS15). Male offspring were allowed to acquire METH SA (0.05 mg/kg/infusion) in 15 2-h daily sessions starting at PND67, followed by extinction training and cue-induced reinstatement of METH-seeking behavior. Rats were then assessed for MeCP2 levels in the NAc core by immunohistochemistry. The MS180 group self-administered significantly more METH and acquired SA earlier than the MS15 group. No group differences in extinction or cue-induced reinstatement were observed. MS15 rats had significantly elevated MeCP2-immunoreactive cells in the NAc core as compared to MS180 rats. Together, these data suggest that MS has lasting influences on METH SA as well as epigenetic processes in the brain reward circuitry.

Keywords: **maternal separation, Mecp2, methamphetamine, early life stress, self-administration, nucleus accumbens, epigenetics**

INTRODUCTION

Methamphetamine (METH) is an extremely potent and highly addictive psychostimulant and neurotoxic drug (Xie and Miller, 2009). METH abuse has many detrimental consequences for the individual and for society as a whole. For the individual, chronic abuse has negative neuropsychological and psychiatric effects, as well as modifying the healthy brain's functional and structural reward and learning neurocircuitry (Darke et al., 2008; Krasnova and Cadet, 2009; Taylor et al., 2013). METH abuse has been identified as both a strong risk factor for violence and high-risk sexual behaviors. In one study of a population between the ages of 18 and 25, 34.9% self-reported violent behavior while under the influence of METH, such as domestic violence, gang-related violence, and random acts of violence (Sommers et al., 2006). Individuals on METH often engage in unprotected vaginal and anal sex and also have sex with multiple partners (Springer et al., 2007). It is apparent that chronic METH use has a multitude of deleterious effects on both the users and society as a whole.

Since METH use has been associated with a variety of negative health and social consequences, it is important to identify risk-factors associated with its abuse. Clinical research has shown early life stress, particularly childhood abuse and neglect, is a reliable risk factor that influences adult drug abuse (Anda et al., 2006; Messina et al., 2008). Childhood abuse or neglect is highly prevalent with ∼1.5 million cases reported in 2010 (Child Maltreatment 2010, U.S. Department of Health and Human Services) and exposure to childhood abuse and household dysfunction has been related to an earlier onset of METH use in both men and women (Messina et al., 2008). There is substantial evidence that early life stress produces long-lasting changes in the brain, including regions that mediate reward-seeking and executive control, which may ultimately predispose the individual to increased propensity toward illicit drug use and addiction (Matthews et al., 2001; Meaney et al., 2002). Stressors during adulthood have also been implicated in affecting drug and alcohol self-administration (SA) (Piazza et al., 1990; Breese et al., 2011).

The rodent maternal separation (MS) model of early life stress is a commonly used paradigm to investigate the influences of early life events on addictive behaviors. In this paradigm, rodents undergo daily separation from maternal care during critical postnatal development and later assessed for propensity toward addiction-like behaviors in adulthood. For example, pups undergoing MS for several hours exhibit depression-like symptoms, high anxiety-like behavior, exaggerated neuroendocrinological responses to stress, and have a high preference for ethanol (Huot et al., 2001). MS has been reported to also alter the reinforcing effects of cocaine, amphetamine, and morphine (Vazquez et al., 2005; Moffett et al., 2006; Der-Avakian and Markou, 2010). However, only a few reports have been published on the effects of MS on adult METH-seeking behavior. In one study, MS failed to produce a significant increase in adolescent METH conditioned place preference (CPP) (Faure et al., 2009), while another study demonstrated that MS attenuated METH CPP in adolescents (Dimatelis et al., 2012a). MS has also been shown to produce a sex- and dose-dependent increase in locomotor and stereotypy responses to METH in adolescent rats (Pritchard et al., 2012). To our knowledge, however, there are no reports to date on the effect of MS on adult intravenous (i.v.) METH SA, extinction, and reinstatement. Given the negative impact of METH abuse and the relationship observed between MS and other drugs of abuse, more research in this area is warranted.

Emerging evidence suggests a strong role of epigenetics in regulating gene transcription based on early experiences that in turn modulate brain systems and behavior into adulthood. Many neural systems implicated in drug addiction are influenced by MS, such as the hypothalamic pituitary adrenal (HPA) axis (Plotsky and Meaney, 1993), endocannabinoid system (Romano-López et al., 2012), monoaminergic systems (Matthews et al., 2001; Ploj et al., 2003; Dimatelis et al., 2012b), and growth factors such as BDNF (Bolaños and Nestler, 2004; Lippmann et al., 2007). Recent studies implicate epigenetic modifications as a mechanism behind these changes in rodents, non-human primates, and humans (McGowan et al., 2009; Murgatroyd et al., 2009; Kinnally et al., 2011). For example, Murgatroyd et al. (2009) showed that MS induced hypomethylation of the arginine-vasopressin (Avp) enhancer, subsequently causing upregulation of Avp expression and a hyper-responsive HPA axis. Additionally, maternal care has been implicated in DNA methylation and corresponding changes in glucocorticoid receptor (GR) expression levels in the hippocampus (Weaver et al., 2004). Furthermore, adult rats exposed to early life stress have demonstrated reduced BDNF in the prefrontal cortex correlated with hypermethylation of the BDNF IV promoter region (Roth et al., 2009). Indeed, these studies suggest that early life experiences are influencing epigenetic markers that modulate multiple brain systems implicated in drug vulnerability.

Interestingly, epigenetic factors are also altered by drug exposure and can influence drug intake, behavioral, and neural responses (Renthal and Nestler, 2008; Robison and Nestler, 2011; Lewis and Olive, in press). For example, trimethylation of histone H3 lysine 4 (H3K4) at the promoter region of a chemokine receptor type 2 (CCR2), a gene implicated in locomotor sensitization, has been associated with METH-induced hyperlocomotion in mice (Ikegami et al., 2010). Additionally, cocaine increases methyl CpG binding protein 2 (MeCP2) expression in multiple brain regions of the rat (Cassel et al., 2006) and MeCP2 has been implicated in cocaine and amphetamine reward and reinforcement (Deng et al., 2010; Im et al., 2010). Specifically, Deng et al.

(2010) found that virally mediated ablation of MeCP2 expression in the nucleus accumbens (NAc) increased the conditioned rewarding effects of amphetamines, whereas overexpression of MeCP2 in the NAc decreased amphetamine reward. Furthermore, Im et al. (2010) showed that cocaine intake was reduced after knockdown of MeCP2 expression in the dorsal striatum. Hence, recent studies suggest that the predisposition of one's epigenetic phenotype may influence their behavioral response to drugs of abuse while exposure to drugs of abuse also modulates their epigenetic phenotype.

Although MS and psychostimulants have been shown to individually affect epigenetic factors such as MeCP2, and MeCP2 has been implicated in drug seeking behavior, it is yet to be determined if MS and, specifically, METH also interact to affect epigenetic factors. Therefore, the goal of the present study was to investigate the relationship between early life stress, METH SA, extinction and reinstatement, and MeCP2 expression in the NAc. We hypothesized that MS would increase susceptibility to the acquisition of METH SA, impair extinction learning, and increase cue-induced reinstatement. We also predicted that MeCP2 expression in the NAc would be negatively correlated with levels of METH SA.

MATERIALS AND METHODS

All experimental and surgical procedures were carried out in adherence to the National Institutes of Health *Guide for the Care and Use of Laboratory Animals* (National Research Council, 1996) and approved by the Institutional Animal Care and Use Committee of Arizona State University.

ANIMALS AND MATERNAL SEPARATION PROCEDURES

Pregnant dams were purchased from Charles River Laboratories and arrived on gestational day 12 (GD12). Dams were housed individually in standard polycarbonate cages in a temperature and humidity controlled room with food and water available *ad libitum*. Beginning on GD20 (range of gestation 21–23 days) cages were checked for delivery of pups three times a day. Litters were culled to a maximum size of 12 immediately after discovery. Litter sizes ranged from 10 to 12 with one litter at eight due to pup attrition. The litter sex ratios were left natural with an average of 7/6 male/female ratio across all litters. Day of birth was considered postnatal day 0 (PND0).

Litters were randomly assigned to one of two conditions: MS for 180 min per day (MS180) or the handled group, 15 min per day (MS15). After pup attrition due to filicide, and exclusion of animals that lost catheter patency during the experiment, the MS15 ($n = 9$) condition had three litters with one to four male pups per litter and the MS180 ($n = 17$) group had five litters with two to five male pups per litter that were used in the behavioral testing. The separation procedure began on PND2. At 8:00 a.m. (reverse light cycle, lights off at 7:00 a.m.) the dam was removed from the home cage and placed into a new cage with fresh bedding. The pups were then removed and placed into a separation cage kept in an isolated room. Heat lamps were set over the separation cages and maintained at 30 ± 0.5 to 32 ± 0.5 °C to control for hypothermic conditions. The pups were left unattended during the corresponding separation period then returned to the home-cage immediately prior to the dams return.

During PND15–19 litters were left undisturbed, weaned on PND21 into same sex group housing, and pair housed with a sibling on PND45. After separation procedures rats were left undisturbed with the exception of once a week cage cleaning performed by Department of Animal Care and Treatment employes. Females were not used for the remainder of the study.

SURGICAL PROCEDURES

Male rats were implanted with i.v. catheters into the jugular vein on PND60 ± 1 day. Rats were anesthetized with isoflurane (2% v/v, Butler Schein Animal Health, Dublin, OH, USA) vaporized in oxygen at a flow rate of 2 l/min. Rats received pre-incision injections of buprenorphine (0.05 mg/kg, s.c., Reckitt Benckiser, Richmond, VA, USA) and meloxicam (1 mg/kg, s.c., Boehringer Ingelheim, St. Joseph, MO, USA). Surgical sites were shaved and cleaned with 1% iodine. A ~2 cm incision was made in order to isolate the right or left jugular vein. A sterile silastic catheter filled with 100 U/ml heparin was inserted 2.5 cm into the vein. The catheter was secured to the surrounding tissue with sutures, and the opposite end of the catheter was tunneled subcutaneously to the dorsum where it exited the skin between the scapulae. The catheter was secured to the surrounding tissue by sutures and a mesh collar attached to a threaded vascular access port (Plastics One, Roanoke, VA, USA). The wound was then treated with 0.2 ml bupivacaine hydrochloride (0.25% v/v), closed with nylon sutures (Ethicon, San Lorenzo, Puerto Rico) and topically treated with topical lidocaine and a triple antibiotic gel. The access port was sealed with a piece of Tygon tubing closed at one end and a threaded protective cap (Plastics One). Rats were given small portions of sweetened cereal to facilitate postsurgical rehabilitation. Following surgical procedures, rats were allowed at least 7 days of recovery and received daily i.v. infusions of 0.2 ml Timentin and 0.2 ml heparin to minimize infections and maintain catheter patency.

SELF-ADMINISTRATION APPARATUS

Behavioral testing was conducted in SA chambers (ENV-008; Med Associates Inc., St. Albans, VT, USA) that were interfaced to a PC computer and located in sound attenuating melamine enclosures equipped with ventilation fans. The chambers (28 cm × 27 cm × 22 cm) consisted of two aluminum walls and two clear Plexiglas walls. The ceiling was also constructed of Plexiglas with a 3-cm diameter hole cut in the center to allow a drug delivery tether to pass through. The floor consisted parallel stainless steel rods (0.48 cm diameter) placed 1.6 cm apart. Each chamber contained a house light located 1.25 cm from the ceiling, a Sonalert speaker that provided an auditory stimulus (~65 dB, 2900 Hz) during drug infusion, one retractable response lever, one stationary response lever, and two 2.5 cm stimulus cue lights located above each response lever. The retractable lever was designated the active lever as an additional cue for drug availability. Response levers were located 7 cm above the floor of the chamber. Centered between the levers was a 5 cm × 5 cm food pellet receptacle. Each chamber was outfitted with a single-speed automated drug infusion pump (PHM-100; Med Associates). Tygon microbore tubing (0.5 mm ID) was used to connect the syringe containing the drug solution to a single-channel liquid swivel that was mounted to the top of the chamber enclosure. The swivel was then connected to the vascular access port using Tygon microbore tubing that was protected by a stainless steel tether (Plastics One, Roanoke, VA, USA). All experimental parameters were controlled using Med PC IV software (Med Associates).

METHAMPHETAMINE SELF-ADMINISTRATION, EXTINCTION, AND CUE-INDUCED REINSTATEMENT

Beginning on PND67 male rats underwent 2 h daily SA sessions whereby presses on one of the levers (designated the active lever) resulted in delivery of METH (0.1 mg/kg per infusion, delivered in a volume of 0.06 ml over a 2-s period) on an fixed ratio 1 (FR1) schedule of reinforcement. Each METH infusion delivery was followed by a 20-s timeout period, during which additional active lever presses were recorded but produced no drug infusions. Each infusion was accompanied by concurrent illumination of a stimulus light located directly above the active lever, and presentation of an auditory stimulus for 2 s. SA sessions were conducted 7 days per week for 15 consecutive days. METH hydrochloride (Sigma Aldrich, St. Louis, MO, USA) was dissolved in 0.9% sterile saline for i.v. SA.

Next, all animals were subjected to extinction training, whereby presses on the active lever no longer produced any programed consequences (i.e., no tone/light presentation and no activation of the syringe pump). Extinction training sessions were 2 h in length and were conducted for 15 consecutive days. On the day immediately following the last extinction session, all rats underwent cue-induced reinstatement, whereby presses on the active lever produced the tone and light cue previously presented during METH infusion, but did not deliver any drug solution. Presses on the inactive lever did not produce any programed consequences throughout the experiment.

TISSUE PREPARATION AND IMMUNOHISTOCHEMISTRY

Immunochemistry procedures were carried out according to standard procedures. Brain tissues were collected on the day following the reinstatement test session. Rats were deeply anesthetized with 150 mg/kg i.p. sodium pentobarbital and perfused transcardially with ice-cold 0.1 M phosphate buffered saline (PBS) followed by ice-cold 4% w/v paraformaldehyde (PFA) in PBS, pH 7.4. Brains were removed, post-fixed in 4% PFA overnight and stored in 30% w/v sucrose in PBS. Brains were sectioned (35 μm thickness) in the coronal plane on a cryostat (Leica CM1900, Bannockburn, IL, USA). Sections were then rinsed 3 × 10 min in PBS containing 0.1% v/v Tween 20 (PBST) followed by incubation in PBST containing 5% v/v normal donkey serum for 1 h. Sections were then incubated overnight under gentile agitation at 4° C in PBST containing a rabbit anti-MeCP2 polyclonal antibody (PA1-887; 1:200 dilution; Thermo Scientific) and then rinsed 3 × 10 min in PBS. Sections were then incubated in PBS containing Alexa Fluor 488 conjugated donkey anti-rabbit IgG antisera (1:200; Jackson ImmunoResearch, West Grove, PA, USA) and then rinsed 3 × 10 min in PBS. Sections were mounted on microscope slides using VectaShield mounting media (Vector Labs, Burlingame, CA, USA), coverslipped, and stored in darkness until imaging.

IMMUNOREACTIVITY ANALYSIS

Investigator was blind to treatment condition during microscopical analysis. Sections were visualized at 200× magnification using a Leica DMLB epifluorescence microscope equipped with a digital camera that was interfaced to a PC. Digital images of the selected area were obtained using Leica IM50 software and counted by two observers blind to treatment conditions using the ImageJ Tool software package (Rasband, W.S., ImageJ, U.S. National Institutes of Health, Bethesda, MD, USA). The average background removed by the software was 50. A total of six sample areas of the NAc were counted for each subject (i.e., one sample area/two hemispheres/three sections). NAc core area was chosen based on the corpus callosum as a landmark. Care was taken to ensure that the sections for each subject that were labeled came from the same anatomical level within each plane. The counts from all six sample areas from a particular region were averaged to provide a mean number of immunoreactive cells per animal to be used as an $n = 1$ for statistical analysis (Thiel et al., 2009). Inter rater reliability was 89%.

DATA ANALYSIS

The alpha level was set at 0.05 for all statistical analyses and analyzed using IBM SPSS Statistics 20 software. A repeated-measures ANCOVA with litter as the factor and rearing condition as the covariate was used to test for litter effects. Separate repeated-measures ANOVAs with rearing condition as a between-subjects factor and session as a within-subjects factor were used to analyze active and inactive lever presses during SA and extinction. The correlation between METH-seeking behavior and MeCP2 expression within the NAc was calculated using Pearson's product correlation.

RESULTS

LITTER EFFECTS

A repeated-measures ANCOVA was conducted by litters and controlling for rearing condition on the number of METH infusions per session over 15 days revealed no significant pre-existing differences between litters ($p = 0.23$).

METH SELF-ADMINISTRATION

A total of $n = 4$ animals were removed from the MS15 and MS180 groups respectively due to loss of catheter patency. Repeated-measures ANOVA revealed a significant main effect of rearing condition on the number of METH infusions per session [$F(1,24) = 9.83$, $p = 0.004$] (see **Figures 1** and **2**), as well as the number of total active lever presses per session [$F(1,24) = 13.79$, $p = 0.001$], MS180 had more active lever presses and received more infusions than MS15. No group differences in the total number of inactive lever presses were observed [$F(1,17) = 38.76$, $p = 0.425$]. However, in both rearing conditions we noted a time-dependent increase in inactive lever pressing across SA sessions (see **Table 1**), and we attribute this to be a result of non-specific motor activity that resulted from increasing level of METH SA.

EXTINCTION

For both groups, extinction training produced a significant reduction in the number of active lever presses when comparing the average of the final 2 days of Ext to the average of the final 2 days

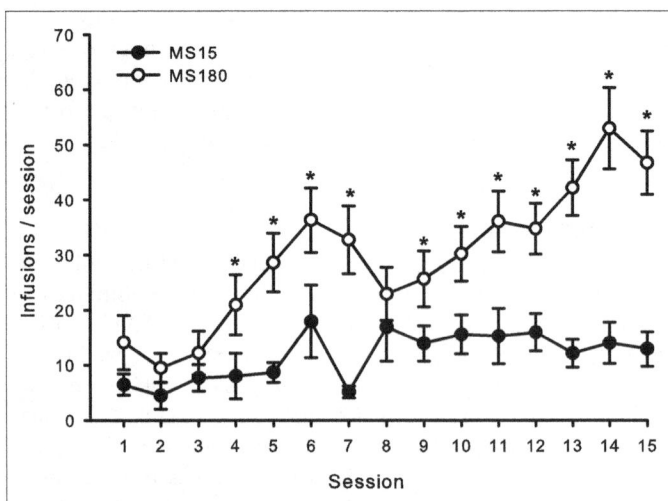

FIGURE 1 | Average number of METH SA infusions per 2-h session for 15 consecutive days in MS15 ($n = 9$) and MS180 ($n = 17$) rats. Data points represent group mean ± SEM. *$p < 0.05$ vs. MS15.

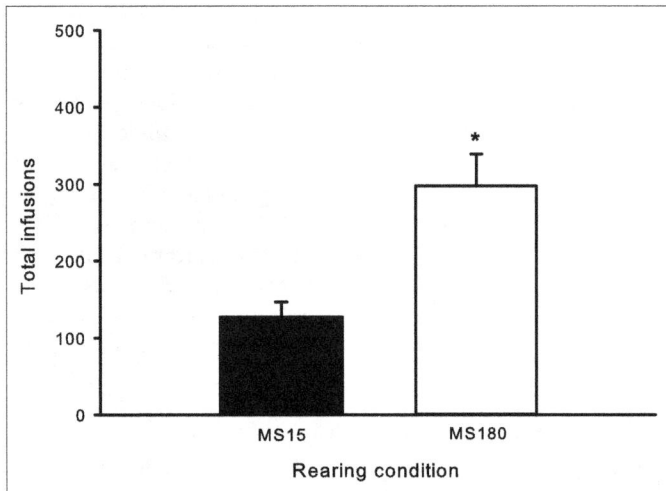

FIGURE 2 | Total number of METH infusions earned across 15 daily 2-h sessions in MS15 ($n = 9$) and MS180 ($n = 17$) rats. Data points represent group mean ± SEM. *$p < 0.05$ vs. MS15.

of SA ($n = 26$) [$t(50) = 5.10$, $p < 0.0001$]. Repeated-measures ANOVA revealed no significant group differences (MS15 $n = 9$, MS180 $n = 17$) in rate of extinction of active lever pressing [$F(1,20) = 0.94$, $p = 0.34$] (see **Figure 3**). However, a significant group difference in the number of inactive lever presses during extinction training [$F(1,24) = 5.47$, $p = 0.028$] was observed, with rats in the MS15 group emitting more inactive lever presses over the 15-day extinction period compared to the MS180 group (see **Table 1**).

CUE-INDUCED REINSTATEMENT

Cue-induced reinstatement was observed in both groups as assessed by the number of active lever presses (averaged across the final 2 days of Ext) compared to active lever presses during the reinstatement session [$t(50) = -4.46$, $p < 0.0001$]. However, there

Table 1 | Mean ± SEM active or inactive lever presses across 15 METH SA sessions (in 5 session bins), 15 extinction sessions, and the cue-induced reinstatement session.

	MS15	MS180
SELF-ADMINISTRATION		
Active lever presses (sessions 1–5)	35 ± 11	85 ± 15
Active lever presses (sessions 6–10)	51 ± 11	111 ± 19
Active lever presses (sessions 11–15)	70 ± 14	213 ± 23
Inactive lever presses (sessions 1–5)	122 ± 46	73 ± 18
Inactive lever presses (sessions 6–10)	97 ± 25	101 ± 25
Inactive lever presses (sessions 11–15)	144 ± 36	167 ± 36
EXTINCTION		
Active lever presses	147 ± 22	151 ± 10
Inactive lever presses	302 ± 100	117 ± 16[*]
REINSTATEMENT		
Active lever presses	18 ± 4	24 ± 3
Inactive lever presses	7 ± 3	8 ± 2

[*]Indicates $p < 0.05$ vs. inactive lever presses during extinction in the MS15 group.

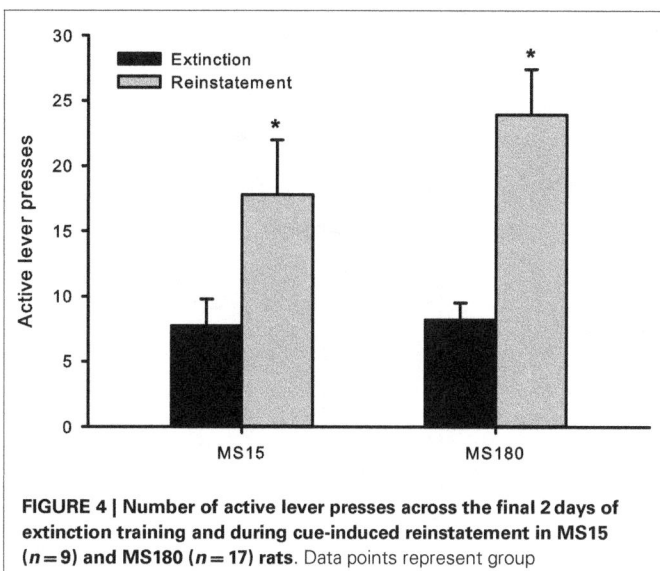

FIGURE 4 | Number of active lever presses across the final 2 days of extinction training and during cue-induced reinstatement in MS15 ($n = 9$) and MS180 ($n = 17$) rats. Data points represent group mean ± SEM. *$p < 0.05$ vs. extinction.

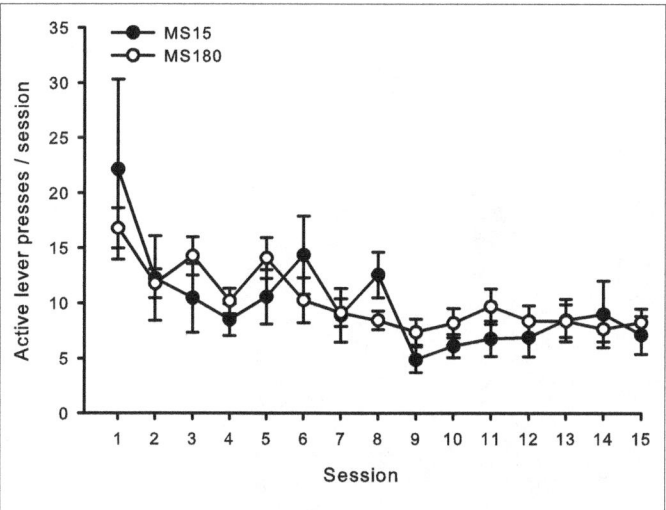

FIGURE 3 | Average number of active lever presses per 2-h session for 15 consecutive days during extinction in MS15 ($n = 9$) and MS180 ($n = 17$) rats. Data points represent group mean ± SEM. No significant differences between rearing conditions were observed.

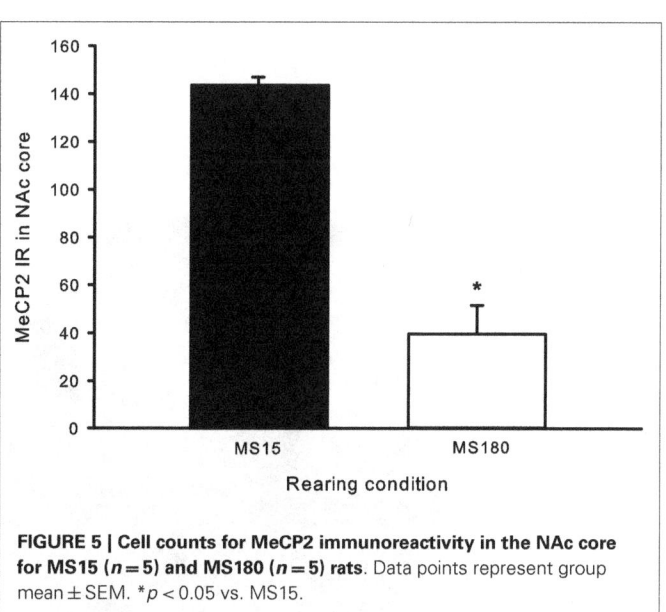

FIGURE 5 | Cell counts for MeCP2 immunoreactivity in the NAc core for MS15 ($n = 5$) and MS180 ($n = 5$) rats. Data points represent group mean ± SEM. *$p < 0.05$ vs. MS15.

was no significant difference between the groups for the number of active lever presses during reinstatement testing [$F(1,24)$ 1.134, $p = 0.298$] (see **Figure 4**).

MeCP2 IMMUNOREACTIVITY

A total of ten pups from five different litters (three per rearing condition) were used in the analysis of the MeCP2 data. There was a highly significant difference in MeCP2 immunoreactivity between MS15 rats and MS180 rats in the NAc core, $p < 0.001$, with MS15 expressing more labeled profiles than did MS180 (see **Figure 5**). There was also a negative correlation between MeCP2 immunoreactivity and number of total active lever presses during 15 days of SA, $r = -0.839$, $p = 0.003$ ($n = 5$ per rearing condition)

(see **Figure 6**). Rats emitting fewer lever presses expressed higher numbers of labeled profiles in the NAc core (**Figure 7**).

DISCUSSION

Early life maternal care is known to influence a multitude of neurological, endocrine, epigenetic, and behavioral outcomes in adulthood (Francis et al., 1999; Roth, 2012). Our findings contribute to the literature by suggesting that MS causes alterations that influence vulnerability to drug abuse (Moffett et al., 2007), in this case METH SA. For the first time, our study suggests that either repeated and prolonged MS leads to increased vulnerability to METH intake or that minimal MS protects against adult METH SA vulnerability. This is evidenced by our findings that MS180 rats showed higher levels of METH SA over 15 daily sessions compared to MS15. These findings are in agreement with

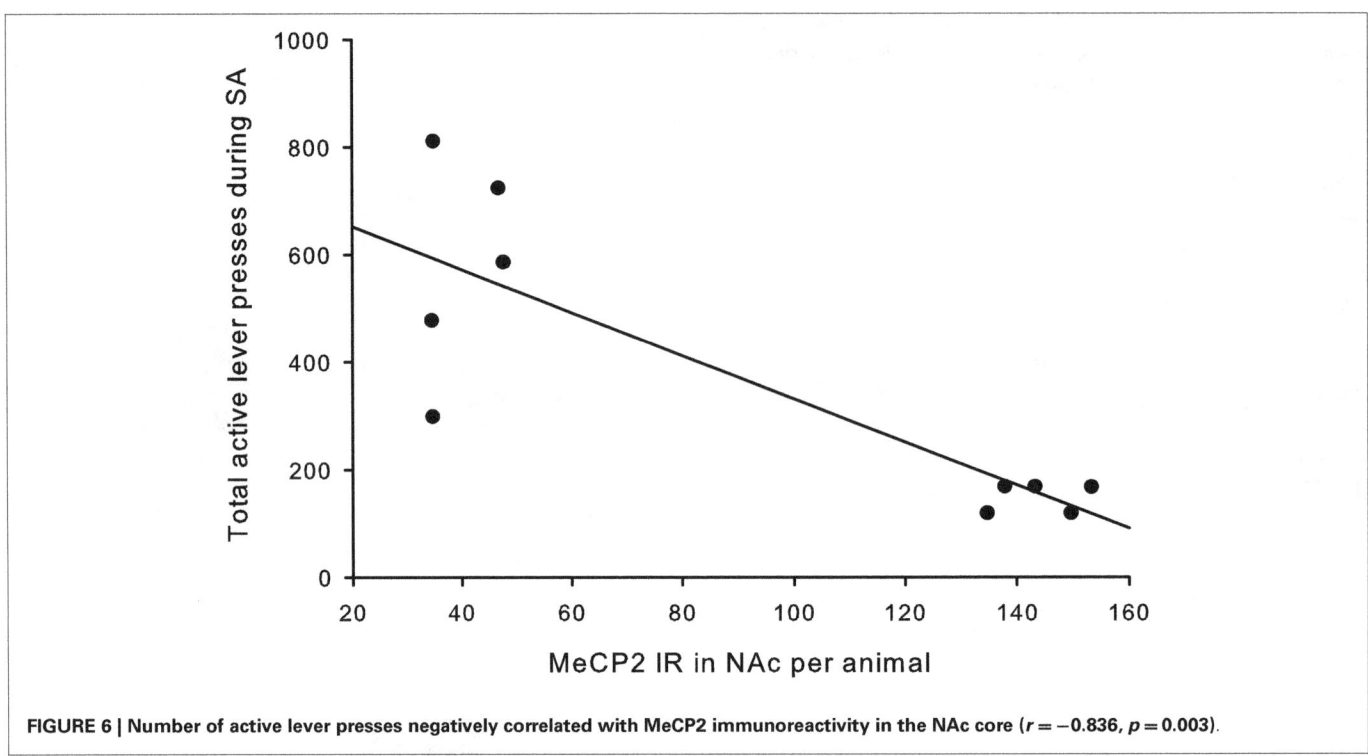

FIGURE 6 | Number of active lever presses negatively correlated with MeCP2 immunoreactivity in the NAc core ($r = -0.836$, $p = 0.003$).

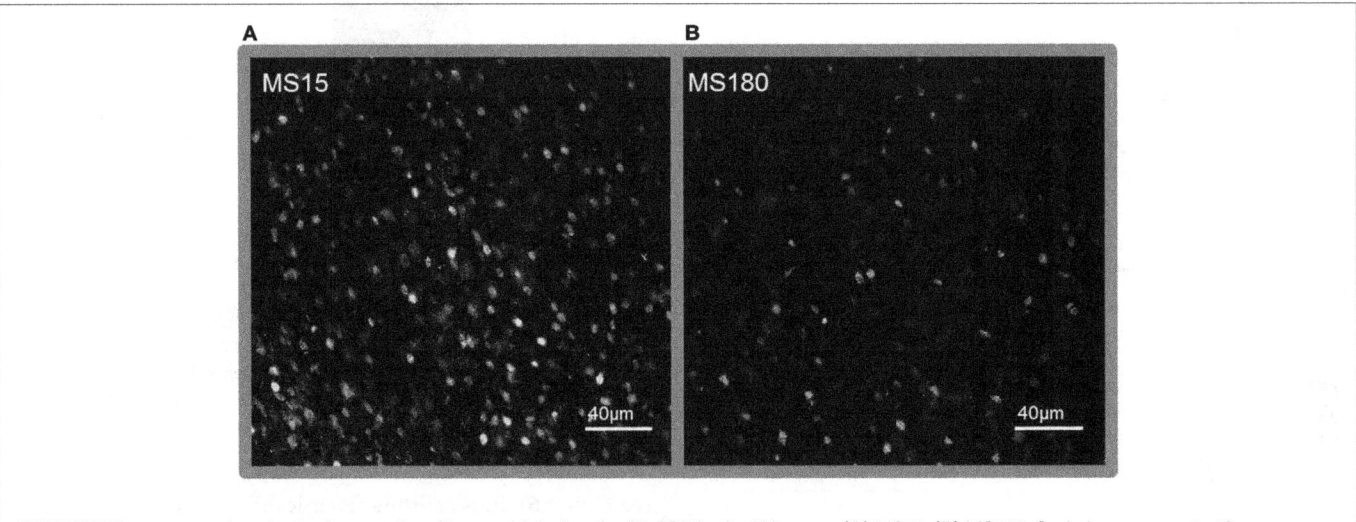

FIGURE 7 | Representative photomicrographs of immunolabeling for MeCP2 in the NAc core. **(A)** MS15, **(B)** MS180. Scale bar represents 40 μm.

previous studies examining effects of MS on intake of cocaine, morphine, amphetamine, and ethanol (Huot et al., 2001; Vazquez et al., 2005; Moffett et al., 2006; Der-Avakian and Markou, 2010). Additionally, we noted that MS15 rats demonstrated a preference for the inactive lever over the active lever during SA. While the reason for this is currently unknown, a possible explanation for this counterintuitive observation is different non-specific behavioral response to METH SA or enhanced operant sensation seeking in the MS15 group.

The possible protective or resilient effect in the MS15 group provides an interesting comparison. MS15 adults have shown

reduced responding for cocaine when compared to non-separated controls (Flagel et al., 2003; Moffett et al., 2006). Since our data set does not include a non-handled control it is difficult to distinguish whether the SA behavior is reflective of increased vulnerability in the MS180, protective effects in MS15, or both, but the robust differences are clear. The effects of brief and prolonged MS we found on METH SA fits the inverted U-shape resilience function usually found in drug abuse-related behaviors after MS (Neisewander et al., 2012). It has been postulated that the protective effects seen in the MS15 group may be due to the increased maternal care post separation (Marmendal et al., 2004; Francis and Kuhar, 2008).

Many have argued that the MS15 rearing condition is more ethologically relevant than the standard non-separated controls since food foraging and other activities would necessitate the dam to leave the litter for brief amounts of time.

The current literature on MS and drug reward, reinforcement, and SA demonstrates that MS180 and MS15 tend to be the most divergent groups when compared to the various controls. For this reason, in the present study, we did not include a non-separated control group in order to increase validity and reliability in our data and improve interpretation in comparison with other studies. Additionally, there are large inconsistencies across laboratories with regards to procedures for breeding, culling, fostering, litter sex ratios, separation duration and days, the order in which dams and pups are returned to the home cage, controlled temperature settings outside of the home cage, PND of weaning, and post-weaning housing conditions prior to and during manipulations. Furthermore, the use of control groups (including MS0, non-handled, and Animal Facility Reared) is highly variable. The issues concerning different control groups and variations in procedures have previously been discussed by others (Matthews et al., 1999, 2001). Jaworski et al. (2005) provides a well laid out table comparing different experimental and control groups commonly used. Recently, a trend toward comparing only two groups has emerged. For example, Matthews et al. (2001) used a MS2 and MS360, Ploj et al. (2003) only used MS15 and MS360, and Murgatroyd et al. (2009) used non-disturbed and MS180 with mice. Our current paradigm met the goal of optimizing the differences between conditions and is consistent with the type of two group design that is currently gaining momentum in this field.

For almost a decade, it has been known that maternal care during early neurological development influences DNA methylation that is directly responsible for HPA reactivity to stress throughout the lifespan. Weaver et al. (2004), showed that offspring of low licking/grooming and arch-back nursing (LG-ABN) mothers had higher levels of GR DNA methylation, decreased expression of the GR gene, a heighted HPA stress response, and displayed more fear-like behavior. Since this pioneering study, many laboratories have demonstrated various alterations in DNA methylation in adulthood following early life stress. For example, early life stress has been associated with increased global methylation, as well as increased methylation at the regulatory region of serotonin transporter (5-HTT), and higher behavioral stress responses in female macaques (Kinnally et al., 2011). Early life stress has also been found to induce hypomethylation of the Avp enhancer in male mice with a subsequent increased HPA reactivity (Murgatroyd et al., 2009). Although the brain region, gene, and direction in which DNA methylation is altered by early life stress is diverse, the outcome tends to remain constant, with a hyperactive HPA stress response and/or increased behavioral stress reactivity in adulthood. Since an overactive HPA axis and early life stress are strongly associated with a higher risk for drug addiction, additional research is needed to investigate if early life stress mediates epigenetic factors influencing the reward network that may predispose the animal to a higher propensity toward drug intake.

Methyl CpG binding protein 2 is a methylated DNA binding protein that attracts histone deacetylases (HDACs) and is commonly associated with specific gene silencing and repression of transcription (Jones et al., 1998), although it may also act to mediate transcription on a genome wide manner as well (Skene et al., 2010). Interestingly, drug exposure mediates levels of MeCP2 in various brain regions and manipulating MeCP2 levels prior to drug exposure can affect the drugs rewarding properties (Cassel et al., 2006; Deng et al., 2010; Im et al., 2010). Therefore we investigated if early life stress mediated MeCP2 levels in the NAc core, a brain region associated with the initial rewarding effects of drugs of abuse (Taylor et al., 2013). We observed group differences in MeCP2 immunoreactivity in the NAc core, such that MS15 rats expressed significantly higher levels of MeCP2 compared to MS180 rats.

Our results suggest a difference in DNA methylation in the NAc; however, the precise gene(s) where methylation has occurred and is bound by MeCP2 was not determined. Previous studies have suggested that MS rats may have altered DA, NE, and 5-HT function and GABA and glutamate levels in the NAc (Hall et al., 1999; Matthews et al., 2001; Romano-López et al., 2012). It has also been demonstrated that NAc protein expression is extensively changed after both MS and METH exposure (Dimatelis et al., 2012b). Therefore, the difference in methylated DNA may be associated with any number of genes involved in these systems in the NAc, and identification of methylated genes is worthy of further investigation. It is important to note that Romano-López et al. (2012) did not find a difference in MeCP2 levels in the NAc between their separated and non-separated pups using immunoblotting techniques. Thus, quantification by immunohistochemistry may not reveal the same results as by immunoblotting. Additionally, the differences in separation procedures and drug exposure potentially played a role in these contrary results.

The negative correlation between active lever presses and MeCP2 immunoreactivity in the NAc fits with Deng et al.'s (2010) study in which MeCP2 in the NAc had an inverse relationship with amphetamine CPP. This data warrants future directions in order to explicate this relationship, for example, additional studies are needed to determine the influence of rearing condition on MeCP2 levels in the NAc in drug-naïve animals as well as the influence of varying levels of METH exposure. Also worthy of future studies is the possibility that an enriched environment (EE) during adolescence could reverse the detrimental effects of MS on METH SA in adulthood and if it has a mediating effect on MeCP2 levels in the NAc. EE during an abstinence phase of cocaine showed protective effects to cue-induced reinstatement (Thiel et al., 2009) and reduced CPP to cocaine (Solinas et al., 2010). More recently, it was demonstrated that EE during different developmental time points can protect against METH SA acquisition and cue-induced reinstatement (Lü et al., 2012).

Few studies have investigated the effect of MS on drug relapse paradigms yet, there is little data that suggests early life stress may increase relapse vulnerability (Neisewander et al., 2012). Contrary to existing literature and our predictions that MS would influence extinction rates and cue-induced reinstatement, we failed to detect an effect. It is possible that we may have detected an extinction or reinstatement effect if the rats were trained on a progressive ratio or a higher FR of reinforcement since these schedules produce higher response rates. On the other hand, failing to find an effect may be indicative that rearing condition only influenced the initial rewarding or reinforcing effects of METH as opposed to the subsequent course of addiction, abstinence, and relapse. Also, we only tested for cue-induced reinstatement, future research is necessary to determine group differences in stress and drug induced reinstatement.

In summary, we observed that early life stress in the form of extended MS produced an increased vulnerability to adult METH SA in adult male rats or that a minimal daily MS led to resilience in adult METH SA. Increases in METH intake were paralleled by decreased MeCP2 immunoreactivity in the NAc core. Surprisingly,

extinction and cue-induced reinstatement were unaffected by MS. These results suggest the possibility that early life stress may contribute to vulnerability toward METH intake. Further studies are needed to establish a contributory role for changes in MeCP2 levels in the NAc core or other brain regions in these behavioral effects.

ACKNOWLEDGMENTS

This work was supported by Public Health Service grant DA025606 to M. Foster Olive.

REFERENCES

Anda, R. F., Felitti, V. J., Bremner, J. D., Walker, J. D., Whitfield, C., Perry, B. D., et al. (2006). The enduring effects of abuse and related adverse experiences in childhood a convergence of evidence from neurobiology and epidemiology. *Eur. Arch. Psychiatry Clin. Neurosci.* 256, 174–186. doi:10.1007/s00406-005-0624-4

Bolaños, C. A., and Nestler, E. J. (2004). Neurotrophic mechanisms in drug addiction. *Neuromolecular Med.* 5, 69–83. doi:10.1385/NMM:5:1:069

Breese, G. R., Sinha, R., and Heilig, M. (2011). Chronic alcohol neuroadaptation and stress contribute to susceptibility for alcohol craving and relapse. *Pharmacol. Ther.* 129, 149–171. doi:10.1016/j.pharmthera.2010.09.007

Cassel, S., Carouge, D., Gensburger, C., Anglard, P., Burgun, C., Dietrich, J., et al. (2006). Fluoxetine and cocaine induce the epigenetic factors MeCP2 and MBD1 in adult rat brain. *Mol. Pharmacol.* 70, 487–492. doi:10.1124/mol.106.022301

Darke, S., Kaye, S., McKetin, R., and Duflou, J. (2008). Major physical and psychological harms of methamphetamine use. *Drug Alcohol Rev.* 27, 253–262. doi:10.1080/09595230801923702

Deng, J. V., Rodriguiz, R. M., Hutchinson, A. N., Kim, I.-H., Wetsel, W. C., and West, A. E. (2010). MeCP2 in the nucleus accumbens contributes to neural and behavioral responses to psychostimulants. *Nat. Neurosci.* 13, 1128–1136. doi:10.1038/nn.2614

Der-Avakian, A., and Markou, A. (2010). Neonatal maternal separation exacerbates the reward-enhancing effect of acute amphetamine administration and the anhedonic effect of repeated social defeat in adult rats. *Neuroscience* 170, 1189–1198. doi:10.1016/j.neuroscience.2010.08.002

Dimatelis, J. J., Russell, A., Stein, D. J., and Daniels, W. M. (2012a). The effects of lobeline and naltrexone on methamphetamine-induced

place preference and striatal dopamine and serotonin levels in adolescent rats with a history of maternal separation. *Metab. Brain Dis.* 27, 351–361. doi:10.1007/s11011-012-9288-8

Dimatelis, J. J., Russell, V. A., Stein, D. J., and Daniels, W. M. (2012b). Effects of maternal separation and methamphetamine exposure on protein expression in the nucleus accumbens shell and core. *Metab. Brain Dis.* 27, 363–375. doi:10.1007/s11011-012-9295-9

Faure, J., Stein, D. J., and Daniels, W. (2009). Maternal separation fails to render animals more susceptible to methamphetamine-induced conditioned place preference. *Metab. Brain Dis.* 24, 541–559. doi:10.1007/s11011-009-9158-1

Flagel, S. B., Vazquez, D. M., and Robinson, T. E. (2003). Manipulations during the second, but not the first, week of life increase susceptibility to cocaine self-administration in female rats. *Neuropsychopharmacology* 28, 1741–1751. doi:10.1038/sj.npp.1300228

Francis, D. D., and Kuhar, M. J. (2008). Frequency of maternal licking and grooming correlates negatively with vulnerability to cocaine and alcohol use in rats. *Pharmacol. Biochem. Behav.* 90, 497–500. doi:10.1016/j.pbb.2008.04.012

Francis, D. D., Champagne, F. A., Liu, D., and Meaney, M. J. (1999). Maternal care, gene expression, and the development of individual differences in stress reactivity. *Ann. N. Y. Acad. Sci.* 896, 66–84. doi:10.1111/j.1749-6632.1999.tb08106.x

Hall, F. S., Wilkinson, L. S., Humby, T., and Robbins, T. W. (1999). Maternal deprivation of neonatal rats produces enduring changes in dopamine function. *Synapse* 32, 37–43. doi:10.1002/(SICI)1098-2396(199904)32:1<37::AID-SYN5>3.3.CO;2-W

Huot, R. L., Thrivikraman, K. V., Meaney, M. J., and Plotsky, P. M.

(2001). Development of adult ethanol preference and anxiety as a consequence of neonatal maternal separation in Long Evans rats and reversal with antidepressant treatment. *Psychopharmacology (Berl.)* 158, 366–373. doi:10.1007/s002130100701

Ikegami, D., Narita, M., Imai, S., Miyashita, K., Tamura, R., Narita, M., et al. (2010). Epigenetic modulation at the CCR2 gene correlates with the maintenance of behavioral sensitization to methamphetamine. *Addict. Biol.* 15, 358–361. doi:10.1111/j.1369-1600.2010.00219.x

Im, H. I., Hollander, J. A., Bali, P., and Kenny, P. J. (2010). MeCP2 controls BDNF expression and cocaine intake through homeostatic interactions with microRNA-212. *Nat. Neurosci.* 13, 1120–1127. doi:10.1038/nn.2615

Jaworski, J. N., Francis, D. D., Brommer, C. L., Morgan, E. T., and Kuhar, M. J. (2005). Effects of early maternal separation on ethanol intake, GABA receptors and metabolizing enzymes in adult rats. *Psychopharmacology (Berl.)* 181, 8–15. doi:10.1007/s00213-005-2232-4

Jones, P. L., Veenstra, G. J., Wade, P. A., Vermaak, D., Kass, S. U., Landsberger, N., et al. (1998). Methylated DNA and MeCP2 recruit histone deacetylase to repress transcription. *Nat. Genetics* 19, 187–191.

Kinnally, E. L., Feinberg, C., Kim, D., Ferguson, K., Leibel, R., Coplan, J. D., et al. (2011). DNA methylation as a risk factor in the effects of early life stress. *Brain Behav. Immun.* 25, 1548–1553. doi:10.1016/j.bbi.2011.05.001

Krasnova, I., and Cadet, J. L. (2009). Methamphetamine toxicity and messengers of death. *Brain Res. Rev.* 60, 379–407. doi:10.1016/j.brainresrev.2009.03.002

Lippmann, M., Bress, A., Nemeroff, C. B., Plotsky, P. M., and Monteggia, L. M. (2007). Long-term

behavioural and molecular alterations associated with maternal separation in rats. *Eur. J. Neurosci.* 25, 3091–3098. doi:10.1111/j.1460-9568.2007.05522.x

Lü, X., Zhao, C., Zhang, L., Ma, B., Lou, Z., Sun, Y., et al. (2012). The effects of rearing condition on methamphetamine self-administration and cue-induced drug seeking. *Drug Alcohol Depend.* 124, 288–298. doi:10.1016/j.drugalcdep.2012.01.022

Marmendal, M., Roman, E., Eriksson, C. J. P., Nylander, I., and Fahlke, C. (2004). Maternal separation alters maternal care, but has minor effects on behavior and brain opioid peptides in adult offspring. *Dev. Psychobiol.* 45, 140–152. doi:10.1002/dev.20027

Matthews, K., Dalley, J. W., Matthews, C., Tsai, T. H., and Robbins, T. W. (2001). Periodic maternal separation of neonatal rats produces region- and gender-specific effects on biogenic amine content in postmortem adult brain. *Synapse* 40, 1–10. doi:10.1002/1098-2396(200104)40:1<1::AID-SYN1020>3.0.CO;2-E

Matthews, K., Robbins, T. W., Everitt, B. J., and Caine, S. B. (1999). Repeated neonatal maternal separation alters intravenous cocaine self-administration in adult rats. *Psychopharmacology (Berl.)* 141, 123–134. doi:10.1007/s002130050816

McGowan, P. O., Sasaki, A., D'Alessio, A. C., Dymov, S., Labonté, B., Szyf, M., et al. (2009). Epigenetic regulation of the glucocorticoid receptor in human brain associates with childhood abuse. *Nat. Neurosci.* 12, 342–348. doi:10.1038/nn.2270

Meaney, M. J., Brake, W., and Gratton, A. (2002). Environmental regulation of the development of mesolimbic dopamine systems: a neurobiological mechanism for vulnerability to drug abuse? *Psychoneuroendocrinology* 27, 127–138. doi:10.1016/S0306-4530(01)00040-3

Messina, N., Marinelli-Casey, P., Hillhouse, M., Rawson, R., Hunter, J., and Ang, A. (2008). Childhood adverse events and methamphetamine use among men and women childhood adverse events and methamphetamine use among men and women. *J. Psychoactive Drugs* 5, 399–409. doi:10.1080/02791072.2008.1040 0667

Moffett, M. C., Harley, J., Francis, D., Sanghani, S. P., Davis, W. I., and Kuhar, M. J. (2006). Maternal separation and handling affects cocaine self-administration in both the treated pups as adults and the dams. *J. Pharmacol. Exp. Ther.* 317, 1210–1218. doi:10.1124/jpet.106.101139

Moffett, M. C., Vicentic, A., Kozel, M., Plotsky, P., Francis, D. D., and Kuhar, M. J. (2007). Maternal separation alters drug intake patterns in adulthood in rats. *Biochem. Pharmacol.* 73, 321–330. doi:10.1016/j.bcp.2006.08.003

Murgatroyd, C., Patchev, A. V., Wu, Y., Micale, V., Bockmühl, Y., Fischer, D., et al. (2009). Dynamic DNA methylation programs persistent adverse effects of early-life stress. *Nat. Neurosci.* 12, 1559–1566. doi:10.1038/nn.2436

National Research Council. (1996). *Guide for the Care and Use of Laboratory Animals Institute of Laboratory Animal Resources.* Washington: National Academy Press.

Neisewander, J., Peartree, N., and Pentkowski, N. (2012). Emotional valence and context of social influences on drug abuse-related behavior in animal models of social stress and prosocial interaction. *Psychopharmacology (Berl.)* 224, 33–56. doi:10.1007/s00213-012-2853-3

Piazza, P. V., Deminiere, J. M., Le Moal, M., and Simon, H. (1990). Stress- and pharmacologically-induced behavioral sensitization increases vulnerability to acquisition of amphetamine self-administration. *Brain Res.* 514, 22–26. doi:10.1016/0006-8993(90)90431-A

Ploj, K., Roman, E., and Nylander, I. (2003). Long-term effects of maternal separation on ethanol intake and brain opioid and dopamine receptors in male wistar rats. *Neuroscience* 121, 787–799. doi:10.1016/S0306-4522(03)00499-8

Plotsky, P. M., and Meaney, M. J. (1993). Early, postnatal experience alters hypothalamic corticotropin-releasing factor (CRF) mRNA, median eminence CRF content and stress-induced release in adult rats. *Brain Res. Mol. Brain Res.* 18, 195–200. doi:10.1016/0169-328X(93)90189-V

Pritchard, L. M., Hensleigh, E., and Lynch, S. (2012). Altered locomotor and stereotyped responses to acute methamphetamine in adolescent, maternally separated rats. *Psychopharmacology (Berl.)* 223, 27–35. doi:10.1007/s00213-012-2679-z

Renthal, W., and Nestler, E. J. (2008). Epigenetic mechanisms in drug addiction. *Trends Mol. Med.* 14, 341–350. doi:10.1016/j.molmed.2008.06.004

Robison, A. J., and Nestler, E. J. (2011). Transcriptional and epigenetic mechanisms of addiction. *Nat. Rev. Neurosci.* 12, 623–637. doi:10.1038/nrn3111

Romano-López, A., Méndez-Díaz, M., Ruiz-Contreras, A. E., Carrisoza, R., and Prospéro-García, O. (2012). Maternal separation and proclivity for ethanol intake: a potential role of the endocannabinoid system in rats. *Neuroscience* 223, 296–304. doi:10.1016/j.neuroscience.2012.07.071

Roth, T. L. (2012). Epigenetics of neurobiology and behavior during development and adulthood. *Dev. Psychobiol.* 54, 590–597. doi:10.1002/dev.20550

Roth, T. L., Lubin, F. D., Funk, A. J., and Sweatt, J. D. (2009). Lasting epigenetic influence of early-life adversity on the BDNF gene. *Biol. Psychiatry* 65, 760–769. doi:10.1016/j.biopsych.2008.11.028

Skene, P. J., Illingworth, R. S., Webb, S., Kerr, A. R. W., James, K. D., Turner, D. J., et al. (2010). Neuronal MeCP2 is expressed at near histone-octamer levels and globally alters the chromatin state. *Mol. Cell* 37, 457–468. doi:10.1016/j.molcel.2010.01.030

Solinas, M., Thiriet, N., Chauvet, C., and Jaber, M. (2010). Prevention and treatment of drug addiction by environmental enrichment. *Prog. Neurobiol.* 92, 572–592. doi:10.1016/j.pneurobio.2010.08.002

Sommers, I., Baskin, D., and Baskin-Sommers, A. (2006). Methamphetamine use among young adults: health and social consequences. *Addict. Behav.* 31, 1469–1476. doi:10.1016/j.addbeh.2005.10.004

Springer, A. E., Peters, R. J., Shegog, R., White, D. L., and Kelder, S. H. (2007). Methamphetamine use and sexual risk behaviors in U.S. high school students: findings from a national risk behavior survey. *Prev. Sci.* 8, 103–113. doi:10.1007/s11121-007-0065-6

Taylor, S. B., Lewis, C. R., and Olive, M. F. (2013). The neurocircuitry of illicit psychostimulant addiction: acute and chronic effects in humans. *Subst. Abuse Rehabil.* 4, 29–43.

Thiel, K. J., Sanabria, F., Pentkowski, N. S., and Neisewander, J. L. (2009). Anti-craving effects of environmental enrichment. *Int. J. Neuropsychopharmacol.* 12, 1151–1156. doi:10.1017/S1461145709990472

Vazquez, V., Penit-Soria, J., Durand, C., Besson, M. J., Giros, B., and Daugé, V. (2005). Maternal deprivation increases vulnerability to morphine dependence and disturbs the enkephalinergic system in adulthood. *J. Neurosci.* 25, 4453–4462. doi:10.1523/JNEUROSCI.4807-04.2005

Weaver, I. C. G., Diorio, J., Seckl, J. R., Szyf, M., and Meaney, M. J. (2004). Early environmental regulation of hippocampal glucocorticoid receptor gene expression: characterization of intracellular mediators and potential genomic target sites. *Ann. N. Y. Acad. Sci.* 1024, 182–212. doi:10.1196/annals.1321.099

Xie, Z., and Miller, G. M. (2009). A receptor mechanism for methamphetamine action in dopamine transporter regulation in brain. *J. Pharmacol. Exp. Ther.* 330, 316–325. doi:10.1124/jpet.109.153775

18

Emerging role for corticotropin releasing factor signaling in the bed nucleus of the stria terminalis at the intersection of stress and reward

Yuval Silberman[1] and Danny G. Winder[1,2] ∗

[1] *Neuroscience Program in Substance Abuse, Department of Molecular Physiology and Biophysics, Vanderbilt Brain Institute, Nashville, TN, USA*
[2] *Kennedy Center for Research on Human Development, Vanderbilt Brain Institute, Nashville, TN, USA*

Edited by:
Nicholas W. Gilpin, LSUHSC-New Orleans, USA

Reviewed by:
Chamindi Seneviratne, University of Virginia, USA
John Mantsch, Marquette University, USA
Sunmee Wee, The Scripps Research Institute, USA

∗Correspondence:
Danny G. Winder, Department of Molecular Physiology and Biophysics, 702 Light Hall, Vanderbilt University School of Medicine, Nashville, TN 37232, USA
e-mail: danny.winder@vanderbilt.edu

Stress and anxiety play an important role in the development and maintenance of drug and alcohol addiction. The bed nucleus of the stria terminalis (BNST), a brain region involved in the production of long-term stress-related behaviors, plays an important role in animal models of relapse, such as reinstatement to previously extinguished drug-seeking behaviors. While a number of neurotransmitter systems have been suggested to play a role in these behaviors, recent evidence points to the neuropeptide corticotropin releasing factor (CRF) as being critically important in BNST-mediated reinstatement behaviors. Although numerous studies indicate that the BNST is a complex brain region with multiple afferent and efferent systems and a variety of cell types, there has only been limited work to determine how CRF modulates this complex neuronal system at the circuit level. Recent work from our lab and others have begun to unravel these BNST neurocircuits and explore their roles in CRF-related reinstatement behaviors. This review will examine the role of CRF signaling in drug addiction and reinstatement with an emphasis on critical neurocircuitry within the BNST that may offer new insights into treatments for addiction.

Keywords: extended amygdala, reinstatement, relapse, excitatory transmission, addiction

INTRODUCTION

Alcohol and drug addiction are chronically relapsing disorders in which alcohol/drug use progresses from initial stages of limited, non-dependent intake to later stages of uncontrolled abuse (Koob, 2009; Koob and Volkow, 2010). One prominent theory posits that initial periods of use are driven primarily by the positive reinforcing value of drugs and alcohol (euphoria) while later stages of alcohol/drug addiction are driven by negative reinforcement (relief of withdrawal-induced negative affective states) (Koob and Volkow, 2010). The primary reinforcing effects of alcohol and other drugs are thought to occur by increased dopamine (DA) signaling that leads to enhanced activity of the mesocorticolimbic pathway, which in turn likely leads to escalated craving (Wise, 1980; Di Chiara and Imperato, 1988; Di Chiara, 2002; Volkow et al., 2003). Escalated alcohol/drug taking and prolonged binge episodes are thought to result in adaptation to the mesocorticolimbic pathway that results in devaluation of natural rewards, diminished cognitive control of behaviors, and increased salience of drug-related stimuli (Koob and Le, 2001; Koob and Volkow, 2010). During this time, the dorsal striatum, which typically plays a limited role in the acute reinforcing effects of drugs, becomes engaged after prolonged drug exposures and promotes compulsive drug-seeking typical in addiction (Everitt et al., 2008). For more complete reviews of mesocorticolimbic function in the initiation of drug addiction refer to (Feltenstein and See, 2008; Koob and Volkow, 2010).

Stressors and negative affective states, such as anxiety and depression, are often cited by recovering addicts as key instigators of drug craving and relapse (Sinha, 2007). Drug/alcohol binges are typically followed by various lengths of drug-withdrawal periods and numerous studies have shown that repeated binge/withdrawal episodes can recruit and sensitize brain regions associated with negative affective states, such as those that comprise the extended amygdala (for review see Koob, 2008; Koob and Volkow, 2010). Once recruited during withdrawal, brain regions associated with negative affect can remain hypersensitive even after extended periods of abstinence (Santucci et al., 2008). Furthermore, relief of negative emotional states is thought to be a critical component of alcohol/drug seeking during withdrawal (Koob, 2009). This suggests that brain regions associated with stress reactivity and negative affect, particularly the extended amygdala, become hypersensitive following repeated binge/withdrawal cycles and may mediate the transition to long-term addictive behaviors via negative reinforcement.

Altogether, these ideas support an important role of stress-related neurocircuitry in the progression of addiction and in relapse. Clinical studies on relapse have been paralleled and now extended in preclinical studies utilizing reinstatement models (Shaham et al., 2003). In this manuscript, we will review recent findings on the neurocircuitry of drug-seeking behaviors with a specific focus on those systems involved in enhanced drug-seeking during stress-induced relapse. We will also highlight potential mechanisms by which stress-related neurocircuitry may modulate drug-seeking behaviors that could be used for potential treatment targets for alcoholism and drug addiction.

NEUROCIRCUITRY INVOLVED IN DRUG SEEKING DURING WITHDRAWAL AND REINSTATEMENT

Reinstatement models typically involve training an animal to work to receive a drug or alcohol for a given period of time, then extinguishing that behavior before triggering the animal to seek out drugs again (Shaham et al., 2003; Epstein et al., 2006). Typical triggers of reinstatement are (1) re-exposure to the same or related drug previously administered (drug-induced reinstatement), (2) giving the animal drug-associated stimuli or cues (cue-induced reinstatement), or (3) exposure to a variety of stressors (stress-induced reinstatement). Work from reinstatement models has shown distinct roles of multiple brain regions and neurotransmitter systems in each type of reinstatement.

NEUROCIRCUITRY OF DRUG-INDUCED REINSTATEMENT

A great deal of research has shown that increased activity of brain regions projecting to the mesocortical DA system is a critical factor in drug-induced reinstatement models (for review see Kalivas and Volkow, 2005; Feltenstein and See, 2008). One pathway shown to be critical to drug-induced reinstatement is a glutamatergic projection from the medial prefrontal cortex to the nucleus accumbens (Stewart and Vezina, 1988; Cornish and Kalivas, 2000; McFarland and Kalivas, 2001). Furthermore, limbic areas like the basolateral amygdala (BLA) may play a role in drug-induced reinstatement by enhanced activity of its glutamatergic projections to mesocorticolimbic system (McFarland and Kalivas, 2001; Fuchs and See, 2002). Therefore drug-induced reinstatement likely occurs via increased glutamatergic transmission to enhance mesocorticolimbic pathway activity, likely from cortical and limbic areas as well as by direct action of the drug of abuse on mesocorticolimbic DA receptors (for review see, Feltenstein and See, 2008).

NEUROCIRCUITRY OF CUE-INDUCED REINSTATEMENT

In addition to its role in drug-induced reinstatement, numerous studies have shown an important role for the BLA in cue-induced reinstatement. Exposure to drug-associated cues results in increased DA release and increased c-fos activation in the BLA following withdrawal (Neisewander et al., 1998; Weiss et al., 2000). Furthermore, intra-BLA injections of DA receptor antagonists block cue-induced reinstatement (See et al., 2001). Stimulation of the BLA has been shown to increase DA efflux in the nucleus accumbens via a glutamate receptor-dependent mechanism (Howland et al., 2002) suggesting an important role of glutamatergic afferents to the mesolimbic DA system in cue-induced reinstatement. The medial prefrontal cortex (Van den Oever et al., 2010) and the central nucleus of the amygdala (Radwanska et al., 2008) have also been shown to be important in cue-induced reinstatement.

Overall, these findings suggest that DA or glutamatergic neurotransmission in the mesocorticolimbic pathway or its afferents could be targets for therapies to reduce relapse in recovering addicts. However, use of dopaminergic agonists has yet to be proven effective for long-term relapse treatment (Lingford-Hughes et al., 2010) and may be problematic in regards to abuse liability (Shorter and Kosten, 2011). In addition, therapeutics targeting DA receptors may be problematic because of potential side effects due to interactions with motor systems or interactions with the cardiovascular system since modulating DA receptor activity can have effects on hemodynamics and cardiovascular function (Zeng et al., 2007; Banday and Lokhandwala, 2008). Furthermore, drugs targeting glutamatergic transmission given orally may also cause problematic side-effects as modulating glutamate receptors can adversely affect many other brain regions not involved in reinstatement. These findings leave the field open to the need of more selective DA or glutamatergic drugs or drugs targeting different receptor systems.

EXTENDED AMYGDALA NEUROCIRCUITRY IN STRESS-INDUCED REINSTATEMENT

Stress-induced reinstatement may be a critical model for finding suitable therapeutic targets for two important reasons. First, recovering addicts can work to modify their behavior to avoid drug re-exposure and exposure to drug-related cues as often as possible while stress in daily human life is virtually inevitable. Situations like family issues, finding and maintaining work, and even traffic in daily commutes can be stressful events to any person and may be sensitized in recovering addicts. Therefore, it is not surprising that stress is a major trigger for relapse in addicted patients (Sinha, 2007) and may make therapies targeting this system more likely to be effective in preventing relapse. Second, the neuromodulatory systems involved in stress-induced reinstatement described below may make for better pharmacotherapeutic targets due to their limited abuse liability and potentially less significant side effect profiles.

A great deal of work has examined stress-induced relapse in the preclinical setting, and a variety of stressors have been shown to reinstate drug-seeking behaviors or preference. These include footshock, restraint stress, and forced swim stress (Shaham et al., 2003; Tzschentke, 2007; Shalev et al., 2010). These studies have revealed key neurobiological mechanisms of stress-induced reinstatement, with a particular focus on the effects of two stress-related neuromodulatory systems, norepinephrine (NE) and corticotropin releasing factor (CRF), in two related brain regions of the extended amygdala, the central nucleus of the amygdala and bed nucleus of the stria terminalis (BNST) (Shaham et al., 2003; Epstein et al., 2006; Sofuoglu and Sewell, 2009; Erb, 2010; Haass-Koffler and Bartlett, 2012).

Withdrawal from chronic drug abuse can lead to NE dysfunction in the clinical population that is associated with increased vulnerability to anxiety (McDougle et al., 1994). Numerous preclinical studies have also shown drug-withdrawal-induced increases in anxiety-like behaviors and withdrawal-induced escalation in drug intake can be ameliorated by blockade of β- and α1-adrenergic receptors (ARs) (Rudoy and Van Bockstaele, 2007; Wee et al., 2008; Rudoy et al., 2009; Forget et al., 2010; Verplaetse et al., 2012). Importantly, ICV injection of NE increases fos expression in the BNST (Brown et al., 2011) and β-AR antagonists microinjected into the extended amygdala can block stress-induced reinstatement (Leri et al., 2002) suggesting that dysfunction of NE systems in the extended amygdala is likely a key factor in enhanced drug-seeking following stress.

CENTRAL AMYGDALA NEUROCIRCUITRY IN ADDICTION

The central amygdala (CeA) appears to contribute to the use of a number of different drugs. Acute and chronic alcohol/drug exposures and withdrawal increase CRF biosynthesis in the CeA (Merlo et al., 1995; Rodriguez de et al., 1997; Richter and Weiss, 1999; Maj et al., 2003; George et al., 2007; Zorrilla et al., 2012) and the CeA sends a CRF-containing projection to the BNST that is critical for stress-induced reinstatement (Erb et al., 2001). Therefore, an understanding of drug/alcohol interactions with CeA CRF neurocircuitry may provide an insight into an important interface between stress and addiction A series of studies have shown that EtOH enhances GABAergic neurotransmission in the CeA via a CRF type 1 receptor (CRFR1)-dependent mechanism (Roberto et al., 2003, 2010; Nie et al., 2009). Mice exposed to chronic intermittent ethanol (CIE) exhibit higher levels of EtOH drinking, increased GABA release, and heightened CeA CRFR1 sensitivity during withdrawal, suggesting a key role of CRF-GABA interaction in the CeA in the development of EtOH dependence (Roberto et al., 2004, 2010). Furthermore, treating mice with CRFR1 antagonists blocked the ability of CIE to increase alcohol drinking (Roberto et al., 2010). CIE-induced increases in alcohol self-administration are also blocked by an intra-CeA microinjection of a non-selective CRFR antagonist (Funk et al., 2006a). CeA CRF neurocircuitry is also activated during binge-like EtOH self-administration prior to the development of dependence and binge-like EtOH consumption can be reduced by intra-CeA microinjections of CRFR1 antagonists (Lowery-Gionta et al., 2012). Since CRFR1 antagonists can block stress-induced increases in EtOH self-administration (Hansson et al., 2006; Marinelli et al., 2007; Lowery et al., 2008), these findings indicate that changes in CeA CRF signaling may play an important role in the development and maintenance of EtOH addiction and in relapse.

In addition to its effects on CeA GABAergic neurotransmission and its functional role in EtOH induced alterations to CeA activity, CRFR1 can also enhance CeA glutamatergic neurotransmission. CRFR1 activation increases glutamate release from specific presynaptic sources in the CeA (Liu et al., 2004; Silberman and Winder, 2013) and can induce long-term potentiation of the BLA-CeA pathway (Fu et al., 2007). This effect can be manipulated by chronic drug exposures as withdrawal from chronic intermittent cocaine can enhance CRFR1 induced long-term potentiation of CeA synaptic transmission (Fu et al., 2007), suggesting that CeA CRF signaling is important for cocaine related behaviors and may play an important role in the development of cocaine addiction. Blockade of CeA CRFR1 can also attenuate dysphoria associated with nicotine withdrawal (Bruijnzeel et al., 2012). These findings suggest that changes in CeA CRF neurotransmission may play a role in addiction to multiple drug types. However, although CRF-producing neurons do exist in the CeA, it is not yet clear if these neurons are the source of extracellular CRF in the CeA as our recent studies suggests that CRF neurons in the CeA may be predominantly projection type (Silberman et al., 2013). Indeed, some evidence indicates that other brain regions may be the major source of extracellular CRF in the CeA (Uryu et al., 1992). It is also not yet clear how alcohol/drugs might alter the activity of CeA CRF neurons that project to the BNST. Future research will be needed to determine how CeA CRF signaling to the BNST is altered by chronic alcohol or drug exposure that may make them more sensitive to stress to promote CRF release in the BNST to initiate reinstatement.

BED NUCLEUS OF THE STRIA TERMINALIS NEUROCIRCUITRY IN STRESS-INDUCED REINSTATEMENT

Alcohol and other drugs of abuse can also modulate CRF activity in the BNST. Protracted withdrawal from cocaine, heroin, and alcohol can result in a dysregulation of the intrinsic excitability of some BNST neurons via a CRF-mediated mechanism (Francesconi et al., 2009), suggesting that repeated activation of BNST CRF receptors likely plays a critical role in the development of drug-withdrawal symptomology. Furthermore, microinjections of CRFR1 antagonists into the BNST can block stress-induced reinstatement of drug-seeking (Erb and Stewart, 1999; Erb et al., 2001) while microinjections of CRF into the BNST can drive reinstatement for drug-seeking (Erb and Stewart, 1999). Together, these findings suggest that CRFR1 within the BNST is a critical component of stress-induced reinstatement behaviors.

While the above studies have shown a clear role of BNST CRF signaling in stress-induced reinstatement of cocaine seeking, it less clear what role CRF signaling in the BNST plays in alcohol addiction. For instance, although intra-CeA injections of CRF antagonists post CIE can block CIE-induced increases in EtOH self-administration, post-CIE intra-BNST injections of the same antagonist does not block enhanced drinking (Funk et al., 2006a). However, a series of studies indicate that BNST CRF signaling becomes enhanced during exposure to stressors that elicit reinstatement to ethanol seeking (Le et al., 2000; Funk et al., 2006b). Interestingly, cycles of stressors can substitute for cycles of intermittent EtOH exposures to increase withdrawal-induced anxiety, an effect that is also CRF receptor dependent (Breese et al., 2004). Furthermore, recent studies indicate that intra-BNST injections of CRF before ethanol exposure sensitized ethanol-withdrawal-induced anxiety while intra-BNST CRFR1 antagonist injections prior to stress blocked increases of anxiety-like behavior during ethanol withdrawal (Huang et al., 2010). Therefore, it is likely that the combination of repeated EtOH exposure and stressors (environmental stress or drug-withdrawal stress) sensitizes BNST CRF activity to promote anxiety-like behaviors in withdrawal. This sensitized BNST CRF activity may increase the likelihood of stress-induced reinstatement of ethanol and other drugs of abuse.

MECHANISMS OF NE/CRF INTERACTIONS IN STRESS-INDUCED REINSTATEMENT

Together, the findings reviewed above indicate that both NE and CRF in the extended amygdala are key components of both acute drug-withdrawal syndromes and reinstatement. Although we now have a better understanding of the neurocircuitry and neurotransmitter systems involved in stress-induced reinstatement, it is still unclear how chronic exposure to drugs modulates NE/CRF-related neurocircuitry in the extended amygdala to sensitize stress pathways and precipitate reinstatement. For these reasons, our lab and others have recently focused on this neurocircuitry to elucidate the major neuronal mechanisms involved in enhanced stress sensitivity following chronic drug exposure and role of this circuitry in the addiction process.

NE/CRF INTERACTIONS IN THE BNST PROMOTE REINSTATEMENT TO DRUG SEEKING

While the work described in the previous section indicates an important role of NE and CRF signaling in modulation of BNST activity in stress-induced reinstatement behaviors, the mechanisms by which stress-related signaling modulates extended amygdala activity and how this modulated activity drives alcohol/drug seeking is not well understood. One clue as to the mechanism of BNST NE and CRF signaling is that pretreatment with a CRFR antagonist can block reinstating effects of AR stimulation while blockade of adrenergic signaling does not alter CRF-induced reinstatement (Brown et al., 2009). Given the likely role of β-AR receptors in the BNST in stress-induced reinstatement (Leri et al., 2002), these findings suggests that β-AR and CRF systems may interact in the BNST to initiate drug-seeking behavior following stress exposure and that β-ARs and CRFRs may work in a serial fashion to enhance BNST activity. To confirm this mechanism, our lab examined the role of β-ARs and CRFRs on glutamatergic transmission in the BNST (Nobis et al., 2011). In these studies, the β-AR agonist, isoproterenol, and CRF increased the frequency of spontaneous glutamatergic neurotransmission in the BNST. Interestingly, the effect of both drugs was blocked by pretreatment with a CRFR1 antagonist. The effects of CRF and isoproterenol were occluded during acute withdrawal from chronic cocaine exposure, suggesting that serial NE-CRF signaling in the BNST is engaged *in vivo* during drug exposures (Nobis et al., 2011).

POTENTIAL ROLE FOR CRF-PRODUCING NEURONS WITHIN THE BNST IN STRESS-INDUCED REINSTATEMENT

While it has been established that elevated CRF levels in the BNST are important for stress-induced reinstatement, one remaining question is the source of elevated extracellular CRF in the BNST in response to stress exposure. CRF could be released from local neuronal sources, from extrinsic CRF projections from the CeA, or both (Veinante et al., 1997; Erb et al., 2001). To further explore this question, we hypothesized that if β-ARs enhance BNST CRF levels by modulating the activity of local CRF neurons, then isoproterenol would be expected to alter the activity of BNST neurons that produce CRF. On the other hand, if β-AR activation resulted in increased CRF from CeA sources, then the activity of BNST CRF neurons might not be altered by isoproterenol. To test this hypothesis, we recorded the activity of CRF-producing neurons in the BNST in a novel CRF-reporter mouse line (Silberman et al., 2013). To develop this line, we crossed two commercially available mouse lines from Jackson Laboratories, the *CRF-ires-cre* (strain B6(Cg)-Crhtm1(cre)Zjh/J) line and the ROSA-tomato [strain B6.Cg-t(ROSA)26Sor < tm14(CAG-tdTomato)Hze > /J] line. Crossing these two lines of mice resulted in offspring where a red fluorescent protein (*tomato)* was targeted to *cre* containing neurons, which in this case were neurons that produced *cre* under the control of the endogenous *Crf* promoter/enhancer elements (CRF-*tomato* mice). The *CRF-tomato* mice were found to have high levels of *tomato* expression in brain areas known to be dense in CRF-producing neurons, like the paraventricular nucleus of the hypothalamus,

the CeA, and the BNST, while brain regions that are known to have little CRF-producing neurons, like the cortex and striatum, were shown to have sparse *tomato* expression.

We then preformed whole-cell patch clamp electrophysiology experiments on CRF-*tomato* neurons in the BNST. These studies indicate that there are several different subtypes of BNST CRF neurons based on electrophysiological characteristics. Three of the subtypes were similar to those previous shown to exist in the rat BNST (Hammack et al., 2007) while the two remaining subtypes have not previously been characterized. Research is currently ongoing in our lab to determine if distinct CRF neuronal subtypes play dissociable roles in BNST-mediated behaviors and if they are can be distinguished based on their projection targets or other neurochemical markers.

Regardless of these characteristic differences in CRF neuron subtypes, isoproterenol application resulted in a significant depolarization of BNST CRF neurons, an effect that was significantly correlated with increased input resistance. These data suggest a role of β-ARs in the direct depolarization of BNST CRF neurons through closure of a leak or voltage-gated channel. Such a depolarization could increase release of CRF from these neurons, although this has yet to be directly tested. Together, these data suggest that stress-induced increases in NE signaling in the BNST leads to enhanced local CRF neuron activity in the BNST which likely leads to enhanced CRF release. Enhanced extracellular CRF levels in the BNST in turn leads to enhanced glutamatergic activity in the BNST and thus increased BNST excitation (see summary **Figure 1**). This enhanced level of BNST CRF may be further modulated by CRF afferents from the CeA (Erb et al., 2001). Overall, CRF-mediated enhancement of excitatory drive in the BNST is likely a key participant in stress-induced reinstatement. The following section will further describe this proposed BNST neurocircuit and its sensitivity to drug-related permutations as a critical factor precipitating reinstatement to drug-seeking behaviors following withdrawal.

POTENTIAL ROLE OF BNST PROJECTIONS TO THE VTA IN STRESS-INDUCED REINSTATEMENT

Although the above described studies show a clear role for NE/CRF interactions in enhancing BNST excitability, it is not clear how enhanced BNST excitability leads to increased drug-seeking behavior following stress. As mentioned earlier, mesolimbic circuit activation is a critical component of drug-seeking behavior in all types of reinstatement models. Therefore, it is hypothesized that BNST afferents to the VTA may be an important pathway in initiation of drug-seeking behaviors following stress. The following sections will explore this possibility.

NEUROANATOMICAL AND FUNCTIONAL EVIDENCE FOR BNST-VTA CIRCUITRY IN DRUG-SEEKING BEHAVIORS

A series of neuroanatomical studies showed that the BNST sends a dense set of projections to the VTA (Georges and Aston-Jones, 2001, 2002; Dong and Swanson, 2004, 2006a,b). Disconnection of this pathway reduces cocaine preference (Sartor and Aston-Jones, 2012) and BNST neurons projecting to the VTA become activated during reinstatement to cocaine seeking (Mahler and Aston-Jones, 2012), suggesting BNST projections to the VTA are important in multiple drug-related behaviors such as preference and drug

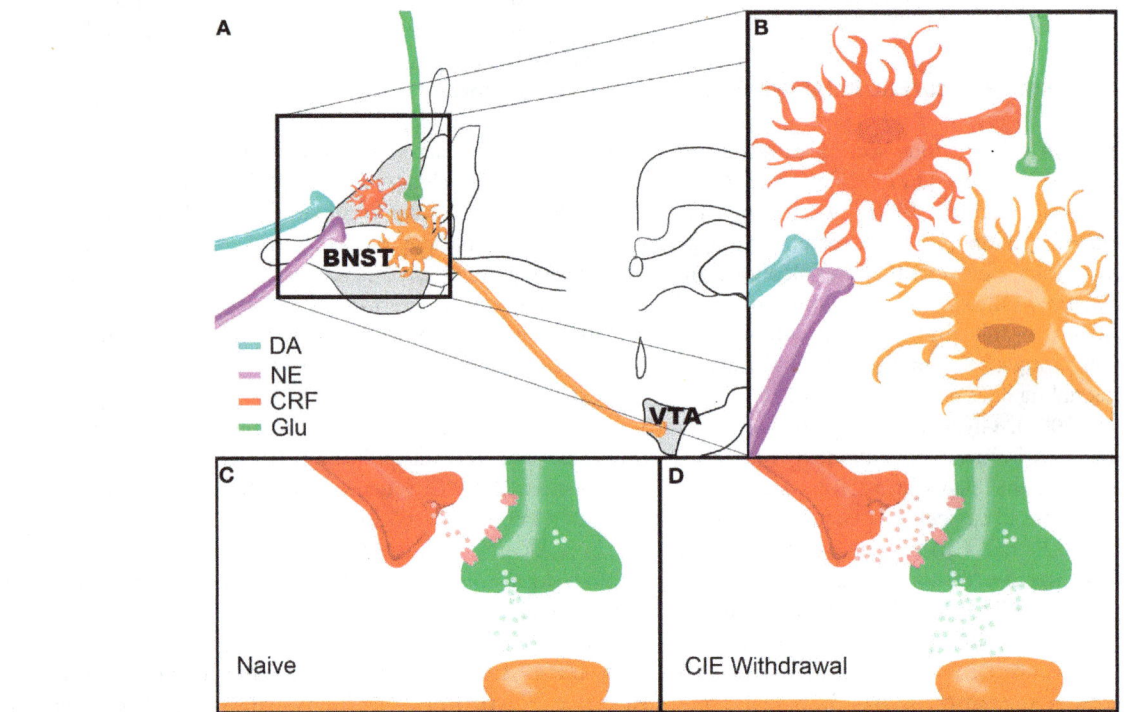

FIGURE 1 | Model of Chronic Intermittent Ethanol-Withdrawal Modulation of BNST CRF Circuitry. (A) Dopamine and norepinephrine afferents synapse onto CRF-producing neurons in the BNST which in turn influence neurotransmitter release from glutamatergic afferents onto BNST neurons projecting to the VTA. **(B)** Close up view of proposed neurocircuitry described in **(A)**. **(C,D)** Model of CRF modulation of glutamatergic transmission onto a VTA-projecting BNST neuron in a drug-naïve state **(C)** or during acute ethanol withdrawal following CIE **(D)**. Note that there are higher levels of CRF and glutamate release during withdrawal compared to the drug-naïve state. Figure reprinted from (Silberman et al., 2013).

seeking during reinstatement. Initial *in vivo* electrophysiology studies showed that electrical and pharmacological stimulation of the BNST can elicit increased firing of putative DA neurons in the VTA (Georges and Aston-Jones, 2001). This pathway was further characterized showing that antagonism of glutamatergic receptors in the VTA can block BNST stimulation mediated enhancement of VTA DA neuron firing while having minimal effects on putative VTA GABA neuron firing (Georges and Aston-Jones, 2002). Together, these anatomical and electrophysiology studies suggest that the BNST may regulate the activity of the VTA DA neurons during reinstatement.

More recent studies using optogenetic strategies suggest that parallel circuitry in the BNST can mediate distinct aspects of anxiety-like behaviors (Kim et al., 2013). These studies show that selective inactivation of cells in the region of the oval subnucleus of the dorsal BNST (ovBNST) is correlated to a reduction in anxiety-like behaviors and that ovBNST neurons inhibit the activity of the anterodorsal subregion of the BNST (adBNST). These studies further show that the adBNST contains neurons that project to the VTA, parabrachial nucleus, and lateral hypothalamus and that selective stimulation of these pathways may promote different aspect of anxiolysis, as measured by increased open arm time in an elevated plus maze and reduction in respiratory rates. Our recent evidence further suggests that these divergent projections likely arise from distinct subpopulations of neurons in the adBNST (Silberman et al., 2013). Kim et al. (2013) propose this

arrangement of BNST neuronal signaling may facilitate modular circuit adaptations in response to environmental stimuli by independent tuning of divergent projection neuron populations. Especially relevant to this review, optogenetic stimulation of adBNST terminals in the VTA can elicit realtime place preference, suggesting that increased activity of certain BNST projection neurons are critical for regulation of VTA-mediated reward behavior (Jennings et al., 2013).

While the BNST contains multiple subnuclei and a variety of neuronal cell types based on immunohistochemical and electrophysiological characteristics (Egli and Winder, 2003; Dumont and Williams, 2004; Hammack et al., 2007; Kash et al., 2008), studies indicate that BNST neurons that project to the VTA may be sensitive to modulation by drugs of abuse (Dumont et al., 2008). Interestingly, more recent work has shown that BNST neurons that project to the VTA are more likely to become activated following a stressor than other BNST neurons (Briand et al., 2010). Together, these findings suggest that certain subpopulations of BNST neurons, i.e., VTA-projecting neurons, are particularly important to enhanced drug seeking following stress exposures.

CRFR1 MEDIATES ETHANOL-WITHDRAWAL-INDUCED INCREASES IN GLUTAMATERGIC TRANSMISSION ONTO BNST NEURONS PROJECTING TO THE VTA

In combination with previous evidence of the importance of BNST CRF signaling to stress-induced reinstatement, we hypothesized that CRF modulation of BNST neurons projecting to the VTA may be uniquely sensitive to drug-induced alterations in excitability. To test this hypothesis we have recently performed a series of experiments to determine the effect of CRF on glutamatergic transmission onto VTA-projecting BNST neurons and determine whether chronic drug exposures can modulate this system. VTA-projecting BNST neurons were identified by microinjecting retrograde fluorescent microspheres into the VTA and labeled neurons in the BNST were recorded using whole-cell electrophysiology methods (Silberman et al., 2013). In these studies, we showed that CRF, via activation of CRFR1, can enhance glutamate release onto BNST neurons projecting to the VTA. Combined with our data showing that β-AR activation depolarizes BNST CRF neurons, the above findings indicate that stress, via release of NE in the BNST, can increase BNST CRF activity to, in turn, increase glutamatergic signaling onto VTA-projecting BNST neurons (**Figures 1A,B**).

We then tested whether this pathway is modulated by abused drugs by exposing VTA-retrograde tracer mice to the CIE vapor exposure paradigm (CIE). This repeated ethanol exposure/withdrawal paradigm has been shown to increase anxiety-like behaviors during withdrawal (Kash et al., 2009) and increase voluntary ethanol drinking post-withdrawal (Becker and Lopez, 2004), suggesting that this paradigm is an important tool in assessing neurobiological changes in negative reinforcement pathways, such as the BNST, following drug exposure. Interestingly, we found that basal glutamatergic tone was increased in excitatory synapses that regulate VTA-projecting BNST neurons during the acute withdrawal phase after a 2 week CIE cycle. Also, from this enhanced basal glutamatergic tone, exogenous application of CRF could no longer enhance glutamatergic transmission as it could in drug-naïve or sham exposed mice. This functional occlusion of exogenous CRF suggests that CRF receptors may already be maximally active during acute drug-withdrawal time points, perhaps due to highly elevated extracellular CRF levels and sensitize BNST CRF circuitry. This may be one reason why post-CIE CRFR1 antagonist injections into the BNST do not block CIE-induced increases in ethanol self-administration (Funk et al., 2006a) and suggests that CRFR1 antagonist treatment prior to CIE may normalize BNST CRF circuitry during acute ethanol withdrawal. To examine this hypothesis, we exposed a second cohort of VTA-tracer mice to CIE with the inclusion of daily injections of a CRFR1 antagonist prior to ethanol vapor exposure. Pretreatment with a CRFR1 antagonist completely abolished the effects of CIE on increasing basal glutamatergic function during acute withdrawal timepoints. Together, these findings indicate that CIE modulates BNST CRF neurocircuitry *in vivo* and that this neurocircuit becomes hyperactive during CIE withdrawal (**Figures 1C,D**). An important caveat to these findings is that the role of BNST CRF sensitivity has mainly been examined during acute withdrawal phases and has provided potentially conflicting results. It will be important in future studies to examine the mechanisms by which sensitized BNST CRF circuitry may promote increased stress-induced drug-seeking behavior during later time points in extended withdrawal.

Although more work will be needed to conclusively show a role of this circuit in reinstatement behaviors, the recruitment of the catecholamine-CRF-glutamate circuit in the BNST to drive increased VTA activity is one promising mechanism by which

stress can enhance drug seeking in reinstatement models. Interestingly, while the above described studies focused on the effect of ethanol on BNST CRF circuitry other work indicates that cocaine (Nobis et al., 2011) and opiates (Wang et al., 2006; Jaferi et al., 2009) may also stimulate BNST CRF neurocircuitry *in vivo*. Together, these findings suggest that modulation of BNST CRF may be a common pathway for stress-induced reinstatement for multiple classes of abused drugs. Therefore, therapeutics targeting this system may be useful for the effective long-term prevention of stress-induced relapse in addiction to many types of drugs.

PROPOSED MODEL OF BNST/VTA CIRCUITRY IN STRESS-INDUCED REINSTATEMENT

The studies described above suggest a critical role of increased activity of BNST neurons that project to the VTA in the neurophysiological response to stress and drug addiction. However, the mechanism by which activation of BNST projection neurons may modulate VTA activity is not clear.

MULTIPLE SUBTYPES OF BNST NEURONS PROJECT TO THE VTA

Some electrophysiological studies indicate that BNST projections to the VTA are likely to be glutamatergic, as they enhance VTA neuron firing (Georges and Aston-Jones, 2001, 2002). However, more recent work indicates that BNST projections to the VTA may be either glutamatergic or GABAergic (Jennings et al., 2013). Other recent studies utilizing fluorescence *in situ* hybridization and retrograde labeling techniques show that there are three types of VTA-projecting neurons in the BNST. The vast majority of these neurons (~90%) are GAD+/VGlut− while other subtypes are VGlut2+/GAD− or VGlut3+/GAD+ (Kudo et al., 2012). This suggests that most VTA-projecting neurons in the BNST are GABAergic, while a minority of outputs may be glutamatergic or contain a mixture of transmitters. Our recent work shows that VTA-projecting BNST neurons can be divided into three classes based on electrophysiological responses to hyperpolarizing and depolarizing current injections (Silberman et al., 2013). Although it has yet to be tested, it is tempting to think that the differences in GAD and VGlut2/3 expression in BNST neuron subtypes may be related to differences in their electrophysiological firing properties. Still other studies suggest that at least some of the BNST neurons projecting to the VTA contain CRF (Rodaros et al., 2007). This is an important consideration as elevated CRF levels in the VTA can drive DA neuron activity after exposure to drugs of abuse by a number of mechanisms (Wise and Morales, 2010). Determining the contribution of these unique BNST projection neuron subtypes to stress-induced drug-seeking behavior may be useful in targeting future treatments for relapse prevention.

EVIDENCE FOR SUBTYPE SPECIFIC BNST INNERVATION OF VTA GABA AND VTA DA NEURONS

Overall these findings indicate that the BNST sends a mixture of neurotransmitters to the VTA. However, what is less clear is whether distinct types of BNST projection neurons synapse to different VTA neurons. Recent evidence indicates that selective optogenetic stimulation of VTA GABA neurons disrupts reward consumption (van Zessen et al., 2012) and increased conditioned place aversion (Tan et al., 2012). Furthermore, selective optogenetic stimulation of VTA DA neurons can enhance positive reinforcing actions in an operant food seeking task and can reactivate previously extinguished food seeking behavior in the absence of cues (Adamantidis et al., 2011). Interestingly, recent immunoelectron microscopy work indicates that vGLUT containing BNST projection neurons may selective target VTA DA neurons while GABAergic BNST projection neurons may specifically target GABA neurons in the VTA [(Kudo et al., 2012) although see also (Jennings et al., 2013)]. Together, these findings may indicate that enhanced activity of BNST projections to the VTA during reinstatement may stimulate VTA DA neurons via increasing local glutamatergic levels while at the same time disinhibiting VTA DA neuron firing by inhibiting local GABA release (see model, **Figure 2**). This may be one mechanism by which drug-withdrawal enhances burst firing of VTA DA neurons (Hopf et al., 2007), an effect that is important in drug-seeking behaviors (Wanat et al., 2009), and may be especially important in stress-induced reinstatement models.

The precise role of distinct VTA-projecting BNST neurons in reinstatement is not yet fully understood. For instance, although evidence suggests that BNST neurons that project to the VTA can be mainly GABAergic, but also glutamatergic or potentially both (Kudo et al., 2012), it is not clear if these pathways have an equal distribution of synaptic strength. Furthermore, some BNST projections to the VTA may contain CRF (Rodaros et al.,

2007) but it is not clear which of the VTA-projecting neurons described by Kudo et al. or Jennings and Sparta et al. are also CRF positive. If so, this may suggest that a single population of VTA-projecting BNST neurons may have divergent modes of action in reinstatement related behaviors based on which neurotransmitter is released at specific time points relative to reinstatement trigger exposure. Lastly, most of the electrophysiology studies described in this review focused on neurocircuitry in the dorsal subregion of the BNST while most of the behavioral work has focused on activity of the ventral BNST subregion. This is an important consideration as the dorsal BNST, which has a high proportion of GABAergic interneurons, sends afferents to the ventral BNST, which has a higher proportion of projection neurons (Dong et al., 2001). This suggests that the dorsal BNST might coordinate overall BNST output via modulation of ventral BNST projection neurons, potentially via BNST CRF interneuron activity. It is not yet clear if interneurons or VTA-projecting neurons from the dorsal and ventral BNST are equally mutable to chronic drug exposures/withdrawal cycles. While more conclusive research will be needed to test these intriguing possibilities, these findings may indicate dissociable roles of BNST projection neuron subtypes in mediating various aspects of drug-seeking behavior during reinstatement that could potentially be targeted individually for pharmacotherapies for relapse prevention in the future.

POTENTIAL ROLE OF BNST CRF SIGNALING IN CUE-INDUCED REINSTATEMENT
EVIDENCE FOR DIRECT AND INDIRECT DOPAMINERGIC ACTIVATION OF BNST IN CUE-INDUCED REINSTATEMENT

In addition to its role in stress-induced reinstatement described above, recent evidence may suggest that BNST CRF neurocircuitry could also play a role in cue-induced reinstatement. BLA DA receptor activation is critical for cue-induced reinstatement (See et al., 2001) and DA can increase BLA activity, but only after chronic drug exposure (Li et al., 2011). Since the BLA sends direct projections to the BNST as well as via indirect projections through the CeA (Davis et al., 2010), DA induced activation of the BLA may enhance BNST excitability to precipitate reinstatement following a cue exposure. In addition, drugs of abuse and other rewarding stimuli can also directly increase extracellular DA levels in the BNST (Carboni et al., 2000; Park et al., 2012). Previous work in our lab shows that DA can enhance glutamate release in the BNST via activation of CRFR1 (Kash et al., 2008). This effect is further confirmed by our more recent work indicating that DA can depolarize BNST CRF neurons (Silberman et al., 2013). Together, these findings suggest both direct and indirect mechanisms for DA induced increases in BNST excitability and point to a potential role of BNST DA circuitry in cue-induced reinstatement via modulation of BNST CRF circuitry.

Importantly, behavioral evidence also shows a potential role for the BNST in cue-induced reinstatement models. For instance, recent findings indicate that pharmacological inactivation of the BNST can reduce cue-induced reinstatement (Buffalari and See, 2011). In addition, much like earlier studies showing selective increases in c-fos in VTA-projecting BNST neurons following stress-induced reinstatement, recent findings show that increased c-fos activation in VTA-projecting BNST neurons is correlated

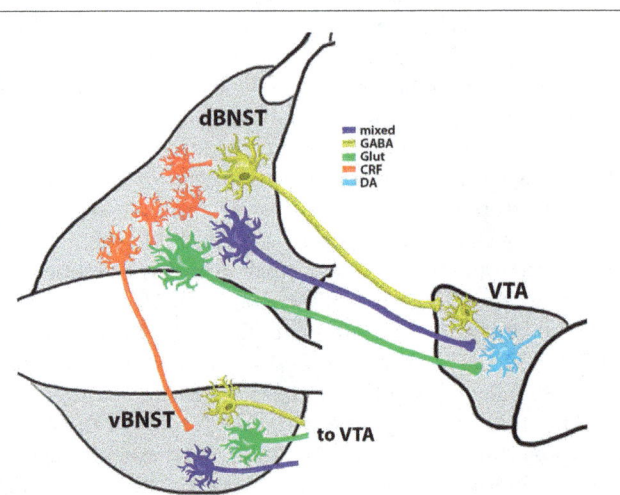

FIGURE 2 | Summary Model of Reinstatement Related BNST and VTA Connectivity. CRF+ neurons modulate the activity of VTA-projecting BNST neurons. Evidence (Kudo et al., 2012) shows that at least three types of VTA-projecting neurons are located in the BNST: (1) a GABAergic projection (~90% of all BNST projection neurons) that selectively innervates VTA GABA neurons to provide disinhibition of VTA DA neurons; (2) a glutamatergic (Glut) projection that selectively targets VTA DA neurons; and (3) a mixed GABA/Glut projection that also targets VTA DA neurons. These projection neuron populations may exist in both the dorsal and ventral BNST subregions (d and vBNST, respectively) and each projection pathway may have distinct and coordinated responses to chronic drug exposure, withdrawal, and reinstatement. Coordinated activity of dBNST and vBNST projection neurons is likely regulated by dBNST interneurons, of which CRF+ neurons may be a critical component. This local CRF neuron coordination of BNST activity might also be altered by chronic exposure and withdrawal and may be an important target for the prevention of relapse-like behaviors.

to enhanced cocaine-seeking following an exposure to a drug-associated cue (Mahler and Aston-Jones, 2012). Together with our electrophysiology data, these findings suggest that DA may increase extracellular CRF levels in the BNST via enhancing the activity of local BNST CRF neurons, which in turn increases glutamate release onto VTA-projecting BNST neurons, leading to increased VTA DA firing to reinstate drug-seeking behaviors.

EVIDENCE FOR CONVERGENCE OF CUE-INDUCED AND STRESS-INDUCED REINSTATEMENT PATHWAYS IN THE BNST

Interestingly, while clinical evidence shows that exposing recovering addicts to drug-associated cues results in enhanced feelings of craving, recent findings indicate that these same cues also increase feelings of negative affect (Fox et al., 2007). Therefore, drug-associated cues could act as a psychological stress by activating stress-related neurocircuitry. This suggests that drug-associated cues may concurrently increase both DA and NE signaling in these patients. Our data suggest that DA and NE can additively enhance BNST excitability (Nobis et al., 2011), suggesting a convergence of cue-induced (dopaminergic) and stress-induced (noradrenergic) reinstatement pathway influences on BNST excitability. Preclinical studies also suggest a link between cue and stress-induced reinstatement (Buffalari and See, 2009) suggesting that simultaneous exposure to drug-cues and stress can greatly increase the risk of relapse in recovering addicts. Together, these findings indicate that BNST CRF signaling is an important potential target for convergent influences of both cue and stress-induced reinstatement pathways.

SUMMARY AND POTENTIAL TREATMENTS

The findings reviewed here suggest that a catecholamine-CRF-glutamatergic signaling pathway in the BNST plays an important role in the reinstatement to drug-seeking behavior, an important animal model of relapse to alcohol/drug addiction. While this pathway is clearly important in stress-related behaviors, especially in stress-induced reinstatement, further studies suggests that this pathway may also be important in cue-induced reinstatement. Therefore, pharmacotherapies targeting this pathway may be useful in the prevention of relapse to both drug-associated cues and stressors. Unfortunately, relapse can be a life-long struggle in recovering addicts, which means that pharmacotherapies to prevent relapse likely need to be taken daily for extended periods of time. Therefore these therapies need to be well-tolerated and devoid of harsh side-effects. As described earlier, agonist therapies targeting the DA aspect of this pathway may be problematic from the side-effect standpoint due to effects on the cardiovascular system and abuse liability. DA antagonist therapies are also problematic for their potential for extra-pyramidal (Peacock et al., 1999) and anhedonic side effects (Stein, 2008). Recent studies have looked into the effect of β-AR antagonists to reduce the probability of relapse in the clinical population (Hughes et al., 2000; Kampman et al., 2001; Schwabe et al., 2011). Overall, these studies have shown β-AR antagonist to potentially be useful in the clinical setting, especially for reducing stress-induced changes in habitual behaviors and in those patients that have more severe withdrawal symptoms. However, it is unclear if treatment with β-AR antagonists would have an effect on cue-induced relapse.

Since DA and β-AR activation enhances BNST activity via CRFR1 activation, then CRFR1 antagonists might be a better alternative for the effective long-term prevention of both cue and stress-induced relapse. CRFR1 antagonists have been shown to reduce ethanol intake following withdrawal in a number of pre-clinical studies (Funk et al., 2007; Logrip et al., 2011). To date, there have been no studies examining the effectiveness of CRFR1 antagonists in relapse prevention in the clinical setting. However, this class of drugs has been studied in the clinical setting to treat anxiety disorders and other stress-related disorders. While these studies have shown limited effectiveness of CRFR1 antagonists in treating general anxiety disorder (Coric et al., 2010) or irritable bowel syndrome (Sweetser et al., 2009), these compounds can produce significant signal reductions in the amygdala during pain expectation in humans (Hubbard et al., 2011). These findings suggest that CRFR1 antagonists may be useful in reducing negative affect in response to specific psychological stimuli. Importantly, these drugs are very well tolerated in the above mentioned studies and have been shown to cause no significant side-effects (Kunzel et al., 2003; Schmidt et al., 2010). However, to date many CRF antagonists have been shown to have undesirable lipophilic or pharmacokinetic profiles limiting their bioavailability and efficacy in clinical trials (Zorrilla and Koob, 2010). CRF antagonists with better pharmacokinetics may prove useful in the treatment of addiction in the future through interference with the proposed BNST CRF reinstatement circuit described here. Overall, CRF circuitry within the BNST is a critical locus for interactions between stress and reward signaling in addiction and may be an important target requiring further study for the treatment of relapse and addiction.

REFERENCES

Adamantidis, A. R., Tsai, H. C., Boutrel, B., Zhang, F., Stuber, G. D., Budygin, E. A., et al. (2011). Optogenetic interrogation of dopaminergic modulation of the multiple phases of reward-seeking behavior. J. Neurosci. 31, 10829–10835. doi:10.1523/JNEUROSCI.2246-11.2011

Banday, A. A., and Lokhandwala, M. F. (2008). Dopamine receptors and hypertension. Curr. Hypertens. Rep. 10, 268–275. doi:10.1007/s11906-008-0051-9

Becker, H. C., and Lopez, M. F. (2004). Increased ethanol drinking after repeated chronic ethanol exposure and withdrawal experience in C57BL/6 mice. Alcohol. Clin. Exp. Res. 28, 1829–1838. doi:10.1097/01.ALC.0000149977.95306.3A

Breese, G. R., Knapp, D. J., and Overstreet, D. H. (2004). Stress sensitization of ethanol withdrawal-induced reduction in social interaction: inhibition by CRF-1 and benzodiazepine receptor antagonists and a 5-HT1A-receptor agonist. Neuropsychopharmacology 29, 470–482. doi:10.1038/sj.npp.1300419

Briand, L. A., Vassoler, F. M., Pierce, R. C., Valentino, R. J., and Blendy, J. A. (2010). Ventral tegmental afferents in stress-induced reinstatement: the role of cAMP response element-binding protein. J. Neurosci. 30, 16149–16159. doi:10.1523/JNEUROSCI.2827-10.2010

Brown, Z. J., Nobrega, J. N., and Erb, S. (2011). Central injections of noradrenaline induce reinstatement of cocaine seeking and increase c-fos mRNA expression in the extended amygdala. Behav. Brain Res. 217, 472–476. doi:10.1016/j.bbr.2010.09.025

Brown, Z. J., Tribe, E., D'Souza, N. A., and Erb, S. (2009). Interaction between noradrenaline and corticotrophin-releasing factor in the reinstatement of cocaine seeking in the rat. Psychopharmacology (Berl.) 203, 121–130. doi:10.1007/s00213-008-1376-4

Bruijnzeel, A. W., Ford, J., Rogers, J. A., Scheick, S., Ji, Y., Bishnoi,

M., et al. (2012). Blockade of CRF1 receptors in the central nucleus of the amygdala attenuates the dysphoria associated with nicotine withdrawal in rats. *Pharmacol. Biochem. Behav.* 101, 62–68. doi:10.1016/j.pbb.2011.12.001

Buffalari, D., and See, R. (2011). Inactivation of the bed nucleus of the stria terminalis in an animal model of relapse: effects on conditioned cue-induced reinstatement and its enhancement by yohimbine. *Psychopharmacology (Berl.)* 213, 19–27. doi:10.1007/s00213-010-2008-3

Buffalari, D. M., and See, R. E. (2009). Footshock stress potentiates cue-induced cocaine-seeking in an animal model of relapse. *Physiol. Behav.* 98, 614–617. doi:10.1016/j.physbeh.2009.09.013

Carboni, E., Silvagni, A., Rolando, M. T., and Di, C. G. (2000). Stimulation of in vivo dopamine transmission in the bed nucleus of stria terminalis by reinforcing drugs. *J. Neurosci.* 20, RC102.

Coric, V., Feldman, H. H., Oren, D. A., Shekhar, A., Pultz, J., Dockens, R. C., et al. (2010). Multicenter, randomized, double-blind, active comparator and placebo-controlled trial of a corticotropin-releasing factor receptor-1 antagonist in generalized anxiety disorder. *Depress. Anxiety* 27, 417–425. doi:10.1002/da.20695

Cornish, J. L., and Kalivas, P. W. (2000). Glutamate transmission in the nucleus accumbens mediates relapse in cocaine addiction. *J. Neurosci.* 20, RC89.

Davis, M., Walker, D. L., Miles, L., and Grillon, C. (2010). Phasic vs. sustained fear in rats and humans: role of the extended amygdala in fear vs. anxiety. *Neuropsychopharmacology* 35, 105–135. doi:10.1038/npp.2009.109

Di Chiara, G. (2002). Nucleus accumbens shell and core dopamine: differential role in behavior and addiction. *Behav. Brain Res.* 137, 75–114. doi:10.1016/S0166-4328(02)00286-3

Di Chiara, G., and Imperato, A. (1988). Drugs abused by humans preferentially increase synaptic dopamine concentrations in the mesolimbic system of freely moving rats. *Proc. Natl. Acad. Sci. U.S.A.* 85, 5274–5278. doi:10.1073/pnas.85.14.5274

Dong, H. W., Petrovich, G. D., Watts, A. G., and Swanson, L. W. (2001). Basic organization of projections from the oval and fusiform nuclei of the bed nuclei of the stria terminalis in adult rat brain. *J. Comp. Neurol.* 436, 430–455. doi:10.1002/cne.1079

Dong, H. W., and Swanson, L. W. (2004). Organization of axonal projections from the anterolateral area of the bed nuclei of the stria terminalis. *J. Comp. Neurol.* 468, 277–298. doi:10.1002/cne.10949

Dong, H. W., and Swanson, L. W. (2006a). Projections from bed nuclei of the stria terminalis, anteromedial area: cerebral hemisphere integration of neuroendocrine, autonomic, and behavioral aspects of energy balance. *J. Comp. Neurol.* 494, 142–178. doi:10.1002/cne.20790

Dong, H. W., and Swanson, L. W. (2006b). Projections from bed nuclei of the stria terminalis, dorsomedial nucleus: implications for cerebral hemisphere integration of neuroendocrine, autonomic, and drinking responses. *J. Comp. Neurol.* 494, 75–107. doi:10.1002/cne.20790

Dumont, E. C., Rycroft, B. K., Maiz, J., and Williams, J. T. (2008). Morphine produces circuit-specific neuroplasticity in the bed nucleus of the stria terminalis. *Neuroscience* 153, 232–239. doi:10.1016/j.neuroscience.2008.01.039

Dumont, E. C., and Williams, J. T. (2004). Noradrenaline triggers GABAA inhibition of bed nucleus of the stria terminalis neurons projecting to the ventral tegmental area. *J. Neurosci.* 24, 8198–8204. doi:10.1523/JNEUROSCI.0425-04.2004

Egli, R. E., and Winder, D. G. (2003). Dorsal and ventral distribution of excitable and synaptic properties of neurons of the bed nucleus of the stria terminalis. *J. Neurophysiol.* 90, 405–414. doi:10.1152/jn.00228.2003

Epstein, D., Preston, K., Stewart, J., and Shaham, Y. (2006). Toward a model of drug relapse: an assessment of the validity of the reinstatement procedure. *Psychopharmacology (Berl.)* 189, 1–16. doi:10.1007/s00213-006-0529-6

Erb, S. (2010). Evaluation of the relationship between anxiety during withdrawal and stress-induced reinstatement of cocaine seeking. *Prog. Neuropsychopharmacol. Biol. Psychiatry* 34, 798–807. doi:10.1016/j.pnpbp.2009.11.025

Erb, S., Salmaso, N., Rodaros, D., and Stewart, J. (2001). A role for the CRF-containing pathway from central nucleus of the amygdala to bed nucleus of the stria terminalis in the stress-induced reinstatement of cocaine seeking in rats. *Psychopharmacology (Berl.)* 158, 360–365. doi:10.1007/s002130000642

Erb, S., and Stewart, J. (1999). A role for the bed nucleus of the stria terminalis, but not the amygdala, in the effects of corticotropin-releasing factor on stress-induced reinstatement of cocaine seeking. *J. Neurosci.* 19, RC35.

Everitt, B. J., Belin, D., Economidou, D., Pelloux, Y., Dalley, J. W., and Robbins, T. W. (2008). Review. Neural mechanisms underlying the vulnerability to develop compulsive drug-seeking habits and addiction. *Philos. Trans. R. Soc. Lond. B Biol. Sci.* 363, 3125–3135. doi:10.1098/rstb.2008.0089

Feltenstein, M. W., and See, R. E. (2008). The neurocircuitry of addiction: an overview. *Br. J. Pharmacol.* 154, 261–274. doi:10.1038/bjp.2008.51

Forget, B., Wertheim, C., Mascia, P., Pushparaj, A., Goldberg, S. R., and Le, F. B. (2010). Noradrenergic alpha1 receptors as a novel target for the treatment of nicotine addiction. *Neuropsychopharmacology* 35, 1751–1760. doi:10.1038/npp.2010.42

Fox, H. C., Bergquist, K. L., Hong, K. I., and Sinha, R. (2007). Stress-induced and alcohol cue-induced craving in recently abstinent alcohol-dependent individuals. *Alcohol. Clin. Exp. Res.* 31, 395–403. doi:10.1111/j.1530-0277.2006.00320.x

Francesconi, W., Berton, F., Repunte-Canonigo, V., Hagihara, K., Thurbon, D., Lekic, D., et al. (2009). Protracted withdrawal from alcohol and drugs of abuse impairs long-term potentiation of intrinsic excitability in the juxtacapsular bed nucleus of the stria terminalis. *J. Neurosci.* 29, 5389–5401. doi:10.1523/JNEUROSCI.5129-08.2009

Fu, Y., Pollandt, S., Liu, J., Krishnan, B., Genzer, K., Orozco-Cabal, L., et al. (2007). Long-term potentiation (LTP) in the central amygdala (CeA) is enhanced after prolonged withdrawal from chronic cocaine and requires CRF1 receptors. *J. Neurophysiol.* 97, 937–941. doi:10.1152/jn.00349.2006

Fuchs, R. A., and See, R. E. (2002). Basolateral amygdala inactivation abolishes conditioned stimulus- and heroin-induced reinstatement of extinguished heroin-seeking behavior in rats. *Psychopharmacology (Berl.)* 160, 425–433. doi:10.1007/s00213-001-0997-7

Funk, C. K., O'Dell, L. E., Crawford, E. F., and Koob, G. F. (2006a). Corticotropin-releasing factor within the central nucleus of the amygdala mediates enhanced ethanol self-administration in withdrawn, ethanol-dependent rats. *J. Neurosci.* 26, 11324–11332. doi:10.1523/JNEUROSCI.3096-06.2006

Funk, D., Li, Z., and Le, A. D. (2006b). Effects of environmental and pharmacological stressors on c-fos and corticotropin-releasing factor mRNA in rat brain: relationship to the reinstatement of alcohol seeking. *Neuroscience* 138, 235–243. doi:10.1016/j.neuroscience.2005.10.062

Funk, C. K., Zorrilla, E. P., Lee, M. J., Rice, K. C., and Koob, G. F. (2007). Corticotropin-releasing factor 1 antagonists selectively reduce ethanol self-administration in ethanol-dependent rats. *Biol. Psychiatry* 61, 78–86. doi:10.1016/j.biopsych.2006.03.063

George, O., Ghozland, S., Azar, M. R., Cottone, P., Zorrilla, E. P., Parsons, L. H., et al. (2007). CRF-CRF1 system activation mediates withdrawal-induced increases in nicotine self-administration in nicotine-dependent rats. *Proc. Natl. Acad. Sci. U.S.A.* 104, 17198–17203. doi:10.1073/pnas.0707585104

Georges, F., and Aston-Jones, G. (2001). Potent regulation of midbrain dopamine neurons by the bed nucleus of the stria terminalis. *J. Neurosci.* 21, RC160.

Georges, F., and Aston-Jones, G. (2002). Activation of ventral tegmental area cells by the bed nucleus of the stria terminalis: a novel excitatory amino acid input to midbrain dopamine neurons. *J. Neurosci.* 22, 5173–5187.

Haass-Koffler, C. L., and Bartlett, S. E. (2012). Stress and addiction: contribution of the corticotropin releasing factor (CRF) system in neuroplasticity. *Front. Mol. Neurosci.* 5:91. doi:10.3389/fnmol.2012.00091

Hammack, S. E., Mania, I., and Rainnie, D. G. (2007). Differential expression of intrinsic membrane currents in defined cell types of the anterolateral bed nucleus of the stria terminalis. *J. Neurophysiol.* 98, 638–656. doi:10.1152/jn.00382.2007

Hansson, A. C., Cippitelli, A., Sommer, W. H., Fedeli, A., Bjork, K., Soverchia, L., et al. (2006). Variation at the rat Crhr1 locus and sensitivity to relapse into alcohol seeking induced by environmental stress. *Proc. Natl. Acad. Sci. U.S.A.* 103, 15236–15241. doi:10.1073/pnas.0604419103

Hopf, F. W., Martin, M., Chen, B. T., Bowers, M. S., Mohamedi, M. M., and Bonci, A. (2007). Withdrawal from intermittent ethanol exposure increases probability of burst firing in VTA neurons in vitro. *J. Neurophysiol.* 98, 2297–2310. doi:10.1152/jn.00824.2007

Howland, J. G., Taepavarapruk, P., and Phillips, A. G. (2002). Glutamate receptor-dependent modulation of dopamine efflux in the nucleus accumbens by basolateral, but not central, nucleus of the amygdala in rats. *J. Neurosci.* 22, 1137–1145.

Huang, M. M., Overstreet, D. H., Knapp, D. J., Angel, R., Wills, T. A., Navarro, M., et al. (2010). Corticotropin-releasing factor (CRF) sensitization of ethanol withdrawal-induced anxiety-like behavior is brain site specific and mediated by CRF-1 receptors: relation to stress-induced sensitization. *J. Pharmacol. Exp. Ther.* 332, 298–307. doi:10.1124/jpet.109.159186

Hubbard, C. S., Labus, J. S., Bueller, J., Stains, J., Suyenobu, B., Dukes, G. E., et al. (2011). Corticotropin-releasing factor receptor 1 antagonist alters regional activation and effective connectivity in an emotional-arousal circuit during expectation of abdominal pain. *J. Neurosci.* 31, 12491–12500. doi:10.1523/JNEUROSCI.1860-11.2011

Hughes, J. R., Stead, L. F., and Lancaster, T. (2000). Anxiolytics for smoking cessation. *Cochrane Database Syst. Rev.* 4:CD002849. doi:10.1002/14651858.CD002849

Jaferi, A., Lane, D. A., and Pickel, V. M. (2009). Subcellular plasticity of the corticotropin-releasing factor receptor in dendrites of the mouse bed nucleus of the stria terminalis following chronic opiate exposure. *Neuroscience* 163, 143–154. doi:10.1016/j.neuroscience.2009.06.029

Jennings, J. H., Sparta, D. R., Stamatakis, A. M., Ung, R. L., Pleil, K. E., Kash, T. L., et al. (2013). Distinct extended amygdala circuits for divergent motivational states. *Nature* 496, 224–228. doi:10.1038/nature12041

Kalivas, P. W., and Volkow, N. D. (2005). The neural basis of addiction: a pathology of motivation and choice. *Am. J. Psychiatry* 162, 1403–1413. doi:10.1176/appi.ajp.162.8.1403

Kampman, K. M., Volpicelli, J. R., Mulvaney, F., Alterman, A. I., Cornish, J., Gariti, P., et al. (2001). Effectiveness of propranolol for cocaine dependence treatment may depend on cocaine withdrawal symptom severity. *Drug Alcohol Depend.* 63, 69–78. doi:10.1016/S0376-8716(00)00193-9

Kash, T. L., Baucum, A. J., Conrad, K. L., Colbran, R. J., and Winder, D. G. (2009). Alcohol exposure alters NMDAR function in the bed nucleus of the stria terminalis. *Neuropsychopharmacology* 34, 2420–2429. doi:10.1038/npp.2009.69

Kash, T. L., Nobis, W. P., Matthews, R. T., and Winder, D. G. (2008). Dopamine enhances fast excitatory synaptic transmission in the extended amygdala by a CRF-R1-dependent process. *J. Neurosci.* 28, 13856–13865. doi:10.1523/JNEUROSCI.4715-08.2008

Kim, S. Y., Adhikari, A., Lee, S. Y., Marshel, J. H., Kim, C. K., Mallory, C. S., et al. (2013). Diverging neural pathways assemble a behavioural state from separable features in anxiety. *Nature* 496, 219–223. doi:10.1038/nature12018

Koob, G. F. (2008). A role for brain stress systems in addiction. *Neuron* 59, 11–34. doi:10.1016/j.neuron.2008.06.012

Koob, G. F. (2009). Brain stress systems in the amygdala and addiction. *Brain Res.* 1293, 61–75. doi:10.1016/j.brainres.2009.03.038

Koob, G. F., and Le, M. M. (2001). Drug addiction, dysregulation of reward, and allostasis. *Neuropsychopharmacology* 24, 97–129. doi:10.1016/S0893-133X(00)00195-0

Koob, G. F., and Volkow, N. D. (2010). Neurocircuitry of addiction. *Neuropsychopharmacology* 35, 217–238. doi:10.1038/npp.2009.110

Kudo, T., Uchigashima, M., Miyazaki, T., Konno, K., Yamasaki, M., Yanagawa, Y., et al. (2012). Three types of neurochemical projection from the bed nucleus of the stria terminalis to the ventral tegmental area in adult mice. *J. Neurosci.* 32, 18035–18046. doi:10.1523/JNEUROSCI.4057-12.2012

Kunzel, H. E., Zobel, A. W., Nickel, T., Ackl, N., Uhr, M., Sonntag, A., et al. (2003). Treatment of depression with the CRH-1-receptor antagonist R121919: endocrine changes and side effects. *J. Psychiatr. Res.* 37, 525–533. doi:10.1016/S0022-3956(03)00070-0

Le, A. D., Harding, S., Juzytsch, W., Watchus, J., Shalev, U., and Shaham, Y. (2000). The role of corticotrophin-releasing factor in stress-induced relapse to alcohol-seeking behavior in rats. *Psychopharmacology (Berl.)* 150, 317–324. doi:10.1007/s002130000411

Leri, F., Flores, J., Rodaros, D., and Stewart, J. (2002). Blockade of stress-induced but not cocaine-induced reinstatement by infusion of noradrenergic antagonists into the bed nucleus of the stria terminalis or the central nucleus of the amygdala. *J. Neurosci.* 22, 5713–5718.

Li, Z., Luan, W., Chen, Y., Chen, M., Dong, Y., Lai, B., et al. (2011). Chronic morphine treatment switches the effect of dopamine on excitatory synaptic transmission from inhibition to excitation in pyramidal cells of the basolateral amygdala. *J. Neurosci.* 31, 17527–17536. doi:10.1523/JNEUROSCI.3806-11.2011

Lingford-Hughes, A., Watson, B., Kalk, N., and Reid, A. (2010). Neuropharmacology of addiction and how it informs treatment. *Br. Med. Bull.* 96, 93–110. doi:10.1093/bmb/ldq032

Liu, J., Yu, B., Neugebauer, V., Grigoriadis, D. E., Rivier, J., Vale, W. W., et al. (2004). Corticotropin-releasing factor and Urocortin I modulate excitatory glutamatergic synaptic transmission. *J. Neurosci.* 24, 4020–4029. doi:10.1523/JNEUROSCI.5531-03.2004

Logrip, M. L., Koob, G. F., and Zorrilla, E. P. (2011). Role of corticotropin-releasing factor in drug addiction: potential for pharmacological intervention. *CNS Drugs* 25, 271–287. doi:10.2165/11587790-000000000-00000

Lowery, E. G., Sparrow, A. M., Breese, G. R., Knapp, D. J., and Thiele, T. E. (2008). The CRF-1 receptor antagonist, CP-154,526, attenuates stress-induced increases in ethanol consumption by BALB/cJ mice. *Alcohol. Clin. Exp. Res.* 32, 240–248. doi:10.1111/j.1530-0277.2007.00573.x

Lowery-Gionta, E. G., Navarro, M., Li, C., Pleil, K. E., Rinker, J. A., Cox, B. R., et al. (2012). Corticotropin releasing factor signaling in the central amygdala is recruited during binge-like ethanol consumption in C57BL/6J mice. *J. Neurosci.* 32, 3405–3413. doi:10.1523/JNEUROSCI.6256-11.2012

Mahler, S. V., and Aston-Jones, G. S. (2012). Fos activation of selective afferents to ventral tegmental area during cue-induced reinstatement of cocaine seeking in rats. *J. Neurosci.* 32, 13309–13326. doi:10.1523/JNEUROSCI.2277-12.2012

Maj, M., Turchan, J., Smialowska, M., and Przewlocka, B. (2003). Morphine and cocaine influence on CRF biosynthesis in the rat central nucleus of amygdala. *Neuropeptides* 37, 105–110. doi:10.1016/S0143-4179(03)00021-0

Marinelli, P. W., Funk, D., Juzytsch, W., Harding, S., Rice, K. C., Shaham, Y., et al. (2007). The CRF1 receptor antagonist antalarmin attenuates yohimbine-induced increases in operant alcohol self-administration and reinstatement of alcohol seeking in rats. *Psychopharmacology (Berl.)* 195, 345–355. doi:10.1007/s00213-007-0905-x

McDougle, C. J., Black, J. E., Malison, R. T., Zimmermann, R. C., Kosten, T. R., Heninger, G. R., et al. (1994). Noradrenergic dysregulation during discontinuation of cocaine use in addicts. *Arch. Gen. Psychiatry* 51, 713–719. doi:10.1001/archpsyc.1994.03950090045007

McFarland, K., and Kalivas, P. W. (2001). The circuitry mediating cocaine-induced reinstatement of drug-seeking behavior. *J. Neurosci.* 21, 8655–8663.

Merlo, P. E., Lorang, M., Yeganeh, M., Rodriguez de, F. F., Raber, J., Koob, G. F., et al. (1995). Increase of extracellular corticotropin-releasing factor-like immunoreactivity levels in the amygdala of awake rats during restraint stress and ethanol withdrawal as measured by microdialysis. *J. Neurosci.* 15, 5439–5447.

Neisewander, J. L., Fuchs, R. A., O'Dell, L. E., and Khroyan, T. V. (1998). Effects of SCH-23390 on dopamine D1 receptor occupancy and locomotion produced by intraaccumbens cocaine infusion. *Synapse* 30, 194–204. doi:10.1002/(SICI)1098-2396(199810)30:2<194::AID-SYN9>3.0.CO;2-7

Nie, Z., Zorrilla, E. P., Madamba, S. G., Rice, K. C., Roberto, M., and Siggins, G. R. (2009). Presynaptic CRF1 receptors mediate the ethanol enhancement of GABAergic transmission in the mouse central amygdala. *ScientificWorldJournal* 9, 68–85. doi:10.1100/tsw.2009.1

Nobis, W. P., Kash, T. L., Silberman, Y., and Winder, D. G. (2011). beta-Adrenergic receptors enhance excitatory transmission in the bed nucleus of the stria terminalis through a corticotrophin-releasing factor receptor-dependent and cocaine-regulated mechanism. *Biol. Psychiatry* 69, 1083–1090. doi:10.1016/j.biopsych.2010.12.030

Park, J., Wheeler, R. A., Fontillas, K., Keithley, R. B., Carelli, R. M., and Wightman, R. M. (2012). Catecholamines in the bed nucleus of the stria terminalis reciprocally respond to reward and aversion. *Biol. Psychiatry* 71, 327–334. doi:10.1016/j.biopsych.2011.10.017

Peacock, L., Hansen, L., Morkeberg, F., and Gerlach, J. (1999). Chronic dopamine D1, dopamine D2 and combined dopamine D1 and D2 antagonist treatment in *Cebus apella* monkeys: antiamphetamine effects and extrapyramidal side effects. *Neuropsychopharmacology* 20, 35–43. doi:10.1016/S0893-133X(98)00049-9

Radwanska, K., Wrobel, E., Korkosz, A., Rogowski, A., Kostowski, W., Bienkowski, P., et al. (2008). Alcohol relapse induced by discrete cues activates components of AP-1 transcription factor and ERK pathway in the rat basolateral and central amygdala. *Neuropsychopharmacology* 33, 1835–1846. doi:10.1038/sj.npp.1301567

Richter, R. M., and Weiss, F. (1999). In vivo CRF release in rat amygdala is increased during cocaine withdrawal in self-administering rats. *Synapse* 32, 254–261. doi:10.1002/(SICI)1098-2396(19990615)32:4<254::AID-SYN2>3.0.CO;2-H

Roberto, M., Cruz, M. T., Gilpin, N. W., Sabino, V., Schweitzer, P., Bajo, M., et al. (2010). Corticotropin releasing factor-induced amygdala gamma-aminobutyric Acid release plays a key role in alcohol dependence. *Biol. Psychiatry* 67, 831–839. doi:10.1016/j.biopsych.2009.11.007

Roberto, M., Madamba, S. G., Moore, S. D., Tallent, M. K., and Siggins, G. R. (2003). Ethanol increases GABAergic transmission at both pre- and postsynaptic sites in rat central amygdala neurons. *Proc. Natl. Acad. Sci. U.S.A.* 100, 2053–2058. doi:10.1073/pnas.0437926100

Roberto, M., Madamba, S. G., Stouffer, D. G., Parsons, L. H., and Siggins, G. R. (2004). Increased GABA release in the central amygdala of ethanol-dependent rats. *J. Neurosci.* 24, 10159–10166. doi:10.1523/JNEUROSCI.3004-04.2004

Rodaros, D., Caruana, D. A., Amir, S., and Stewart, J. (2007). Corticotropin-releasing factor projections from limbic forebrain and paraventricular nucleus of the hypothalamus to the region of the ventral tegmental area. *Neuroscience* 150, 8–13. doi:10.1016/j.neuroscience.2007.09.043

Rodriguez de, F. F., Carrera, M. R., Navarro, M., Koob, G. F., and Weiss, F. (1997). Activation of corticotropin-releasing factor in the limbic system during cannabinoid withdrawal. *Science* 276, 2050–2054. doi:10.1126/science.276.5321.2050

Rudoy, C. A., Reyes, A. R., and Van Bockstaele, E. J. (2009). Evidence for beta1-adrenergic receptor involvement in amygdalar corticotropin-releasing factor gene expression: implications for cocaine withdrawal. *Neuropsychopharmacology* 34, 1135–1148. doi:10.1038/npp.2008.102

Rudoy, C. A., and Van Bockstaele, E. J. (2007). Betaxolol, a selective beta(1)-adrenergic receptor antagonist, diminishes anxiety-like behavior during early withdrawal from chronic cocaine administration in rats. *Prog. Neuropsychopharmacol. Biol. Psychiatry* 31, 1119–1129. doi:10.1016/j.pnpbp.2007.04.005

Santucci, A. C., Cortes, C., Bettica, A., and Cortes, F. (2008). Chronic ethanol consumption in rats produces residual increases in anxiety 4 months after withdrawal. *Behav. Brain Res.* 188, 24–31. doi:10.1016/j.bbr.2007.10.009

Sartor, G. C., and Aston-Jones, G. (2012). Regulation of the ventral tegmental area by the bed nucleus of the stria terminalis is required for expression of cocaine preference. *Eur. J. Neurosci.* 36, 3549–3558. doi:10.1111/j.1460-9568.2012.08277.x

Schmidt, M. E., Andrews, R. D., van der Ark, P., Brown, T., Mannaert, E., Steckler, T., et al. (2010). Dose-dependent effects of the CRF(1) receptor antagonist R317573 on regional brain activity in healthy male subjects. *Psychopharmacology (Berl.)* 208, 109–119. doi:10.1007/s00213-009-1714-1

Schwabe, L., Hoffken, O., Tegenthoff, M., and Wolf, O. T. (2011). Preventing the stress-induced shift from goal-directed to habit action with a beta-adrenergic antagonist. *J. Neurosci.* 31, 17317–17325. doi:10.1523/JNEUROSCI.3304-11.2011

See, R. E., Kruzich, P. J., and Grimm, J. W. (2001). Dopamine, but not glutamate, receptor blockade in the basolateral amygdala attenuates conditioned reward in a rat model of relapse to cocaine-seeking behavior. *Psychopharmacology (Berl.)* 154, 301–310. doi:10.1007/s002130000636

Shaham, Y., Shalev, U., Lu, L., de Wit, H., and Stewart, J. (2003). The reinstatement model of drug relapse: history, methodology and major findings. *Psychopharmacology (Berl.)* 168, 3–20. doi:10.1007/s00213-002-1224-x

Shalev, U., Erb, S., and Shaham, Y. (2010). Role of CRF and other neuropeptides in stress-induced reinstatement of drug seeking. *Brain Res.* 1314, 15–28. doi:10.1016/j.brainres.2009.07.028

Shorter, D., and Kosten, T. R. (2011). Novel pharmacotherapeutic treatments for cocaine addiction. *BMC Med.* 9:119. doi:10.1186/1741-7015-9-119

Silberman, Y., Matthews, R. T., and Winder, D. G. (2013). A corticotropin releasing factor pathway for ethanol regulation of the ventral tegmental area in the bed nucleus of the stria terminalis. *J. Neurosci.* 33, 950–960. doi:10.1523/JNEUROSCI.2949-12.2013

Silberman, Y., and Winder, D. G. (2013). Corticotropin releasing factor and catecholamines enhance glutamatergic neurotransmission in the lateral subdivision of the central amygdala. *Neuropharmacology* 70C, 316–323. doi:10.1016/j.neuropharm.2013.02.014

Sinha, R. (2007). The role of stress in addiction relapse. *Curr. Psychiatry Rep.* 9, 388–395. doi:10.1007/s11920-007-0050-6

Sofuoglu, M., and Sewell, R. A. (2009). Norepinephrine and stimulant addiction. *Addict. Biol.* 14, 119–129. doi:10.1111/j.1369-1600.2008.00138.x

Stein, D. J. (2008). Depression, anhedonia, and psychomotor symptoms: the role of dopaminergic neurocircuitry. *CNS Spectr.* 13, 561–565.

Stewart, J., and Vezina, P. (1988). A comparison of the effects of intra-accumbens injections of amphetamine and morphine on reinstatement of heroin intravenous self-administration behavior. *Brain Res.* 457, 287–294. doi:10.1016/0006-8993(88)90698-1

Sweetser, S., Camilleri, M., Linker Nord, S. J., Burton, D. D., Castenada, L., Croop, R., et al. (2009). Do corticotropin releasing factor-1 receptors influence colonic transit and bowel function in women with irritable bowel syndrome? *Am. J. Physiol. Gastrointest. Liver Physiol.* 296, G1299–G1306. doi:10.1152/ajpgi.00011.2009

Tan, K. R., Yvon, C., Turiault, M., Mirzabekov, J. J., Doehner, J., Labouebe, G., et al. (2012). GABA neurons of the VTA drive conditioned place aversion. *Neuron* 73, 1173–1183. doi:10.1016/j.neuron.2012.02.015

Tzschentke, T. M. (2007). Measuring reward with the conditioned place preference (CPP) paradigm: update of the last decade. *Addict. Biol.* 12, 227–462. doi:10.1111/j.1369-1600.2007.00070.x

Uryu, K., Okumura, T., Shibasaki, T., and Sakanaka, M. (1992). Fine structure and possible origins of nerve fibers with corticotropin-releasing factor-like immunoreactivity in the rat central amygdaloid nucleus. *Brain Res.* 577, 175–179. doi:10.1016/0006-8993(92)90554-M

Van den Oever, M. C., Spijker, S., Smit, A. B., and De Vries, T. J. (2010). Prefrontal cortex plasticity mechanisms in drug seeking and relapse. *Neurosci. Biobehav. Rev.* 35, 276–284. doi:10.1016/j.neubiorev.2009.11.016

van Zessen, R., Phillips, J. L., Budygin, E. A., and Stuber, G. D. (2012). Activation of VTA GABA neurons disrupts reward consumption. *Neuron* 73, 1184–1194. doi:10.1016/j.neuron.2012.02.016

Veinante, P., Stoeckel, M. E., and Freund-Mercier, M. J. (1997). GABA- and peptide-immunoreactivities co-localize in the rat central extended amygdala. *Neuroreport* 8, 2985–2989. doi:10.1097/00001756-199709080-00035

Verplaetse, T. L., Rasmussen, D. D., Froehlich, J. C., and Czachowski, C. L. (2012). Effects of prazosin, an alpha1-adrenergic receptor antagonist, on the seeking and intake of alcohol and sucrose in alcohol-preferring (P) rats. *Alcohol. Clin. Exp. Res.* 36, 881–886. doi:10.1111/j.1530-0277.2011.01653.x

Volkow, N. D., Fowler, J. S., and Wang, G. J. (2003). The addicted human brain: insights from imaging studies. *J. Clin. Invest.* 111, 1444–1451. doi:10.1172/JCI18533

Wanat, M. J., Willuhn, I., Clark, J. J., and Phillips, P. E. (2009). Phasic dopamine release in appetitive behaviors and drug addiction. *Curr. Drug Abuse Rev.* 2, 195–213. doi:10.2174/1874473710902020195

Wang, J., Fang, Q., Liu, Z., and Lu, L. (2006). Region-specific effects of brain corticotropin-releasing factor receptor type 1 blockade on footshock-stress- or drug-priming-induced reinstatement of morphine conditioned place preference in rats. *Psychopharmacology (Berl.)* 185, 19–28. doi:10.1007/s00213-005-0262-6

Wee, S., Mandyam, C. D., Lekic, D. M., and Koob, G. F. (2008). Alpha 1-noradrenergic system role in increased motivation for cocaine intake in rats with prolonged access. *Eur. Neuropsychopharmacol.* 18, 303–311. doi:10.1016/j.euroneuro.2007. 08.003

Weiss, F., Maldonado-Vlaar, C. S., Parsons, L. H., Kerr, T. M., Smith, D. L., and Ben-Shahar, O. (2000). Control of cocaine-seeking behavior by drug-associated stimuli in rats: effects on recovery of extinguished operant-responding and extracellular dopamine levels in amygdala and nucleus accumbens. *Proc. Natl. Acad. Sci. U.S.A.* 97, 4321–4326. doi:10.1073/pnas.97.8.4321

Wise, R. A. (1980). Action of drugs of abuse on brain reward systems. *Pharmacol. Biochem. Behav.* 13(Suppl. 1), 213–223. doi:10.1016/S0091-3057(80) 80033-5

Wise, R. A., and Morales, M. (2010). A ventral tegmental CRF-glutamate-dopamine interaction in addiction. *Brain Res.* 1314, 38–43. doi:10.1016/ j.brainres.2009.09.101

Zeng, C., Zhang, M., Asico, L. D., Eisner, G. M., and Jose, P. A. (2007). The dopaminergic system in hypertension. *Clin. Sci.* 112, 583–597. doi:10.1042/CS20070018

Zorrilla, E. P., and Koob, G. F. (2010). Progress in corticotropin-releasing factor-1 antagonist development. *Drug Discov. Today* 15, 371–383. doi:10. 1016/j.drudis.2010.02.011

Zorrilla, E. P., Wee, S., Zhao, Y., Specio, S., Boutrel, B., Koob, G. F., et al. (2012). Extended access cocaine self-administration differentially activates dorsal raphe and amygdala corticotropin-releasing factor systems in rats. *Addict. Biol.* 17, 300–308. doi:10.1111/j.1369-1600.2011.00329.x

Permissions

The contributors of this book come from diverse backgrounds, making this book a truly international effort. This book will bring forth new frontiers with its revolutionizing research information and detailed analysis of the nascent developments around the world.

We would like to thank all the contributing authors for lending their expertise to make the book truly unique.

They have played a crucial role in the development of this book. Without their invaluable contributions this book wouldn't have been possible. They have made vital efforts to compile up to date information on the varied aspects of this subject to make this book a valuable addition to the collection of many professionals and students.

This book was conceptualized with the vision of imparting up-to-date information and advanced data in this field. To ensure the same, a matchless editorial board was set up. Every individual on the board went through rigorous rounds of assessment to prove their worth. After which they invested a large part of their time researching and compiling the most relevant data for our readers.

The editorial board has been involved in producing this book since its inception. They have spent rigorous hours researching and exploring the diverse topics which have resulted in the successful publishing of this book. They have passed on their knowledge of decades through this book. To expedite this challenging task, the publisher supported the team at every step. A small team of assistant editors was also appointed to further simplify the editing procedure and attain best results for the readers.

Apart from the editorial board, the designing team has also invested a significant amount of their time in understanding the subject and creating the most relevant covers. They scrutinized every image to scout for the most suitable representation of the subject and create an appropriate cover for the book.

The publishing team has been an ardent support to the editorial, designing and production team. Their endless efforts to recruit the best for this project, has resulted in the accomplishment of this book. They are a veteran in the field of academics and their pool of knowledge is as vast as their experience in printing. Their expertise and guidance has proved useful at every step. Their uncompromising quality standards have made this book an exceptional effort. Their encouragement from time to time has been an inspiration for everyone.

The publisher and the editorial board hope that this book will prove to be a valuable piece of knowledge for researchers, students, practitioners and scholars across the globe.

List of Contributors

Danae Campos-Melo, Danny Galleguillos, Natalia Sánchez, Katia Gysling and María E. Andrés
Nucleus Millennium in Stress and Addiction, Department of Cellular and Molecular Biology, Faculty of Biological Sciences, Pontificia Universidad Católica de Chile, Santiago, Chile

Kate Hutton-Bedbrook and Gavan P. McNally
School of Psychology, The University of New SouthWales, Sydney, NSW, Australia

Subhashini Srinivasan
Ernest Gallo Clinic and Research Center at the University of California San Francisco, Emeryville, CA, USA

Masroor Shariff and Selena E. Bartlett
Translational Research Institute and Institute for Health and Biomedical Innovation, Queensland University of Technology, Brisbane, QLD, Australia

Helena J.V. Rutherford and Linda C. Mayes
Yale Child Study Center, Yale University, New Haven, CT, USA

Sarah K. Williams
Department of Psychiatry, University of North Carolina-Chapel Hill, Chapel Hill, NC, USA

Sheryl Moy and Josephine M. Johns
Department of Psychiatry, University of North Carolina-Chapel Hill, Chapel Hill, NC, USA
Carolina Institute for Developmental Disabilities, University of North Carolina-Chapel Hill, Chapel Hill, NC, USA

Scott P. Goulding, Adam T. Gould, Kevin D. Lominac, Karen K. Szumlinski
Department of Psychology, Neuroscience Research Institute, University of California at Santa Barbara, Santa Barbara, CA, USA

Ilona Obara
Department of Psychology, Neuroscience Research Institute, University of California at Santa Barbara, Santa Barbara, CA, USA
School of Medicine, Pharmacy and Health, Queen's Campus, University of Durham, Stockton on Tees, UK

Jia-Hua Hu, Ping Wu Zhang, Marlin Dehoff, Bo Xiao, and Paul F.Worley
Department of Neuroscience, Johns Hopkins University School of Medicine, Baltimore, MD, USA

Georg von Jonquieres and Matthias Klugmann
Translational Neuroscience Facility, School of Medical Sciences, UNSW Kensington Campus, University of New SouthWales, Sydney, NSW, Australia

Peter H. Seeburg
Department of Molecular Neurobiology, Max Planck Institute Medical Research, Heidelberg, Germany

Krista M. Lisdahl, Erika R. Gilbart, Natasha E.Wright and Skyler Shollenbarger
Department of Psychology, University of Wisconsin-Milwaukee, Milwaukee, WI, USA

Diana Martinez
New York State Psychiatric Institute, Columbia University, New York, NY, USA

Pierre Trifilieff
NutriNeuro, UMR 1286 INRA, University Bordeaux 2, Bordeaux, France

George F. Koob
Committee on the Neurobiology of Addictive Disorders, The Scripps Research Institute, La Jolla, CA, USA

Chitra D. Mandyam
Committee on the Neurobiology of Addictive Disorders, The Scripps Research Institute, La Jolla, CA, USA

Lydia O. Ayanwuyi, Francisca Carvajal, Jose M. Lerma-Cabrera, Esi Domi, Massimo Ubaldi,Roberto Ciccocioppo and Andrea Cippitelli
Pharmacology Unit, School of Pharmacy, University of Camerino, Camerino, Italy

Karl Björk and Markus Heilig
Laboratory of Clinical and Translational Studies, National Institutes of Health, National Institute on Alcohol Abuse and Alcoholism, Bethesda, MD, USA

Marisa Roberto
Committee on the Neurobiology of Addictive Disorders, The Scripps Research Institute, La Jolla, CA, USA

Oscar V.Torres, Luis A. Natividad, Luis M. Carcoba and Laura E. O'Dell
Department of Psychology, The University of Texas at El Paso, El Paso, TX, USA

Purva Bali and Paul J. Kenny
Laboratory of Behavioral and Molecular Neuroscience, Department of Molecular Therapeutics, The Scripps Research Institute – Florida, Jupiter, FL, USA
Laboratory of Behavioral and Molecular Neuroscience, Department of Neuroscience, The Scripps Research Institute – Florida, Jupiter, FL, USA

Luciana G. Gentil
Department of Biological Sciences, The University of Texas at El Paso, El Paso, TX, USA

Ami Cohen and Olivier George
Committee on the Neurobiology of Addictive Disorders, The Scripps Research Institute, La Jolla, CA, USA

J. T. Gass and L. J. Chandler
Department of Neurosciences, Medical University of South Carolina, Charleston, SC, USA

Martin Zack
Cognitive Psychopharmacology Laboratory, Neuroscience Department, Centre for Addiction and Mental Health, Toronto, ON, Canada

Robert E. Featherstone
Translational Neuroscience Program, Department of Psychiatry, School of Medicine, University of Pennsylvania, Philadelphia, PA, USA

Sarah Mathewson and Paul J. Fletcher
Biopsychology Section, Neuroscience Department, Centre for Addiction and Mental Health, Toronto, ON, Canada

Linzy M. Hendrickson, Melissa J. Guildford and Andrew R.Tapper
Department of Psychiatry, Brudnick Neuropsychiatric Research Institute, University of Massachusetts Medical School,Worcester, MA, USA

Candace R. Lewis, Kelsey Staudinger, Lena Scheck and M. Foster Olive
Department of Psychology, Arizona State University, Tempe, AZ, USA

Yuval Silberman
Neuroscience Program in Substance Abuse, Department of Molecular Physiology and Biophysics, Vanderbilt Brain Institute, Nashville, TN, USA

Danny G. Winder
Neuroscience Program in Substance Abuse, Department of Molecular Physiology and Biophysics, Vanderbilt Brain Institute, Nashville, TN, USA
Kennedy Center for Research on Human Development, Vanderbilt Brain Institute, Nashville, TN, USA

Index

A

Acetylcholine Receptors, 19, 23, 91, 147, 153, 158, 160, 162, 164-165, 197, 207-212

Adrenocorticotropic Hormone, 20, 39, 111, 136

Amygdala, 6-7, 12-13, 32, 34, 36, 38-40, 42-47, 57-58, 61, 64, 67, 69, 73, 75, 83, 86, 90-92, 94, 96-97, 99-103, 135-137, 140-143, 145, 154-156, 162-163, 166, 171-174, 229-233

Anterior Cingulate, 34, 48, 63-64, 68, 169, 180, 189

B

Basolateral Amygdala, 20, 40, 86, 92, 108, 111, 115-116, 172, 177, 179, 223, 230-232

C

Cardiovascular Tone, 20, 22

Central Nervous System, 1, 12, 20, 39, 56, 92, 111, 114, 133-134, 153, 156, 197, 208

Chronic Constriction Injury, 47, 49, 51-53, 56

Cocaine Dependence, 78-80, 83-85, 87-88, 92, 96, 195, 208

Cognitive Inhibition, 62, 64-65, 67-68

Conditioned Place-preference, 47, 56

Conditioned Stimulus, 16, 168, 184-185, 187-191, 230

Corticotropin Releasing Factor, 1, 12-13, 37, 105, 125, 145, 222

D

Dentate Gyrus, 13, 75, 108-109, 112-114, 116, 172

Dopamine, 2-5, 7-14, 21, 26, 28, 32, 36, 42-46, 53, 57-58, 71, 78-89, 91-92, 94, 123-125, 129, 157-161, 163-164, 166-167, 177, 180-182, 194-197, 199, 207-212, 226, 229-233

Dopamine Signaling, 5, 14, 78-84, 129, 209

Dynorphin, 78, 80-90, 92, 96, 99-101, 103, 105, 126, 154-156, 162-165

E

Ethanol, 8, 13, 21-22, 24, 26-29, 58, 90-91, 93-99, 103-106, 108-116, 124-126, 137, 143-145, 156, 158, 163, 165, 172, 177, 197, 199-214, 218, 220-221, 224, 226-227, 229-232

Extracellular Dopamine, 78-81, 84, 88-89, 98, 194, 233

Extrahypothalamic Stress Systems, 108

F

Functional Magnetic Resonance Imaging, 32, 61

G

Gene Expression, 1-2, 5-6, 8-10, 12, 21, 26, 37, 43, 45, 57, 72, 84-88, 92, 127-128, 131, 133, 135-136, 140-142, 144, 146, 158, 174-175, 180, 220-221, 232

Gene Knock-out, 48

Generic Control, 49

G (right column)

Gestation Days, 31

Glucocorticoid, 9, 11-14, 19-26, 28-29, 108-109, 111-112, 115, 136, 214, 220-221

Glutamate Neuroadaptations, 48

Gray Matter, 59, 61, 63-65, 70

H

Habitual Behavior, 30, 171

Hippocampus, 2, 20-23, 25, 27-29, 32, 34, 38-40, 43-44, 61, 70, 73, 75-76, 83, 91-92, 108-116, 128, 134, 152, 154-155, 171-176, 178-180, 199

Homer Proteins, 47, 49, 53

Hypodopaminergic State, 78, 80, 83

Hypothalamus, 1, 4, 6, 12, 20, 22-23, 25-26, 28, 30, 32-34, 36, 38, 45, 91-92, 97, 125, 135-137, 141-143, 156, 172, 175-176, 178-180, 199, 225-226, 232

Hypothalamus-pituitary-adrenal, 1

I

Immunoblotting, 48-51, 53, 219

Inflammatory Pain, 48, 57

K

Kappa Opioid Receptor, 78, 84, 86

L

Lateral Habenula, 35, 37, 44, 199-200, 206-207, 210

Locomotor Activity, 5, 7-9, 48-49, 133, 145, 149, 158, 161, 166, 181, 184-185, 191, 195, 202

M

Maternal Behavior, 30-32, 43-46

Mesocorticolimbic Circuit, 47-48

Metabotropic Glutamate Receptors, 47, 57, 205

Microglial Proliferation, 110

Mifepristone, 19, 24, 26, 29, 115

N

Negative Reinforcement, 30, 38, 90-91, 93, 101, 107, 148, 222, 227

Neurochemical Elements, 90

Neuron-glia Interactions, 45, 109

Neuropathic Pain, 47-49, 56-58

Neuropeptide Y, 22, 90, 92, 99, 106, 113, 144, 155-156, 158, 161, 165-166

Neuropsychology, 43, 59, 115-116

Neurotoxic Effects, 59-60

Nicotinic Acetylcholine Receptors, 19, 158, 160, 197, 207-209

CPSIA information can be obtained
at www.ICGtesting.com
Printed in the USA
BVHW012038300822
645853BV00002B/61